AFFIRMING
DIVERSITY

AFFIRMING DIVERSITY

THE SOCIOPOLITICAL CONTEXT OF MULTICULTURAL EDUCATION

FIFTH EDITION

Sonia Nieto

University of Massachusetts, Amherst

Patty Bode

Tufts University *in affiliation with*
The School of the Museum of Fine Arts, Boston

PEARSON

Boston   New York   San Francisco
Mexico City   Montreal   Toronto   London   Madrid   Munich   Paris
Hong Kong   Singapore   Tokyo   Cape Town   Sydney

*This book is dedicated to all the students and teachers with whom
we have had the privilege to work.*

Series Editor: Kelly Villella Canton
Developmental Editor: Christien Shangraw
Series Editorial Assistant: Angela Pickard
Marketing Manager: Weslie Sellinger
Production Editor: Annette Joseph
Editorial Production Service: Marty Tenney,
  Modern Graphics, Inc.

Composition Buyer: Linda Cox
Manufacturing Buyer: Linda Morris
Electronic Composition: Modern Graphics, Inc.
Interior Design: The Davis Group
Cover Administrator: Linda Knowles

For related titles and support materials, visit our online catalog at www.ablongman.com.

Between the time website information is gathered and then published, it is not unusual
for some sites to have closed. Also, the transcription of URLs can result in typographical
errors. The publisher would appreciate notification where these errors occur so that
they may be corrected in subsequent editions.

ISBN-10: 0-205-52982-8
ISBN-13: 978-0-205-52982-7

Library of Congress Cataloging-in-Publication Data

Nieto, Sonia.
   Affirming diversity : the sociopolitical context of multicultural education / Sonia
Nieto, Patty Bode.—5th ed.
      p. cm.
   Includes bibliographical references and index.
   ISBN-10: 0-205-52982-8
   ISBN-13: 978-0-205-52982-7
      1. Multicultural education—United States—Case studies. I. Bode, Patty. II. Title.
LC1099.3.N54 2008
370.1170973—dc22
                                                                              2007007640

Printed in the United States of America

10 9 8 7 6 5 4 3 2 1   RRD-VA 11   10   09   08   07

This book's front cover art is made up of self-portraits from students of Josie Kealty and
Allyson Simes at Framingham High School, Framingham, MA: Cherry Au, Erica Bort-
nick, Aaron Everett, Joseph Kenny, David Kiser, Davone Mature, Dany Mbako, Ronald
Ortiz, Suheily Rodriguez, Emily Roskey, Adam Skaggs, Nicholas Sulfaro.

About the Authors

SONIA NIETO

Sonia Nieto is Professor Emerita of Language, Literacy, and Culture, University of Massachusetts, Amherst. She has taught students at all levels from elementary through graduate school and she continues to speak and write on multicultural education, the education of Latinos, and other culturally and linguistically diverse student populations. Other books include *The Light in Their Eyes: Creating Multicultural Learning Communities* (1999), *What Keeps Teachers Going?* (2003), and two edited volumes, *Puerto Rican Students in U.S. Schools* (2000) and *Why We Teach* (2005). She has received many awards for her advocacy and activism, including the 1997 Multicultural Educator of the Year Award from the National Association for Multicultural Education, an Annenberg Institute Senior Fellowship (1998–2000), the Outstanding Language Arts Educator of the Year from the National Council of Teachers of English (2005), and honorary doctorates from Lesley University (1999) and Bridgewater State College (2004).

PATTY BODE

Patty Bode is the Director of Art Education for Tufts University in affiliation with the School of the Museum of Fine Arts, Boston. Her research interests include multicultural theory and practice in teacher preparation, the arts in urban education, and the role of visual culture in the expression of student knowledge. She has published and lectured on retheorizing identity and curriculum, redefining multicultural education, and critical art pedagogy. Years of experience as an activist public school teacher and teacher educator inform her art making, research, and teaching. She has received awards for efforts in anti-racist curriculum reform and bridging theory and practice in multicultural education, including the 2005 *Multicultural Educator of the Year Award* from the National Association for Multicultural Education.

Contents

2 About Terminology   32

3 Multicultural Education and School Reform   42

PART TWO

DEVELOPING A CONCEPTUAL FRAMEWORK FOR MULTICULTURAL EDUCATION   63

6 Culture, Identity, and Learning   169

PART THREE

IMPLICATIONS OF DIVERSITY FOR TEACHING AND LEARNING IN A MULTICULTURAL SOCIETY   317

9 Learning From Students   319

10 Adapting Curriculum for Multicultural Classrooms   367

11 Affirming Diversity: Implications for Teachers, Schools, and Families 407

Foreword

Since the publication of the fourth edition of *Affirming Diversity*, there has been much turbulence on the global stage. The 9/11 attacks were quickly followed by the invasions of Afghanistan and Iraq, where armed conflict continues (as of this writing) and sectarian violence has spiraled out of control. The bombings in Madrid and London that killed hundreds of people bring home the fragility of life even in the most affluent regions of the world.

During this same period, in an almost surreal juxtaposition, education in the United States has been pushed further than perhaps ever before into a sanitized and disconnected state. As a result of the high-stakes testing regime ushered in by the federal No Child Left Behind (NCLB) Act of 2001, many schools have "drawn their blinds" and turned their backs on the world outside the classroom. Schooling has been reduced to the transmission of scripted skills and facts to the exclusion of inquiry, critical literacy, and social awareness. In schools across the country, instruction focuses relentlessly on teaching to the test. This is particularly the case in schools in low-income areas, which are considered most at risk of failing to demonstrate "adequate yearly progress." Ryan Monroe (2006), an English as a second language (ESL) teacher in a Maryland public school, calculated that during the 2004/2005 school year, English language learning (ELL) students in the fifth grade classroom where he was assigned took five different standardized tests, some of them more than once. He notes the instructional consequences: "During the course of the year, my students missed 33 days of ESL classes, or about 18 percent of their English instruction, due to standardized testing." This calculation does not include the extensive time that many schools devote to preparing their students to take these tests.

In addition to the loss of instructional time, a further consequence of the current educational regimen is the fact that discussion of issues that matter—for example, students' experiences and perceptions, social realities in communities and the country as a whole, world events, and issues crucial to becoming an informed citizen such as the roots of conflict and inequality—are assigned to the dubious category of off-task behavior. In some school districts, even recess has been sacrificed on the altar of adequate yearly progress.

As summarized in Chapter 1 of this fifth edition of *Affirming Diversity*, despite the fact that NCLB *has* put the achievement of minority groups and English language learners (ELL) on the accountability map, criticism of NCLB has been extensive (see also Bibliography at the end of this foreword). *Affirming Diversity* provides us with a powerful set of conceptual tools to counter the current attempts to constrict the instructional space. A central message throughout the book is that *teachers have choices*. Despite the pressures that are being applied to exclude critical literacy and student experience from classroom instruction, we always have at least some degree of freedom in how we interact with students, how we connect with their cultural experiences and language talents, how we involve parents in their children's learning, how we adapt content to link with students' prior knowledge, and in the levels of cognitive engagement we try to evoke through our instruction. Alternative modes of assessment (such as portfolio assessment) can also present a counter-discourse to the inaccurate and misleading accounts of students' progress and efforts often reflected in standardized test scores. In articulating our choices, both individually and collectively, we rediscover our own identities as educators and also become aware of the identity options that our instruction opens up (or shuts down) for our students.

Sonia Nieto and Patty Bode open up a dialogical sphere of both affirmation and resistance: affirmation of students' and teachers' identities and resistance to coercive and misguided top-down control. When we realize that we *do* have choices, and when we explicitly articulate these choices, we take the first steps toward *empowerment*, which can be defined as the collaborative creation of power. Disempowered teachers are not in a position to create contexts of empowerment for their students. We need to understand and rediscover the power that we bring to the classroom, not as instructional technicians who simply read scripts, but as *educators* whose instructional choices exert a dramatic impact on the lives of our students.

Affirming Diversity challenges us, as educators, to make explicit the image of our students and of our society that is implied by our interactions in the school context. What kind of people do we hope our students will grow up to be? What kinds of abilities and knowledge are accessible to them in our classroom? What kind of society do we hope they will create? The answers to all these questions are written in the daily record of our interactions with our students. Our interactions with students and communities constitute a moral enterprise, whether we define it as such or not.

Students' and teachers' voices occupy a central place in this book. They complement and illustrate the theoretical analyses and remind us that the interactions between educators and students dramatically affect not only the acquisition of knowledge and skills but also the creation of both students' and teachers' identities. Unfortunately in many classrooms, the curriculum has been sanitized such that opportunities for critical reflection on personal and collective identity and on issues of social justice are minimized. The image of our students and society implied by this pedagogical orientation is an image of compliant consumers who gratefully accept their place within the existing power structure and who can easily be manipulated to exercise their democratic rights to preserve that power structure.

A radically different image is implied by the pedagogical orientations articulated in *Affirming Diversity*. Students are viewed as critical thinkers capable of, and responsible for, creating change through action both in their own lives and in the broader society. Their interactions in school provide opportunities to collaborate across cultural and linguistic boundaries in the generation, interpretation, and application of knowledge. The curriculum orients students toward critical reflection on issues of social justice and identity (both personal and collective).

The image of students and society implied in these educational interactions is that of individuals who have developed respect for both their own cultural identities and the identities of others; who are capable of collaborating with others in the democratic pursuit of social justice; and who see themselves as members of a global community with shared economic, scientific, and environmental interests. As such, the directions highlighted in *Affirming Diversity* respond much more adequately to the challenges of the 21st century than the introverted xenophobic focus of those who argue, explicitly or implicitly, for a monolingual, monocultural education.

The alternative to multicultural education is monocultural education. The history of monocultural education is written in the "certainties" of the Crusades and the Inquisition; the smug brutalities of slavery; the casual eradication of language, culture, and identity in boarding schools inflicted on Native American children; and the contemporary claims of fundamentalist groups, from various religious persuasions, to have exclusive access to ultimate truths. Surely, 9/11 should have brought home to us the destructive power of monocultural, fundamentalist, belief systems. Surely, it should have been a wake-up call to figure out ways of living together in a global context in which cross-cultural contact and population mobility are at an all-time high in human history. Surely, it should have been an urgent reminder that education is a microcosm of the society we hope our students will form. Yet, within our classrooms we see reiterations of *us versus them* (right versus wrong) ideologies, insistence on monocultural certainties as opposed to multicultural inquiry, and frazzled impatience at suggestions that we consider the gap between teaching to the test and education for national and global citizenship. Multicultural education is still as likely to be seen as a threat to fundamental (fundamentalist?) values of our society as it is an invitation to critical self-reflection and dialogue.

Affirming Diversity not only constitutes an eloquent and forceful statement about the importance of multicultural education to our society, it also affirms the central role that individual educators play in nurturing and shaping the lives and identities of our youth. To be a teacher is to be a visionary: As we interact with our students, we envisage what contributions they will play in shaping a better society and we orchestrate our classroom interactions to enable our students to realize these possibilities. This book encourages us to recognize that power relations in the broader society often operate to constrict our vision of what we can achieve with our students. *Affirming Diversity* challenges us to make choices in our classrooms that resist the perpetuation of coercive relations of power. It affords both the insight and inspiration to enable us to create interactions with our students that are respectful, intellectually challenging, and empowering for both them and us.

Affirming Diversity not only opens up a world of ideas and the sharing of experiences but also unlocks an internal switch. It opens a door to dialogue. It is through dialogue that we create understanding and initiate action. As you read this book, talk back to it. As you listen to the experiences and perspectives of the teachers and students who speak from the pages about their educational experiences and the choices they have made, talk back to them about your experiences and choices—those you have made in the past and will make in the future.

Affirming Diversity is both medium and message. The medium of change is dialogue, both internally within ourselves and with our colleagues. Our dialogue, however, must be informed by accurate information. The fact, for example, that NCLB has produced no improvement in students' overall educational progress nor closed the "achievement gap" across social groups, provides a basis for thinking critically about what alternative educational directions might be pursued. *Affirming Diversity* does not supply prescriptions or formulaic solutions, but it does present empirical research and invites us to think and talk about our own identities as educators and the potential and consequences of the choices we make on a daily basis. As such, it represents a powerful source of inspiration, ideas, and solidarity for all of us who see social justice and equity as important core values within our educational systems. *Affirming Diversity* also highlights the fact that our global society can use all of the multilingual and multicultural intelligence it can get. The consequences of squandering the intellectual, linguistic, and cultural resources that our students bring to school can be seen in our domestic prisons, in our battlefields abroad, and in the spiritual malaise that afflicts our society. This book does not provide a map, but it does provide inspiration: It breathes new life into those of us who believe that education is important. If we believe that education is fundamentally a spiritual endeavour rather than just an economic or bureaucratic exercise, then this book points the way.

Jim Cummins
University of Toronto

Bibliography

Cummins, J., Brown, K., and Sayers, D. *Literacy, Technology, and Diversity: Teaching for Success in Changing Times* (Boston: Allyn and Bacon, 2006).

Monroe, J. R., "Standardized Testing in the Lives of ELL Students: A Teacher's Firsthand Account." Available at: www.elladvocates.org/documents/nclb/Monroe_Standardized_Testing_for_ELLs.pdf; accessed November 25, 2006.

Preface

hy students succeed or fail in school has been the subject of much research and debate, particularly for students whose racial, ethnic, linguistic, or social class backgrounds differ from that of the dominant group. In this book, we consider these matters in relation to a comprehensive understanding of multicultural education. Rather than focus only on individual experience or psychological responses to schooling, we explore how societal and educational structures, policies, and practices affect student learning, and we suggest some ways that teachers, individually and collectively, can provide high-quality education in spite of obstacles that may get in the way. That is, we place multicultural education within a broad sociopolitical context that considers not just education but also the social, economic, and political context of the world in which we live.

In this fifth edition of *Affirming Diversity*, we continue to explore such matters as diversity, equity, and equality. We believe they are more significant than ever before, both in our own society and around the globe. Regional wars, the U.S. invasion and subsequent war in Iraq, interethnic and interracial strife here and abroad, global warming, the devastation of the environment—all of these are front-page headlines that cannot be separated from schooling in a democratic society. They call for a different way to interact in the world. At the same time, education around the world is increasingly defined by policies far removed from the daily classroom life of most students and teachers but nevertheless having enormous consequences for teachers, students, and communities. High-stakes testing, a standardization of the curriculum, vouchers, "choice," charter schools, and a marketization of schooling are all having a tremendous impact on public schools.

Given the situation briefly sketched above, we believe teachers and prospective teachers need, more than ever, to understand how the larger societal context affects students, particularly those who are most marginalized in both their schools and in society in general. Why do some students succeed academically while others fail? What do race/ethnicity, social class, language, and other differences have to do with academic success? What is the real significance of the "achievement gap"? How does the societal context influence what happens in your school? Do your school's and your school system's policies and practices exacerbate and perpetuate inequality? Can teachers and other educators turn this situation around? If so, how? *Affirming Diversity* is an attempt to answer these questions—and more—that both new and veteran teachers face every day in increasingly diverse classrooms and in schools that are becoming more bureaucratic and standardized.

ABOUT THIS BOOK

This book explores the meaning, necessity, and benefits of multicultural education for students from all backgrounds through research that explores the following:

- Influences on schooling such as:
  - Racism and other biases and expectations of students' achievement
  - School organization and educational policies and practices
  - Cultural and other differences such as ethnicity, race, gender, language, sexual orientation, and social class
  - The sociopolitical context of schools and society
- A conceptual framework for multicultural education based on that investigation
- Case studies and snapshots—in the words of a selected group of students from a variety of backgrounds—about home, school, and community experiences and about how these have influenced the students' school achievement.

The book presents data on the multicultural nature of schools and society, including information about different cultural groups, their experiences in schools, and the issues and challenges they face. Relevant research on the success or failure of students in schools is also presented.

Affirming Diversity consists of 11 chapters organized in three parts. Part 1 sets the stage for understanding the *sociopolitical context of multicultural education*. In addition, we define the terminology used in the text and we offer a comprehensive definition of multicultural education. Part 2 develops the conceptual framework for multicultural education, emphasizing institutional and cultural factors in schooling and individual and group responses to education. This section explores the multiple forces that may affect the school achievement of students from a variety of backgrounds.

To provide insights into the interrelated roles that discrimination, school policies and practices, and culture play in the education of students in the classroom, we present 16 case studies and 6 snapshots. Incorporated throughout Parts 2 and 3, the case studies and snapshots highlight salient issues discussed in particular chapters, and they provide a concrete means for addressing issues of diversity and success or failure in the schools. We hope that the case studies and snapshots will help you more fully understand the lives and school experiences of a variety of young people who are representative of our nation's growing diversity.

Part 3 focuses on the implications of the case studies and snapshots for teaching and learning in a multicultural society such as ours. We use themes that emerged from our interviews with the students in the case studies and snapshots to emphasize factors that may affect learning for different students. In Chapter 10, three specific curriculum ideas for elementary, middle, and high schools are comprehensively described. These examples embody what the previous chapters have defined as multicultural education, that is, education that affirms diversity, encourages critical thinking, and leads to social justice and action. Chapter 11 offers suggestions for developing environments that foster high-quality education, concentrating on multicultural education as a process. In addition, we propose a model of multicultural education that affirms all students.

Each chapter concludes with (1) a series of problems or situations for you to think about and (2) suggestions for classroom activities and community actions. There are no immediate or easy answers to many of the dilemmas you face with your students every day. The purpose of posing particular problems and proposing activities to address them is to suggest that careful attention needs to be paid to the many manifestations of inequality in our schools and that productive resolutions can be achieved when teachers, students, and parents reflect critically on these problems and work together to solve them.

 # WHAT'S NEW IN THE FIFTH EDITION?

Readers of previous editions will notice many changes in this fifth edition, the most significant of which is that *Affirming Diversity* now has a co-author. In what follows, both Sonia Nieto, the original author, and Patty Bode, the new co-author, will introduce this new change.

SONIA

I first wrote *Affirming Diversity* over 15 years ago and I have been gratified by the enormous and generous response of readers to the text through its first four editions. Because it has been the basis for much of my work in the profession, as well as my visibility in the field, *Affirming Diversity* has had a huge impact on my own life. It is, therefore, a book that is close to my heart. Because I am committed to continuing it, I decided a number of years ago to find a colleague who might become my co-author for this and subsequent editions, someone who would keep the spirit of the book alive for many years to come. From the moment I made this decision, it was clear that Patty Bode would be the perfect person for the job.

An artist, researcher, and teacher, Patty is currently a faculty member and Director of Art Education at Tufts University in affiliation with the School of the Museum of Fine Arts, Boston. Before that, she was an art teacher for over 15 years in public elementary and middle schools. She and I have known one another for many years, first when she was a master's, and later, a doctoral student in my program. I was fortunate to be her advisor both times. We have become close friends and colleagues, and our families have also become close over the years. Patty and I have worked together on many projects, including the fourth edition of *Affirming Diversity*, for which she provided all the children's artwork, among other contributions.

She is widely respected in both the multicultural education and art education arenas and has brought her artistic eye, critical mind, and passion for social justice to this edition, as she does to everything. I am thrilled that she has joined me in keeping *Affirming Diversity* fresh, timely, and relevant to our times.

PATTY

The first four editions of *Affirming Diversity* played a transformative role in my research, teaching, and worldview. I am honored to be part of this fifth edition and am eternally grateful to Sonia for inviting me to participate in the continual metamorphosis of the book. Through the work on the text, I see students calling out for teachers who can cross racial, cultural, and social class borders and who can overcome curriculum constraints and resist bureaucratic expectations to create meaningful, high-achieving learning communities. As a teacher, I recognize the struggle that arises from competing messages from academic, political, and popular culture about what counts as knowledge and what defines teaching. The vision we assert in this book hopes to activate antiracist critical pedagogy in classrooms. For all students and their families and teachers, I hope that this new edition of *Affirming Diversity* contributes to creating change.

CHANGES IN THE TEXT

A New Structure   A major change we have made in the text is the addition of two new chapters, which also necessitated a change in the structure of the text. Based on feedback from reviewers and instructors who have used the book over the years, we decided to add a chapter defining what we mean by the *sociopolitical context of education*, since this concept provides the foundation for the entire book. This is now Chapter 1, followed by a chapter on terminology, as before. Part 1 closes with Chapter 3 (formerly Chapter 9), Multicultural Education and School Reform, where we define *multicultural education*. We thought it made sense to bring together in one place all three chapters that concern defining the parameters of diversity and multicultural education.

New Curricular Adaptations   Chapter 10, Adapting the Curriculum for Multicultural Classrooms, is the other new chapter. Many readers have asked us for more concrete examples of multicultural education in the classroom. The models and units presented include: (1) studying "the other" by focusing on specific cultures and geographic regions in a curriculum unit called *Cambodia and the Cambodian American Experience*; (2) changing structures for more equitable curriculum in a curriculum unit called *Transforming Pedagogy by Detracking Math*; (3) designing a social justice thematic approach and a related curriculum unit called *Expanding Definitions of Family*. A fourth unit can be found on the Companion Website at www.ablongman.com/nieto5e with art and additional interactive materials. That unit focuses on responding to current events and institutional racism in a unit called *Hurricane Katrina and the Opportunity for Change*.

A New Feature   To provide even more specific applications for classrooms and schools, we have integrated the former Chapter 11 (Multicultural Education in Practice) into the chapters in Parts 2 and 3 of the text. To do so, we have created a new feature, "What You Can Do," that expands the suggestions in the previous editions for classroom, school, and community action projects and research ideas.

New Case Studies and Snapshots   A third major change is the addition of new case studies and snapshots. Given the rapidly changing demographics and realities of young people and their families, we thought it was important to include case studies and snapshots of current students whose lives are quite different from the lives of their peers of even just a decade ago. New case studies include those of Latrell Elton, an African American student from Atlanta (following Chapter 8); Rashaud Kates, an African American student from a mid-size city in Georgia (following Chapter 4); Yahaira León, a Puerto Rican/Dominican student currently living in Philadelphia (following Chapter 6); Alicia Montejo, a Mexican American student from Colorado (following Chapter 7); Christina Kamau, a Kenyan immigrant living in the Midwest (following Chapter 9); and Savoun Nouch, a Cambodian American student most recently from Providence, Rhode Island, who attended schools in California for most of his life (following Chapter 9). The case studies they have replaced will now be on a Web page especially created for the text: **www.ablongman.com/nieto5e.** The Web page will include not only previous cases but also the updates (formerly included in the book's epilogue) on students we have highlighted in previous editions. We hope you will take advantage of this new feature and use it to view some of the older case studies and catch up with where the students, now all adults, are in their lives.

In addition to the new case studies, the text includes two new snapshots, shorter versions of case studies, that are found throughout the text: Nini Rostland, a biracial Black South African/White American young woman living in Iowa (in Chapter 8), and Eugene Crocket, a young man who was adopted by two gay dads attending school in a mid-size town in New England (in Chapter 10).

SUPPLEMENTS

Instructor's Manual   The manual contains a sample syllabus, course suggestions, an overview of MyLabSchool, and for each chapter: Overview, Problem Posing, Response Journal Prompts, Whole Class/Group Work assignments, Student as Teacher assignments, a Critical Pedagogy in Action assignment, instructions for projects to be included in student portfolios and used as assessments, handouts to accompany all assignments, essay questions, and annotated video and book resources. Instructors may request the IM from their local Allyn and Bacon representatives. It is available in print or easy download from Allyn and Bacon' Instructor's Resource Center at **www.ablongman.com/irc.**

PowerPoint™ Presentation   Instructors may also download book-specific PowerPoint slides from the Instructor Resource Center at **www.ablongman.com/irc.**

They outline the key points of each chapter, and are customizable so that professors may add or delete material as they see fit. Your local representative can provide a password and instructions for using the IRC.

Companion Website   Students and instructors may access the text's Companion Web site at **www.ablongman.com/nieto5e** for chapter Summaries, Learning Objectives, concept cards, Internet Resources (Web links), Critical Thinking Scenarios, and follow-up material related to the text's Case Studies and Snapshots. The book's glossary, appendix, and an additional curriculum model to supplement Chapter 10 also appear in PDF on the site.

mylabschool Where the classroom comes to life!   Allyn and Bacon's teacher education website at **www.mylabschool.com** contains a collection of tools to expand students' course knowledge and to help prepare them for licensure exams and their teaching careers. Instructors may choose to order access codes to this website packaged with this book at no additional cost, or students may choose to purchase access on their own. The site includes video clips from real classrooms that include annotations and reflection questions; an extensive archive of text and multimedia cases that provide valuable perspectives on real classrooms and real teaching challenges; Allyn and Bacon's Lesson and Portfolio Builder application, which includes an integrated state standards correlation tool; research paper guidelines in Research Navigator™, which provides access to three exclusive databases of credible and reliable source material, including EBSCO's ContentSelect Academic Journal Database, *New York Times* Search by Subject Archive, and Link Library. MyLabSchool also includes a *Careers* section with resources for Praxis exams and licensure preparation, professional portfolio development, job searches, and interview techniques.

ACKNOWLEDGMENTS

We are deeply appreciative of the many individuals who have helped us with the fifth edition of *Affirming Diversity*. We are particularly indebted to the students and families who participated in the interviews for the case studies and snapshots; their voices anchor the work of this book. For their dedicated research assistance and overall commitment to the mission of the book, we thank Kathryn C. Boelter and Rachel Ilana Shuman. We also thank Ruth Harman for her heartfelt dedication and research assistance with collection of data and statistics. For help with interviews of young people for the new case studies and snapshots we are most grateful to the interviewers. Carlie Tartakov has been an active contributor since the first edition of the book. She is responsible for thorough and compelling interviews of four participants, two of whom are new to this edition. John Raible has contributed three thoughtful interviews; two in the fourth edition and a new one for this edition. More insights and rich interviews for this edition were contributed by Keonilrath Bun, Jason Irizarry, Stephanie Schmidt, and Vera Stenhouse. In addition, Carlie Tartakov, Diane Sweet, and Paula Elliott were able to locate and reinterview the young people they first interviewed more than a decade ago; these updates are on the accompanying Web page. We are indebted to Linda Howard, Fern Sherman, Nadia Bara, and Avi Abramson for taking the time to let us know how they are doing after all these years.

We are grateful to Kristen French, who wrote the Instructor's Resource Manual, a guide characterized by both a critical edge and helpful pedagogical suggestions.

We also thank the teachers who submitted their students' artwork that appears on the cover and at the opening of some parts and some chapters: Liz Brennan, Layla Cady, Kristen DiMenno, Tara Farley, Rosalie Sidoti-Iacono, Josie Kealty, Julie Sawyer, Ben Sears, Rachel Shuman, Allyson Simes, and Gina Simm. We deeply appreciate the talent and generosity of the students who allowed us to reproduce their art. We are also indebted to the professional artists who contributed their artwork: Sezin Aksoy, Michael E. Coblyn, Winston Chmielinski, and Julia Katz. Their art informs each section and emphasizes the role of visual culture in multicultural education.

Professional colleagues who have read and commented on the various iterations of this text have helped to strengthen it, and we are thankful to all of them. For this fifth edition, we thank the following reviewers: Yolanda Abel, Johns Hopkins University; Heewon Chang, Eastern University; Diana Ciesko, Valencia Community College; Marta Cronin, Indian River Community College; Heather W. Hackman, Saint Cloud State University; Sumi Hagiwara, Montclair State University; Margaret King, Ohio University; Gale Seiler, University of Maryland, Baltimore.

Their detailed comments and suggestions for improving the book were enormously helpful. We know that the fifth edition is better as a result.

At Allyn and Bacon, we are grateful for the support and encouragement we received from our editor, Kelly Villella Canton, and our development editor, Christien Shangraw. They were a joy to work with, and we have appreciated their support and encouragement throughout this process.

Once again, we owe a heartfelt thank you to Jim Cummins, a scholar of rare genius and a wonderful friend, for writing the inspiring foreword to this fifth edition. Jim has been a consistent and enthusiastic supporter of this book for many years. His willingness to write the foreword for this fifth edition means a great deal to us.

We would not be where we are without our families. Sonia particularly wants to acknowledge Angel, her partner of 40 years, for his unconditional love and support, and her daughters Alicia and Marisa for teaching her how to be a mother. Her grandchildren—Jazmyne, Corissa, Terrance, Monique, Tatiana, Celsito, Aliya, Clarita, Lucia, and Mariya—are a source of joy and inspiration.

Patty wants to thank Mark, her life partner, for his love, humor, and encouragement, and her sons, Bob, Ryan, and Keo for revealing the adventures of life's ongoing journey. Her parents, George and Joann Bode, were her first teachers and continue to provide loving guidance.

S.N., P.B.

PART 1

SETTING THE STAGE
Multicultural Education Within a Sociopolitical Context

"At its best, multiculturalism is an ongoing process of questioning, revising, and struggling to create greater equity in every nook and cranny of school life . . . It is a fight for economic and social justice. . . . Such a perspective is not simply about explaining society, it is about changing it."

—Rethinking Schools
15, no. 1 (Fall 2000)

To set the stage for understanding multicultural education within a broad societal context, and to help you think about the implications of this context for students of diverse backgrounds, the three chapters in Part 1 introduce a number of foundational concepts. In Chapter 1 we describe key assumptions that undergird this text and define what we mean by the *sociopolitical context of education*. Chapter 1 also introduces other fundamental definitions and parameters of multicultural education and then presents demographic data about both the general population and the population in U.S. schools, with implications of these data for education. We briefly describe a key approach we have employed in this text, namely, the use of *case studies* and *snapshots* that reflect some of the tremendous diversity that currently exists in our schools.

In Chapter 2 we discuss terminology—the names used to describe people, which are of major significance in multicultural education—and we explain some of our choices in terminology.

Using the discussion in Chapters 1 and 2 as a foundation, Chapter 3 defines *multicultural education* and describes its essential components. Because we view multicultural education as far more than simply altering the curriculum to reflect more Brown and Black faces or adding assembly programs on diversity, Chapter 3 provides examples of what we mean by a *critical* multicultural perspective.

Student artists from Malden High School, Malden, Massachusetts, as they appear in the photography portraits on page 1: Shinichi Harimoto, Tina Chen, Jessica Chan, Antonio Antenor, Elsa Basile, Janie Do, Loan Nguyen, Adrian Aquino, Darren Jones, Dominika Hudcova, Chelsea Choate, Leonardo Fonseca, Ming Tseng, Sardi Pronja, Rassan Charles, Ariel Lefkovith, Jennifer Tran, Crystal Pray, Marc Manson-Hing, Sara Veliz, Karen Chen, Pearl Chan, Lina Lui, Rubia Iwano, Toa Rivera, Katelyn Cody, Sandra Wong, Lauren Hastings, Erica Femino, Tiffany Cabral, Joel Kayima, Cassie McIver. Photos and design by art teachers: Alison Fine, Rosalie Iacono-Sidoti, Kristen DiMenno.

Understanding the Sociopolitical Context of Multicultural Education

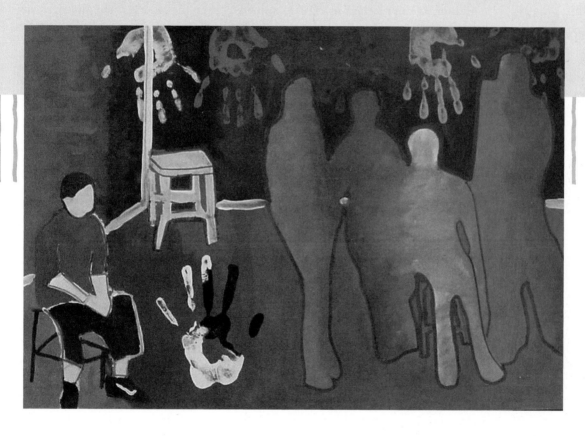

Elena Cutting and Niroshan Amarsiriwardena in Tara Farley's art class, *Collaborative poetry painting*. Tempera, 2005.

"As a nation, we have been counting on education to solve the problems of unemployment, joblessness, and poverty for many years. But education did not cause these problems, and education cannot solve them. An economic system that chases profits and casts people aside (especially people of color) is culpable."

— *Jean Anyon,*
Radical Possibilities, 2005

Decisions made about education are often viewed as if they were politically neutral. Yet, as we hope to make clear in this chapter and throughout the text, such decisions are never politically neutral. Rather, they are tied to the social, political, and economic structures that frame and define our society. The *sociopolitical context* of society includes laws, regulations, policies, practices, traditions, and ideologies.

To put it another way, multicultural education, or any kind of education for that matter, cannot be understood in a vacuum. Yet in many schools, multicultural education is approached as if it is divorced from the policies and practices of schools and from the structures and ideologies of society. This kind of thinking results in a singular focus on cultural artifacts, such as food and dress, or on ethnic celebrations. It can become "fairyland" multicultural education, disassociated from the lives of teachers, students, and communities. This is multicultural education *without* a sociopolitical context. In this book, however, we are interested in how the sociopolitical context of the United States, and indeed of our global society, shapes schools and therefore also shapes the experiences of the children and adults who inhabit schools.

ASSUMPTIONS UNDERLYING THIS TEXT

It is important that we begin by clarifying a number of assumptions underlying the concepts described in this book.

IDENTITY, DIFFERENCE, POWER, AND PRIVILEGE ARE ALL CONNECTED

Race, ethnicity, social class, language use, gender, sexual orientation, religion, ability, and other social and human differences are a major aspect of the sociopolitical context that we will address in this book—that is, one's identity frames (although it does not necessarily *determine*) how one experiences the world. Identities always carry some baggage; they are perceived in particular ways by a society and by individuals within that society. An accent, for instance, may invoke positive or negative images, depending on one's social class, race, country of origin, and variety of language. As a consequence, in the context of U.S. society, someone who is French and speaks with a Parisian accent, for example, is generally viewed more positively than someone from Senegal who also speaks French.

At the same time, multicultural education does not simply involve the affirmation of language and culture. Multicultural education confronts not only issues of difference but also issues of power and privilege in society. This means challenging racism and other biases as well as the inequitable structures, policies, and practices of schools and, ultimately, of society itself. Affirming language and culture can help students become successful and well-adjusted learners, but unless language and cultural issues are viewed critically through the lens of equity and social justice, they are unlikely to have a lasting impact in promoting real change.

Educational failure is an issue too complex and knotty to be "fixed" by any single program or approach. Viewing multicultural education per se as "the answer" to school failure is simplistic because other important social and educational issues that affect the lives of students are thereby ignored. Multicultural education does not exist in a vacuum but must be understood in its larger personal, social, historical, and political context. However, if it is broadly conceptualized and implemented, multicultural education can have a substantive, positive impact on the education of most students. To be effective, multicultural education needs to move beyond diversity as a passing fad. It needs to take into account our history of immigration as well as the social, political, and economic inequality and exclusion that have characterized our past and present, particularly our educational history. These issues are too often ignored in superficial approaches to multicultural education.

MULTICULTURAL EDUCATION IS INCLUSIVE OF MANY DIFFERENCES

Another key issue in multicultural education is the groups that are included. This book's framework and approach to multicultural education are broadly inclusive: They are based on the belief that multicultural education is for *everyone* regardless of ethnicity, race, language, social class, religion, gender, sexual orientation, ability, or other differences. One book, however, cannot possibly give all of these topics the central importance they deserve. This book uses race, ethnicity, and language as the major lenses to view and understand multicultural education. While we address other differences in one way or another, we give special emphasis to these. Both multicultural and bilingual education were direct outgrowths of the civil rights movement, and they developed in response to racism, ethnocentrism, and language discrimination in education. These inequities continue to exist, especially for American Indian, Latino, and African American youngsters, and they are central to this book's perspective and approach.

Nevertheless, we believe that multicultural education includes everyone, and we have made an attempt in this text to be inclusive of many differences. Having a broad definition of multicultural education raises another dilemma. One reason that multicultural education is such a challenging topic for some educators is that they have a hard time facing and discussing racism. For example, whenever we bring up racism with a group of predominantly White teachers, we find that too often they want to move on immediately to, say, sexism or classism without spending much time on racism. Sexism and classism are certainly worthy of study and attention—in fact, they must be part of a multicultural agenda—but the discomfort of many White teachers in talking about racism is very evident. Racism is an excruciatingly difficult issue for many people. Given our nation's history of exclusion and discrimination, this is not surprising, but it is only through a thorough exploration of discrimination based on race that we can understand the genesis as well as the rationale for a more inclusive framework for multicultural education that includes language, social class, sexual orientation, gender, ethnicity, religion, and other differences.

TEACHERS ARE NOT THE VILLAINS

Another belief that informs this book's perspective and approach is that teachers cannot be singled out as the villains responsible for students' failure. Although some teachers bear responsibility for having low expectations because they are racist and elitist in their interactions with students and parents and thus provide educational environments that discourage many students from learning, most do not do this consciously. Most teachers are sincerely concerned about their students and want very much to provide them with the best education possible. Nonetheless, because of their own limited experiences and education, they may know very little about the students they teach. As a result, their beliefs about students of diverse backgrounds may be based on spurious assumptions and stereotypes. These things are true of all teachers, not just White teachers. In fact, a teacher's being from a non-White ethnic group or background does not guarantee that he or she will be effective with students of diverse backgrounds or even with students of his or her own background. Furthermore, teachers are often at the mercy of decisions made by others far removed from the classroom; they generally have little involvement in developing the policies and practices of their schools and frequently do not even question them.

Teachers also are the products of educational systems that have a history of racism, exclusion, and debilitating pedagogy. As a consequence, their practices may reflect their experiences, and they may unwittingly perpetuate policies and approaches that are harmful to many of their students. We cannot separate schools from the communities they serve or from the context of society in general. Oppressive forces that limit opportunities in the schools reflect such forces in the society at large. The purpose of this book is not to point a finger, but to provide a forum for reflection and discussion so that teachers take responsibility for their own actions, challenge the actions of schools and society that affect their students' education, and help bring about positive change.

QUALITY PUBLIC EDUCATION IS A CAUSE WORTH FIGHTING FOR

Another key assumption of this book is that public education is worth defending and fighting for. In spite of all its shortcomings, and although it has never lived up to its potential, public education remains a noble ideal because it is one of the few institutions that at least articulates the common good, if not always achieves it. Public education remains the last and best hope for many young people for a better life. Yet, during an era characterized by rigid standardization and restructuring, the public schools have often been a target of scorn and disrespect in the press and among politicians. In spite of this, the public still believes in the promise of public education. A study published by the Public Education Network and *Education Week* reported the finding that Americans are at least five times more likely to cite public schools (rather than places of worship, hospitals, or libraries) as the most important institutions in their communities. Moreover, more than 90 percent of the people polled maintained that a quality public education is every child's birthright, and the great majority claimed that education is their greatest priority.[1] Given this unambiguous and overwhelming support for public education, it is clear that public schools can provide all children with a good education and it is within the ability of teachers, administrators, and the public at large to ensure that they do so.

DEFINING THE SOCIOPOLITICAL CONTEXT OF MULTICULTURAL EDUCATION

Now that we have explained some of the assumptions underlying this text, we want to define what we mean by the *sociopolitical context of education*. As you will see in the remainder of this chapter, understanding this term is crucial to a critical view of multicultural education. A significant aspect of the sociopolitical context concerns the unexamined ideologies and myths that shape commonly accepted ideas and values in a society. The chapter provides a number of examples of how unexamined ideologies and myths contribute to the sociopolitical context.

MYTHS ABOUT IMMIGRATION AND DIFFERENCE

Because immigration is one of today's most contentious issues, it offers a particularly vivid example of the sociopolitical context. Immigration is no longer a romantic phenomenon of the past: Current headlines and other media reports scream about "illegal aliens," about electric fences along the U.S.–Mexico border, and about the self-appointed vigilante Minutemen adamant on guarding our borders, albeit illegally. The United States is not just a nation of past immigrants, often romantically portrayed, but also a nation of new immigrants who daily disembark on our shores, cross our borders, or fly into our metropolitan areas. For the most part, new immigrants, particularly those from Latin America, Asia, and Africa, are neither warmly welcomed nor given easy access to the resources in the United States. While we define ourselves as "a nation of immigrants," there is waning support for new immigrants.

Myths about U.S. immigration die hard. Even the widely accepted fact that immigrants came to North America and never returned to their countries of origin is not entirely true. According to Irving Howe, one-third of European immigrants who came to the United States between 1908 and 1924 eventually made their way back home, thus shattering a popular myth.[2] In addition, and in spite of conventional wisdom to the contrary, most European immigrants did *not* succeed academically. In his research, Richard Rothstein found that during the immigration period from 1880 to 1915, few Americans succeeded in school, least of all immigrants; immigrants of all backgrounds did poorly. Instead, it was the children and grandchildren of European immigrants who fared well in school, but the myth that first-generation immigrants "made it," at least in terms of academics, is firmly established in the public psyche. Because schools have traditionally perceived their role as that of an assimilating agent, the isolation, rejection, and failure that have frequently accompanied immigration have simply been left at the schoolhouse door.

U.S. history is also steeped in slavery and conquest. Millions of descendants of Africans, American Indians, Mexicans, Puerto Ricans, and others colonized within and beyond U.S. borders have experienced political and economic oppression and, in schools, disparagement of their native cultures and languages. But the history of racism and exploitation experienced by so many of our people, including their children, is rarely taught. Instead, conventional curricula and pedagogy have been based on the myth of a painless and smooth assimilation of immigrants.

The research reported in this book suggests that we need to make the history of all groups visible by making it part of the curriculum, instruction, and schooling in general. The words of the students in the case studies and snapshots included in this book provide eloquent testimony for the need to do so. For instance, Manuel Gomes, the young man who is the subject of one of the case studies that follow Chapter 7, claimed that he "[could not] be an American" because it would mean forsaking his Cape Verdean background. Vanessa Mattison, a young woman fiercely devoted to social justice and equality but with little awareness of the United States' history of racism and inequity, knew nothing about her European American past and even felt uncomfortable discussing it. Vanessa's case study follows Chapter 4. James Karam, whose case study is at the end of Chapter 6, is a Lebanese Christian student whose culture was totally missing in the school's curriculum and extracurricular activities. James learned to appreciate any references to his background, even if negative. In light of the racial and ethnic profiling that has increased since September 11, 2001, it is clear that such invisibility is no longer acceptable, if indeed it ever was.

Immigration and colonization experiences are a significant point of departure for our journey into multicultural education. This journey needs to begin with teachers, who themselves are frequently unaware of or uncomfortable with their own ethnicity. By reconnecting with their own backgrounds and with the suffering as well as the triumphs of their families, teachers can lay the groundwork for students to reclaim their histories and voices. This book invites you to begin the journey.

EDUCATIONAL STRUCTURES

The ideologies underlying educational structures exemplify how the sociopolitical context is operational at the school level. Schools' and the larger society's assumptions about people form a belief system that helps create and perpetuate structures that reproduce those assumptions. For example, if we believe that intelligence is primarily inherited, we will design schools that support this belief. On the other hand, if we believe that intelligence is largely created by particular social and economic conditions, our schools will look quite different. Likewise, if we believe that some cultures are inherently superior to others, our schools will replicate the cultural values that are assumed to be superior while dismissing others.

At a personal level, we take in the ideologies and beliefs in our society and we act on them *whether we actively believe them or not.* In the case of the ideology of racism, for example, Beverly Daniel Tatum has aptly described it as "smog in the air."

Sometimes it is so thick it is visible, other times it is less apparent, but always, day in and day out, we are breathing it in. None of us would introduce ourselves as "smog-breathers" (and most of us don't want to be described as prejudiced), but if we live in a smoggy place, how can we avoid breathing the air?[3]

The "smog" is part of the sociopolitical context in which we live and in which schools exist. This context includes not only racism but also other biases based on human and social differences, including social class, language, sexual orientation, gender, and other factors. Pretending that the smog doesn't exist, or that it doesn't influence us, is to negate reality. A good example can be found in school funding: In their yearly report on funding of public schools, the Education Trust has consistently shown that low-income students and students of color are badly shortchanged by most states, proving once again that race and social class still matter a great deal in our nation. In their 2005 report, the Trust found that in the United States, as a whole, we spend $900 a year *less* on each student in public school districts with the largest number of poor students.[4] In another investigation, the *Christian Science Monitor* found that the difference in annual spending between the wealthiest and the poorest school districts has grown to a staggering $19,361 per student.[5] Surely, no one can pretend that this difference does not matter.

School-Level Policies and Practices   School funding is generally a state- and district-level issue. How does the sociopolitical context affect policies and practices at the school level? Let's take a very concrete example: Schools that enforce an "English-only" policy are, willingly or not, sending students a message about the status and importance of languages other than English. In some of these schools, students are forbidden to speak their native language not only in classrooms, but even in halls, the cafeteria, and the playground. To students who speak a language other than English, the message is clear: Your language is not welcome here; it is less important than English. While the policy may have been well intentioned and created out of a sincere effort to help students learn English, the result is deprecation of students' identities, intentional or not. In some instances, these kinds of policies are not innocent at all, but instead reflect a xenophobic reaction to hearing languages other than English in our midst. In either case, the result is negative and an example of how ideologies help create structures that benefit some students over others.

Another obvious example is the curriculum: If the content of school knowledge excludes the history, art, culture, and ways of knowing of entire groups of people, these groups themselves are dismissed as having little significance in creating history, art, culture, and so on. The sociopolitical context also undergirds other school policies and practices, including pedagogy, ability grouping, testing, parent outreach, disciplinary policies, and the hiring of teachers and other school personnel. We return to this issue in Chapter 5.

To correct the educational short-changing of diverse student populations, the curriculum and pedagogy must be changed in individual classrooms. But on a broader level, changes must go beyond the classroom: Schools' policies and practices and the societal ideologies that support them must also be confronted and transformed. That is, we need to create not only *affirming classrooms* but also an *affirming society* in which racism, sexism, social class discrimination, heterosexism, and other biases are no longer acceptable. This is a tall order, but if multicultural education is to make a real difference, working to change society to be more socially equitable and just must go hand-in-hand with changes in curricula and classroom practices.

GOALS OF MULTICULTURAL EDUCATION

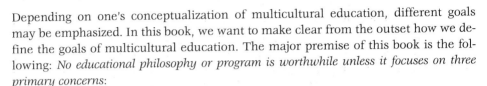

Depending on one's conceptualization of multicultural education, different goals may be emphasized. In this book, we want to make clear from the outset how we define the goals of multicultural education. The major premise of this book is the following: *No educational philosophy or program is worthwhile unless it focuses on three primary concerns*:

- Tackling inequality and promoting access to an equal education
- Raising the achievement of all students and providing them with an equitable and high-quality education
- Giving students an apprenticeship in the opportunity to become critical and productive members of a democratic society

We believe that multicultural education must *confront inequality and stratification in schools and in society*. Helping students get along, teaching them to feel better about themselves, and "sensitizing" them to one another are worthy goals of good educational practice, including multicultural education. But if multicultural education does not tackle the far more thorny questions of stratification and inequity, and if viewed in isolation from the reality of students' lives, these goals can turn into superficial strategies that only scratch the surface of educational failure. Simply wanting our students to get along with and be respectful of one another makes little difference in the options they will have as a result of their schooling. Students' lives are inexorably affected by economic, social, and political conditions in schools and society—that is, by the sociopolitical context in which they live and learn—and this means that we need to consider these conditions in our conceptualization and implementation of multicultural education.

Learning is an equally central goal of multicultural education. Unless learning is at the very core of a multicultural perspective, having "feel-good" assemblies or self-concept–building classroom activities will do nothing to create equitable school environments for students. Considering the vastly unequal learning outcomes among students of different backgrounds (see the subsequent discussion of the "achievement gap" in this chapter), it is absolutely essential that learning be placed at the center of multicultural education. Otherwise, too many young people will continue to face harrowing life choices because they are not receiving a high-quality, rigorous education.

Learning to take tests or getting into a good university cannot be the be-all and end-all of an excellent education. A third and equally crucial goal of multicultural education is to *promote democracy by preparing students to contribute to the general well-being of society, not only to their own self-interests*. Multicultural educator Will Kymlicka has expressed this sentiment in the following way: "We need to continually remind ourselves that multiculturalism is not just about expanding individual horizons, or increasing personal intercultural skills, but is part of a larger project of justice and equality."[6]

DEFINING KEY TERMS IN MULTICULTURAL EDUCATION

We now turn to some central definitions that help explain the approach we use in this book.

EQUAL EDUCATION AND EQUITABLE EDUCATION: WHAT'S THE DIFFERENCE?

Two terms often associated with multicultural education are *equality* and *equity*, which are sometimes erroneously used interchangeably. Both equal education and educational equity are fundamental to multicultural education, yet they are quite different. As educator Enid Lee has explained, "Equity is the process; equality is the result."[7] That is, *equal education* may mean simply providing the same resources and opportunities for all students. While this alone would afford a better education for a wider range of students than is currently the case, it is not enough. Achieving educational equality involves providing an *equitable education*. *Equity* goes beyond equality: It means that all students must be given the *real possibility of an equality of outcomes*. A high-quality education is impossible without a focus on equity. Robert Moses, who began the highly successful Algebra Project, which promotes high-level math courses for Urban Black and Latino middle school and high school students, has gone so far as to suggest that quality education for all students is a civil rights issue.[8]

SOCIAL JUSTICE

Frequently invoked but rarely defined, *social justice* is another term associated with an equitable education. In this book, we define it as *a philosophy, an approach, and actions that embody treating all people with fairness, respect, dignity, and generosity*. On a societal scale, this means affording each person the real—not simply a stated or codified—opportunity to achieve their potential by giving them access to the goods, services, and social and cultural capital of a society, while also affirming the culture and talents of each individual and the group or groups with which they identify.

In terms of education, in particular, social justice is not just about "being nice" to students, or about giving them a pat on the back. Social justice in education includes four components. First, it challenges, confronts, and disrupts misconceptions, untruths, and stereotypes that lead to structural inequality and discrimination based on race, social class, gender, and other social and human differences. This means that teachers with a social justice perspective consciously include topics that focus on inequality in the curriculum, and they encourage their students to work for equality and fairness both in and out of the classroom.

Second, a social justice perspective means providing all students with the resources necessary to learn to their full potential. This includes *material resources* such as books, curriculum, financial support, and so on. Equally vital are *emotional resources* such as a belief in all students' ability and worth; care for them as individuals and learners; high expectations and rigorous demands of them; and the necessary social and cultural capital to negotiate the world. These are not just responsibilities of individual teachers and schools, however. Beyond the classroom level, achieving social justice requires reforming school policies and practices so that all students are provided an equal chance to learn. This entails critically evaluating policies such as high-stakes testing, tracking, student retention, segregation, and parent and family outreach, among others.

Social justice in education is not just about *giving* students resources, however. A third component of a social justice perspective is *drawing on* the talents and strengths that students bring to their education. This requires a rejection of the deficit perspective that has characterized much of the education of marginalized students, to a shift that views all students—not just those from privileged backgrounds—as having resources that can be a foundation for their learning. These resources include their languages, cultures, and experiences.

A fourth essential component of social justice is creating a learning environment that promotes critical thinking and supports agency for social change. Creating such environments can provide students with an apprenticeship in democracy, a vital part of preparing them for the future. Much more will be said throughout the text about how to go about creating such a learning environment.

THE "ACHIEVEMENT GAP"

Another term that needs defining is *achievement gap*. This term has evolved over the past couple of decades to describe the circumstances in which some students, primarily those from racially, culturally, and linguistically marginalized and poor families, achieve less than other students. Although research has largely focused on Black and White students, the "achievement gap" is also evident among students of other ethnic and racial backgrounds.[9]

There is no denying that the "achievement gap" is real: In 2006, *Quality Counts*, the tenth annual report on the results of standards-based education, examined scores on the National Assessment of Educational Progress (NAEP) from 1992 through 2005. The report concluded that although student achievement in general had improved, the gap between African American and Hispanic students compared to White students remains very large. Specifically, the gap is the equivalent of two grade levels or more, almost what it was in 1992. For example, while 41 percent of Whites are reading at grade level, only 15 percent of Hispanics and 13 percent of African Americans are at grade level. The gap worsens through the years: Black and Hispanic 12th graders perform at the same level in reading and math as White eighth graders.[10] The gap is not only deplorable but is also an indictment of our public education system.

However, in spite of the fact that the "achievement gap" is a reality, some-times this term is a misnomer because it places undue responsibility on students alone. As a result, we believe that what has become known as the *achievement gap* can also appropriately be called the *resource gap* or the *expectations gap* because student achievement does not come out of the blue but is influenced by many other factors—that is, student achievement is related directly to the conditions and contexts in which students learn. For instance, because some schools are well en-dowed in terms of materials and resources, the students in these schools have mul-tiple means to help them learn. On the other hand, schools that serve students living in poverty, which tend to have fewer resources, provide fewer opportuni-ties for robust student learning.

Of course, material resources alone are not the answer to the problem of achievement. The expectations that teachers and schools have of students are also important, and these unfortunately are sometimes related to students' racial and so-cial class backgrounds. Educator Mano Singham has cited research that concludes that the impact of teacher expectations is *three times greater* for Black and Latino stu-dents than for White students.[11] This too is part of the sociopolitical context of the "achievement gap."

The problem with the term "achievement gap" is that it suggests that students alone are responsible for their learning, as if school and societal conditions and con-texts did not exist. The result is that the problem is defined as a "minority" problem rather than as a problem of unequal schooling. For all these reasons, we use the term *achievement gap* with caution and always in quotation marks.

At the same time, the research on the "achievement gap" cannot be ignored, be-cause it has uncovered salient differences in the learning outcomes for students of various backgrounds. According to Joseph D'Amico, the two major causes of the "achievement gap" are *sociocultural and school-related factors*. Sociocultural factors in-clude poverty, ethnicity, low level of parental education, weak family-support sys-tems, and students' reactions to discrimination and stereotyping.[12] One school-related factor is low expectations, particularly in schools that serve students who are both economically disadvantaged and from ethnic and racial minority back-grounds. A common response among educators and the public has been to focus on the first set of factors (that is, on sociocultural "problems" and "deficits") more than on school-related factors. Turning this thinking around would be a better policy be-cause educators can do little to change the life circumstances of students but can do a great deal to change the context of schools.

For example, according to D'Amico, some schools are successful with students of color, students living in poverty, and students who live in difficult circumstances. What makes the difference? Schools that have narrowed the "achievement gap" are characterized by well-trained and motivated teachers who are teaching in their sub-ject area; a curriculum that is culturally sensitive, challenging, and consistent with high academic standards; and a school culture that reflects a focus on high academic achievement among all students.[13]

Addressing school-related issues alone, however, will not completely do away with the "achievement gap" because poverty plays a large part in the differential learning of students. Recently, this argument has been made convincingly by several noted scholars, including Jean Anyon, who cites a wealth of research and other data to come to the following chilling conclusion:

> Thus, in my view, low-achieving urban schools are not primarily a consequence of failed educational policy, or urban family dynamics, as mainstream analysts and public policies typically imply. Failing public schools in cities are, rather, a logical consequence of the U.S. macroeconomy—and the federal and regional policies and practices that support it.[14]

Likewise, in a comprehensively researched article on the effects of poverty on learning and achievement, David Berliner makes the argument that poverty *alone* places severe limits on what can be accomplished through educational reform efforts, especially those associated with the No Child Left Behind legislation.[15] His conclusion is that the most powerful policy for improving our nation's school achievement would be a reduction in family and youth poverty.

The suggestion that poverty and other social ills negatively affect learning is unsettling and a reminder that schools alone cannot tackle the inequality and stratification that exist in society. Richard Rothstein, an economist who has studied this issue extensively, has suggested that school reform efforts alone will not turn things around. He advocates three approaches that must be pursued if progress is to be made in narrowing the "achievement gap": promoting school improvement efforts that raise the quality of instruction; giving more attention to out-of-school hours by implementing early childhood, after-school, and summer programs; and implementing policies that would provide appropriate health services and stable housing and narrow the growing income inequalities in our society. He contends that only by implementing all these measures would poor children be better prepared for school.[16]

Although it is true that the "achievement gap" is strongly related to poverty, race and ethnicity are also prominent issues to consider in understanding the gap. Joseph D'Amico found that the gap may be even greater among students of color with *high* socioeconomic status. In addition, he found that although the "achievement gap" between Black and White students was reduced by about half between 1970 and 1988, there has been a marked reversal of this trend since 1988.[17]

Perhaps the most dramatic example of the "achievement gap" can be found in high school dropout rates. Researcher Gary Orfield has cited a few hundred high schools in the nation—all overwhelmingly "minority," low income, and located in urban centers—where the dropout rate has reached catastrophic proportions. He calls these high schools "dropout factories." According to Orfield, the dropout rate of African American and Latino students is a civil rights crisis because it affects these communities disproportionately. Moreover, less money per student is spent in these "dropout factory" schools than in schools in other areas—sometimes a difference of over $2,000 less per student.[18] The fact that these schools are, for the most part, located in poor communities that serve African American and Latino students, that they employ more inexperienced teachers than in wealthier districts, and that less money is spent in them, cannot be dismissed as coincidence.[19] This is also part of the sociopolitical context of education.

DEFICIT THEORIES AND THEIR STUBBORN DURABILITY

Why schools fail to meet their mission to provide all students with an equitable and high-quality education has been the subject of educational research for some time. As the "achievement gap" grows, theories about cultural deprivation and genetic inferiority are once again being used to explain differences in intelligence and achievement, and the implications of these deficit theories continue to influence educational policies and practices. Deficit theories assume that some children, because of genetic, cultural or experiential differences, are inferior to other children—that is, that they have deficits that must be overcome if they are to learn. One problem with such hypotheses is that they place complete responsibility for children's failure on their homes and families, effectively absolving schools and society from responsibility. Whether the focus is on the individual or the community, the result remains largely the same: blaming the victims of poor schooling rather than looking in a more systematic way at the role played by the schools in which they learn (or fail to learn) and by the society at large. All these factors need to be explored together.

Another problem with deficit theories is their focus on conditions that are outside the control of most teachers, schools, and students. Deficit theories foster despair because they suggest that students' problems are predetermined and thus there is no hope for changing the circumstances that produced them in the first place. Teachers and schools alone cannot alleviate the poverty and other oppressive conditions in which students may live. It is far more realistic and promising to tackle the problems that teachers and schools *can* do something about by providing educational environments that encourage all students to learn. This is why school policies and practices and teachers' attitudes and behaviors, rather than the supposed shortcomings of students, are the basis for the kinds of transformations suggested in this book. (A more complete discussion of deficit theories and other theories that explain differential learning appears in Chapter 8.)

U.S. SCHOOLS AND SOCIETY: A DEMOGRAPHIC MOSAIC

In order to understand the sociopolitical context of multicultural education, we need to know something about the changes in the United States in the recent past, and how these changes have transformed our schools. In what follows, we provide a mosaic of the rich diversity of the population in the nation as well as in our public schools as a framework for understanding this context. We focus on population statistics, immigration, language diversity, and other differences that characterize U.S. schools and society in this decade, the first of the 21st century.

We begin with an overview of the U.S. population in terms of race and ethnicity. As we see in Table 1.1, in 2004 the population of the United States numbered over 293 million. This was the most complete official data available as this book went to press. The overall population has increased steadily since then. For instance, on October 12,

TABLE 1.1
Resident Population by Sex, Race, and Hispanic Origin Status: 2000 to 2004[1]

Characteristic	Number (1,000)					Percent change 2000 to 2004
	2000[2] (April 1)	2001	2002	2003	2004	
Both Sexes						
Total	**281,425**	**285,102**	**287,941**	**290,789**	**293,655**	**4.3**
One race	277,527	281,048	283,761	286,481	289,217	4.2
White	228,107	230,506	232,348	234,199	236,058	3.5
Black or African American	35,705	36,249	36,667	37,082	37,502	5.0
American Indian and Alaska Native	2,664	2,711	2,749	2,787	2,825	6.0
Asian	10,589	11,107	11,512	11,919	12,326	16.4
Native Hawaiian and Other Pacific Islanders	463	475	485	495	506	9.3
Two or more races	3,898	4,054	4,180	4,308	4,439	13.9
Race alone or in combination:[3]						
White	231,436	233,978	235,935	237,901	239,880	3.6
Black or African American	37,105	37,744	38,238	38,732	39,232	5.7
American Indian and Alaska Native	4,225	4,280	4,323	4,366	4,409	4.4
Asian	12,007	12,586	13,041	13,498	13,957	16.2
Native Hawaiian and Other Pacific Islanders	907	927	944	960	976	7.7
Not Hispanic or Latino	246,118	248,042	249,464	250,887	252,333	2.5
One race	242,712	244,506	245,824	247,141	248,478	2.4
White	195,577	196,320	196,822	197,325	197,841	1.2
Black or African American	34,314	34,813	35,196	35,577	35,964	4.8
American Indian and Alaska Native	2,097	2,130	2,155	2,181	2,207	5.2
Asian	10,357	10,867	11,267	11,667	12,068	16.5
Native Hawaiian and Other Pacific Islanders	367	376	383	391	398	8.5
Two or more races	3,406	3,536	3,641	3,747	3,855	13.2
Race alone or in combination:[3]						
White	198,477	199,338	199,935	200,534	201,148	1.3
Black or African American	35,499	36,078	36,526	36,972	37,426	5.4
American Indian and Alaska Native	3,456	3,491	3,518	3,546	3,574	3.4
Asian	11,632	12,196	12,639	13,083	13,530	16.3
Native Hawaiian and Other Pacific Islanders	752	767	779	791	803	6.8
Hispanic or Latino	35,306	37,060	38,477	39,902	41,322	17.0
One race	34,815	36,543	37,937	39,340	40,739	17.0
White	32,530	34,186	35,526	36,873	38,217	17.5
Black or African American	1,391	1,436	1,470	1,505	1,539	10.6
American Indian and Alaska Native	566	582	594	606	618	9.1
Asian	232	240	246	252	258	10.9
Native Hawaiian and Other Pacific Islanders	95	99	102	105	107	12.6
Two or more races	491	518	539	561	583	18.7
Race alone or in combination:[3]						
White	32,959	34,641	36,000	37,368	38,732	17.5

Black or African American	1,606	1,666	1,713	1,760	1,806	12.5
American Indian and Alaska Native	770	789	805	820	835	8.6
Asian	375	390	402	414	427	13.8
Native Hawaiian and Other Pacific Islanders	155	160	165	169	174	12.0
Male						
Total	**138,056**	**140,013**	**141,519**	**143,024**	**144,537**	**4.7**
One race	136,146	138,023	139,465	140,906	142,352	4.6
White	112,478	113,798	114,810	115,820	116,832	3.9
Black or African American	16,972	17,246	17,455	17,662	17,873	5.3
American Indian and Alaska Native	1,333	1,357	1,376	1,396	1,415	6.2
Asian	5,128	5,380	5,578	5,776	5,975	16.5
Native Hawaiian and Other Pacific Islanders	235	242	247	252	257	9.4
Two or more races	1,910	1,990	2,054	2,119	2,185	14.4
Race alone or in combination:[3]						
White	114,116	115,508	116,578	117,647	118,720	4.0
Black or African American	17,644	17,966	18,214	18,461	18,713	6.1
American Indian and Alaska Native	2,088	2,116	2,138	2,160	2,182	4.5
Asian	5,834	6,118	6,341	6,565	6,789	16.4
Native Hawaiian and Other Pacific Islanders	456	466	475	483	491	7.7
Not Hispanic or Latino	119,894	120,919	121,675	122,428	123,190	2.7
Hispanic or Latino	18,162	19,094	19,844	20,597	21,347	17.5
Female						
Total	**143,368**	**145,089**	**146,422**	**147,765**	**149,118**	**4.0**
One race	141,381	143,025	144,296	145,576	146,865	3.9
White	115,628	116,708	117,538	118,379	119,225	3.1
Black or African American	18,733	19,003	19,212	19,420	19,630	4.8
American Indian and Alaska Native	1,331	1,354	1,372	1,391	1,410	5.9
Asian	5,461	5,727	5,935	6,143	6,352	16.3
Native Hawaiian and Other Pacific Islanders	227	233	238	243	248	9.2
Two or more races	1,987	2,064	2,126	2,189	2,253	13.4
Race alone or in combination:[3]						
White	117,321	118,470	119,357	120,254	121,160	3.3
Black or African American	19,461	19,778	20,024	20,271	20,520	5.4
American Indian and Alaska Native	2,137	2,164	2,185	2,206	2,227	4.2
Asian	6,173	6,468	6,701	6,933	7,168	16.1
Native Hawaiian and Other Pacific Islanders	451	461	469	477	485	7.6
Not Hispanic or Latino	126,224	127,123	127,789	128,460	129,143	2.3
Hispanic or Latino	17,144	17,967	18,633	19,305	19,975	16.5

[1]281,425 represents 281,425,000. As of July, except as noted. Data shown are modified race counts; see text, this section.
[2]See footnote 3. Table 11. [3]In combination with one or more other races. The sum of the five race groups adds to more than the total population because individuals may report more than one race.
Source: U.S. Census Bureau, "Annual Estimates of the Population by Sex, Race and Hispanic or Latino Origin for the United States: April 1, 2000 to July 1, 2004 (NC-EST2004-03)"; published 9 June 2005; www.census.gov/popest/national/asrh/NC-EST2004-srh.html

2006, a press release from the U.S. Census Bureau reported that the nation's population would reach 300,000,000 on October 17.[20] Nevertheless, we use this table because the Census Bureau had not yet published a more complete list documenting the growth of all the subgroups reported in Table 1.1.

Of the total population, the largest "minority" group (more on this terminology in Chapter 2) is Hispanic/Latino (over 41 million residents), followed by Blacks or African Americans (37.5 million)(see Figure 1.1). Growth among different segments of the population has not, however, been proportionate: According to the U.S. Census Bureau, from 2000 to 2004, the number of Whites increased by 3.5 percent and the African American population increased by 5 percent. By far, the largest increases were in the Latino population, which had grown by 17 percent, and the Asian population, which had grown by 16.4 percent.

Even more dramatic than current population statistics are projections for the coming years: The U.S. Census Bureau estimates that from 2000 to 2050, the total population will have grown from 282.1 million to 419.9 million. Again, however, the growth will not be even: The White population is expected to grow to 210.3 million, an increase of 7 percent, although it is expected to *decrease* in the decade from 2040–2050. Whites are thus expected to comprise only 50.1 percent of the total U.S. population by 2050, compared with 69.4 percent in 2000. The African American

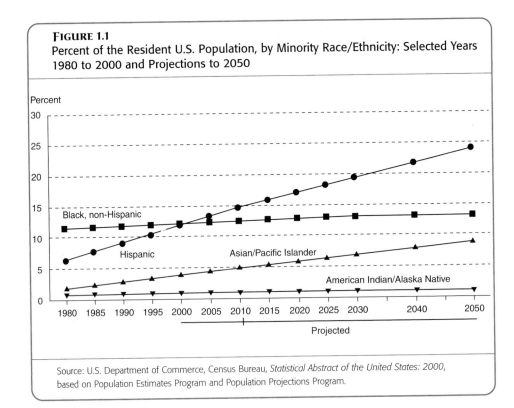

FIGURE 1.1
Percent of the Resident U.S. Population, by Minority Race/Ethnicity: Selected Years 1980 to 2000 and Projections to 2050

Source: U.S. Department of Commerce, Census Bureau, *Statistical Abstract of the United States: 2000,* based on Population Estimates Program and Population Projections Program.

TABLE 1.2
Immigration: 1901 to 2004[1]

Period	Number	Rate[2]	Year	Number	Rate[2]
1901 to 1910	8,795	10.4	1990	1,536	6.1
1911 to 1920	5,736	5.7	1991	1,827	7.2
1921 to 1930	4,107	3.5	1992	974	3.8
			1993	904	3.5
1931 to 1940	528	0.4	1994	804	3.1
1941 to 1950	1,035	0.7	1995	720	2.7
1951 to 1960	2,515	1.5	1996	916	3.4
			1997	798	2.9
1961 to 1970	3,322	1.7	1998	654	2.4
1971 to 1980	4,493	2.1	1999	647	2.3
1981 to 1990	7,338	3.1	2000	850	3.0
			2001	1,064	3.7
1991 to 2000	9,095	3.4	2002	1,064	3.7
2001 to 2004	3,780	3.3	2003	706	2.4
			2004	946	3.2

[1]In thousands, except rate (8,795 represents 8,795,000). For fiscal years ending in year shown; see text, Section 8. For definition of immigrants, see text of this section. Data represent immigrants admitted. Rates based on Census Bureau estimates as of July 1 for resident population through 1929 and for total population thereafter (excluding Alaska and Hawaii prior to 1959)

[2]Annual rate per 1,000 U.S. population. Rate computed by dividing sum of annual immigration totals by sum of annual U.S. population totals for same number of years.

Source: U.S. Department of Homeland Security, Office of Immigration Statistics, *2004 Yearbook of Immigration Statistics*. See also http://uscis.gov/graphics/shared/statistics/yearbook/index.htm.

population is expected to grow to 61.4 million, increasing from 12.7 percent to 14.6 percent of the total population. In contrast, the Latino population is expected to grow to 102.6 million, or 24.4 percent of the total U.S. population, nearly doubling its current percentage of 12.6. Asians are also expected to increase substantially in number, from 10.7 million to 33.4 million, an increase from 3.8 percent to 8 percent of the total U.S. population.

In addition, legal immigration has grown enormously in the past three decades, as is evident in Table 1.2. As we can see in this table, legal immigration hit a peak in 1991 in terms of numbers (although not in terms of percentage of total population, which peaked at the beginning of the 20th century), reaching more than 1.8 million. By 2004, it had fallen to 946,000, still a sizable number.

Another noteworthy indication of the growing diversity in the United States is the current number of foreign-born or first-generation U.S. residents, which in the year 2000 reached the highest level in U.S. history—56 million, or triple the number in 1970. And unlike previous immigrants, who were primarily from Europe, more than half of the new immigrants are from Latin America, and 25 percent from Asia.[21]

The growth in immigration has been accompanied by an increase in linguistic diversity. Currently, 18 percent of the total U.S. population speak a language other than English at home. Spanish is the language spoken by half of these, although there are also many other languages spoken in U.S. homes (more information on linguistic diversity is given in Chapter 7).

The impact of the growing cultural, racial, national origin, and linguistic diversity is clearly visible in our nation's public schools in several ways. First, the sheer number of students in U.S. public schools is growing: In 2003, 49.5 million students were enrolled in public elementary and secondary schools in the United States, an increase of more than 2 million since 2001.[22] Second, the nature of the student population is quite different from what it was just a few decades ago. In 1970, at the height of the public school enrollment of the "baby boom" generation, White students comprised 79 percent of total enrollment, followed by African Americans at 14 percent, Hispanics at 6 percent, and Asians, Pacific Islanders, and other ethnic groups at 1 percent. These statistics have vastly changed: In 2003, 60 percent of students in U.S. public schools were White, 18 percent were Hispanic, 16 percent were African American, and 4 percent were Asian and other races. The Census Bureau's population projections indicate that the student population will continue to diversify in the coming years. Third, our public schools' growing diversity is clearly evidenced by the number of students who are foreign born or have foreign-born parents. As of 2003, over 49 million students, or 31 percent of those enrolled in U.S. elementary and secondary schools, were foreign born or had at least one parent who was foreign born.

At the same time that diversity in schools around the country is growing, racial and ethnic segregation has been on the rise. That is, students in U.S. schools are now more likely to be segregated from students of other races and backgrounds than at any time in the recent past. Indeed, according to Gary Orfield, much of the progress made in integrating the nation's schools during previous decades was eradicated by the end of the 1990s. For Blacks, the 1990s witnessed the largest backward movement toward segregation since the *Brown v. Board of Education* Supreme Court decision, and the trend is continuing. For Latinos, the situation has been equally dramatic: Latinos are now the most segregated of all ethnic groups in terms of race, ethnicity, and poverty.[23] Despite this trend, there is growing evidence that schools with diverse student populations are good for students of all backgrounds.[24]

In addition, many young people live in poverty. Race and ethnicity have a strong link to poverty. The percentage of all people in the United States living below the poverty level is currently 12.4. However, while only about 8.3 percent of Whites live in poverty, nearly 25 percent of African Americans and Native Americans and 22 percent of Hispanics live in poverty.[25] In terms of the school-aged population, 40 percent of all U.S. children live in low-income families, and 18 percent live in poor families, which translates into the sobering reality that *almost half of all children in the United States live in some degree of poverty.* Even more disturbing, although the number of children living in poverty had declined from 1990–2000, it has been rising steadily since then.[26]

At the same time that the number of students of color, those who speak languages other than English and those who live in poverty has increased, the nation's teachers have become more monolithic, monocultural, and monolingual. For example, as of 2003, 90 percent of public school teachers were White, 6 percent were African American, and fewer than 5 percent were of other racial/ethnic backgrounds.[27]

One implication of the tremendous diversity previously described is that all teachers, regardless of their own identities and experiences, need to be prepared to effectively teach students of all backgrounds. One way to do so is to learn about the social, cultural, and political circumstances of real students in real schools. In the following section, we briefly discusses the case study approach used in this book to help readers think about how they can best translate the information into their classroom practices.

THE USE OF CASE STUDIES

An essential element of the sociopolitical context of education concerns students—who they are, how they identify, what their families are like, how they live, the values they hold dear, what helps them learn, and their desires and hopes for the future. Because of the importance of student voices in understanding the sociopolitical context of education, case studies and snapshots are used throughout this book to provide descriptions and stories of students of diverse backgrounds. (See the Appendix for more information on the selection of students for the case studies and snapshots and the approach to selecting the themes illustrated by them.)

WHAT ARE CASE STUDIES?

The case study approach fits within the general framework of qualitative research. Case studies have earned a solid reputation in social science research during the past several years because of the sense of empathy they promote. Sharan Merriam describes the essential characteristics of a qualitative case study as *particularistic* (focusing on one person or social unit), *descriptive* (because the result is a rich, thick portrait), and *heuristic* (because it sharpens the reader's understanding, leading to discovering new meanings).[28] A case study is also *inductive* because generalizations and hypotheses emerge from examination of the data. In this book, we use *ethnographic case studies*, that is, case studies that include a sociocultural analysis of each of the students, all of whom are presented contextually within their cultural and social environment.

The case studies and snapshots differ in terms of length and treatment: Snapshots are short and written mostly in the words of the young people, with a brief analysis, while case studies are longer and offer more in-depth analysis. Case studies are placed at the ends of Chapters 4 through 9, and snapshots are placed within chapters to highlight particular issues discussed in the chapters.

The young people in the case studies and snapshots are actual students who were interviewed about their experiences in school, the importance of culture and language in their lives, what they like and dislike about school, teachers who made a difference in their lives, and what they expect to get out of school. The students are described within a variety of settings—home, school, community, and city or town in which they live—because, by looking at each of these settings, we gain a clearer, more complete picture of their lives.

The students have multiple identities. As young men and women from a number of racial, ethnic, linguistic, social class, and cultural groups, they have had many different life experiences. They live in various geographic locations: from large cities to small rural areas. They are first-, second-, or third-generation Americans, or their ancestors may have been here for many hundreds of years or even forever. Some are from economically poor families, while others are from struggling working-class, middle-class, or well-to-do families. Most are heterosexual, and others are gay and lesbian. They range in age from 13 to 19. When first interviewed, some of them were almost ready to graduate from high school, a few were in middle or junior high school, and the others were at various levels of high school. They range from monolingual English-speaking youths to fluent bilinguals. Their families vary from very large (11 children) to very small (one child) in both one- and two-parent households. Their parents' educational backgrounds vary as well, from no high school education to postgraduate degrees.

In spite of the vast differences in their experiences and backgrounds, most (although not all) of the students in these case studies share one characteristic: They are successful in school. Although there may be disagreements about what it means to be successful (research by Michelle Fine, for example, suggested that, in some ways, the most "successful" students are those who drop out of school[29]), most of the students have been able to develop both academic skills and positive attitudes about themselves and about the value of education. They generally have good grades, most have hopes (but not always plans) of attending college, and they have fairly positive perceptions of school.

Beyond Generalizations and Stereotypes

Inclusion of case studies and snapshots is not for the purpose of generalization to all students in U.S. schools. No educational research, whether qualitative or quantitative, can do so. The students in the case studies and snapshots in this book are not *samples*, as might be the case with quantitative research, but *examples* of a wide variety of students. Case studies can help us look at specific examples so that solutions for more general situations can be hypothesized and developed. For example, James Karam, the Lebanese Christian student whose case study follows Chapter 6, does not reflect the experiences of all Lebanese students in U.S. schools. However, describing James's experience within its sociocultural framework can help us understand other Lebanese students. Whereas quantitative methods can yield some important data about Lebanese students in general (for example, their numbers in the United States or their relative levels of achievement), it is only through a qualitative approach that we can explore more deeply, for example, the impact of "invisible minority" status on James.

No case study of a single individual can adequately or legitimately portray the complexity of an entire group of people. (Neither, of course, can any quantitative approach claim to do this.) Although some Mexican Americans prefer to learn collaboratively, and some African American students may perceive school success as "acting White" (these issues are discussed further in Chapters 8 and 9), many do not. To reach such conclusions contradicts one of the very purposes of case studies, which is to challenge stereotypes.

The case studies are meant to encourage you to ask questions rather than to make assumptions about what it means to be from a large family, to be raised by two dads, to be Vietnamese, middle class, lesbian, African American, Cape Verdean, or anything else. It is far easier to pigeonhole people according to our preconceptions and biases, but the deeper struggle is to try to understand people on their own terms. Some of the experiences, feelings, and statements of the young people described in the case studies and snapshots may surprise you and shake some deep-seated beliefs. So much the better if they do. On the other hand, they may reflect some of your own experiences or your knowledge of young people of diverse racial and sociocultural backgrounds. In either case, what these students say should be understood within the context of their particular school, family, and community experiences.

LEARNING FROM THE CASE STUDIES AND SNAPSHOTS

Although the students in all the case studies and snapshots are wonderful and engaging, they are not exceptional in the sense that they are totally unlike other young people. We did not have to go to extraordinary measures to find them. Young people such as these are all around us. They are the young people in our local urban, rural, or suburban schools; they can be found on our sports teams, in our communities, and in our places of worship. They are in our English and math classes, bilingual and monolingual programs, and special education and gifted and talented programs. All we have to do is speak to them and listen to what they have to tell us. You will probably find the stories of the students in your own classrooms, whether they are succeeding in school or not, just as fascinating as the stories in the case studies and snapshots.

We hope that you will read each of these stories critically and with the goal of understanding how the experiences and thoughts of young people can influence classroom discourse and strategies as well as school policies and practices in general. These young people challenge us to believe that all students in our nation's classrooms are capable of learning. Although their stories demonstrate the indomitable strength of youth, they also reveal the tremendous fragility of academic success, which is so easily disrupted by a poor teacher, a negative comment, or an environment that denies the importance of one's experiences. In the end, all their voices challenge us as teachers and as a society to do the very best we can to ensure that educational equity is not an illusion but an achievable goal.

MULTICULTURAL EDUCATION, BACKLASH, AND NO CHILD LEFT BEHIND

Since its beginnings in the 1970s, multicultural education has been criticized for many reasons. While some of the criticisms have been warranted and have, in fact, helped the field develop more solidly, many of the arguments against multicultural education have been deeply ideological. That is, multicultural education has come under fire precisely because it has challenged the status quo, encouraged the emergence of previously silenced and marginalized voices, and championed the transformation of curriculum and the use of alternative pedagogies.

ERODING THE TRADITIONAL EDUCATIONAL CANON

One argument against multicultural education is that it can easily slide into a separatist monoculturalism that pits Europeans and European Americans against people of other backgrounds, creating a divisive "us versus them" mentality. This argument assumes that no "us versus them" mentality currently exists and that there already is unity among all people in our country—both clearly erroneous assumptions. There are tremendous divisions among people in the United States, and glossing over these differences will not make them go away. On the contrary, supporters of multicultural education assume that a curriculum that is more multicultural is also more complicated and truthful and will, in the long run, help develop citizens who think critically, expansively, and creatively.

In terms of its impact on schooling, opponents have been especially nervous about how a multicultural perspective might translate into curriculum changes. Those who fear that the traditional educational canon is being eroded have vociferously criticized it because, they claim, a multicultural curriculum will do away with our "common culture." The ramifications of this stance can be seen in efforts to do away with specific courses at high schools and universities and, in the aftermath of September 11, 2001, in claims that it is now more important than ever to focus on a rigidly defined version of American history.

In countering this argument, we need to remember that the history of other groups of people in the United States is not foreign; it is *American history*. Our history was never exclusively a European saga of immigration and assimilation, although that is, of course, an important part of the American story. But our collective consciousness began with—and continues to be influenced by—Indigenous Americans as well as by those who were forcibly brought from Africa into slavery. No one in our nation has been untouched by African American, Native American, Mexican American, and Asian American histories and cultures (among many other groups, including women, European American immigrants, and working class people). The influence of these groups can be seen in our history, popular culture, civic engagement, and arts.

The trajectory of U.S. history has been characterized largely by the quest for equality, and this is no more evident than in the case of those who have been most marginalized by our society. The words *freedom, liberty*, and *equality* would have much less power today were it not for the protracted struggles against the abolition of slavery and for universal suffrage and civil rights, some of which continue today. Although these words were originally meant to apply to only land-owning White males early in our history, they came to be meaningful for others because of campaigns to extend these ideals to all people. Whether or not we acknowledge it in our history books, our culture and history have been shaped by the fusion of many people of different backgrounds.

THE "BACK TO BASICS" ARGUMENT

The backlash against multicultural education has also been evident in claims that a focus on diversity is a diversion from the "basics." This has especially been the case since the educational reform movement that began in 1983 after the publication of *A Nation at Risk*.[30] One vivid example of the back-to-basics argument is E. D. Hirsch's 1987 book *Cultural Literacy: What Every American Needs to Know*, which includes a list of several thousand terms and concepts that the author considers essential for every educated person to know or, at least, to recognize and be familiar with.[31] Many critics have charged that both the book and the list are provincial and Eurocentric, with little attention given to the arts, history, or culture of those from groups other than the so-called mainstream. Since publication of Hirsch's book, several hundred schools around the nation have been structured and organized according to the "cultural literacy" model promoted by Hirsch, further promulgating a notion of cultural literacy that flies in the face of the rapidly changing demographics—not to mention the rich multicultural history—of our nation. There are also numerous spin-off publications, sold at supermarkets, that focus on different grade levels, making Hirsch's cultural literacy model and ideas a virtual cottage industry that is hard to ignore.

While many of us might welcome a generally agreed-upon definition of the educated person, this is a complex issue that cannot be solved by a prescribed list, or even a prescribed curriculum. In a recent book, Eugene Provenzo challenged Hirsch's views by publishing his own book, *Critical Literacy: What Every American Ought to Know*, a critique of both Hirsch and the simplistic ideas behind the cultural literacy model that he promotes.[32]

NCLB AND THE CHALLENGE OF WORKING WITHIN THE STANDARDS

The most recent iteration of the back-to-basics argument has occurred since the passage of the No Child Left Behind (NCLB) law in 2001, particularly because along with higher standards, the law requires that each state have an annual testing program of children in reading and math.[33]

NCLB is a response to several issues plaguing our educational system. First, NCLB needs to be understood as a response to the deplorable history of educational inequality in our nation. As you will see in demographic data, research studies, and our own case studies throughout this text, educational inequality has been a fact of life for many children in our schools, but especially for students of color and poor children. Parents, educators, and other defenders of public education have long advocated for addressing this inequality. It is not surprising, then, that many advocates of equal education initially supported NCLB and that it remains popular with some.

At the same time, conspicuous among the most ardent supporters of NCLB are those who support privatization of schools, including vouchers, charter schools, and so forth. Thus, the goals of various groups promoting NCLB are not the same and, in some cases, may be contradictory. In the years since NCLB was first passed, it has lost favor with a great many people for many reasons, including its single-minded focus on tests as the primary criterion for viewing academic progress, as well as the dismal results this focus has produced so far.

Teaching to the Test and High Standards   As a result of the law, there has been immense pressure on teachers and administrators to "teach to the test" and to devote a lion's share of the school day to reading and mathematics. The effects have been mixed. While test scores are rising in some districts, one recent comprehensive survey found that the law's pressure on teachers has led to increased stress on the job and a negative effect on staff morale. The same survey found that 71 percent of surveyed school districts reported having reduced instructional time in at least one other subject to make time for reading and mathematics.[34] The arts, social studies, and even science have been reduced or eliminated in some schools. Recess and physical education have also been curtailed in many schools. And although multicultural education is not a subject area, it too has been one of the casualties of this pressure. One reason is that, as a consequence of NCLB, the testing frenzy has had a chilling effect on schools' and teachers' autonomy to develop and implement curricula, and this includes multicultural curricula.

Most state standards do not preclude the possibility of including multiple perspectives in the curriculum. In fact, there is no contradiction between high standards and multicultural education. Quite the opposite is the case: Since its very beginning, one of the major arguments in support of multicultural education has been that some students—particularly students of color and poor students of all backgrounds—have been the victims of an inferior education, often based on their race/ethnicity, social class, first language, and other differences. Multicultural education, through a rich curriculum and rigorous demands, was seen as an antidote to this situation. Nonetheless, the pressure that teachers and administrators are under to meet "adequate yearly progress" (AYP), as defined by standardized tests, has resulted in little support for the arts and even for such subjects as social studies and science, much less for innovation and creativity in curriculum and instruction.

Effects of NCLB   There has been a great deal of criticism of NCLB and its negative effects, particularly on students living in poverty, those whom the law was purportedly intended to help. For instance, *The Boston Globe* reported in 2005 that the Massachusetts high school dropout rate had experienced the largest increase in 14 years and that the class graduating in 2007 was expected to have a dropout rate of 31 percent. Hispanics and other immigrants have been the most severely affected. The high dropout rate included thousands of students who failed the state's high-stakes exam, the Massachusetts Comprehensive Assessment System (MCAS).[35] Rather than helping such students, the MCAS has clearly had an adverse effect.

FairTest, a national advocacy group that promotes fair and open testing, has been especially critical of NCLB. It maintains, for instance, that NCLB is based on two false assumptions: one, that boosting standardized test scores should be the primary goal of schools; and two, that schools can be best improved by threatening teachers and administrators with severe penalties. In its analysis of the law, FairTest concludes that NCLB has failed to address the underlying problems of school achievement, namely, family poverty and inadequate school funding.[36] In addition, because test scores have been rising in some states, there is increasing criticism that tests are becoming easier rather than that achievement is improving.[37] FairTest has also reported on two research studies that found striking evidence that exit exams actually decrease high school completion rates, increase GED test-taking, and exacerbate inequalities in educational attainment.[38]

The Civil Rights Project at Harvard University has also been critical of NCLB. In a 2006 report, the author of one study, Jaekyung Lee, compared findings of the National Assessment of Education Progress (NAEP) to state assessment results and concluded that although students were showing improvement in state exams in both math and reading, they were not showing similar gains on the NAEP, the only independent national test that randomly samples students across the country.[39] As a result, Lee concluded that state-administered tests tend to significantly inflate proficiency levels and deflate racial and social achievement gaps in the state. That is, the higher the stakes of state assessments, the greater the discrepancies between NAEP and state results. These discrepancies are especially significant for students living in poverty and for Black and Latino students.

There are also ethical concerns associated with the NCLB law. In 2006, the National Council of Churches Committee on Public Education and Literacy took a strong stand against NCLB. Its statement, titled "Ten Moral Concerns in the Implementation of the *No Child Left Behind Act*," affirms:

> Now several years into *No Child Left Behind's* implementation, it is becoming clear that the law is leaving behind more children than it is saving. The children being abandoned are our nation's most vulnerable children—children of color and poor children in America's big cities and remote rural areas—the very children the law claims it will rescue.[40]

The statement concludes with an indictment of the testing policies that have resulted in leaving so many children behind:

> We people of faith do not view our children as products to be tested and managed but instead as unique human beings to be nurtured and educated. We call on our political leaders to invest in developing the capacity of all schools. Our nation should be judged by the way we care for our children.[41]

NCLB has also had devastating effects on teachers' sense of professionalism. Many teachers are now reluctant to engage in interesting projects with their students, or even to collaborate with peers because of criticisms they are likely to receive from administrators, who are also under tremendous pressure to keep their schools out of the headlines for failing to meet AYP. The result in many schools around the country is that teachers are expected to follow a rigidly prescribed curriculum, particularly in reading and math, with little room for innovation or collaboration. What are teachers to do?

Teachers' Responsibilities Within NCLB   In terms of teachers' responsibilities, we must once again consider the sociopolitical context of education. Curriculum and pedagogy, along with other school policies and practices, as we shall see in Chapter 5, are as much *political* issues as they are educational issues. The same is true of standards. Every curriculum decision also says something about the values, expectations, hopes, and dreams that a teacher has for his or her students. If this is the case, it becomes the responsibility of teachers to help define the curriculum and not simply to be automatons who implement a rigidly prescribed curriculum.

In a recent book about this topic, Christine Sleeter suggests that there is a difference between a *standards-driven* and a *standards-conscious* curriculum. A standards-driven curriculum, according to her, begins with the standards and draws the "big ideas" from them for further design and implementation. A standards-conscious curriculum, on the other hand, uses the standards as a *tool* rather than as either the starting point or the underlying ideology for the development of big ideas. In her book, *Un-Standardizing Curriculum: Multicultural Teaching in the Standards-Based Classroom*, Sleeter provides powerful vignettes of teachers who face the same pressures to "teach to the test" as all teachers. In spite of this pressure, rather than following the standards uncritically, these teachers developed standards-based curricula that are both creative and critical.[42] Another example of using the standards in inventive ways is Mary Cowhey's *Black Ants and Buddhists: Thinking Critically and Teaching Differently in the Primary Grades*.[43] A first- and second-grade teacher, Cowhey uses the standards to develop curriculum that is inspiring, demanding, and multicultural.

These books, and a growing number of others, are challenging the notion that standards will necessarily lead to standardization. They provide vivid examples of how powerful learning and imagination can be promoted even within a testing and accountability context that tends to leave little room for these things.

THE COMPLEX NATURE OF SCHOOLING AND THE ROLE OF TEACHERS

We believe that multicultural education has tremendous promise and a great deal to offer public schools in the 21st century. However, we do not see it as a panacea, nor should you. As we hope we have made clear in this chapter, our schools reflect the sociopolitical context in which we live. This context is unfair to many young people and their families and the situations in which they live and go to school, but teachers and other educators do not simply have to go along with this reality. We believe that one of our primary roles as educators is to interrupt the cycle of inequality and oppression. Developing a multicultural approach can help, but it cannot eliminate the inequities in our schools. No program, philosophy, or approach can do this. It will take courage, creativity, hard work, and on-going collaboration with like-minded educators and others to change things. We can begin the process by teaching well and with heart and soul, by asking questions, and by seeking social justice in our schools.

Writing a book that might offer useful insights into education in a highly complex and diverse society is an exceedingly difficult task. The major pitfall in writing a book about multicultural education is that the information presented can be overgeneralized to the point that it becomes just another harmful stereotype. For example, after reading the case study of the Vietnamese student Hoang Vinh in Chapter 6, one might conclude that Vietnamese students are always successful in school because their culture reinforces academic success. However, this conclusion would be simplistic because it neglects issues such as the effect of societal expectations on school achievement as well as many other factors. Similarly, based on the case study of Paul Chavez in Chapter 8, one may also conclude that all Chicanos are gang members, or based on the case studies of Avi Abramson and James Karam in Chapters 5 and 6, respectively, that all Jewish and Arab students are religious. None of these conclusions is warranted by the case studies, yet that is the danger of using individual examples. Therefore, we urge you to read the case studies, the snapshots, and the entire book with a critical eye and a thoughtful mind.

In this book we have tried to consider schooling as a dynamic process in which competing interests and values are at work every day in complex and contradictory ways. Expectations of students and the community are often pitted against expectations of teachers and schools; the organization and policies of schools are sometimes diametrically opposed to what is developmentally appropriate for young people; and racial, gender, class, and language stratification are frequently used to explain the success or failure of students. Through the study of the many complex forces that influence young people, we can begin to understand the lives of the students who comprise our multicultural society.

Summary

In this chapter, we have attempted to provide a definition and description of the *sociopolitical context of multicultural education*. As described, comprehending the sociopolitical context requires (1) an understanding of the social, economic, political, and ideological underpinnings of the society and of education within the society, (2) the goals of multicultural education, and (3) knowledge of the current demographics of our nation. By studying these issues through ethnographic "lenses," specifically through case studies of students who reflect the tremendous diversity of our school-age population, we can understand the effect of the sociopolitical context on various segments of the population as well as on the nation as a whole. We also considered a topic that is both current and controversial in schools and communities around the nation: the No Child Left Behind (NCLB) law and its implications for education in a multicultural society.

Companion Website

For access to additional case studies, weblinks, concept cards, and other material related to this chapter, visit the text's companion website at **www.ablongman.com/nieto5e**.

Notes to Chapter 1

1. Public Education Network and *Education Week, Action for All: The Public's Responsibility for Public Education* (Washington, DC: Author, 2001).

2. Irving Howe, *World of Our Fathers* (New York: Simon & Schuster, 1983).

3. Beverly Daniel Tatum, *"Why Are All the Black Kids Sitting Together in the Cafeteria?" and Other Conversations About Race* (New York: HarperCollins, 1997): 6.

4. The Education Trust, *The Funding Gap 2005* (Washington, DC: Author, 2005).

5. Nam Y. Huh, "Does Money Transform Schools?" *The Christian Science Monitor*, August 9, 2005. Available at: www.csmonitor.com/2005/0809/p01.S03-ussc.html

6. Will Kymlicka, "Foreword." In *Diversity and Citizenship in Education: Global Perspectives*, edited by James A. Banks (San Francisco: Jossey-Bass, 2004): xiii–xviii.

7. Enid Lee, "Equity and Equality." From a keynote speech at the annual Connecticut National Association for Multicultural Education (NAME) Conference, October 2004.

8. Robert P. Moses, "Quality Education is a Civil Rights Issue." In *Minority Achievement*, edited by David T. Gordon (Cambridge, MA: Harvard Education Letter Focus Series 7, 2002): 26–27.

9. Edmund W. Gordon, "Bridging the Minority Achievement Gap." *Principal* (May 2000): 20–23.

10. *Quality Counts at 10: A Decade of Standards-Based Education,* 2006. Available at: www.edweek.org/ew/articles/2006/01/05/17overview.h25.html

11. Mano Singham, "The Achievement Gap: Myths and Realities." *Phi Delta Kappan* 84, no. 8 (April 2003): 586–591.

12. Joseph J. D'Amico, "A Closer Look at the Minority Achievement Gap." *ERS Spectrum* (Spring 2001): 4–10.

13. *Ibid.*

14. Jean Anyon, *Radical Possibilities: Public Policy, Urban Education, and a New Social Movement* (New York: Routledge, 2005): 2.

15. David C. Berliner, "Our Impoverished View of Educational Reform." *Teachers College Record.* Available at: www.tcrecord.org/content.asp?contentID+12106

16. Richard Rothstein, *Class and Schools: Using Social, Economic, and Educational Reform to Close the Black-White Achievement Gap.* (New York: Teachers College Press, and Washington, DC: Economic Policy Institute, 2004).

17. D'Amico, "A Closer Look at the Minority Achievement Gap."

18. Gary Orfield, "Losing Our Future: Minority Youth Left Out." In *Dropouts in America: Confronting the Graduate Rate Crisis,* edited by Gary Orfield (Cambridge, MA: Harvard Education Press, 2004): p. 1–11, 9.

19. Pamela M. Prah, "Schools With Poor, Minority Students Get Less State Funds." Available at: www.stateline.org

20. "Nation's Population to Reach 300,000,000 on Oct. 17." *U.S. Census Bureau News*, October 12, 2006. Washington, DC: Author, Public Information Office.

21. U.S. Census Bureau, *Profile of the Foreign-Born Population in the United States: 2000* (Washington, DC: U.S. Department of Commerce, 2002).

22. All the data cited in this paragraph are from the following U.S. Census Bureau publication: Hyon B. Shin, "School Enrollment: Social and Economic Characteristics of Students—October 2003." In *Current Population Reports* (Washington, DC: U.S. Census Bureau, 2005).

23. Gary Orfield, *Schools More Separate: Consequences of a Decade of Resegregation* (Cambridge, MA: The Civil Rights Project, Harvard University, 2001).

24. Kugler, Eileen Gale. *Debunking the Middle-Class Myth: Why Diverse Schools are Good for All Kids* (Lanham, MD: Scarecrow Press, 2002).

25. U.S. Census Bureau, "Income, Poverty, and Health Insurance Coverage in the United States." In *Current Population Survey, 2003 to 2005 Annual Social and Economic Supplements* (Washington, DC: Author, 2005).

26. National Center for Children in Poverty, *Basic Facts About Low-Income Children: Birth to Age 18.* Available at: www.NCCP.org

27. National Collaborative on Diversity in the Teaching Force, *Assessment of Diversity in America's Teaching Force: A Call to Action* (Washington, DC: Author, October 2004).

28. Sharan B. Merriam, *Case Study Research in Education: A Qualitative Approach* (San Francisco: Jossey-Bass, 1998): 27.

29. Michelle Fine, *Framing Dropouts: Notes on the Politics of an Urban High School* (Albany: State University of New York Press, 1991).

30. National Commission on Excellence in Education, *A Nation at Risk: The Imperative for Education Reform* (Washington, DC: U.S. Government Printing Office, 1983).

31. E. D. Hirsch, *Cultural Literacy: What Every American Needs to Know* (Boston: Houghton Mifflin, 1987).

32. Eugene F. Provenzo, Jr., *Critical Literacy: What Every American Ought to Know* (Boulder, CO: Paradigm, 2005).

33. *No Child Left Behind Act of 2001*, Public Law 107-110.

34. Center on Education Policy, *From the Capital to the Classroom: Year 4 of the No Child Left Behind Act* (Washington, DC: Author, 2006).

35. Maria Sacchetti and Tracy Jan, "High School Dropout Rate Reaches Highest in 14 Years." *The Boston Globe*, October 22, 2005. Available at: www.boston.com/news/local/massachusetts/articles/2005/10/22/high_school_dropout_rates_reaches_highest_in_14-years?/mode+PF

36. Monty Neill, Lisa Guisbond, and Bob Schaeffer (with James Madison and Life Legeros), *Failing Our Children: How "No Child Left Behind" Undermines Quality and Equity in Education* (Cambridge, MA: The National Center for Fair and Open Testing, 2004). See also Deborah Meier, Alfie Kohn, Linda Darling-Hammond, Theodore R. Sizer, George Wood, et al., *Many Children Left Behind: How The No Child Left Behind Act Is Damaging Our Children and Our Schools* (Boston: Beacon Press, 2004).

37. Michael Winerip, "One Secret to Better Test Scores: Make State Reading Tests Easier." *The New York Times*, October 5, 2005. Available at: www.nytimes.com/2005/10/05/education/05education.html

38. "Exit Exams Decrease Graduation Rates," *FairTest Examiner*, August 2006. Available at: www.fairtest.org

39. Jaekyung Lee, *Tracking Achievement Gaps and Assessing the Impact of NCLB on the Gaps: An In-Depth Look into National and State Reading and Math Outcome Trends* (Cambridge, MA: The Civil Rights Project, 2006).

40. National Council of Churches, "Ten Moral Concerns in the Implementation of the *No Child Left Behind Act*: A Statement of the National Council of Churches Committee on Public Education and Literacy, 2006." Available at: www.ncccusa.org

41. *Ibid.*

42. Christine E. Sleeter, *Un-Standardizing Curriculum: Multicultural Teaching in the Standards-Based Classroom* (New York: Teachers College Press, 2005).

43. Mary Cowhey, *Black Ants and Buddhists: Thinking Critically and Teaching Differently in the Primary Grades* (Portland, ME: Stenhouse, 2006).

2

About Terminology

Julia Katz, *Portraits*
Charcoal and mixed media, 2005.

"It kind of makes me mad that they always try to put people into a certain box. You have to check a box every time you fill out a form. I don't fit in a box."

—Nini Rostland, interviewee

anguage is always changing. Because it mirrors social, economic, and political events, it is a key barometer of a society at any given time. Terms in a language may become obsolete; it could not be otherwise because language is a reflection of societal changes. Throughout the years, the shift in terminology related to groups of people, for example, from *Negro* to *Black* to *Afro-American* and more recently to *African American*, is a case in point. Such changes often represent deliberate attempts by a group to name or rename itself. This decision is political as well as linguistic, and it responds to the need for group self-determination and autonomy. Terms also evolve as an attempt to be more precise and correct. In this sense, the term *African American* implies culture rather than simply color. It recognizes that the notion of race, in spite of its significance in a society rigidly stratified along these lines, is neither accurate nor does it capture the complexity of a people. On the other hand, the term *Black* is more comprehensive because it includes people of African descent from all around the world.

Terminology is particularly important in multicultural education. In our society, we have not always been appropriate or sensitive in our use of words to describe people. In its most blatant form, this insensitivity is apparent in the racial and ethnic epithets that even our youngest children seem to know and use. It is also evident in more subtle examples, such as observations made by Gordon Allport many years ago: (1) that the refusal of southern newspapers to capitalize *Negro* was meant to diminish the stature of Blacks and (2) that certain words develop stereotypical ethnic connotations (for example, "inscrutable" is almost automatically associated with Asians and "rhythm" with African Americans).[1] Although words per se may not be negative, they can become code words for belittling the experience of an entire group of people and, hence, are disparaging.

THE CONUNDRUM OF RACE

The concept of race has received a great deal of criticism because, in a biological sense, race does not exist at all. There is no scientific evidence that so-called racial groups differ in biologically or genetically significant ways. Differences that do exist are primarily social, that is, they are based on one's experiences within a particular cultural group. Thus, it is now generally accepted that the very concept of race is a social construction, that is, a racial group is socially and not biologically determined. There is really only one "race"—the human race. In the words of Linda Howard, one of the interviewees in the case studies that follow Chapter 4, "I'm human. That's my race; I'm part of the human race." Linda identified as Black American and White American, but she was correct in seeing herself as part of the human race. Even as a young woman, she knew that, historically, the concept of race has been used to oppress entire groups of people for their supposed differences.

Nevertheless, although race as a notion is dubious at best, racism is not. Consequently, the problem with using terms that emphasize only culture is that the very real issue of racism in our society is then obscured. Our use of terminology in this text is in no way meant to do so, but rather to stress that the notion of race alone does not define people. For example, African Americans and Haitians are both Black. They share some basic cultural values and are both subjected to racist attitudes and behaviors in the United States, but the particular life experiences, native language usage, and ethnicity of each group is overlooked or even denied if we simply call both groups *Black* rather than also identifying them ethnically.

We have decided to use terms that refer specifically to so-called racial groups when such terms are warranted. In speaking of segregated schools, for example, it makes sense to refer to *Black* and *White* students rather than to *African American* and *European American* students because color is the salient issue. In this way, we hope to underscore the fact that there are always differences of opinion about the use of various terms.

We have capitalized the terms *White* and *Black* because they refer to groups of people, as do terms such as *Latino, Asian,* and *African.* As such, they deserve to be capitalized. Although these are not the scientific terms for so-called racial groups, terms such as *Negroid* and *Caucasian* are no longer used in everyday speech or are rejected because of their negative connotations.

Because race is a social construction, some scholars who write about it have made the decision to use the term only in quotation marks ("race") to underscore its social construction. We have decided not to do so in this book for a couple of reasons. First, it can be reasonably argued that all differences are socially constructed (social class, gender, ethnicity, sexual orientation, and so on) and that to separate race from the others is arbitrary. The second reason is a more practical one: Because of the many references to race, gender, social class, ethnicity, and other differences in this text, readers would find it disconcerting to confront a flurry of quotation marks around words in paragraph after paragraph about "race," "gender," "social class," and so forth.

MAKING CHOICES ABOUT WHAT TERMS TO USE

To be both sensitive and appropriate in the use of language, we prefer some words or terms over others. We are not suggesting that the terms we have chosen to use are "politically correct" or that they are the only ones that should be used, nor do we want to impose our usage on others. Rather, in what follows, we explain our thinking to help you reflect on and decide what terminology is most appropriate for you to use in your context.

Our choice of terms used in this book is based largely on the answers to two questions:

1. What do the people themselves want to be called?

2. What is the most accurate term?

The terms used stem from the answers to these questions, based on our conversations with people from various groups, our reading of current research, and our listening to debates regarding the use of terms. Language is always tentative, and so are the terminology choices we have made here. New terms evolve every day. Such is the inexactitude of language that it can never completely capture the complexity of our lives.[2]

MULTIPLE TERMS FOR SIMILAR GROUPS

In some cases, we have chosen to use two terms or more, sometimes interchangeably, because each may have meanings important in particular contexts. Terminology choices change through the years because of changing usage.

NATIVE AMERICANS, AMERICAN INDIANS

For example, in this book we use the terms *Native American*, *Indian*, *American Indian*, and *Indigenous people* to refer to the many indigenous nations in the Western Hemisphere. During the 1960s, *Native American* became the preferred term because it reflected a people's determination to name themselves and to have others recognize them as the original inhabitants of these lands. During the late 1980s and 1990s, the use of this term declined, and the terms *American Indian*, *Indian*, and *Native* people were more common. We have decided to use these terms most often because we have noted that people from these groups generally use them as well. Also, *Native American* may be confusing because it sometimes refers to a citizen of the United States whose early ancestors came from Europe but who is native to this land (i.e., born in the United States). Because *Indian* also refers to people from India, if we use this term, we usually add the qualifier *American*. More recently, the term *Native American* has again become popular in some quarters. For instance, Fern, one of the young women in the case studies, deliberately refers to herself in this way, reminding us that, even among people from the same group, different terms are used.

LATINOS, HISPANICS, AND OTHERS

Although some people have definite and strong preferences for the terms *Latino* and *Hispanic*, we have used these terms more or less interchangeably to refer to people of Latin American and Caribbean Spanish-speaking heritage. We generally prefer the term *Latino*, but *Hispanic* is more widespread and well known. Unlike the terms *European*, *African*, *Latin American*, or *Asian*, however, *Hispanic* does not refer to a particular continent or country (i.e., there is no continent named Hispania). The term *Latino*, on the other hand, has the disadvantage of having a sexist connotation when used to refer to both males and females together. Some have argued that *Latino* is far more accurate, and others have staunchly defended the use of *Hispanic*. The debate is complicated by the tremendous diversity within the Latino/Hispanic community itself. Martha Gimenez has suggested that neither *Hispanic* nor *Latino* is appropriate or desirable as an overarching term because both terms give South Americans a "contrived Hispanic ethnicity," since South Americans, in general, have not faced the kinds of oppressive conditions in the United States that Mexicans and Puerto Ricans have encountered.[3] Gimenez has instead suggested categories that would differentiate these groups according to the various groups' experience in the United States: first, Puerto Ricans and Mexicans, the two "minority" groups who have been historically oppressed in the United States; followed by Cuban immigrants; Central American refugees; Central American immigrants; and South American immigrants. Gimenez's thinking is that because each group has a particular historical context, use of these categorizations reflects the relative status, time in the United States, race, and other differences among these groups. Although helpful, her analysis does not include Dominicans, a group with a growing presence in the United States.

When the more specific ethnic name is available, we use neither *Latino* nor *Hispanic*. For example, none of the Latino students in the case studies in this book refer to themselves as *Latino, Latina,* or *Hispanic*: Alicia Montejo defines herself as *Mexican*; Paul Chavez uses both *Chicano* and *Mexican American*; and Yahaira León identifies as both *Dominican* and *Puerto Rican*. Whenever possible, these distinctions need to be made; otherwise, fundamental differences in ethnicity, national origin, self-identification, and time in this country are easily overlooked.

Chicano, a term popular in the late 1960s and early 1970s, is preferred by some people of Mexican origin, while *Mexican American* is preferred by others. *Chicano,* an emphatically self-affirming and political term reflecting the culture and realities of urban, economically oppressed Mexican Americans in U.S. society, grew out of the Brown Power Movement in the 1960s. Although used by many scholars and activists, the less political term *Mexican American* is more common in other segments of the community.

Puerto Ricans also use different terms for specific situations to describe or refer to themselves. For example, while *Puerto Rican* is the general term used by most people, a growing number of second- and third-generation Puerto Ricans prefer the term *Nuyorican* (an amalgam of *New Yorker,* the preferred destination of Puerto Ricans in the 20th century, and *Puerto Rican*). More recently, the term *Diasporican* has gained popularity, as it acknowledges two realities: First, most Puerto Ricans in the United States no longer live in New York but are dispersed throughout the Northeast and, increasingly, throughout the country; and second, the immigration of Puerto Ricans represents a true diaspora because more Puerto Ricans currently live in the United States than on the island of Puerto Rico.[4] The term *Boricua,* derived from *Boriquén,* the name given to the island by the Taínos, its original inhabitants, is an affectionate term for *Puerto Rican* and also used quite often.

WHITES (EUROPEAN AMERICANS)

White people, as the majority in U.S. society, seldom think of themselves as ethnic; they tend to reserve this term for other, more easily identifiable groups. Nevertheless, the fact is that we are all ethnic, whether or not we choose to identify in this way or not. Because Whites in U.S. society tend to think of themselves as the norm, they often view other groups as ethnic and therefore somewhat exotic and colorful. By using the term *European American,* we hope to challenge Whites to see themselves as ethnic. Although "whiteness" is an important factor, it hides more than it reveals: There is a tremendous diversity of ethnic backgrounds among Whites, and this is lost if race or color is used as the only identifier. The term *European American* also implies culture, something that many European Americans lament they do not have. This is nonsense, of course. Everybody has a culture, whether clearly manifested in its more traditional forms or not.

The term *European American*, like all terms, has its drawbacks. For one, although it is more specific than *White*, it is still overly inclusive of a great many ethnic backgrounds that may have little in common other than race or color. (A similar criticism applies to terms such as *African*, *Asian*, or *Latin American*.) Another drawback to the use of the term *European American* is that many European Americans are a mixture of several European ethnic groups. A person may be German, Irish, and Italian (they may affectionately refer to themselves as "*Heinz 57*") and not speak any of the languages or follow any of the traditions associated with any of these cultures. It is reasonable to ask, in such cases, why they should be called *European American* when they are essentially "as American as apple pie." (Of course, the same can be said of African Americans, Latinos, and Asian Americans whose families have been in the United States for any length of time and for Native Americans, the original inhabitants of the continent.) European Americans may never have even visited Europe, for example, or may not identify at all with a European heritage. Nevertheless, we have chosen to use the term *European American* because the tradition, values, and behaviors of White Americans are grounded in European mores and values. Although they may be estranged from their European heritage and may have drastically changed and adapted to U.S. mainstream culture, their roots are still European.

We do not use the terms *Anglo* and *Anglo-American*, except when speaking specifically of those with an English heritage, because these are inaccurate terms for referring to Whites in the United States. Many Whites are not English in origin but rather come from a wide variety of ethnic groups from European societies. Classifying all Whites as Anglos is even more of an overgeneralization than calling them European Americans. If used to contrast English speakers from speakers of other languages, the term *Anglo-American* is equally inaccurate because African Americans, among others whose native language is English, are not included in this classification. In addition, it is a term rejected by some, not the least of whom are many Irish Americans, who are often understandably offended at being identified with an English heritage.

PEOPLE OF COLOR

We generally use terms related to specific ethnic backgrounds; however, if an overarching term is needed for so-called "minorities," we prefer to use *people of color*. The term *people of color* encompasses those who have been labeled "minority," that is, American Indians, African Americans, Latinos, and Asian Americans, and it emerged from these communities themselves. It also implies important connections among the groups and underlines some common experiences in the United States. We prefer the term *people of color* because *minority* is a misnomer; it is never used to describe groups such as Swedish Americans, Albanian Americans, or Dutch Americans. Yet, strictly speaking, these groups, which represent numerical minorities in our society, should also be referred to in this way. Historically, the term has been used to refer only to racial minorities, implying a status less than that accorded to other groups. Conversely, using the term *people of color* might imply that Whites are somehow colorless, yet, as we know, almost everyone is mixed, including many Europeans. In fact, some individuals who identify as people of color may actually be lighter in color than some European Americans, reinforcing the fact that such terms are political rather than descriptive.

Even when groups are no longer a "minority," the dominant discourse insists tenaciously on maintaining the "minority" status of some groups. The result is convoluted language that maintains a pejorative connotation. For example, schools in which African American and Latino students become the majority are commonly referred to as "*majority minority*" schools rather than "*primarily Black and Latino*" schools. The connection between name and low status in the use of this term is quite clear. We have also chosen to use the term *people of color* because we find it a better alternative to negatively charged words such as *disempowered* or *dominated*—terms that are accurate in a socioeconomic sense but incomplete because they emphasize only victimization.

The term *people of color* is not without its problems, however. In spite of the wide acceptance of the term and its use by many people (and in this book), we find it increasingly unsatisfactory on several counts. One problem is the implication of a common historical experience among all groups and individuals included under this designation. Aside from a mutual history of oppression at the hands of those in power (not an insignificant commonality), a shared historical experience among these disparate groups is an illusion. A presumed common experience also suggests that there is no conflict among these groups. As we know, such conflicts not only exist, but they have resulted in periodic outbreaks of serious interethnic violence. These have emanated not only from a shared oppression and the competition for scarce resources that results from political domination, but also from deep-seated cultural and social differences among the groups themselves.

People of color is also inaccurate when referring, for example, to Latinos of European background, as is the case with many Argentinians and Cubans, and light-skinned Latinos in general. When these Latinos refer to themselves in this way, they risk implying that they have experienced the same level of virulent racism as their darker skinned compatriots.

At the moment, there is no completely adequate language for such a huge conglomeration of groups. Whenever possible, and for the sake of clarity, we prefer to identify people by their specific ethnic or racial group, thus avoiding the lumping together of people of different groups.

PROBLEMS WITH LUMPING GROUPS TOGETHER

Overarching terms cause a number of problems. The term *European American*, for example, implies that all those who are White are also European American. This is not always true, as in the case of Jews: Many are European American (Polish, German, English, etc.), but many are not. More important, in the context of the Holocaust, the historical experience of Jews is quite different from that of many other European Americans. The same can be said of Romany people (commonly called *Gypsies*), who also were victims of the Holocaust. Language remains imprecise in capturing these differences.

Although some groups, such as Latinos, share a great many cultural attributes, they are also quite different from one another. A Peruvian and a Dominican, for example, may both speak Spanish, practice the Catholic religion, and share deeply rooted family values. However, the native language of some Peruvians is not Spanish, and Dominicans have an African background not shared by most Peruvians. These differences, among many others, often go unacknowledged when we speak simply of *Latinos* or *Hispanics*. Within the context of the U.S. experience, Latinos differ in many respects, including race, social class, level of education, and length of time in this country. Each of these factors may make a dramatic difference in the school achievement of children from distinct groups.

The same discussion applies to the terms *Native Americans* and *Asian Americans*, each of which includes groups with tremendously distinct histories and cultures. Again, although they may share some basic cultural values and historical experiences, specific ethnic characteristics and historical frames of reference are lost when we lump these people together. A Bolivian, for example, may refer to herself first as a Bolivian and then as a Latina. The same can be said for a Navajo, who may identify first with his Nation and second with American Indians as a larger group, or a Pakistani who prefers *Pakistani* to the all-encompassing term *Asian*.

At the same time, it is also true that there are many commonalities among all Indigenous groups just as there are among most Latino groups or people of African descent. These may include a worldview, a common historical experience, and shared conditions of life in the United States. Where such commonalities exist, we sometimes use the more generalized term. In addition, we are restricted by the fact that much of the research literature documenting the experiences of both American Indian and Hispanic groups does not distinguish the ethnic groups within them. As a result, we are sometimes obliged to use the generic term in spite of our preference to disaggregate along ethnic lines.

A similar argument can be made for Asian and Asian American ethnic groups. These classifications include an incredibly diverse array of groups, such as Chinese, Japanese, Vietnamese, Cambodian, Filipino, Native Hawaiian, Pakistani, and Indian. To believe that one designation could possibly be sufficient to cover them all is foolhardy, because they differ not only in history and culture but also in language, unlike Latinos, most of whom share at least a common language. Like Latinos, Asians also differ in social class, length of time in the United States, immigrant experience, and educational background and experiences, and these differences invariably influence the educational achievement of the children in these groups.[5] The term *Pacific Islander* is now used together with *Asian* to provide a more specific term for a number of groups. It is preferred by most Asians and Pacific Islanders to the outdated and exotic term *Oriental* or even *East Indian*, but still fails to account for all differences.

Finally, a word about the terms *America* and *American*. Because *America* refers to the entire Western Hemisphere, whenever possible we will refer to our country as the United States. Also, although *American* has been limited by common use within our borders to mean U.S. citizens, this is not only inaccurate but also offensive to millions of North, Central, and South Americans who consider themselves as American as people living within the United States. Nevertheless, because the term *American* is in common use in the United States, we use it at times to refer to citizens and residents of the United States.

SUMMARY

The language choices we have made throughout this book are meant, first and foremost, to affirm diversity. We have attempted to identify people as they would want to be identified. We have also used terms that emphasize what people are rather than what they are not—that is, we have avoided terms such as *non-White* and *non-English-speaking*. Readers familiar with the first four editions of this text will note that we have made some changes in terminology throughout the years, and we expect to continue to do so. Language that refers to human beings is inaccurate and imprecise, and although we have strived to be both precise and sensitive, our choices are certainly open to debate.

Language can capture only imperfectly the nuances of who we are as people, and, like multicultural education itself, it is in constant flux. For example, the great increase in the number of biethnic, multiethnic, biracial, and multiracial people in our society, and their insistence on identifying as such, is a reminder that words cannot totally describe the multifaceted identities of human beings. The expansion of terms associated with sexual orientation is another example. Only a few years ago, *lesbian* and *gay* were the only terms known by the general public, but now *bisexual*, *transsexual*, *transgender*, and other terms describing sexual orientation are making their way into the general vocabulary. The acronym *LGBT* to represent the lesbian, gay, bisexual, and transgender community is now widely used (see Appendix for definitions). Many young people are refusing to accept rigid categorizations based on one culture, race, or other kind of social grouping, claiming instead what Gloria Anzaldúa and others have called a "hybrid identity"[6] and one that is constantly changing. A number of examples of these hybrid identities are included in the case studies and snapshots in subsequent chapters.

Language carries great weight in education because it affects the lives of students. As educators, we need to be careful about what terms we use and how, since our choices may send negative messages that can have long-term effects. We therefore need to pay close attention and be sensitive to the connotations and innuendos of our talk.

◆◆◆ Companion Website

For access to additional case studies, weblinks, concept cards, and other material related to this chapter, visit the text's companion website at **www.ablongman.com/nieto5e**.

Notes to Chapter 2

1. Gordon W. Allport, *The Nature of Prejudice* (Reading, MA: Addison-Wesley, 1954).

2. For a useful dictionary on the evolution of ethnic and racial terms and the biases they contain, see *The Color of Words* by Philip H. Herbst (Yarmouth, ME: Intercultural Press, 1997).

3. Martha E. Gimenez, " 'Latino/Hispanic': Who Needs a Name? The Case Against a Standardized Terminology." In *Latinos and Education: A Critical Reader*, edited by Antonia Darder, Rodolfo D. Torres, and Henry Gutiérrez (New York: Routledge, 1997): 225–239.

4. The term "DiaspoRican" was popularized by Nuyorican poet Mariposa. See J. M. Valldejuli and Juan Flores. "New Rican Voices: Un Muestrario/A Sampler at the Millennium." *Journal of the Center for Puerto Rican Studies*, v. 12, n. 1 (2000), 49–96. The term also has been taken up in fields such as education. See René Antrop-González and Anthony De Jesús, "Toward a Theory of *Critical Care* in Urban Small School Reform: Examining Structures and Pedagogies of Caring in Two Latino Community-Based Schools." *International Journal of Qualitative Studies in Education*, v. 19, n. 4 (2006), 409–433.

5. For a helpful discussion of these differences, see Valerie Ooka Pang, Peter N. Kiang, and Yoon K. Pak, "Asian Pacific American Students: Challenging a Biased Educational System." In *Handbook of Research on Multicultural Education*, 2nd ed., edited by James A. Banks and Cherry A. McGee Banks (San Francisco: Jossey-Bass, 2004): 542–563.

6. Gloria Anzaldúa, *Borderlands/La Frontera: The New Mestiza* (San Francisco: Aunt Lute Press, 1987).

3

Multicultural Education and School Reform

Rachel Ilana Shuman, *Providence/Hope*. Mixed media collage, 2005.

"We don't need multicultural education here; most of our students are White."

"I don't see color. All my students are the same to me."

"We shouldn't talk about racism in school because it has nothing to do with learning. Besides, it'll just make the kids feel bad."

"Let's not focus on negative things. Can't we all just get along?"

"I want to include multicultural education in my curriculum, but there's just no time for it."

"Oh, yes, we have multicultural education here: We celebrate Black History Month, and there's an annual Diversity Dinner."

"Multicultural education is just therapy for Black students."

"Multicultural education became irrelevant after 9/11. It's divisive because it focuses on differences. Now, more than ever, we need to stress our similarities."

In discussing multicultural education with teachers and other educators over many years, we have heard all these comments and other similar remarks. Statements such as these reflect a profound misconception of multicultural education.

When multicultural education is mentioned, many people first think of lessons in human relations and sensitivity training, units about ethnic holidays, education in inner-city schools, or food festivals. If multicultural education is limited to these issues, the potential for substantive change in schools is severely diminished. Moreover, those who called for an end to multicultural education after September 11, 2001, missed the boat. Rather than eliminating it, we believe that 9/11 underscored the need to emphasize multicultural education more than ever. In fact, we believe that nothing is more divisive than a monocultural education, because such an education excludes so many people and perspectives from schools' curricula and pedagogy.

When broadly conceptualized, multicultural education can lead to more understanding and empathy. It can also help to address the four areas of potential conflict and inequity to be addressed in Part 2—namely, racism and discrimination, structural conditions in schools that may limit learning, the impact of culture on learning, and language diversity. However, it is necessary to stress that multicultural education is not a panacea for all educational ills. Because schools are part of our communities, they reflect the stratification and social inequities of the larger society. As long as this is the case, no school program alone, no matter how broadly conceptualized, can change things completely without addressing inequalities in the larger society. It will not cure underachievement, eliminate boring and irrelevant curriculum, or stop vandalism. It will not automatically motivate families to participate in schools, reinvigorate tired and dissatisfied teachers, or guarantee a lower dropout rate.

Despite these caveats, when multicultural education is conceptualized as broadbased school reform, it can offer hope for real change. Multicultural education in a sociopolitical context is both richer and more complex than simple lessons on getting along or units on ethnic festivals. By focusing on major conditions contributing to underachievement, a broadly conceptualized multicultural education permits educators to explore alternatives to a system that promotes failure for too many of its students. Such an exploration can lead to the creation of a richer and more productive school climate and a deeper awareness of the role of culture and language in learning. Seen in this comprehensive way, educational success for all students is a realistic goal rather than an impossible ideal.

This chapter proposes a definition of multicultural education based on the context and terminology demonstrated in the preceding chapters and analyzes the seven primary characteristics included in the definition. These characteristics underscore the role that multicultural education can play in reforming schools and providing an equal and excellent education for all students. This definition of multicultural education emerges from the reality of persistent problems in our nation's schools, especially the lack of achievement among students of diverse backgrounds. A comprehensive definition emphasizes the context and process of education rather than viewing multicultural education as an add-on or luxury disconnected from the everyday lives of students.

In spite of some differences among major theorists, during the past 30 years there has been remarkable consistency in the educational field about the goals, purposes, and reasons for multicultural education.[1] But no definition of multicultural education can truly capture all its complexities. The definition we present here reflects one way of conceptualizing the issues; it is based on our many years of experience as students, teachers, researchers, and teacher educators. We hope that it will serve to encourage further dialogue and reflection among readers. So, although we propose seven characteristics that we believe are essential in multicultural education, you might come up with just three, or with 15. The point is not to develop a definitive way to understand multicultural education but instead to start you thinking about the interplay of societal and school structures and contexts and how they influence learning.

What we believe *is* essential is an emphasis on the sociopolitical context of education and a rejection of the notion that multicultural education is either a superficial addition of content to the curriculum, or, alternatively, the magic pill that will do away with all educational problems. In the process of considering our definition of multicultural education, it is our hope that you will develop your own ideas, priorities, and perspective.

A Definition of Multicultural Education

We define multicultural education in a sociopolitical context as follows: Multicultural education is a process of comprehensive school reform and basic education for all students. It challenges and rejects racism and other forms of discrimination in schools and society and accepts and affirms the pluralism (ethnic, racial, linguistic, religious, economic, and gender, among others) that students, their communities, and teachers reflect. Multicultural education permeates schools' curriculum and instructional strategies as well as the interactions among teachers, students, and families and the very way that schools conceptualize the nature of teaching and learning. Because it uses critical pedagogy as its underlying philosophy and focuses on knowledge, reflection, and action (praxis) as the basis for social change, multicultural education promotes democratic principles of social justice.

The seven basic characteristics of multicultural education in this definition are as follows:

1. Multicultural education is antiracist education.
2. Multicultural education is basic education.
3. Multicultural education is important for all students.
4. Multicultural education is pervasive.
5. Multicultural education is education for social justice.
6. Multicultural education is a process.
7. Multicultural education is critical pedagogy.

Multicultural Education
Is Antiracist Education

Antiracism, indeed antidiscrimination in general, is at the very core of a multicultural perspective. It is essential to keep the antiracist nature of multicultural education in mind because, in many schools, even some that espouse a multicultural philosophy, only superficial aspects of multicultural education are apparent. Celebrations of ethnic festivals are the extent of multicultural education programs in some schools. In others, sincere attempts to decorate bulletin boards with what is thought to be a multicultural perspective end up perpetuating the worst kind of stereotypes. Even where there are serious attempts to develop a truly pluralistic environment, it is not unusual to find incongruencies. In some schools, for instance, the highest academic tracks are overwhelmingly White, the lowest are populated primarily by students of color, and girls are nonexistent or invisible in calculus and physics classes. These are examples of multicultural education without an explicitly antiracist and antidiscrimination perspective.

Because many people erroneously assume that a school's multicultural program automatically takes care of racism, we stress that multicultural education *must be consciously antiracist*. Writing about multicultural education over 25 years ago, when the field was fairly new, Meyer Weinberg asserted:

> Most multicultural materials deal wholly with the cultural distinctiveness of various groups and little more. Almost never is there any sustained attention to the ugly realities of systematic discrimination against the same group that also happens to utilize quaint clothing, fascinating toys, delightful fairy tales, and delicious food. Responding to racist attacks and defamation is also part of the culture of the group under study.[2]

Being antiracist and antidiscriminatory means being mindful of how some students are favored over others in school policies and practices such as the curriculum, choice of materials, sorting policies, and teachers' interactions and relationships with students and their families. Consequently, to be inclusive and balanced, multicultural curriculum must, by definition, be antiracist. Teaching does not become more honest and critical simply by becoming more inclusive, but this is an important first step in ensuring that students have access to a wide variety of viewpoints. Although the beautiful and heroic aspects of our history should be taught, so must the ugly and exclusionary. Rather than viewing the world through rose-colored glasses, antiracist multicultural education forces teachers and students to take a long, hard look at everything as it was and is, instead of just how we wish it were.

Too many schools avoid confronting in an honest and direct way the negative aspects of history, the arts, and science. Michelle Fine has called this the "fear of naming," and it is part of the system of silencing in public schools.[3] To name might become too messy, or so the thinking goes. Teachers often refuse to engage their students in discussions about racism because it might "demoralize" them. Too dangerous a topic, it is often left untouched.

Related to the fear of naming is the insistence of schools on "sanitizing" the curriculum, or what Jonathon Kozol many years ago called "tailoring" important men and women for school use. Kozol described how schools manage to take the most exciting and memorable heroes and bleed the life and spirit completely out of them because it can be dangerous, he wrote, to teach a history "studded with so many bold, and revolutionary, and subversive, and exhilarating men and women." He described how, instead, schools drain these heroes of their passions, glaze them over with an implausible veneer, place them on lofty pedestals, and then tell "incredibly dull stories" about them.[4] Although he wrote these words many years ago, Kozol could just as well be writing about education in today's U.S. schools.

The process of sanitizing is nowhere more evident than in depictions of Martin Luther King, Jr. In attempting to make him palatable to the U.S. mainstream, schools have made King a milquetoast. The only thing most children know about him is that he kept "having a dream." School bulletin boards are full of ethereal pictures of Dr. King surrounded by clouds. If children get to read or hear any of his speeches at all, it is his "I Have a Dream" speech. As inspirational as this speech is, it is only one of his notable accomplishments. Rare indeed are allusions to his early and consistent opposition to the Vietnam War; his strong criticism of unbridled capitalism; and the connections he made near the end of his life among racism, capitalism, and war. This sanitization of Martin Luther King, a man full of passion and life, renders him an oversimplified, lifeless figure, thus making him a "safe hero."

Most of the heroes we present to our children are either those in the mainstream or those who have become safe through the process of what Kozol referred to as "tailoring." Others who have fought for social justice are often downplayed, maligned, or ignored. For example, although John Brown's actions in defense of the liberation of enslaved people are considered noble by many, in our history books he is presented, at best, as somewhat of a crazed idealist. Nat Turner is another example. The slave revolt that he led deserves a larger place in our history, if only to acknowledge that enslaved people fought against their own oppression and were not simply passive victims. However, Turner's name and role in U.S. history are usually overlooked, and Abraham Lincoln is presented as the Great Emancipator as if he single-handedly was responsible for the abolition of slavery (and with little acknowledgment of his own inconsistent ideas about race and equality). Nat Turner is not considered a safe hero; Abraham Lincoln is.

To be antiracist also means to work affirmatively to combat racism. It means making antiracism and antidiscrimination explicit parts of the curriculum and teaching young people skills in confronting racism. A school that is truly committed to a multicultural philosophy will closely examine both its policies and the attitudes and behaviors of its staff to determine how these might discriminate against some students. The focus on school policies and practices makes it evident that multicultural education is about more than the perceptions and beliefs of individual teachers and other educators. Multicultural education is antiracist because it exposes racist and discriminatory practices in schools.

Racism is seldom mentioned in school (it is bad, a dirty word) and, therefore, is not dealt with. Unfortunately, many teachers think that simply having lessons in getting along or celebrating Human Relations Week will make students nonracist or nondiscriminatory in general. But it is impossible to be untouched by racism, sexism, linguicism, heterosexism, ageism, anti-Semitism, classism, and ethnocentrism in a society characterized by all of them. To expect schools to be an oasis of sensitivity and understanding in the midst of this stratification is unrealistic. Therefore, part of the mission of the school becomes creating the environment and encouragement that legitimates talk about inequality and makes it a source of dialogue. Teaching the missing or fragmented parts of our history is crucial to achieving this mission.

Although White students may be uncomfortable by discussions about race, Henry Giroux has suggested that bringing race and racism into full view can become a useful and positive pedagogical tool to help students locate themselves and their responsibilities concerning racism.[5] In addition, Beverly Daniel Tatum's groundbreaking work on bringing discussions of race out of the closet proposes discussing race and racism within the framework of racial and cultural identity theory. Doing so, she contends, can help students and teachers focus on how racism negatively affects all people and can provide a sense of hope for positive changes.[6]

What about teachers? Because many teachers have had little experience with diversity, discussions of racism often threaten to disrupt their deeply held ideals of fair play and equality. Most teachers are uneasy with these topics, and therefore fruitful classroom discussions about discrimination rarely happen. If this continues to be the case, neither unfair individual behaviors nor institutional policies and practices in schools will change. Students of disempowered groups will continue to bear the brunt of these kinds of inequities. The dilemma is how to challenge the silence about race and racism so that teachers can enter into meaningful and constructive dialogue with their students. In speaking specifically about confronting this issue in teacher education, Marilyn Cochran-Smith writes, "To teach lessons about race and racism in teacher education is to struggle to unlearn racism itself—to interrogate the assumptions that are deeply embedded in the curriculum, to our own complicity in maintaining existing systems of privilege and oppression, and to grapple with our own failure."[7]

For example, in research with teachers from around the country, Karen McLean Donaldson found that many teachers were in denial about racism and its effects in schools. On the other hand, those who became active in antiracist projects broadened their understanding and were able to use their new skills in creating affirming learning environments for all their students.[8]

One of the reasons schools are reluctant to tackle racism and discrimination is that these are disturbing topics for those who have traditionally benefited by their race, gender, and social class, among other advantageous differences. Because instruction in, and discussion of, such topics place people in the role of either the victimizer or the victimized, an initial and logical reaction, for example, of European American teachers and students in discussing race, is to feel guilty. But being antiracist does not mean flailing about in guilt and remorse. Although this reaction may be understandable, remaining at this level is immobilizing. Teachers and students need to move beyond guilt to a state of invigorated awareness and informed confidence in which they take personal and group action for positive change rather than hide behind feelings of remorse.

The primary victims of racism and discrimination are those who suffer its immediate consequences, but racism and discrimination are destructive and demeaning to everyone. Keeping this in mind, it is easier for all teachers and students to face these issues. Although not everyone is directly guilty of racism and discrimination, we are all responsible for it. What does this mean? Primarily, it means that working actively for social justice is everyone's business. Yet it is often the victims of racism and other kinds of discrimination who are left to act on their own. Fern Sherman's case study, which follows Chapter 5, is a good example. Being the only Native American student in her entire school was difficult. For one, it meant that Fern felt a tremendous responsibility to confront, on her own, the racism she saw in texts and in the curriculum. Having allies to support her would have shifted the responsibility from her shoulders to others so that it could become a shared responsibility. Everybody loses out when a particular group of students is scapegoated. Rebecca Florentina's case study, which follows Chapter 6, is another example. As a lesbian, Rebecca felt the need to personally confront the heterosexual biases in her school, but this should have been viewed as everyone's responsibility. Indeed, we will have come a long way when everybody feels this same obligation.

Multicultural Education Is Basic Education

Given the recurring concern for teaching the "basics," multicultural education must be understood as basic education. Multicultural literacy is just as indispensable for living in today's world as reading, writing, arithmetic, and computer literacy. When multicultural education is peripheral to the core curriculum, it is perceived as irrelevant to basic education. One of the major stumbling blocks to implementing a broadly conceptualized multicultural education is the ossification of the "canon" in our schools.

The canon, as understood in contemporary U.S. education, assumes that the knowledge that is most worthwhile is already in place. This notion explains the popularity of E. D. Hirsch's series *What Every* [*First, Second, Third . . .*] *Grader Needs to Know*.[9] Geared primarily to parents, this series builds on the fear that their children simply will not measure up if they do not possess the core knowledge (usually in the form of facts) that they need to succeed in school. According to this rather narrow view, the basics have, in effect, already been defined, and the knowledge taught is inevitably European, male, and upper class in origin and conception. In a recent response to Hirsch's view of cultural literacy, Eugene Provenzo faults Hirsch for a limited and rigid understanding of cultural literacy that is ultimately impoverished, elitist, antidemocratic, and even un-American in that it excludes so much that is uniquely American.[10]

The idea that there is a static and sacred knowledge that must be mastered is especially evident in the arts and social sciences. For instance, art history classes rarely consider other countries besides France's, Italy's, and sometimes England's Great Masters, yet surely other nations besides Europe have had great masters. "Classical music" is another example. What is called "classical music" is actually European classical music. Africa, Asia, and Latin America define their classical music in different ways. This same ethnocentrism is found in our history books, which portray Europeans and European Americans as the "actors" and all others as the recipients, bystanders, or bit players of history. The canon, as it currently stands, however, is unrealistic and incomplete because history is never as one-sided as it appears in most of our schools' curricula. We need to expand the definition of *basic* education by opening up curricula to a variety of perspectives and experiences.

This is not to say that the concern that the canon tries to address is not a genuine one. Modern-day knowledge is so dispersed and compartmentalized that our young people learn very little about commonalities in our history and culture. There is little core knowledge to which they are exposed and this can be problematic, but proposing static curricula, almost exclusively with European and European American referents, does little to expand our actual common culture.

At the same time, it is unrealistic, for a number of reasons, to expect perfectly "equal treatment" about all groups of people in school curricula and instruction. A "force-fit," which tries to equalize the number of African Americans, women, Jewish Americans, gays, and so on in the curriculum, is not what multicultural education is about. A great many groups have been denied access to participation in history. Thus, their role has not been equal, at least if we consider history in the traditional sense of great movers and shakers, monarchs and despots, and makers of war and peace. But, even within this somewhat narrow view of history, the participation of people of diverse backgrounds and social identities has nevertheless been appreciable. These heretofore ignored participants deserve to be included. The point is that those who have been important and/or prominent in the evolution of our history, arts, literature, and science, yet invisible, should be made visible. Recent literature anthologies are a good example of the inclusion of more voices and perspectives than ever before. Did these people become "great writers" overnight, or was it simply that they were "buried" for too long?

We are not recommending simply the "contributions" approach to history, literature, and the arts.[11] Such an approach can easily become patronizing by simply adding bits and pieces to a preconceived canon. Rather, missing from most curricula is a consideration of how generally excluded groups have made history and affected the arts, literature, geography, science, and philosophy on their own terms.

The alternative to multicultural education is monocultural education, which reflects only one reality and is biased toward the dominant group. Monocultural education is the order of the day in most of our schools. What students learn represents only a fraction of what is available knowledge, and those who decide what is most important make choices that are influenced by their own limited background, education, and experiences. Because the viewpoints of so many are left out, monocultural education is, at best, an incomplete education. It deprives all students of the diversity that is part of our world.

No school can consider that it is doing a proper or complete job unless its students develop multicultural literacy. What such a conception means in practice will no doubt differ from school to school, but at the very least, we should expect all students to be fluent in a language other than their own, aware of the literature and arts of many different peoples, and conversant with the history and geography not only of the United States but also of African, Asian, Latin American, and European countries. Through such an education, we should expect students to develop social and intellectual skills that help them understand and empathize with a wide diversity of people. Nothing can be more basic than this.

MULTICULTURAL EDUCATION IS IMPORTANT FOR ALL STUDENTS

There is a widespread perception—or rather, misperception—that multicultural education is only for students of color, for urban students, or for so-called "disadvantaged" or "at-risk" students. This belief probably grew from the roots of multicultural education: the Civil Rights and Equal Education Movements of the 1960s. During that era, the primary objective of multicultural education was to address the needs of students who historically had been most neglected or miseducated by the schools, especially students of color. Those who first promoted multicultural education firmly believed that attention needed to be given to developing curriculum and materials that reflected these students' histories, cultures, and experiences. This thinking was historically necessary and is understandable even today, given the great curricular imbalance that continues to exist in most schools.

More recently, a broader conceptualization of multicultural education has gained acceptance. It is that all students are miseducated to the extent that they receive only a partial and biased education. Although it is true that the primary victims of biased education are those who are invisible in the curriculum, everyone misses out when education is biased. Important female figures, for example, are still largely absent in curricula, except in special courses on women's history that are few and far between. Working-class history is also absent in virtually all U.S. curricula. The children of the working class are deprived not only of a more forthright education but, more important, of a place in history, and students of all social class backgrounds are deprived of a more honest and complete view of our past. Likewise, there is a pervasive and impenetrable silence concerning gays and lesbians in most schools, not just in the curriculum but also in extracurricular activities. The result is that gay and lesbian students are placed at risk in terms of social well-being and academic achievement.[12]

Teachers in primarily White schools might think that multicultural education is not meant for their students. They could not be more wrong. White students receive only a partial education, which helps to legitimate their cultural blindness. Seeing only themselves, they may believe that they are the norm and thus most important and everyone else is secondary and less important. A recent book that challenges this perception (*What If All the Kids Are White?*) provides excellent strategies and resources for teachers working in mostly White communities.[13]

Males also receive an incomplete education because they (not to mention their female peers) learn little about women in their schooling. The children of the wealthy learn that the wealthy and the powerful are the real makers of history, the ones who have left their mark on civilization. Heterosexual students receive the message that gay and lesbian students should be ostracized because they are deviant and immoral. Only the able-bodied are reflected in most curricula, save for exceptions such as Helen Keller, who are presented as either bigger than life or as sources of pity. The humanity of all students is jeopardized as a result.

Multicultural education is, by definition, *inclusive*. Because it is *about* all people, it is also *for* all people, regardless of their ethnicity, ability, social class, language, sexual orientation, religion, gender, race, or other difference. It can even be convincingly argued that students from the dominant culture need multicultural education more than others because they are generally the most miseducated or uneducated about diversity. For example, European American youths often think that they do not even have a culture, at least not in the same sense that easily culturally identifiable youths do. At the same time, they feel that their ways of living, doing things, believing, and acting are "normal." Anything else is "ethnic" and exotic.

Feeling as they do, young people from dominant groups are prone to develop an unrealistic view of the world and of their place in it. These are the children who learn not to question, for example, the name of "flesh-colored" bandages, even though they are not the flesh color of 75 percent of the world's population. They do not even have to think about the fact that everyone, Christian or not, gets holidays at Christmas and Easter and that the holidays of other religions are given little attention in our calendars and school schedules. They may automatically assume that all children are raised by heterosexual biological parents and may be surprised to learn that many children are instead raised by just one parent, adoptive parents, grandparents, or lesbian or gay parents. Whereas children from dominated groups may develop feelings of inferiority based on their schooling, dominant group children may develop feelings of superiority. Both responses are based on incomplete and inaccurate information about the complexity and diversity of the world, and both are harmful.

In spite of this, multicultural education continues to be thought of by many educators as education for the "culturally different" or the "disadvantaged." Teachers in predominantly European American schools, for example, may feel it is not important or necessary to teach their students anything about the Civil Rights Movement. Likewise, only in scattered bilingual programs in Mexican American communities are students exposed to literature by Mexican and Mexican American authors, and ethnic studies classes are often only offered at high schools with a high percentage of students of color. These are ethnocentric interpretations of multicultural education.

The thinking behind these actions is paternalistic as well as misinformed. Because anything remotely digressing from the "regular" (European American) curriculum is automatically considered soft by some educators, a traditional response to making a curriculum multicultural is to water it down. Poor pedagogical decisions are then based on the premise that so-called disadvantaged students need a watered-down version of the "real" curriculum, whereas more privileged children can handle the "regular" or more academically challenging curriculum. But, rather than dilute it, making a curriculum multicultural inevitably enriches it. All students would be enriched by reading the poetry of Langston Hughes or the stories of Gary Soto, by being fluent in a second language, or by understanding the history of Islam.

MULTICULTURAL EDUCATION IS PERVASIVE

Multicultural education is neither an activity that happens at a set period of the day nor another subject area to be covered. Having a "multicultural teacher" who goes from class to class in the same way as the music or art teacher is not what multicultural education should be about either. If this is a school's concept of multicultural education, it is little wonder that teachers sometimes decide that it is a frill they cannot afford.

A true multicultural approach is pervasive. It permeates everything: the school climate, physical environment, curriculum, and relationships among teachers and students and community.[14] It is apparent in every lesson, curriculum guide, unit, bulletin board, and letter that is sent home; it can be seen in the process by which books and audiovisual aids are acquired for the library, in the games played during recess, and in the lunch that is served. *Multicultural education is a philosophy, a way of looking at the world*, not simply a program or a class or a teacher. In this comprehensive way, multicultural education helps us rethink school reform.

What might a multicultural philosophy mean in the way that schools are organized? For one, it would probably mean the end of rigid forms of ability tracking, which inevitably favors some students over others. It would also mean that the complexion of the school, both literally and figuratively, would change. That is, schools would be desegregated rather than segregated along lines of race and social class as they are now. In addition, there would be an effort to have the entire school staff be more representative of our nation's diversity. Pervasiveness would be apparent in the great variety and creativity of instructional strategies, so that students from all cultural groups, and females as well as males, would benefit from methods other than the traditional. The curriculum would be completely overhauled and would include the histories, viewpoints, and insights of many different peoples and both males and females. Topics usually considered "dangerous" could be talked about in classes, and students would be encouraged to become critical thinkers. Textbooks and other instructional materials would also reflect a pluralistic perspective. Families and other community people would be visible in the schools because they offer a unique and helpful viewpoint. Teachers, families, and students would have the opportunity to work together to design motivating and multiculturally appropriate curricula.

In other less global but no less important ways, the multicultural school would probably look vastly different. For example, the lunchroom might offer a variety of international meals, not because they are exotic delights but because they are the foods people in the community eat daily. Sports and games from all over the world might be played, and not all would be competitive. Letters would be sent home in the languages that the particular child's family understands. Children would not be punished for speaking their native language. On the contrary, they would be encouraged to do so, and it would be used in their instruction as well. In summary, the school would be a learning environment in which curriculum, pedagogy, and outreach are all consistent with a broadly conceptualized multicultural philosophy.

MULTICULTURAL EDUCATION IS EDUCATION FOR SOCIAL JUSTICE

All good education connects theory with reflection and action, which is what Brazilian educator Paulo Freire defined as *praxis*.[15] Developing a multicultural perspective means learning how to think in more inclusive and expansive ways, reflecting on what is learned, and applying that learning to real situations. Nearly a century ago, educational philosopher John Dewey described what happens when education is not connected to reflection and action when he wrote "information severed from thoughtful action is dead, a mind-crushing load."[16] Multicultural education invites students and teachers to put their learning into action for social justice (for a definition of social justice, see Chapter 1). Whether debating a difficult issue, developing a community newspaper, starting a collaborative program at a local senior center, or organizing a petition for the removal of a potentially dangerous waste treatment plant in the neighborhood, students learn that they have power, collectively and individually, to make change.

This aspect of multicultural education fits in particularly well with the developmental level of young people who, starting in the middle elementary grades, are very conscious of what is fair and unfair. If their pronounced sense of justice is not channeled appropriately, the result can be anger, resentment, alienation, or dropping out of school physically or psychologically.

Preparing students for active membership in a democracy is also the basis of Deweyian philosophy and it has frequently been cited by schools as a major educational goal. But few schools serve as sites of apprenticeship for democracy. Policies and practices such as inflexible ability grouping, inequitable testing, monocultural curricula, and unimaginative pedagogy contradict this lofty aim. The result is that students in many schools perceive the claim of democracy to be a hollow and irrelevant issue. Henry Giroux, for example, has suggested that what he calls "the discourse of democracy" has been trivialized to mean such things as uncritical patriotism and mandatory pledges to the flag that the 9/11 disaster has exacerbated.[17] In some schools, democratic practices are found only in textbooks and confined to discussions of the American Revolution, and the chance for students to practice day-to-day democracy is minimal.

The fact that controversial topics such as power and inequality are rarely discussed in schools should come as no surprise. As institutions, schools are charged with maintaining the status quo, and discussing such issues might seem to threaten the status quo. But schools are also expected to promote equality. Exposing the contradictions between democratic ideals and actual manifestations of inequality makes many people uncomfortable, including some educators. Still, such matters are at the heart of a broadly conceptualized multicultural perspective because the subject matter of schooling is society, with all its wrinkles and warts and contradictions. Ethics and the distribution of power, status, and rewards are basic societal concerns; education *must* address them.

Although the connection between multicultural education and students' rights and responsibilities in a democracy is unmistakable, many young people do not learn about these responsibilities, about the challenges of democracy, or about the central role of citizens in ensuring and maintaining the privileges of democracy. Results from a recent study about the First Amendment, in which over 112,000 high school students were surveyed, is a chilling example of how little students understand about democracy. The project, which was funded by the John S. and James L. Knight Foundation, found that when the First Amendment was quoted to students, more than one-third of them felt that it went too far in the rights it guarantees. The report concluded that "It appears, in fact, that our nation's high schools are failing their students when it comes to instilling in them appreciation for the First Amendment."[18] In this situation, social justice becomes an empty concept.

Multicultural education can have a great impact in helping to turn this situation around. A multicultural perspective presumes that classrooms should not simply allow discussions that focus on social justice, but also welcome them and even plan actively for such discussions to take place. These discussions might center on issues that adversely and disproportionately affect disenfranchised communities—poverty, discrimination, war, the national budget—and what students can do to address these problems. Because all of these problems are pluralistic, education must be multicultural.

Multicultural Education Is a Process

Curriculum and materials represent the content of multicultural education, but multicultural education is, above all, a process, that is, it is ongoing and dynamic. No one ever stops becoming a multicultural person, and knowledge is never complete. This means that there is no established canon that is set in stone. Second, multicultural education is a process because it primarily involves relationships among people. The sensitivity and understanding teachers show their students are more crucial in promoting student learning than the facts and figures they may know about different ethnic and cultural groups. Also, multicultural education is a process because it concerns such intangibles as expectations of student achievement, learning environments, students' learning preferences, and other cultural variables that are absolutely essential for schools to understand if they are to become successful with all students. More detail on this is given in Chapter 4.

The dimension of multicultural education as a process is too often relegated to a secondary position, because content is easier to handle and has speedier results. For instance, staging an assembly program on Black History Month is easier than eliminating tracking: The former involves adding extracurricular content, and, although this is important and necessary, it is not as decisive at challenging fundamental perceptions about ability, social class, and race through the elimination of tracking. Another example: Changing a basal reader is easier than developing higher expectations for all students. The former involves substituting one book for another; the latter involves changing perceptions, behaviors, and knowledge, not an easy task. As a result, the processes of multicultural education are generally more complex, more politically volatile, and even more threatening to vested interests than introducing "controversial" content.

Because multicultural education is a process, it must debunk simplistic and erroneous conventional wisdom as well as dismantle policies and practices that are disadvantageous for some students at the expense of others. Through their teacher education programs, future teachers need to develop an awareness of the influence of culture and language on learning, the persistence of racism and discrimination in schools and society, and instructional and curricular strategies that encourage learning among a wide variety of students. Teachers' roles in the school also need to be redefined, because empowered teachers help to create learning environments in which students are empowered. Also, the role of families needs to be expanded so that the insights and values of the community can be accurately reflected in the school. Nothing short of a complete restructuring of curricula and the organization of schools is required. The process is complex, problematic, controversial, and time consuming, but it is one in which teachers and schools must engage to make their schools truly multicultural.

MULTICULTURAL EDUCATION IS CRITICAL PEDAGOGY

Knowledge is neither neutral nor apolitical, yet it is generally treated by teachers and schools as if it were. Consequently, knowledge taught in our schools tends to reflect the lowest common denominator—that which is sure to offend the fewest (and the most powerful) and is least controversial. Students may leave school with the impression that all major conflicts have already been resolved, but history, including educational history, is still full of great debates, controversies, and ideological struggles. These controversies and conflicts are often left at the schoolhouse door.

Every educational decision made at any level, whether by a teacher or by an entire school system, reflects the political ideology and worldview of the decision maker. Decisions to dismantle tracking, discontinue standardized tests, lengthen the school day, use one reading program rather than another, study literature from the Harlem Renaissance or Elizabethan period (or both), or use learning centers rather than rows of chairs, all reflect a particular view of learners and of education.

All the decisions we, as educators, make, no matter how neutral they seem, may have an impact on the lives and experiences of our students. This is true of the curriculum, books, and other materials we provide for them. State and local guidelines and mandates may limit what particular schools and teachers choose to teach, and this too is a political decision. What is excluded is often as revealing as what is included. Much of the literature taught at the high school level, for instance, is still heavily male-oriented, European, and European American. The significance of women, people of color, and those who write in other languages (even if their work has been translated into English) is diminished, unintentionally or not.

A major problem with a monocultural curriculum is that it gives students only one way of seeing the world. When reality is presented as static, finished and flat, the underlying tensions, controversies, passions, and problems faced by people throughout history and today disappear. To be informed and active participants in a democratic society, students need to understand the complexity of the world and the many perspectives involved. Using a critical perspective, students learn that there is not just one way (or even two or three) of viewing issues.

To explain what we mean by "using a critical perspective," we will be facetious and use the number 17 to explain it: Let's say there are at least 17 ways of understanding reality, and, until we have learned all of them, we have only part of the truth. The point is that there are multiple perspectives on every issue, but most of us have learned only the "safe" or standard way of interpreting events and issues.

Textbooks in all subject areas exclude information about unpopular perspectives or the perspectives of disempowered groups in our society. These are the "lies my teacher told me" to which James Loewen refers in his powerful critique of U.S. history textbooks.[19] For instance, Thanksgiving is generally presented as an uncomplicated celebration in which Pilgrims and Indians shared the bounty of the harvest, but it is unlikely that the Wampanoags experienced Thanksgiving in this manner. One way to counter simplistic or one-sided views is to provide alternative or multiple views of the same topic. A good example is a book published by the Boston Children's Museum that presents a multiplicity of perspectives on Thanksgiving, including the Wampanoag perspective.[20] Likewise, few U.S. history texts include the perspective of working-class people, although they were and continue to be the backbone of our country. To cite another example, the immigrant experience is generally treated as a romantic and successful odyssey rather than the traumatic, wrenching, and often less-than-idyllic situation it was (and still is) for so many. The experiences of non-European immigrants or those forcibly incorporated into the United States are usually presented as if they were identical to the experiences of Europeans, which they have not at all been. We can also be sure that, if the perspectives of women were taken seriously, the school curriculum would be altered dramatically. The historian Howard Zinn provides one of the few examples of such a multifaceted, multicultural, and complex history. In his classic, *A People's History of the United States* (most recently updated in 2005), we clearly see a history full of passion and conflict with voices rarely included in traditional history texts.[21] All students need to understand these multiple perspectives and not only the viewpoints of dominant groups. Unless they do, students will continue to think of history as linear and fixed and to think of themselves as passive and unable to make changes in their communities and the larger society or even in their personal interactions.

According to James Banks, the main goal of a multicultural curriculum is to help students develop decision-making and social action skills.[22] By doing so, students learn to view events and situations from a variety of perspectives. A multicultural approach values diversity and encourages critical thinking, reflection, and action. Through this process, students are empowered. This is the basis of critical pedagogy. Its opposite is what Paulo Freire called "domesticating education,"—education that emphasizes passivity, acceptance, and submissiveness. According to Freire, education for domestication is a process of "transferring knowledge," whereas education for liberation is one of "transforming action."[23] Education that is liberating encourages students to take risks, to be curious, and to question. Rather than expecting students to repeat teachers' words, it expects them to seek their own answers.

How are critical pedagogy and multicultural education connected? They are what Geneva Gay has called "mirror images."[24] That is, they work together, according to Christine Sleeter, as "a form of resistance to dominant modes of schooling."[25] Critical pedagogy acknowledges rather than suppresses cultural and linguistic diversity. It is not simply the transfer of knowledge from teacher to students, even though that knowledge may challenge what students previously learned. Critical literacy, which developed from critical pedagogy and focuses specifically on language, has a similar goal. According to educational researcher Barbara Comber, "When teachers and students are engaged in critical literacy, they will be asking complicated questions about language and power, about people and lifestyle, about morality and ethics, about who is advantaged by the way things are and who is disadvantaged."[26]

A multicultural perspective does not simply operate on the principle of substituting one "truth" or perspective for another. Rather, it reflects on multiple and contradictory perspectives to understand reality more fully. The historian Ronald Takaki expressed it best when he said, "The multiculturalism I have been seeking is a serious scholarship that includes all American peoples and challenges the traditional master narrative of American history." He concludes that "[t]he intellectual purpose of multiculturalism is a more accurate understanding of who we are as Americans."[27] This means that, in our pluralistic society, teachers and students need to learn to understand even those viewpoints with which they may disagree—not to practice "political correctness," but to develop a critical perspective about what they hear, read, or see. Individuals with this kind of critical perspective can use the understanding gained from mindful reflection to act as catalysts for change.

Ira Shor has proposed that critical pedagogy is more difficult precisely because it moves beyond academic discourse: "Testing the limits by practicing theory and theorizing practice in a real context is harder and more risky than theorizing theory without a context."[28] Yet the typical curriculum discourages students from thinking critically. In this sense, critical pedagogy takes courage. What does it mean to teach with courage? A few examples are in order. For teachers Darcy Ballentine and Lisa Hill, the purpose of teaching reading to their second, third, and fourth graders meant challenging the children to take up "brave books" that included what the teachers called "dangerous truths." These books broached topics such as racism and inequality, issues generally avoided in children's books (although certainly present in the lives of many children). Ballentine and Hill reflected on their experience in this way: "In the year that we taught these two texts, as well as many other brave books, our children's voices—in discussion, in explanations of their art, and in their dramatic enactments—continually reminded us that the risks we were taking in our teaching made sense."[29]

More recently, teacher Vivian Vasquez, in her book *Negotiating Critical Literacies with Young Children*, documented her experiences in using a critical literacy approach with three- to five-year-olds. Among the many examples she cites, one concerns what happened when the children in her class realized that a classmate had not eaten at the annual school barbecue because he was a vegetarian and only hot dogs and hamburgers had been served. On their own initiative—but having learned to think critically about social action—the students drew up a petition about providing vegetarian alternatives and gave it to the event committee. The next year, vegetarian alternatives were provided. In her beautiful and hopeful book, Vasquez demonstrates that critical literacy is not about despair and anger but rather about joy and inclusion. She also affirms that even the youngest children can learn to think critically and positively about their ability to effect change through their actions.[30]

History is generally written by the conquerors, not by the vanquished or by those who benefit least in society. The result is that history books are skewed in the direction of dominant groups in a society. When American Indian people write history books, they generally say that Columbus *invaded* rather than *discovered* this land, and that there was no heroic *westward expansion,* but rather an *eastern encroachment.* Mexican Americans often include references to Aztlán, the legendary land that was overrun by Europeans during this encroachment. Many Puerto Ricans remove the gratuitous word *granted* that appears in so many textbooks and explain that U.S. citizenship was instead *imposed*, and they emphasize that U.S. citizenship was opposed by even the two houses of the legislature that existed in Puerto Rico in 1917. African American historians tend to describe the active participation of enslaved Africans in their own liberation, and they often include such accounts as slave narratives to describe the rebellion and resistance of their people. Working class people who know their history usually credit laborers rather than Andrew Carnegie with the tremendous building boom that occurred in the United States, and the rapid growth of the U.S. economy, during the late 19th century and the 20th century. And Japanese Americans frequently cite racist hysteria, economic exploitation, and propaganda as major reasons for their internment in U.S. concentration camps during World War II.

Critical pedagogy is also an exploder of myths. It helps to expose and demystify as well as demythologize some of the truths that we take for granted and to analyze them critically and carefully. Justice for all, equal treatment under the law, and equal educational opportunity, although certainly ideals worth believing in and striving for, are not always the reality. The problem is that we teach them as if they are, and were always, real and true, with no exceptions. Critical pedagogy allows us to have faith in these ideals while critically examining the discrepancies between the ideal and the reality.

Because critical pedagogy begins with the experiences and viewpoints of students, it is by its very nature multicultural. The most successful education is that which begins with the learner and, when a multicultural perspective underpins education, students themselves become the foundation for the curriculum. However, a liberating education also takes students beyond their own particular and therefore limited experiences, no matter what their background.

Critical pedagogy is not new, although it has been referred to by other terms in other times. In our country, precursors to critical pedagogy can be found in the work of African American educators such as Carter Woodson and W. E. B. DuBois.[31] In Brazil, the historic work of Paulo Freire influenced literacy and liberation movements throughout the world. Even before Freire, critical pedagogy was being practiced in other parts of the world. Almost half a century ago, Sylvia Ashton-Warner, teaching Maori children in New Zealand, found that the curriculum, materials, viewpoints, and pedagogy that had been used in educating them were all borrowed from the dominant culture. Because Maori children had been failed dismally by New Zealand schools, Ashton-Warner developed a strategy for literacy based on the children's experiences and interests. Calling it an "organic" approach, she taught children how to read by using the words they wanted to learn. Each child would bring in a number of new words each day, learn to read them, and then use them in writing. Because Ashton-Warner's approach was based on what children knew and wanted to know, it was extraordinarily successful. In contrast, basal readers, having little to do with Maori children's experiences, were mechanistic instruments that imposed severe limitations on the students' creativity and expressiveness.[32]

Other approaches that have successfully used the experiences of students are worth mentioning. The superb preschool curriculum developed nearly two decades ago by Louise Derman-Sparks and the Anti-Bias Curriculum Task Force is especially noteworthy. Another recent example is Mary Cowhey's approach. A first- and second-grade teacher, Cowhey has written about how she uses critical pedagogy to help create a strong community as well as to teach her students to question everything they learn. Catherine Compton-Lilly, in her role as a first-grade teacher and later a reading teacher, uses a critical perspective to develop classroom strategies to "change the world" by confronting assumptions about race, poverty, and culture. Instructional strategies based on students' languages, cultures, families, and communities are also included in wonderful books by the educational organizations Rethinking Schools and Teaching for Change. Ira Shor's descriptions of the work he does in his own college classroom are further proof of the power of critical pedagogy at all levels. In the same category, Enid Lee, Deborah Menkart, and Margo Okazawa-Rey have developed an exceptional professional development guide for teachers and preservice teachers.[33]

SUMMARY

Multicultural education represents a way of rethinking school reform because it responds to many of the problematic factors leading to school underachievement and failure. When implemented comprehensively, multicultural education can transform and enrich the schooling of all young people. Because multicultural education takes into account the cultures, languages, and experiences of all students, it can go beyond the simple transfer of skills to include those attitudes and critical, analytical abilities that have the potential to empower students for productive and meaningful lives.

This discussion leads us to an intriguing insight: In the final analysis, multicultural education as defined here is simply good pedagogy. That is, all good education takes students seriously, uses their experiences as a basis for further learning, and helps them to develop into informed, critically aware, and empowered citizens. What is multicultural about this? To put it simply, in our multicultural society, all good education needs to take into account the diversity of our student population. Multicultural education is good education for a larger number of our students. Is multicultural education just as necessary in a monocultural society? In response, we might legitimately ask whether even the most ethnically homogeneous society is truly monocultural, considering the diversity of social class, language, sexual orientation, physical and mental ability, and other human and social differences that exist in all societies. Our world is increasingly interdependent, and all students need to understand their role in a global society, not simply in their small town, city, or nation. Multicultural education is a process that goes beyond the changing demographics in a particular country. It is more effective education for a changing world.

◆◆◆ To Think About

1. What do you see as the difference between a broadly conceptualized multicultural education and multicultural education defined in terms of "holidays and heroes"?

2. Do you believe it is important for antiracism and antidiscrimination, in general, to be at the core of multicultural education? Why or why not?

3. Would you say that European American students are miseducated if they are not exposed to a multicultural curriculum? What about males if they do not learn about women in history? Why?

4. Think of a number of curriculum ideas that conform to the definition of multicultural education as social justice. How might students be engaged through the curriculum to consider and act on issues of social justice? Give some specific examples.

5. How do you define multicultural education? Explain your definition.

◆◆◆ Activities for Personal, School, and Community Change

1. Prepare a public presentation on the benefits of multicultural education for your colleagues, a group of new teachers, or a group of parents. What might you include in your presentation to convince skeptics that multicultural education, broadly defined and implemented, is necessary for your school?

2. Ask to be on your school's hiring committee when the next teaching position becomes available. How can you use your influence to define the job qualifications and job description in a way that includes multicultural education? What should these be?

3. With a group of colleagues, develop an art, science, or math project that builds on multicultural education as critical pedagogy. How would you do this? In what activities would students be involved? How would these activities motivate them to think critically? Discuss the results with your colleagues.

◆◆◆ Companion Website

For access to additional case studies, weblinks, concept cards, and other material related to this chapter, visit the text's companion website at **www.ablongman.com/nieto5e**.

Racism, Discrimination, and Expectations of Students' Achievement

Winston Chmelinski. *Trust me.* Acrylic painting, 2006.

"[Racists have power] only if you let them! We'll stick with [the example of] striped shirts: If I go where everyone is wearing solids, and I'm wearing a stripe, and someone comes up to me and tells me, 'You don't belong here; you're wearing stripes,' I'll say, 'I belong anywhere I want to belong.' And I'll stand right there! But there are some people who just say, 'Oh, okay,' and will turn around and leave. Then the racist has the power."

— Linda Howard, interviewee

65

Linda Howard, one of the interviewees whose case study follows this chapter, was directly harmed by racism in and out of school, and she developed a sophisticated understanding of it on both an individual and an institutional level. As you will see in her case study, Linda thought very deeply about racism. Regrettably, too many teachers and other educators have not. In this chapter, we explore the impact that racism, other biases, and expectations of student abilities may have on achievement. We focus on racism as an example of bias but also discuss other kinds of personal and institutional discrimination. These include discrimination on the basis of gender (sexism), ethnic group (ethnocentrism), social class (classism), language (linguicism),[1] sexual orientation and lesbian, gay, bisexual, and transgender (LGBT) identities (heterosexism), age (ageism), and discrimination against Jews (anti-Semitism), against Arabs (anti-Arab discrimination), and against people with disabilities (ableism), among other differences.

RACISM AND DISCRIMINATION: DEFINITIONS AND DIMENSIONS

Although the terms *racism* and *prejudice* are often used interchangeably, they do not mean the same thing. Gordon Allport, in his groundbreaking work on the nature of prejudice, quotes a United Nations document that defines discrimination as "any conduct based on a distinction made on grounds of natural or social categories, which have no relation either to individual capacities or merits, or to the concrete behavior of the individual person."[2] This definition is helpful but incomplete for two reasons. For one, it fails to describe the harmful *effects* of such conduct; for another, it fails to move beyond the individual level. More broadly speaking, *discrimination* (whether based on race, gender, social class, or other differences) denotes negative or destructive *behaviors* that can result in denying some groups life's necessities as well as the privileges, rights, and opportunities enjoyed by other groups. Discrimination is usually based on prejudice, that is, the attitudes and beliefs of individuals about entire groups of people. These attitudes and beliefs are generally, but not always, negative. Attitudes alone, however, are not as harmful as the behaviors, policies, and practices that result from such attitudes.

Our society, among many others, categorizes people according to both visible and invisible traits, uses such classifications to assign behavioral and cognitive traits to these categories, and then applies policies and practices based on these categories that jeopardize some people and benefit others.[3] In the United States, the conventional norm used to measure all other groups is European American, upper-middle class, English-speaking, heterosexual, able-bodied, and male. Classifications based on race, ethnicity, gender, social class, and other physical or social differences are omnipresent. Frequently, they result in gross exaggerations and stereotypes: Girls are not as smart as boys; African Americans have rhythm; Asians are studious; Poles are simple-minded; Jews are smart; and poor people need instant gratification. Although some of these may appear to be "positive" stereotypes, both "negative" and "positive" stereotypes have negative results because they limit our perception of entire groups of people. There are two major problems with categorizing people in this way. First, people of all groups begin to believe the stereotypes, and, second, both material and psychological resources are doled out accordingly.

Racism and other forms of discrimination are based on assumptions that one ethnic group, class, gender, or language is superior to all others. Researcher Carol Lee describes these assumptions as "folk theories about groups in the human family that are inextricably tied to relationships of power and dominance."[4] Discrimination based on perceptions of superiority is part of the structure of schools; the curriculum; the education most teachers receive; and the interactions among teachers, students, and the community. But, discrimination is not simply an individual bias; it is above all an *institutional practice*. It is for this reason that individual effort alone is not generally enough to counteract racism and other negative institutional practices. In our society, the metaphor of "pulling yourself up by your bootstraps" is powerful, it fails to explain how structural inequality gets in the way of individual efforts.

Individual and Institutional Dimensions of Racism and Discrimination

Too often, prejudice and discrimination are viewed by many people as *individuals'* negative perceptions toward members of other groups. Consequently, most definitions of racism and discrimination obscure the institutional nature of oppression. Although the beliefs and behaviors of individuals may be very hurtful and psychologically damaging, institutional discrimination—that is, the systematic use of economic and political power in institutions (such as schools) that leads to detrimental policies and practices—does far greater damage. These policies and practices have a destructive effect on groups that share a particular identity (be it racial, ethnic, gender, or other). The major difference between individual and institutional discrimination is the wielding of *power*. It is primarily through the power of the people who control institutions, such as schools, that oppressive policies and practices are reinforced and legitimated. Linda Howard, the young interviewee introduced at the beginning of this chapter, understood this distinction. In her case study, she distinguishes between prejudice and racism in this way: "We all have some type of person that we don't like, whether it's from a different race, or from a different background, or they have different habits." But she goes on to explain, as we saw in her quote at the beginning of the chapter, that a racist is someone who has the *power* to carry out his or her prejudices.

Here's another example: Let's say that you are prejudiced against tall people. Although your bias may hurt tall individuals because you refuse to befriend them or because you make fun of them, you can do very little to limit their options in life. If, however, you belong to a group of powerful "non-talls" and you limit the access of tall people to certain neighborhoods, prohibit them from receiving quality health care through particular policies, discourage or outlaw intermarriage between "talls" and people of short or average height, develop policies against the employment of "talls" in high-status professions, and place all children who are the offspring of "talls" (or who show early signs of becoming above average in height) in the lowest ability tracks in schools, then your bias would have teeth and its institutional power would be clear. The following discussion focuses primarily on this kind of discrimination, that is, *institutional discrimination*.

Institutional discrimination generally refers to how people are excluded or deprived of rights or opportunities as a result of the normal operations of the institution. Although the individuals involved in the institution may not themselves be prejudiced or have any racist intentions, or even awareness of how others may be harmed, the result may nevertheless be racism. Intentional and unintentional racism may be different, but because they both result in negative outcomes, in the end it does not really matter whether racism and other forms of discrimination are intentional. Rather than trying to figure out whether the intent of a discriminatory action was to do harm or not, educators' time would do better spent addressing the *effects* of racism.

THE SYSTEMIC NATURE OF DISCRIMINATION

When we understand racism and other forms of discrimination as a *systemic* problem, not simply as an individual dislike for a particular group of people, we can better understand the negative and destructive effects it can have. Vanessa Mattison, whose case study is one of those that follows this chapter, provides a good example of a young person struggling to reconcile our country's lofty ideals of equality and fair play with the reality of the injustice she saw around her. Vanessa was committed to promoting social justice, but she saw it primarily as working to change the attitudes and behaviors of individuals. She had not yet made the connection between racism and institutional oppression, and she did not grasp that institutional racism is far more harmful than individual biases or acts of meanness. But she was beginning to see that certain norms existed that were unfair to Blacks, women, and gays and lesbians. In her words, "There's all these underlying rules that if you're not this, you can't do that."

This is meant neither to minimize the powerful effects of individual prejudice and discrimination, which can be personally painful, nor to suggest that discrimination is perpetrated only by certain groups, for example, by Whites toward Blacks. There is no monopoly on prejudice and individual discrimination; they may be directed at any group and even occur within groups. However, in our society, interethnic and intraethnic biases and personal prejudices, while negative and hurtful, simply do not have the long-range and life-limiting effects of institutional racism and other kinds of institutional discrimination.

As an illustration of institutional racism in schools, let us look at how testing practices are used. What places some students at a disadvantage is not just that particular teachers have prejudiced attitudes about them; teachers may have negative attitudes or may, in fact, like the students very much. Instead, what places the students at jeopardy is the fact that they are labeled, grouped, and tracked, sometimes for the length of their schooling, or even denied a high school diploma, because of their score on a high-stakes test. In this case, it is institutions—school systems and the testing industry—that have a major negative impact.

Prejudice and discrimination, then, are not just personality traits or individual psychological dysfunctions; they are also a manifestation of economic, political, and social power. The institutional definition of racism is not always easy to accept because it goes against deeply held ideals of equality and justice in our nation. According to Beverly Tatum, "An understanding of racism as a system of advantage presents a serious challenge to the notion of the United States as a just society where rewards are based solely on one's merits."[5] Racism as an institutional system implies that some people and groups benefit and others lose. Whites, whether they intend to or not, benefit in a racist society; males benefit in a sexist society. Discrimination always helps somebody—those with the most power—which explains why racism, sexism, and other forms of discrimination continue in spite of the fact that everyone claims to be against them.

According to the late Meyer Weinberg, a well-known historian whose research focused on school desegregation, racism is a system of privilege and penalty. That is, one is rewarded or punished in housing, education, employment, health, and in other institutions by the simple fact of belonging to a particular group, regardless of one's individual merits or faults. He wrote, "Racism consists centrally of two facets: First, a belief in the inherent superiority of some people and the inherent inferiority of others; and second, the acceptance of distributing goods and services—let alone respect—in accordance with such judgments of unequal worth." In addressing the institutional nature of racism, he added, "Racism is always collective. Prejudiced individuals may join the large movement, but they do not cause it." According to this concept, what Weinberg called the "silence of institutional racism" and the "ruckus of individual racism" are mutually supportive.[6] It is sometimes difficult to separate one level of racism from the other, because they feed on and inform one another. What is crucial, according to Weinberg, is understanding that the doctrine of White supremacy is at the root of racism.

THE HISTORY AND PERSISTENCE OF RACISM IN U.S. SCHOOLS

As institutions, schools respond to and reflect the larger society. Therefore, it is not surprising that racism finds its way into schools in much the same way that it finds its way into other institutions, such as housing, employment, and the criminal justice system. In schools, overt expressions of racism may be less common today than in the past, but racism does not exist only when schools are legally segregated or racial epithets are used. Racism is also manifested in rigid ability tracking, low expectations of students based on their identity, and inequitably funded schools, among other policies and practices.

Racism and other forms of discrimination—particularly sexism, classism, ethnocentrism, and linguicism—have a long history in our schools, and their effects are widespread and long lasting. The most blatant form of discrimination is the actual withholding of education, as was the case historically with African Americans and sometimes with American Indians. To teach enslaved Africans to read was a crime punishable under the law, and it became a subversive activity that was practiced by

Blacks in ingenious ways.[7] Another overt form of discrimination is segregating students, by law or custom, according to their race, ethnicity, or gender, as was perpetrated at one time or another against African American, Mexican American, Japanese, and Chinese students as well as against females. Yet another form is forcing a group into boarding schools, as was done to American Indian students well into the twentieth century. In such groups, children were encouraged to adopt the ways of the dominant culture in sundry ways, from subtle persuasion to physical punishment for speaking their native language.[8] All of these are bitter reminders of the inequities of U.S. educational history.

Unfortunately, the discrimination that children face in schools is not a thing of the past. School practices and policies continue to discriminate against some children in very concrete ways. Recent studies have found that most students of color are in schools that are still segregated by race and social class, and the situation is worsening rather than improving. The result is that today, students of all races are less likely to interact with those of other backgrounds than at any time in the past three decades.[9] At the impetus of the Civil Rights Movement, many school systems throughout the United States were indeed becoming desegregated, but less than rigorous implementation of desegregation plans, "White flight" (that is, the movement of Whites to rural and suburban areas and to private schools), and housing patterns succeeded in resegregating many schools. Segregation invariably results in school systems that are "separate and unequal" because segregated schools are funded differently. In general, fewer resources are provided to schools in poor communities, and vastly superior resources provided to schools in wealthier communities.

Segregation often results in students' receiving differential schooling on the basis of their social class, race, and ethnicity. In addition, schools that serve students of color tend to provide curricula that are watered down and at a lower level than those of schools that serve primarily White middle-class students. Also, teachers in poor urban schools tend to have less experience and less preparation than those who teach in schools that serve primarily European American and middle-class students. Even when they are desegregated, many schools resegregate students through practices such as rigid ability tracking. Consequently, desegregating schools, in and of itself, does not guarantee educational equity.

MANIFESTATIONS OF RACISM AND DISCRIMINATION IN SCHOOLS

Racism and discrimination are manifested in numerous school practices and policies. Policies that are likely to jeopardize educationally marginalized students are most common in precisely the institutions in which those students are found. For example, studies have found that some policies have especially negative consequences for African American, Latino, and American Indian students. This is the case, for instance, with rigid ability tracking and high-stakes tests.[10]

It is sometimes difficult to separate what is racist or discriminatory from what appear to be neutral school policies and practices or behaviors of individual teachers. An early study cited by Ray McDermott helps illustrate this point.[11] Through filmed classroom observations, the study found that a White teacher tended to have much more

WHAT YOU CAN DO

MAKE DIFFERENCES AND SIMILARITIES AN EXPLICIT PART OF YOUR CURRICULUM

From preschool through high school, you can create a physical environment that affirms differences. This environment might include a variety of pictures and posters, wall hangings from different cultures, children's artwork, maps and flags from around the world, bulletin boards of special days that feature multicultural themes, exhibits of art from around the country and the world, and a well-stocked multicultural library in which all manner of differences are evident. The game corner can include a variety of games, from checkers to Parcheesi to Mankala to dominoes. Different languages can also be featured on bulletin boards and posters, with translations in English.

frequent eye contact with her White students than with her Black students. Was this behavior the result of racism? Was it because of cultural and communication differences? Or was poor teacher preparation responsible for her behavior?

In another example of how difficult it is to separate racism from individual teachers' behaviors or seemingly neutral policies, Patricia Gándara found in a study of 50 low-income and high-achieving Mexican Americans that most were either light-skinned or European in appearance. Few of the sample, according to Gándara, looked "classically Mexican in both skin color and features."[12] Does this mean that teachers intentionally favored these students because of their light skin? Did teachers assume that light-skinned students were smarter?

These questions are impossible to answer in any conclusive way, although it is probable that institutional racism and teachers' biases both played a role in negative outcomes such as those detailed in the two studies described. The results, however, are very clear. In the study cited by McDermott, the Black children had to try three times harder to catch the teacher's eye for signs of approval, affection, and encouragement. In Gándara's study, the light-skinned students were able to derive significantly more benefits from their schooling than their dark-skinned peers.

Thus, it is clear that racism and other forms of institutional discrimination play a part in students' educational success or failure. In general, African American, Latino, American Indian, and poor children continue to achieve below grade level, drop out in much greater numbers, and go to college in much lower proportions than their middle-class and European American peers. Three concrete examples illustrate this point. Black and Latino students are chronically underrepresented in programs for the gifted and talented; they are only half as likely as White students to be placed in a class for the gifted though they may be equally gifted. Just as troubling, one study found that school districts with more White teachers had a greater rate of minority enrollment in special education; on the other hand, the placement of White students in special education was unrelated to the racial composition of the faculty. In another example, Latino students drop out of school at a rate higher than any other major ethnic group, and, in some places, the rate is as high as 80 percent.[13] To comprehend the enormity of this situation, one needs to imagine a school in which

80 of every 100 students enrolled do not make it to high school graduation. This would be completely unacceptable in middle-class and wealthy communities, yet it is not unusual in poor communities. In addition, schools are frequently unsafe for LGBT students. A report by Human Rights Watch found that verbal, physical, and sexual harassment of LGBT students is widespread in U.S. schools and that many teachers and administrators fail to deal effectively with these incidents.[14]

If educational failure were caused only by students' background and other social characteristics, it would be difficult to explain why similar students are successful in some classrooms and schools and not in others. In his extensive review of schools where the "achievement gap" has narrowed, Joseph D'Amico described a number of differences between schools that primarily serve middle-class or affluent European American students and those that primarily serve students of color and students living in poverty. He found that schools with a narrow "achievement gap" have highly competent, dedicated, and well-trained teachers who have higher expectations for all students; a curriculum that is both culturally sensitive and challenging; and a school community that emphasizes high achievement.[15]

Even when schools are successful at narrowing the "achievement gap," however, they alone cannot solve all the problems created by an inequitable and unequal society. As we saw in Chapter 1, the sociopolitical context of education includes many matters other than schools and teachers, and these too have an impact on student learning. For example, discrimination based on social class is also prevalent in our public schools, and social class and race are often intertwined. In her research, Jean Anyon has found that differences in academic achievement are due primarily to the kinds of schools students attend, the length of time they stay in school, the curriculum and pedagogy to which they are exposed, and societal beliefs concerning their ability. As a result, unequal opportunities to learn can produce significant differences in academic achievement by low-income urban versus affluent suburban students, and the consequences may be dramatic in terms of future life options. Using extensive data from numerous studies, Anyon has concluded that compound educational and political inequality in the occupations, salaries, and housing of the urban poor and the affluent reinforce political and economic differences.[16] Her work suggests that while school reform is both important and necessary, what schools can accomplish is limited if larger macroeconomic policies having to do with employment, housing patterns, health, and other issues, do not change.

Rather than eradicate social class differences, then, it appears that schooling reflects and duplicates (or even exacerbates) them. This finding was confirmed by Samuel Bowles and Herbert Gintis in their ground-breaking class analysis of schooling more than three decades ago.[17] Bowles and Gintis compared the number of years of schooling of students with the socioeconomic status of their parents and found that students whose parents were in the highest socioeconomic group tended to complete the most years of schooling. They concluded that schooling, in and of itself, does not necessarily move poor children out of their parents' low economic class. More often, schooling maintains and solidifies class divisions. Tragically, as researchers Jean Anyon, David Berliner, Richard Rothstein, and others have more recently documented, this outcome is still true.[18]

Intentional or not, racism, classism, and other forms of discrimination are apparent in the quality of education that students receive. For instance, even when teachers believe they are being fair, the results may be unfair. A study by Janet Ward Schofield found that teachers who claimed to be "colorblind" suspended African American males at highly disproportionate rates.[19] Another graphic example of discrimination based on both race and class is found in the vastly different resources given to schools, depending on the socioeconomic level of the student population served. As Jonathon Kozol states in his most recent searing indictment of public education, the resegregation of students of different backgrounds is akin to apartheid, the heinous policy that legally separated people according to race in South Africa (similar to Jim Crow, the United States's racist laws and actions during the late 19th century and first part of the 20th century, which continued until the 1950s).[20] Recent research by Gary Orfield and Chungmei Lee support this contention: According to them, because African Americans and Latinos are segregated as much by poverty as they are by race and ethnicity, segregation is an overriding contributor to the tremendous standardized tests disparities that exist between the races.[21]

The effect of discrimination on students is most painfully apparent when students themselves have the opportunity to speak. For example, Junia Yearwood, a high school teacher of students of diverse racial backgrounds, decided to find out for herself how they experienced school. She asked them to write down the answers to two questions: "What is the best thing a teacher has ever said to you?" and "What is the worst thing a teacher has ever said to you?" What she found through her research is a clear indication of the power of words to either make or break students' attitudes about school. This is part of what Junia wrote:

> There was no dearth of examples of experiences of degradation offered by my students. They said that teachers called them, among many other words, "stupid," "slow," "ignorant," "fat," "dumb," "punk." They said that teachers made comments such as "You'll never amount to anything," "Shut up," "You can't even pass a test," "Even if you study, you'll still fail," "That was a dumb answer," and "You are the worst student." One said that when he failed a test, the teacher said, "I'm not surprised," and another volunteered that his fourth grade teacher had said, "I should put you in kindergarten." Another student said a teacher had told him that in a couple of years, he would be either dead or in jail.[22]

In another example, a study conducted by Karen McLean Donaldson in an urban high school in the Northeast discovered that an astounding 80 percent of students surveyed said they had experienced or witnessed racism or other forms of discrimination in school. She found that students were affected by racism in three major ways: (1) White students experienced guilt and embarrassment when they became aware of the racism to which their peers were subjected, (2) students of color sometimes felt they needed to compensate and overachieve to prove they were equal to their White classmates, and (3) at other times, students of color claimed their self-esteem was badly damaged.[23] However, self-esteem is a complicated issue that includes many variables. It does not come fully formed out of the blue but is *created* in particular contexts and responds to conditions that vary from situation to situation. Teachers' and schools' complicity in creating negative self-esteem cannot be discounted. This point was illustrated by Lillian, a young woman in a study of an urban high school conducted by Nitza Hidalgo. Lillian commented, "That's another problem I have, teachers, they are always talking about how we have no type of self-esteem or anything like that. . . . But they're the people that's putting us down. That's why our self-esteem is so low."[24]

RACISM, DISCRIMINATION, AND SILENCE

Well-meaning teachers are sometimes unintentionally discriminatory when they remain silent about race and racism. They may fear that talking about race will only exacerbate the problem of racism. As a consequence, most schools are characterized by a curious absence of talk about differences, particularly about race.[25] Such silences about racism are sometimes thought to be appropriate because they demonstrate that

WHAT YOU CAN DO

START EARLY

Focusing on human differences and similarities can begin as early as the preschool years, for example, talking about skin color, hair texture, and other physical differences and similarities. Rather than telling White children that it is not polite to say that Black children have "dirty" skin, use this remark and others like it as a basis for making skin differences an explicit part of the curriculum. Use individual photographs of the children, pictures from magazines of people from all over the world, stories that emphasize the similarities in human feelings across all groups, and dolls that represent a variety of races, ethnicities, and genders.

Patty Bode, one of the authors of this text and a former art teacher, uses a color theory lesson to focus attention on skin color. One year, Patty developed a school-wide activity in which every student and staff member in the school was engaged, from cooks to teachers to the principal and custodian. She had everyone mix the primary colors to match their particular skin color and then make hand prints. In the process, they engaged in dialogue about race, the words we use to describe people of different backgrounds, discrimination and racism, and other issues rarely discussed in most schools. When they were finished, Patty hung all the handprints (more than 500) in the halls of the schools. It

was a powerful graphic representation of diversity and inclusiveness.

CONTINUE THROUGH THE GRADES

When used critically, festivals can also become an important element of the curriculum. Although we need to avoid creating a superficial view of diversity based only on festivals, Deborah Menkart has suggested that even using the traditional idea of "heritage months" can become a positive approach in diversifying the curriculum.* In addition to heritage months and festivals, foods can also become a rich resource in the curriculum. Mark Zanger, in a thoroughly researched and excellent resource on foods from around the world, suggests that food can be used as the basis for many creative projects related to culture and immigration.†

In addition, there are many ways in which you can work with your students and colleagues to develop a "school culture" that truly represents your community. Some activities and rituals, such as selecting local or national school heroes from a variety of backgrounds, can be conducted as school-wide projects. Other activities could be having all students learn songs, poems, or speeches from several cultures and having all students take part in local history projects that explore the lives, experiences, and ac-

teachers are "colorblind," that is, fair and impartial when it comes to judging people based on their race. They insist that they see no difference in their students, in spite of their students' obvious differences in race and ethnicity. This patronizing stance facilitates the denial of racism because, according to Pearl Rosenberg, ". . . people who are colorblind have an optical defect that limits their ability to see."[26] Mica Pollock refers to the purposeful suppressing of words associated with race as "colormuteness." Colormuteness is a result of people's uneasiness with directly addressing issues of race. She writes, "Given the amount of worrying that race-label use seems to require in America, it is perhaps unsurprising that many Americans have proposed we solve our 'race problems' by talking as if race did not matter at all."[27] In her study of a California high school, Pollock found that consciously suppressing words associated with race can paradoxically cause educators to replicate the very inequities they say they want to erase.

complishments of many different people. You might develop a "Classtory" (i.e., a history of the class) that includes the pictures and biographies of each member of the class, including information about their ethnicity, the languages they speak, and the things they like to do with friends and family.

With older students, focusing on multicultural literature that depicts the reality of women and men of many groups is an effective strategy. (See the Appendix for a list of professional resources in multicultural literature.) Curriculum that discusses the history and culture of particular groups is also helpful, especially when used in an interdisciplinary and crosscultural approach.

DIRECTLY CONFRONT RACISM AND DISCRIMINATION

Focusing on similarities and differences alone does not guarantee that racism will disappear. In fact, a focus on similarities and differences can become an excuse for not delving more deeply into racism. Because racism and other biases are generally hushed up or avoided in schools, they can become uncomfortable topics of conversation. Directly confronting racism and discrimination can be a healthy and caring way to address these difficult issues.

Even young children can take part in discussions on racism and discrimination. Although many teachers believe that young children should not be exposed to the horrors of racism at an early age, they overlook the fact that many children suffer the effects of racism or other forms of discrimination every day. Discussing these issues in developmentally appropriate ways helps even the youngest children tackle racism and other biases in productive rather than negative ways.

The name-calling that goes on in many schools also provides a valuable opportunity for you to engage in dialogue with your students, as well as with other teachers, administrators, and families. Rather than addressing name-calling as isolated incidents or as the work of a few troublemakers, as is too often done, discussing it openly and directly helps students understand these incidents as symptoms of systemic problems in society and schools. Making explicit the biases that are implicit in name-calling can become part of "circle" or "sharing" time or can form the basis for lessons on racism, sexism, ableism, or other biases.

*Deborah J. Menkart, "Deepening the Meaning of Heritage Months," Educational Leadership 56, no. 7 (1999): 19–21.
†Mark H. Zanger, The American Ethnic Cookbook for Students (Phoenix, AZ: Oxyx Press, 2001).

In the United States, colorblindness and colormuteness begin in early childhood, when children are admonished not to say anything about racial differences, among other differences, because "it's not nice." We learn early on that even admitting that we notice race is wrong. The process of reinforcing colorblindness and colormuteness continues with teacher preparation. Preservice teachers, especially Whites, are often reluctant to mention race, and they become uncomfortable when the issue of racism is broached. They also find it difficult to consider their individual or collective role in perpetuating or helping to overcome it. Rosenberg provides numerous examples of how preservice teachers with whom she has worked over the years are hesitant to ask questions from their field experiences that relate to race, for instance, "Why are all the after-school detention kids students of color?"[28] She suggests that addressing such questions in teacher education programs would help future teachers understand the legacy of racism and inequality in our schools and our nation.

Silence and denial about racism are also prevalent when student teachers become teachers. That this attitude can be taken to an extreme is evident in research by Ellen Bigler: When she asked a middle school librarian in a town with a sizable Puerto Rican community if there were any books on the Hispanic experience, the librarian answered that carrying such books was inadvisable because it would interfere with the children's self-identification of themselves as "American."[29] This assimilationist kind of thinking assumes that the only way to deal with differences is to pretend they don't exist. Yet, the reluctance to discuss race can result in overlooking or denying issues of power that are embedded in race.

In spite of the prevalence of colorblindness and colormuteness, professional education can help teachers learn to view, discuss, and deal with racial and other differences in a more honest way. For example, Sandra Lawrence and Beverly Tatum, in a study on the effects of an antiracist professional development course on teachers, found that most of the White teachers involved had never explicitly discussed race prior to the course. One of the teachers said, "I am 35 years old and I never really started thinking about race too much until now."[30] By the end of the course, most of the teachers acknowledged the necessity of addressing issues of race, difference, and privilege at individual, classroom, and institutional levels. One teacher explained, "Throughout this course, I have been coming to terms with my own personal and group responsibility in allowing racism to persist."[31]

Failure to discuss racism, unfortunately, will not make it go away. Racism, classism, and other forms of discrimination play a key role in creating and maintaining inappropriate learning environments for many students. A related phenomenon concerns the impact of teachers' expectations on student achievement.

EXPECTATIONS OF STUDENTS' ACHIEVEMENT

Much research has focused on teachers' interactions with their students, specifically teacher expectations. The term *self-fulfilling prophecy*, coined by Robert Merton in 1948, means that students perform in ways that teachers expect.[33] Student perform-

SNAPSHOT

Kaval Sethi

Kaval Sethi,[1] a junior in high school at the time of his interview, and his sister, a junior in college, were born and raised in the United States shortly after their parents moved from Bombay, India. They lived in a wealthy suburb of Long Island in New York. Kaval, a hopeful and positive young man, had attended school in the same district since kindergarten. He was in honors classes in all subjects and had a 3.7 cumulative average; in addition, he was taking four advanced placement (AP) classes. Kaval was active in a number of school activities, including the math club and jazz band. In the community, he was involved in his local *Gurudwara*, the Sikh house of worship, and he volunteered in the soup kitchen affiliated with the Gurudwara. Besides his native English language, he also spoke Punjabi and Hindi.

As a Sikh, Kaval wore a *Dastaar* (turban) and kept a beard, requirements for men who follow the Sikh religion. These things made him visibly different from other young men, and he was sometimes made fun of or singled out by other students.

Kaval Sethi was keenly aware of how his ethnicity and social class affected his life. During his interview, he talked about both the social class and economic privileges he enjoyed and the marginalization he experienced because of his religious affiliation. Kaval openly discussed the challenges faced by Sikhs and others after the events of September 11, 2001.

I am an Indian American. My Sikh identity is very important to me. I like to keep my beard and keep my turban, and I don't cut my hair. Sikhism defines my religion, how I act religiously, and how I act in my morals. When I say [I am] Indian American, that is how I am culturally. My cultural character: the food I eat, the kinds of friends I have, the things I do. I am very Indian, but I mix a lot of American values into my culture.

Sikhism defines a lot about my life. I am Sikh, and my religion prohibits cutting hair. I want everyone to know that I am Sikh. I am just as different as everyone else. I am part of your culture—but I'm different as well.

I visited India recently. The life that they live isn't much different from mine. It's a little tougher. I guess it's not as much technology. I was very comfortable in India. [There], they realize you are a foreigner, and *you* realize you are a foreigner. I know that [in the United States], other people see me differently from another person. You don't get that feeling when you walk around India, but as soon as you speak to an American, they know you are an American.

My parents worked hard to get where they are. They owe it all to education. They find it very important. *I* find it very important; I just don't find *high school* important. My dad came when he was 17, and he went to college in New York. . . . My mom's first time coming to America was when she first got married to my dad. They worked very hard to get where they are right now. They also learned a lot of things by living life, not just by going to school. From my family, basically I've learned my whole moral character. My parents have taught me to be morally strong.

Some people are concerned [about Sikhs coming into the school]. I guess that is because they are confused about our affiliations. We are not Muslims. Some people confuse us with terrorists. In our school, some kids ask me, "Are you Muslim?" And I say, "No, I'm not Muslim. I'm Sikh." Not a lot of people know about it, but I think it's like the fifth largest religion in the world.

A White American in America does not have to deal with the prejudice that Sikhs have. I had a lot of bad experiences as a little child. [Other kids] would make fun of me . . . because I was different. They used to call me names. Some kids did not make fun of me, and I would hang out with them. By the time people understood, they stopped.

Sikhs are singled out because we wear turbans. I am the only kid in my class who wears a turban. I guess originally, at first, on the day [after September 11], some people were feeling kind of prejudiced against me because of Osama bin Laden and how closely Sikhs resemble Osama bin Laden, because Sikhs wear beards and turbans. So originally, people would be kind of antagonistic, but that really subsided very quickly 'cause they understood that I was a Sikh and I wasn't really a harm to them.

Definitely my English and social studies teachers know plenty about Sikhism. My math and science teachers really don't understand it. They *do* ask questions. Over the years, the math and science teachers have asked plenty of questions about Sikhism, and I've answered them. My teachers are [mostly] fair. . . . some teachers had prejudices against

(*continued*)

me. I want them to know about my religion, some basic facts, so they can better relate to me. If they relate to me, I can be more open.

I'm very much into music. I play music and trumpet. I'm into economics and business—and science. Probably biology will be my major in college. I'm into environmental topics. I'm part of the Environmental Action Committee. I'm very much into preserving the environment. . . . I'm also into jazz.

I go to Gurudwara [the temple]. I like to help out as much as possible there. I try to help clean up after *langar* (it's like a free kitchen; on Sunday they have it after the religious service). I like helping at that. I like to help out in things that I can help out in.

Now I am confident. A few years ago I would be shy. I am extremely independent. . . . If I want to do it, I will do it. I am very proud of myself—of what I can accomplish.

COMMENTARY

Sikhs, particularly males, have been targets of anti-Muslim and xenophobic sentiments because of their mistaken association with Islam. Sikh Americans have been verbally and physically as-

saulted, and some even murdered. Many persons with Brown skin endured hostility and threats after September 11th, but Sikh males and Muslims women wearing the *hijeb* have the physical markers in addition to the phenotypic ones that make them targets of bigotry and fear. Kaval felt that most teachers were not prejudiced, but he longed for more awareness and understanding from them because, for the most part, they failed to address these issues, either through private conversations or in the curriculum.[32]

[1]We are grateful to Khyati Joshi, who found and interviewed Kaval. She also provided us with important background information about Asian and Indian Americans in general, and the Sikh American community specifically. Khyati also suggested other sources of information. The websites www.sikhcoalition.org and www.sikhmediawatch.org provide up-to-date information about the Sikh American community. For information concerning hate crimes, see the website www.aaldef.org; see also Khyati Y. Joshi, *New Roots in America's Sacred Ground: Religion, Race, and Ethnicity in Indian America* (New Brunswick, NJ: Rutgers University Press, 2006).

ance is based on both overt and covert messages from teachers about students' worth, intelligence, and capability. The term did not come into wide use until 1968, when a classic study by Robert Rosenthal and Lenore Jacobson provided the impetus for subsequent extensive research on the subject.[34] In this study, several classes of children in grades one through six were given a nonverbal intelligence test (the researchers called it the *Harvard Test of Influenced Acquisition*), which researchers claimed would measure the students' potential for intellectual growth. Twenty percent of the students were randomly selected by the researchers as "intellectual bloomers," and their names were given to the teachers. Although the students' test scores actually had nothing at all to do with their potential, the teachers were told to be on the alert for signs of intellectual growth among these particular children. Overall, these children—particularly in the lower grades—showed considerably greater gains in IQ during the school year than did the other students. They were also rated by their teachers as being more interesting, curious, and happy and were thought to be more likely to succeed later in life.

Rosenthal and Jacobson's research on teacher expectations caused a sensation in the educational community, and controversy surrounding it continues to the present. From the beginning, the reception to this line of research has been mixed, with both supporters and detractors, but one outcome was that the effect of teachers' expectations on the academic achievement of their students was taken seriously for the first time. Before this research, students' failure in school was usually ascribed wholly to individual or family circumstances. Now, the possible influence of teachers' attitudes and behaviors and the schools' complicity in the process had to be considered as well. The most compelling implications were for the education of those students most seriously disadvantaged by schooling, that is, for students of color and the poor. For instance, teachers' beliefs that their students are "dumb" can become a rationale for providing low-level work in the form of elementary facts, simple drills, and rote memorization. Students are not immune to these messages.[35]

Early research by Ray Rist on teachers' expectations is also worth mentioning here. In a ground-breaking study, he found that a kindergarten teacher had grouped her class by the eighth day of class. In reviewing how she had done so, Rist noted that the teacher had already roughly constructed an "ideal type" of student, most of whose characteristics were related to social class. By the end of the school year, the teacher's differential treatment of children based on whom she considered "fast" and "slow" learners became evident. The "fast" learners received more teaching time, more reward-directed behavior, and more attention. The interactional patterns between the teacher and her students then took on a castelike appearance. The result, after three years of similar behavior by other teachers, was that teachers' behavior toward the different groups influenced the children's achievement. In other words, the teachers themselves contributed to the creation of the "slow" learners in their classrooms.[36] In the research by Rist, all the children and teachers were African American, although they represented different social classes, but similar results have been found with poor and working-class children regardless of race.[37]

Some of the research on teacher expectations is quite old. Although it is reasonable to expect that, with the increasing diversity in our schools, it no longer holds true, there are still numerous examples of teachers' low expectations of students. In fact, in a reprint of his classic 1970 study in the year 2000, Ray Rist came to the conclusion that much of the reality of education for Black youth had changed very little during the intervening 30 years. For Rist, the issues of color and class inequality evidence the "profound disconnect between the rhetoric and the reality of American society." He concluded the following:

> The sobering reality is that when it comes to both color and class, U.S. schools tend to conform much more to the contours of American society than they transform it. And this appears to be a lesson that we are not wanting to learn.[38]

Given the increasing diversity in our public schools, the problem is even more acute because many teachers know little or nothing about the background of their students. Consequently, teachers may consider their students' identity to be at fault. In a recent study, Marcos Pizarro interviewed over 200 Chicano students about their experiences in school. The students were a diverse group: Some were successful students, while others had been largely unsuccessful in school; some lived in small towns and others lived in large cities; they represented different social classes; they were high school, community college, and university students;

and some were high school dropouts. As a result of these interviews, Pizarro concluded that the students were "profiled" by their teachers, and that this "profiling" had a significant effect on their schooling experiences and outcomes. He found that the students were profiled according to skin color, social class, dress, specific behaviors, linguistic abilities, friendship groups, and so on. The result is that they were judged by these characteristics, which usually had little to do with their intellectual abilities. While the profiling might have been unintentional and unconscious, the results could be devastating:

> These processes are significant because teachers represent both authority figures and the gatekeepers into the realm of knowledge and success. When these authority figures base their actions on stereotypes, the impact of those actions is overwhelming for many students. Just as the police often use racial profiles to determine who are potential criminals and who does not need to be pulled over, teachers use racial profiles to determine who will and will not benefit from opportunities to excel in school.[39]

In spite of some very negative experiences, however, Pizarro found some students who had been extremely successful. Significantly, the most successful students were those who had been mentored through the various transitions of their schooling by teachers and other authority figures who linked the students' identities with their schooling. That is, when teachers viewed students' identities in a positive way and connected the students' identities with success in learning, the result was students who were self-assured in their own identities and dedicated to their schooling.

The issue of labeling is key here. Rubén Rumbaut found that the self-esteem of immigrant students is linked to how they are labeled by their schools. Specifically, he found that students' self-esteem is diminished when they are labeled "limited English proficient."[40] If this is the case with a seemingly neutral term, more loaded labels no doubt have a much greater impact, but explicit labeling may not even be needed. According to Claude Steele, the basic problem that causes low student achievement is what he terms *stereotype threat*, based on the constant devaluation faced by Blacks, other people of color, and females in society. In schools, this devaluation occurs primarily through the harmful attitudes and beliefs that teachers communicate, knowingly or not, to their students. Steele maintains, "Deep in the psyche of American educators is a presumption that black students need academic remediation, or extra time with elemental curricula to overcome background deficits."[41] Building on this line of research among young children, the most recent confirmation of the importance of affirming students' identities comes from a widely reported randomized, double-blind study by Geoffrey Cohen and his associates.[42] The researchers asked a randomly selected group of African American and European American students to complete a writing assignment in which they were to choose either their most or least important value among a list that included relationships with friends or family, or being good at art. Although the children completed this brief 15-minute assignment near the beginning of the school year, the result was dramatic: The academic performance of the African American students who had written about their most important value was raised and the racial "achievement gap" was reduced by 40 percent. No effect was seen, up or down, among the European American students. In other words, the intervention benefited targeted students without jeopardizing non-targeted students.

Extensive research by Milbrey McLaughlin and Joan Talbert in high schools around the country confirms the importance of having high expectations for students. The researchers described how many of the teachers in the schools responded to "nontraditional" students (including the growing population of students of color) by lowering their expectations and watering down the curriculum. They also found that the teachers who water down the curriculum usually place the responsibility for low achievement squarely on the students themselves. This pattern was most evident in low-track classrooms. On the other hand, the researchers found that teachers who modified the curriculum without lowering their expectations of students, and who worked to establish strong teacher-student relationships, were better able to reach their students, even those who came from economically disadvantaged backgrounds.[43] Similar findings from numerous studies have been reported consistently over the past several years. In a review of these studies, Christine Sleeter came to the conclusion that the research confirms that "students from communities that have been historically underserved can achieve *when the teachers and school believe they can and take responsibility to make it happen.*"[44]

Although disadvantage may contribute to the problem, Claude Steele contends that Blacks underachieve even when they have sufficient material resources, adequate academic preparation, and a strong value orientation toward education. To prove his point, he reviewed a number of programs that have had substantial success in improving the academic achievement of Black students without specifically addressing either their culturally specific learning orientations or socioeconomic disadvantage. What made the difference? In these programs, student achievement was improved simply by treating students as if they were talented and capable. Steele concludes, "That erasing stigma improves black achievement is perhaps the strongest evidence that stigma is what depresses it in the first place."[45]

Teachers' attitudes about the diversity of their students develop long before they become teachers. In a review of related literature, Kenneth Zeichner found that teacher education students, who are mostly White and monolingual, generally view diversity of student backgrounds as a problem.[46] He also found that the most common characteristics of effective teachers in urban schools are (1) a belief that their students are capable learners and (2) an ability to communicate this belief to the students. Martin Haberman reached a similar conclusion, identifying a number of functions of successful teachers of the urban poor. Most significantly, he found that successful teachers did not blame students for failure and had consistently high expectations of their students.[47] Rashaud Kates, whose case study follows this chapter, offers compelling evidence of this reality. According to Rashaud, many teachers do not expect Black students to achieve academically. He said, "People are already judging you when you're African American. I would tell teachers about African American students, 'Everybody's not bad; have high expectations'."

What happens when teachers develop high expectations of their students? In an inspiring example of how changing the expectations of students can influence achievement in a positive direction, Rosa Hernandez Sheets recounted her own experience with five Spanish-speaking students who had failed her Spanish class. Just one semester after placing them in what she labeled her "advanced" class, the very same students, who had previously failed, passed the AP Spanish language exam, earning college credits while just sophomores and juniors. A year later, they passed the AP Spanish literature exam. As a result of the change in her pedagogy, during a three-year period, Latino and Latina students who had been labeled "at risk" were performing at a level commonly expected of honors students.[48] Another example can be found in the work of Cynthia Ballenger, a teacher of Haitian American children in a Massachusetts preschool. As Ballenger herself states, "I began with these children expecting deficits, not because I believed they or their background were deficient—I was definitely against such a view—but because I did not know how to see their strengths." Through her work with the children and their families, Ballenger documents how her beliefs and practices shifted as she began to build on the strengths and experiences that the children brought to school, strengths that had not previously been evident to her.[49] Clearly, such expectations can have an immense impact on young people: In a nationwide Gallup Youth Survey that asked 13- to 17-year-old students if they worked harder for some teachers than for others, 75 percent of the students responded that they did. The most common reason they gave was that they liked some teachers more than others. The report concluded, "Responses to the question asking why some classes make teens feel more involved than others do . . . underscore the idea that effective schooling relies almost entirely on creative and passionate teachers."[50]

Research on teachers' expectations is not without controversy. First, it has been criticized as unnecessarily reductionist because, in the long run, the detractors claim, what teachers expect matters less than what teachers do. Second, the critics say that the term "teachers' expectations" and the research on which it is based imply that teachers have the sole responsibility for students' achievement or lack of it and that this is both an unrealistic and an incomplete explanation for student success or failure. The study by Rosenthal and Jacobson, for example, is, in fact, a glaring indication of the disrespect with which teachers have frequently been treated in research, and it raises serious ethical issues about how research is done. Blaming teachers, or "teacher bashing," provides a convenient outlet for complex problems, but it fails to take into account the fact that teachers function within contexts in which they usually have little power.

There are, of course, teachers who have low expectations of students from particular backgrounds and who are, in the worst cases, insensitive and racist. But, placing teachers at the center of expectations of student achievement shifts the blame entirely to some of those who care most deeply about students and who struggle every day to help them learn. The use of the term *teachers' expectations* distances the school and society from their responsibility and complicity in student failure. The truth is that, teachers, schools, students, communities, and society all interact to produce failure.

Low expectations mirror the expectations of society. It is not simply teachers who expect little from poor, working-class, and culturally dominated groups. The first President Bush, when he was running for president, visited Garfield High School in East Los Angeles, a school made famous by the extraordinary efforts of Jaime Escalante and other teachers in propelling an unprecedented number of students to college in spite of poverty and discrimination. Rather than build on the message that college is both possible and desirable, Bush focused instead on the idea that a college education is not really needed for success. He told the largely Mexican American student body that "we need people to build our buildings . . . people who do the hard physical work of our society."[51] It is doubtful that he would even have considered uttering these same words at Beverly Hills High School, a short distance away. A message of low expectations delivered to students who should have heard precisely the opposite is thus replicated even by those at the highest levels of a government claiming to be equitable to all students.

Although this incident happened more than a decade ago, the kind of thinking it embodies is not a relic of the past. More recently, a state appeals court in New York ruled that youngsters who drop out of the New York City schools by eighth grade have nevertheless received "a sound basic education." This astonishing ruling resulted in overturning a 2001 landmark decision that had found the state's formula for funding public schools unfair because it favored those who live in suburban areas. The majority opinion in the 2002 appeals court case, written by Judge Alfred Lerner, said in part that "the skills required to enable a person to obtain employment, vote, and serve on a jury, are imparted between grades 8 and 9." And although Judge Lerner conceded that so little education would probably qualify people for only the lowest-paying jobs, he added, "Society needs workers at all levels of jobs, the majority of which may very well be low-level."[52] One wonders if Judge Lerner would want this same level of education for his own children, or if he would think it fair and equitable for them.

The Complex Connections Between Diversity and Discrimination

Societal inequities are frequently reinforced in school policies and practices. Consequently, institutional racism and other biases are apparent in schools as well as in the general society. Let us take the example of language. The fact that when they start school some children do not speak English, cannot be separated from how their native language is viewed by the larger society or from the kinds of programs available for them in schools. Each of these programs—whether English as a second language (ESL), English immersion, or two-way bilingual education—has an underlying philosophy with broad implications for students' achievement or failure, as discussed in Chapter 7. As a consequence, each approach may have a profound influence on the quality of education that language-minority children receive. However, linguistic and other differences do not exist independently of how they are perceived in the general society or by teachers: There is a complex relationship between a student's race, culture, native language, and other unique characteristics *and* with institutional discrimination, school practices, and teacher and societal expectations.

Social class provides another example of the complex links between difference and discrimination. In spite of the enduring belief in our society that social class mobility is available to all, classism is a grim reality because *economic inequality is now greater in the United States than in many other wealthy nations in the world.* Given the vastly unequal resources of families at different socioeconomic levels, it should come as no surprise, then, that social class and educational attainment are strongly correlated.[53] In addition, social class inequality is especially pronounced and severe among children of color. Linked to this reality is the widely accepted classist view among many educators that poverty *causes* academic failure. Although poverty *can* have an adverse or even a devastating effect on student achievement, the belief that poverty and educational failure go hand in hand is questionable. Important research by Denny Taylor and Catherine Dorsey-Gaines provides evidence that poverty alone is not an adequate explanation for students' failure to learn. In their work with Black families living in urban poverty, Taylor and Dorsey-Gaines found inspiring cases of academically successful students. They discovered children who consistently did their homework, made the honor roll, and had positive attitudes about school. The parents of these children motivated them to learn and study, had high hopes for their education, were optimistic about the future, and considered literacy an integral part of their lives—this in spite of such devastating conditions as family deaths; no food, heat, or hot water; and a host of other hostile situations.[54]

We need to reiterate that the economic situation of students of color and other students living in poverty has often been used as an explanation for academic failure, but, as Janine Bempechat suggests, it is far more productive to investigate how high-achieving students in these groups are successful *in spite of* poverty and discrimination, among other problems.[55] In her research among both high- and low-achieving poor students, Bempechat found that the high achievers in all ethnic groups believed that success is due to hard work. She concluded that teachers need to help low achievers understand that poor performance does not result from a lack of ability as much as from lack of trying: If students believe they do not have the ability, it makes little sense for them to invest any effort at all in their learning. Examples such as these demonstrate that, although poverty is certainly a disadvantage, it is not an insurmountable obstacle to learning.

However, lest we fall into the trap of expecting all parents to be heroic in their efforts to help their children succeed in spite of all these obstacles, we should point out that parents, no matter how much they try, cannot by themselves tackle all the odds. Thus, making the honor roll in a substandard school is vastly different from making the honor roll in an academically rigorous school with highly prepared teachers. We also need to ask what *kind* of homework the parents are getting their children to do. Is it simply to copy endless lists of spelling words, or is it to think critically about a particular subject or do an imaginative and engaging project? One major explanation for low academic achievement is the lack of equitable resources given to students of different social classes and racial and ethnic backgrounds. For instance, one of the most disturbing findings concerning students' access to qualified teachers is this: Many more teachers with little academic preparation and little experience are teaching in schools serving poor children than in those serving middle-class children.[56] Thus, it is clear that the sociopolitical contexts of the schools attended by children of different social and economic classes are vastly unequal, and parents, no matter how noble and inspired, cannot change this by themselves. Therefore, schools need to take some of the responsibility for creating conditions that promote active and engaged student learning.

Although, in the ideal sense, education in the United States is based on the lofty values of democracy, freedom, and equal access for all, these examples point out how this has not been the case in reality. Historically, our educational system proposed to tear down the rigid systems of class and caste on which education in most of the world was (and still is) based and to provide all students with an equal education. Education was to be, as Horace Mann claimed, "the great equalizer," but, as some educational historians have demonstrated, the common school's primary purposes were to replicate inequality and to control the unruly masses.[57] Thus, the original goals of public school education were often at cross-purposes.

In the United States, mass public education began in earnest in the 19th century through the legislation of compulsory education, and its most eloquent democratic expression is found in the early 20th century philosophy of John Dewey.[58] In his utopian view, schools could be the answer to social inequality. Over time, however, schools have become one of the major "sorting" mechanisms of students of different backgrounds. The contradiction between the Deweyian hope for education as a social equalizer and the actual unequal outcomes of schooling is with us even today. The commitment to educational equity that Dewey articulated continues through policies such as desegregation, multicultural and nonsexist education, and through legislation and policies aimed at eradicating existing inequalities. At the same time, the legacy of inequality also continues through policies and practices that favor some students over others, including unequal funding, rigid tracking, racial and ethnic and social class segregation, and unfair tests. As a result, schools have often been sites of bitter conflict.

Race is another pivotal way in which privilege has been granted on an unequal basis. Based on his research, the historian David Tyack asserts that the struggle to achieve equality in education is nothing new and that race has often been at the center of this struggle. He adds, "Attempts to preserve white supremacy and to achieve racial justice have fueled the politics of education for more than a century."[59] On the other hand, those interested in equal education have not sat idly by. Assertive action on the part of parents, students, teachers, and other allies has been crucial in challenging the schools to live up to their promise of equality. Schools were not racially desegregated simply because the courts ordered it, and gender-fair education was not legislated only because Congress thought it was a good idea. In both cases, as in many others, educational opportunity was expanded because many people—including parents, students, teachers, and communities—engaged in struggle, legal or otherwise, to bring about change.

Although, in theory, education is no longer meant to replicate societal inequities but rather to reflect the ideals of democracy, we know that such is not the reality. Our schools have consistently failed to provide an equitable education for students of all backgrounds and situations. The complex interplay of student differences, institutional racism and discrimination, teacher and societal biases that lead to low expectations, and unfair school policies and practices *all* play a role in keeping it this way.

SUMMARY

Racism is unfortunately not a vestige of the past. Even in 2005, in the aftermath of Hurricane Katrina—a hurricane with tragic consequences for many people living in New Orleans and other Gulf Coast areas—racism was painfully obvious in how African Americans were treated. A study by the *Washington Post* confirmed the explicit racism in this situation, a racism that likely was not even perceived by those taking part in the study. Shanto Iyengar, director of the Political Communication Lab at Stanford University, asked more than 2,300 individuals to go to a website that featured a news article about the effects of the hurricane. The article was accompanied by a photograph of an individual. Unbeknownst to the participants, the race, gender, and occupation of the featured person varied, so that while participants read the same article, it could be about an African American male or female, a White male or female, or a Latino/a. After they had read the article, participants were asked to determine how much government aid the victim should receive. If race did not matter, there would be no difference in the allocations. Race, however, did indeed matter: Participants were willing to give assistance to a White victim for about a year, but the average for African Americans was a month shorter. In addition, African Americans would receive $1,000 less than Whites, and the darker the skin, the less the victim received. According to the article, the "penalty" for being Black was not just a psychological one but also a monetary one.[60]

Focusing on the persistence of racism and discrimination and low expectations is in no way intended to deny the difficult family and economic situation of many poor children and children of color, or its impact on their school experiences and achievement. Many people of color in the United States also live in poverty, and the two cannot be separated. Moreover, poverty can lead to such problems as drug abuse, violence, and other social ills as well as poor medical care, deficient nutrition, and a struggle for the bare necessities for survival—and *all* of these conditions harm children's lives, including their school experiences. The fact that poor children and their families do not have the resources and experiences that economic privilege would give them is also detrimental.

However, blaming poor people and people from dominated racial or cultural groups for their educational problems is not the answer to solving societal inequities. Teachers can do nothing to change the conditions in which their students may live today, but they *can* work to change their own biases and the institutional structures that act as obstacles to student learning and to the possibilities for their students' futures. Although some teachers and other educators might prefer to think that students' lack of academic achievement is due solely to conditions inside their homes or inherent in their cultures, clearly, racism and other forms of institutional discrimination play a central role in educational failure, as does the related phenomenon of low expectations.

◆◆◆ To Think About

1. Let's say that you are a high school teacher and you are having a discussion with your students about the benefits of education. This is your dilemma: Horace Mann's claim that education is "the great equalizer" has been criticized as simplistic or unrealistic. At the same time, a focus on racism, discrimination, and teachers' expectations can be criticized as being overly deterministic in explaining school failure, leading children to lose faith that education can make any difference at all. What is the appropriate approach to take with your students? Should you emphasize the tremendous opportunities that are available in our country? Should you instead focus on the barriers to taking advantage of opportunities, particularly for some segments of the population? Try role playing this situation: As the teacher, lead your students in an attempt to find the most beneficial stance.

2. Think about schools with which you are familiar. Have you seen evidence of racism or other forms of discrimination? Was it based primarily on race, gender, class, language, sexual orientation, or other differences? How was it manifested?

3. How would you go about "erasing stereotype threat" for students of color, as Claude Steele suggests? Think of some strategies in specific situations.

4. There has been some controversy surrounding research on teachers' expectations. Review some of the debate in the sources cited in this chapter. Think about your own experiences as a student. Describe a time when teachers' expectations did or did not make a difference in your life.

◆◆◆ Activities for Personal, School, and Community Change

1. Develop a lesson for your classroom that directly focuses on racism and/or discrimination. If you teach one of the lower grades, you may want to use a children's book. (See some of the resources recommended in the Appendix.) With older students, you can base the lesson on some current event or on a personal experience that one of the students has had. Write and reflect on the outcome of the lesson. Was it difficult for you to plan? To implement? Why? What was the reaction of students? What have you learned from this?

2. Ask one of your trusted colleagues to visit your classroom and observe your teaching for several days with the purpose of pointing out how you might unintentionally demonstrate low or high expectations for students. After debriefing your colleague, draw up a plan of action to address any instances she or he may have witnessed.

3. Begin a study group in your school to learn more about the effects of discrimination and racism on students and teachers. Plan to meet once a week or once a month for a specific amount of time (half a year, a year, or whatever time frame makes sense in your specific context). Select appropriate books from the references cited in this chapter, watch related videos together, and write together about ways to combat these kinds of discrimination in school (for videos and other resources, see the listings for the nonprofit organizations Teaching for Change and Rethinking Schools in the Appendix).

 Companion Website

For access to additional case studies, weblinks, concept cards, and other material related to this chapter, visit the text's companion website at **www.ablongman.com/nieto5e**.

Notes to Chapter 4

1. According to Tove Skutnabb-Kangas, *linguicism* can be defined as "ideologies and structures which are used to legitimate, effectuate and reproduce an unequal division of power and resources (both material and non-material) between groups which are defined on the basis of language (on the basis of their mother tongues)." See "Multilingualism and the Education of Minority Children." In *Minority Education: From Shame to Struggle*, edited by Tove Skutnabb-Kangas and Jim Cummins (Clevedon, England: Multilingual Matters, 1988): 13.

2. Gordon Allport, *The Nature of Prejudice* (Reading, MA: Addison-Wesley, 1954): 52.

3. See, for example, Stephen Jay Gould, *The Mismeasure of Man* (New York: W. W. Norton, 1981) (revised and expanded ed., 1996) for a history of racism in intelligence measurement, and Steven Selden, *Inheriting Shame: The Story of Eugenics and Racism in America* (New York: Teachers College Press, 1999) for a comprehensive treatment of the eugenics movement.

4. Carol D. Lee, "Why We Need To Re-Think Race and Ethnicity in Educational Research," *Educational Researcher* 32, no. 5 (June/July 2003): 3–5, p. 3.

5. Beverly Daniel Tatum, "Talking about Race, Learning about Racism: The Application of Racial Identity Development Theory in the Classroom." *Harvard Educational Review* 62, no. 1 (Spring 1992): 6.

6. Meyer Weinberg, "Introduction." In *Racism in the United States: A Comprehensive Classified Bibliography*, compiled by Meyer Weinberg (New York: Greenwood Press, 1990): xii–xiii.

7. Weinberg, *Racism in the United States: A Comprehensive Classified Bibliography*. See also Joel Spring, *Deculturalization and the Struggle for Equality: A Brief History of the Education of Dominated Cultures in the United States*, 5th ed. (New York: McGraw-Hill, 2006).

8. Weinberg, *Racism in the United States: A Comprehensive Classified Bibliography*; Joel Spring, *Deculturalization and the Struggle for Equality: A Brief History of the Education of Dominated Cultures in the United States*, 5th ed. See also the documentation of educational discrimination against Mexican Americans in Rubén Donato, *The Other Struggle for Equal Schools* (New York: State University of New York Press, 1997) and José F. Moreno, ed., *The Elusive Quest for Equality: 150 years of Chicano/Chicano Education* (Cambridge, MA: Harvard Educational Review, 1999). For the history of educational discrimination against Native Americans, see K. Tsianina Lomawaima and Teresa L. McCarty, "When Tribal Sovereignty Challenges Democracy: American Indian Education and the Democratic Ideal." *American Educational Research Journal* 39, no. 2 (Summer 2002): 279–305. For the history of gender-segregated schooling, see Myra Sadker and David Sadker, "Gender Bias: From Colonial America to Today's Classrooms." In *Multicultural Education: Issues and Perspectives*, 5th ed., edited by James A. Banks and Cherry A. McGee Banks (New York: John Wiley & Sons, 2005).

9. For example, Gary Orfield and his associates found that the period from 1991 through 1994 saw the largest backward movement toward segregation for Blacks since the 1954 *Brown v. Topeka Board of Education* decision. They also reported that Latino students have become the most segregated of all groups. See Gary Orfield and John T. Yun, *Resegregation in American Schools* (Cambridge, MA: Civil Rights Project at Harvard University, 1999). For the consequences of this segregation, see Gary Orfield and Chungmei Lee, *Why Segregation Matters: Poverty and Educational Inequality* (Cambridge, MA: Civil Rights Project at Harvard University, 1999). Available at: http://civilrightsproject.harvard.edu/research/deseg/deseg05.phpmimetext/

10. On the subject of rigid tracking, see, for example, Jeannie Oakes, Amy Stuart Wells, Makeba Jones, and Amanda Datnow, "Detracking: The Social Construction of Ability, Cultural Politics, and Resistance to Reform." *Teachers College Record* 98, no. 3 (1997): 482–510; and on the impact of high-stakes testing on students of color, see George Madaus and Marguerite Clarke, "The Adverse Impact of High-Stakes Testing on Minority Students: Evidence from One Hundred Years of Test Data." In *Raising Standards or Raising Barriers? Inequality and High-Stakes Testing in Public Education*, edited by Gary Orfield and Mindy L. Kornhaber (New York: The Century Foundation Press, 2001).

11. Ray P. McDermott, "The Cultural Context of Learning to Read." In *Papers in Applied Linguistics: Linguistics and Reading Series* 1, edited by Stanley F. Wanat (Washington, DC: Center for Applied Linguistics, 1977).

12. Patricia Gándara, *Over the Ivy Walls: The Educational Mobility of Low-Income Chicanos* (Albany: State University of New York Press, 1995).

13. See Matthew Ladner and Christopher Hammons, "Special but Unequal: Race and Special Education." In *Rethinking Special Education for a New Century*, edited by Chester E. Finn, Andrew J. Rotherham, and Charles R. Hokanson (Washington, DC: Thomas B. Fordham Foundation, 2001); Beth Harry and Janette Klingner, *Why Are So Many Minority Students in Special Education?* (New York: Teachers College Press, 2006).

14. Michael Bochniek and A. Widney Brown, *Hatred in the Hallways: Violence and Discrimination Against Lesbian, Gay, Bisexual, and Transgender Students in U.S. Schools* (New York: Human Rights Watch, 2001).

15. Joseph J. D'Amico, "A Closer Look at the Minority Achievement Gap." *ERS Spectrum* (May 2000): 4–10.

16. Jean Anyon, *Radical Possibilities: Public Policy, Urban Education, and a New Social Movement* (New York: Routledge, 2005).

17. Samuel Bowles and Herbert Gintis, *Schooling in Capitalist America: Educational Reform and the Contradictions of Economic Life* (New York: Basic Books, 1976).

18. See, for instance, Anyon, *Radical Possibilities: Public Policy, Urban Education, and a New Social Movement*; David C. Berliner, "Our Impoverished View of Educational Reform." *Teachers College Record*, available at: http://www.tcrecord.org/content.asp?contentID+12106; Richard Rothstein, *Class and Schools: Using Social, Economic, and Educational Reform to Close the Black-White Achievement Gap* (New York: Teachers College Press, and Washington, DC: Economic Policy Institute, 2004).

19. Janet Ward Schofield, "The Colorblind Perspective in School: Causes and Consequences." In *Multicultural Education: Issues and Perspectives*, 5th ed., edited by James A. Banks and Cherry A. McGee Banks (New York: Wiley, 2005).

20. Jonathon Kozol, *The Shame of the Nation: The Restoration of Apartheid Schooling in America.* (New York: Crown, 2005).

21. Orfield and Lee, *Why Segregation Matters: Poverty and Educational Inequality*.

22. Junia Yearwood, "Words that Kill." In *What Keeps Teachers Going?*, Sonia Nieto (New York: Teachers College Press, 2003).

23. Karen B. McLean Donaldson, *Through Students' Eyes: Combating Racism in United States Schools* (Westport, CT: Praeger, 1996).

24. Nitza M. Hidalgo, " 'Free Time, School Is Like a Free Time': Social Relations in City High School Classes" (Unpublished Doctoral Dissertation, Graduate School of Education, Harvard University, Cambridge, MA 1991): 95.

25. See, for example, Michelle Fine, *Framing Dropouts: Notes on the Politics of an Urban High School* (Albany: State University of New York Press, 1991); Christine E. Sleeter, "White Racism." *Multicultural Education* 1, no. 4 (Spring 1994): 5–8, 39.

26. Pearl M. Rosenberg, "Color Blindness in Teacher Education: An Optical Illusion." In *Off White: Readings on Power, Privilege, and Resistance*, edited by Michelle Fine, Lois Weis, Linda Powell Pruitt, and April Burns (New York: Routledge, 2004): 257–272, p. 257, p. 262.

27. Mica Pollock, *Colormute: Race Talk Dilemmas in an American School* (Princeton, NJ: Princeton University Press, 2004): 2.

28. Pearl M. Rosenberg, "Color Blindness in Teacher Education: An Optical Illusion." pp. 257, 262.

29. Ellen Bigler, *American Conversations: Puerto Ricans, White Ethnics, and Multicultural Education* (Philadelphia: Temple University Press, 1999).

30. Sandra M. Lawrence and Beverly Daniel Tatum, "White Educators as Allies: Moving From Awareness

to Action." In *Off White: Readings on Power, Privilege, and Resistance*, edited by Michelle Fine, Lois Weis, Linda Powell Pruitt, and April Burns (New York: Routledge, 2004): 363–372, p. 362.

31. *Ibid.*, 368.

32. Khyati Y. Joshi, *New Roots in America's Sacred Ground: Religion, Race, and Ethnicity in Indian America* (New Brunswick, NJ: Rutgers University Press, 2006).

33. Robert Merton, "The Self-Fulfilling Prophecy." *Antioch Review* 8 (1948): 193–210. Nancy Schniewind and Ellen Davidson. *Open Minds to Equality: A Sourcebook of Learning Activities to Affirm Diversity and Promote Equality.* 3rd ed. (Milwaukee, WI: Rethinking Schools, 2006).

34. Robert Rosenthal and Lenore Jacobson, *Pygmalion in the Classroom* (New York: Holt, Rinehart and Winston, 1968).

35. See, for instance, Richard E. Snow, "Unfinished Pygmalion." *Contemporary Psychology* 14 (1969): 197–200; Samuel S. Wineburg, "The Self-Fulfillment of the Self-Fulfilling Prophecy: A Critical Appraisal." *Educational Researcher* 16, no. 9 (December 1987): 28–37; Robert Rosenthal, "Pygmalion Effects: Existence, Magnitude, and Social Importance." *Educational Researcher* 16, no. 9 (December 1987): 37–44; Jacquelynne Eccles and Lee Jussim, "Teacher Expectations II: Construction and Reflection of Student Achievement." *Journal of Personality and Social Psychology* 63, no. 6 (December 1992): 947–961.

36. Ray C. Rist, "Student Social Class and Teacher Expectations: The Self-Fulfilling Prophecy in Ghetto Education." In *Challenging the Myths: The Schools, the Blacks, and the Poor*, edited by Susan Stodolsky. Reprint Series no. 5 (Cambridge, MA: Harvard Educational Review, 1971).

37. See the review of this research in Jean Anyon, "Inner Cities, Affluent Suburbs, and Unequal Educational Opportunity." In *Multicultural Education: Issues and Perspectives*, updated 4th ed. edited by James A. Banks and Cherry A. McGee Banks (New York: John Wiley & Sons, 2003).

38. Ray C. Rist, "Author's Introduction: The Enduring Dilemmas of Class and Color in American Education." *Harvard Educational Review*, HER Classic Reprint 70, no. 3 (Fall 2000): 257–301.

39. Marcos Pizarro, *Chicanas and Chicanos in School: Racial Profiling, Identity Battles, and Empowerment* (Austin: University of Texas Press, 2005).

40. Rubén G. Rumbaut, "The Crucible Within: Ethnic Identity, Self-Esteem, and Segmented Assimilation Among Children of Immigrants." In *Origins and Destinies: Immigration, Race, and Ethnicity in America*, edited by Silvia Pedraza and Rubén G. Rumbaut (Belmont, CA: Wadsworth, 1996).

41. Claude M. Steele, "Race and the Schooling of Black Americans." *The Atlantic Monthly* (April 1992): 68–78.

42. Geoffrey L. Cohen, Julio Garcia, Nancy Apfel, and Allison Master, "Reducing the Racial Achievement Gap: A Social-Psychological Intervention." *Science* 313, no. 5791 (September 2006): 1307–1310.

43. Milbrey W. McLaughlin and Joan E. Talbert, *Professional Communities and the Work of High School Teaching* (Chicago: University of Chicago Press, 2001).

44. Christine E. Sleeter, *Un-Standardizing Curriculum: Multicultural Teaching in the Standards-Based Classroom* (New York: Teachers College Press, 2005): 128.

45. Steele, "Race and the Schooling of Black Americans," p. 77.

46. Kenneth Zeichner, "Educating Teachers to Close the Achievement Gap: Issues of Pedagogy, Knowledge, and Teacher Preparation." In *Closing the Achievement Gap: Reframing the Reform*, edited by Belinda Williams (Washington, DC: Association for Supervision and Curriculum Development, 2003).

47. Martin Haberman, "Selecting 'Star' Teachers for Children and Youth in Urban Poverty." *Phi Delta Kappan* 76, no. 10 (June 1995): 777–781.

48. Rosa Hernandez Sheets, "From Remedial to Gifted: Effects of Culturally Centered Pedagogy." *Theory into Practice* 34, no. 3 (Summer 1995): 186–193.

49. Cynthia Ballenger, *Teaching Other People's Children: Literacy and Learning in a Bilingual Classroom* (New York: Teachers College Press, 1999): 3.

50. Steve Crabtree, "Teachers Who Care Get Most From Kids." Available at: www.detnews.com/2004/schools/0406/04/a09-173712.htm

51. As quoted in the Tomás Rivera Center *Newsletter* 2, no. 4 (Fall 1989): 9.

52. Juan González, "Schools Ruling Defies Logic." [New York] *Daily News*, Thursday, June 27, 2002.

53. See, for example, Samuel Bowles and Herbert Gintis, *Schooling in Capitalist America*; also see Gregory Mantsios, "Class in America: Myths and Realities," *Detroit News*, June 4, 2004; and Paula S. Rothenberg, ed., *Race, Class, and Gender in the United States*, 5th ed. (New York: Worth Publishers, 2001).

54. Denny Taylor and Catherine Dorsey-Gaines, *Growing Up Literate: Learning from Inner-City Families* (Portsmouth, NH: Heinemann, 1988).

55. Janine Bempechat, "Learning from Poor and Minority Students Who Succeed in School." *Harvard Education Letter* 15, no. 3 (May/June 1999): 1–3.

56. Jane L. David and Patrick M. Shields, *When Theory*

Hits Reality: Standards-Based Reform in Urban Districts, Final Narrative Report. (Menlo Park, CA: SRI International, 2001).

57. Michael B. Katz, *Class, Bureaucracy, and the Schools: The Illusion of Educational Change in America* (New York: Praeger, 1975). See also Joel Spring, *The American School: 1642–2004,* 6th ed. (New York: McGraw-Hill College, 2005).

58. John Dewey, *Democracy and Education* (New York: Free Press, 1916).

59. David Tyack, "Schooling and Social Diversity: Historical Reflections." In *Toward a Common Destiny: Improving Race and Ethnic Relations in America,* edited by Willis D. Hawley and Anthony W. Jackson (San Francisco: Jossey-Bass Publishers, 1995): 4.

60. Richard Morin, "The Color of Disaster Assistance." *Washington Post,* June 9, 2006. Available at: www.washingtonpost.com/wp-dyn/content/article/2006/06/08/AR2006060801768/html

Chapter 4 Case Studies

Linda Howard

Unless you're mixed, you don't know what it's like to be mixed.

Jefferson High School is a large, comprehensive high school in Boston. It has a highly diverse population of students from throughout the city, including African American, Puerto Rican and other Latino, Haitian, Cape Verdean, Vietnamese, Cambodian, Chinese American, other Asian American, and European American students. This is the high school from which Linda Howard,[1] a 19-year-old senior, had just graduated. Linda was the class valedictorian, was awarded a four-year scholarship to a prominent university in New England, and was looking forward to her college education. She was already thinking about graduate school, and although she had not yet decided what she wanted to study, she was contemplating majoring in education or English.

Frequently taken for Puerto Rican or Cape Verdean because of her biracial background (her father is African American, and her mother is European American), she resented these assumptions by those who did not know her. Linda's insistence about being recognized as biracial and multicultural sometimes put her in a difficult situation, especially with friends who pressured her to identify with either her Black or her White heritage. She remained steadfast in proclaiming her biracial identity in spite of the difficulty it caused her. Her friends were a mosaic of the varied backgrounds of her school and of the community in which she lived. Her best female friend was Puerto Rican, and her boyfriend Tyrone was West Indian.

Linda had an uneven academic career. At Tremont School, a highly respected magnet elementary school in the city, she was very successful. The school's population was diverse, with children of different backgrounds from all over the city. She loved that school and has good memories of caring teachers there. By the time she reached junior high, she was held back twice, in both seventh and eighth grades, because she had been in an accident and had missed a great deal of school during her recuperation. By the end of her second eighth grade, she had improved her grades significantly. After the eighth grade, Linda transferred to Academic High, her present school, which she attended for two years before transferring to Jefferson High. She was a highly successful student, although she felt that Jefferson High was "too easy." The normal load for most students is four academic courses and two electives, but Linda had taken six academic courses per semester.

Linda was recognized as a gifted student by her teachers. She was a talented singer and she even hoped to someday make a living as a musician. She inherited her love of music from her father, who had given up a career in music. The entire family sang together, and Linda claimed to be the best singer—when her father was not around. She was a member of the school choir and also studied music on her own. Music gave her great solace and motivated her to do her best. Linda was also gifted in language. She frequently wrote poems to express her feelings.

At the time of her interviews, Linda lived with her mother, father, one older brother, and two younger brothers in a middle-class, predominantly Black community in Boston. Her family had moved there from a public housing project 14 years before and bought their first home two years later. She still called the housing project and neighborhood where she grew up "part of my community, part of my heritage." Both of Linda's parents were working professionals, although that had not always been the case. She was proud of the fact that her father started in the telephone company as a lineman some 20 years earlier and now had a white-collar job. Her mother was a human services administrator.

Being both outgoing and personable, Linda had a great many friends. Showing her more playful side, she told us she and some of them "cruise around, find cute guys, and yell out the window, 'Yo, baby!' That's how we hang!" Tyrone was her "very best friend." They had known each other for seven years and were actually engaged when she was 15. She broke off the engagement because she felt that she had her life ahead of her and needed to plan for college and a career. One month before being interviewed, they had broken up completely but were still good friends. Linda said that she would do anything in the world for Tyrone.

Linda was very aware of her values and of the role her family played in their formation. Her interviews highlighted a number of issues central to understanding these values: her struggle concerning identity and racism, the importance of teachers' caring and their role in students' learning, and the great value of education in her life and her parents' influence over this factor.

Identity, Racism, and Self-Determination

My parents are Black and White American. I come from a long heritage. I am of French, English, Irish, Dutch, Scottish, Canadian, and African descent.

I don't really use race. I always say, "My father's Black, my mother's White, I'm mixed." But I'm American; I'm human. That's my race; I'm part of the human race.

After all these years, and all the struggling (because when [my parents] got married it was a time right before desegregation), people from all sides were telling them, "No, you'll never make it. You'll never make it. White and Black don't belong together in the same house." And after 20 years, they're still together and they're still strong. Stronger now than ever, probably. That's what I like the most about them. They fought against all odds, and they won.

It's hard when you go out in the streets and you've got a bunch of White friends and you're the darkest person there. No matter how light you are to the rest of your family, you're the darkest person there, and they say you're Black. Then you go out with a bunch of Black people, and you're the lightest there, and they say, "Yeah, my best friend's White." But I'm not. I'm both.

I don't always fit in—unless I'm in a mixed group. That's how it's different. Because if I'm in a group of people who are all one race, then they seem to look at me as being the other race. . . . whereas if I'm in a group full of [racially mixed] people, my race doesn't seem to matter to everybody else. . . . Then I don't feel like I'm standing out. But if I'm in a group of totally one race, then I sort of stand out, and that's something that's hard to get used to.

It's hard. I look at history, and I feel really bad for what some of my ancestors did to some of my other ancestors. Unless you're mixed, you don't know what it's like to be mixed.

My boss, who was a teacher of mine last year, just today said something about me being Puerto Rican. I said, "We've been through this before. I am not Puerto Rican. I am Black and White." I may look Hispanic, but this is what I mean. And this is a person who I've known for a whole year and a half now. [I felt] like I was insignificant. If, after all this time, he didn't know, and we discussed it last year. . . . It was insulting. I usually don't get insulted by it. I say, "Oh, no, I'm not Spanish. I'm Black and White." And people say, "Oh really? You are? I thought you were Spanish."

[Teachers should not] try to make us one or the other. And God forbid you should make us something we're totally not. . . . Don't write down that I'm Hispanic when I'm not. Some people actually think I'm Chinese when I smile. . . . Find out. Don't just make your judgments. And I'm not saying judgment as insulting judgments. But some people, they don't realize that there are so many intermarried couples today. You have to ask people what they are. If you really want to know, you have to ask them. You don't just make assumptions. 'Cause you know what happens when you assume. . . . If you're filling out someone's report card form and you need to know, then ask.

I don't know how to put this . . . race hasn't really been a big factor for me. Because in my house, my mother's White; my father's Black; I was raised with everybody. Sometimes I don't even notice. I see people walking down the street. I don't care what they are; they're people.

My culture is my family. I have an enormous family. I have three brothers, two parents, and my father has ten brothers and sisters, and all of my aunts and uncles have children. That to me is my culture . . . I was born and raised in America. I'm fourth-generation American, so it's not like I'm second generation, where things were brought over from a different country or brought and instilled in me. I'm just American, and my culture is my family, and what we do as a family. Family is very important to us. . . . My family is the center of my life.

I've had people tell me, "Well, you're Black." I'm not Black; I'm Black and White. I'm Black and White American. "Well, you're Black!" No, I'm not! I'm both. It's insulting, when they try and . . . bring it right back to the old standards, that if you have anybody in your family who's Black, you're Black. . . . I mean, I'm not ashamed of being Black, but I'm not ashamed of being White either, and, if I'm both, I want to be part of both. And I think teachers need to be sensitive to that.

I would say I have more Black culture than White . . . because I know all about fried chicken and candied yams and grits and collard greens and ham hocks and all that because that's what we eat . . . My father had to teach my mother how to cook all that stuff [laughs]. But that's just as far as food goes . . . But as far as everything else, my family is my culture.

See, the thing is, I mix it at home so much that it's not really a problem for me to mix it outside. But then again, it's just my mother and my grandmother on the "White side," so it's not like I have a lot to mix.

I don't think [interracial identity is] that big of a problem. It's not killing anybody. At least as far as I know, it's not. It's not destroying families and lives and stuff. It's a minor thing. If you learn how to deal with it at a young age, as I did, it really doesn't bother you the rest of your life, like drugs. . . .

In the city, I don't think there's really much room for racism, especially anymore, because there's just so many different cultures. You can't be a racist. . . . I think it's *possible*, but I don't think it's logical. I don't think it was ever logical. It's possible. It's very possible, but it's sort of ridiculous to give it a try.

I think we're all racist in a sense. We all have some type of person that we don't like, whether it's from a different race, or from a different background, or they have different habits.

But to me a *serious racist* is a person who believes that people of different ethnic backgrounds don't belong or should be in *their* space and shouldn't invade *our* space: "Don't come and invade my space, you Chinese person. You belong over in China or you belong over in Chinatown."

Racists come out and tell you that they don't like who you are. Prejudiced people [on the other hand] will say it in like those little hints, you know, like, "Oh, yes, some of my best friends are Black." Or they say little ethnic remarks that they know will insult you, but they won't come out and tell you, "You're Black. I don't want anything to do with you." Racists, to me, would come out and do that.

Both racists and prejudiced people make judgments, and most of the time they're wrong judgments, but the racist will carry his one step further. . . . A racist is a person that will carry out their prejudices.

[Racists have power] only if you let them! We'll stick with [the example of] striped shirts: If I go where everyone is wearing solids, and I'm wearing a stripe, and someone comes up to me and tells me, "You don't belong here; you're wearing stripes," I'll say, "I belong anywhere I want to belong." And I'll stand right there! But there are some people who just say, "Oh, okay," and will turn around and leave. Then the racist has the power.

I wrote a poem about racism. I despise [racism]. . . .

> Why do they hate me?
> I'll never know
> Why not ride their buses
> in the front row?
> Why not share their fountains
> or look at their wives?
> Why not eat where they do
> or share in their lives?
> Can't walk with them
> Can't talk with them unless I'm a slave
> But all that I wonder is who ever gave
> them the right to tell me
> What I can and can't do
> Who I can and can't be
> God made each one of us
> just like the other
> The only difference is,
> I'm darker in color.

I had a fight with a woman at work. She's White, and at the time I was the only Black person in my department. Or I was the only person who was at *all* Black in my department. And she just kept on laying on the racist jokes. At one point, I said, "You know, Nellie, you're a racist pig!" And she got offended by *that*. And I was just joking, just like she'd been joking for two days straight—all the racist jokes that she could think of. And we got into a big fight over it. She threw something at me, and I was ready to kill her. . . . There's only so far you can carry this. She started to get down and dirty. . . . She was really getting evil. . . . They locked her out of the room, and they had to hold me back because I was going to throttle her.

She thought I was upset because she tossed the water at me. I said, "You know, Nellie, it's not the water. It's all these remarks you've been saying. And you just don't seem to have any regard for my feelings."

I remember one thing she was talking about. She said, "I'm not racist, just because I was jumped by eight Black girls when I was in the seventh grade, I'm not racist." After [30] years, why was she still saying they were eight *Black* girls? That to me was insulting. That was then; this is now. I didn't do it to you. I didn't jump you. It wasn't my father who jumped you; it wasn't my aunt who jumped you. . . . I told her I didn't want it taken out on me, that's the thing. I don't want anybody's racism taken out on me.

I've got a foot on both sides of the fence, and there's only so much I can take. I'm straddling the fence, and it's hard to laugh and joke with you when you're talking about the foot that's on the other side.

She couldn't understand it. We didn't talk for weeks. And then one day, I had to work with her. We didn't say anything for the first . . . like two hours of work. And then I just said, "Smile, Nellie, you're driving me nuts!" and she smiled and laughed. And we've been good friends ever since. She just knows you don't say ethnic things around me; you don't joke around with me like that because I won't stand for it from you anymore. We can be friends; we can talk about anything else—except race.

Teachers, Role Models, and Caring

My first-grade teacher and I are very close. As a matter of fact, she's my mentor. I'm following in her footsteps. I'm going to study elementary education. She's always been there for me. After the first or second grade, if I had a problem, I could always go back to her. Through the whole rest of my life, I've been able to go back and talk to her. She's a Golden Apple Award winner, which is a very high award for elementary school teachers. She keeps me on my toes. When I start getting down, she peps me back up, and I get back on my feet.

All of my teachers were wonderful. I don't think there's a teacher at the whole Tremont School that I didn't like. It's just a feeling you have. You know that they really care for you. You just know it; you can tell. Teachers who don't have you in any of their classes or haven't ever had you, they still know who you are. . . . The Tremont School in itself is a community. I love that school! I want to teach there.

I knew [Academic High] would be a hard school, but I didn't know it would be so . . . they're just so rigid. The teachers, there's no feeling. Like I said, the Tremont was a community for me, and I loved it. I'm that type of person; I'm an outgoing person, and I like to be able to talk to anybody and not feel that I can't talk to someone. If I have to spend six hours a day in school, I want to feel that I can talk to my teachers. At Academic, I didn't feel that at all. I hated it, absolutely hated it. They let me know that I wasn't high anymore. I was average. They slapped me with it. My first report card, oh goodness, it was terrible. I don't remember exactly what grades they were; I just do remember it was the first time in my life I had seen an F or a D under my name.

I think you have to be creative to be a teacher. You have to make it interesting. You can't just go in and say, "Yeah, I'm going to teach the kids just that; I'm gonna teach them right out of the book and that's the way it is, and don't ask questions." Because then you're gonna lose their interest. . . . Because I know there were plenty of classes where I lost complete interest. But those were all because the teachers just [said], "Open the books to this page." They never made up problems out of their head. Everything came out of the book. You didn't ask questions. If you asked them questions, then the answer was, "In the book." And if you asked the question and the answer wasn't in the book, then you shouldn't have asked that question!

Mr. Benson, he cared; he was the only one of the two Black teachers [at Jefferson High School]. He was not enough. The other Black teacher, he was a racist, and I didn't like him. I belonged to the Black Students' Association, and he was the advisor. And he just made it so obvious . . . he was all for Black supremacy. A lot of times, whether they deserved it or not, his Black students passed, and his White students, if they deserved an A, they got a B. He was insistent that only Hispanics and Blacks be allowed in the club. He had a very hard time letting me in because I'm not all Black. . . . I just really wasn't that welcome there.

He never found out what I was about. He just made his judgments from afar. He knew that I was Black and White, and I looked too White for him, I guess. But we never discussed it.

At Jefferson, just about the whole school is like a big community. There are very few White, Caucasian, whatever you want to call them, us [laughing]. There are very few, but they don't cluster together. It's all integrated. . . . Nobody gets treated differently. We're all the same.

I've enjoyed all my English teachers at Jefferson. But Mr. Benson, my English Honors teacher, he just threw me for a whirl! I wasn't going to college until I met this man. He was one of the few teachers I could talk to. Instead of going to lunch, I used to go to Mr. Benson's room, and he and I would just sit and talk and talk and talk. My father and Mr. Benson share a lot of the same values. And every time I've heard Mr. Benson talk, all I could think about was Daddy: "Oh, that's exactly what my father says!" . . . "Education, get your education and go far." "Whether you're flipping burgers at the local joint or you're up there working on Wall Street, be proud of yourself."

'Cause Mr. Benson, he says, I can go into Harvard and converse with those people, and I can go out in the street and rap with y'all. It's that type of thing. I love it. I try and be like that myself. I have my street talk. I get out in the street and I say "ain't" this and "ain't" that and "your momma" or "wha's up?" But I get somewhere where I know the people aren't familiar with that language or aren't accepting that language, and I will talk properly. . . . I walk into a place, and I listen to how people are talking, and it just automatically comes to me.

Mr. Benson is the same as I am. Well, his mother was Black and his father was White, so Mr. Benson and I could relate on all the problems that you face in the world. Like when you go to fill out any kind of form and they ask you, "Black, White, Chinese, Hispanic, Other." I check off "Other" and I'll write it down. And then Mr. Benson told me that he found out that when you write it down, they put you under "Black" because it all comes back to the old laws about, if you had any Black blood in you, you were Black.

I wrote a poem about it. It was just a bunch of questions: "What am I?" I had filled out a whole bunch of college essays, and I was tired of having to write out "Other: Black American and White American." And I went to him and I said, "Mr. Benson, what do you do when you get all these forms and they ask you "Black, White, or Other?" And he said, "You might as well just fill out "Black" because that's what they'll do to you." That just drives me nuts! And we got on this big conversation about it.

He came from the lower class in Chicago and worked his way, and he studied every night, six hours a night. He got into Harvard, and he went to Harvard, and now he's back helping the people who needed help. Because the way he sees it, he could go and he could teach at Phillips Academy, and he could teach at Boston Latin, which he did for awhile. But those people don't need his help. That's how he sees it. They're gonna learn with or without him. He wanted to come back to a small community, the underprivileged community, and help those people. That's what made me admire him the most because I like to help people.

The teacher who didn't really help me at all in high school was my computer lit. teacher. Because I have no idea about computer literacy. I got A's in that course. Just because he saw that I had A's and that my name was all around the school for all the "wonderful things" I do, he just automatically assumed. He didn't really pay attention to who I was. The grade I think I deserved in that class was at least a C, but I got A just because everybody else gave me A's. But everybody else gave me A's because I earned them. He gave me A's because he was following the crowd. He just assumed, "Yeah, well, she's a good student." And I showed up to class every day. . . . He didn't help me at all because he didn't challenge me. Everybody else challenges me; I had to earn their grades. I didn't have to earn his grade. I just had to show up.

If I were to teach math, I'd turn all the math problems into games. I had a teacher who did that. I *hated* math up until the second time I was in the seventh grade. . . . I despised math until I met Ms. Morgan. And from that point on, I have never received less than a B in math. She turned every math problem . . . every type of math problem was a game, so that school is never, "This is the way it is, and that's just it. Just learn it." I'd make everything exciting and fun, or I'd try to. That makes school enjoyable.

Family Values and Education

In the Tremont and in the Williams [schools], I was the top of my class, well, not top of my class, but I was very high up in the ranks. . . . That all comes from family. My mother's been reading me books since probably the day I was born, up until school age . . . any book with a serious message for children. My mother's always been very big on that, to make sure that reading was important. I still love to read . . . mysteries, human interest stories. It made a difference in elementary school. It really did. And, actually, it made a difference in high school, after I left Academic High, because I graduated first in my class.

My parents know that the further I go in school, the better life I'll have. Because they had to struggle to get where they are today. They had to struggle to make themselves comfortable. Going to school is going to be a struggle. But as long as I'm in school, my parents will always be there for me.

The first five years of your life, that's when you develop the most. Before you go to school, you've already got your personality. If you have parents who are showing you the right values (not "*the* right values" because everybody's values to them are right . . .), whatever values they've given you are what you carry for the rest of your life.

That's the way my family has raised me. . . . They really taught me not to judge. You just accept [people] the way they are. With my family, if you go to church, you go to church; if you don't, you don't. My grandmother says, "Jesus still loves you and I still love you, whether you go to church or not." It's that kind of thing. You just learn to accept people.

Sexuality—I don't judge, I try not to, anyway. I'm sure subconsciously I do . . . I don't come out and say, "Ugh, he's gay." My neighborhood is thoroughly mixed and sexually open. And they're my neighbors. I don't differentiate them. And that's something I wish a lot of people would do. Because I think it's wrong. Because if you were to take people and differentiate because of their preferences, be it sexual or anything, *everybody's* different. I prefer a certain type of music; you prefer a different type of music. Does that mean we have to hate each other? Does that mean you have to pick on me and call me names? That's the way I see it.

I'm not going to be exactly like my parents. I grew up with basic values. And I follow those basic values. And if you think about it, the choices I make have something to do with my values. And the only place I got my values from was [home]. So, I may change things around, flip them over, just adjust them a bit. But they still come down to my home values, my basic values, and my basic values came from home.

[My parents] have always taken good care of me. They're always there for me, all the time, if I need to talk. And they make it so obvious that they love me, you know, with these ridiculous curfews that I have [*laughs*]. I know it's for the better, although I can't stand it; I know there's a reason behind it, some twisted reason! . . . Just a regular night out, I have to be in at midnight. If it's a party, I don't have to be in 'til two. All my friends stay out 'til three and four in the morning. But that's because their parents can go to sleep. My parents can't sleep if I'm not home. That's what I like the most about them.

I was reading an article the other day about how the family dinner has sort of been tossed out the window in today's society. My family sits down to dinner together four out of seven nights a week, all six of us. Dinner's at six. If it's late, then everybody waits. You don't just eat on your own. I've noticed a lot of people, my boyfriend, for one, they never eat together. I've had all kinds of friends who always say, "Your family *eats* [together]?" And that's different from other families.

It's very important to my parents, and it'll be important to me. Because that's the time when we sit down and say, "How was your day? What'd you do? How are you feeling? Do you have a headache? Did you have a rough day? Did you have a good day?" You know? And that's about the only time the whole family can sit together and talk and discuss.

I have wonderful parents, although I don't tell them [*laughing*]. [*Do they know?*] Probably.

My father and my mother had to work [their way] up. My father has been working for the telephone company for 20 years. He started off cutting lines and working underground. Now he sits in his office. He's a businessman these days, and he had to work his way up. Whereas if I go and get myself a college education, I'm not going to have to start splicing lines if I want to work at the telephone company. I'm going to start with the knowledge that I don't have to splice a line. I could start in the office with my father.

A lot of us [Black kids] just don't have the home life. I really do think it begins when you're a baby! My mother, like I said, I believe she read to me from the day I was born; I'm sure of it. A lot of people just didn't have that. Their parents both had to work; they didn't have anybody at home to read to them. They just sat in front of the tube all day. When they came home from school, their homework was just tossed aside, and they sat in front of the television until Mom and Dad came home. Then Mom and Dad rushed them through dinner, got them to bed, and this and that. A lot of them just didn't come from the right background to have—not the smarts, but to be educated enough to pass that test [to get into Academic High]. Because the Academic test isn't a test of how much you know; it's more of a test of how well can you solve problems. . . . The Black population wasn't very high there.

I blew two years. I learned a lot from it. As a matter of fact, one of my college essays was on the fact that, from that experience, I learned that I don't need to hear other people's praise to get by. All I need to know is in here [*pointing to her heart*] whether I tried or not.

It's not the school you go to. It's what you want to get out of it and what you take from it.

If I know I did my hardest, if I know I tried my very best and I got an F, I'd have a beef with the teacher about it, but if that's what I got, that's what I got. If that's seriously what I earned after all my efforts, then I'll have to live with it.

[Grades] are not that important. To me, they're just something on a piece of paper.

. . . [My parents] feel just about the same way. If they ask me, "Honestly, did you try your best?" and I tell them yes, then they'll look at the grades and say okay. . . . The first thing my father always looked at was conduct and effort. If all the letter grades in the academic grades said F's, and I had A's in conduct and effort, then my father would just see the F's, and say "Oh, well . . . "

[The reason for going to school is] to make yourself a better person. To learn more, not only about the world and what other people have gathered as facts, but to learn more about yourself.

The more that there are opportunities for you to learn, you should always take them. I just want to keep continuously learning, because when you stop learning, then you start dying.

I've got it all laid out. I've got a four-year scholarship to one of the best schools in New England. All I've gotta do is go there and make the grade.

If I see the opportunity to become a leader, I'll do it. I'll just go and take over. . . . I like the recognition.

I'm ready now. I can face the challenge. I'm ready to go out in the world and let [that] university know who I am!

 # Commentary

Issues of identity were clearly at the core of Linda's striving to carve out a place for herself in her family, community, and school. Although she had reached quite a sophisticated understanding of race, racial awareness, racism, and identity, some feelings of ambivalence, conflict, and pain were still apparent. Being "mixed," to use Linda's term, is the reality of more and more students in U.S. schools. According to recent national census data, nearly 6.8 percent of people under the age of 18 are of mixed heritage.[2] In spite of this reality, many schools are unaware of the strains, dilemmas, and benefits that biracial identity poses for children.

It is likely that most people in the United States are a mixture of several racial heritages, but this is either not known or not readily acknowledged. According to some estimates, Blacks in the United States are, on average, about 20 percent White, and Whites are about 1 percent Black.[3] Although this assertion is impossible to prove, *miscegenation*, or racial mixing, is far more common than generally admitted in our society. Discomfort with this issue is understandable, given the history of rape and subjugation forced on African American women, especially during slavery. This is an example of the legacy of racism; so is the "one-drop" rule—the idea that one drop of Black blood makes a person Black—to which Linda alluded. In fact, the "one-drop" rule was reaffirmed as late as 1982 in a court decision in Louisiana, in which $\frac{1}{32}$ African ancestry was sufficient to keep "Black" on an individual's birth certificate.[4]

This classification, which has not been practiced in other societies, was not always the case in the United States. Rather, it emerged some time in the early 18th century.[5] The classification was to the benefit of the institution of slavery because, with this logic, people could still be enslaved even if they were mostly White. Like race itself, this was a social and political construction rather than a biological one.

Although during the first half of the 20th century, interracial marriages in the United States had declined dramatically from earlier times, they began to increase after the Civil Rights Movement. Between 1970 and 1980, the number of interracial marriages doubled, from 310,000 to 613,000; by 1991, the number had climbed to 994,000. As documented in *Of Many Colors*, a book of portraits and interviews of multiracial and multiethnic families, it is estimated that there are more than a million interracial marriages. This still represents a small percentage of all marriages in the United States.[6]

Considering the racist underpinnings of group and self-identification in the United States, the dilemmas Linda faced were difficult indeed. One study of biethnic and biracial students' self-concept found that the school environment was hostile to them through an insistence that these students deny part of their heritage. Moreover, the students who were interviewed felt that their schools did not promote the inclusion of biethnic and biracial students, and in fact, hindered their self-identification.[7] According to Maria Root, the existing psychological models of racial and cultural identity development have not yet caught up with the reality of a rapidly expanding multiracial and multiethnic population. As a result, young people are still adversely affected by mixed-race heritage. If they are of mixed heritage, particularly if that includes European American background, these youngsters are often seen as "less authentic" African Americans, Asian Americans, or Latinos. Thus, she claims, "Authenticity tests are a form of racial hazing and illogically enforce a limited, superficial solidarity."[8] On the other hand, the situation is complex because mixed-race identity also has its advantages. As author Alejandra Lopez has suggested,

> . . . though being of mixed heritage can have its disadvantages at times (affected by situational, regional, and cultural contexts), its growing prevalence, acceptability, and even trendiness influence the ways in which people make decisions about how to racially identify themselves and their children.[9]

Lopez concludes that the increasing prevalence of mixed-race identity demands (1) a more critical exploration of how educators talk about race and ethnicity and (2) a clearer understanding of the fluidity and hybridity of such identity.

In spite of—or perhaps because of—the relative invisibility of mixed-race people, especially at the time she was first interviewed in 1990, Linda identified most strongly with her family. As she said, "My culture is my family." And because her family was mixed, so was her culture. Hers was a particularly courageous stand in a society that forces an individual to choose one identity over the other or fits a person into one that she or he would not necessarily choose. The simple act of naming herself was a powerful experience for Linda.

Except for her time at Academic High, a very competitive and highly regarded high school where she was made to feel unintelligent, Linda loved school for the most part. Having teachers who understood and cared was also meaningful for Linda. Fortunately, there were a number of such teachers in each of her schools. Of course, Linda did not expect all her teachers to be biracial like herself, but she did expect them all to be sensitive and accepting of who she was, rather than imposing their own ideas about identity on her. The teachers who stood out were not only those with whom she could identify culturally but also those who made learning fun, engaging, and challenging.

Linda Howard, an extraordinary young woman, was ambitious, certain of her talents, and ready for the future. No doubt, her strong family bonds, love of learning, and steadfast identification as Black and White all contributed to her academic success. Her teachers and schools were not always able to understand or support her, which emphasizes the importance of a school's social context and the degree to which it can insulate students from racism and influence students' self-esteem.

◆◆◆ Reflect on This Case Study

1. Linda Howard insists on identifying as biracial. She also says that she is just "a member of the human race" and that race is not very important to her. Nevertheless, she obviously spent a great deal of time thinking about race, as some of her anecdotes and poems make clear. Are these assertions contradictory? Why or why not?

2. If you were one of Linda's teachers, how might you affirm her identity? Give specific examples.

3. What can you learn, for your own teaching, from the teachers who have been most influential in Linda's life? What are the implications for curriculum? For pedagogy? For relationships with students?

4. Linda's family is, as she says, "the center" of her life. How do you think this has helped Linda become a successful student? Does this mean that students whose families are different from hers cannot be successful? Give some examples of academically successful students who have had different experiences from Linda's.

5. Can issues of race and identity be handled by schools, or are these issues too complicated for them? What skills do you think you need if you are to face these issues effectively?

Rashaud Kates

I am African American. My culture is important to me. It is who I am.

Rashaud Kates,[1] a soft-spoken African American high school student in a mid-sized town on the southern coast of Georgia, was getting ready to start his senior year of high school at the time of this interview.

Rashaud lived with his mother, since his parents had recently divorced, but his father continued to figure prominently in his life. He had older siblings from his mom's first marriage who lived on their own. One sister, with whom he spent a great deal of time, lived nearby. His family lived within very modest means in a humble neighborhood close to his school that he described as "safe and quiet." His father, a former U.S. Marine, worked for a law enforcement training center. His mother was a housekeeper and also worked at his church.

The school that Rashaud was attending is a comprehensive high school for grades 9–12 with approximately 1600 students. He was a high-achieving student who cared deeply about his grades, especially as they reflected his parents' pride and his collegiate future. Co-curricular activities also played a significant role in his school life. He was a member of the after-school club Future Business Leaders of America.[2] Rashaud also played on the school basketball team and looked forward to playing varsity his senior year. The school population was racially diverse: 55 percent White students, 42 percent Black students, and small percentages of Hispanic, Native American, and Asian students. Just under 40 percent of the students received meal assistance.

Rashaud's school life can be viewed through the lens of the broader context of Black students in U.S. schools. The data on the schooling experience of many African American students, especially young men, reflect the "crisis in Black education" cited by scholars of the American Educational Research Association (AERA) Commission on Research in Black Education (CORIBE).[3] In several studies, the commission documents the overwhelming unequal learning opportunities for students of African heritage and calls for a transformative research agenda.[4] Disparities in graduation rates, resources, and access to qualified teachers; racial bias in special education; and cultural alienation in curriculum and instruction are among the many rigorously documented characteristics that contribute to systemic inequality for many students of color, especially low-income African American youth.[5]

These realities permeate the lives of many students. Nevertheless, Rashaud, his family, and many of his teachers demonstrated resolve in overcoming institutional discriminatory structures to cultivate a bright future. Rashaud's deep family roots, connections to school, and abiding trust in the promise of education undergird all three themes that emerged in his case study: *determined responsibility, plans for the future*, and *the enduring influence of teachers' expectations*, with which we begin.

The Enduring Influence of Teachers' Expectations

Being an African American student, to me, really it's kinda' tense. People look at you every way, to see if you're doing stuff wrong, but really you don't [do anything wrong]. If you were somebody else, they really wouldn't look at you like that. People are already judging you when you're African American. I would tell teachers about African American students, "Everybody's not bad; have high expectations."

I am African American. My culture is important to me. It is who I am. The school does Black History Month. That's about the only time [the school recognizes my culture]. There are mostly White teachers in my school. If a student is trying to do what they need to do, that's all that really matters. It shouldn't matter if the teacher is a different race. The thing that might hold me back from getting a good education, sometimes is that when I first meet a teacher, the teacher thinks I'm bad 'cause I'm Black. I overcome it by just being me, just who I am; then they see me a regular person.

Sometimes I think it's just the way things are, but you could really do something about it if people would just stop acting up and stuff. Then teachers would be able to understand that everybody ain't bad or whatever. My advice for other African American boys entering our school is, "Don't act like everybody else, like the kids who are acting up. You gotta work hard, study, and stayed focused."

I had teachers who I learned a lot from. Ms. Teshek in fourth grade. She joked a lot, she used to have us laughing all the time . . . it was really fun . . . she was really fun, we laughed a lot in fourth grade. We learned more from her, because it made us pay more attention. She taught everything . . . math, reading, science, and everything.

Another teacher in middle school, Ms. Hollis, . . . she was a seventh grade teacher; she taught math. She was strict. To me, it was good; to other people it might have been bad. It was good, because that's how my daddy is about my grades and stuff, so I was just used to it. She used to have a ruler she carried around, and she used to hit the desk all the time to let you know that she was expecting something out of you. A teacher needs to let you know that they expect a lot. It makes you work harder. When a teacher is strict like that, they are doing it because they care about you. I did well in math that year. See, with my daddy, if I get a D or something on my progress report, I get a punishment or something until I get my grades up. Sometimes he gave me a bit of money if I did real good. If I didn't get a good progress report, there would be punishment.

Also, in middle school, Ms. Ketchem, in English—she spent time with me after class, to teach me stuff. In English I did good because she helped me so much. Sometimes after school, sometimes during the lunch break, mostly after school, whenever she could, she would help me know where to put the commas and stuff like that.

Another teacher is from a class I took during tenth-grade year called "Entrepreneurship"; I just really liked it. We made business plans and discussed them, and all this stuff. [We learned about] developing a business; I made a clothing store. I learned so much; I was in FBLA [Future Business Leaders of America]. I joined last year as a junior. It was fun; I felt like a real businessman. We would go and volunteer a lot. We volunteered at Ronald McDonald house in Savannah and we went to a couple of nursing homes. We try to think about how we can help. Mr. Richards runs FBLA, [the] same teacher who taught Entrepreneurship. He helps me think about college. I want to take another business class, but I don't know if I can.

My favorite subject is math . . . learning about money . . . knowing about money. Maybe Ms. Hollis from seventh grade had something to do with that. If you do well in math you can manage your money better. My least favorite is history. I don't really see a point in knowing what happened in 1720 or whatever . . . all those dates. If I could tell the teacher what I want to learn, I would want to know about the wars. Now they only teach about World War II. We never make it to the subject of the war in Iraq or even the Vietnam War. Never make it to that. It never comes up. The war now is never discussed.

If I were principal of the school. . . . I would listen to the students' suggestions. We do go to the principal about a lot of stuff. I don't feel like they really listen. For the prom, it was suggested to have a DJ instead of the band, and they didn't listen to that. Then, they only had one pep rally for the whole year. It was for football season. They didn't listen about that. She was all right as a principal, she just didn't listen to us too much.

Some teachers need to be more laid back. Some of them are always on you for the small stuff. Not the way Ms. Hollis was, because she was on us to get good grades. Some teachers are just always, always on you for nothing.

Determined Responsibility

Now, I'm an OK student. I messed up my A/B honor roll last year. In ninth and tenth grade I was on the A/B honor roll. But last year in eleventh grade, because of literature class, I messed up at the end of the year. I don't know, I was just slackin'. I got a C. I just slacked; I was disappointed. I do think I'll get back on honor roll senior year because I'm going to work hard. If I feel myself slacking, if my grades start to go, I'll go to the teachers and ask if I can do some make-up work or something . . . ask for help and make up work.

I have friends who are successful students. My friend Carl is successful. He got all his stuff together. He is supposed to apply for college. He wants to be a producer to do music and stuff. He is successful because he really works. I know. I see him after school in the library. He is always working.

The way to succeed is through determination. You gotta be determined to do it. If you're not, you won't get it done. Determination means a lot. You need an education to better yourself in life. To get an education, to broaden life, it makes more opportunities and stuff. I think I am accomplishing that.

My parents want to see me successful and get a chance to start my business . . . to be secure financially. My brother didn't graduate from high school. My parents check my grades. They tell me what they are thinking. It matters to me, because if they didn't care, I wouldn't care. Since they do, I really do. I really want to make them proud. I think I am getting what I need out of school. Sometimes I wish I could get more out of it. Like some of the classes. Like the literature.

I wish I could get more out of the literature. We were learning about allegory and all that, which I liked and then literature class changed. It doesn't seem [to mean] much about anything. There's not really any stories or literature about African Americans in our school.

Plans for the Future

Freshman year I did not play basketball because everybody was telling me it was the hardest year. I was worried about grades, so I didn't play basketball. I did good in school, so sophomore and junior year I played JV. So I started and I got to play a lot. Senior year will be my varsity year. I'd like to play in college.

Guidance counselors are talking about college. They told me to take the SAT test, and I did. They are telling us to take all the tests. They told me I can go to the community college down here, but I really want to go to Georgia State. I have looked at the college application. For financing college, I am going to try to apply for scholarships. I have been on the Internet looking. In the guidance office, I heard about some scholarships.

If I don't get on the basketball team, I'll still go to college. Sports at college are like this: I would like to play sports so I gotta keep my grades up to be able to play sports, so it helps. But if I don't play sports, I will still be keeping my grades up. The [Georgia State] basketball team is good—I want to play sports, but I gotta keep the grades up too.

When I am done with college I want to start my own business. I am not too sure yet what business. I am just interested in the business world. I am going to apply to Alabama State, too. That's about all I'm looking at right now. The college here is a community college. A four-year college would be better.

My parents don't say too much about college. They don't really know what to say about it; they haven't been to college. They don't know what it is like. Maybe they worry about money; they just don't talk about college. They want me to go.

◆◆◆ Commentary

Rashaud had a great deal in common with many high school students. He enjoyed sports and after-school clubs. He worked at his church and did not have much time for TV but enjoyed watching sports news shows when he had the chance. He liked reading mysteries, listening to R&B and eating chili-cheese-dogs and hamburgers. He cared about school achievement and realized the importance of good grades for his collegiate future. Juggling academic achievement with co-curricular activities, part-time employment, family commitments, and participation in a faith community is a balancing act for many American teens.

In addition to the stringent pressures faced by Rashaud (and other conscientious high school students), he knew that he had to overcome the persistence of institutionalized racism in schools. He put it plainly, "The teacher thinks I'm bad 'cause I'm Black." Rashaud's encounters with negative discriminatory expectations echo the experiences of many African American students reported in other studies. The prevalence of these experiences make it clear that Rashaud has articulated a phenomenon that reaches beyond individual bias; however, Rashaud viewed changing this dynamic as the responsibility of the students "who act up." He took up the challenge to disprove the bias of some teachers by just "being himself." The overwhelming social message that individual effort may defeat powerful structural obstacles runs deep.

Rashaud did not entertain the possibility that the institutional structures need to be changed. The destructive effect of institutionalized racism on students' perceptions of their racial identities is not always obvious to students like Rashaud who develop achievement strategies to counteract the racism.

A study by Ann Arnett Ferguson describes how certain forms of punishment in schools perpetuate the identity of "troublemakers and potential inmates," especially among African American boys, while she makes an argument for change in approach to classroom strategies.[6] Reports by other researchers—Angel Love and Ann Cale Kruger, for example—stress the importance of educating teachers to examine their beliefs related to knowledge, race and culture, teaching practices, teaching as a profession, and expectations of students.[7] The results of such teacher education could change both the students' and teachers' views of the prospects for Rashaud and his peers.

Most students are not taught to critically assess the hierarchies of institutional discrimination and cultural bias that exist in many schools. Rashaud's case points up that he and other students appear to maintain faith in the notion of American meritocracy, believing that determination and hard work alone will bring them success, even when inequities stare them in the face. Prudence Carter's study noted the persistence of this hopeful yet seemingly contradictory mindset—that is, that many African American students acknowledge the existence of racism and its influence on their lives and schooling, while on the other hand, they are frequently emphatic that their potential success or failures are contingent upon their own personal determination and hard work.[8]

In contrast to the disparaging incidents and situations he faced, Rashaud also remembered a number of teachers who had positively influenced his learning. His description of the warmth and humor of his fourth grade teacher appeared to be in direct opposition with the seventh grade math teacher's ruler-banging strategies, yet he asserted that both styles contributed to his success. We question whether Rashaud's appreciation of the math teacher's rigorous expectations could be developed in a less punitive way (without the ruler banging), but the point remains that a range of approaches may lead to academic achievement, which is another implication of Angel Love and Ann Cale Kruger's study. They point out that there may be numerous pathways to teaching African American children successfully and that successful teachers may hold an eclectic array of beliefs.[9]

It is notable that Rashaud reported the invisibility of his ancestors' cultural, economic, and historical experiences in the curriculum. He also described the school's ignoring of students' voices, even in matters that appeared to be relatively minor to address, such as the prom music and pep rallies. Reports and stories about students like Rashaud underscore the significance of providing curricula, as well as teaching methods, in which students see reflections of themselves and their heritage. Rashaud explicitly yearned for more curriculum, in both social studies and literature courses, that reflected the cultural perspectives of his ancestors as well as his current social and political realities.

He may have been edging toward school disengagement with his report of "slackin'" in the literature course, but his resolve to strengthen his grade in the class appeared to draw from a matrix of other support systems. Despite the variety of factors that may have been impeding or promoting his success, Rashaud's sense of self-determination mattered a great deal. His effort to maintain a high level of school engagement may be attributed to a web of intricate factors, not the least of which were his parents' supportive expectations, his views on a productive future, the efforts of many dedicated (if not always culturally responsive) teachers, and his involvement in co-curricular activities.

While Rashaud stated that he was receiving some guidance counseling about the local community college, he appeared to have been left on his own to navigate applying to comprehensive four-year institutions and seeking out scholarships—a high hurdle, to be sure. Several researchers highlight the necessity of mentors to support students of color in this process, which is so vital to socioeconomic upward mobility.[10] Prudence Carter refers to such mentors as "Multicultural Navigators."[11] Especially for African American males in under-resourced schools and communities, multicultural navigators may have an enduring imprint on a student's future. To be guided by an adult who is fluent in the social and cultural capitals of college admissions and scholarship acquisition can make the difference between discouraged confusion and confident assertion for a student. Moreover, since the challenges do not end at the college admissions office door, a mentor's sustained support may help a young person to endure the academic rigors of higher education and stay in college and facilitate the youth's passage into independent adulthood.

Rashaud's family was explicitly supportive of his aspirations but may not have had access to the experiences needed to provide multicultural navigation. Rashaud may still have been able to break through the institutional barriers, even in the absence of a specific mentor or a school program or structure to facilitate college entrance. Will Rashaud's commitment to academic achievement, determination to disprove stereotypes, engagement in community service, and athletic skills be enough for him to gain admission to a realm that few people in his daily life have entered? Will he sustain his vision of his future? If so, what resources will he be able to access to pursue his hopeful vision as a successful businessperson? More to the point, how many peers of African heritage will he see in his college classes and in his potential business meetings? Will Rashaud be a celebrated exception or part of revolutionary change?

Joyce King and the CORIBE scholars (see notes 3 and 4) call for educators to keep watch and take action against the diminishment of humanity and thereby advance the broader picture of human freedom that is so crucial in the education of African American youth.[12] Rashaud's accomplishments, combined with his indomitable outlook, are a reminder to all educators about the imperative of their call.

◆◆◆ Reflect on This Case Study

1. Rashaud did not see his racial identity or culture reflected in the school curriculum. What may have been preventing the school from being more culturally responsive? What are some strategies the school administration and teachers could have implemented to affirm Rashaud's identity and that of his peers?

2. As a teacher, what is your responsibility for ensuring that all students achieve? What might you do when a student exhibits behavior that Rashaud described as "slackin'" in literature class? Whose responsibility is it to ensure student engagement?

3. What are the respective roles of the school and individual teachers in supporting students through the college admissions process? When does this support begin? How might this support be shaped for first-generation college-bound students from communities with less experience in the cultural capital of college admissions?

VANESSA MATTISON

A good education is like growing, expanding your mind and your views.

At the time of her interview, Vanessa Mattison[1] was 17 years old. Her family had been in the United States for many generations. European American in background, Vanessa lived in Welborn Hills, a small, rural hill town in western New England, but she had had a number of experiences that helped make her far more worldly than others in her circumstances. By 17, she had traveled to Africa, the Caribbean, and Mexico. Her travels opened her eyes to some of the realities beyond her small community, which was made up of several diverse groups of people: farming families who have lived in the area for generations; newer families with more formal education and more liberal values who had left urban areas in search of a more rural and simple lifestyle; and working-class families, who made their living in the retail and light industries of the surrounding towns and small cities. Although Vanessa's family did not fit neatly into any category, it probably had the most in common with the second group. For example, they read not only *Newsweek* but also *Greenpeace*; they were vegetarians; they listened to Bob Dylan, Joan Baez, and reggae and blues music; and they traveled from time to time. A number of the other families from Welborn Hills also routinely traveled outside the United States, but others had never even been to Boston or New York, both just a few hours away by car. In the town's only elementary school, as well as in the regional secondary school that the town's students attended, the class conflict between the more liberal and educated families and the families that had lived here for generations was almost palpable.

Only a tiny minority of the residents of Welborn Hills were people of color. The same was true of Hills Regional High School, a school for grades 7 through 12, with a population of approximately 700 students, which served a number of rural towns, including Welborn Hills. For many of the European American students, access to understanding cultural differences and to meeting and being friends with people different from themselves depended on class and educational privilege—that is, only students like Vanessa who had had the privilege of traveling, had any inkling of the influence of racism or cultural differences on those different from themselves.

Taking classes in Spanish, calculus, sociology, humanities, art, and "contemporary problems," Vanessa was on an academic track. She was successful and engaged in school and was looking forward to being the first in her family to go to college. Socially active and involved in sports, Vanessa was self-confident and open to new ideas. She had many friends, both male and female, from a variety of cultural backgrounds. Soft-spoken and thoughtful in her replies, Vanessa had deeply held beliefs about the value of all people, peace, social justice, and environmental concerns.

Vanessa lived with both parents in a modest home, and she described them as economically lower middle-class. Her sister, age 21, lived in a nearby town. Her father, who had been raised in the area, was a craftsperson, and her mother a paralegal. Although both parents had finished high school, neither had gone to college. Vanessa said her family was different from others because her parents were still together and everyone in her family was happy and got along. She took pride in the fact that her parents stood up for what they believed in. At the time she was interviewed, their courage of conviction was taking the shape of protest against the First Gulf War, which had just begun.

Having never needed to identify ethnically or racially because she had always been considered the "norm," it became clear from the outset that Vanessa was embarrassed and uncomfortable with the issue of self-identification and culture. In spite of her greater awareness of culture and cultural differences than the majority of her peers, it was a difficult issue for her. She wanted to grapple with it, however. In fact, she agreed to be interviewed precisely because the project sounded "interesting and important," and she made time for it in her busy schedule. *Discomfort with issues of cultural, racial, and linguistic differences* is the major theme that emerged from the interview with Vanessa. The other issues focused on the *promise, sometimes unfulfilled, of education* and on *what teachers can do to make school more fun for students.*

The Discomfort of Differences

[*How do you describe yourself?*] I generally don't. . . . Wait, can you explain that? Like, what do you want to know?

Well, I would [describe myself as White], but it doesn't matter to me, so that's why I said it's a tough question. 'Cause I usually just describe myself as, like, what I believe in or something like that. Rather than, like, what culture I am, whether I'm Black or White. 'Cause that doesn't matter.

[I'm] . . . well, Scottish, French and German, I guess. My family all speak English at home, though I'm taking Spanish. I guess I'm middle class or lower class. It depends on how you think of it. I guess the German part might have come in the 20th century. I'm not really sure, that's just a general guess. . . . I wasn't really interested. I don't really know if we have that many connections back to who was where when and what happened.

I don't have any [religious beliefs]. I've never gone to church. We never, like, read the Bible as a family or anything. I think both of my parents used to go to church. I think they were Catholic. . . . They probably didn't think it was as important to their life as the people who had wanted them to go. . . . I don't really know much about it. But if I had a choice, I probably wouldn't want to go to church because I think that I'd rather formulate my own ideas than being told that the

Earth was created in seven days and God did this and He did this. I don't know. He seems like just too almighty of a person to me. I just don't believe it.

I guess . . . obviously I just made it seem like [culture] wasn't [important]. It's just that, like, all the stuff that's happened to people because of their culture, like the slaves and Jewish people. Culture, what you look like, whether you're Black or White could matter less to me. It's the person who you are . . . it's not what your appearance depicts.

I don't think it's fair. I don't think that one person should have an easier time just because of the color of their skin, or their race, or 'cause they belong to a particular church or something.

People like Blacks still don't have as many rights as the White man. I'm saying "man" because women don't have their rights either. The "superiority game . . . " 'Cause people just have it stuck in their head that that's the way it is and . . . I don't really know how to change it . . . I try and change it, speak out against it.

[Other cultures] are not that well represented [in my school] because there's not that many people who live around here. The majority is probably White. But they're represented in a small margin. . . . We've read books, and we've seen movies. I think we saw part of the freedom marches in the South and stuff like that. And we saw *Gandhi*, although that isn't really to this culture.

Each of us that go to [our school] is important . . . because it adds what you could say would be a culture. Just like our community, the school community.

Well, I guess people's backgrounds *do* [matter] because that's what makes them what they are.

[Culture] is like a conglomeration of language, the way you speak, the way you are . . . things that are important to you. . . . Well, the culture of the United States is kind of like norms, things that happen a lot. Like if you were to go to another country, it might strike you as weird because you don't do it at home that way.

I don't agree with a lot of our culture. I don't agree with how it's so rushed and how if you're Black, you're supposedly not as good or you're not as fit for the job or something like that. And if you're a woman, it's the same thing. And, like, you can't be gay without being put down. I don't know, there's all these underlying rules about if you're not this, you can't do that.

It seems weird . . . because people came over from Europe, and they wanted to get away from all the stuff that was over there. And then they came here and set up all the stuff like slavery, and I don't know, it seems the opposite of what they would have done. It was probably like burned into their head already from where they were: If you were lower class, then you usually weren't taught to read or educated. . . . They might not have come over thinking that's what they had in mind, but since that's what they had always known, that's what they did.

Like [the first president] Bush said in his speech a little while ago that "We're doing all we can to fight racism" and blah, blah, blah, when the Supreme Court just made the ruling about schools and busing, which was basically turning back a decision they had made a long time ago.

When I see racism, I often think that I wish I was Black or I wish I was the group that was being discriminated against. You know how some women say, "I hate men"? I don't know, but I'm sure that Black people said this, when they were slaves, like "I hate White people." I don't want to be thought of like that because I'm not against them. I think they're equal. And also after they've been put through so much awfulness, I think that every White person should be in their shoes.

When I was in second grade, there was somebody coming into our class who was going to be Black. He was like a new student and somebody said something about it, and me and a couple of my other friends got really mad at him. "It doesn't matter what color they are. They could be orange or yellow or brown. It doesn't matter, they're just a person."

For strength and inspiration, I usually look to Martin Luther King, Jr. I like Gandhi too, because I believe in nonviolence. And I believe they helped to strengthen the basis for my belief, and they gave specific examples of how it could work. I just believe in nonviolence as a way to get what you want . . . and peace. I don't believe if you punch somebody, then, yeah, they may do what you want them to do, but they're not going to be doing it because they want to. They're just going to be doing it because of fear. I don't think fear is a good policy.

Education and Values

Supposedly education is what this country is built on, but there's no money for it.

Money is being cut out of all the schools. We lost a bunch of programs. We don't have as many teachers. We're going to lose more money, and it seems like the government's always promoting it as this great big deal. Then, where's the money for it? They're not supporting it. . . . [In my school] they still have, for seventh and eighth grade, sewing and cooking and art. Music is still there, and sports was supported by the public this year through bottle drives and a big fundfest. I don't know what's going to happen next year. I hope it's still supported.

[My parents] feel the same way, . . . that the government needs to step in and help and that it's sad that it's going downhill. I think they think it's important to learn. Because they want me to be able to do what I want to do, and not, as I said before, get locked in a corner.

I've learned a lot of my morals [from my parents], like nonviolence and expressing myself, and striving for what I want, being able to have the confidence to reach what I want.

They're caring, and they're willing to go against the norm. They're willing to protest, that's a good word for it, for what they believe in . . . People drive by the [peace] vigils and give us the finger.

I think [Dad] values being able to survive on his own. Like moving away from your family and growing up and having your own job and supporting yourself and being able to get around, and not always having to have people do things for you. . . . He's fun and supportive.

[Mom] also strives for what her goals are and believes in self-support, working for what's yours.

It's not a broken-up family. My parents are together, and they're happy, and there isn't any fighting. Everybody gets along. A lot of my friends [are from divorced families]. There's a lot of support that I don't see in other families. . . . We don't always go with the flow. You know, like most people supposedly right now are for the [First] Gulf War. We're not, so we stand in the minority. . . . I personally don't believe in violence to solve things. I don't think that killing a zillion million people for oil is a good reason either. And you can't bring peace to somewhere that's not your culture and has a different government, and you especially can't do it through war. That's not going to solve things. And it would take a lot of talking and rearranging their entire society to get them to be like us, which I don't think is what they should be, 'cause they're not and they never have been and probably won't be.

[My parents want me to go to school] so I can be educated and get a job. So I can have options and not get stuck. . . . Probably because they didn't go to college and they'd like me to. That's just a guess . . . [But I would like] a little less pressure . . . like around college and school.

[I want to] go to college to help people. I want to be a psychologist or do social work, work with the environment. I'm not sure.

I guess [grades are important] because they've kind of become that way. . . . I think education is if you learn personally. That's not what the school thinks. It's not like if you get an A or an F, but if you learn. It's not just for the grades. . . . If I get grades that aren't real good, [my parents] are not real excited. And they always make sure that I'm doing my homework. They tell me to get off the phone.

I'm happy. Success is being happy to me. It's not like having a job that gives you a zillion dollars. It's just having self-happiness.

A good education is like when you personally learn something . . . like growing, expanding your mind and your views.

Making School More Fun

[In elementary school I liked] recess, 'cause it was a break between doing stuff. Everything wasn't just pushed at you. And art, which was really fun. . . . It was a safe place, and I liked the teachers and the people that went there. . . . I liked that on Valentine's Day and Christmas and birthdays they had [parties] for us. They mixed school and fun.

I did the work, I understood it, and I was interested.

My favorite [subject] is art because of the freedom to express myself, to paint and draw. Humanities is my worst 'cause it's just lectures and tests.

I play field hockey and I've done track and I've done tennis, because it's a way of releasing energy and feeling good about yourself and being in shape. . . . I'm in a peer-education group. It's a group of 18 seniors who set up programs to educate the other students in the school on issues like alcoholism, drunk driving, stereotyping, a bunch more. It's kind of like, since they're students and they're projecting to a student audience, it's easier for some people to relate.

We did a skit on [stereotyping]. We had jocks, hippies, snobs, burnouts, and a nerd. And we did these little scenarios like the snob liked this guy who was a hippie and all her friends were like, "Oh, my God! You like *him*?! He's such a hippie!" And then, like, the hippie friends said the same thing about the snob, and then, like, everything stopped and the two people who liked each other got up and said, "I wish my friends would understand. . . . " And then the person who was narrating said, "Well, here's one way in which the situation could be fixed." So they went back where they were and said, "Okay, yeah, well, I guess we should give them a chance." Most of the ideas came from us except for the one I just explained to you. Me and two other people basically wrote the whole skit. We just did it for the seventh and eighth grade. We thought that would be the most effective place 'cause that's where it basically starts. They liked it.

It's important for teachers to get to know all the students and know where they're coming from and why they may react a certain way to certain things because then it'll be easier to get through. And there won't be as many barriers because they'll already know. . . . Maybe if school didn't just start off on the first day with homework, maybe if it started off with just getting to know each other, even if you're in a class that's already known each other.

You could have games that could teach anything that they're trying to teach through notes or lectures. Well, like, if you're doing Spanish, you can play Hangman or something. You can play word games where you have to guess the word. Like they give you a definition and it makes you remember the words. Or if somebody acts out a word, you remember it better than someone just looking it up or writing it down.

Make it more entertaining 'cause people learn a lot from entertainment. If you see a play, you'll probably remember it more than a lecture, [or] if you see a movie, play a game, or something. Work those more into what they're doing. . . . I think that some books should be required just to show some points of view.

Some [teachers], based on [students'] reputation, may not be as patient with some people. [Students get reputations] basically through grades and troublemaking, like if you get in trouble with the system and get detentions.

[Unhelpful teachers are] ones that just kind of just move really fast, just trying to get across to you what they're trying to teach you . . . not willing to slow down because they need to get in what they want to get in.

[Most teachers] are really caring and supportive and are willing to share their lives and are willing to listen to mine. They don't just want to talk about what they're teaching you; they also want to know you.

 ## Commentary

Coming face to face with racial, class, cultural, and other differences was difficult for Vanessa because she had not often needed to consider these things. One gets the sense that, for her, "culture," "ethnicity," and "race" were what *other* people had, and Vanessa sometimes seemed offended at having to talk about them. It was almost as if she considered it rude to broach questions of race and culture—that discussing them meant you were a racist (what Mica Pollock defines as "colormuteness").[2] In this, Vanessa was similar to other young people of European descent for whom ethnicity is inconsequential. In a study assessing the salience of identity for young people of various backgrounds, the researcher found that most African American, Mexican American, and Asian American young people rate ethnicity as important to their identity, but only 25 percent of White students do.[3]

Vanessa took the approach that cultural and racial differences are not significant. She was, in fact, simply reflecting the value of being colorblind, which we all have been led to believe is both right and fair. In this framework, differences are seen as a *deficit* rather than as an *asset*. Being White and having Christian parents, Vanessa rarely had been confronted with her cultural identity. She considered herself the "norm," "just a person." As is the case for most White Americans, she had the privilege of seeing herself as just an individual, an opportunity not generally afforded to those from other groups.

Because Vanessa associated culture, race, and other differences with oppression and inequality, these issues were difficult for her to address. For one, Vanessa viewed cultural and other differences as *causing* oppression ("like all the stuff that happened to people because of their culture, like the slaves and the Jewish people"). For another, she was offended by the unfairness with which differences are treated. The fact that some people are penalized for being who they are, while others are rewarded for it, made it difficult for her to confront differences.[4] Not wanting to benefit from racism, Vanessa found it easier to avoid or downplay the issue. Her growing awareness of sexism, revealed through comments such as, "I'm saying 'man' 'cause women don't have their rights either" may have helped her make the connection between the two issues.[5]

Vanessa was struggling to understand the contradictions between the ideals she had been taught and the discrimination she saw around her. She was beginning to link issues such as peace and social justice with those of racism and other biases. Although she associated herself with her race only when confronted with the example of racism exhibited by other White people, it was at such times that Vanessa clearly saw the need for Whites to stand up and take responsibility. She also understood that being White generally meant having more opportunities, which she resented as unfair.

Through dialogue with Vanessa, it became clear that few of these issues had ever been addressed in any of her classes. When asked if she had learned history and other subject matter in school from the perspectives of different groups of people, she answered that everything was taught from what she called "a general perspective." Because the viewpoints of others are invisible in the traditional curriculum, many students think of the one reality that is taught as the "general" reality and the experiences of others as little more than ethnic add-ons to "real" knowledge.

In spite of her lack of awareness of diverse perspectives, Vanessa was becoming keenly aware of, and committed to, social issues. For example, she spoke out against discriminatory statements and in this way tried to change things. Vanessa had exhibited such outspokenness since second grade. Even in that incident, however, she and her friends thought that, by overlooking racial differences, they would be helping the new boy in class. Being colorblind was, to them, the logical response.[6]

Although she believed that education should be a major priority in our society if we want to give all students an equal education, Vanessa was aware that the societal commitment simply is not there. She felt that education, although compulsory, is often not engaging. Vanessa viewed education as crucial, but she wished it were more interesting and interactive. Her perception of schooling as boring and "flat," especially at the secondary level, and her suggestion that teachers should make school more entertaining and fun for all students, corroborate what has been found to be the general attitude of students in many schools around the United States.[7]

Vanessa's parents also understood that education would give Vanessa options they themselves had not had. They were involved in school activities (her mother served on the local school committee, and both parents had volunteered time to the schools), and they also demonstrated their concerns in many other ways. Their involvement, in Vanessa's words, "shows that they care."

Related to the value of education are the other values that Vanessa learned from her parents: self-reliance, self-confidence, and independent thought. These values obviously helped her develop her own persona in a school setting that was both conformist and conservative. A strong and forthright young woman with deeply held values and beliefs, Vanessa, although still uncomfortable with issues of diversity in a comprehensive way, was clearly committed to struggling with them. The interviews themselves seemed to have served as a catalyst to her thinking more extensively about diversity, racism, and identity. For example, after stating how *unimportant* race and culture were to her, she quietly admitted, "Well, I guess people's backgrounds *do* [matter] because that's what makes them what they are." Given the strength and support of her family, her searching soul, and her grounding in peace and social justice, she was a wonderful example of a young person ready to, in her words, "expand my mind and my views."

Reflect on This Case Study

1. Why do you think White people in the United States generally do not identify with any particular racial or ethnic group? What can teachers do to help White students identify with their cultural heritage?

2. What kinds of school experiences would have made Vanessa more comfortable with diversity?

3. As a teacher, what is your responsibility for introducing your students to diversity? What strategies and activities might you use? How would these differ in a primarily White school, compared to a more culturally and racially heterogeneous school?

4. What is the role of values in education? Should schools teach values? Why or why not? Should some of Vanessa's family's values be included? Why or why not?

5. Vanessa gave several suggestions for making school more entertaining and fun. In a group, develop suggestions for teachers that would make school more interesting and engaging for students. Focus on a particular grade level and subject area.

Notes to Chapter 4 Case Studies

Linda Howard

1. I appreciate the work of Paula Elliott in conducting and analyzing the extensive interviews that were the basis for this case study. Paula is an assistant professor at Wheelock College, where she teaches prospective and practicing teachers. Her research interests focus on the experiences of educators of color in preservice and in-service programs that explicitly address racism, racial identity development, and the process of teaching and learning.

2. U.S. Census Bureau, *Census 2000 Summary File 1* (Washington, DC: Department of Commerce, 2002).

3. Joel Williamson, *New People: Miscegenation and Mulattos in the United States* (New York: Free Press, 1980).

4. Robin Lin Miller and Mary Jane Rotheram-Borus, "Growing Up Biracial in the United States." In *Race, Ethnicity, and Self: Identity in Multicultural Perspective,* edited by Elizabeth Pathy Salett and Diane R. Koslow (Washington, DC: National Multicultural Institute, 1994).

5. Williamson, *New People: Miscegenation and Mulattos in the United States.*

6. Gigi Kaeser and Peggy Gillespie, *Of Many Colors: Portraits of Multiracial Families* (Amherst, MA: University of Massachusetts Press, 1997).

7. Marta I. Cruz-Janzen, "*Curriculum and the Self-Concept of Biethnic and Biracial Persons,*" diss., College of Education, University of Denver, April 1997.

8. Maria P. P. Root, "Multiracial Families and Children: Implications for Educational Research and Practice." In *Handbook of Research on Multicultural Education,* edited by James A. Banks & Cherry A. McGee Banks (San Francisco: Jossey-Bass, 2004): 112.

9. Alejandra Lopez, "Mixed-race School-age Children: A Summary of Census 2000 Data." *Educational Researcher* 32, no. 6 (August/September 2003): 25–27.

Rashaud Kates

1. We would like to thank Joan Nichols, a high school art teacher in Georgia, who assisted us in arranging Rashaud's interview.

2. For more information on Future Business Leaders of America, visit their national website: www.fbla .pbl.org.

3. For more information on the American Educational Research Association Commission on Research in Black Education, see the website www.aera.net.

4. Joyce E. King, ed. *Black Education: A Transformative Research and Action Agenda for the New Century* (Washington, DC/Mahwah, NJ: AERA/Lawrence Erlbaum, 2005).

5. *Ibid.*, 11–12.

6. Ann Arnett Ferguson, *Bad Boys: Public School in the Making of Black Masculinity* (Ann Arbor: University of Michigan Press, 2001).

7. Angela Love and Ann Cale Kruger, "Teacher beliefs and student achievement in urban schools serving African American students." *Journal of Educational Research* 99, no. 2 (November–December 2005): 87(12).

8. Prudence L. Carter, *Keepin' It Real: School Success Beyond Black and White* (New York: Oxford University Press, 2005).

9. Love and Cale Kruger, "Teacher beliefs and student achievement in urban schools serving African American students."

10. See Ricardo D. Stanton-Salazar, *Manufacturing Hope and Despair: The School and Kin Support Networks of U.S.-Mexican Youth* (New York: Teachers College Press, 2001): 251; also see Gilberto Q. Conchas, *The Color of Success: Race and High-Achieving Urban Youth* (New York: Teachers College Press, 2006): 113–115.

11. Carter, *Keepin' It Real: School Success Beyond Black and White.*

12. King, *Black Education*, 2005, 11–12.

Vanessa Mattison

1. We are grateful to Maya Gillingham for the interviews and the background for Vanessa's case study. Maya is a therapeutic body worker and holistic health educator, diversity trainer, and group facilitator. She lives with her partner, Chino, and their daughter, in Oakland.

2. Mica Pollock, *Colormute: Race Talk Dilemmas in an American School* (Princeton, NJ: Princeton University Press, 2004).

3. See Jean D. Phinney, "A Three-Stage Model of Ethnic Identity Development in Adolescence." In *Ethnic Identity Formation and Transmission Among Hispanics and Other Minorities*, edited by Martha E. Bernal and George P. Knight (Albany: State University of New York Press, 1993).

4. See Beverly Daniel Tatum, *"Why Are All the Black Kids Sitting Together in the Cafeteria?" and Other Conversations About Race* (New York: HarperCollins, 1997).

5. See Peggy McIntosh, "White Privilege and Male Privilege: A Personal Account of Coming to See Correspondences Through Work in Women's Studies," (Working Paper no. 189, Wellesley College Center for Research on Women, Wellesley, MA, 1988).

6. For a helpful discussion about the kinds of actions Whites can take to fight racism, see Andrea Ayvazian, "Interrupting the Cycle of Oppression: The Role of Allies as Agents of Change." In *Race, Class, and Gender in the United States*, 4th ed., edited by Paula S. Rothenberg (New York: Worth, 2001).

7. See, for example, Bruce L. Wilson and H. Dickson Corbett, *Listening to Urban Kids: School Reform and the Teachers They Want* (Albany: State University of New York Press, 2001).

Structural and Organizational Issues in Schools

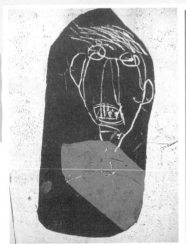

"I've noticed if you're getting D's and F's, they don't look up to you; they look down. And you're always the last on the list for special activities, you know?"

— Fern Sherman, interviewee

Andrea D. Cardoso and Brianna Millor-Hammond in Liz Brennan's and Layla Cady's art class. *Self-portraits.* Relief prints, 2006.

Nearly a century ago, John Dewey warned, "Democracy cannot flourish where the chief influences in selecting subject matter of instruction are utilitarian ends narrowly conceived for the masses, and, for the higher education of the few, the traditions of a specialized cultivated class."[1] As Dewey feared, our public schools, as currently organized, are not fulfilling the promise of democracy. Certain school policies and practices exacerbate the inequality that exists in society. Although some of these policies and practices may have evolved in an attempt to deal more equitably with student diversity, just the opposite may be the result. This is the case with *tracking*, which often is meant to help those students most in academic need. Some practices are so integral to the schooling experience that they are hardly disputed even though there may be little evidence for their effectiveness. This is the case with *retention,* or holding students back a grade. Some may not be official policies, but rather unquestioned practices that can lead to disempowerment. This is the case with the limited roles that teachers, students, and parents have in school.

Policies and practices can end up becoming rigid structures that are difficult to change. Many of these structures, unfortunately, run counter to the grand and noble purposes that Dewey described, yet they have come to define schooling itself. These include the general similarity of curriculum and schedules, particular patterns of resource allocation, and an unswerving faith in test scores as measures of ability or success. The case studies that follow this chapter provide other examples of organizational practices and policies that can harm students. Avi Abramson, for example, was adamant that teachers' pedagogy can either motivate or turn off students. For Fern Sherman, the content of the curriculum sometimes made her feel alienated and angry. As these cases demonstrate, all school policies and practices need to be critically evaluated if we are serious about developing the kind of public education that Dewey deemed necessary.

It is legitimate to ask how structural and organizational issues such as school policies and practices are related to multicultural education. When multicultural education is thought of as simple additions of ethnic content to the traditional curriculum, a discussion of school policies and practices may seem irrelevant. However, when defined comprehensively, multicultural education questions the total context of education, including curriculum, student placement, physical structure of schools, school climate, pedagogical strategies, assumptions about student ability, hiring of staff, and parent involvement, among other issues. In this sense, organizational structures are central to the development of a comprehensive multicultural education.

The following discussion provides examples of classroom and school-based policies and practices that may reinforce social inequities by inhibiting the educational success of some students. Because the focus is on the classroom and school rather than society, the impression may be that issues such as school financing, residential housing patterns, unemployment opportunities, racism and other institutional biases, and the ideological underpinnings of education are not as important. On the contrary, as we made clear in Chapter 1, all of these larger structural issues are profoundly implicated in school failure. We urge you to keep these societal issues in mind to understand how they directly influence inequities at the classroom and school levels.

Because larger structural issues have been discussed in previous chapters, this chapter focuses on school and classroom-based policies and practices. Each of the following is briefly described and examined:

- Tracking
- Retention
- Standardized testing
- Curriculum
- Pedagogy
- Physical structure
- Disciplinary policies
- Limited role of students
- Limited role of teachers
- Limited family and community involvement

TRACKING

One of the most inequitable and, until two decades ago, relatively undisputed practices in schools is tracking. The term *tracking* generally refers to the placement of students into groups that are perceived to be of similar ability (homogeneous groups) within classes (e.g., reading groups in self-contained classes), into classroom groups according to perceived abilities and subject areas (e.g., a low-level math group in seventh grade), or into groups according to specific programs of study at the high school level (e.g., academic or vocational).[2] In most schools, some kind of tracking is as much a part of school as are bells and recess.

Tracking may begin at the very earliest grades and decisions about student placement may be made on tenuous grounds. These can include social indicators such as information provided on registration forms, initial interviews with parents, and teachers' prior knowledge about specific students. Furthermore, research over many years has confirmed that tracking is frequently linked with racial, ethnic, and social-class differences. For example, research by Jeannie Oakes and Gretchen Guiton found that economically advantaged Whites and Asians in three high schools that they studied had much greater access to high-status, academically rigorous courses than Latinos whose achievement was similar.[3]

Tracking decisions are rarely innocent and their effects are not benign; on the contrary, they can have devastating consequences. Students in elementary school may be targeted for years to come, sometimes for their entire academic careers and beyond. As they get older, students may need to make decisions about future programs of study. For example, they may need to decide on a vocational school, an academic track, a secretarial or "business" track, or what is sometimes called a "general" track. Through their choices, they may pursue a college education, a low-paying job, or almost certain joblessness. Thus, at young ages, students are expected to make choices that can virtually chart the course of their entire lives. Young people 13 or 14 years of age are hardly prepared to make such monumental decisions on their own, and many parents are unable to help them. In addition, most schools lack adequate staffs to help students and their families make these decisions. Because of the labeling that low-track students often experience, they may not feel capable of handling more demanding programs of study.

Another consequence of tracking is that students may develop enduring classroom personalities and attitudes. They may begin to believe that their placement in these groups is natural and a true reflection of whether they are "smart," "average," or "dumb." Although students may feel that they themselves are deciding which courses to take, these decisions may actually have been made for them years before by the first teacher who placed them, for example, in the "Crows" rather than the "Blue Jays" reading group. The messages children internalize because of grouping practices are probably more destructive than we realize, and their effects more long lasting than we care to admit.

A further result of tracking is that students who most need excellent and experienced teachers have the least access to them. Considering the way in which scheduling decisions are made, teachers with the most experience are frequently given the "plum" assignments, and this usually means teaching high-ability classes. For example, in their research in high schools around the country, Milbrey McLaughlin and Joan Talbert found that teachers assigned to low-track classes were often poorly prepared in their subject matter and new to teaching.[4]

Tracking leaves its mark on pedagogy as well. Students in the lowest levels are the most likely to be subjected to rote memorization and static teaching methods, as their teachers often feel that these are the children who most need to master the "basics." Until the basics are learned, the thinking goes, creative methods are a frill that these students can ill afford. Children living in poverty and those most alienated by the schools are once again the losers, and the cycle of school failure is repeated. The students most in need are placed in the lowest level classes and exposed to the drudgery of drill and repetition, school becomes more boring and senseless every day, and the students become discouraged and drop out.

This is not to imply that students at the top ability levels always receive instruction that is uplifting, interesting, and meaningful. They too are exposed to methods and materials similar to those used for students at the bottom levels. If innovative methods and appealing materials exist at all, however, they tend to be found at the top levels. Knowledge becomes yet another privilege of those who are already privileged.

The effectiveness of tracking is questionable. In her 1985 pioneering research study of 25 junior and senior high schools around the country, Jeannie Oakes found that the results of tracking were almost exclusively negative for most students. Many other studies since then have been consistent with this finding. In a recent edition of her groundbreaking study, Oakes reviewed the field over the past 20 years and concluded that tracking as a practice is still largely grounded in ideologies that maintain race and social class privilege.[5] If the purpose of tracking is to provide access to opportunity for those who have most been denied this access, it has failed badly. In many instances, it has had the opposite effect.

Despite the extensive evidence that it does not work for most students, tracking is in place in most schools throughout the United States. Although its effects may be contrary to statements about its intended outcomes, tracking has been an immutable part of the culture of middle and secondary schools for many years, partly because the culture of the school is resistant to change. Once an idea has taken hold in schools, it seems to develop a life of its own, regardless of its usefulness or effectiveness. Moreover, schools respond poorly to pressure for change, particularly if it comes from those most jeopardized but least powerful.

If tracking were unanimously acknowledged as placing all students at risk, it would have been eliminated long ago. The truth is that powerful vested interests are at play in preserving it. Although tracking affects most students negatively, it may help a few. The evidence is mixed, but there is some indication that high-achieving students benefit from being tracked in honors and high-level classes. It is not surprising, then, that it is frequently the parents of high-achieving students who are most reluctant to challenge tracking because they perceive it as beneficial to their children. In addition, as mentioned previously, tracking decisions and race are often linked. This was found to be the case in a three-year longitudinal case study by Oakes and her colleagues. In their review of ten racially and socioeconomically mixed secondary schools participating in detracking reform, the researchers concluded that one of the greatest barriers to detracking was the resistance of powerful parents, most of whom were White. Through strategies such as threatening to remove their children from the school, the parents of students who traditionally benefited from tracking made detracking difficult, if not impossible.[6]

As we have seen, tracking is largely propped up and sustained by social class interests. Because it sorts and classifies students, tracking helps prepare them for their place in the larger society. Students in the top tracks generally end up attending college and having a better shot at becoming professionals; those in the bottom tracks frequently drop out or, if they do finish high school, become unskilled workers. Without lapsing into a mechanistic explanation for a complex process, it is nevertheless true that some students benefit and others lose because of tracking. Teachers and schools may compound the problem by seeing tracking as the only alternative to handling student differences and as a "natural" and even "neutral" practice.

We want to make it clear, however, that grouping per se is not always a negative practice. Good and experienced teachers have always understood that short-term and flexible grouping can be very effective in reviewing a particular skill or teaching intensively a missing piece of social studies or math or science. Grouping in such instances can be effective in meeting temporary and specific ends. But because rigid ability-group tracking is linked with, and supported by, particular classist and racist ideologies, grouping of any kind needs to be done with great care.

What are the alternatives to tracking? One approach is to "detrack," that is, to do away with tracking based on so-called ability differences. However, detracking alone will do little unless accompanied by a change in the school's culture and norms. In one study of six racially mixed high schools undergoing detracking, Susan Yonezawa, Amy Stuart Wells, and Irene Serna found that the schools' low- and middle-track students, mostly Latino and African American, resisted entering high-track classes even when they were academically capable of taking them because they "hungered for 'places of respect'—classrooms where they were not racially isolated and their cultural backgrounds were valued."[7] Because tracking is supported by a complex set of structures that reinforce cultural assumptions and influence students' identities, the authors concluded that "freedom of choice" for students to select their own classes is by itself an empty concept *without* altering the other structures and ideologies that help perpetuate existing track hierarchies. They suggest that, to work, tracking needs to be accompanied by "safe spaces" such as ethnic studies classes that can make students feel valued. Anne Wheelock, who also has written extensively on the subject of tracking, has suggested that detracking combined with strategies such as cooperative learning, peer tutoring, multilevel teaching, shared decision making with students, and de-emphasizing the use of textbooks, while challenging racist and classist notions of ability, can also result in inspired stories of improved learning and intergroup relations.[8]

Although students differ from one another in many ways, and such differences need to be taken into account in order to provide students with a high-quality education, tracking alone has not proved to be the answer. At the same time, tracking alone cannot be blamed for inequality in learning. Singling out any particular policy or practice as the culprit is an insufficient explanation for schools' lack of success with particular students. In his extensive review of educational research, Joseph D'Amico found that other aspects of schools play a crucial role: the quality of teaching and the attitudes of teachers, the nature of the curriculum and instruction, the level of material resources available to students and teachers, and class size (among others).[9] Thus, it is a constellation of factors that create school failure, and the discussion that follows considers some of these factors.

RETENTION

Retention, or the practice of holding students back a grade, is another common practice in schools. Like tracking, retention is intertwined with other policies and practices that exacerbate inequality. For instance, it is related to testing because retention decisions are often made as a result of test scores. This is especially evident in the high-stakes testing context of the past several years.

One review of the literature on the effect of retention begins with the pointed question, "Making students repeat a grade hasn't worked for 100 years, so why it is still happening?" Susan Black, the author, goes on to say that according to some estimates, almost 2.5 million children are retained in U.S. classrooms and low-income students, boys, and students of color are overrepresented in this number. Aside from a short-term benefit for some students—a benefit that has been found to have no lasting effects—there is no evidence that retention brings children up to grade level. On the contrary, Black reviewed several decades of research that showed retention fails to improve achievement. Also, retention is linked in a very obvious way with dropping out of school: Students who are retained once are 40–50 percent more likely to drop out of school than those who have never been retained; for those retained twice, the risk is 90 percent.[10]

Students are typically retained in a particular grade when a determination is made, usually by the teacher (sometimes in consultation with counselors, the principal, and parents) that a student is incapable of performing the work that is required in the coming grade. As in the case of tracking, these decisions are generally made with good intentions: Often, teachers want to protect students from further failure or believe that, during the following year (in the same class), students will learn the material that they have not yet learned. As in the case of tracking, this reasoning is often erroneous. The largest number of students is retained in first grade, although researchers have found that first graders usually benefit the least from the practice.[11] In addition, as more pressure is placed on kindergarten to become more like first grade, there is a related pressure for kindergarten teachers to have their students "ready to learn" in first grade. As a consequence, more retentions are occurring in kindergarten. Yet, as one large study found, there is no evidence whatsoever that a policy of grade retention in kindergarten improves average achievement in math or reading. In fact, the evidence points in the opposite direction: Children who are retained actually learn less than they would have, had they been promoted.[12]

What, then, is the alternative? Considering the widespread public opposition to "social promotion"—promoting students to the next grade even if they have not learned the subject matter of their current grade—it is unrealistic to expect that retention as a policy will be abandoned. It is also unfair to simply move students on to the next grade even if they are unprepared for it and to expect them to catch up on their own. Because of this dilemma, more schools are implementing alternative intervention programs such as mandatory summer school and after-school tutoring programs. However, these measures are likely to produce few results unless accompanied by comprehensive school-wide reform involving other practices and policies. For example, extracurricular activities have been found to have a positive influence on student retention.[13] The connection between academic success and cocurricular and extracurricular activities is also clear in the case studies in this book, yet poor urban schools, where the need is greatest, have fewer of these activities.

STANDARDIZED TESTING

Another practice that impedes equity in schools is the uncritical use of standardized testing, particularly when employed to sort students rather than to improve instruction. Originally designed almost a century ago to help identify children who were labeled "mentally retarded", the use of standardized tests expanded greatly afterward, influenced by the tremendous influx of new immigrants into the country. As a result, the original aims of standardized tests were subverted to include rationalization of racist theories of genetic inferiority.[14] An extensive review of how test use changed during this period is not called for here. Nonetheless, it should be pointed out that standardized tests have frequently been used as a basis for segregating and sorting students, principally those whose cultures and languages differ from the mainstream. Moreover, the relationship between IQ tests and repressive and racist social

WHAT YOU CAN DO

BECOME INFORMED

In collaboration with colleagues, use professional days to visit schools that have successfully implemented detracking. Recommend that staff development sessions address directly tracking, detracking, and alternative kinds of grouping. It would be critical for schools considering detracking to view the video *Off-Track* (developed by Michelle Fine and her colleagues and available from Teachers College Press). In it, students and staff address the benefits and challenges of detracking. In addition, as part of a team of colleagues, you might ask for the opportunity to prepare seminars in which staff members share ideas for detracking or for creative grouping in classrooms.

DETRACK EXTRACURRICULAR ACTIVITIES

Tracking also occurs in extracurricular activities. As the case studies and snapshots demonstrate, extracurricular activities were significant in the academic success of most of the students interviewed or described. Nevertheless, extracurricular clubs

or organizations are often seen by students as exclusive clubs with limited membership. The school newspaper, for instance, is generally an activity in which highly intellectual and academically successful students engage, whereas sports is usually often the major domain of less academically oriented students. School activities and clubs frequently perpetuate the social class groupings that students develop instead of helping to counter the stereotypes on which they are based.

Although the message "You need not apply" is not purposely given, many students infer it from the recruitment policies and activities of some clubs and organizations. You can help make clubs and other organizations appealing to a wider range of students by, for instance, becoming a faculty sponsor for a group and actively recruiting and encouraging students of diverse backgrounds to join. Also, you could print recruitment materials in a number of languages, post them in neighborhood centers, and do outreach with families of students underrepresented in extracurricular activities to encourage their children to join.

theories and policies is not a historical relic. Unfortunately, there are contemporary examples of this relationship.[15]

Testing and tracking have often been symbiotically linked. Joel Spring has used a variety of primary sources ranging from real estate publications to newspaper accounts to demonstrate these links.[16] Lewis Terman, a psychologist who experimented with intelligence tests at the beginning of the 20th century, stated, with absolute conviction, after testing only two American Indian and Mexican American children, "Their dullness seems to be racial, or at least inherent in the family stock from which they came. . . . Children of this group should be segregated in special classes . . . they cannot master abstractions, but they can often be made efficient workers."[17] The same reasoning was used on other occasions to explain the "inferior" intelligence of Blacks, Jews, and Italians; practically every new ethnic group that has come to the United States has fared badly on standardized tests.[18]

Although today comments about specific groups tend not to be as blatantly racist as Lewis Terman's, the kind and number of standardized tests to which we continue to subject our students are staggering. This situation is especially related to the No Child Left Behind (NCLB) law that mandates annual mandatory testing in reading and math and—starting in the 2007–2008 school year, in science—at least once in elementary, middle, and high school. The testing requirement is based on the dubious reasoning that more tests will somehow lead to more learning and higher standards. Students now spend entire days, sometimes weeks, taking standardized tests. On top of the actual testing days, a great deal of time is spent on teaching children *how* to take tests, time that could be better spent in teaching, and the students' learning, actual content. In fact, Barbara Miner, writing for *Rethinking Schools*, has estimated that 17 tests—not including city and classroom-based test—are now required by NCLB each year.[19] One teacher we know told us that in her school, every year the fourth graders need to take a whopping 35 standardized tests!

In addition, the fact that textbook companies and other companies that develop tests earn huge profits from test construction and dissemination is often unmentioned, yet it, too, is a reality. The Government Accounting Office (GAO) reported that states would spend somewhere between $1.9 billion to $5.3 billion between 2002 and 2008 to implement NCLB-mandated tests. These, according to Barbara Miner, are just the *indirect* costs; if teacher time was added, the figure would be many times higher. Moreover, Miner found that the private testing companies that control the market operate with little or no public accountability, which is ironic considering the calls for "accountability" in schools.[20]

Despite its purported intent, NCLB has focused little attention on changes in curriculum or instructional practices, on improvements in teacher education, or on equalizing funding for school districts. Richard Elmore, a respected educational researcher whose work has centered on school improvement, has called this legislation "the single largest—and the single most damaging—expansion of federal policy over the nation's education system."[21] In reviewing the history of this legislation, Elmore argues that a school's ability to make improvements has much more to do with the beliefs and practices of the people in the school than with a demand that students in those schools reach a particular performance level on tests. According to him, the work of improving schools consists of improving "capacity," that is, the knowledge and skills of teachers, by increasing their command of content and how to teach it.

A concern for equity is a common reason cited for "high stakes" testing, that is, for linking test scores to the success of schools, teachers, and students. Certainly, equity is a significant concern because, as we have seen, schools for poor children of diverse backgrounds are often inferior to others; however, there is little evidence to support the contention that standardized tests lead to greater achievement. A number of reviews of testing legislation and practice have concluded that, rather than improving learning outcomes, such legislation is actually having a detrimental impact because gross inequities in instructional quality, resources, and other support services are being ignored. Researchers and educators concerned with social justice in education have become alarmed at these results. For instance, in a comprehensive volume devoted to the topic of standardized tests and equity, its editors, Gary Orfield and Mindy Kornhaber, conclude that "high-stakes tests, even those intended to raise standards for all students, can and have created barriers, especially for the nation's most vulnerable students."[22] Moreover, the efficacy of using such tests to improve student learning has been called into serious question. In a large multi-state study on the impact of high-stakes testing funded by the Rockefeller Foundation, researchers Audrey Amrein and David Berliner came to the conclusion that if the intended goal of using high-stakes tests is to increase student learning, then it is not working. Evidence from the study of 18 states is that in almost every case, student learning was *unchanged* or actually *went down* when high-stakes testing policies were instituted.[23] Also, as pointed out in the discussion of retention, because more states are now requiring that students pass a standardized test before they can graduate from high school, tests are resulting in increased urban dropout rates.

Standardized test scores are also inequitable because they correlate highly with family income. This reality exposes the myth that in the United States there is equality of opportunity regardless of social class and race. In a review of abundant national and international studies, David Berliner found overwhelming evidence of a positive and high relationship between social class and test scores.[24] This correlation has consistently been shown to be the case with the Scholastic Achievement Test (SAT), a test that is required for admission to most colleges and universities. Even the College Board, which administers the SAT, has demonstrated the correlation between income and scores: In their own analysis, the College Board found that a student whose family makes less than $10,000 a year scores nearly 250 points less on the SAT than a student whose family earns more than $100,000 a year.[25]

In addition, standardized testing affects other practices that impede equity. For example, testing may have a harmful effect on curricula by limiting teachers' creativity. This is because teachers in schools in which children have poor test scores may be forced to "teach to the test" rather than create curricula that respond to the real needs of learners. The result may be "dumbing down" or restricting the curriculum to better reflect the content and approach of tests. This is precisely the conclusion reached by Linda McNeil, who investigated the so-called Texas miracle (that is, the claim that student achievement in Texas increased as a result of more rigorous testing). What she found was that, instead, the testing mandates narrowed the curriculum and created conditions hostile to learning. In addition to reducing teacher motivation, more standardized testing led to higher dropout rates among students.[26] Other research corroborates this conclusion. One study found that the most pervasive finding on the effects of high-stakes testing on instruction has been the narrowing of the curriculum.[27] In addition, a national survey of 12,000 teachers reported that the extent of curriculum narrowing due to testing was directly associated with the nature of the stakes involved—that is, the higher the stakes, the greater the teachers' focus on tested content.[28]

Pedagogy may also be negatively affected by standardized testing. Many critics of high-stakes testing have found that when standardized tests were required, there was a decline in the use of such innovative approaches as student-centered discussions, essay writing, research projects, and laboratory work.[29] Because of the growing pressure to raise test scores, teachers may reason that they have little time for innovative approaches. This, in turn, affects teacher autonomy because it removes curriculum decision making from the teacher to the school, district, city, or even state level. The result is that the further the curriculum is from the teacher and the school, the less it reflects the lives of the students in the school.

Regrettably, the concern for engagement in meaningful activities is missing in many state-mandated testing programs, and students who are most vulnerable are once again the major victims. In a vicious cycle of failure, students perceived as needing more help are placed in classes in which the curriculum is diluted and higher levels of thinking are not demanded and in which instruction is bland and formulaic. As a result, the academic achievement of students may fall even further behind. Michael Sadowski, who has done a careful review of the issues, asks the timely question, "Are high-stakes tests worth the wager?"[30]

Although standardized tests ostensibly are used to provide teachers and schools with information about the learning needs of students, in fact they are often used to sort students further. John Dewey minced no words in expressing his views of rigid assessments: "How one person's abilities compare in quantity with those of another is none of the teacher's business. It is irrelevant to his work," Dewey wrote. He went on to state, "What is required is that every individual shall have opportunities to employ his own powers in activities that have meaning."[31]

In spite of the shortcomings of high-stakes standardized testing, we need to understand why there is so much popular support for them. For one, many people view standardized tests as highly objective and reliable measures of what students know, even if this is not the case. In addition, parents whose children attend poor schools have become weary of the poor achievement of their children. It is true that many teachers who work in poor urban and rural schools are highly competent and devoted to their students; they demonstrate their care through high expectations and rigorous demands. On the other hand, as we saw in Chapter 4, in schools where few teachers know much about the students they are teaching, expectations of student achievement are likely to be quite low. As a result, some schools have been chronically underserved for many years, with very little actual teaching taking place. It is little wonder that some children in these circumstances have failed to learn and that their parents have become staunch advocates of stringent accountability measures, including standardized testing. As we have seen, however, standardized tests alone rarely guarantee equality; in fact, they may exacerbate inequality.

There is, nevertheless, a need to have reliable and effective assessment of student learning. Teachers and schools must be held accountable for what students learn or fail to learn, especially in the case of those who have received low-quality schooling. This means that schools, districts, states, and the federal government need to rethink testing policies and practices so that they are more equitable. One response has been to promote alternative assessments, for example to replace or at least complement norm-referenced tests with *performance-based assessments*, also called *authentic assessments*. Some examples of more authentic assessment are portfolios, performance tasks, and student exhibitions. The alternative assessment movement represents an important shift in thinking about the purpose and uses of tests, from sorting and separating students toward ensuring more equitable opportunities for all children to learn at high levels of achievement.

However, even if performance-based assessments are positive alternatives to norm-referenced assessments, they are not necessarily more equitable, especially if they are used in the same way as externally developed and mandated tests.[32] Once again, *how* assessment is used is just as important as *what kind* of assessment is used.

THE CURRICULUM

Broadly defined, *curriculum* is the organized environment for learning. This means that it concerns *what* should be learned and *under what conditions* it is to be learned. Although it may seem that this is a fairly clear-cut process, it is not. Because curriculum defines what is deemed important for students to know, it also involves the knowledge, attitudes, and traditions valued in society. Thus, curriculum is an inherently *political* matter. To illustrate this point, we turn to curriculum theorist Michael Apple, who has suggested a number of essential questions to keep in mind when thinking about the curriculum—questions that are particularly significant within a multicultural framework. Some of them are: "Whose knowledge is it? Who selected it? Why is it organized and taught in this way?"[33] If we consider these issues when developing or implementing the curriculum, it becomes clear that any curriculum is deeply ideological. Because only a tiny fraction of the vast array of available knowledge finds its way into state curriculum standards and frameworks, district guides, textbooks, and teachers' instructional manuals, it is obvious that the curriculum is never neutral. Instead, it represents what is perceived to be consequential and necessary knowledge, generally by those who are dominant in a society. Furthermore, curriculum decisions in public schools are usually made by those furthest from the lives of students—namely, central and state boards of education, with little input from teachers, parents, and students.

The curriculum lets students know whether the knowledge they and their communities value has prestige within the educational establishment and beyond. The problem is that the curriculum is often presented as if it were the whole, unvarnished, and uncontested truth. It is more appropriate to think of curriculum as a decision-making process. If we think of it in this way, we realize that *somebody* made decisions about what to include. For example, it is rare for Black English to be incorporated into the established curriculum. It only becomes part of the curriculum when students who speak Black English are corrected by their teachers. Hence, even when present in the curriculum, Black English tends to be viewed in a negative light. As a result, students may pick up the powerful message that the language variety they speak has little value in our society. On the other hand, if teachers were to use students' language—including Black English, or *Ebonics*—as a bridge to Standard English or to discuss critical perspectives about the role that language and culture play in their lives, the value of students' identity is affirmed. This is the case with Bob Fecho, who used his students' vernacular to discuss broader issues about language and power in his urban high school English classroom.[34] Unfortunately, however, talk about such issues is frequently silenced, and in this way, the curriculum serves as a

WHAT YOU CAN DO

BE PROACTIVE ABOUT TESTS

Tests exert a powerful influence on most educational decisions. Yet, as we have seen, they correlate more with family income than with intelligence or ability. The specific strategies that each teacher, school, and school district chooses to engage in may vary, depending on how they use tests, whether the tests are grossly biased or not, and the testing skills that students already have. There are two basic strategies: Either challenge the use of tests, or focus attention on test taking and how to use it to the advantage of the students. In fact, these need not be either-or strategies. We know of one teacher, for instance, who campaigns against standardized tests because he knows they unfairly jeopardize his students. At the same time, he developed after-school tutorial sessions in which he teaches his students specific test-taking skills so that they might be more successful in taking these required tests.

In affluent schools and neighborhoods, students often learn specific test-taking skills that help them do very well on tests. A recent study found that test coaching, contrary to previous

claims, boosted math SAT scores by 18 points.* More affluent families also have the means to pay for tutoring and other classes to help their children do well on tests. Less affluent students, especially students living in poverty, do not generally have the same kind of access to learning these skills.

With a group of interested colleagues and parents, you can approach the local school committee and ask that standardized tests be kept to a minimum, that the results be used in more appropriate ways, and that students not be placed at risk because of the results of such tests. Like the previously mentioned teacher, you might decide that given the pervasiveness of testing and the power it exerts on the options of young people, your energy might be better spent in teaching students how to take tests more critically and effectively. To help even the playing field, you can start an after-school test-tutoring program for students in your school. Try to get funding from your school system or PTA, or even from a local business.

*Jack Kaplan, "The Effectiveness of SAT Coaching on Math SAT Scores," Chance 18, no. 2 (2005).

primary means of social control. Often, students learn that what is meaningful at home is negated in school.

The life of the school is often separate and distinct from the life of the community in ways that are abundantly clear as soon as one steps inside the school; and this is especially evident in schools in urban and poor rural areas. As an example, it is not unusual to see urban classrooms in which young children learn about "community helpers" without ever studying about people in their own communities. They learn about police officers, fire fighters, and mail carriers, all of whom may live outside their immediate neighborhood. Students learn about doctors and lawyers and people who own large businesses, but they may never have met one of these people in their own neighborhood. The people the children do see every day—the owner of the corner "bodega," the local factory worker, or community service providers—are rarely mentioned as "community helpers." In like manner, the curriculum hardly ever includes the study of non-Christian holidays or history, and this fact helps explain why Avi Abramson, whose case study follows this chapter, had a hard time adjusting to public school.

racism had a positive impact on the racial attitudes of both White students and students of color.[39]

That contentious and difficult issues need to be confronted honestly and directly is the underlying premise behind the Facing History and Ourselves (FHAO) School. The school, located in New York City, promotes in-depth examination of some of history's most troubling incidents (the Nazi Holocaust, the Armenian genocide, and U.S. slavery, to name a few) as a key to encouraging young people to work for a socially just and democratic society. FHAO, a nonprofit organization with headquarters in Brookline, Massachusetts, and regional offices around the country and connections around the world, advances the idea that young people are capable of reflecting critically on such issues as scapegoating, racism, and personal and collective responsibility in order to become productive and concerned adults. One article described the curriculum as deeply connected with the pedagogy and underlying assumptions about young people:

> Facing History's approach is more than curriculum, however; it's a method of inquiry. The emphasis is not on lectures or memorizing names and dates. Students read memoirs, write essays, create artwork, debate in class, take field trips, and meet activists and Holocaust survivors. They work on small group projects to learn teamwork and keep journals to discover their own hearts, minds, and voices.[40]

This stance makes learning more complex and knotty, to be sure, but it also makes learning more meaningful for students. Maxine Greene, addressing the matter of complexity in the aftermath of 9/11 said, "The curriculum has to leave so many questions open so that children will explore and wonder and not believe there is a final answer, because they can only be devastated when they find out there isn't."[41] Murray Levin, an educator who taught at Harvard University and Boston University and later at the Greater Egleston Community School in Boston, provides a vivid example. Levin believed that even the most marginalized students learn when education is meaningful to their lives. The title of his book documenting the experiences he had at the school is *'Teach Me!' Kids Will Learn When Oppression Is the Lesson*.[42] We would do well to heed these words.

The relationship between curriculum and democracy is significant, especially in this post-9/11 era. In light of our nation's expressed support for equality and fair play, students need to learn that patriotism means standing up for individual and collective freedom, and this is sometimes unpopular. Actions that we now recognize as patriotic may have been very unpopular at the time they took place. For example, the general public largely reviled the actions of those who took part in the Civil Rights Movement, yet today the view that all Americans deserve equal rights is largely accepted, at least in principle. The same is true of women's rights, considered a radical idea just a few decades ago. The issue of gay rights, still controversial in many quarters, hopefully will follow the same course.

Students need to learn that putting democracy into action may mean taking unpopular stands. There is frequently a tremendous chasm between expounding on democracy and actual democratic actions in schools. Providing students with both the *rhetoric* and the *reality* of democracy may help them to become agents of positive social change. However, curriculum transformation is needed if we believe that one of the basic purposes of schooling is to prepare young people to become productive and critical citizens of a democratic society.

Democratic principles are thwarted by the lack of access to knowledge in other ways as well. For example, sometimes the curriculum is "watered down" by teachers who believe that such accommodations will better meet the needs of learners from socioeconomically disadvantaged backgrounds. On the face of it, this practice may seem equitable, but the truth is that it may reflect teachers' lower expectations of some students. All children can benefit from high expectations and a challenging curriculum, but some students are regularly subjected to diluted, undemanding, and boring educational programs because teachers and schools do not tap into their strengths and talents. Typically, though, what students want are *more* demands rather than fewer, as you can see in the case studies in this book. In fact, according to researcher Linda Darling-Hammond, "unequal access to high-level courses and challenging curriculum explains much of the so-called 'achievement gap.'"[43]

For instance, sociologists have found patterns of disproportionately low achievement and participation in science, math, and other high-status courses among female students, students of color, and students of low-income families.[44] Low-income students and students from inner city and poor rural schools, therefore, generally have fewer opportunities to learn, and as we have already seen, they also have fewer material resources, less engaging learning activities in their classrooms, and less qualified teachers.

Textbooks, a considerable component of the curriculum in most schools, may also be at odds with democratic and pluralistic values. Textbooks tend to reinforce the dominance of the European American perspective and to sustain stereotypes of groups outside the cultural and political mainstream. This situation is not new. A 1949 comprehensive analysis of 300 textbooks revealed that many of them perpetuated negative stereotypes of "minority" groups.[45] This finding has been reiterated time and again in more recent years.[46] A similar situation has been documented in children's literature, which, until just a few decades ago, largely omitted or stereotyped the lives and experiences of African American, Latino, Asian American, American Indian, and other groups.[47]

Even in recent textbooks, the lack of adequate representation of women and people of color is striking; critical and nondominant perspectives are also largely missing. According to James Loewen, most history textbooks are filled with half-truths or myths. Loewen points out how both textbooks and public monuments have perpetuated the myths that are the basis for much of the U.S. history taught in school.[48]

PEDAGOGY

Pedagogy refers to the strategies, techniques, and approaches used by teachers in their classrooms, that is, *teachers' practices*. It means more than these things, however. Pedagogy also includes how teachers perceive the nature of learning and what they do to create conditions that motivate students to become critical thinkers. For example, most classrooms, through their practices, reflect the belief that learning can best take place in a competitive atmosphere—that is, the most prevalent approaches used in the classroom stress individual achievement and extrinsic motivation. These include ability grouping, testing of all kinds, and rote learning. Although learning in such classrooms can be fun or interesting, students may learn other unintended lessons as well: that learning equals memorization, that reciting what teachers want to hear is what education is about, and that independent thinking has no place in the classroom.

The observation that schools are tedious places where little learning takes place and where most students are not challenged to learn is hardly new. It is particularly true of secondary schools, where subject matter dominates pedagogy and classes are too often driven by standardized tests as "gatekeepers" to promotion and/or accreditation. The case studies of both Avi Abramson and Fern Sherman provide enlightening examples of pedagogy that is engaging or boring. Avi contrasted teachers that "teach from the point of view of the kid" with those who "just come out and say, 'All right, do this, *blah, blah, blah.*' " Fern mentioned that she would have liked more "involved activities" in which more students take part, "not making only the two smartest people up here do the whole work for the whole class."

Avi and Fern's impressions are confirmed by research. In his comprehensive and classic study on secondary schools, John Goodlad found that textbooks were used frequently and mechanistically, whereas other materials were used infrequently, if at all; that teaching methods varied little from the traditional "chalk and talk" methodology commonly used over 100 years ago; and that routine and rote learning were favored over creativity and critical thinking.[49] Most students today would likely agree. In a three-year study of students in Philadelphia middle schools, Bruce Wilson and H. Dickson Corbett discovered that, more than anything, students wanted teachers who taught content meaningful to their lives and who had high expectations of them.[50] Specifically, students most frequently mentioned projects and experiments as the kind of work they liked doing best and that most helped them learn. Rather than focusing only on just teachers' personalities or their sense of humor, students cared about *how* their teachers taught.

Martin Haberman uses the term *pedagogy of poverty* to refer to a basic urban pedagogy that encompasses a body of specific strategies that are limited to asking questions, giving directions, making assignments, and monitoring seatwork. Unsupported by research, theory, or even the practice of the best urban teachers, this pedagogy of poverty is based on the dubious assumption that children of culturally, racially, and linguistically diverse backgrounds and poor students cannot learn in creative, active, and challenging environments. Suggesting instead that exemplary pedagogy in urban schools actively involves students in real-life situations and allows them to reflect on their own lives, Haberman finds that good teaching is taking place when, among other things, the following occur:

- Students are involved with issues they perceive as vital concerns (e.g., rather than avoid controversies as censorship of school newspapers or dress codes, students use these opportunities for learning).

WHAT YOU CAN DO

USE THE CURRICULUM CRITICALLY

Use the current curriculum as the basis for helping students develop a more critical perspective and better research skills. For example, when studying the Revolutionary War, have students investigate the experiences of African Americans, American Indians, women, working people, loyalists, and others whose perspectives have traditionally been excluded from the curriculum. When studying the Industrial Revolution, ask students to explore the role of the nascent workers' movement and of children and young women factory workers, as well as the impact of European immigration on the rise of cities. Students can also concentrate on the emergence of scientific discoveries through inventions by African Americans, women, and immigrants during the late 19th century.

When teaching different mathematical operations, ask students to investigate how they are done in other countries. A variety of materials, such as an abacus and other counting instruments, can be demonstrated. If traditional U.S. holidays are commemorated in the curriculum, try to include other perspectives as well. For example, for Columbus Day, discuss the concept of "discovery" with students so that they understand that this was the perspective of the Europeans, not the Indians. Alternative activities can focus on October 12th as the encounter of two worldviews and histories rather than on the "discovery" of one world by another. (*Rethinking Columbus*,* from Rethinking Schools, is an excellent publication that includes many lesson plans and other resources for classrooms.) Thanksgiving, considered by many American Indians to be a day of mourning, is another holiday that can be presented through multiple perspectives.

Create an emerging multicultural curriculum by using the experiences, cultures, and languages of every student in your class. Encourage them to "bring their identities" into the classroom, for example, by inviting their parents to teach the class about their particular talent, job, or interest. These talents do not have to be culture specific: For instance, a parent who is a seamstress might teach the children how to sew a hem. Although a talent may not be particular to a specific ethnic heritage, it helps students to see that people from all backgrounds have skills and worthwhile experiences.

Activities such as these are particularly effective at the early elementary level, but they can be equally relevant for secondary students studying specific subjects. For example, if older students are learning calligraphy, invite a local Chinese artist to give them some pointers, or, if they are learning about operating a small business, invite a local store owner to speak to them.

Oral history projects that focus on students and their family experiences are another good way to make the curriculum multicultural. Ask students to collect stories, poems, and legends from their families, either tape recorded or written down, to create a multicultural library. More elaborate activities might include dramatizations for the school assembly, videotaping parents and other community members reciting the poems and stories, and readings by older students to children in the younger grades.

*Bill Bigelow and Bob Peterson, Rethinking Columbus: The Next 500 Years, 2nd ed. (Milwaukee, WI: Rethinking Schools, 1998).

- Students are involved with explanations of differences in race, culture, religion, ethnicity, and gender.
- Students are helped to see major concepts, big ideas, and general principles rather than isolated facts.

- Students are involved in planning their education.
- Students are involved in applying ideals such as fairness, equity, and justice to their world.
- Students are actively involved in heterogeneous groups.
- Students are asked to question common sense or widely accepted assumptions.[51]

Expanding pedagogical strategies alone, however, will not change how and what students learn in school. Let us take the example of cooperative learning, generally praised as a useful instructional strategy. In reviewing virtually hundreds of studies of cooperative learning over the past three decades, Laurel Shaper Walters concluded that there is a positive correlation between cooperative learning and student achievement.[52] In spite of its commendable qualities, however, cooperative learning should be viewed as no more than a means to an end. Cooperative learning is based on the premise that using the talents and skills of all students is key to designing successful learning environments. But, if it is viewed unproblematically, cooperative learning has little chance of changing the fundamental climate of learning in the classroom. In this regard, research by Mary McCaslin and Thomas Good found that small-group work too often allowed some students to become even more passive and dependent learners than if they were in whole-class settings.[53] This is a good reminder that particular methods can become, in the words of María de la Luz Reyes, "venerable assumptions" that take on a life of their own, disconnected from their educational purposes or sociopolitical context.[54]

Another pedagogical approach growing in popularity is *constructivism*.[55] This approach is based on the notion that students' background knowledge can be enormously significant in their learning and that their interpretations of new information is influenced by their prior knowledge and experiences. Through this approach, teachers encourage students to use what they know to develop deeper understandings rather than simply to learn random and unrelated facts. Constructivist teaching is characterized by such practices as inquiry activities, problem-posing strategies, and dialogue among peers. In this approach, learning is viewed as an interactive rather than a passive process, and students' creativity and intelligence are respected. Although this sounds promising, constructivism—or any other approach, for that matter—is not necessarily effective with all students and cannot be simply "applied" as if it is the answer to all learning problems. In a critique of constructivism, Virginia Richardson, who is herself a proponent of the approach, claims that using it indiscriminately may be counterproductive. One problem in doing so is that it ignores the fact that the approach reflects a dominant view of pedagogy: Constructivism does not take into account the experiences and wishes of those who would rather learn differently. Richardson writes, "The most serious problem with the use of the constructive pedagogy construct occurs when it becomes valued as best practice for everyone."[56]

Who has access to constructivist teaching? Although conventional wisdom might lead us to believe that only students in high-ability groups receive this kind of instruction, the opposite has actually been found. In their investigation of the use of constructivist versus didactic teaching, Becky Smerden and her colleagues found that *less able* students in science classes received *more* constructivist instruction than did more able students. The researchers did not greet this finding with optimism. Instead, they were troubled by this finding because they discovered that a great many of the teachers who used this type of instruction in lower level courses were not trained in science and did not have certification as science teachers. Because they had a weak base of scientific knowledge, they used constructivism to cover this fact. If this is the case, the researchers concluded, methods alone do not guarantee high-quality educational experiences for students.[57]

We need to view all approaches and methods with a critical eye, even with skepticism, because no method will solve learning problems for all students. This is the problem with any pedagogical approach that is uncritically elevated to the level of "best practice" as if a particular practice is appropriate for all students in all contexts. Lilia Bartolomé suggests that, instead of devotion to a particular instructional strategy, teachers need to develop a "humanizing pedagogy" that values students' cultural, linguistic, and experiential backgrounds.[58] To underscore the secondary place of particular strategies, Jim Cummins cautions that "good teaching does not require us to internalize an endless list of instructional techniques. Much more fundamental is the recognition that human relationships are central to effective instruction."[59]

CLIMATE AND PHYSICAL STRUCTURE

Climate refers to the nature of the environment. In schools, the climate can either encourage or stifle learning. In urban areas, and increasingly in some suburban areas as well, for instance, it is not unusual to find schools with police officers standing guard. In some schools, students are frisked before entering. Teachers sometimes feel afraid unless they lock their classrooms. Climate is often, although not always, associated with the *physical structure* of schools, that is, the architecture, classroom resources, cleanliness, order, and even such things as the color of the paint in the hallways and the condition of the plumbing in the bathrooms. The physical structure of schools can also either promote or inhibit educational equity. In some schools, desks are nailed to the floor; halls and classrooms are airless and poorly lit; and shattered glass can be found in courtyards where young children play. To understand the connection that exists between climate and physical structures, we turn to Ron Berger, a long-time teacher, who describes how the various elements of a school's culture affect students:

> The aspects of a school that most clearly engrave the school experience on children are often in the "other stuff" category: the physical appearance of the school building, outside and in; the manner in which school property and personal property are respected and cared for in the school; the levels of physical safety and emotional safety that children and adults in the building feel; the way routines of arrival, class transitions, lunch times, and dismissal are handled; the ways authority is exercised; the tone of courtesy, kindness, and acceptance in peer culture; the ways in which students' achievements are shared with the school community and outside of it; the

aspects of the school that define it in the larger community. These things are every bit as important as curriculum.[60]

One dramatic example of how school climate can influence student behavior was reported by Valerie Lee and David Burkam. Using a sample of 3,840 students in 190 urban and suburban high schools, they found that the structures and organization of high schools may influence students' decisions to stay in school or drop out. Some of the conditions that fostered staying in school were school size of fewer than 1,500 students, a curriculum offering mainly academic courses and few nonacademic courses, and positive relationships between students and their teachers. Lee and Burkam concluded that explanations for dropping out that rely solely on students' social background and school behaviors are inadequate.[61]

In addition, a survey of the literature associated with school facilities reported that there is indeed a relationship between poor student achievement and the condition of school buildings. These conditions include poor lighting, inadequate ventilation, inadequate or too much heating, school safety, class size, and air quality.[62] Also, disturbing statistics about the physical condition of schools have been reported: One in four U.S. schools is overcrowded and 3.5 million children attend public schools that are in very poor or even nonoperative condition—this in the wealthiest country in the world.[63] Add the lack of relevant and culturally appropriate pictures, posters, and other instructional materials, and we are left with environments that are scarcely inviting centers of learning.

In many instances, of course, schools are uninviting, fortresslike places precisely because school officials are trying to protect students and teachers against vandalism, theft, and other acts of violence. Although violence in schools has diminished

WHAT YOU CAN DO

PUNCH UP YOUR PEDAGOGY!

The case studies and snapshots in this book highlight the fact that the standard pedagogy used in many schools is unappealing to most students. Although textbooks may be important teaching and learning tools, they often become the entire curriculum and are used as the only basis for pedagogy, to the exclusion of materials that may be more appealing. Go beyond textbooks and use additional resources to make the curriculum more inviting for students, for example, audiovisual materials such as camcorders and cameras, guest speakers, and alternative reading material. To create a real sense of history among students, use primary documents and involve students more directly as "history sleuths" to uncover history.

Develop a variety of approaches that will engage students. Although a straight lecture, what has been called "chalk and talk," may be appropriate sometimes, it treats students as passive learners and receptacles of knowledge. It is also culturally inappropriate for many students. To help students become more active learners as well as to provide a multiculturally sensitive learning environment, encourage group work, individualized tasks, collaborative research, peer tutoring, cross-age tutoring, group reflection, dialogue, and action projects in the school and community. The last of these might include volunteer activities at a local senior center or day-care center or a letter-writing campaign about a community issue (e.g., the need for a traffic light at a nearby intersection).

in the past several years, it is still a major problem. The violent crime victimization rate at school declined from 48 per 1,000 in 1992 to 28 per 1,000 in 2003. In spite of this decline, students 12 years of age or older were victims of about 740,000 violent crimes such as bullying, and another 1.2 million were victims of theft.[64] Moreover, a recent survey of 32,000 students in 108 urban schools found that 25 percent of the students surveyed said they felt uncertain about their safety in school, and fully half indicated that they had seen other students being bullied at least once a month.[65]

Schools alone are not to blame for violence, however. Violence in schools is a reflection of the violence that takes place in society, and teachers and administrators often struggle heroically to contain it and to make schools places of learning and joy. Yet, frequently it is students from these very schools who do the damage. Boredom and rage are implicated in these actions, particularly when schools show little regard for students by silencing their voices and negating their identities in the curriculum. Destructiveness and violence by students sometimes represent a clear message that school structures are incompatible with students' emotional and physical needs. For instance, the U.S. Department of Education reported that large and impersonal schools, and those with hostile and authoritarian teachers and administrators, were more likely to be vandalized than schools characterized by cooperation among teachers and administrators and clear expectations for students.[66]

The resemblance of some schools to factories or prisons has been mentioned many times over the years.[67] The size of schools alone is enough to give them this institutional look. High schools hold sometimes 2,000, 3,000, or even 4,000 students, and it is easy to understand the students' and teachers' feelings of alienation and insecurity that can result. Also, schools that are in good repair may help to retain both teachers and students. One study found that facility quality was an important predictor of the decision of teachers to stay or leave, probably even more important than a pay increase.[68] Another project has experimented with the color of walls: Publicolor, a program in which students are encouraged to paint over the industrial shades of their schools' walls, has been found to lower dropout rates, decrease discipline problem, and increase attendance.[69]

Because school size makes a difference in student learning, many schools are developing schools within schools, teams, or other approaches to encourage more familylike environments and closer relationships among students and teachers. School size may also influence students' feelings of belonging, and thus their engagement with learning. One recent study concluded that elementary schools of fewer than 400 students tend to display stronger collective teacher responsibility for student learning and greater student achievement in math.[70] Small classes also have been proven to have an effect on student learning. A widely cited study by Jeremy Finn and his associates found that when students started early and continued in small classes or classes with teachers' aides for at least three years, they performed significantly better in all grades than students in full-size classes or without teachers' aides. In addition, those benefits lasted: Students who attended small classes in grades K–3 continued to perform better in all subjects up to the eighth grade.[71] Class size alone, however, may not be the most important factor in influencing student engagement in learning. Simply making schools smaller will not have a major impact if the climate within schools remains unchanged.[72]

Not all schools are large and impersonal, however. In general, the farther away from urban or poor rural communities, the less institutional the appearance of the school. Suburban schools or schools in wealthy towns tend to look strikingly different from schools that serve the poor. Not only do the former usually have more space, bigger classrooms, and more light, but they also have more material supplies and generally are in better physical condition, partly because the level of financing for the education of poor students is lower than for children in more affluent districts. Wealthier schools tend to have smaller classes as well, another condition that is related to higher quality education for students.

The physical environment of schools can also reflect the expectations that educators have of the capabilities of students. If students are perceived to be deficient, the educational environment may reflect a no-nonsense, back-to-basics drill orientation. However, if students are perceived as intelligent and motivated and as having an interest in the world around them, the educational environment tends to reflect an intellectually stimulating and academically challenging orientation, a place where learning is considered joyful rather than tedious. Given this reality, we might well ask what would happen if the schools attended by youngsters in poor urban and rural areas were to miraculously become like the schools that middle-class and wealthy youngsters attend. Might there be a change in educational outcomes if all students had access to generously endowed, smaller, and more democratically run schools? We cannot know the answer to this question until we try such an approach, but one thing is for certain: The physical environment in many schools provides a stark contrast to the stated purposes of teaching and learning. When schools are not cared for, when they become fortresses rather than an integral part of the community they serve, and when they are holding places instead of learning environments, the contradiction between goals and realities is a vivid one. This chasm between ideal and real is not lost on the students.

DISCIPLINARY POLICIES

Disciplinary policies, especially in middle and secondary schools, may be at odds with the developmental level of students and, as a result, can aggravate the sense of alienation felt by some students. Research that supports this hypothesis is compelling. Two decades ago, using longitudinal data from the national High School and Beyond study, researchers Gary Wehlage and Robert Rutter found that certain conditions in the schools themselves can *predict* the dropping-out behavior of students.[73] These conditions include disciplinary policies perceived by students to be unfair and ineffective, especially those that are imposed rather than negotiated. Consequently, there is a serious problem with what Wehlage and Rutter refer to as the *holding power* of school.

They concluded that certain student characteristics *in combination with* certain school conditions are responsible for students' decisions to drop out.

Interpretations of student behavior may be culturally or class biased, and this poses an additional barrier to enforcing disciplinary policies fairly. For example, students in poor schools who insist on wearing highly prized leather jackets in class may be doing so because of a well-founded fear that they will be stolen if left in the closet. Latino children who cast their eyes downward when being scolded probably are not being defiant but simply behaving out of respect for their teachers, as they were taught at home. African American students are especially vulnerable to unfair policies if they follow particular styles. For example, in her study of an urban school undergoing restructuring, Pauline Lipman described the case of an African American male student who was given a 10-day in-school suspension for wearing his overall straps unsnapped, a common style among African American males, whereas White students who wore their pants with large holes cut in the thighs, a widespread style among White students, were not even reprimanded.[74]

Students living in poverty and students of color are also more likely to be suspended and to be victims of corporal punishment. This inequity is frequently related to poor communication among administrators, teachers, and students. For example, in a two-month investigation, the *Seattle Post-Intelligencer* found that Black students were two and a half times more likely to be suspended or expelled than other students. Although common explanations for this situation include poverty and broken homes,

WHAT YOU CAN DO

ENLIVEN YOUR ENVIRONMENT

There are some things in your physical environment that you can do little about but there are others that you can change, both inside classrooms and out.

Make your classroom inviting and comfortable. Ask parents, students, and colleagues to help with ideas and resources. In the younger grades, create engaging activity corners, a cozy place to read, comfortable chairs or a couch, and a place for group work. In the older grades, have a quiet place for individual work and a space for collaborative research. From time to time, place seats in a horseshoe arrangement in order to create a more amenable space for dialogue. From preschool through high school, posters, maps, pictures, books, and music help create a sense of belonging in a classroom.

Outside the classroom, graffiti and garbage around a school, or broken toilets and nonfunctioning science labs, give the message that the children who attend that school are not valued. Help organize families, colleagues, and children for clean-up brigades. If there are more serious problems, inform parents and other community members about some of the policies and practices that make school uninviting so that they can organize to help solve these problems. These issues can be brought up at parent–teacher association (PTA), school board, and even city council meetings. Unless demands are made to change the negative messages these school-environment problems send, children will continue to be the victims.

the investigation found that Black students were far more likely than others to be suspended or expelled *regardless of their home lives and poverty*. In this case, too, school climate and size can make a difference. The report of this investigation cited one school that had become a "small school" by creating a more intimate and sensitive environment. The result was that suspensions and expulsions had been reduced across the board, although a racial gap still existed. "A school culture that prides itself on being color-blind," the report concluded, "might be better off taking a hard look at race."[75]

Discipline can be an issue even among more economically privileged students who are culturally different from the mainstream. For instance, Avi Abramson, one of the case studies that follows this chapter, pointed out how he was the subject of several anti-Semitic incidents. Because teachers were uncertain how they should respond, Avi felt that he had to take matters into his own hands. One time, he said, "I went up to the teacher and I said to her, 'I'm either gonna leave the class or they leave.' "

A lack of awareness of cultural and social factors on the part of teachers and schools can lead to misinterpretations and faulty conclusions. Although it is usually students who experience the least success in school who bear the brunt of rigid school policies, all students who differ from the cultural mainstream are jeopardized.

The Limited Role of Students

That many students are alienated, uninvolved, and discouraged by school is abundantly clear. This fact is most striking, of course, in dropout rates, the most extreme manifestation of disengagement from schooling. Students who drop out are commonly uninvolved and passive participants in the school experience.

Usually, schools are not organized to encourage active student involvement. Although school is a place where a lot of talk goes on, it is seldom student talk, and teachers and other staff lose out on an opportunity to learn firsthand from students about their educational experiences and what could improve them. Students and teachers who spend the most time in schools and classrooms often have the least opportunity to talk about their experiences.

Although it is true that students are nominally represented in the governance structure of many schools, often this representation is merely window dressing that has little to do with the actual management of the school. Rather than being designed to prepare students for democratic life, most schools are more like benign dictatorships in which all decisions are made for them, albeit in what schools may perceive to be students' best interests. They are more often organized around issues of control than of collaboration or consultation. That is, students are expected to learn what is decided, designed, and executed by others. Often, it is not the teacher or even the school that determines the content but some mythical "downtown," school board, or state education department.

In the classroom itself, the pedagogy frequently reflects what Paulo Freire called *banking education*, that is, a process by which teachers "deposit" knowledge into students, who are thought to be empty receptacles. It is education that promotes powerlessness. In a characterization of what happens in most schools, Freire contrasted the expected roles of the teacher and the students:

- The teacher teaches, and the students are taught.
- The teacher knows everything, and the students know nothing.
- The teacher thinks, and the students are thought about.
- The teacher talks, and the students listen—meekly.
- The teacher disciplines, and the students are disciplined.
- The teacher chooses and enforces his or her choice, and the students comply.
- The teacher acts, and the students have the illusion of acting through the action of the teacher.
- The teacher chooses the program content, and the students (who were not consulted) adapt to it.
- The teacher confuses the authority of knowledge with his or her own professional authority, which he or she sets in opposition to the freedom of the students.
- The teacher is the subject of the learning process, while the pupils are mere objects.[76]

What impact does involvement of students have on their school experiences and achievement? Little research has been done on this issue, but researcher Ernest Morrell, in a multiyear critical ethnographic study of—and *with*—urban students, sought to understand the relationship between apprenticing urban youth as critical researchers of their realities and the development of their academic literacy. Working on a college access project with students of color from Pacific High School (a pseudonym) during two summers, they took on the issue of the tremendous disparity that existed in the high school, based on ethnicity and social class background, effectively making it seem like two separate high schools. Morrell saw students develop from novices to productive writers, researchers, and speakers at national education conferences who published their research as a form of social action. He concluded,

> Through their writings, presentations, personal conversations, and subtle interrogations, the project participants forced nearly all of the major power brokers at the school and in the district to respond to the two-school situation at Pacific Beach High School and to design and implement strategies to overcome the problem.[77]

In addition, students became more passionate learners. Some who had never dreamed about going to college were so changed by this experience that they were determined to do so. Unfortunately, however, as Morrell found, such changes cannot be sustained in the absence of a broader political movement in which students, families, and educators mobilize to radically alter the status quo in schools and districts. Nevertheless, the message should not be lost on teachers and schools: When students

WHAT YOU CAN DO

CREATE INCLUSIVE
DISCIPLINARY PRACTICES

Investigate how disciplinary policies and practices affect students of different groups unfairly by looking at rates of detention, suspension, and assignments to "special" classes or alternative programs in your school. If students in these programs are overwhelmingly from one social or racial group or gender, ask the principal to set up study or inquiry groups to look into this problem. Suggest appropriate steps to address the problem directly.

At the classroom level, ask your students to help design disciplinary policies. Think about how to involve all your students as class citizens. At the school level, rather than rely on those who happen to be on the student council—generally a rather limited group of students—suggest a forum in which a broad range of student voices are heard. This forum can include academic classes, assemblies, and other student activities such as sports and clubs.

---

are involved in directing their own education in some way, they are more enthusiastic learners.

THE LIMITED ROLE OF TEACHERS

As a group, teachers are shown little respect by our society and are usually poorly paid and infrequently rewarded. In school, they are sometimes the victims of physical and verbal threats and attacks, and they feel a lack of parental support and involvement. Moreover, teachers are traditionally discouraged from becoming involved in decision-making processes in the schools. Moreover, they have become more alienated in the current climate of reform because more decisions about curriculum and instruction are being made by others, while accountability is being more and more determined by high-stakes tests and imposed standards. Alienated and discouraged teachers can hardly be expected to help students become empowered, critical thinkers. Michelle Fine, for instance, reported research findings that teacher disempowerment correlates highly with disparaging attitudes toward students—that is, the more powerless teachers feel, the more negative they are toward their students. In contrast, teachers who feel that they have autonomy in their classrooms and in decisions about curriculum generally also have high expectations of their students.[78]

New structures such as teacher-led schools, job sharing, and time, on a weekly basis, for professional development and other activities may help make teachers more active players in their schools. In addition, a number of recent studies have found that, in order to create a sense of teaching as intellectual work, it is vital to develop schools as professional communities of practice.[79] Changing the nature of professional development in schools so that teachers take more responsibility for their own learning is imperative, but the professional climate in schools is only one aspect of a larger problem. Teachers are disempowered for many reasons, and these do not correspond simply to school structures. Their disempowerment also has a lot to do with their status within the professional hierarchy. For example, many teachers become angry at the lack of respect with which they are treated by administrators and the general public. They also resent the fact that they are frequently overlooked when it comes to making decisions about curriculum and instruction. More recently, with the growing standardization of curriculum in public schools and the greater use of high-stakes tests, teachers have even less say on these issues than before. Restructuring schools to be more respectful of teachers' professionalism is, therefore, crucial if they are to become places where teachers feel engaged and empowered.

Nevertheless, restructuring and greater teacher efficacy, by themselves, are no guarantee that schools will become more effective learning environments for students. For example, in research on a restructuring school, Pauline Lipman found that even in an environment where teachers were included in developing policies, some policies remained largely untouched. Tracking was never challenged, disciplinary practices primarily continued to jeopardize students of color, and a general silence concerning issues of racism and inequality pervaded the school.[80] It is clear, then, that making the school environment better for teachers will not necessarily make it better for students. Structural changes to broaden the roles, responsibilities, and status of teachers need to be accompanied by changes in (1) the general public's attitudes about teachers' professionalism, (2) teachers' beliefs about their own capabilities, and (3) the dynamic possibilities for learning that students' diversity creates. Thus, in spite of the restrictions imposed by high-stakes standardized testing and the bureaucratization of schools, when teachers deliberately choose to work together to promote change, and when they focus on learning about their students' realities, tremendous positive changes can begin to take shape.

LIMITED FAMILY AND COMMUNITY INVOLVEMENT

The findings of research on the effectiveness of family and community involvement are clear. In programs with strong family involvement, students are consistently better achievers than in otherwise identical programs with less family involvement. In addition, students in schools that maintain frequent contact with their communities outperform students in other schools. These positive effects persist well beyond the short term.[81]

There are many definitions of parent involvement, and each is more or less effective, depending on the context. Becoming involved in activities such as attendance at parent–teacher conferences, participation in parent–teacher associations (PTAs), and influence over children's selection of courses can help improve student achievement. But involvement of this kind is becoming more and more scarce in a society increasingly characterized by one-parent families or two-parent families in which both work outside the home. Thus, defining involvement only in these traditional ways is problematic. PTA meetings held during the day, parent–teacher conferences held during school hours, and the ubiquitous parent-sponsored cake sale are becoming relics of the past. Currently, most families, regardless of cultural or economic background, find it difficult to attend meetings or to otherwise become involved in the governance of the school or in fund-raising.

Cultural and economic differences also influence family involvement. Families of linguistically and culturally diverse communities and from working-class neighborhoods frequently have difficulty fulfilling the level and kind of parent involvement expected by the school, such as homework assistance and family excursions. Not taking part in these activities should not be interpreted as noninvolvement or apathy, however. Families of all backgrounds generally have high expectations and aspirations for their children, although school personnel may not realize this. In addition, there is a general lack of awareness among school staff concerning the cultural and linguistic resources of families of diverse backgrounds. One study found that when Mexican American families were encouraged to participate in a home-school partnership, their involvement with school increased and their children's engagement with learning also increased. Similar conclusions have been reached in studies of families of other backgrounds.[82]

Family involvement is a complex issue, and teachers and other educators are often intimidated by family involvement or are reluctant to reach out to families. For one, most educators have had little preparation for working with families.[83] Also, families and school personnel may have little knowledge of one another's realities. One interesting poll found that there was a wide gap in the way parents and principals perceived their relationship: Although 93 percent of the principals said that their relationships with parents was "satisfactory," only 64 percent of the parents polled expressed the same feeling.[84] Furthermore, teachers and other school staff often do not understand the cultural values of different families and the goals that parents have for their children; typical involvement strategies may further estrange families who already feel disconnected from the school. This was one of the conclusions reached by Guadalupe Valdés in a study of ten Mexican immigrant families in the Southwest. She found that although the beliefs and practices of the families were perfectly reasonable in their former cultural contexts, they did not always work in their new setting. Schools do not always know how to negotiate these different worlds, and common strategies such as "parenting classes" tend to worsen the situation. In the words of Valdés,[85]

> Relationships between parents and schools do, in fact, reflect the structural locations of these individuals in the wider society. Simply bringing parents to schools will not change the racist or classist responses that teachers may have toward them and their behaviors. Parenting classes alone will not equalize outcomes.

In spite of the challenges of parent involvement—especially when it comes to poor and immigrant families—it still represents a potential avenue for bringing community values, lifestyles, and realities into the school. When families become in-

WHAT YOU CAN DO

VIGOROUSLY PROMOTE FAMILY OUTREACH

First, recognize and acknowledge that most families are involved in the education of their children through the values they foster at home and in the implicit and explicit expectations they have of their children. At the same time, encourage families to become more involved in the day-to-day life of the school if they can.

Most important, communicate with families regularly through a weekly or monthly newsletter, phone calls, meetings at school or home, or a combination of these methods. Mary Cowhey, a teacher we know, visits every family of her students in the two weeks prior to the beginning of school. She says she learns more about her students, about who loves them, and about what's important to them through these visits than any other way.

When school meetings are to take place, ask administrators to provide child care, translation of the proceedings into languages spoken by the families, and transportation. Encourage family members to bring activities and materials that are significant to them and their children into the classroom.

volved, it also means that their language and culture and the expectations they have for their children can become a part of the dialogue, and it is through dialogue that true change can begin to happen.

SUMMARY

The organization and structures of schools often are contrary to the needs of students, the values of their communities, and even to one of the major articulated purposes of schooling—to provide equal educational opportunity for all students. The result is that policies and practices in schools more often than not reflect and maintain the status quo and the stratification of the larger society. But schools by themselves cannot change this situation. Witness the sobering words of Jeannie Oakes and her colleagues. In a longitudinal study of 16 schools around the country undergoing reform, these researchers reached the reluctant conclusion that the educational reforms they studied "did little to interrupt or disrupt the course of the nation's history, flaws, and inequity, its hegemony and racism." They added, "Asking to disrupt a nation is a tall order—one that, we have become convinced, schools will eagerly follow but should not be expected to lead."[86]

In spite of our fondest wishes, therefore, schools cannot, by themselves, become an oasis of equity in a land of inequity. This does not mean, however, that the situation is hopeless. On the contrary, there is much for teachers and other educators to do, both in classrooms and out. This is the subject of subsequent chapters.

 **To Think About**

1. Ability-group tracking decisions are often based on ideologies concerning intelligence. The "nature versus nurture" argument in explaining intelligence has been raging for many years. That is, while some people believe that intelligence is primarily dependent on genetic makeup ("nature"), others believe that the environment ("nurture") plays a more important role. What are your thoughts on this debate? Why? What is the basis for your conclusions?

2. Think about the curriculum in classrooms where you have been a student. How have your experiences and culture and those of your classmates been included? If they have not, what do you think the effect has been on you and others? In a journal, write to a former teacher and tell her or him what kinds of changes in the curriculum would have made you a more enthusiastic and engaged student.

3. Design a school for either the elementary or secondary level that would provide a suitable environment for learning. Explain why you've designed it in the way that you have.

4. The criticism has been made that because schools do not provide opportunities for either teachers or students to exercise critical thinking or leadership, they subvert the very purpose of education as preparation for civic life and democratic participation. Do you believe this to be the case? How? Discuss some ways in which schools might provide more opportunities for teachers and students to be more fully engaged.

5. Research the disciplinary policies in your district. How do suspensions compare across racial, ethnic, and gender groups? How would you interpret these data? If there are inequities, what can you do—alone, with colleagues, or with parents and other community members—to address them?

 Activities for Personal, School, and Community Change

1. Observe a number of similar classrooms, some that are tracked and others that are not. What are the differences in these classrooms? Be specific, citing student engagement with work, expectations of student achievement, level of academic difficulty, and teacher-student and student-student relationships. What are your conclusions about tracking? What can you do about it?

2. Get some evaluation checklists for textbooks at your library or, working with colleagues, design your own. Review and evaluate the textbooks used in your local school. Are they biased against students of any group? How? Give specific examples based on the checklists you have used.

3. Observe a classroom and indicate the kind of pedagogical strategies used by the teacher. Are all students engaged in learning? Who are not, and what might engage them?

4. With a group of colleagues, prepare a workshop for other teachers on retention and alternatives to it. Present some actual data from your school or district about the effects of retention.

◆ ◆ ◆   Companion Website

For access to additional case studies, weblinks, concept cards, and other material related to this chapter, visit the text's companion website at **www.ablongman.com/nieto5e**.

Notes to Chapter 5

1. John Dewey, *Democracy and Education* (New York: Free Press, 1916): 175.

2. For the purpose of consistency, the term *tracking* rather than *ability grouping* will be generally used in the discussion that follows.

3. Jeannie Oakes and Gretchen Guiton, "Matchmaking: The Dynamics of High School Tracking Decisions." *American Educational Research Journal* 32, no. 1 (Spring 1995): 3–33. For a comprehensive review of this history, see Jeannie Oakes, *Keeping Track: How Schools Structure Inequality*, 2nd ed. (New Haven, CT: Yale University Press, 2005).

4. Milbrey W. McLaughlin and Joan E. Talbert, *Professional Communities and the Work of High School Teaching* (Chicago: University of Chicago Press, 2001).

5. Jeannie Oakes, *Keeping Track: How Schools Structure Inequality* (New Haven, CT: Yale University Press, 1985). See also *Keeping Track: How Schools Structure Inequality*, 2nd ed., 2005.

6. This research is reviewed in the new edition of *Keeping Track*. See Note 5.

7. Susan Yonezawa, Amy Stuart Wells, and Irene Serna, "Choosing Tracks: 'Freedom of Choice' in Detracking Schools." *American Educational Research Journal*, 39, no. 1 (Spring 2002): 37–67.

8. Anne Wheelock, *Crossing the Tracks: How "Untracking" Can Save America's Schools* (New York: New Press, 1992).

9. Joseph J. D'Amico, "A Closer Look at the Minority Achievement Gap." *ERS Spectrum* (Spring 2001): 4–10.

10. Susan Black, "Second Time Around." *American School*, 191, no. 11 (November 2004). Available at: www.asbj.com/researcharchive/index.html

11. Karen Kelly, "Retention vs. Social Promotion: Schools Search for Alternatives." *Harvard Education Letter* 15, no. 1 (Jan/Feb 1999): 1–3.

12. Guanglei Hong and Stephen W. Raudenbush, "Effects of Kindergarten Retention Policy on Children's Cognitive Growth in Reading and Mathematics." *Educational Evaluation and Policy Analysis* 27, no. 3 (Fall 2005): 205–224.

13. See, for instance, Nilda Flores-González, "The Structuring of Extracurricular Opportunities and Latino Student Retention." *Journal of Poverty* 4, nos. 1, 2 (2000): 85–108.

14. See Steve Selden, *Inheriting Shame: The Story of Eugenics and Racism in America* (New York: Teachers College Press, 1999).

15. For a more recent example of how IQ tests are used to "prove" the social and intellectual inferiority of some groups, see Richard J. Herrnstein and Charles Murray, *The Bell Curve: Intelligence and Class Structure in American Life* (New York: Free Press, 1994).

16. Joel Spring, *American Education*, 12th ed. (New York: McGraw-Hill, 2006).

17. Lewis Terman, *The Measurement of Intelligence* (Boston: Houghton Mifflin, 1916).

18. See examples of the connection between IQ testing and eugenics in Selden, *Inheriting Shame: The Story of Eugenics and Racism in America* and in Stephen Jay Gould, *The Mismeasure of Man*, revised and expanded ed. (New York: W. W. Norton, 1996).

19. Barbara Miner, "Testing Companies Mine for Gold." *Rethinking Schools* 19, no. 2 (Winter 2004): 5–7.

20. *Ibid.*

21. Richard F. Elmore, "Testing Trap," *Harvard Magazine* (September–October 2002). Available at: www.harvardmagazine.com/on-line/o902140.html

22. Gary Orfield and Mindy L. Kornhaber, eds., *Raising Standards or Raising Barriers? Inequality and High-Stakes Testing in Public Education* (New York: The Century Foundation Press, 2001).

23. Audrey I. Amrein and David C. Berliner, "High-Stakes Testing, Uncertainty, and Student Learning," *Education Policy Analysis Archives* 10, no. 18 (2002). Available at: http://epaa.asu.edu/epaa/v10n18/

24. David C. Berliner, "Our Impoverished View of Educational Reform." *Teachers College Record*. Available at: www.tcrecord.org/content.asp?contentID=12106

25. College Board, "2004 College Bound Seniors' Test Scores: SAT." In *College-Bound Seniors 2004: A Profile of SAT Program Test Takers* (New York: Author, 2005).

26. Linda McNeil, *Contradictions of School Reform: Educational Costs of Standardized Testing* (New York: Routledge, 2000).

27. James W. Pellegrino, Naomi Chudowsky, and Robert Glaser, *Knowing What Students Know: The Science and Design of Educational Assessment* (Washington, DC: National Academy Press, 2001).

28. Joseph J. Pedula, Lisa M. Abrams, George F. Madaus, Michael K. Russell, Miguel A. Ramos, and Jing Miao, *Perceived Effects of State-Mandated Testing Programs on Teaching and Learning: Findings from a National Survey of Teachers* (Boston: National Board on Educational Testing and Public Policy, Boston College, 2003).

29. Many recent books and monographs have weighed in on the debate about standardized tests. Most have come out squarely against the overuse and misuse of high-stakes standardized tests. Besides Linda McNeil's *Contradictions of School Reform*, some of the most important titles are Kathy Swope and Barbara Miner, *Failing Our Kids: Why the Testing Craze Won't Fix Our Schools* (Milwaukee: Rethinking Schools, 2000); Deborah Meier, *In Schools We Trust: Creating Communities of Learning in an Era of Testing and Standardization* (Boston: Beacon Press, 2003); M. Gail Jones, Brett D. Jones, and Tracy Hargrove, *The Unintended Consequences of High-Stakes Testing* (Lanham, MD: Rowman & Littlefield, 2003); and Sharon Nichols and David C. Berliner, *The Inevitable Corruption of Indicators and Educators Through High-Stakes Testing.* (Tempe, AZ: Educational Policy Studies Laboratory, Educational Policy Research Unit, Arizona State University, March 2005). Available at: http://edpolicylab.org

30. Michael Sadowski, "Are High-Stakes Tests Worth the Wager?" In *Minority Achievement*, edited by David T. Gordon (Cambridge, MA: *Harvard Education Letter* Focus Series no. 7, 2002).

31. Dewey, *Democracy and Education*, 172.

32. Several of the chapter authors in Gary Orfield and Mindy Kornhaber's *Raising Standards or Raising Barriers?* discuss alternatives to high-stakes standardized tests and also offer some caveats about them.

33. Michael W. Apple, *Identity and Curriculum*, 3rd ed. (New York: RoutledgeFalmer, 2004).

34. Bob Fecho, *Is This English? Race, Language, and Culture in the Classroom* (New York: Teachers College Press, 2003). See also Lisa Delpit and Joanne Kilgour Doudy, eds., *The Skin That We Speak: Thoughts on Language and Culture in the Classroom* (New York: New Press, 2002).

35. James A. Banks, *An Introduction to Multicultural Education*, 4th ed. (Boston: Allyn and Bacon, 2007).

36. Judith Solsken, Jo-Anne Wilson Keenan, and Jerri Willett, "Interweaving Stories: Creating a Multicultural Classroom Through School/Home/University Collaboration." *Democracy and Education* (Fall 1993): 16–21.

37. Michelle Fine, *Framing Dropouts: Notes on the Politics of an Urban Public High School* (Albany: State University of New York Press, 1991): 33.

38. *Ibid.*, 37.

39. J. M. Hughes and Rebecca S. Bigler, "Addressing Race and Racism in the Classroom." In *Lessons in Integration: Realizing the Promise of Racial Diversity in American Schools* by Gary Orfield and Erica Frankonburg, eds. (Charlottesville: University of Virginia Press, 2007).

40. Fran Smith, "Candor in the Class." Available at: http://edutopia.or/magazine/ed1article.php?id=Art _1499&issue_apr_06

41. Maxine Greene, "Reflections: Implications of September 11th for Curriculum." In *Division B: Curriculum Studies Newsletter* (Washington, DC: American Educational Research Association, Fall 2001).

42. Murray Levin, *'Teach Me!' Kids Will Learn When Oppression Is the Lesson* (Lanham, MD: Rowman & Littlefield, 2001).

43. Linda Darling-Hammond, "New Standards and Inequalities: School Reform and the Education of African American Students." In *Black Education: A Transformative Research and Action Agenda for the New Century*, edited by Joyce E. King (Mahwah, NJ: Lawrence Erlbaum; and Washington, DC: American Educational Research Association, 2005).

44. For an excellent analysis of this phenomenon, see Kathleen Demarrais and Margaret LeCompte, *The Way Schools Work: A Sociological Analysis of Education*, 4th ed. (Boston: Allyn and Bacon, 2007).

45. Study by the American Council on Education in 1949; cited by Gordon Allport, *The Nature of Prejudice* (Reading, MA: Addison-Wesley, 1954): 202.

46. See Christine E. Sleeter, *Un-Standardizing the Curriculum: Multicultural Teaching in the Standards-Based Classroom* (New York: Teachers College Press, 2005) for a recent review.

47. Violet J. Harris, ed., *Using Multiethnic Literature in the K–8 Classroom* (Norwood, MA: Christopher-Gordon, 1997); Arlette Willis, ed., *Teaching and Using Multicultural Literature in Grades 9–12: Moving Beyond the Canon* (Norwood, MA: Christopher-Gordon, 1998).

48. James W. Loewen, *Lies My Teacher Told Me: Everything Your American History Textbook Got Wrong* (New York: New Press, reissue edition, 2005); and James W. Loewen, *Lies Across America: What Our Historic Sites Got Wrong* (New York: New Press, 2000).

49. John Goodlad, *A Place Called School*, 20th Anniversary ed. (New York: McGraw-Hill, 2004).

50. Bruce L. Wilson and H. Dickson Corbett, *Listening to Urban Kids: School Reform and the Teachers They Want* (Albany: State University of New York Press, 2001).

51. Martin Haberman, "The Pedagogy of Poverty versus Good Teaching." *Phi Delta Kappan* 73, no. 4 (December 1991): 290–294.

52. Laurel Shaper Walters, "Putting Cooperative Learning to the Test." *Harvard Education Letter* 16, no. 3 (May/June 2000): 1–7.

53. Mary McCaslin and Thomas L. Good, "Compliant Cognition: The Misalliance of Management and Instructional Goals in Current School Reform." *Educational Researcher* 21, no. 3 (April 1992): 4–17.

54. For a discussion of these issues, see María de la Luz Reyes, "Challenging Venerable Assumptions: Literacy Instruction for Linguistically Different Students." *Harvard Educational Review* 62, no. 4 (Winter 1992): 427–446.

55. D. C. Phillips, ed. *Constructivism in Education.* National Society for the Study of Education Yearbook, 99, issue 1. (Chicago: University of Illinois at Chicago, 2000).

56. Virginia Richardson, "Constructivist Pedagogy," *Teachers College Record* 105, no. 9 (December 2003): 1623–1640, p. 1635.

57. Becky A. Smerden, David T. Burkham, and Valerie E. Lee, "Access to Constructivist and Didactic Teaching: Who Gets it? Where is it Practiced?" *Teachers College Record* 101, no. 1 (Fall 1999): 5–34.

58. Lilia I. Bartolomé, "Beyond the Methods Fetish: Toward a Humanizing Pedagogy." *Harvard Educational Review* 64, no. 2 (Summer 1994): 173–194.

59. Jim Cummins, *Negotiating Identities: Education for Empowerment in a Diverse Society* (Ontario: California Association for Bilingual Education, 1996): 73.

60. Ron Berger, "What Is a Culture of Quality?" In *Going Public With Our Teaching: An Anthology of Practice*, edited by Thomas Hatch, Dilruba Ahmed, Ann Lieberman, Deborah Faigenbaum, Melissa Eiler White, and Desiree H. Pointer Mace (New York: Teachers College Press, 2005): 35.

61. Valerie E. Lee and David T. Burkam, "Dropping Out of High School: The Role of School Organization and Structure." *American Educational Research Journal* 40, no. 2 (Summer 2003): 353–393.

62. "Public School Facilities: Providing Environments That Sustain Learning." *ACCESS* (Quarterly Newsletter of the Advocacy Center for Children's Educational Success With Standards), 4, no. 1 (Winter 2004): 1.

63. Sara Mead, "Schoolings' Crumbling Infrastructure: Addressing a Serious and Unappreciated Problem," 2005. Available at: www.edweek.org/ew/articles/2005/06/15/a40mead.h24.html

64. Jill DeVoe, Peter Katharin, Margaret Noonan, Thomas Snyder, and Katrina Baum, *Indicators of School Climate and Safety: 2005* (Washington, DC: Bureau of Justice Statistics, and the National Center for Education Statistics, 2005).

65. Brian K. Perkins, *Where We Learn: The CUBE Survey of Urban School Climate* (Washington, DC: Urban Achievement Task Force, Council of Urban Boards of Education and the National School Boards Association, 2006).

66. Many of these ideas are addressed in an informative article by Susan Black, "The Roots of Vandalism," *American School Board Journal* (July 2002). Available at: www.asbj.com/current/research.html

67. David B. Tyack, *The One Best System: A History of American Urban Education* (Cambridge, MA: Harvard University Press, 1974); Michael B. Katz, *Class, Bureaucracy, and the Schools: The Illusion of Educational Change in America* (New York: Praeger, 1975).

68. Jack Buckley, Mark Schneider, and Yi Shang. "Fix It and They Might Stay: School Facility Quality and Teacher Retention in Washington, DC." *Teachers College Record* 107, no. 4 (May 2005): 1107–1123.

69. "Do Brighter Walls Make Brighter Students?" Available at: www.cnn.com/2005/EDUCATION/12/19/paint.in.schools.ap/index.html

70. Valerie E. Lee and S. Loeb, "School Size in Chicago Elementary Schools: Effects on Teachers' Attitudes and Students' Achievement," *American Educational Research Journal* 37 (2000): 3–31.

71. Jeremy D. Finn, Susan B. Gerber, Charles M. Achilles, and Jayne Byrd-Zaharias, "The Enduring Effects of Small Classes." *Teachers College Record* 103, no. 2 (April 2001): 145–183.

72. For the benefits and potential pitfalls of small schools, see Deborah Meier, " 'As Though They Owned The Place': Small Schools as Membership Communities." *Phi Delta Kappan* 87, no. 9 (May 2006): 657–662.

73. Gary G. Wehlage and Robert A. Rutter, "Dropping Out: How Much Do Schools Contribute to the Problem?" In *School Dropouts: Patterns and Policies*, edited by Gary Natriello (New York: Teachers College Press, Columbia University, 1986).

74. Pauline Lipman, "Restructuring in Context: A Case Study of Teacher Participation and the Dynamics of Ideology, Race, and Power." *American Educational Research Journal* 34, no. 1 (1997): 3–37.

75. "School Discipline: An Uneven Hand," *Seattle Post-Intelligencer*, July 1, 2002. Available at: www.seattlepi.nwsource.com/disciplinegap/

76. Paulo Freire, *Pedagogy of the Oppressed* (New York: Seabury Press, 1970): 59.

77. Ernest Morrell, *Becoming Critical Researchers: Literacy and Empowerment for Urban Youth* (New York: Peter Lang, 2004).

78. See Fine, *Framing Dropouts: Notes on the Politics of an Urban Public High School.*

79. See, for example, Sonia Nieto, *What Keeps Teachers Going?* (New York: Teachers College Press, 2003) and McLaughlin and Talbert, *Professional Communities and the Work of High School Teaching.*

80. Pauline Lipman, *Restructuring in Context.*

81. For the literature on the importance of family–school partnerships, see Anne T. Henderson and Karen L. Mapp, *A New Wave of Evidence: The Impact of School, Family, and Community Connections on Student Achievement* (Austin, TX: Southwest Educational Development Laboratory, 2002).

82. Concha Delgado-Gaitan, *Involving Latino Families in Schools: Raising Student Achievement Through Home-School Partnerships* (Thousand Oaks, CA: Corwin

Press, 2004). See also Carmen I. Mercado and Luis Moll, "Student Agency Through Collaborative Research in Puerto Rican Communities." In *Puerto Rican Students in U.S. Schools*, edited by Sonia Nieto (Mahwah, NJ: Lawrence Erlbaum, 2000).

83. Joyce L. Epstein's *School, Family, and Community Partnerships: Preparing Educators and Improving Schools* (Boulder, CO: Westview, 2001), a textbook for courses that focus on family involvement, fills this void.

84. Harris Interactive, Inc., *Survey of the American Teacher: An Examination of School Leadership* (Rochester, NY: Author, 2003). Available at: www .metlife.com/Applications/Corporate/WPS/DCA/Pagegenerator/0,1674,P2315,00.htm/

85. Guadalupe Valdés, *Con Respeto: Bridging the Distance Between Culturally Diverse Families and Schools* (New York: Teachers College Press, 1996): 39.

86. Jeannie Oakes, Karen Hunter Quartz, Steve Ryan, and Martin Lipton, *Becoming Good American Schools: The Struggle for Civil Virtue in Education Reform* (San Francisco: Jossey-Bass, 2000): xxi.

CHAPTER 5 CASE STUDIES

AVI ABRAMSON

Some teachers teach from the point of view of the kid. They don't just come out and say, "All right, do this, blah, blah, blah." They're not so one-tone voice.

Talbot is a small, quiet, and aging working-class town in eastern Massachusetts a few miles from the busy metropolis of Boston. Its total area is a mere 1.6 square miles, and it has a population of approximately 20,000. With the exception of salt marshes and surplus federal installations, there is little vacant land in Talbot.

One gets a sense of the community's aging by its housing. More than half of the dwellings are at least 75 years old, and this is partly due to the nature of the population. In the past two decades, the number of youths has been declining, with younger adults and families moving to more prosperous areas. The older residents remain, continuing to live in homes that long ago lost their newness and modern veneer. Both public and parochial school enrollment have been dwindling over the past two decades. One of the three elementary schools was turned into condominiums. The one high school in town, Talbot High School, has approximately 700 students.

Avi Abramson,[1] the subject of this case study, lived in Talbot at the time of his interview over a decade ago. Talbot was home to many Italians and Irish and to smaller concentrations of other European American immigrants. The percentage of people of color was quite low—only a handful of families. Although there had been a thriving community in Talbot just a generation before, the number of Jewish families was very small at the time of Avi's interview. There were two synagogues in town, one known as the "big synagogue" and the other as the "small synagogue." Many Jewish families moved to other communities, and the remaining Jews were mostly senior citizens; many of them were religiously observant and went to temple regularly. According to Avi, many people in his community were close to 85 years of age. The high school had no more than ten Jewish students.

Avi had lived in Talbot almost all his life, except for a year when his family moved to North Carolina. He went to first and second grade in public school, then went to a Jewish day school until eighth grade. When interviewed, he was 16 years old and a senior at Talbot High School. As he explained during his interviews, Avi had not always been a successful student, and he had had a hard time adjusting to public school because the curriculum was so different from what he had experienced in the Jewish day school. His plans were to go to college the following year, and he had given some thought to becoming either a history teacher or a graphic designer. Because both his parents had been teachers and because drawing was one of his hobbies, these choices were not unexpected.

Avi lived on the water-tower hillside of this quaint old town in a quiet neighborhood of single and multifamily homes. During the Christmas season, his house was easily spotted: It was the only one on the street without Christmas lights. He described his town as peaceful, and he said he enjoyed living there. Avi and his family developed good relationships with their neighbors, whom he described with fondness ("Everybody looks out for each other," he said). Nevertheless, he clearly longed to live in a community where he was not perceived as being so "different."

Avi lived with his mother and a brother who was 10 years his elder. His older sister lived in New York City with her husband and two children. Avi's father had originally come from Israel and had met his Jewish American wife in the United States, where he had remained. He had died after a long illness six years before Avi's interview. He had been a much-loved teacher in various Hebrew schools. Avi's mother was also a Hebrew teacher, and, although she loved teaching, there was not much call for Hebrew teachers in the area, so she began studying computers to prepare for a new career.

Exuding a warm glow of familiarity and old, comfortable furniture, Avi's home was filled with the aroma of latkes (potato pancakes) during the Hanukkah season and of many other Jewish foods at other times of the year. Books and artifacts were everywhere, reflecting the family's respect for tradition and history.

In many ways, Avi was a typical American teenager. He had a girlfriend and enjoyed frequent telephone conversations with friends. His bedroom was crammed with posters, comic books, encyclopedias, track team gear, woodworking projects, Star Trek memorabilia, drawing pads full of his own comics, and, underneath it all, bunk beds. However, in other ways, Avi was different from many other American youths. His serious, wise demeanor was evident in the profound respect and love that he had for his culture and religion. Few young people of any religion would dedicate every Saturday, as he did, to leading the last elderly remnants of his community in their Sabbath prayers at the small synagogue (what one might call a "role model in reverse"). He enjoyed speaking Hebrew, loved the Jewish holidays, and devoted a great deal of time to religious and cultural activities. An energetic and thoughtful young man, he enjoyed school as well as sports and other hobbies. But Avi was not what one would call a "nerd." Although he was serious about his studies, he had not always excelled in school and did not spend an inordinate amount of time studying.

Three basic themes were revealed in Avi's interviews. One was his *sense of responsibility*—to himself, his family, and his community—as well as his persistence in fulfilling this responsibility. This trait was especially evident in the respect and care with which he treated his culture and religion. *The joy and pain of maintaining them* was another theme frequently discussed by Avi. *The role of positive pressure,* from peers and family, and through activities such as track, was the third.

Independent Responsibility and Persistence

I'm fairly religious. I mean, I work in a temple on Saturdays, so I keep myself Orthodox. I try to keep the law, you know, for Shabbos [Yiddish for Sabbath], 'cause I'm reading the Torah [holiest book for Jews], so it would be nice if the person who's reading at least [should follow it]; if you're reading the law, then you might as well follow it. Set an example, in a way. Again, I don't know how much of a role model I can be to 85-year-olds [*laughs sadly*].

I'm currently working, or helping out, in Temple Solomon, with their services. A lot of people here too, they come to temple but some of them don't understand exactly what they're doing. They come, and if there weren't certain people here, they wouldn't know what to do and they wouldn't come at all, probably. So, I guess one of the reasons why I probably do what I'm doing is . . . well, I enjoy it 'cause I enjoy doing the services. I enjoy being that kind of leader. To help them.

I was going to temple every Saturday when I was little. I didn't follow along, but I just listened to them every time, and I got the tune and everything. It wasn't hard for me at all to learn the service for my Bar Mitzvah 'cause I already knew half of it in my head. Yeah, it's fun . . . it is.

The Price of Maintaining Language and Culture

There were more [Jews] years ago. Yeah, and now everybody has aged, and all the young ones are gone and left. So, there's not too many young ones coming up, 'cause there's not too many families—young families. The average age is probably 50s.

[In school] I'm the only, really, person that I guess follows the [Jewish Orthodox] laws. So I wouldn't go out on a Friday night or something like that. Right now, most people know that I don't usually come out on a Friday night. But when I started high school, people used to say sometimes, "Ya coming out tonight?" I'm like, "No, I can't. . . . " In a way, it brought me away from those people. I mean, I have different responsibilities than most people.

If I miss track and say, "'cause it's not exactly the holiday, it's the day before and I have to go home and prepare," most people won't understand. "What do you mean, you have to prepare?" or, "I thought the holiday was tomorrow?" Most other religions don't have so many holidays during the year, so there's not that much preparation that they have to do, I guess.

[*How would you feel if you lived in a place where everybody was Jewish?*] [I'd] have a good feeling every day, 'cause everybody knows there's a holiday. It would be fun, 'cause I mean, it wouldn't be boring on Shabbos 'cause when you can't . . . really do anything, there's always somebody around. That's why I go to [Jewish] camp, too.

There's not too many other Jewish children around [here]. I'm sure there's some families. I know there are a few families that live in Talbot, but they aren't religious or they . . . just don't have time to send their children to temple.

We just had Simchas Torah here the other day. . . . It was really pathetic. I mean, on Thursday night, there were four little kids there, and there were less than 20 people all together. And then, Friday morning, there were 11 men at the big shul [temple], and there were 10 at the little shul.

When I have kids, I want to bring them up in a Jewish community. And from the looks of it here, there might be a Jewish community. I mean, there is one now, but it's dwindling away, or starting to rebuild itself. But it will probably take a while before it actually becomes a large Jewish community again, when people start coming and bringing their children to the temple and actually doing something.

And I'd like to be in a place myself, even if I'm not married, I'd like to be in a place where I could walk to the temple on Saturday, or I could just go down the street and I won't have to travel so far to where I could get some good kosher meat. Or things like that. Some place where there's always something to do, [so] you don't have to travel too far.

If the other people that are out there, if the reason that they don't come is also probably 'cause their parents [don't] . . . 'cause I remember, I was just speaking to a friend of mine last week who's Jewish, and I said to him, "When was the last time you were in temple? I'm just curious." I was just joking around with him, of course. And, he was like, "Yeah, I haven't been there in a while, you know. It's pretty sad. My parents don't follow anything, so I don't," he basically said.

A couple of years ago, I had some anti-Semitic things happen. But that was cleared up. I mean, it wasn't cleared up, but they, I don't know. . . . There's a few kids in school that I still know are anti-Semites. Basically Jew haters.

I was in a woods class, and there was another boy in there, my age, and he was in my grade. He's also Jewish, and he used to come to the temple sometimes and went to Hebrew school. But then, of course, he started hanging around with the wrong people, and some of these people were in my class, and I guess they were making fun of him. And a few of them started making swastikas out of wood. So I saw one and I said to some kid, "What are you doing?" and the kid said to me, "Don't worry. It's not for you. It's for him." And I said to him, "*What?!?*" And he walked away. And after a while, they started bugging me about it, and they started saying remarks and things and. . . . Finally, it got to a point where I had them thrown out of class . . . 'cause I just decided to speak up.

And there was one kid that I didn't have thrown out because I didn't think he was as harmful as they were. But it turned out, as the year went on, I had a little incident with him too.

It was one of the last days of school, and I was wearing shorts, and it was hot out, you know. And I came into the class and I said to myself, "This is it. If he says something to me today, I'm gonna go hit him." So I walked in there and I was just walking around, and he started bugging me again, so I did the same thing. I just went up to him and I pushed him, and he must've been 300 pounds. And I just started pushing him and I said, "Come on, let's go already. I'm sick of you. . . ." I don't remember exactly what happened, but I know I got pulled away. And he walked by me again and he goes, "You ready for the second Holocaust?"

And then I think I had him thrown out. Yeah, you see, I went up to the teacher and I said to her, "I'm either gonna leave the class or they leave."

It was funny 'cause one of the kids I got thrown out actually wasn't that harmful. I don't know, he was just like a little follower on the side. And it turns out last year, I was on the track team and he decided to do track, and I became friends with him. And I got to know him, and . . . apparently his grandfather had converted to Judaism before he died. This year, I'm pretty good friends with him, and every time I'm talking to him, he's always mentioning Judaism. And he's very interested in Judaism and he told me that he would like to convert himself. He just asked me last week if he could come to the temple.

He understands a lot now. So, I mean, he was hanging around with the wrong [crowd]. They didn't care. I mean, they weren't doing anything in the class, anyways. They were just sitting around. Yeah, druggies basically.

[*Do your teachers understand your culture?*] Yeah, when I tell them I'm gonna be out of school for the holidays and they say, "Okay, don't worry. Make up, don't worry." They know about Rosh Hashanah and Yom Kippur [major Jewish holidays], but they don't know about Succos. There's the first day and the last day. After Yom Kippur, I say I'm gonna be out these other days and they go, "Oh, I thought the holidays were over with," and I go, "No, there's a few more." But they're nice about it anyway. I mean, sometimes, once in a while, someone gets a little frustrated. You know, if I come in the next day after a holiday and I'm not ready for the test 'cause I couldn't write or do anything to study for it, but I make up my work in pretty good time. And I don't usually have any trouble.

[*How do you celebrate holidays with your family?*] With pride and tradition! [*laughs*] I usually have to stay around here 'cause I work in the temple. But if we can, we invite somebody over for the Seder [Passover dinner]. It's nice to have people over for the holidays. It makes the holiday more enjoyable.

I like the taste of chicken on a Friday night—that I've waited for all week long. It's just not the same on Wednesday night. You can't even smell it the same. It's different. I like deli stuff: corned beef, a nice sandwich, a little pickle, you know. I like kugel too. All the Jewish food's good. On like Shavuos or Pesach or Succos, we usually get special fruits, like the new spring fruits, the first fruits of the harvest.

[Pesach, or Passover] is my favorite holiday. I love the preparation for it. I don't like it after the third day because there's no more seders, and there's nothing left to do except for waiting it out. I mean, it wouldn't be so bad. . . . You see, if I have to go to school, I have to go to school in the middle. But if I didn't have to go to school, then I could sit home and kind of enjoy it. But I have to go to school, and I just say it's not the same when you see other food that you can't eat. I mean, it would be a whole different feeling if you saw so many other people eating matzoth or whatever.

When I went to [Jewish] day school, it was nice to have people who were Jewish around you. I mean, it made you understand. When I came [to public school] in the ninth grade, it was hard 'cause I didn't hardly know anybody, and I didn't know what to expect 'cause it was such a different curriculum. I didn't know anybody, like I said, and you just walked around, you know, tried to speak to people, see who you could make friends with, who was right to make friends with.

The Role of Positive Pressure

[Good grades] give you confidence, show you what you're doing. . . . and [help you] keep on going.

I haven't done really bad in a while. . . . I mean occasionally, I'll do bad on a test or something, but I'll just bring it back up after. 'cause I'll feel bad after. "Ugh, I really did bad. I should have done really well." And I just try and do it better the next time. . . . Let myself slip a little bit and then I'll go back. I'll take a break and go on.

Growing up at an early age, [my parents taught me] like what was right and wrong and the basics of Judaism. . . . One summer, my mother was teaching me Hebrew. My mother actually taught . . . sat me down and actually taught me.

She's fair. . . . She doesn't keep me bound, keep me in. You know, "Stay here; don't go anywhere. You can't go out if you have to." She trusts me. . . . Most of the time, I can see why she wouldn't want me to do some things.

Most [teachers] are understanding. I mean, if you don't know how to do something, you can always just go ask them. And ask them again and again and again [*he singles out one particular teacher, a math teacher he had in ninth grade*] 'cause I never really did good in math 'til ninth grade and I had him. And he showed me that it wasn't so bad, and after that I've been doing pretty good in math and I enjoy it.

There's some teachers that understand the kids better than other teachers. . . . They teach from the point of view of the kid. They don't just come out and say, "All right, do this, *blah, blah, blah.*" I mean, in a way, they like, sometimes joke around with the kid. They try to act like the student. . . . They're not so *one-tone voice*.

[A bad teacher is] one who just . . . for example, some student was doing really bad on his tests, test after test after test. The teacher would just correct them and that's it. Wouldn't say anything to the student. . . .

I try to run [track] as often as I can. I mean, during the season you kinda have to run every day just to keep in shape. But I like to run anyways, 'cause when you run you think about everything and just . . . it gives you time, in a way, [to] relax, and just get your mind in a different place.

I do a lot of drawing. I've been drawing for years. Just sometimes—it's nothing special. Sometimes it's just doodling or drawing strange designs or things like that. But I enjoy it. It relaxes me to sit down, flip on my radio, anything I want to listen to and just draw away. It just puts you away from the rest of the world.

Some of my friends have an influence on me, too, to do well in school. My friends from camp, I mean, they all do pretty good in school and we're all close friends. Whenever one of us gets in, if we ever got into some sort of trouble, we'd bail each other out of it. Because, well, I mean, we all trust each other, basically. We keep in touch a lot. We'll always be friends.

I run up my phone bill talking to them 'cause they're all out of state. [My mother] tells me to write letters [*laughs*]. But sometimes it's hard 'cause sometimes, in a way, I live off my friends. They're like a type of energy, like a power source.

◆◆◆ Commentary

When asked to describe himself, Avi said he was "fun loving and religious," adjectives that might not ordinarily be juxtaposed in this way, yet, curiously, his description was an apt one. Deeply involved in his religion, as was apparent from his earnest and responsible attitude about his work at the synagogue, he was also a gregarious and playful teenager who enjoyed camp, sports, and practical jokes. A little digging may reveal how Avi was able to develop these seemingly divergent qualities.

Because both of his parents were teachers, and given the immensely important role of scholarship within religious education in the Jewish culture, it was no surprise that Avi had done well in school. However, the perception that all Jewish children are good students, what has often been called a "positive stereotype," has placed an undue burden on many youths. Like the "model minority" myth surrounding the academic achievement of Asian students, the consequences of this "positive stereotype" are negative in that they treat a whole class of students in the same way, without allowing for individual differences.

The enormous commitment he had to his religious community in the "small synagogue" was evident. Avi spoke Hebrew and worked hard at it. He studied the Torah and was open about the love he had for his culture and religion. But the price Avi was paying for upholding his religion and culture was often steep. The mismatch of his culture with that of the school was evident in many ways, especially when it came to organizational policies and practices. For example, during his interviews, Avi said that he had accepted that most of his teachers and classmates did not pronounce his name correctly. He appreciated that most of them tried to be understanding about the Jewish holidays, although they usually did not understand what holiday observance meant within the religious context of Judaism. His days off were always at odds with those of the other students, and the curriculum was at odds with his experience. Because remaining somewhat unassimilated is a hard choice, Avi's desire to move from Talbot when he had his own family was not surprising.

Other problems Avi talked about concerned his social life and the lack of friends in his community. For a teenager, making the decision between staying home on Friday evening with family or going out with friends can be difficult. Incidents of anti-Semitism in school were also painful reminders that being different from the majority can still be dangerous in our society. The decisiveness with which he handled these particular incidents revealed his self-confidence and desire to take control of his life (by "having them taken out of the class"), although in his hesitant explanation, it was also evident that he felt powerless ("But that was cleared up. I mean, it wasn't cleared up, but they, I don't know . . ."). The incidents also revealed his own stereotypes and social class biases about those he called "druggies."

Straddling two worlds, Avi was constantly confronted with the need to accommodate the outside world. This is a challenge historically faced by most immigrants. As expressed by Stephan Brumberg in describing the experience of Jewish immigrants in New York City at the turn of the century, "In the immigrant world, learning to live simultaneously in two worlds may have been required for successful adaptation."[2] What is unique in Avi's case is that this balancing act was increasingly taking place with those who had been here for more than one or two generations, not simply with new arrivals.

Jewish culture is intertwined with religion and tradition, rather than with nationality as in other groups, and this may make maintaining cultural ties more difficult. Although our society claims to be secular, clearly it is not. Rather, it is openly a Christian nation, as can be seen in the abundance of Christian symbols and artifacts, from the daily prayer in Congress to the crèches that adorn small towns in New England, where Avi comes from, at Christmas. Added to this is the weight of centuries of oppression, minority status, and marginality to which Jews have been subjected. Even in societies where they have been assimilated, Jews have often been victimized and treated as scapegoats.[3] Given this long history of oppression, Jews throughout the world have had to think long and hard about the balance between the degree of accommodating to host societies and maintaining their cultural traditions. The results have ranged widely—from becoming completely assimilated and losing all traces of their roots to remaining within religious and cultural enclaves removed from any but the most basic and necessary exchanges with non-Jews.[4]

Pressure toward assimilation and the accommodations made to it are only one reflection of the diversity in the Jewish community in the United States, which has often been portrayed in a unidimensional manner. However, Jews differ in religiosity, tradition, political viewpoints, language, and social class, among other characteristics. The religious tenets in Judaism itself—that is, Orthodox, Reform, and Conservative elements—reflect this diversity. In addition, some Jews who are not religious at all—secular Jews—are still profoundly Jewish in terms of cultural values. Some Jews speak Hebrew and others speak Yiddish, although others speak neither. Jews differ in their viewpoints on relations with the Arab world and on Zionism.

Besides his religion and track, another source of positive pressure for Avi were his Jewish friends, who are, in his eloquent phrase, "a type of energy . . . like a power source." That peers can have this kind of influence on young people is often overlooked by schools and parents, yet it is the very reason for the existence of such institutions as Portuguese American schools, Hebrew camps, and Saturday culture schools in the Chinese community.

Avi Abramson was straddling two worlds, trying to be both an American and a Jew. He was maintaining a difficult balancing act between complete assimilation into the mainstream of U.S. life and holding onto his religion and culture. This is not easy, even for seasoned adults. For Avi, it meant not giving in to assimilationist forces while also accommodating those parts of his life to U.S. society that would not compromise his values. With the help of his family, friends, and religious community, and with the support of his non-Jewish community, he would no doubt be able to do it.[5]

◆◆◆ Reflect on This Case Study

1. What, in your view, keeps Avi Abramson so involved in his synagogue?
2. Do you think Avi's school life would be different if he were not on the track team? How? What implications can you draw from this for schools?
3. The United States officially supports "separation of church and state," but is it possible for teachers to affirm Avi's culture and background without bringing religion into the school? Think about some ways this might be done. If you do not believe it is possible, list some of the ways that the separation of church and state is violated in schools and other institutions. What is the alternative to this practice?
4. Friends are, in Avi's words, "like a power source." How can teachers use this power source to good advantage? Think of strategies that teachers and schools might develop to build on positive peer pressure.
5. It is obvious that Avi has little respect for those he calls "the druggies." Do schools help perpetuate stereotypes about students in different social groups? How? If you were a teacher in his school, what might you do about this problem? What if you were the principal?

FERN SHERMAN

If there's something in the history book that's wrong,
I should tell them that it is wrong.

Springdale, a small city in Iowa, is surrounded by farm country. With a population of close to 50,000, the city is a haven from the problems of more populated midwestern cities, yet it affords the advantages of a large university and other cultural activities. The city is not very ethnically diverse: Most of the residents of Springdale identify as "American," with no ethnic classification. Many have been here for several generations. The African American community numbers just over 1,000 and there are fewer than 800 Latinos. There are slightly more than 3,000 Asians, the largest non–European American group. The number of Native Americans in the entire city is minuscule, totaling only about 60.

When she was first interviewed, Fern Sherman[1] was 14 years old and an eighth grader in the middle school in town. Of Chippewa, Ponca, Norwegian, German, and English heritage, Fern identified as Native American. She and her sisters were registered as both Turtle Mountain Chippewa and Northern Ponca, an Indian Nation that was reinstated after being "terminated" (no longer recognized by the federal government) in 1966. Tribal affiliation designations are so complex and bureaucratic that Fern and her sisters were classified as $^{237}/_{512}$, or slightly over half Indian. This kind of identification is arbitrary and clearly a social construct, having little to do with self-identification. American Indians are unique in having this kind of definition in the United States.[2]

The American Indian community is extremely heterogeneous. In 2002, the U.S. Census Bureau reported that it numbered almost 2.5 million, nearly triple the 1970 U.S. census.[3] About 500 Nations are recognized by the federal government, of which more than 200 have a land base or reservation. There are others that are not officially recognized. About two-thirds of all American Indians now live away from reservations in other communities, primarily in urban areas. Although a growing number speak only English, one-third regularly speak another language as well. Currently, more than 200 languages are spoken, and some are still vigorously maintained. For example, more than 70 percent of Navajo children enter school speaking Navajo as their native language. Several Indian Nations have declared their languages to be official, designating English as a "foreign language."[4] American Indians are also very diverse in cultural traditions, physical appearance, religion, and lifestyle. In spite of these vast differences, a pan-Indian identity has emerged in the past several decades, probably the result of several factors: the many values shared by most Native peoples; the need to develop greater political strength; and intermarriage among Native groups, as was the case in Fern's family.

There are currently more than half a million American Indian/Alaska Native students (the designation used by the Census Bureau) in U.S. public schools.[5] Fern was the only Native American in her entire school, although she said she wished there were more. Before moving to Springdale, she had attended a tribal reservation school for kindergarten and first grade, and later a public school where there were a large number of Indian students. In that school, there had been some Indian teachers, an Indian Club, an Indian education program with special tutors, and other support services. In both of those schools, Fern and her sisters had felt comfortable and accepted, which had not always been the case after they moved to Springdale.

Fern lived with her father, two sisters, and young nephew. Her father was a professor of political science at the local university, and her mother, who lived in another city, was a truck driver. Her parents had been separated for years, and Fern and her sisters rarely saw their mother, who had taken little responsibility for their upbringing and education. Two of Fern's other sisters lived with their mother. Instrumental in raising her nephew, Daryl, who was two years old when she was interviewed, Fern had seen firsthand what raising a child was like and wanted to delay having children of her own for a long time. She said, "I want to get my life started and on the go before I have a family."

Fern's sisters, Juanita and Rose, were 16 and 17 years old at the time of the interview. Despite not being their biological father, Mr. Sherman had taken responsibility for raising Juanita and Rose as well as his own daughter. Both of the older girls had a history of alcohol and drug abuse. Rose was in an out-of-state treatment center but was expected to move back home in a few months; Juanita was living at an alcohol and drug abuse residential center. She had begun drinking a number of years earlier because, according to her father, "She just never fit in." Isolated and alone at school, she sought relief through alcohol.

Mr. Sherman had worked valiantly to help Juanita and Rose overcome their addiction. Having seen firsthand the results of drug and alcohol abuse, he was convinced that they are linked to poor self-esteem and lack of success in school. As a result, he had pushed his daughters to excel in school. Having lived through the nightmare of addiction with his family, he thought a lot about the role that schools should play. He ruefully asked, "Do we have to intervene in every Indian kid's life that goes into these school systems in such drastic manners?" Although he did not place the blame entirely on teachers for his children's problems, he thought there were too many misunderstandings in school that could lead to failure. Getting a good education was an essential that he felt his children could not afford to neglect. As a result, he was tireless in his pressure on them to study, get good grades, and prepare for college. At the time of the interview, Fern was in eighth grade and doing very well academically. Her father was keeping his fingers crossed that she would continue to do so, although his agonizing experiences with his other daughters had tempered his optimism.

Becoming aware and proud of their heritage was another message that Mr. Sherman had given his daughters. They did not speak a language other than English at home, but he sometimes taught them words in Ponca. They perceived his pressure on them to succeed and to identify as Native American as sometimes overbearing, but they also appreciated him for giving them strength in their culture and the determination to get ahead.

Fern and her family lived in a middle-class neighborhood close to the university. Although it was a friendly and close-knit community, like many suburbs it provided little recreation for youths. Although they were the only Native American family in the area, Fern described her community as a "really nice neighborhood" and "one big happy family." She said that her neighbors were always there to help one another out and that they were understanding and kind.

Saying that the middle school she attended was "kinda stuck on itself," Fern nevertheless acknowledged that it was a good school. She was taking classes in science, math, English, home economics, art, physical education, and family and consumer science, her favorite subject because it included experiences in childcare. Her grades were very good, although not necessarily reflective of her interests. Her highest grade was in English, her least favorite subject; and her worst grade, C, was in her favorite subject, science. Her grades were, however, a reflection of the particular teachers who taught these subjects that year. Fern was very active in school activities such as chorus, cooking club, and sports and in out-of-school activities such as dance.

Aware of the role of teachers' expectations on her achievement, Fern spoke about her reaction to different teachers and schools. Family pressures and responsibilities, the isolation she felt as the only Native American student in her school, and identifying as a successful student were the other dominant themes that emerged during Fern's interviews.

The Role of Teachers' Expectations

I'd rather go through school and get A's and B's than D's and F's. . . . In Springdale, I've noticed if you're getting D's and F's, they don't look up to you; they look down. And you're always the last on the list for special activities, you know?

Most of my friends were from the same culture or background [in my former school in South Dakota] 'cause there are a lot of Native Americans there. And you weren't really treated different there. You were all the same and you all got pushed the same and you were all helped the same. And one thing I've noticed in Springdale is they kind of teach 25 percent and they kinda leave 75 percent out. . . . [Teachers] really push us hard, but, if we're getting bad grades, they don't help us as much.

Being at the top of my class, always being noticed as a top person, grade-wise [made me feel good]. I mostly got straight A's and B's until I moved to Springdale. And I got like a C and D the first semester, in science and math here because they just push you to your limits. I mean, it's just incredible the way they think you're like "Incredible Woman" or something.

I don't like being pushed to my limit. I mean, I think you should have a little bit of lee-way. Like, this past week, I had three different reports due in three different classes. I think [teachers] should have at least a little bit of communication, not to give you three reports due in the same week.

I like going to math or, like, science to do different experiments. I've always liked science, but it's not really my best subject. I like American history because sometimes I'll know more than the teacher just because my dad has taught me stuff. I don't really like English . . . because I hate when they make you cut off at 400 words. If you can't write what you're gonna write, why write it?

In science, if you don't understand something, and the science teacher doesn't get in until 8:00 and the bell rings at 8:10 . . . In 10 minutes, you can't learn something. . . . Like, if you don't have your assignment done, and you need help on it, you have 10 minutes to go in, get help, get it done. Because if it's not done by class time, you'll have detention.

[*What would you do to make school more interesting?*] More like involved activities in class, you know? . . . 'cause, like, when you're sitting in class, and the teacher is lecturing, I usually feel like falling asleep, 'cause it's just blah. And in chorus, there's, like, this rap about history, you know? It's really fun. . . . More like making the whole class be involved, not making only the two smartest people up here do the whole work for the whole class.

Family Pressure, Expectations, and Responsibilities

I try [to do well in school] for my dad, but I mostly do it for myself. [My sisters] are always like, "Yeah, you're daddy's girl, just 'cause you get A's and B's." It's how they put me down for what I'm doing, for how I'm succeeding.

He's always involved in what's happening in school, unlike most parents. . . . My dad is just always [at school]. He's always been there, every school activity, I mean, unless our car breaks down. . . . I sure remember, we were having a musical and it was set up with, like, 300 kids. And our car had a flat tire. And so my dad put this air stuff in so he could get me to the musical [*laughing*]. And he went and got the tire fixed and he made the guy give him a ride back to school so he could see it! . . . He's always been involved, so I really don't know what it's like to not be involved.

He thinks [school] is heaven! When he was young, he only got A's and B's. C was an F to him. And I sometimes have to stop him and say, "Hey, I'm not you!" But I'm glad he's pushing me.

Just from my family breaking up so many times, I've learned to always stick with it. I've learned really to stick with my family. I've always been told to love everybody the same in your family, but sometimes that's really hard for me because I've always been so close to Juanita. So, I really feel that Juanita's my mom. . . . My dad's probably the first person I go to, and Juanita's probably someone I can go to, you know, for "woman help."

[Dad] always tries to comfort me, telling me that he's always there for me. He can always arrange for me to talk to somebody if I'm hurting. But I try to explain to him that he's the only person I really need. He's always been understanding. . . . [When things go bad], I talk to my dad.

My dad is more or less a brick wall that you can't get through [*laughing*]. He's really set, like you always get those stupid lectures: "Well, my dad did it this way. . . ." But, Dad, *you're* not your dad. I know I might grow up and treat my children a little bit the same way as my dad, but knowing how much it hurts me inside when he says, "Well, you know, I was a straight A student when I was little. . . ." I'm not gonna do that to my kids because it just makes them want to fail more. When you're mad at your parents, you try to find something to get them back with. And I think grades are a very good way to get them back with.

He's a kid at heart. He doesn't try to be "Macho Parent" or "Mercedes Man." He doesn't try to fit in with people. He's himself, and he's always been himself. And if people don't like the way he is, tough Sherlock!

He's a one-of-a-kind dad. I'll always love him for what he is. I've really not known [my mother] that much. From just what my dad's told me and what I've seen, she is really hard to get along with. She's, like, very emotional. She makes all these excuses . . . "Yeah, my phone bill's really high. I'm sorry I can't call you." Well, if the stupid boyfriend's more important than calling her own daughter, you know, that's not my fault. She's always been mean, in my eyes, but nice when she's face to face with me.

I think I'm gifted to have a family like this, but I'm glad we're not a Leave-it-to-Beaver-Cleaver family. I've got friends that their families are perfect, no problems. But I'm sure there *are* problems inside the locked doors, but not really showing it. But in my family, if I'm angry, I'm going to go out and tell them. I hate people who try to hide it.

You know how counselors say "dysfunctional" and "functional" families? I think every family's dysfunctional, in their own way. I mean, every family is gonna have a fight about what they're gonna eat for supper, or who gets the family car tonight, or whatever.

The Isolation of Being Native American

Sometimes I get sick of hearing about [being Native American]. I mean, like my dad just goes on and on, and finally, I just space out and pretend like I'm listening to him. Because I've already heard all of it. And he always tries to make me what I'm not . . . make me more Native American. And since I'm the only Native American in the Springdale school district almost, he tries to make me go to the principal and say, "We need this." There's no use, because there's no other Native Americans to help me!

I'm really not noticed as a Native American until something . . . like the ITBS test. The woman was giving us our codes. She called "Native Americans," and she goes, "Well, I don't think there is any." And the whole auditorium goes, "Fern!" I think it's really neat. I don't hide it. I express it.

[South Dakota] was more like everybody was a family. You would go to your backyard and have a banquet with the whole neighborhood, you know? It was like the whole town was one big family.

[My teachers don't understand my culture.] Like if I say, "This isn't done in my culture. This isn't the way it's done. . . ." Like, talking about abortion in history or something. For Native Americans, abortion is just . . . like, you should really put the mother in jail for it. Because the baby is alive, just like we are. And that's the way I feel. And when they sit there and say, "It's the mother's right to do it," well, I don't think it's the mother's right because it's not the baby's fault the mother doesn't want it. And so, when I try to tell them, they just, "Oh, well, we're out of time." They cut me off, and we've still got half an hour! And so that kinda makes me mad.

If there's something in the history book that's wrong, my dad always taught me that, if it's wrong, I should tell them that it is wrong. And the only time I ever do is if I know it's exactly wrong. Like we were reading about Native Americans and scalping. Well, the French are really the ones that made them do it so they could get money. And my teacher would not believe me. I finally just shut up because he just would not believe me. . . . Just my arguments with them, they just cut it off.

[Other people] are not going to understand me as much, if I start talking about spirituality. But I don't feel like people put me down or put me up for being Indian. I always get good praises from people, you know. "I'm glad you're sticking in there, not being ashamed of being Native American."

We do have different values. We do have different needs, and we do have different wants. I mean, I'm sure every family needs love. Love is a very, very top thing in our list of needs. For White people, it's usually shelter over their heads. For Native Americans, usually number one . . . family love.

It can be different. Like my family sits down and eats corn soup and fried dough. It would be different from, "Well, my family goes out for pizza."

I don't know why other Native Americans have dropped out of Springdale schools. Maybe it's because I just haven't been in high school yet. But I remember one time, my sister came home and she was just mad. They said that "Geronimo was a stupid chief riding that stupid horse," and my sister got mad!

I've always been taught to be kind to elders, to always look up to them. And my dad's always taught me that everybody's really the same. I mean, there's no difference between Black and White. . . . Really everybody's the same to me, because we're all the same blood, you know?

Identifying as Successful

I found school fun. I liked to do homework. I got moved: I didn't go to kindergarten. I went straight from Head Start to first grade because I was too bored in the classes, and I wouldn't do the work because I fought with the teachers and told them I already did it because I had done it the year before. And so my dad made them move me out because there was no use for me to stay back if I wasn't gonna learn anything new.

I like sports a lot . . . volleyball and basketball. I like sports and I'm just glad they offer them 'cause some schools don't have enough funding. Basketball is mostly my sport. I compare it to stuff, like, when I can't get science, or like in sewing, I'll look at that machine and I'll say, "This is a basketball; I can overcome it. . . ."

One [of my friends], she's really understanding. If I have family problems, she's always there to talk to. We're really close. We're, like, involved in the same sports, and we love basketball. Natalie, I can always talk to. . . . I mean, she's like free counseling!

I've, like, always wanted to be president of the United States, but I figured that was too hard [*laughs*]. . . . I don't know, I kinda wanna be a fashion lawyer. I've always wanted to be president and I think it's just because, like, I'll see so many mess-ups and . . . I don't know, just George Bush [the elder] right now. . . . I was infatuated with Ronald Reagan the whole time he was in office. And, like, I'd make posters for Dad and tell him, "Yeah, this is me." And I just like the idea of being head honcho!

[*What is the reason for going to school?*] To learn and make something out of yourself when you're older, so you're not just, I don't know, a person on welfare or something.

I sure remember the day I got my first B; I started crying. Most of my friends, you know, get A's and B's, and everything. And it's not to impress them; it's to show them that I'm just as good, you know? It's mostly just for me, to make me know that I'm just as good as anybody else and that I can really do it.

I'm ambitious. I always want to get things done. Like, say, I'm running for copresident for the school, I want to get my campaign done [way] ahead, not the day before.

I succeed in everything I do. If I don't get it right the first time, I always go back and try to do it again.

◆◆◆ Commentary

Teachers' expectations play an important role in the academic achievement of many students, including Native American students. They certainly had an impact on Fern's school achievement. Although she said she did not like being pushed, it was obvious that when teachers held high expectations, she was able to live up to them. Although Fern was a successful student, the dropout rate for Native American students as a whole is estimated to be among the highest of any other group—more than

30 percent.[6] This percentage is misleading, however, because many students drop out before even reaching high school, as early as elementary school.

Fern's father, who promoted both academic achievement and ethnic pride and awareness for his daughters, was obviously the major influence in her life. Having been a successful student himself, he knew the value of education. And, as an American Indian, he was convinced that the only way to progress, both individually and for the community, was by getting a good education. These are the messages Fern had been listening to since early childhood and they had a profound impact on her. She said that she tried to be successful for herself, her father, and her friends ("to show them that I'm just as good"). The need to excel on an individual basis contradicts a deeply held cultural value of collective progress in American Indian communities. Striving to excel for one's family, Nation, or community is a much better way of motivating children, which is why Fern's father stressed "making Grandmother proud." Providing a learning environment that emphasizes cooperative learning rather than individual competition is one important, culturally appropriate strategy for schools to consider. Others include using traditional ways of knowing in constructing the curriculum and providing meaningful activities that affirm and build on students' culture.[7]

Being the only American Indian student in school is a theme that came up repeatedly during Fern's interviews. At times, she felt that the pressure of being the only one was unbearable, especially when her father expected her to confront every issue dealing with Native people head on. At other times, being the only one meant being unique and special (she identified being singled out for this kind of interview as one of the benefits). Although some teachers, such as her English teacher, made accommodations in the content and structure of their curricula, most others did not. For instance, her feeling that a Native American perspective was missing from school curricula was likely correct. Also, when giving students writing assignments about their families, her English teacher allowed each student ample flexibility to discuss differences, and, although Fern loved science, she felt that her teacher was not very helpful and probably the "last person for me to go talk to." Being the only Native American in her school also meant always being different. Fern was an extremely strong young woman, but this kind of pressure is exceedingly difficult for adolescents experiencing the traumas of identification and peer acceptance.

Education was sometimes used to separate American Indian children physically, emotionally, and culturally from their families. A particularly graphic example of this practice is the 1895 *Annual Report* of the Indian commissioner to the Secretary of the Interior, in which the government's intent in educating Indian children was described as "to free the children from the language and habits of their untutored and oftentimes savage parents."[8] Such blatant expressions of racism probably would not be used today, but many of the patronizing attitudes stemming from this belief are still apparent in the curriculum and texts used in schools.

According to Sharon Nelson-Barber and Elise Trumbull Estrin, a majority of teachers do not recognize the knowledge or learning strategies that American Indian students bring to science and math; because of this, teachers miss out on ways to involve students more meaningfully in their learning.[9] Ironically, however, traditional

American Indian ways of knowing, such as modeling and providing time for observation and practice, are consistent with current constructivist notions of learning.[10] When schools are culturally aware and make sense to students, the students tend to succeed. Teresa McCarty's in-depth study of Rough Rock Community School in Arizona is moving testimony to this truth.[11] This school, in existence for over 40 years, has been a model and inspiration for many other schools for Indigenous groups that are attempting to create affirming and high-quality learning environments.

American Indian children are faced with other difficult situations as well. Suicide is much more prevalent among reservation Indians than in the general population; the rate of adult unemployment among American Indians is extraordinary, reaching as high as 50 percent; health care, particularly on reservations, is either completely absent or inadequate; infant mortality is higher among American Indians than the national average; there are widespread nutritional deficiencies in this group; and alcoholism may affect the lives and functioning of more than 60 percent of all American Indian children.[12] Struggling against these odds is an awesome responsibility; school sometimes takes a back seat. Fern developed a number of successful strategies to deal with these overwhelmingly negative barriers to success: She was unabashedly ambitious and she wanted to succeed in school and beyond and was quite certain that she would ("I succeed in everything I do," she said confidently). In fact, when asked what she likes most about herself, she was quick to single out her ambition.

In helping to raise her nephew, supporting her sister Juanita during a difficult time, adjusting to a school where she was culturally different from all her peers, and confronting the dual challenges of academic success and parental pressures, no matter how positive they may be, Fern Sherman was contending with tremendous responsibilities at an early age.

◆◆◆ Reflect on This Case Study

1. Fern's feeling of isolation in a city with so few American Indians affected her life in a great many ways. When have you been the only ___ (fill in the blank) in a particular setting? What impact did this have on you? Describe how you felt in school, at home, and in your community. What might have made you feel less isolated? What are the implications of this situation for you as a teacher?

2. What is meant by the statement that tribal affiliation is a "social construction"? Who determines what a person is? Why do you think that identity has been determined *for* some people in our society, while other people have been able to determine their own identity?

3. Based on Fern's case study, what do you think are some of the pressures that can lead to alcohol and drug abuse for young people? What specific situations in the American Indian community can exacerbate this problem? What can schools do to help alleviate it?

4. If you could talk with Fern about remaining a successful and confident student, what would you say?

5. What approaches might work to lower the dropout rate of American Indian students? What can schools, communities, and families do together to help?

6. Work together with a small group of your colleagues and plan a science lesson in which you incorporate some American Indian ways of knowing (you may want to read the article by Nelson-Barber and Estrin cited in the case study). How might it differ from another science lesson? Would Indian students be the only ones to benefit from such lessons? Why or why not?

Notes to Chapter 5 Case Studies

Avi Abramson

1. We appreciate Diane Sweet's work in finding and interviewing Avi and in providing extensive background information for this case study. Diane teaches courses in language and writing at the Wentworth Institute of Technology in Massachusetts.

2. Stephan F. Brumberg, *Going to America, Going to School: The Jewish Immigrant Public School Encounter in Turn-of-the-Century New York City* (New York: Praeger, 1986): 2.

3. See Meyer Weinberg's extensive history of anti-Semitism in 12 countries, *Because They Were Jews: A History of Anti-Semitism* (Westport, CT: Greenwood Press,

1986); Chapter 12 deals with the United States. See also Leonard Dinnerstein, *Anti-Semitism in America* (New York: Oxford University Press, 1994).

4. For an examination of the pressure Jews feel to become assimilated in U.S. society, see Seymour Martin Lipset and Earl Raab, *Jews and the New American Scene* (Cambridge, MA: Harvard University Press, 1995) and Alan M. Dershowitz, *The Vanishing American Jew* (New York: Simon & Schuster, 1998).

5. For an update on Avi's life, see the *Epilogue* on the *Affirming Diversity* Web page.

Fern Sherman

1. We wish to thank Carlie Collins Tartakov for the extensive interviews with Fern Sherman, her sister Juanita, and their father. After 23 years of teaching in elementary schools in California and Massachusetts, Carlie became a faculty member in the Department of Curriculum and Instruction at Iowa State University, from which she recently retired.

2. Cornel Pewewardy, "Will the 'Real' Indians Please Stand Up?" *Multicultural Review* (June 1998): 36–42.

3. U.S. Census Bureau, *Census 2000 Summary File 1* (Washington, DC: U.S. Department of Commerce, 2002).

4. The Northern Ute Nation, for example, declared English a foreign language in 1984; see Jon Reyhner, "Native American Languages Act Becomes Law." *NABE*

News 14, no. 3 (December 1, 1990).

5. National Center for Education Statistics, *State Nonfiscal Survey of Public Elementary/Secondary Education* (Washington, DC: U.S. Department of Education, 2001).

6. See K. Tsianina Lomawaima, "Educating Native Americans." In *Handbook of Research on Multicultural Education*, 2nd ed. edited by James A. Banks and Cherry A. McGee Banks (San Francisco: Jossey-Bass, 2004). See also Donna Deyhle and Karen Swisher, "Research in American Indian and Alaska Native Education: From Assimilation to Self-Determination." In *Review of Research in Education*, 22, edited by Michael W. Apple (Washington, DC: American Educational Research Association, 1997).

7. See, for example, Deyhle and Swisher, "Research in American Indian and Alaska Native Education: From Assimilation to Self-Determination"; Sharon Nelson-Barber and Elise Trumbull Estrin, "Bringing Native American Perspectives to Mathematics and Science Teaching." *Theory into Practice* 34, no. 3 (Summer 1995): 174–185; and K. Tsianina Lomawaima and Teresa L. McCarty, "When Tribal Sovereignty Challenges Democracy: American Indian Education and the Democratic Ideal," *American Educational Research Journal* 39, no. 2 (Summer 2002): 279–305.

8. As cited in Jon Reyhner, "Bilingual Education: Teaching the Native Language." In *Teaching the Indian Child: A Bilingual/Multicultural Approach*, edited by Jon Reyhner (Billings: Eastern Montana College, 1992): 39.

9. Nelson-Barber and Estrin, 1995.

10. *Ibid.*

11. Teresa L. McCarty, *A Place to Be Navajo: Rough Rock and the Struggle for Self-Determination in Indigenous Schooling* (Mahwah, NJ: Lawrence Erlbaum, 2002). See also Reyhner, "Bilingual Education: Teaching the Native Language."

12. See, for example, Mei L. Castor, Michael S. Smyser, Maile M. Taualii, Alice N. Park, Shelley A. Lawson, and Ralph A. Forquera, "A Nationwide Population-Based Study Identifying Health Disparities Between American Indians/Alaska Natives and the General Populations Living in Select Urban Counties," *American Journal of Public Health* 96, no. 8 (2006): 1478–1484; for the latest data, including on reservations, see the National Council of Urban Indian Health Services website (www.ncuih.org).

Culture, Identity, and Learning

6

Michael Coblyn. *Blessed Mother, study.* Charcoal and watercolor on mylar, 2003.

"[Teachers] just understand some things outside, but they cannot understand something inside our hearts."

—*Hoang Vinh, interviewee*

Young people whose languages and cultures differ from the dominant group often struggle to form and sustain a clear image of themselves. In addition, they struggle to have teachers understand who they really are—to help teachers "understand something inside our hearts," in the poignant words of Hoang Vinh—because teachers and schools commonly view students' differences as deficiencies. The case studies of Yahaira León, James Karam, Hoang Vinh, and Rebecca Florentina that follow this chapter provide diverse and moving examples of how students' identities may be devalued. In spite of being proud of themselves and their families and communities, at one time or another, all of these young people felt the need to hide or de-emphasize their identity, culture, or language in school. Yet this de-emphasis may have had negative consequences for their learning. This chapter explores the influence that culture and identity may have on student learning, and it reviews a number of promising pedagogical and curricular adaptations that teachers and schools can make.

Many teachers and schools, in an attempt to be colorblind, do not want to acknowledge cultural or racial differences. "I don't see Black or White," a teacher will say, "I see only *students*." This statement assumes that to be colorblind is to be fair, impartial, and objective because to see differences, in this line of reasoning, is to see defects and inferiority. Although it sounds fair and honest and ethical, the opposite may actually be true. When used to mean *nondiscriminatory* in attitude and behavior, *colorblindness* is not a bad thing. On the other hand, colorblindness may result in *refusing to accept differences* and therefore accepting the dominant culture as the norm. In the case of lesbian, gay, bisexual, and transgender (LGBT) students, this attitude may be expressed as "I don't care what they do in their private lives; I just don't want them to broadcast it." This may sound accepting and nondiscriminatory, but the same statement is not generally made about heterosexual students. In both cases, these attitudes result in denying the identities of particular students, thereby making them invisible.

A good example of using the concept of colorblindness to deny differences was provided by the U.S. Supreme Court in the *Lau* decision of 1974.[1] The San Francisco School Department was sued on behalf of Chinese-speaking students who, parents and other advocates charged, were not being provided with an equal education. The school department countered by claiming that they were providing these students with an equal education because the students received *exactly the same* teachers, instruction, and materials as all others. The U.S. Supreme Court, in a unanimous decision, ruled against the school department. The Court reasoned that giving non-English-speaking students the same instruction, teachers, and materials as English-speaking students flew in the face of equal educational opportunity because Chinese-speaking students could not benefit from instruction provided in English. The dictum "Equal is not the same" is useful here. It means that treating everyone in the same way will not necessarily lead to equality; rather, it may end up perpetuating the inequality that already exists. Learning to affirm differences rather than deny them is what a multicultural perspective is about. In contrast, the general tendency throughout U.S. history (and this is also true of the histories of most countries) has been to attempt to do away with differences, an approach based on the notion that unity creates harmony whereas diversity breeds instability and discord. Color-blindness has often meant viewing everyone as "the same," but, as established in the *Lau* decision, "equal is not the same."

What are the educational implications of "Equal is not the same"? First, it means *acknowledging the differences that children bring to school* such as their gender, race, ethnicity, language, social class, sexual orientation, abilities and talents, among others. The refusal to acknowledge differences often results in schools and teachers labeling children's behavior as "deficient." In other cases, it results in making students "invisible," as happened with James Karam, one of the students in the case studies following this chapter.

Second, it means *admitting the possibility that students' identities may influence how they experience school* and, hence, how they learn. Being aware of the connections among culture, identity, and learning should in no way devalue children's backgrounds or lower our expectations of them, yet this is precisely why so many educators have a hard time accepting "Equal is not the same." That is, they are reluctant to accept this notion because they may feel that, in doing so, they must lower their expectations or "water down" the curriculum so that all children can learn. Yet neither of these practices is necessary.

Third, *accepting differences also means making provisions for them.* When students' cultural and linguistic backgrounds are viewed as a strength on which educators can draw and build, pedagogy changes to incorporate students' lives. This approach is based on the best of educational theory, that is, that individual differences must be taken into account in teaching and that education must begin "where children are at." Yet these ideas are often overlooked when it comes to cultural and linguistic differences. The fact that Yahaira León, whose case study immediately follows this chapter, was fluent in two languages was rarely viewed as anything but a liability by most of her teachers. If we are serious about providing all students with educational equity, then students' cultures and identities need to be seen not as a burden, a problem, or even a challenge, but rather as assets upon which to build.

DEFINING CULTURE

Before we can ask schools to change in order to teach all students, we need to understand the differences that students bring with them to school. Culture is one of these differences, and we define it as follows: *Culture consists of the values, traditions, worldview, and social and political relationships created, shared, and transformed by a group of people bound together by a common history, geographic location, language, social class, religion, or other shared identity.* Culture includes not only tangibles such as foods, holidays, dress, and artistic expression but also less tangible manifestations such as communication style, attitudes, values, and family relationships. These features of culture are often more difficult to pinpoint, but doing so is necessary if we want to understand how student learning may be affected.

Power is implicated in culture as well. That is, members of the dominant group in a society traditionally think of dominant cultural values as "normal," while they view the values of subordinated groups as deviant or even wrong. The difference in perception is due more to the power of each of these groups than to any inherent goodness or rightness in the values themselves. For instance, U.S. mainstream culture stresses the necessity for youngsters to become independent at an early age, whereas other cultures emphasize interdependence as a major value. Neither of these values is innately right or wrong; each has developed as a result of the group's history, experiences, and needs. However, people with a U.S. mainstream frame of reference may view as abnormal, or at the very least curious, the interdependent relationships of Latino children and parents, for instance. They may characterize Latino children as overly dependent, too attached to their parents and siblings, and needing more attention than other children. For their part, Latino families may view U.S. mainstream culture as strange and cold for its insistence on independence at what they consider too young an age. However, the difference in these perceptions is that the values of Latinos do not carry the same weight or power as those of the dominant group.

In this text, we are concerned primarily with the *sociocultural* and *sociopolitical* dimensions of identity rather than with individual psychological identity formation. Thus, we focus on such issues as *power, institutional arrangements in schools,* and *the impact of ideology on culture* as well as *students' lived realities and experiences in families and communities.* This is not to dismiss the importance of individual identity development. On the contrary, it is imperative that teachers understand how children develop their social and cultural selves and how this process interacts with issues of race, ethnicity, gender, and other variables. The work of such scholars as Beverly Daniel Tatum, Gary Howard, Bailey Jackson, and others focuses specifically on such matters. All teachers should become familiar with these theories as well as the sociocultural and sociopolitical perspectives underlying this text.[2]

We are always on shaky ground when considering cultural differences. The danger of considering culture lies in overgeneralizing its effects. Overgeneralizations can lead to gross stereotypes, which in turn may lead to erroneous conclusions concerning entire groups of people, not to mention the abilities and intelligence of individual students. We have all seen some of the more disastrous consequences of overgeneralizations: checklists of cultural traits of different ethnic groups, the mandate to use certain pedagogical strategies with students of particular backgrounds, and treatises on "indisputable" student behaviors. Culture, in such instances, is treated as a *product* rather than a *process*, and it is viewed as unchanging and unchangeable. Viewing culture in this way can also lead to *essentializing* culture, that is, ascribing particular immutable characteristics to it. This may result in thinking of culture as inherent in individuals and groups. Kris Gutierrez and Barbara Rogoff describe it as believing that individuals and groups are "carriers of culture—an assumption that creates problems, especially as research on cultural styles of ethnic (or racial) groups is applied in schools."[3] They suggest using instead a cultural-historical approach that recognizes the histories and valued practices of cultural groups. Rather than thinking of culture as "pure," unadulterated, and unaffected by other circumstances and contexts, they view learning as a process that takes place within ongoing activity. Gutierrez and Rogoff thus distinguish between *understanding cultural practices* and *locating cultural characteristics*, because the latter can be problematic.

Using the previous example, we would be in error to view Latino culture as *always* interdependent, regardless of the situation. It would be a mistake to believe this because culture is too complex and too varied for us to conclude that all those who share a particular background behave in the same way or believe the same things.

HYBRIDITY: ANOTHER WAY OF UNDERSTANDING CULTURE

One problem with a static view of culture is that it fails to recognize that our society is more heterogeneous than ever. As you can see in the case studies and snapshots of young people in this book, many of them have multiple identities: Rebecca is not only a lesbian but *also* Italian American; Linda is *both* Black and White; Yahaira is Dominican *and* Puerto Rican; David is Jewish *and* adopted. In the case of these young people, *all* of their identities are significant to them. With multiple identities of this kind growing ever more rapidly, it is impossible to speak about culture as it is lived today, in this context, as if it were unitary. A major premise of this book is that a static view of culture contradicts the very notion of multicultural education as presented here.

This brings us to a discussion of *hybridity*, that is, the fusion of various cultures to form new, distinct, and ever-changing identities. Hybridity is a reality in our own country as well as internationally. It refers not simply to mixed-race and ethnic identity, although this is certainly a growing reality. Because about 4 percent of youth under age 18 in the United States are of mixed heritage and the number is growing rapidly, Alejandra Lopez argues that we need to learn to talk about identity in different ways, "allowing for fluidity and multiplicity in racial-ethnic identification."[4]

Some examples can help explain this kind of fluidity. In an ethnographic study of a large, urban, and culturally diverse high school, Laurie Olen described how immigrant students felt "caught in the middle," not really fitting into any category. She found that the "sides" were constantly shifting: While identity was sometimes defined in terms of nationality, at other times it was defined in terms of culture, religion, race, or language and sometimes as a combination of these.[5] In another example, Pedro Noguera's research with Mexican American students in East Oakland illustrates how context influences identity. When they were in elementary school, the Mexican American children were described by African American classmates— and frequently referred to themselves—as "White." However, in the new social contexts of adolescence and middle school, they began to view themselves as Mexican Americans, among other identities.[6] Daniel Yon's research in a Toronto high school illustrates similar complexities: He found, for example, that a Serbian identified as "Spanish," while a White male identified strongly with Guyanese. Yon refers to the shifting notions of identity as "elusive culture" that is, a view of culture as an ongoing process that includes not only race and ethnicity but also popular culture.[7]

Hybridity, then, also refers to *how* people identify, regardless of which ethnic or racial group they may belong to. It recognizes that there are many other identities besides race and ethnicity; these may include gender, sexual orientation, geographic location, and professional affiliation, among many others. That is, hybridity refers to the fact that, in Nadine Dolby's words, identity is not "an absolute state of being" but rather a variable that is constantly shifting and changing.[8] For example, urban youth often identify with a culture that is an amalgam of various ethnic, racial, and other identifications. Hip-hop culture is a good example of this: Incorporating music, dance, visual culture, as well as a working-class and often marginalized urban perspectives, it represents a unique culture that is not tied to any one ethnic or racial group. In fact, it is not unusual in many suburban, primarily White middle schools and high schools to see young people identifying principally with urban hip-hop culture, even though many of these young people have never lived in cities or known people of color. Recognizing the complexity in culture allows us to understand the many and varied identities taken on by young people.

INFLUENCE OF CULTURE ON LEARNING

Learning is at the core of our discussion of culture. That is, we are not interested in exploring culture simply for the sake of developing awareness of cultural differences, or sensitivity to students of diverse backgrounds. These are also important goals, but considering the troubling history of underachievement and marginalization of students of particular backgrounds in our schools—especially students of color and poor students of all backgrounds—educators must first examine how culture may influence learning and achievement in school.

In this book, we suggest looking at culture through an anthropological lens. Much of the research reported here, and from which part of the conceptual framework for multicultural education has been developed, is *ethnographic research*—that is, educational research based on anthropological constructs that include methods such as field work, interviews, and participant observation. More than 30 years ago, Ray McDermott defined ethnography as "any rigorous attempt to account for people's behavior in terms of their relations with those around them in different situations."[9] In educational anthropology, this means looking at schools as cultural sites and at teachers and students as cultural agents. This area of research has profoundly affected educational thinking in the past 30 years, especially in educational settings characterized by cultural diversity.[10]

While culture is integral to the learning process, it may affect individuals differently. For instance, while it may be true that Appalachian people share a rich heritage that includes a strong sense of kinship, the culture may not have the same effect on every child.[11] In other words, *culture is not destiny*. Given differences in social class and family structure, individual psychological and emotional differences and experiences, birth order, residence and a host of individual distinctions, it would be folly to think that culture alone accounts for all human differences. Anyone who has children can confirm this truth: Two offspring from the same parents, with the same culture and social class, and raised in substantially the same way, can turn out to be as different as night and day. Hence, culture is neither static nor deterministic; it gives us just one way in which to better understand differences among students. The assumption that culture is the primary determinant of academic achievement can be oversimplistic, dangerous, and counterproductive because, although culture may *influence*, it does not *determine* who we are.

Everyone has a culture, but many times, members of the culturally dominant group of a society do not even think of themselves as cultural beings. For them, culture is something that other people have, especially people who differ from the mainstream in race or ethnicity. This thinking is reflected in the case of Vanessa Mattison at the end of Chapter 4. The problem with conceptualizing culture in this way is that it tends to "exoticize" those people who are not in the cultural mainstream. A more complicated view of culture is needed, especially among teachers whose classrooms are becoming more diverse every day. There are vast differences among learners within ethnic groups, and these differences may be due not just to culture but also to social class, language spoken at home, number of years or generations in the United States, and simple individual differences.

Let us take the example of social class, an aspect of identity that may be as important as ethnicity in influencing learning. Because membership within a particular social group is based on economic factors as well as cultural values, the working class may differ from the middle class not only in particular values and practices but also in the amount and kinds of economic resources they have at their disposal. Because of these differences, gross generalizations may be made, thus perpetuating what has been called "the culture of poverty," that is, a view of poverty that sees the poor as having no culture or having a culture that is without any merit whatsoever. Thus, the "culture of poverty" pathologizes the values and actions of working class and poor people.

An example is the work of Ruby Payne, an educator whose ideas on poverty have been propagated throughout the country.[12] Her framework for understanding poverty has been wholeheartedly accepted by some and harshly criticized by others. Paul Gorski, an educational researcher, has been particularly critical of Payne's framework.[13] According to him, Payne fails to base her arguments on creditable research; she also neglects addressing such issues as the root causes of poverty and the tendency for students living in poverty to become the victims of substandard schooling, as described in Chapter 5. While Payne asserts that people in poverty do not value education—a claim unfortunately voiced by many educators who work with poor children—Gorski reviews research that refutes this claim. A major problem with Payne's analysis is that it supports a deficit perspective of students and families living in poverty. Such a perspective leaves little hope for students' academic success or for high expectations of them on the part of teachers and schools. Far better analyses of poverty, which educators need to become acquainted with, are grounded in an understanding of the larger structural issues that create and sustain poverty.[14] Rather than rely on frameworks such as Payne's, teachers would do better to reject deficit perspectives and instead work to create learning environments that are as challenging and nurturing for students living in poverty as they are for more economically privileged students.

Notwithstanding these caveats about overdetermining its significance, we want to emphasize that culture *is* important. One reason for insisting on the significance of culture is that some people, primarily those from dominated and disenfranchised groups within society, have been taught that they have no culture. This has resulted in, among other things, what Felix Boateng has called *deculturalization*, that is, a process by which people are first deprived of their own culture and then conditioned into embracing other cultural values.[15] This is how the patronizing term *cultural deprivation* has come to imply that a group is without culture altogether, although in reality what it means is that some people do not share in the culture of the dominant group. Everybody has a culture—that is, everybody has the ability to create and recreate ideas and material goods and to affect their world in a variety of ways.

Multicultural education is one way of counteracting the notion that culture is reserved for the privileged. For example, Hoang Vinh, although only 18 years old when he was interviewed, had a more sophisticated understanding of culture than many adults do. As you will see in his case study, Vinh described Vietnamese cultural values, behaviors, and expectations without falling into simplistic explanations for complex phenomena. He was also very accurate in pointing out cultural differences between his teachers in Vietnam and the United States: He said that one of his teachers, Ms. Mitchell, expected all students to do things in the same way but that people from other countries "have different ideas, so they might think about school in different ways. . . . So she has to learn about that culture." As one example, he described how his English teachers praised him for his fluency in English, although he felt that instead they should have been telling him to study more. He concluded, "But that's the way the American culture is. But my culture is not like that."

Cultural differences in learning may be especially apparent in three areas: *learning styles* or *preferences, interactional* or *communication styles,* and *language differences.* Examples of the first two areas are explored next in this chapter. Language and language issues are considered more fully in Chapter 7 although it should be understood that language is a major component of culture and is also part of the discussion here.

LEARNING STYLES AND PREFERENCES

Learning style is usually defined as the way in which individuals receive and process information.[16] Exactly how culture influences learning is unclear. Early research on learning style maintained that mothers' (or primary caregivers') child-rearing practices are, in large part, responsible for the learning styles that children develop. The case was made that the values, attitudes, and behaviors taught at home become the basis for how children learn to learn.[17] In spite of the advances made in understanding how culture might influence learning, the linear process implied by this theory is not convincing. In fact, some of the early research in this field concentrated on ethnic and racial differences in learning, a perspective that can skirt dangerously close to racist perceptions of differences in IQ.

We prefer the term *learning preferences* because it is a more flexible way of approaching differences in learning. A focus on rigid learning styles is problematic because of its tendency to dichotomize learning (see note 17); it is doubtful that a process as complex as learning can be characterized as having only two poles. A good example is the case of Hoang Vinh, who loved working in cooperative groups, a learning preference that is not usually associated with Vietnamese students. Thus, although learning-style research can be helpful in identifying learning differences related to ethnicity and culture, it also runs the risk of oversimplification and stereotyping and can be used as a rationale for poor or inequitable teaching.

A graphic example of the misapplication of learning-style theory can be found in an early research study in this field by Flora Ida Ortiz. She found that teachers used the "cooperative" attribute from the learning-style literature concerning Hispanics to justify a number of clearly discriminatory pedagogical decisions.[18] Teachers rationalized that Hispanics would be more likely to feel uncomfortable in the limelight or in leadership roles. They also reasoned that Hispanic children liked to share books because of their preference for working cooperatively. As a result, in integrated classrooms in which Hispanic children were present, teachers seldom granted them solo performances in plays or leadership activities in other situations. Teachers placed them in activities the students themselves had not chosen, whereas other children were allowed choices, and teachers had them share books when there were not enough to go around, whereas the non-Hispanic students could have individual copies. The result of these actions was that Hispanic students had less access to materials and a less enriching curriculum than others. Consequently, any negative preconceived notions of children's ability that teachers may have had were reinforced by faulty interpretations of research. It is a good example of the truism, "A little knowledge is a dangerous thing."

Similarly, in a comprehensive review of research on American Indian and Alaska Native education, Donna Deyhle and Karen Swisher concluded that learning-style research can point to meaningful adaptations that may improve the educational outcomes of these students, but they also warned of the detrimental consequences of viewing learning-style research uncritically. Specifically, they pointed out that the depiction of the "nonverbal" Indian child is reinforced when teachers read that American Indian students prefer observation to performance. Deyhle and Swisher conclude:

> The power relations in the classroom, rather than the Indian child as culturally or inherently "nonverbal," are central to understanding the nonparticipatory behavior observed in many Indian classrooms. In these "silent" classrooms, communication is controlled by the teacher, who accepts only one correct answer and singles out individuals to respond to questions for which they have little background knowledge.[19]

An example of debilitating power relations can be seen in the case study of James Karam that follows this chapter. Although the Arabic language and Lebanese culture were very important to James, they were virtually invisible in his school. As a result, he learned to de-emphasize them in the school setting. (Needless to say, this kind of "invisibility" of Arab Americans and their culture disappeared after the events of 9/11.)

Thus, child-rearing practices alone, although they may influence children's learning preferences, do not offer a sufficient explanation. Other circumstances such as power relationships and status differentials are also at work, and these may be even more substantial than child-rearing practices. These power differentials are evident in Rebecca Florentina's comments, summarized in her case study following this chapter. Quite astute in understanding how curriculum and pedagogy can malign students' identities, Rebecca suggested that the major problem in health class was the curriculum and that one way to address this problem was to "get the health teachers to put better curriculum for teaching about same sex, transgender, anything, you know?"

Although not specifically related to cultural differences, Howard Gardner's theory of "multiple intelligences" (MI) has implications for culturally compatible education.[20] According to this theory, each human being is capable of at least eight relatively independent forms of information processing, and each of these is a specific "intelligence." These intelligences include logical-mathematical, linguistic (the two most emphasized in school success), musical, spatial, bodily kinesthetic, interpersonal, naturalistic, and intrapersonal. Accordingly, Gardner defines *intelligence* as the ability to solve problems or develop products that are valued in a particular cultural setting. The salience of cultural differences in intelligence is evident. Gardner's research has demonstrated that individuals differ in the specific profile of intelligences that they exhibit, and these differences may be influenced by what is valued in their culture. Because a broader range of abilities is acknowledged in this conception of intelligence, previously discounted talents of individuals can be considered in a new light.

The theory of multiple intelligences may have significant implications for multicultural education because this theory goes beyond the limited definition of intelligence valued in most schools. For one, it breaks out of the rigid definition of intelligence as book knowledge or doing well on standardized tests. As a result, the theory may be particularly helpful in challenging current assessment practices that focus almost exclusively on logical-mathematical and linguistic intelligence. The danger, as always, lies in extrapolating from individual cases to an entire group. Although it may be true, for example, that a certain culture—because of its social, geographic, or political circumstances—is more highly developed in one kind of intelligence than other cultures, educators should not conclude that all the group's members will manifest this intelligence equally. They should also not assume that individuals from this culture are *primarily* or *only* intelligent in one way and, therefore, unable to develop intelligence in other areas.

COMMUNICATION STYLE

Cultural influences can be found in interactional or communication styles, that is, the ways individuals interact with one another and the messages they send, intentionally or not, in their communications. According to Geneva Gay, communication is much more than the content and structuring of written and spoken language. She states,

> Sociocultural context and nuances, discourse logic and dynamics, delivery styles, social functions, role expectations, norms of interaction, and nonverbal gestures are as important (if not more so) than vocabulary, grammar, lexicon, pronunciation, and other linguistic structural dimensions of communication.[21]

WHAT YOU CAN DO

RESPECT AND AFFIRM STUDENT DIFFERENCES

Learning how to understand cultural differences does not mean simply learning about culture. Knowing about *Cinco de Mayo* in the Mexican American community or about health practices among Vietnamese will do little to prepare you for day-to-day experiences with students of diverse backgrounds. Because culture is constantly changing, we cannot view it as static and unvarying. A more promising approach is to reflect on how cultural differences may affect your students' learning and to be open to changing your curriculum and pedagogy accordingly. Therefore, when facing cultural differences, always ask yourself the question "Who does the accommodating?" Is it always students from nonmajority cultures?

Here are some specific strategies:

1. To accommodate the learning preferences of all your students, plan a variety of activities so that all students' preferences are accommodated. Students who are comfortable working in groups should have the opportunity to do so and so should students who are not used to this style of working. The point is not to segregate students according to their preferences, but rather to have all students develop skills in a broad range of activities.

2. Investigate out-of-school activities in which your students are engaged (e.g., art, performances, music, athletics). As much as is possible, use such activities in the school to motivate students to learn school-related subjects.

3. Learn to think of yourself as a life-long learner. Listen to and watch a variety of news sources, read books about different cultural and racial experiences, and be open to other experiences that will broaden your outlook beyond your town, cultural group, and nation.

If teachers and schools are unaware of these differences and the impact they can have on learning, the result may be cultural conflict that leads to school failure. School failure, in this case, can be understood as the product of miscommunication between teachers and students and a rational adaptation by students who are devalued by schools. Following this line of thought, unless changes are made in learning environments, school failure may be inevitable.

On the basis of his extensive review of culturally compatible education, Roland Tharp concluded that when schools become more attuned to children's cultures, academic achievement improves.[22] Tharp has suggested at least four cultural variables related to communication that may be at odds with the expectations and structures of schools: *social organization, sociolinguistics, cognition,* and *motivation.* An example or two will suffice to demonstrate the complex interplay among them. Social organization, for instance, refers to the ways classrooms are organized. Tharp suggests that the traditional U.S. whole-class organization, with "rank-and-file" seating and a teacher/leader who instructs or demonstrates, is not necessarily the best arrangement for all children. In the area of sociolinguistics, Tharp explains how short "wait times" (that is, the length of time teachers wait for student responses) may be disadvantageous for American Indian students, who generally take longer to respond to teachers' questions because their culture emphasizes deliberate thought.

How relationships between students and teachers can be either improved or damaged by their interactions is another pertinent area of research. As an example, students and teachers from the same background are often on the same wavelength simply because they have an insider's understanding of cultural meanings and therefore do not have to figure out the verbal and nonverbal messages they are sending. Michele Foster examined how a shared cultural background or shared norms about how language is used in African American communities can benefit classroom interactions. She found that, in classrooms of African American students taught by African American teachers, there are subtle but significant interactional differences from other classrooms. For example, she documented the positive classroom effect of one African American teacher who used Standard English to regulate student behavior, but "performances" (i.e., what Foster described as stylized ways of speaking that resemble African American preaching style) to relate the everyday life experiences of her students to more abstract concepts.[23] Another example of communication style comes from more recent research on urban youth culture: Ernest Morrell and Jeff Duncan-Andrade used their students' involvement with hip-hop culture to successfully engage them in literacy learning.[24]

Carol Lee's research on the literacy practices of African American high school students also showed that cultural resources support learning. In analyzing students' everyday practices, Lee found that African American students who speak Ebonics, or what she calls *African American Vernacular English* (*AAVE*), consistently use irony, satire, and symbolism in their everyday talk, especially in the speech genre *signifying*, that is, ritualistic insults and other word games. Because of their creative use of language, Lee reasoned that building on this kind of knowledge and skills would be an effective basis for a literature curriculum because, in Lee's words, "Use of rhythm, alliteration, metaphor, irony, and satire are routine in the language practices of this speech community."[25] As a result of this understanding, Lee developed the Cultural Modeling Project, a four-year literature curriculum that has been implemented in a large midwestern city. The result: Students at all grade levels have achieved beyond what their standardized reading scores predicted.

Cultural differences probably influence students in more ways than we can imagine. For example, take the case of Susan, a new teacher who was attending a workshop being given by me (Sonia) many years ago. Susan was a young teacher of English as a Second Language (ESL) to Puerto Rican students. Although she was sincerely committed to her students' achievement, she was unaware of many aspects of their culture. The Puerto Rican children, most of whom had recently arrived in the United States, used the communication style typical of their culture. For example, many Puerto Ricans wrinkle their noses to signify "What?" When Susan would ask the children if they understood the lesson, some would invariably wrinkle their noses. Not understanding this gesture, Susan simply went on with the lesson, assuming that their nose wrinkling had no meaning.

Two years after first being exposed to this behavior, while attending a workshop in which we discussed Puerto Rican gestures and the work of Carmen Judith Nine-Curt in the area of nonverbal communication, Susan learned that nose wrinkling

---

WHAT YOU CAN DO

RESEARCH FAMILY "FUNDS OF KNOWLEDGE"

Explore who your students are, what makes them "tick," and the values and life skills of their families. Doing so will help you understand the strengths that families have, rather than focusing on assumed weaknesses or deficits.

If you are an elementary level teacher, make it a point to visit your students' families at least once a year. Focus on learning about what Norma Gonzalez, Luis Moll, and Cathy Amanti have called "families' funds of knowledge"—that is, their skills and competencies—and think about how you can use these in your curriculum. To learn more about doing such research, see their book.*

Considering the large number of students they teach, it is unrealistic to expect secondary school teachers to engage in such research. However, there are other projects that can help you become familiar with your students' cultures and identities. Oral histories are an excellent way to learn about your students' family histories, challenges, and triumphs, and oral histories do not need to be confined to the English or social studies class. Math, health, science, art, and other subject matters are fertile ground for case studies. You'll be surprised at how much you can learn—and use in your curriculum—from conducting this kind of project.

*Norma E. Gonzalez, Luis C. Moll, and Cathy Amanti (eds.), Funds of Knowledge: Theorizing Practices in Households and Classrooms (Mahwah, NJ: Lawrence Erlbaum, 2005).

---

among Puerto Ricans was a way of asking "What?" or "What do you mean?" or of saying, "I don't understand."[26] From then on, Susan understood that, when they exhibited this form of nonverbal communication, her students were asking for help or for further clarification. We all laughed about it that day in the workshop, but this humorous anecdote is not without its serious consequences. Students whose culture, verbal or nonverbal, is unacknowledged or misunderstood in their classrooms are likely to feel alienated, unwelcome, and out of place.

Similar miscommunication happens between teachers and students of other backgrounds as well. Promoting teachers' familiarity with communication differences would go a long way in helping teachers transform their curriculum to address their students' backgrounds more adequately. The communication styles explored here are only the tip of the iceberg, but they help to point out the sometimes subtle ways that culture, if not understood, can interfere with learning.

CULTURAL DISCONTINUITIES AND SCHOOL ACHIEVEMENT

Cultural discontinuities, that is, the lack of congruence between home and school cultures, may cause numerous problems for students from culturally marginalized groups. A review of some of the literature on culture-specific educational accommodations can pinpoint how discontinuities between schools and students may lead to negative academic outcomes.

A classic research study that paved the way for numerous other studies by anthropologists, sociolinguists, and educators was done by Shirley Brice Heath in the Piedmont Carolinas during the 1970s.[27] In exploring the language of Black children at home and at school, she found that different ways of using language resulted in tensions between the children and their mostly White teachers in the classroom. For example, the children were not accustomed to answering questions concerning the attributes of objects (color, size, shape, and so on), the kinds of questions that typically occur in classroom discourse as well as in middle-class homes (i.e., "what color is the car?" "How many dolls are there?"). Instead, the children generally used descriptive language at home mostly for storytelling and other purposes. The result was a communication breakdown, with teachers believing that many of the students were "slow" and students perceiving a lack of support from teachers. Through research coordinated by Heath, the teachers began to experiment with different ways of asking questions. The result was that teachers helped children bridge the gap between their home and school experiences and thus the children's language use in the classroom was enhanced.

The culture and language children bring to school are often disregarded and replaced, and this situation can have dire consequences. In the words of Geneva Gay, "Decontextualizing teaching and learning from the ethnicities and cultures of students minimizes the chances that their achievement potential will ever be fully realized."[28] A teacher's best intentions may be ineffective if students' cultural differences are neglected in curriculum and instruction, and this is underscored by another classic ethnographic research. Susan Philips's research on the Warm Springs Reservation is a powerful example that points out the problems that can emerge when teachers are not familiar with their students' culture.[29] In the case of American Indians, the core values of respect and value for the dignity of the individual, harmony, internal locus of control, cooperation, and sharing inevitably influence students' reactions to their educational experiences. Philips found that students performed poorly in classroom contexts that demanded individualized performance and emphasized competition. On the other hand, their performance improved greatly when the context did not require students to perform in public and when cooperation was valued over competition. As Philips's study demonstrated, cooperative learning, which is compatible with the values of many American Indian families, is an approach worth exploring in classes with American Indian children. It may be helpful in other settings as well. Other research on American Indian students as well as African American students has reached similar conclusions about how cultural incompatibilities can influence student learning.[30]

A very different example might come from the experiences of a newly arrived Vietnamese immigrant attending a U.S. school. Such a child might feel extremely off balance and uncomfortable in a classroom environment in which teachers are informal and friendly, students are expected to ask questions and speak in front of the class, and group work is the order of the day.[31] The cultural discontinuity that exists in an educational environment in which teachers are revered and have a formal relationship with their students, and where learning is based on listening and memorizing, can be a dramatic one. Nevertheless, as we shall see in Hoang Vinh's case study, not all Vietnamese students react this way, because there are countless differences among people from the same cultural group.

Cultural discontinuities, however, do not develop simply because of differing cultural values among groups. There is often a direct connection between culture and the *sociopolitical context of schooling*. One example of the link between sociopolitical context and culture is the remarkable academic success of South Asian students in U.S. schools. The prevailing explanation for their success is that the cultural values of South Asian students are congruent with the academic culture of schools. Although this may be true, it alone is not sufficient to explain their success. The fact that the parents of South Asian students are the most highly educated among all immigrants is also a factor. For instance, Heather Kim has documented that an extraordinary 87 percent of South Asian fathers and 70 percent of South Asian mothers have a college degree or higher, compared to 31 percent of United States parents. The Asian American students who perform best on tests are generally those whose parents have the most education. They comprise the highest proportion of children of immigrants born in the United States, compared to the proportion of children of other immigrant populations.[32] As we can see, culture cannot easily be separated from other issues such as social class, parents' level of education, and students' access to higher education.

The sociopolitical link is further highlighted by research on the practice, in the late 19th and early 20th centuries, of sending American Indian students to distant boarding schools. Attending such schools meant that students were physically separated from their parents and consequently from their cultural connections. Moreover, the very purpose of such schools was to eradicate students' native language and culture in an attempt to "Americanize" them.[33] The dropout rate among these students was very high because of the school-related social and emotional problems they experienced. Although the dropout rate of Native Americans remains high in some areas, it has been reduced dramatically in cases where secondary education has been returned to local communities.[34]

Becoming aware of the sociopolitical context of education is important for other reasons as well. For instance, Deyhle and Swisher, in their research on American Indians, have expressed the concern that educators sometimes use the cultural discontinuity theory to argue only for a culturally compatible curriculum to solve the dropout problem.[35] In so doing, educators may neglect to confront other more pressing problems in American Indian and Alaskan Native schools, such as the lack of equitable financing and appropriate resources. The same concerns apply to students other nonmainstream backgrounds.[36] An example can be found in the case of LGBT students who may not do well in school. The problem is likely not their lack of intelligence or a cultural mismatch with the school, but rather the rejection they experience in school as a result of the school's unwelcoming climate. Changing the curriculum would probably help, but in some cases, LGBT students may decide that dropping out of school is the only recourse they have. Rebecca Florentina, in the case study that follows this chapter, mentions a number of friends who have felt the need to do so.

These examples demonstrate that cultural incompatibilities are varied and complex. Research concerning them is vital if we are to grasp how children from different cultural backgrounds respond to teachers' behaviors and what teachers can do to change how they teach. However, no single solution will bridge the gap between the school and home cultures of all students.

CULTURE-SPECIFIC EDUCATIONAL ACCOMMODATIONS

Various approaches and programs have been designed to provide for the particular educational needs of students from specific cultural groups, and some of these programs have proved to be extremely successful. A number of examples of modifications to make instruction more culturally appropriate reveal the reasoning behind the approach known variously as *culturally compatible, culturally congruent, culturally appropriate, culturally responsive,* or *culturally relevant instruction.*[37]

The Kamehameha Elementary Education Program (KEEP) in Hawaii, which was in existence from the late 1970s to the mid-1990s, is an example of using a culturally specific approach in teaching.[38] KEEP was begun when perceived cultural discontinuities in instruction were identified as a major problem in the poor academic achievement of Native Hawaiian children. As a privately funded, multidisciplinary educational research effort, KEEP's purpose was to explore remedies for Hawaiian children's chronic academic underachievement by changing certain educational practices: changing from a phonics approach to one emphasizing comprehension; from individual work desks to work centers for heterogeneous groups; and from high praise to more culturally appropriate praise, including indirect and group praise. The KEEP culturally compatible kindergarten (K) through grade 3 language arts program met with great success, including significant gains in reading achievement. One explanation for the success of the program is that instruction was modified to more closely match the children's cultural styles. The move from phonics to comprehension, for instance, allowed the students to contribute in a speech style called the *talk-story*, which is a familiar linguistic event in the Hawaiian community. Other instructional changes, including a preference for cooperative work and group accomplishment, were also compatible with Native Hawaiian culture.

There are other challenges in Native Hawaiian education, however, and these often have more to do with the sociopolitical context than with the children's learning preferences. According to Margaret Maaka, "In Hawai'i, a place of many cultures, the English-only ideology is firmly entrenched in all levels of the education system."[39] In the past two decades, a major focus of Native Hawaiian education has been language preservation. In 1896, the Hawaiian language was outlawed as a language of instruction, and as a result, there are fewer Native Hawaiian speakers each year. In 1984, the movement to preserve the Hawaiian language began with the opening of the first Punana Leo Hawaiian language immersion preschool. In addition, the

Kamehameha Schools, which serve students in grades K–12, are recognized for their language-based immersion program to preserve both the Native Hawaiian language and the Hawaiian culture. According to Sarah Keahi, a Native Hawaiian educator, "As indigenous educators, we know that a culture and its language are inseparable, for the language is the vehicle by which the culture is transmitted."[40]

Sometimes, new teachers of students of culturally marginalized backgrounds assume that they cannot expect very much of their students, especially if these students are also economically poor, yet the opposite is true. Research on the pedagogy of teachers of students of diverse backgrounds provides convincing illustrations of how teachers use cultural knowledge and experiences to overcome some of the debilitating and negative messages of schools and society. It also documents how the most effective teachers challenge students rather than let them "slide." Jacqueline Jordan Irvine and James Fraser describe culturally responsive teachers of African American students as "warm demanders," that is, teachers who are affectionate and loving while they are tough and rigorous in their expectations.[41] Gloria Ladson-Billings's research of effective teachers of African American students also documents how successful teachers use students' culture as a bridge to the dominant culture. The pedagogy of the effective teachers she describes is empowering because, rather than simply teach students blind acceptance of the inherent values of the dominant culture, these teachers encourage students to think critically and work actively for social justice.[42] In addition to considering the competencies of teachers who are successful with African American students, these studies document additional effective practices, including teachers' use of interactive rather than didactic methods and the high standards they set for students.

The opposite of culturally relevant teaching happens when teachers create what Joanne Larson and Patricia Irvine have called *reciprocal distancing*. This occurs when the ways in which teachers and students talk about and to each other—ways that often indicate their unique sociocultural realities and knowledge—create distances that can negatively affect students' learning. In a study in an urban school district in the Northeast, Larson and Irvine found that, in spite of teachers' best efforts, their negative or deficit-based beliefs about their culturally and linguistically diverse students might contribute to reciprocal distancing. The researchers cite a specific case concerning a conversation about Dr. Martin Luther King, Jr., in a first-grade classroom. Larson and Irvine found that the teacher continually referred to him without a title, while the students corrected the teacher by saying, "*We* call him Dr. King." Whether teachers meant to or not, through their discourse, they were creating distances that would be difficult to close later on. According to Larson and Irvine, the result was that "linguistically and culturally diverse students learn their place in a stratified society."[43]

This situation, however, is not inevitable. In a case study of a Yup'ik Eskimo teacher teaching Yup'ik students, Jerry Lipka, Gerald Mohatt, and the Ciulistet Group documented how adapting the social interactions, knowledge, and values to the students' culture could be an important way to improve schooling. These researchers concluded that when Yup'ik teachers taught Yup'ik children and related to them in culturally compatible ways, conflict was reduced and school failure was diminished.[44] A major finding of this study was that relationships are at the center of any culturally responsive pedagogy (a topic we return to in more depth in Chapter 8). This is not to suggest that Yup'ik students are successful learners *only* when taught by Yup'ik teachers. Ethnicity is not the only variable here; rather, this case demonstrates that teachers' interactional style and the relationship between the students and teachers helps bolster student success. The good news is that teachers of any background can learn to be culturally responsive.

An illustration in which the cultural identity of teachers and students was not always the same is found in research by Jason Irizarry. Drawing on a larger ethnographic study in the Northeast, he highlighted "Mr. Talbert" (a pseudonym), an African American teacher who had been recommended by parents, community leaders, and other educators as effective with Latino students. Irizarry found that Mr. Talbert used a variety of practices, including *community connections* (sharing personal stories, living in the same community, and knowing what went on in the neighborhood); *language* (that is, supporting various uses of written and spoken language of students including Ebonics, or Black English); and *music* (particularly rap) to relate to his students, while he also demanded high-quality work from them. Although Irizarry was particularly interested in what might "work" for Latino students, what he found instead was a predisposition on the part of Mr. Talbert and the other teachers he studied (who were of Latino, White, and African American backgrounds) to engage with students and their families, to learn about their realities—including how they identify—and to shift their pedagogy accordingly. As a result, the culture of Mr. Talbert's class was negotiated and co-constructed. In the many moving examples provided by Irizarry about how teachers of various backgrounds relate to Latino students, one senses that culturally responsive pedagogy is, more than anything, about *making connections with students*. To describe the practices of particularly effective teachers such as Mr. Talbert, Irizarry coined the term "culturally connected teachers." As one Latino student explained, "Mr. Talbert is the first teacher to ever care about where I'm from and what I'm about. That's love."[45]

Many teachers intuitively and consistently make such modifications, both in their curriculum and in their instructional practices. A good example is a classic study on the subject by Frederick Erickson and Gerald Mohatt. Their research focused on the social relationships in two classrooms of culturally similar American Indian children, one taught by an American Indian and the other by a non-American Indian.[46] Although the classroom organizations differed substantially at the beginning of the year (the American Indian teacher's setup was more consistent with students' cultural understandings), by the end of the year, the non-American Indian teacher had adapted his instructional practices to be more culturally congruent. The non-American Indian teacher, for example, began seating children in table groups rather than individually in rows, and he also began to spend more time on small-group lessons and tutoring than on whole-group lessons. This teacher used what Erickson and Mohatt call *teacher radar* to figure out what he needed to do to connect with his students. The result was a culturally congruent classroom, apparently arrived at intuitively.

A more recent example of developing culturally congruent teaching practices is reported in research by Cynthia Ballenger. A teacher of preschool Haitian children and the only non-Haitian educator in the school, Ballenger documented how she learned to be a culturally responsive teacher from the children themselves. Initially unfamiliar and even uncomfortable with their ways of learning, Ballenger recounts how she expected to see deficits in the children, not because she thought their background was deficient, but because she did not know how to appreciate their strengths. After listening to and learning from the children and other staff members, Ballenger began to adopt some of the styles of the Haitian teachers. She relied on the children's responses to her practices and concluded, "I can tell when I have it more or less right because of the way the children pay attention."[47] The lesson is clear: Heeding what children do and say can make a difference in how teachers interact with them and, consequently, in how well children learn.

These dramatic examples focus on one cultural group in a school, but changes in instruction and curriculum that reflect the *multicultural character* of most schools are also possible. For example, most schools favor a highly competitive and individualistic instructional mode in which only some of the students may be successful. By combining this style with a more cooperative mode, the learning and cultural styles of all children can be respected and valued. The lesson is that, although all schools cannot become *culturally compatible*, they can become *multiculturally sensitive*.

A Critical Appraisal of Culture-Specific Accommodations

In spite of their usefulness, culture-specific accommodations are limited by several factors. First, the diversity of the student population in most schools mitigates culturally specific modifications. Many schools are multicultural, with students from diverse ethnic, social class, and linguistic backgrounds. There are few totally homogeneous schools, and designing a school to be culturally compatible with just one group of students, even if it is the most numerous group, might jeopardize students of other backgrounds—that is, if schools change their instructional strategies to be compatible with students from just one ethnic group, these strategies might be the opposite of what students from other backgrounds need.

Another problem with making educational choices that are solely culturally compatible is that it may lead to segregation being posited as the most effective solution to educational failure. Although segregation might sometimes be warranted, the truth is that history has amply demonstrated that it often leads to inequality. When speaking of culturally dominated groups, "separate but equal" is rarely that; on the contrary, segregation generally means that powerless groups end up with an inferior education because they are given the fewest material resources for their education. Nevertheless, although U.S. courts in the second half of the 20th century upheld integration as a positive goal to strive for because it purportedly leads to increased educational equality, we know that this is not always the result. In fact, as discussed in Chapter 5, segregation is today more prevalent than it has been in decades. Even when schools are desegregated in name, sometimes they are segregated in other ways, especially through tracking in gifted and talented, special education, and other such programs.

We need to distinguish between different kinds of segregation. Segregation imposed by a dominant group is far different from the self-segregation demanded by a dominated, subordinate group that sees through the persistent racism hidden behind the veneer of equality in integrated settings. This is the reasoning behind Afrocentric, American Indian, Latino, or other culturally based schools. Even in these cases, however, culturally separate schools may effectively isolate themselves from receiving some of the benefits of the public school system that might help them meet the needs of the children they serve. Thus, although qualitatively different from segregated schools because they are developed by disempowered communities, culturally homogeneous schools are not always effective. Furthermore, there are numerous cases of students of culturally diverse backgrounds who have been successfully educated in what might be considered culturally incompatible settings. Other factors unrelated to cultural conflict must be involved.

A further problem with culturally congruent education is the implication that all students from a particular group learn in more or less the same way. This assertion is problematic because it *essentializes* culture, that is, it assumes that culture consists of specific elements that can be applied uncritically to all people within particular groups. Thus, essentializing can lead to generalizations and stereotypes that get in the way of viewing students as individuals as well as of members of groups whose cultures are constantly evolving.

In spite of all these caveats, it must be recognized, however, that our public schools are not providing many students—particularly Latino, African American, and American Indian students living in poverty—with the education they deserve. Until they do so, we need to find ways to help these students succeed, and culturally responsive pedagogy, even in segregated settings, is certainly one such approach. Nonetheless, if such programs or schools are based on the notion that culture is unchanging, they are bound to face problems.

SUMMARY

This chapter discussed how culture can influence learning in crucial ways. Using learning-style research, educators began to understand how students of different backgrounds might differ in their learning preferences. More recent methodologies of ethnographic investigation have yielded important findings that can also help teachers and schools recognize the possible impact of culture on learning. Modifications can be made in communication style, program design, and instruction to support the learning of students of diverse backgrounds. However, because using only a cultural analysis concerning learning is limited, the chapter ended with a critical analysis of some of the problems with culture-specific accommodations and an exploration of hybridity, a useful way to understand culture with an increasingly diverse and complex student body.

Ultimately, however, culture matters. Learning cannot take place in settings where students' cultures—broadly defined to include race, ethnicity, social class, language, and other elements such as urban and adolescent identity—are devalued and rejected. Teachers who want to provide all students with a caring and stimulating environment for learning have to take into account their backgrounds and identities. This means learning *about* and *from* their students and those closest to them and making the accommodations necessary to promote their students' learning.

◆◆◆ To Think About

1. What are the advantages of being colorblind? What are the disadvantages? Give some examples of each related to classrooms or schools.

2. What do we mean when we say "Equal is not the same"? To help you consider this question, think about some of the students you know.

3. Can you identify any pedagogical strategies that have seemed to be successful with particular children? How can you use these with students of various cultures?

4. Numerous educators have suggested that traditional seating in rows and conventional "chalk-and-talk" strategies are not appropriate learning environments for a great number of students. What do you think? What does this mean for classroom organization? Is there a difference in the effectiveness of these strategies for elementary versus secondary schools? Suggest some alternatives to the traditional classroom organization and pedagogy that might give more students an equal chance to learn.

5. Given the contradictory messages between home and school that children of various backgrounds receive, it is possible that they will end up rejecting their parents' culture and way of life. What can teachers and schools do to minimize this situation?

◆◆◆ Activities for Personal, School, and Community Change

1. Observe three different students in a classroom. How would you characterize their learning preferences? How do they differ? Do you think these differences have something to do with their gender, race, ethnicity, social class, or other difference? Why or why not? What are the implications for teaching these children?

2. What steps could you take to make your classroom more culturally compatible with the student body? Consider changes in curriculum, organization, use of materials, and pedagogical strategies. Try some of these out and keep a journal of your reflections on the effect they have on students.

3. Consider some of the ways your school can become a culturally welcoming place for students of various backgrounds. For example, what kinds of school-wide rituals can be developed that would make all students feel that they belong? What about parent outreach? What can be done in the hallways and on bulletin boards? Suggest some of these changes to your principal or department head.

Companion Website

For access to additional case studies, weblinks, concept cards, and other material related to this chapter, visit the text's companion website at **www.ablongman.com/nieto5e.**

Notes to Chapter 6

1. *Lau v. Nichols*, 414 U.S. 563. St. Paul, MN: West Publishing (1974).

2. Beverly Daniel Tatum, *"Why Are All the Black Kids Sitting Together in the Cafeteria?" And Other Conversations About Race* (New York: HarperCollins, 1997); Gary Howard, *"We Can't Teach What We Don't Know": White Teachers, Multiracial Schools*, 2nd ed. (New York: Teachers College Press, 2006); Charmaine L. Wijeyesinghe and Bailey W. Jackson, III, eds., *New Perspectives on Racial Identity Development: A Theoretical and Practical Anthology* (New York: New York University Press, May 2001).

3. Kris D. Gutierrez and Barbara Rogoff, "Cultural Ways of Learning: Individual Traits or Repertoires of Practice." *Educational Researcher* 32, no. 5: 19–25, p. 19.

4. Alejandra M. Lopez, "Mixed-Race School-Age Children: A Summary of Census 2000 Data." *Educational Researcher* 32, no. 6 (August/September 2003): 25–37.

5. Laurie Olsen, (1997). *Made in America: Immigrant Students in Our Public Schools* (New York: New Press, 1997): 55.

6. Pedro Noguera, "Joaquín's Dilemma: Understanding the Link Between Racial Identity and School-Related Behaviors." In *Adolescents at School: Perspectives on Youth, Identity, and Education*, edited by Michael Sadowski (Cambridge, MA: Harvard Education Press): 19–30.

7. Daniel A. Yon, *Elusive Culture: Schooling, Race, and Identity in Global Times* (Albany: State University of New York Press, 2000).

8. Nadine Dolby, "Changing Selves: Multicultural Education and the Challenge of New Identities." *Teachers College Record* 102, no. 5 (2000): 898–912.

9. R. P. McDermott, "Social Relations as Contexts for Learning in School." *Harvard Educational Review* 47, no. 2 (May 1977): 198–213.

10. Shirley Brice Heath, "Ethnography in Communities: Learning the Everyday Life of America's Subordinated Youth." In *Handbook of Research on Multicultural Education*, 2nd ed., edited by James A. Banks and Cherry A. McGee Banks (San Francisco: Jossey-Bass, 2004): 146–162.

11. See, for example, Rebecca Eller-Powell, "Teaching for Change in Appalachia." In *Teaching Diverse Populations: Formulating a Knowledge Base*, edited by Etta R. Hollins, Joyce E. King, and Warren C. Hayman (Albany: State University of New York Press, 1994).

12. Ruby Payne, *A Framework for Understanding Poverty* (Highlands, TX: aha! Process, 1996).

13. Paul Gorski, "Savage Inequalities: Uncovering Classism in Ruby Payne's Framework." Essay, Hamline University, St. Paul, MN, 2005. Available at http://www.EdChange.org

14. See, for instance, Richard Rothstein, *Class and Schools: Using Social, Economic, and Educational Reform to Close the Black-White Achievement Gap* (New York: Teachers College Press, and Washington, DC: Economic Policy Institute, 2004); Jean Anyon, *Radical Possibilities: Public Policy, Urban Education, and a New Social Movement* (New York: Routledge, 2005); and Sue Books, ed., *Invisible Children in the Society and Its Schools*, 2nd ed. (Mahwah, NJ: Lawrence Erlbaum, 2003).

15. Felix Boateng, "Combating Deculturalization of the African-American Child in the Public School System: A Multicultural Approach." In *Going to School: The African-American Experience*, edited by Kofi Lomotey (Albany: State University of New York Press, 1990). See also Joel Spring, *Deculturalization and the Struggle for Equality: A Brief History of the Education of Dominated Cultures in the United States*, 5th ed. (New York: McGraw-Hill, 2006).

16. See Karen Swisher and Dilys Schoorman, "Learning Styles: Implications for Teachers." In *Multicultural Education for the 21st Century*, edited by Carlos F. Díaz (New York: Longman, 2001).

17. Witkin, an early theorist in this field, suggested that people are either field independent or field dependent in their learning (see Herman A. Witkin, *Psychological Differentiation* [New York: Wiley, 1962]). According to this theory, the former tend to learn best in situations that emphasize analytic tasks and with materials void of a social context. Individuals who favor this learning mode generally prefer to work alone and are self-motivated. Field-

dependent learners tend to learn best in highly social settings, according to this theory. Manuel Ramirez and Alfredo Castañeda applied Witkin's theory to ethnic groups (see Manuel Ramirez and Alfredo Castañeda, *Cultural Democracy, Bicognitive Development and Education* [New York: Academic Press, 1974]). In research with children of various cultural backgrounds, they concluded that European American students tend to be the most field-independent learners. Mexican American, American Indian, and African American students, by contrast, tend to be closer to "field sensitive" (the term they use for dependent, which may have negative connotations), with Mexican Americans closest to this pole.

18. Flora Ida Ortiz, "Hispanic-American Children's Experiences in Classrooms: A Comparison Between Hispanic and Non-Hispanic Children." In *Class, Race and Gender in American Education*, edited by Lois Weis (Albany: State University of New York Press, 1988).

19. Donna Deyhle and Karen Swisher, "Research in American Indian and Alaska Native Education: From Assimilation to Self-Determination." In *Review of Research in Education* 22, edited by Michael W. Apple (Washington, DC: American Educational Research Association, 1997): 153.

20. Howard Gardner's groundbreaking text on this topic was *Frames of Mind* (New York: Basic Books, 1983). In his 1993 revision, he added to his list of "intelligences" a new naturalistic intelligence, and he conjectured (but stated that it needs further scientific verification) that there may also be a spiritual or existential intelligence. His most recent update on the theory is *Multiple Intelligences: New Horizons* (New York: Basic Books, 2006), in which he reviews the research on MI and includes new material on global applications of his theory.

21. Geneva Gay, *Culturally Responsive Teaching: Theory, Research, and Practice* (New York: Teachers College Press, 2000): 80.

22. Roland G. Tharp, "Psychocultural Variables and Constants: Effects on Teaching and Learning in Schools." *American Psychologist* 44, no. 2 (February 1989): 349–359. (1981): 211–220.

23. Michele Foster, *Black Teachers on Teaching* (New York: The New Press, 1997).

24. Ernest Morrell and Jeff Duncan-Andrade, "Promoting Academic Literacy With Urban Youth Through Engaging Hip-Hop Culture." *English Journal* 9, no. 6 (2002): 88–92.

25. Carol D. Lee, "Intervention Research Based on Current Views of Cognition and Learning." In *Black Education: A Transformative Research and Action*

Agenda for the New Century, edited by Joyce E. King (Washington, DC: American Educational Research Association, and Mahwah, NJ: Lawrence Erlbaum, 2005), 45–71, p. 83.

26. Carmen Judith Nine-Curt, *Nonverbal Communication*, 2nd ed. (Cambridge, MA: Evaluation, Dissemination, and Assessment Center, 1984).

27. Shirley Brice Heath, *Ways with Words* (New York: Cambridge University Press, 1983).

28. Geneva Gay, *Culturally Responsive Teaching: Theory, Research, and Practice* (New York: Teachers College Press, 2000): 23.

29. Susan Urmston Philips, *The Invisible Culture: Communication in Classroom and Community on the Warm Springs Indian Reservation*, reissued with changes (Prospect Heights, IL: Waveland Press, 1993).

30. Deyhle and Swisher, "Research in American Indian and Alaska Native Education: From Assimilation to Self-Determination." For African-centered, or Afrocentric, schooling, see Diane S. Pollard and Cheryl S. Ajirotutu, *African-Centered Schooling in Theory and Practice* (Westport, CT: Bergin and Garvey, 2000).

31. Tam Thi Dang Wei, *Vietnamese Refugee Students: A Handbook for School Personnel* (Cambridge, MA: National Assessment and Dissemination Center, 1980).

32. Heather Kim, *Diversity Among Asian American High School Students* (Princeton, NJ: Educational Testing Service, 1997).

33. David W. Adams, *Education for Extinction: American Indians and the Boarding School Experience, 1875–1928* (Lawrence: University Press of Kansas, 1995).

34. Deyhle and Swisher, "Research in American Indian and Alaska Native Education: From Assimilation to Self-Determination."

35. Deyhle and Swisher, "Research in American Indian and Alaska Native Education: From Assimilation to Self-Determination."

36. For an expanded discussion of these matters, see Sonia Nieto, "Profoundly Multicultural Questions" *Educational Leadership* (December 2002/January 2003): 6–10.

37. See Kathryn H. Au and Alice J. Kawakami, "Cultural Congruence in Instruction"; Gloria Ladson-Billings, *Crossing Over to Canaan: The Journey of New Teachers in Diverse Classrooms* (San Francisco: Jossey-Bass, 2001); Jacqueline Jordan Irvine, ed., *Critical Knowledge for Diverse Teachers and Learners* (Washington, DC: American Association of Colleges for Teacher Education, 1997); and Geneva Gay, *Culturally Responsive Teaching: Theory, Research, and Practice*.

38. Lynn A. Vogt, Cathie Jordan, and Roland G. Tharp,

"Explaining School Failure, Producing School Success: Two Cases." In *Minority Education: Anthropological Perspectives*, edited by Evelyn Jacob and Cathie Jordan (Norwood, NJ: Ablex, 1993).

39. Margaret J. Maaka, "E Kua Takoto te Mānuka T~utahi: Decolonization, Self-Determination, and Education." *Educational Perspectives* 37, no. 1 (2004): 3–13, p. 9.

40. Sarah Keahi, "Advocating for a Stimulating and Language-Based Education: 'If You Don't Learn your Language, Where Can You Go Home To?'" In *Indigenous Educational Models for Contemporary Practice: In Our Mother's Voice*, edited by Maenette Kape'ahiokalani Padeken Ah Nee-Benham and Joanne Elizabeth Cooper (Mahwah, NJ: Lawrence Erlbaum, 2000): 55–60, p. 58.

41. Jacqueline Jordan Irvine and James W. Fraser, "Warm Demanders," *Education Week* 17, no. 35 (May 1998): 56–57.

42. See Gloria Ladson-Billings, *The Dreamkeepers: Successful Teachers of African American Children* (San Francisco: Jossey-Bass, 1994).

43. Joanne Larson and Patricia D. Irvine, "'We Call Him

Dr. King': Reciprocal Distancing in Urban Classrooms." *Language Arts* 76, no. 5 (May 1999): 393–400.

44. Jerry Lipka, Gerald V. Mohatt, and the Ciulistet Group, *Transforming the Culture of Schools: Yup'ik Eskimo Examples* (Mahwah, NJ: Lawrence Erlbaum, 1998).

45. Jason Irizarry, "Ethnic and Urban Intersections in the Classroom: Latino Students, Hybrid Identities, and Culturally Responsive Pedagogy." *Multicultural Perspectives* (forthcoming).

46. Frederick Erickson and Gerald Mohatt, "Cultural Organization of Participation Structures in Two Classrooms of Indian Students." In *Doing the Ethnography of Schooling: Educational Anthropology in Action*, edited by George Spindler (New York: Holt, Rinehart and Winston, 1982).

47. Cynthia Ballenger, *Teaching Other People's Children: Literacy and Learning in a Bilingual Classroom* (New York: Teachers College Press, 1999): 37.

CHAPTER 6 CASE STUDIES

YAHAIRA LEÓN

It's easier to be myself culture-wise.

Fifteen-year old Yahaira León,[1] who was finishing ninth grade at Frontier High School in Philadelphia when she was interviewed, described herself as "half and half" Dominican and Puerto Rican. She continued, "And I guess I could say I'm American too. I was born here." Her parents were also both born in the United States, specifically in New York City, while her grandparents were all born in either Puerto Rico or the Dominican Republic. Yahaira's cultural identity and academic perspectives are influenced by her family life, educational experiences, and sociopolitical history.

The migration of Puerto Ricans and Dominicans from their island nations to New York and the northeastern United States are part of a larger pattern of migratory experiences among many Latino communities in the United States. In spite of sharing the Spanish language, a Caribbean heritage, and the quest for economic opportunities, there are distinct forces at play within each group's political, social, economic, and familial experiences.

The Dominican population in the United States has more than doubled since 1990, making it the fourth largest Latino group in the United States after Mexicans, Puerto Ricans, and Cubans. Like Yahaira's family, most Dominicans in the United States live in the Northeast. In 2006, it was estimated that there were 1.4 million Dominicans in the country, with growth projections of 1.6 million by 2010. About one-third of the growth in the Dominican community is from births in the United States, as in the case of Yahaira and her parents, while approximately 63 percent of the growth is from immigration. These figures are slightly unstable, since it is estimated that up to 15 percent of Dominicans are undocumented.[2] Citizenship is one of the characteristics that differentiate the Dominican community from Puerto Ricans, since Puerto Ricans are citizens of the United States.

The struggle to combat poverty marks the daily realities of many Dominican and Puerto Rican families. Due to their reliance on goods-producing industries in the Northeast that have suffered from de-industrialization, both Puerto Ricans and Dominicans struggle with unemployment in far greater numbers than other Hispanic groups. In 1999, the mean annual per-capita household income of the Dominican population in the United States was $11,065, or approximately half the per-capita income of the average U.S. household that year. These earnings were significantly lower than the per-capita income of the African American population and slightly lower than the income of the average Latino household.[3] Unemployment is a common plight within the Dominican community, and the legal immigration status of some workers keeps them in the lowest income bracket.

Employment prospects and financial status are also linked to educational opportunities. Ramona Hernandez and Francisco L. Rivera-Batiz report that the educational attainment of Dominicans in the United States is changing rapidly. In 2000, for instance, 49 percent of Dominicans 25 years of age or older had not completed high school, compared to 20 percent of the general American population.[4] At the same time, close to 60 percent under age 25 had received some college education, pointing to what Hernandez and Rivera-Batiz describe as an "explosive increase of the educational attainment" of U.S. born Dominicans.[5]

The Dominican Republic's long history of political unrest has left its mark on the economic circumstances, political perspectives, and cultural solidarity of the people. As it became much harder to make a living at farming in the Dominican Republic, people migrated to northeastern cities in the United States to work in factories and tourist industries. Many Dominicans in the United States are referred to by social scientists as *transnational migrants*,[6] that is, those who organize many aspects of their lives—family, religious, political and economic—across national borders. While assimilating into the country that receives them, transnational migrants often also sustain strong ties to their homeland.[7] The transnational dynamic of these immigrants has implications for both the home country and the host country. As the Dominicans in the United States began to send money back to the communities in the Dominican Republic, the standard of living on the island nation improved substantially.[8] However, due to visa and immigration status concerns, U.S. Dominicans may not be able to return to the Dominican Republic as frequently as they desire.

In contrast, patterns of what has been called *circular migration* are not unusual for Puerto Ricans, who frequently first settle in New York—like Yahaira's family did—and later move to other urban areas in the Northeast. Between 1940 and 1970 alone, about 835,000 Puerto Ricans moved to the United States, reflecting one of the most massive outmigrations in the century. In fact, currently more Puerto Ricans live in the United States than in Puerto Rico.[9] Also, although New York City was the primary destination for Puerto Ricans until the 1960s, currently only about 25 percent of the 4,000,000 Puerto Ricans living in the United States are in New York. In fact, one of the most significant findings of the 2000 census concerning Puerto Ricans was that they were increasingly living in relatively small cities such as Milltown, the city where Yahaira was born and where she frequently visits her aunts and cousins on her father's side of the family.

Puerto Rico became a colony of the United States in 1898, which helps explain some of the differences between Puerto Rican migration, or (im)migration, and Dominican immigration.[10] Since 1952, when Puerto Rico was taken over by the United States as a result of the Spanish-American War, it has officially had commonwealth status, although some people maintain that this is a camouflage for what is, in reality, a colony.[11] After 1900, U.S. absentee landlords—and later large corporations—dominated the economy, displacing small farmers and creating the island's economic and political dependence on the United States. Puerto Ricans were made U.S. citizens in 1917—some say, to coincide with the need for soldiers in the armed forces during World War I, for which Puerto Rican men were recruited en masse. Consequently, Puerto Ricans do not need passports or special permission to migrate to the United States. In addition, back-and-forth, or circulatory, migration is a major characteristic of the Puerto Rican community in the United States. This kind of migration stems primarily from the economic dependence of Puerto Rico on the United States. To explain the formidable economic subordination of the island, it is often said that "when the United States sneezes, Puerto Rico catches cold."

Yahaira's family confronts many hardships against the backdrop of these sociopolitical histories of Dominican and Puerto Rican communities in the United States. Due to the constant search for adequate, affordable housing and better employment by Blanca, her single parent, Yahaira had attended eight different schools by ninth grade. Blanca's unwavering hunt for a safe environment, with access to quality education for Yahaira and her sisters, was a Herculean task because of the stratification of U.S. schools by neighborhood real estate taxes. Yahaira recalls frequent transitions as a pervasive part of her childhood: "We moved around a lot. I don't know why, we just moved around a lot. We just had to keep moving."

Yahaira has navigated these challenges while achieving consistent academic success. While the number of transitions to different schools would impede many students, Yahaira was consistently upbeat. She said, "I just have a lot of fun learning 'cause I just liked to learn. I loved school." The three themes that emerged from Yahaira's interview all point to the reasons for her school success: *stability within transition, cultural identity and connection with Mom, and cultural connection and academic challenge.* We will consider Yahaira's experiences starting with stability within transition.

Stability Within Transition

School is, like, my home, well, my second home. But I just love being there. I love reading and learning and everything about it. School was the main place I could read and write without having to worry about anything.

I went to school a lot of places (*laughs*). The high school now—the name is Frontier. It's in downtown Philadelphia. It's a very good school. It's for advanced students. It's just, like, advanced for all areas. I'm learning a lot of new things that I didn't know and I'm advancing on the things I did. I am meeting more and more people who I can connect with and I make a lot more friends. I just have a lot of fun learning. 'Cause I just liked to learn. I always loved school. And well, you don't hear many kids saying that, but I do (*laughs*).

The reason for going to school is to educate your mind. So far, yeah, I am accomplishing that. It is important to me because nowadays, in this economy, you don't get nowhere if you don't have an educated mind. Without that, I can't do nothing. And without an educated mind, I can't get a job, which [means] I can't get money, and I can't support myself when I get older.

Cultural Identity and Connection with Mom

I'd say I'm Puerto Rican and Dominican, because, well, my mom's Dominican and my dad's Puerto Rican. My culture is important because in school they mostly teach us about the English society, the American society. They don' teach us the Hispanic culture or stuff like that, so it's important that I at least know some type of my cultural background, something from there. So whatever I can, I learn from either my family or I try and research it myself.

[What I would like teachers to know about Puerto Rican and Dominican kids is that] we're not the same as every other culture or ethnic group. We have our own ways that should be expressed. We have our own beliefs and customs. If schools would teach about Puerto Rican and Dominican culture, what I would like to learn is, basically, the history and how life is over there now. How it is for the people who have lots of money and compare it to the people who have it a little bit harder lives. How the Dominican Republic and Puerto Rico came to be what they are today—from the different main events that have happened in the history of the countries. I learned a little—just a little bit about it—from my mom and my grandmother but nothing about it in the schools. As a Puerto Rican and Dominican teenager, I'm more educated about my culture. Kids my age who are not Puerto Rican and Dominican might not have the same knowledge of [my] culture.

[The school] does value my culture. In the school I'm going to now it does . . . on certain levels. Every culture is valued in the school. They have African American clubs, Hispanic clubs, but it's not just clubs. The Hispanic club is not just for the Hispanic kids. Anybody could be in the club. 'Cause when we went to the student orientation for the high school, one of the teachers was saying that in the African American group there's a Hispanic president for the group. It's like they're all mixed in and it's not a problem. They all get along together. I'm gonna try to join a club. Probably the Hispanic one and the African American one.

In ninth grade I was in Mock Trial Club. I didn't have time to join the cultural clubs in ninth grade because I was so busy with Mock Trial Club. We met once a week at the beginning of the year, and then when the competition started, it was twice a week and on Saturdays. Also, I have chores at home and responsibilities to babysit my sisters—they're 12 and 7—'cause my mom works all the time and I'm the one that has to watch the girls while she works. Next year I'm gonna do mock trial again and try softball.

So far, I've seen a lot of my friends who are not as successful as I am. I know a lot of people who, at my age, don't really care about school anymore and they're, like, "whatever." I would just tell [new Puerto Rican and Dominican students] to work hard and worry about getting the work done. Don't worry about what's going on with everybody else at school . . . don't be up all in the gossip and just stick to the work and they'll do fine.

[Now, at the high school] I have all really different friends from the type of friends I had last year. They are all really into school. They are all really dedicated to school work and getting things done. They think about college too.

From my family I've learned that not much of my family has graduated. Because, I mean, that just makes it better for me to graduate and shows the family that it can be done. I mean it just takes hard work, and that helps a lot, because then all my younger siblings and younger cousins and nieces and nephews . . . they can see that if they work hard enough, they can do anything.

My mom is involved in my school. She tries her hardest to find out everything that goes on. Every time there's a parent-teacher meeting she goes. When we go to get our report card, she's always asking my teachers how I'm doing and exactly what I do in school. She gets very involved. She likes to know what's going on. My mom tells me repeatedly about school . . . doesn't leave me alone about it. Like everything I do, whether it's good or bad, she tells me and tells me over and over again. "Just fix it, you could do better." If it's something good, "You did great. Don't worry about it." 'Cause sometimes it gets annoying, her being so involved. But, yeah it does matter, 'cause, I mean, without her I probably wouldn't have been so into school and I wouldn't have liked it so much.

My mom is the person I admire the most in the world 'cause without her, I wouldn't be where I am. Without her, I wouldn't even be able to be independent or work out things on my own. I wouldn't be as determined as I am. I think that's enough to make her the most important person in my life.

I have always been living with mom, without dad, since I was 4. I live with my two youngest sisters—they are 7 and 12—and my mother. I am the biggest sister. They look up to me. I want to teach my sisters to always try their hardest at everything else they do—to never settle for less.

Cultural Connection and Academic Challenge

I think my favorite was my fourth grade teacher. She was really nice and she connected very well with the kids in the class. She wasn't the type of teacher that just gives you the work, tells you to do it, leaves it at that. Or the type that doesn't give you enough work and you're, like, sitting there the rest of the day doing nothing. She gave you the right amount of work, let you have the right amount of fun, but still got everything in all together.

I guess teachers understand my culture. Most of my teachers have either been African American or Caucasian. So I really haven't had any Hispanic teachers [until ninth grade] to understand really the culture—but they understand some of it, so that's enough. In the school I went to in eighth grade, almost every teacher spoke Spanish, because almost all the kids there were Hispanic—so they spoke Spanish. Every teacher knew at least some words in Spanish but they also spoke English. That helped because the kids who were just learning English—it was easier for them to communicate with the teachers. In some schools teachers acknowledged Spanish language and in some schools they didn't.

[Something teachers could do better is] involve the culture more into the learning. Like the strategies they use, the methods. If there was more learned or taught about the different cultures, that might help. Like my science teacher [in ninth grade], whenever we had projects he would bring in movies for us to watch, he would bring in cultural movies that would help us learn what we were being taught in the class as well as being able to understand it better through our culture, help us understand the concepts. My science teacher, each day in the class, he takes time to get to know the kids in the classroom a little bit more. He'll sit down and talk with us on a normal basis. Not teacher-to-student but as in a friend-to-friend role. His sister-in-law is Dominican, so we had that in common and I think he knew some Spanish.

The mock trial coach—he builds relationships. [The mock trial coach and the science teacher] learn how to talk to the students. They take the time to learn how life is for each student in the world we are living in. They learn how each student is different and they support each different thing about each student.

Of all my teachers, I think my eighth grade teacher [has been the most helpful] 'cause he was, like, every time I needed something that had to do with school, any time I needed help with anything, he found a way to get me help. Whether it was his subject or not, he'd find somebody to help me and he'd ask my mom—if I needed to—if it was OK to stay after school and get help. In his class I always got top grades 'cause it was my favorite class because it was the reading. That helped a lot.

In my high school, this is a more diverse school. There's more Hispanic kids around. It's easier to be myself culture-wise. A lot of the teachers are more used to working with the Hispanic kids and Black kids, so it's better. They're helping us learn—make it easier by helping us learn within our culture.

I mean that's how school's supposed to be; it's supposed to be hard, not easy. I was in the advanced class in my eighth grade—and we was doing algebra and math and just the basics in reading, science and social studies. But the math was a little bit ahead—well, we got more work than the other classes, so that kind of made it harder, but I still kept my grades up so it was all right.

The first year at the [advanced] high school was actually kind of easy. I just got through the work really easily; it wasn't as hard as I thought it would be. But that is just normal for me. I wish the teacher would challenge me a little bit more. I think they should make the work a little harder. I guess it's kind of hard [for teachers] 'cause I'm the only one in the class that has it so easy, so it's kind of difficult to make things harder for just me and then have the rest of the class have a problem with it.

I don't really read magazines 'cause I just think they're based on nothing. Most of the magazines now are talking about how girls are supposed to be skinny and pretty and their faces are supposed to be a certain way and all this crap, and it's annoying because the beauty you see when you look at people, it's not much. You have to look inside to know, actually know, what the person is. You can't just tell by looking at them. So I don't really look at magazines.

I'm most happy when I'm in my room reading one of my books or watching . . . no not watching . . . just reading one of the books or drawing or writing or something.

I've thought about [what I want to be]. When I was younger, everybody used to tell me be a lawyer because I like to argue and I always have to have the last word. But as I grow older, I think I'd rather be a teacher because, by being a teacher, I can do something that I really love doing and I can still work hard and get what I need to survive. Reading, English language arts are my favorite 'cause there's reading and writing and I love to read and write. That's kind of why I want to be a teacher, so I can be a reading or writing teacher. Since being in Mock Trial at the high school, I'm thinking maybe a lawyer. Probably a lawyer.

All the teachers and counselors are talking to us about college. It was very interesting. I am thinking about being lawyer and Harvard. I just heard from people that it is the most challenging college. I figured since every other grade in school has been easy, I think I should pick a hard college. 'Cause everybody says it's one of the best schools. I don't know. I've just wanted to go there since I was, like, four.

Grades are important to me because with grades—with better grades—I get more successful results. And with even better grades, I can get scholarships to college. My mom thinks grades are important. She looks for mostly A's or B's. She'll settle once in a while for a C but mostly A's or B's.

[To be successful later in life] I need to keep doing what I'm doing now. Working hard to get through whatever I gotta get through.

# Commentary

Yahaira's ideas echo themes that Carmen Rolón found in her study of Puerto Rican girls who achieved academic success.[12] In Rolón's study, it was first, parents—in particular, mothers—who were vehicles of encouragement and achievement. Second, teachers who "respected and affirmed in concrete ways their cultural and linguistic diversity in school"[13] were also significant. Third, Rolón found that "all participants defined college education as their foremost educational goal."[14] In Rolón's study, as well as in Yahaira's words, we hear Latinas describe school as a "second home."[15] In Yahaira's case, caring, supportive teachers and a determined mother motivated her to shape school as an oasis where she could "read and write, without having to worry about anything."

Since Yahaira entered kindergarten fully bilingual in English and Spanish, she was never enrolled in English-language learning programs and achieved well in all school subjects. Despite her fluency in English, she emphasized the link between teachers' "understanding the culture" and affirming Spanish language, whether the teacher knew "at least some words" or was fluent and "speaking to kids and parents." She described teachers who supported her efforts after school and pointed her toward college. She also noted culturally relevant teaching methods and the importance of relationships among teachers and students.

Yahaira's words resonate with Jason Irizarry's study that described teachers who are successful with Latino students as "culturally connected."[16] Irizarry describes cultural connectedness in teachers as a framework for understanding that takes into account the development of hybrid identities that emerge as a result of members of various cultural communities' negotiating their identities and forging new socioculturally situated identities. It also highlights the potential for teachers who are not members of the same racial or ethnic group as that of their students to become "connected" and improve their practice.[17] Significantly, Irizarry points out that teachers do not have to racially match their students in order to develop cultural connectivity with them.

Yet, not all Yahaira's teachers were "culturally connected" and Yahaira was flexible in her expectations. Even more important to Yahaira were teachers' high expectations. Her desire for rigorous work is congruent with Patty Bode's study of urban schools. She found that students felt that teachers should hold students to high expectations. The students articulated an appreciation of teachers who challenge them by pushing them hard and refusing to let them quit.[18] This student attitude is especially salient in discussions about urban schools where most of the students are labeled as "failing," "underperforming" or "below standard" by state mechanisms such as high-stakes standardized testing and federal policies and laws such as No Child Left Behind (NCLB).

Yahaira's hunger to learn more and expand her academic skills had been a consistent theme throughout her school life. She seemed to absolve the schools and teachers by acknowledging the difficulty of challenging one student in a class when others in the class might not be up to the challenge. However, in Gilberto Q. Conchas's study of high-achieving youth of color, he argues that high schools can construct success even for students whose circumstances put them at high risk for school failure.[19]

Yahaira's efforts to achieve academically deserve commendation, since her success could have been disrupted by her family's struggles and the frequent school transitions. The numerous moves may have been less bearable if not for the close-knit extended family to which Yahaira made frequent affectionate references. Collectively, Yahaira's extended family shaped her strong identification with her Spanish language and Puerto Rican and Dominican roots as well as her vision of the future. Her family's nurturing relationships and challenges with hardships formed her perceptions of limitations and possibilities.

Despite the emotional support of extended family on both sides, Yahaira still faced many of the tensions of urban life in the difficult socioeconomic circumstances common to many Latino families. Moreover, her father's long periods of absence—due to his difficulties with the law—rendered his presence in Yahaira's and her sisters' lives elusive.

Hard work and determination are, in many ways, Yahaira's anchors in a tumultuous ocean of school transitions. She viewed hard work as the way to graduate, gain admission to college (preferably Harvard), and achieve career goals. On the subject of her family members and friends who had not graduated from high school, she said, "I mean it just takes hard work." While hard work is an essential ingredient for academic achievement, Yahaira's statement seems to overlook the sociopolitical conditions in which many Puerto Ricans and Dominicans live. Yahaira seems to have accepted the myth of meritocracy; this is no surprise because it seems to have worked in her case.

The complicated forces at play within Yahaira's educational experiences should not be oversimplified as binary perspectives of a cooperative, communal, and so-called Latino perspective in opposition to a utilitarian, competitive American mainstream perspective. Her mother instilled in Yahaira an obvious sense of hard work and determination to achieve and to "never settle for less"; many of Yahaira's teachers drew upon cultural knowledge as a means to academic achievement. An elaborate web of academic culture and family culture is woven into her perspective.

Yahaira expressed her Latina identity in intangible but fundamental ways: her deep feelings for her family, respect for her parents, and her desire to uphold important traditions such as being with family. She also bore a larger share of family obligations than a great many young people from other cultural backgrounds. This is what is referred to in many Latino cultures as *capacidad*, or a combination of maturity, sense of responsibility, and capability. It is a valued cultural trait that Latino parents work hard to inculcate, particularly in their daughters.

Yahaira is very much a product of the intersecting and multiple influences of Puerto Rican, Dominican, and U.S. culture (especially youth culture). She, and many young people like her of various immigrant backgrounds, have created a new culture, one that has elements of the native culture but is also different from it. Yahaira was successfully negotiating the mixed and often conflicting messages of home culture, school culture, and youth culture.

Questions remain, however, about the cost to cultural identity and becoming more fully human when academic accomplishment is perceived primarily as individual hard work.[20] Ricardo D. Stanton-Salazar provides an intricate analysis that integrates the micro, the meso and the macro frameworks of various institutional conditions that "thwart the development of authentic social capital."[21] Stanton-Salazar's research, which focuses primarily on Mexican American youth, applauds and celebrates the accomplishments of some Latino students but asks hard questions about the conditions of the overwhelming majority of Latinos in U.S. schools who are tangled in a web of dehumanizing forces as he explains:

> I speak here of the dehumanizing yet often hidden aspects of class, race, and gender—the inhibiting of cooperative social activity and exchange, shared meaning-making, and assessment of common interest; the undermining of trust in the context of hierarchical power relations; and the inability of both family and school agents to provide developmentally empowering resources.[22]

In general, Yahaira and her mother had been left on their own to tap into some "empowering resources" to construct Yahaira's road to academic success. From many indicators, she appeared to be well on her way to a successful future. When we last checked in with her about her activities after freshman year, she was attending a summer institute at Yale sponsored by the Junior Statesman Foundation.[23] The program develops political and scholarly skills through college level coursework and enrichment activities. Yahaira gained admission to the highly competitive program through a convergence of her Mock Trial coach's dedication, her mother's assertiveness to obtain a scholarship for the costly summer program, and Yahaira's unflagging determination. Such an experience will certainly provide Yahaira a window into her target—an Ivy League college career. As a result of such experiences, navigating higher education may be easier for Yahaira than for other students who do not have a parent or parents with the single-minded determination of Yahaira's mother or the consistent support of teachers like Yahaira's who saw great promise in her.

◆◆◆ Reflect on This Case Study

1. Yahaira's perception is that her school mostly teaches about the "English society, the American society." If she were describing your school or your classroom, would you be satisfied with that portrayal? If not, how might you change Yahaira's experience?

2. How can teachers and schools take advantage of students' desires to learn more about their cultural heritages and histories? For example, Yahaira cited her desire to learn more about "[h]ow the Dominican Republic and Puerto Rico came to be what they are today—from the different main events that have happened in the history of the countries." What could be some responses to such a desire?

3. Yahaira fondly remembered one school where every teacher knew "at least some words in Spanish." What are the implications for educators regarding language and learning? How do you feel about trying to pronounce a few words in lan-

guages other than English, even if you are far from fluent? What are some class-room strategies for affirming multiple languages in the school?

4. The Mock Trial after-school program built on Yahaira's interests and appears to have deeply influenced her choices about her future. What does this tell us about the role of after-school programs in student achievement? What is the role of after-school programs in your school?

5. Yahaira yearns to be challenged more. Can you think of some strategies to en-courage her academic prowess and challenge her intellectual curiosity? How can teachers assess whether they are challenging all students?

JAMES KARAM

I'd like to be considered Lebanese.

Poised between childhood and adulthood, James[1] was a pleasing combination of practical, responsible, wise adult and refreshing, spirited, eager kid. Sixteen years old and a junior in high school when he was interviewed, his maturity was due in no small part to his role as the "responsible" male in the household. His mother and fa-ther were separated, and he was the oldest of three children, a position he generally enjoyed, although he admitted it could be trying at times.

Lebanese Christian, or Maronite, James explained that his father had been born and raised in the United States. His father had met his mother while visiting Lebanon and had brought her back to the United States as his bride. She had lived here for al-most 20 years and had become fluent in English. Although James's parents were separated, both were close to their children and continued to take an active part in their upbringing and education.

According to the U.S. Census Bureau, Arab Americans are people who can trace their heritage to more than 20 countries in North Africa and the Middle East. The 2000 census counted approximately 1.2 million Arab Americans, a siz-able increase in comparison to the 1990 census number of 870,000. However, the Arab-American Institute Foundation estimates that as many as 3.5 million Americans can trace their family lineage to an Arab country.[2] The Lebanese com-munity, part of the larger Arab population in the United States, is little known to the general U.S. population. It is, in this sense, an "invisible minority," about which more is discussed later. There are scattered communities of Lebanese throughout the United States, with large concentrations in several cities, including Springfield, Massachusetts, where James lived. A study of the Arab community in Springfield, conducted almost four decades ago, reported that the first Arab settlers arrived in the 1890s from Lebanon. Most were laborers and worked in the city's factories, for the railroad, or in peddling businesses. They were both Christian and Muslim Lebanese and there generally was little animosity between them. On the contrary, there was a genuine sense of solidarity and cohesiveness in the entire community.[3]

James had attended a Catholic school from kindergarten until third grade but had subsequently gone to a public school. He had been held back in third grade because his family moved out of the state and he had lost a good deal of school time (this still bothered him a great deal, as he said when he was interviewed). Despite this setback, at the time of his interview James was a successful student who had given a lot of thought to his plans after high school. He had worked at keeping his grades high so that he could get into a good college and was fairly certain that he wanted to become a mechanical engineer. His fantasy was to become a professional bike racer, but even if able to pursue this dream, he wanted a college education.

Springfield is a midsize metropolitan city. It is culturally, racially, and economically diverse. At the time of his interview, James was attending one of the high schools in the city, which he described as almost "a little college," and he said he liked all his classes. His classmates reflected many of the cultures and languages of the world, and the school system was intent on incorporating this cultural diversity into the curriculum in many ways, some more successful than others. When James was interviewed, bilingual education was still going strong in Massachusetts (years later, in 2003, it was eliminated), so the school system offered a number of bilingual programs for the Spanish-speaking, Portuguese, Russian, Vietnamese, and Khmer communities. Some of the other activities, such as cultural festivals and international fairs, although a promising start, proved to be somewhat superficial attempts at acknowledging the rich cultural diversity of the city, as James made clear in his interview.

Although he had never studied Arabic formally in school, James was fluent in both English and Arabic because both languages were important to his family. The Maronite church in the city was established in 1905 and was also influential in encouraging the use of Arabic and the maintenance of other Lebanese cultural values in the community. Indicative of the church's role, the Reverend Saab, pastor for more than 50 years, made the following statement concerning his parishioners during his investiture as monsignor: "I did not want them to forget their Lebanese heritage, because this is a wonderful thing."[4] Even when assimilation was generally perceived to be a great value in U.S. society, the Lebanese community was definitely bucking the tide. This was apparent in the large percentage of second- and even third-generation Lebanese in Springfield, both Christian and Muslim, who still spoke Arabic. In the case of the Maronites, the church's role has been not merely to provide a place for worship; rather, it has served as a haven for cultural pride and observance of traditions.

In many other ways, however, the Arab American community has acculturated to the U.S. mainstream. In Springfield, Arabic surnames are now almost nonexistent because most family names have been Anglicized. Actually, were it not for the influence of the church, and to a lesser extent other social and religious organizations and clubs, assimilation might have proceeded much more rapidly. The social class structure has changed as well. The Lebanese community in the city started out as working class, but it is now primarily middle class. In the first decades of the 20th century, the Arab community was similar to many other immigrant communities. It was characterized by large families (an average of ten children), overcrowded flats, congested sidewalks and doorsteps, and dirty, unpaved streets.⁵ Most Arabs in the city now own their own homes and live in middle-class communities.

This was true of James and his family when he was interviewed. He, his mother, 14-year-old brother, and 9-year-old sister lived in a quiet residential neighborhood in the city. His community, primarily European American, was much more homogeneous than the city itself. He said the difference between his neighborhood and the city proper was that there were many trees ("Believe me, I know! I have to rake the leaves every year").

James's perception of himself as a *good student,* as "smart," is an important theme, which will be explored further. In addition, his role as *apprentice in his family* is discussed. The most important theme to emerge, however, was the *invisibility* of James's Lebanese American culture in his high school.

The Invisible Minority

[My elementary school teacher, Mr. Miller] I just liked him. . . . He started calling me "Gonzo" 'cause I had a big nose. He called me *Klinger*—he said 'cause Klinger's Lebanese. You know, the guy on *M.A.S.H?* And then everybody called me *Klinger* from then on. I liked it, kind of . . . everybody laughing at me. Yeah, it doesn't bother me. I don't care if somebody talks about my nose.

We had a foreign language month in school. They had posters and signs and everything. Spanish, French, Spain, Italy—they had all these signs and posters and pictures and stuff all over the school. There was Chinese; they had Japanese; they had Korean. They had lots of stuff.

[*Why didn't they have Arabic?*] I don't know. . . .

[Another time] they made this cookbook of all these different recipes from all over the world, and I would've brought in some Lebanese recipes if somebody'd let me know. And I didn't hear about it until the week before they started selling them. They had some Greek. They had everything, just about. I asked one of the teachers to look at it, and there was nothing Lebanese in there.

[Another time, at the multicultural fair], there was Poland, there was Czechoslovakia, there was Spain, there was Mexico, there was France. There was a lot of different flags. I didn't see Lebanon, though.

I guess there's not that many Lebanese people in . . . I don't know; you don't hear really that much. . . . Well, you hear it in the news a lot, but I mean, I don't know, there's not a lot of Lebanese kids in our school. There's about eight or nine at the most.

I don't mind, 'cause, I mean, I don't know, just, I don't mind it. It's not really important. It *is* important for me. It *would* be important for me to see a Lebanese flag. . . . But you know, it's nothing I would, like, enforce or, like, say something about. If anybody ever asked me about it, I'd probably say, "Yeah, there should be one." You know, if any of the teachers ever asked me, but I don't know. . . .

Some people call me, you know, 'cause I'm Lebanese, so people say, "Look out for the terrorist! Don't mess with him or he'll blow up your house!" or some stuff like that. But they're just joking around, though. I don't think anybody's serious 'cause I wouldn't blow up anybody's house—and they know that. I don't care. It doesn't matter what people say. I just want everybody to know that, you know, it's not true.

On Being a Good Student

I'm probably the smartest kid in my class. It's just, like, usually I can get really into the work and stuff. But everybody else, you know, even the people that do their homework and assignments and stuff, they just do it and pass it in. You know, I like to get involved in it and learn it.

If you don't get involved with it, even if you get perfect scores and stuff, it's not gonna, like, really sink in. You'll probably forget it. You can memorize the words you know, on a test. But you know, if you memorize them, it's not going to do you any good. You have to *learn* them, you know?

I want to make sure that I get my college education. I want to make sure of that. Even if I do get into the career that I specialize in college, I still want to get a college education. . . . I'd love to be an engineer, but my real dream is to be a bike racer. Yeah, it's my love. I love it.

When things go bad, I go ride my bike. That's what I did [once] in the middle of the night. The faster I ride, the harder I pushed, the more it hurt. It made me keep my mind off [things].

[I think I didn't do well in school one year] just because I didn't try. I thought it was too easy so I didn't try. I don't think [Mom] liked that too much. I said, "Mom, I wanna go to summer school, you know, just to bring up my grade." So she paid for it.

In a lot of the things that I do, I usually do good. I don't like it when I don't finish something or when I do real bad. It makes me want to do better. If I ever get a bad grade on a test, it makes me want to do better next time.

Some teachers are just . . . they don't really care. They just teach the stuff. "Here," write a couple of things on the board, "See, that's how you do it. Go ahead, page 25." You know, some teachers are just like that.

Maybe it's not that they don't care. It's just that they don't put enough effort into it, maybe. . . . I don't know.

I like going over it with the class, and you know, letting everybody know your questions. And, you know, there could be someone sitting in the back of the class that has the same question you have. Might as well bring it out.

[Teachers should] make the classes more interesting. . . . Like, not just sit there and say, "Do this and do this and do this." You know, just, like, explain everything, write things on the board.

Apprenticeship within the Family

I speak a mixture of both [Arabic and English]. Sometimes it's just, like, some words come out Arabic and some words come out English. . . . Whichever expresses what I want to say the best, I guess, at the time.

We go to a lot of Lebanese parties and, you know, gatherings and stuff. We go to Catholic-Lebanese church every week. I always want to go to church. Most of my friends don't go to church. A lot of them do, but most of them don't.

My mother's really proud to be Lebanese, and so am I. First thing I'd say is "I'm Lebanese." I'm just proud to be Lebanese. If somebody asked me, "What are you?," everybody else would answer, "I'm American," but I say "I'm Lebanese," and I feel proud of it.

Even though somebody might have the last name like LeMond or something, he's considered American. But you know, LeMond is a French name, so his culture must be French. His background is French. But, you know, they're considered Americans. But I'd like to be considered Lebanese.

My mother's really old-fashioned: "You gotta be in early." "You gotta be in bed at a certain time." That kind of stuff. I guess it'll pay off. When I'm older, I'll realize that she was right, I guess. But right now, I wish I could stay out, like, a little later. I don't mind it, 'cause I don't think I'm really missing much. There must be a reason why. I know a lot of kids that can stay out and, you know, they go out till 12 o'clock, 1 o'clock in the morning. They don't come back home, and their mothers don't even ask them, you know, where they've been or whatever. [My parents are] really loving and caring. . . .

[My parents] basically taught me to be good to people. You know, I've never really been mean to anybody. I don't like fighting. My mother taught me that, mostly. [I] wouldn't want to be a part of any other family, put it that way.

Commentary

Until the events of September 11, 2001, Arab Americans were an invisible minority in the United States. James, however, was interviewed in 1989, and at that time, invisibility was a mark of the community. This became clear not only through discussions with James but also through a review of the literature. Whereas much has been written about numerous other ethnic groups in the United States—even those fewer in number—very little was available about Arab Americans, their culture, school experiences, or learning styles. This situation has changed considerably since 9/11, when Arabs, including Lebanese, inaccurately became linked with extremism and terrorism by many. In reaction to this, a number of educational resources to counteract this perception have been developed.[6] However, compared with most other groups, for whom volumes of information are available (although not necessarily accurate, understood, or used appropriately), Arab Americans still represent a unique case of invisibility because, when represented at all, it is generally in negative ways.

The reasons for this invisibility are varied. For one, the majority of Arabs did not come in a mass influx as the result of famine, political or religious persecution, or war, as have other refugees. Although many Arabs have indeed come to this country under these circumstances in the recent past, previously their numbers had not been conspicuous: Until 2001, Arab immigration to the United States was a relatively "quiet" one. In addition, Arabs' problems of adjustment, although no doubt difficult, had not, until recently, caught the public imagination as had those of other immigrants. Likewise, their children have not faced massive failure in the schools, as is true of the children of other immigrant groups, and for this reason, Arab American children have not been the focus of studies as others have been. Finally, Arabs are not always a racially visible minority, as is usually the case with Asians, Caribbeans, or many Latinos. Many Arab Americans—although certainly not all—can "blend in" with the European American population if they so choose.

Nonetheless, considering the number and diversity of Arabs in the United States and recent events, the simple fact that Arabs and Israelis were involved in a long-standing conflict and were frequently in the news when James was interviewed in 1989, was reason enough for more information about Arab Americans. Beyond the issue of conflict, the reality of the diverse histories and cultures of the approximately 150 million Arabs worldwide deserves some mention on its own merit.

Although it encompasses different religions, socioeconomic classes, and national origins, the Arab community is one of the most heterogeneous in the United States. It is also one of the most misunderstood—shrouded in mystery and consequently in stereotypes. The popular images of Arabs as rich sheikhs, religious zealots, or terrorists are gross stereotypes that do little to create a sense of community among Arabs and non-Arabs in the United States, yet this is sometimes the only "information" the general public has. These are also the images that James and other Arab American children have to struggle against every day. In a poignant account, written more than a quarter century ago, of how this stereotyping affected his own children when they decided not to use their ethnic dress for a multiethnic festival at school, James Zogby, a Lebanese American and currently president of the Arab American Institute, concluded, "Confusion and perhaps fear made them resist any display of pride. What for other students was the joy of ethnicity had become for my Arab-American children the pain of ethnicity."[7] Racist stereotypes of Arabs as barbaric, treacherous, and cruel persist. Yet, according to an article based on actual census figures, the vast majority of Arab Americans are citizens, well educated, and highly diverse.[8]

James had alternately felt invisible or referred to in only negative ways. Because Mr. Miller (the teacher who called him "Gonzo") joked in the same way with many of the other students, and because he allowed them to "make fun" of him too, James liked this attention. It made him feel special in the sense that his background was at least being acknowledged. In spite of what he said, however, the stereotypes about his background had probably taken their toll on James. Although he was quite active in school activities, he was vehement about not wanting to belong to student government. "I hate politics," he said simply.

James was acutely aware of being a good student. He was very confident about his academic success, and his perception of being a successful student was important to him. He was proud, for example, of being persistent, a quality he defined as his best characteristic. At the beginning of his junior year, after summer school, James had broken his foot while playing sports. It had required surgery, and he had been on crutches for several weeks. Because he had missed two weeks of school, he stayed after school every day for a number of weeks, making up labs and quizzes and other assignments. He was struggling with both schoolwork and crutches, but his attitude was positive. "I can't wait to be done with all my makeup work," he said, with a touch of frustration. He got through it, though, as with everything else that he had to do.

James's family played a significant role in the value he placed on education and the need to persevere. Although his family was not typical of the majority of recent immigrants to the United States, who are overwhelmingly Asian and Hispanic, it nevertheless shared some fundamental characteristics. For example, faith in the rewards of education is common among immigrant families, as Laurie Olsen found in her ethnography of recent immigrants in a comprehensive high school in California.[9]

James's favorite teacher was his geometry teacher, the one who he said "takes the time" and who went over everything in class. She was also the faculty adviser for the Helping Hand Club, a community service group in the school and neighborhood. James was quite involved in this group, which helped raise funds for individuals in need, and for charitable organizations. "I like doing that kind of stuff," he said, "helping out."

Other activities also seemed to give James the energy and motivation to keep up with schoolwork. He played soccer and baseball and was on the swim team. He became most enthusiastic, however, when talking about his favorite activity, biking. This sport energized James in many ways. Biking gave him the opportunity to learn about many things: how "practice makes perfect," how to develop and use leadership skills, how it feels to have a setback and not let it be a permanent loss, how to use a hobby to help relieve stress, and how to hone his interpersonal skills. Biking was not just a physical challenge but also an important motivation. James's room was filled with biking magazines, and he said the person he most admired was Greg LeMond, at the time the only U.S. racer who had ever won the Tour de France and the world championship. "I want to be just like him," he said.

Like other parents, James's parents had taught him the values and behaviors they believed most important for his survival and success. In the case of a family culturally different from the mainstream, this role is especially crucial. Teaching children their culture can be called *apprenticeship*. It is a role that is particularly evident among immigrant families who attempt, often against great odds, to keep their native culture alive. For families of the dominant culture, their apprenticeship is usually unconscious, for their children are surrounded by and submerged in the culture every day. They hear the dominant language, see dominant culture behaviors, and take part in all the trappings of everyday life—that is, in mainstream culture. For immigrant families, or even for third- or fourth-generation families who have chosen to maintain aspects of their native culture in some way, the task of their children's apprenticeship is appreciably more difficult. The language they speak at home is not generally echoed in the general population; their values, traditions, and holidays are often at odds with those of the dominant culture; and even the foods they eat or the music they listen to may be absent in the outside world. Because their culture is simply unacknowledged in many ways, these families are engaged in a terribly difficult balancing act of cultural adaptation without complete assimilation.

Although certainly not immune from the difficulties inherent in this role, James had been quite successful at this balancing act. He had a strong and healthy self-image, not only as a student but also as Lebanese. James loved Lebanese food, and he had even learned to cook some of it. The only thing he seemed to dislike, in fact, was Lebanese music, which he called "boring." His house was filled with Lebanese artifacts. A Lebanese pennant was prominently displayed in his room, and his bike-racing helmet had a Lebanese flag on it. James had never been to Lebanon, but he definitely planned to go "when this war is over," as he explained. For the most part, James felt comfortable in two worlds. His apprenticeship had been a largely successful one. He was proud of his culture; he was bilingual; he was not usually embarrassed or ashamed about appearing "different." He considered his family to be "the average American family" in some ways, and he probably considered himself to be an "all-American" kid because he liked to do what he called "normal teenager stuff."

In sum, James Karam had been successful in forging his family, culture, language, hobbies, church, friends, and schoolwork into a unique amalgam, which resulted in a strong self-image and a way of confronting a society not always comfortable with or tolerant of diversity. This achievement had not made him immune, however, to the different and distressing issues that arose because of his ethnic minority status. He had learned, for example, to hide hurt feelings when his culture was disparaged and to treat everything "as a joke." He was quiet, preferring to accept invisibility rather than risk further alienation or rejection. He also learned not to demand that his culture be affirmed. Nevertheless, it was evident that the uncompromising strength of his family, the support he received from his extracurricular activities, and his enduring faith in himself would probably help make the difference between surviving the tension or succumbing to it.

Reflect on This Case Study

1. What invisible minorities are you aware of? Why would you classify them in this way? In terms of visibility, how would you classify Arab Americans since 9/11?
2. Why do you think James was reluctant to bring up his feelings of exclusion from school activities?
3. How would you characterize the role that biking played in James's life? What can teachers and schools learn from this?
4. What advice do you think James would give new teachers about being success-ful teachers? Why?
5. If you knew about James's apprenticeship within the family, how might you use this information in your teaching?

HOANG VINH

For Vietnamese people, [culture] is very important. . . . If we want
to get something, we have to get it. Vietnamese culture is like that. . . .
We work hard, and we get something we want.

At the time he was interviewed, Hoang Vinh[1] was 18 years old. He was born in Viet-nam, in the Xuan Loc province of Dong Nai, about 80 kilometers from Saigon and had been in the United States for three years. Vinh's hands moved in quick gestures as he tried to illustrate what he had to say, almost as if wishing that they would speak for him. Vinh[2] was very conscious of not knowing English well enough to express himself in the way he would have liked and he kept apologizing, "My English is not good." Nevertheless, his English skills were quite advanced for someone who had been in the United States for just a few years.

When he came to the United States, Vinh had first lived in Virginia and then in New England, where he was at the time of his interview. He lived with his uncle, two sisters, and two brothers in a modest house in a residential neighborhood of a pleasant, mostly middle-class college town. The family's Catholicism was evidenced by the statues of Jesus and the Virgin Mary in the living room. Everyone in the family had chores and contributed to keeping the house clean and making the meals. In ad-dition, the older members made sure that the younger children kept in touch with their Vietnamese language and culture. They had weekly sessions in which they wrote to their parents; they allowed only Vietnamese to be spoken at home; and they cooked Vietnamese food, something that even the youngest was learning to do. When Vinh and his siblings received letters from their parents, they read them together. Their uncle reinforced their native literacy by telling them many stories. Vinh also played what he called "music from my Vietnam," to which the entire family listened.

Because Vinh's father had been in the military before 1975 and had worked for the U.S. government, he was considered an American sympathizer. As a result, educational opportunities for his family had been limited after the war. Because they could not leave Vietnam but they wanted their children to have the opportunity for a better education and a more secure future, his parents had sent Vinh and his brothers and sisters to the United States. Vinh and his family had come in what has been called the "second wave" of immigration from Indochina,[3] that is, they came after the huge exodus in 1975. Although Vinh and his family came directly from Vietnam, most of the second-wave immigrants came from refugee camps in Thailand, Malaysia, and elsewhere. This second wave was generally characterized by greater heterogeneity in social class and ethnicity, less formal education, fewer marketable skills, and poorer health than previous immigrants. During the 1980s, when Vinh and his family came to the United States, the school-age Asian and Pacific Islander population between the ages of 5 and 19 grew by an astounding 90 percent. About half of the 800,000 Asian refugees who arrived between 1975 and 1990 were under 18 years of age.[4] The Asian population has grown dramatically since that time. The 2000 census reported that there were 10.2 million Asian and Asian Americans in the United States; of these, 1.1 million were Vietnamese.[5]

Vinh's uncle worked in town and supported all the children in every way he could, taking his role of surrogate father very seriously. Because he wanted to make sure that all the children benefited from their education, he constantly motivated them to do better. During the summers, Vinh worked to contribute to his family here in the United States and in Vietnam, but during the school year he was not allowed to work because of the importance that his parents and uncle placed on his studies ("I just go to school, and, after school, I go home to study," he explained). He used the money he made in the summer to support his family because, he said, "we are very poor." They rarely went to the movies, and they spent little on themselves.

Vinh was starting his senior year in high school at the time he was interviewed. Because the number of Vietnamese speakers in the schools he attended had never been high, Vinh had not been in a bilingual program. Although he had done quite well in school, he enjoyed the opportunity to speak his native language and would no doubt have profited from a bilingual education. Some teachers encouraged Vinh and his Vietnamese classmates to speak Vietnamese during the English as a Second Language (ESL) class to improve their understanding of the curriculum content, but other teachers discouraged the use of their native language. Vinh had recently started an ESL class with a small number of other Vietnamese students and other students whose first language was not English. All of Vinh's other classes were in the "mainstream program" for college-bound students: physics, calculus, French, music, and law. His favorite subject was history because he wanted to learn more about the United States. He was also interested in psychology.

Homework and studying took up many hours of Vinh's time. He placed great value on what he called *becoming educated people,* one of the central themes in his case study. Other themes concerned his *demanding standards*; his attempt to *understand other cultures*, and the *strength one derived from family and culture.*

Becoming "Educated People"

In Vietnam, we go to school because we want to become educated people. But in the United States, most people, they say, "Oh, we go to school because we want to get a good job." But my idea, I don't think so. I say, if we go to school, we want a good job *also*, but we want to become a good person.

[In Vietnam] we go to school, we have to remember *every single word*. We don't have textbooks, so my teacher write on the blackboard. So we have to copy and go home. So, they say, "You have to remember all the things, like all the words." But in the United States, they don't need for you remember all the words. They just need you to understand. But two different school systems. They have different things. I think in my Vietnamese school, they are good. But I also think the United States school system is good. They're not the same. They are good, but good in different ways.

When I go to school [in Vietnam], sometimes I don't know how to do something, so I ask my teacher. She can spend *all the time* to help me, anything I want. So, they are very nice. My teacher, she was very nice. When I asked her everything, she would answer me, teach me something. That's why I remember. But some of my teachers, they always punished me.

[Grades] are not important to me. Important to me is education. I [am] not concerned about [test scores] very much. I just need enough for me to go to college. Sometimes, I never care about [grades]. I just know I do my exam very good. But I don't need to know I got A or B . . . I have to learn more and more. Sometimes, I got C, but I learned very much . . . I learned a lot, and I feel very sorry, "Why I got only C?" But sometimes, if I got B, that's enough. I don't need A.

Some people, they got a good education. They go to school, they got master's, they got doctorate, but they're just helping *themselves*. So that's not good. . . . If I got a good education, I get a good job, not helping only myself. I like to help other people. . . . I want to help other people who don't have money, who don't have a house. . . . The first thing is money. If people live without money, they cannot do nothing. So even if I want to help other people, I have to get a good job. I have the money, so that way I can help them.

Sometimes, the English teachers, they don't understand about us. Because something we not do good . . . like my English is not good. And she say, "Oh, your English is great!" But that's the way the American culture is. But my culture is not like that. If my English is not good, she has to say, "Your English is not good. So you have to go home and study." And she tell me what to study and how to study to get better. But some Americans, you know, they don't understand about myself. So they just say, "Oh! You're doing a good job! You're doing great! Everything is great!" Teachers talk like that, but my culture is different. They say, "You have to do better." So, sometimes when I do something not good, and my teachers say, "Oh, you did great!" I don't like it. I want the truth better.

Some teachers, they never concerned to the students. So, they just do something that they have to do. But they don't really do something to help the people, the students. Some teachers, they just go inside and go to the blackboard. They don't care. So that I don't like.

I have a good teacher, Ms. Brown. She's very sensitive. She understands the students, year to year, year after year. She understands a lot. So when I had her class, we discussed some things very interesting about America. And sometimes she tells us about something very interesting about another culture. But Ms. Mitchell, she just knows how to teach for the children . . . like 10 years old or younger. So some people don't like her. Like me, I don't like her. I like to discuss something. Not just how to write "A" . . . "You have to write like this." So I don't like that. She wants me to write perfectly. So that is not a good way, because we learn another language. Because when we learn another language, we learn to discuss, we learn to understand the word's *meaning*, not about how to *write* the word.

I want to go to college, of course. Right now, I don't know what will happen for the future. If I think of my future, I have to learn more about psychology. If I have a family, I want a perfect family, not really perfect, but I want a very good family. So that's why I study psychology. When I grow up, I get married, I have children, so I have to let them go to school . . . I have good education to teach them. So, Vietnamese want their children to grow up and be polite and go to school, just like I am right now. . . . I just want they will be a good person.

I don't care much about money. So, I just want to have a normal job that I can take care of myself and my family. So that's enough. I don't want to climb up compared to other people, because, you know, different people have different ideas about how to live, so I don't think money is important to me. I just need enough money for my life.

Demanding Standards

I'm not really good, but I'm trying.

In Vietnam, I am a good student. But at the United States, my English is not good sometimes. I cannot say very nice things to some Americans, because my English is not perfect. Sometimes the people, they don't think I'm polite because they don't understand my English exactly. I always say my English is not good, because all the people, they can speak better than me. So, I say, "Why some people, they came here the same year with me, but they can learn better?" So I have to try.

When I lived in Vietnam . . . so I go to school and I got very good credit [grades], but right now, because my English is not good, sometimes I feel very sorry for myself. [My uncle] never told me, "Oh, you do good" or "Oh, you do bad." Because every time I go home, I give him my report card, like from C to A, he don't say nothing. He say, "Next time, you should do better." If I got A, okay, he just say, "Oh, next time, do better than A!" He doesn't need anything from me. But he wants me to be a good person, and helpful. So he wants me to go to school, so someday I have a good job and so I don't need from him anymore.

He encourages me. He talks about why you have to learn and what important things you will do in the future if you learn. I like him to be involved about my school. I like him to be concerned about my credits.

Some people need help, but some people don't. Like me, sometime I need help. I want to know how to apply for college and what will I do to get into college. So that is my problem. I have a counselor, but I never talk to him. Because I don't want them to be concerned about myself because they have a lot of people to talk with. So, sometimes, I just go home and I talk with my brother and my uncle. If I need my counselor every time I got trouble, I'm not going to solve that problem. So, I want to do it by myself. I have to sit down and think, "Why did the trouble start? And how can we solve the problem?" Sometimes, I say, I don't want them to [be] concerned with my problem.

Most American people are very helpful. But because I don't want them to spend time about myself, to help me, so that's why I don't come to them. One other time, I talked with my uncle. He can tell me whatever I want. But my English is not good, so that's why I don't want to talk with American people.

I may need my counselor's help. When I go to college, I have to understand the college system and how to go get into college. The first thing I have to know is the college system, and what's the difference between this school and other schools, and how they compare. . . . I already know how to make applications and how to meet counselors, and how to take a test also.

Sometimes I do better than other people, but I still think it's not good. Because if you learn, you can be more than that. So that's why I keep learning. Because I think, everything you can do, you learn. If you don't learn, you can't do nothing.

Right now, I cannot say [anything good] about myself because if I talk about myself, it's not right. Another person who lives with me, like my brother, he can say something about me better than what I say about myself. Nobody can understand themselves better than other people.

I don't know [if I'm successful] because that belongs to the future. I mean successful for myself [means] that I have a good family; I have a good job; I have respect from other people.

Trying to Understand Other Cultures

I am very different from other people who are the same age. Some people who are the same age, they like to go dancing, they like to smoke, they want to have more fun. But not me. . . . Because right now, all the girls, they like more fun [things] than sit down and think about psychology, think about family. I think it's very difficult to find [a girlfriend] right now. If I find a girlfriend who not agree with any of my ideas, it would not be a good girlfriend. I don't need [her to be] very much like me, but some . . . we would have a little in common. It is not about their color or their language, but their character. I like their character better.

I think it's an important point, because if you understand another language or another culture, it's very good for you. So I keep learning, other cultures, other languages, other customs.

Some [Black] people very good. Most Black people in [this town], they talk very nice. Like in my country, some people very good and some people very bad. I have Chinese, I have Japanese, I have American, I have Cambodian [friends]. Every kind of people. Because I care about character, not about color.

Strength from Culture and Family

Sometimes I think about [marrying] a Vietnamese girl because my son or my daughter, in the future, they will speak Vietnamese. So, if I have an American girlfriend, my children cannot speak Vietnamese. Because I saw other families who have an American wife or an American husband, their children cannot speak Vietnamese. It is very hard to learn a language. In the United States, they have TV, they have radio, every kind of thing, we have to do English. So, that why I don't think my children can learn Vietnamese.

When I sleep, I like to think a little bit about my country. And I feel very good. I always think about . . . my family . . . what gifts they get me before, how they were with me when I was young. Those are very good things to remember and to try to repeat again.

I've been here for three years, but the first two years I didn't learn anything. I got sick, mental. I got mental. Because when I came to the United States, I missed my fathers [parents], my family, and my friends, and my Vietnam. So, every time I go to sleep, I cannot sleep, I don't want to eat anything. So I become sick. I am a very sad person. Sometimes, I just want to be alone to think about myself. I feel sorry about what I do wrong with someone. Whatever I do wrong in the past, I just think and I feel sorry for myself.

I never have a good time. I go to the mall, but I don't feel good. I just sit there. I don't know what to do. Before I got mental, okay, I feel very good about myself, like I am smart, I learn a lot of things. But after I got mental, I don't get any enjoyment. I'm not smart anymore. After I got mental, I don't enjoy anything. Before that, I enjoy lots. Like I listen to music, I go to school and talk to my friends. But now I don't feel I enjoy anything. Just talk with my friends, that's enough, that's my enjoyment.

My culture is my country. We love my country; we love our people; we love the way the Vietnamese, like they talk very nice and they are very polite to all the people. For Vietnamese, [culture] is very important. I think my country is a great country. The people is very courageous.

They never scared to do anything. If we want to get something, we have to get it. Vietnamese culture is like that. We work hard, and we get something we want.

Every culture . . . they have good things and they have bad things. And my culture is the same. But sometimes they're different because they come from different countries. America is so different.

[My teachers] understand some things, just not all Vietnamese culture. Like they just understand some things *outside*. . . . But they cannot understand something inside our hearts.

[Teachers should] understand the students. Like Ms. Mitchell, she just say, "Oh, you have to do it this way," "You have to do that way." But some people, they came from different countries. They have different ideas, so they might think about school in different ways. So maybe she has to know why they think in that way. Because different cultures, they have different meanings about education. So she has to learn about that culture. I think they just *think* that they understand our culture. . . . But it is very hard to tell them, because that's our feelings.

When I came to United States, I heard English, so I say, "Oh, very funny sound." Very strange to me. But I think they feel the same like when we speak Vietnamese. So they hear and they say, "What a strange language." Some people like to listen. But some people don't like to listen. So, if I talk with Americans, I never talk Vietnamese.

Some teachers don't understand about the language. So sometimes, my language, they say it sounds funny. And sometimes, all the languages sound funny. Sometimes, [the teacher] doesn't let us speak Vietnamese, or some people speak Cambodian. Sometimes, she already knows some Spanish, so she lets Spanish [speakers] speak. But because she doesn't know about Vietnamese language, so she doesn't let Vietnamese speak.

[Teachers] have to know about our culture. And they have to help the people learn whatever they want. From the second language, it is very difficult for me and for other people.

I want to learn something good from my culture and something good from American culture. And I want to take both cultures and select something good. If we live in the United States, we have to learn something about new people.

[To keep reading and writing Vietnamese] is very important. So, I like to learn English, but I like to learn my language too. Because different languages, they have different things, special. [My younger sisters] are very good. They don't need my help. They already know. They write to my parents and they keep reading Vietnamese books. . . . Sometimes they forget to pronounce the words, but I help them.

At home, we eat Vietnamese food. . . . The important thing is rice. Everybody eats rice, and vegetables, and meat. They make different kinds of food. The way I grew up, I had to learn, I had to know it. By looking at other people—when my mother cooked, and I just see it, and so I know it.

We tell [our parents] about what we do at school and what we do at home and how nice the people around us, and what we will do better in the future to make them happy. Something not good, we don't write.

They miss us and they want ourselves to live together. They teach me how to live without them.

◆ ◆ ◆ Commentary

Hoang Vinh's experiences in the United States closely paralleled those of other Asian refugees in some respects, but they were quite different in others. His case study gives us many lessons about teachers' expectations, demands on Asian students, and the anguish of cultural clash and language loss. Vinh was emphatic about wanting to become "educated people," which he explained as wanting to know about other people and about the world and wanting to be able to get along with, and help, others. Grades were not as important to Vinh as doing "the best you can." He was convinced that there is a big difference—not just a semantic one, but a cultural one as well—in what it means to "be educated" in the Vietnamese sense and in the United States. His explanation is a good example of what many Asians believe to be one of the main differences between U.S. and Asian cultures. Although U.S. culture is rich materially, it often lacks the spirituality so important in most Asian cultures.[6]

Vietnamese and other Southeast Asian immigrants generally have a substantially higher level of education than other groups, even well-established ones. Their high literacy rate has a significant impact on their schooling in this country. Asians in U.S. schools typically spend much more time on homework than other groups, and literacy and educational activities are undertaken at home as well as at school. The effects of Vinh's family background and early school experiences were evident in his attitudes toward school and in his study habits.

Although Vinh remembered his teachers in Vietnam with some fear because they were strict and demanding, he also recalled them with nostalgia. He also noticed many differences in the educational system in the United States—some positive, others negative. He appreciated, for example, being allowed to use his native language in class and the individual help he received from teachers. Mostly he talked about how he loved working in groups. He mentioned one ESL teacher, his favorite teacher, who often had students work in groups, talking among themselves and coming up with their own solutions and answers. Most of the topics they discussed were related to their lives in the United States, their culture, and their adaptation.

Much of the literature about the traditional learning styles of Vietnamese students emphasizes their passivity and reliance on rote memorization, but Vinh's case dramatizes how important it is to interpret such literature cautiously. For one, there is great diversity among all Asian groups and even within groups. Vinh's predilection for group work, for example, may demonstrate how the *form* of education is not as important as the *process*. That is, group work in this case is the *means* used to facilitate dialogue, which is so important in learning a second language and in learning in general. However, as Vinh's case study indicates, the process may be the crucial factor because it is based on the students' own experiences and engages them meaningfully in their education.

To avoid giving the impression that all Vietnamese students are as concerned with educational success as Vinh was, it must be noted that Vinh was quick to point out that one of his best friends, Duy, was "very lazy." Vinh said Duy did all of his homework but only at school and in a haphazard way. Vinh stated that although Duy was very smart and had a "very good character," he did not care about learning in the same way as Vinh did. Duy had long hair, spent many hours listening to music or thinking about girls, wanted to be "cool," and acted in what Vinh said was "an American way." Unlike Vinh, Duy had a job after school and liked to spend his money at the mall.

Both Duy and Vinh, in different ways, shatter the "model-minority" stereotype. According to this image, all Asian students excel in school, have few adjustment problems, and need little help. This stereotype is widely resented by many Asians and Asian Americans. It is not only inaccurate but can also lead teachers to believe that all Asian American students are cut from the same cloth (notwithstanding the fact that Asian American community in the United States is extremely heterogeneous).[7] The model-minority myth is often used as a standard against which all other groups are measured. This—what Schaefer calls "praising the victim"[8]— may contribute to the interethnic hostilities, already common in schools, that are occurring with more frequency in communities as well. This myth also helps to discredit the legitimate demands for social justice made by other, more vocal groups. The model-minority stereotype also overlooks the great diversity among Asian Americans, a diversity apparent in ethnicity, class, and language, as well as their reasons for being in the United States and their history here. It may place severe demands on students, through teachers who have unreasonable expectations of their academic abilities.

Vinh was extremely hard on himself, and much of this self-assessment was tied to his limited English. The use of the English language as a standard by which to measure one's intelligence is not unusual among immigrant students, who often feel frustrated and angry by the length of time it may take to learn the language. Vinh did not consider himself to be a successful student, often contrasting his academic success in Vietnam with his struggles as a student in the United States.

The tremendous traumas refugees suffer when leaving their country and facing the challenges of a new society are well known. One of the results has been a dramatic incidence in mental health problems among refugees. Moreover, there is evidence that refugees who are unaccompanied minors like Vinh are especially at risk. It has been shown that they experience more depression and other problems such as withdrawal or hyperactivity. These problems may be caused by guilt, homesickness, alienation, and loneliness, which are sometimes aggravated by the hostility and discrimination they, as immigrants, face. Considering the pivotal role of the family in Vietnamese culture, particularly the importance of parents and elders in general, Vinh was bound to suffer mental distress. At the improbable age of 15, he had the formidable task of relocating, along with his siblings, to a foreign country and culture and assuming the role of an "elder" in dealing with a new society. The result was almost inevitable: He became sick. He talked about this period of missing his family and "my Vietnam" with great melancholy.

Although his culture and family provided tremendous emotional support for Vinh, they were largely unacknowledged by the school. Vinh felt that teachers needed to learn about his culture and be sensitive to the difficulty of learning a second language at an older age. Adjusting to his new country posed many challenges for Vinh: learning a new language and writing system; becoming familiar with a new and very different culture; and grieving the loss of parents who, although still living, were no longer with him. In such cases, even an apparent adjustment may be deceiving. For example, a study of a group of Cambodian refugee children found that, as they became more successful at modeling the behavior of U.S. children, their emotional adjustment worsened. In addition, the feeling of being different from other children increased with time in this country.[9] The problems of adolescence are aggravated by immigrant and minority status. Young people like Vinh have a double, sometimes triple, burden compared with other youths. Continuing to rely on his culture was one way Vinh tried to survive this difficult adjustment.

Newcomers must also learn to live in a country that is extremely pluralistic, at times uncomfortably so. The result can be confusion and uncertainty about other cultures outside the mainstream. Immigrants are quick to pick up messages about the valued and devalued cultures in the society. Their preconceived notions about racial superiority and inferiority may also play into this dynamic. The lack of awareness and knowledge of other cultures and their experiences in the United States can worsen the situation. Given no guidance by schools through appropriate curricula or other means, new students are left on their own to interpret the actions of others. Moreover, immigrants are often the target of racist attitudes and even violence by other students.

All of these factors help explain how some attitudes brought by immigrants and then nurtured by prevailing racist attitudes and behaviors in society are played out in schools and communities. Vinh was no exception. His experience with African Americans is an example. He explained that on several occasions he was jumped and robbed when he lived in Virginia. Being a newcomer to the United States, he was perplexed and frustrated by this behavior and came to his own conclusion about why the incident occurred. Vinh saw differences between the Black students in the first school (in Virginia) and those in the mostly middle-class town (in New England) in which he lived at the time he was interviewed. The former, he said, were "very dirty, smoked a lot, and played their music very loud." When asked why he thought this was so, he reflected, "I think that depend on the culture. . . . I don't understand much about Black culture." He added, "Not all Black people [are dirty and loud]. . . . There are good and bad in every group," a cliché often used to soften the impact of gross stereotypes. Vinh was obviously grappling with the issues of race and stereotypes and tried very hard to accept all people for "their character" rather than for the color of their skin or the language they speak. In spite of some of his negative experiences, he had made friends with some of the African American students in the New England school ("Some of them is very cool and very nice").

Schools are expected to take the major responsibility for helping children confront these difficult issues, but often they do not. Given the changing U.S. demographics and the large influx of new immigrants, the rivalry and negative relationships among different groups of immigrants and native-born students will likely be felt even more in the coming years. Interethnic hostility needs to be confronted directly through changes in curriculum and other school policies and practices. Students such as Vinh clearly need this kind of leadership to help them make sense of their new world.

◆◆◆ Reflect on This Case Study

1. Does Vinh's definition of "educated people" differ from yours? If so, how?
2. Vinh resented the false praise he received from some of his teachers. Some students, however, seem to need more praise than others. What does this situation imply for teaching in culturally diverse schools?

3. What did Vinh mean when he said, "I'm not really good, but I'm trying"?
4. Vinh had trouble asking his teachers and counselors for help. Knowing this, what can schools do to help students like Vinh?
5. After reading Vinh's case study, what do you think of the conventional wisdom surrounding the model-minority stereotype?
6. In light of Vinh's interethnic experiences and his perceptions of other cultures, what can schools do to help students from different ethnic and racial groups understand one another better?
7. Because Vinh had never been in schools with high numbers of Vietnamese students, he was never in a bilingual program. Do you think this is an advantage or a disadvantage? Why?

REBECCA FLORENTINA

And all we can do is hope to educate teachers, because there's kids in middle school getting beat up in the hallways because of it, you know?

Rebecca Florentina,[1] 17 and a senior in high school, wore her green hair very short. She had pierced ears and wore pride rings. From time to time, she also wore a t-shirt that said "I'm not a dyke, but my girlfriend is." Rebecca identified as butch lesbian and "came out" in her high school five months before she was interviewed.[2] It wasn't a big public announcement, according to Rebecca. Instead, she came out when she and her girlfriend Stephie started going out. She said, "We would just walk up to somebody and say, 'This is my girlfriend now.' So that's how I came out. I didn't come out like, 'Hey, I'm lesbian!' I came out as 'Hey, this is my girlfriend. Now figure it out.' " Rebecca was just as direct about everything else in her life.

As one of two children (her sister was a sophomore in college) living with a divorced mother, Rebecca appreciated her mother's openmindedness about her identity, her grades, her decisions about college, and her life in general. "Do whatever you want as long as you are happy" is the advice she said her mother always gave her.

A life-long resident of West Blueridge, a small city in Massachusetts known for its liberal attitudes about sexuality, Rebecca didn't contemplate ever moving. She felt safe there, she said, especially as a lesbian. She could hold hands with her girlfriend as they walked down the street and nobody noticed, or, at least, they didn't say anything. For almost a year, she had been involved in Rainbow Youth, a place where LGBT youths went to talk and socialize, a place where, according to Rebecca, she could hang out with her "second family kind of friends."

Rebecca said she also felt safe in her high school, which she characterized as "mostly accepting." A large comprehensive high school with nearly a thousand students, the school is primarily White and middle-class: Only about 10 percent of the students are Latino, and it has a very small African American student body. According to Rebecca, most of her high school's graduates went to college.

Rebecca was particularly close to a couple of teachers in her high school because they had been great allies of the Gay/Straight Alliance (GSA) student group. This club, which had been in existence for several years, is just one of an estimated 200 throughout Massachusetts formed as a result of the Massachusetts' Governor's Commission on Gay and Lesbian Youth. (There are now about 2,600 GSA groups around the country.) The Commission was formed by the governor in reaction to a 1989 federal report on the epidemic of youth suicide among lesbian, gay, transgender, bisexual, and questioning youths. An alarming statistic unearthed by the 1989 federal report was that one-third of all youth suicides were carried out by gay and lesbian youths.[3] Feeling safe in school for LGBT youth has been largely influenced by the presence of GSAs. One large study found that LGBT students in schools with GSAs were three times as likely to feel safe being "out" at school and were much less likely to hear homophobic remarks, compared to students in schools without GSAs.[4]

The Massachusetts' Governor's Commission issued its landmark report in 1993. It was the first of its kind in the nation issued by a state's department of education. It made many recommendations for making schools safe and welcoming for gay and lesbian youths, and four of the recommendations were adopted by the Massachusetts Board of Education:

1. Schools are encouraged to develop policies protecting gay and lesbian students from harassment, violence, and discrimination.
2. Schools are encouraged to offer training to school personnel in violence prevention and suicide prevention.
3. Schools are encouraged to offer school-based support groups for gay, lesbian, and heterosexual students.
4. Schools are encouraged to provide school-based counseling for family members of gay and lesbian students.[5]

Also, in Massachusetts, students cannot be discriminated against on the basis of sexual orientation if they want to start a GSA, and schools must respond to all requests for the formation and funding of GSAs as they do to other extracurricular clubs. As a result of these recommendations, many high schools have received training and support for both students and staff, and they have started to make a positive difference in the climate of high schools throughout the state.[6] The GSA in Rebecca's school was quite active, providing gay and lesbian students with a nurturing environment at the high school. Unfortunately, in 2002, Jane Swift, the outgoing governor of Massachusetts, eliminated funding for this program due, she said, to severe budget constraints and a bad economy. Given this sociopolitical climate, it is no surprise that an obvious theme in Rebecca's interview was the mixed messages she received about safety. It was clear that she was always on guard and that the greater safety she so yearned for was at times elusive. Other themes that emerged were Rebecca's *sense of responsibility to educate others*, her *perseverance and personal motivation*, and her *"invisibility" as an Italian American*.

Mixed Messages: "It's West Blueridge, so it's accepting."

I wouldn't want to be anywhere else. I feel safe here. I feel exceptionally safe here. I take pride in West Blueridge, so it's my community, I guess. It's where I feel the safest. It is what I love. I wouldn't dare move somewhere else. I love it here, but I also don't feel as safe when I go other places, no matter where I go. So even the town down the road, you know? I'll think twice about holding my girlfriend's hand on the streets there. But when I do it in West Blueridge, there's no questions asked. We do it. I mean, who would want to leave a place that makes us feel that safe? There's no fear.

I just think that because it's West Blueridge we get treated so much better than people in other schools. I mean it's obvious, you know. People have gotten killed. [In other places] the comments are like, "Go somewhere else." And people doing double takes and looking at us and giving us weird faces.

I'm in the school's GSA [Gay-Straight Alliance], and that's one reason, you know? The school has a GSA. On a regular basis, there's probably six who go every Friday, which is when we meet, but there's another six or seven who come whenever they can. Not all the time. There's no trans people as far as we know. I think there's two guys, and the rest are female. Our GSA is having a speaker come in. Since our GSA advisor is an administrator, we get exceptions to be able to do this that we might not otherwise. And we're having people come in and talk to the whole school. It's an optional thing. We couldn't make it mandatory. If anybody wants to come, there's going to be a speaker. We're doing a whole week on gay rights and awareness. It's our "Awareness Week." It's going to be during the school. So we'll have rainbow voices. We'll have pins, things like that. We're doing "101 good things about being gay" kind of thing. We're not doing health class–type things. We're doing positive outlook. We're not saying, "this percentage are into drugs; this percent have AIDS." It's kind of like all the good things. We're just making it a happy time. . . . I don't think [any parents have objected]. I think, in West Blueridge, if you don't approve of the lifestyle, you don't say it, because you're going to be offending a heck of a lot of people.

We've gone around and asked teachers to put "Safe Zone" stickers on their door[s]. The majority of them actually have them on their doors. And the teachers don't mind. There's a couple that are kind of iffy. [But] everybody's like, "It's West Blueridge." That's all you have to say, so you don't really get too much [criticism] . . .

I have a teacher who says, "Assuming I'm speaking heterosexually" in class. He's the only person who does it. It made me feel so much safer when I had a different teacher say, in his class the first day, "There will be no swearing, there will be no slurs like "faggot" or whatever in my class." I have two teachers in four years of high school that have ever said something like that, and that was both this year.

I have my band director who says, "All you should be in this room is happy. And leave everything outside. This is a safe place. Let's be happy. Let's play music." I have a psychology teacher who says "heterosexually speaking," so he's not implying that everybody's straight.

[When we "came out"] I don't think we had a bad reaction. My friends were awesome. I didn't lose a single one, you know? So it was pretty cool.

[In the high school], the climate is like, if you're generally like everybody else, you're fine. But if you're totally opposite of what everybody else looks like and acts, you'll get shoved into a locker or something, or told to shut up. But when I walk down the halls, it's fine. There are some groups of people that, you know, you'll walk more quickly by. I don't like to call them cliques, but there are people who congregate in little sections of the hallway. But who doesn't, you know? I do it too.

But our school is, like, it's West Blueridge, so it's accepting. That's what I like about it. Most of the teachers are great. It's very open.

[Students] never say slurs. [They don't say "that's disgusting" or anything like that], but you can tell they're thinking it. You can just tell. And we're, like, okay. But that doesn't . . . that happens like once every two weeks. It's not a big deal, you know? And we're not going to stop being who we are.

I'm in band, and everybody there knows about me and my girlfriend, because we're both in band. And they're all cool with it. And if they're not, they don't say anything. But, like, I wear my sweatshirt all the time. And I'll be reluctant to wear this [t-shirt that says "I'm not a dyke, but my girlfriend is"] in the halls; like, if I'm walking in the halls and some guy who's got his hat twisted up all weird and baggy pants, I'm gonna be reluctant to do that, I think, alone. Because if I go in the bathroom or something, I don't wear this shirt when I'm alone in school.

I don't feel totally safe. But I feel like I have the privilege of feeling more safe than everybody else does. So I'm thankful for what I have, and I just take precautions because that's just me.

You hear ["faggot"] and, like, you can't do anything about it really. It gets said; I probably hear it once every week. I don't know if the teachers hear it. Some girl said, "Oh you faggot" in one of my classes. But I don't know if he heard or not. . . . I think if you had to hold your tongue in class without saying that stuff, it would help a little bit. But when you get out in the halls, it's a totally different atmosphere. People act basically the opposite of how they act in class. It's, like, second nature, you know? They kind of just say it all the time. It makes me angry. I mean, there's nothing you can do, really. I don't think they could do anything. You're not going to stop the kids from doing something they want to do. If I'm in the hall and some other kid's in the hall, and there's no teachers, he can hit me if he wants. Or she.

I think that's all we can do, and I don't think for some people it will help, because if you have this one mindset, you're not going to change it if you don't want to.

[*What advice would you give to a new lesbian student in your school?*] "Join the GSA!" Here are my friends. They're nice, you know? You'll definitely have accepting people who will never turn anybody away. That's why I love them so much. (*pause*) I don't know. Just don't broadcast it, you know? I think we go as far as any straight couple, speaking of myself and my girlfriend. But we don't make out in the halls. That's our personal whatever . . . we don't want to do that. But I don't think we would even, because we would get crap for it. I'd just say "Be who you want to be, and if they don't like it, that's their problem." But most of the people won't mind it.

Educating Others

[I want teachers to know that LGBT students] are just like everybody else. I mean, everybody sees it as somebody who's different and not normal. But it's just your sexuality. I don't identify myself as, like, "Hi, I'm Rebecca and I'm a lesbian." It's, like, this is me, and this is my sexuality. That's as far as I'm going to go with it. I mean, I'll wear a shirt or something. I'm proud of who I am.

It's the teacher who wants to learn from the students, and not just the students who learn from them, that makes a great teacher, and I love that. I would fire the teachers who yelled at their students, because I have teachers who refuse to do that, and the environment is much better. Patience is just taught by being patient yourself. And (*pause*) I have such great teachers right now I can't think of anything bad [to say about them].

My girlfriend and I were mentioned in a newspaper article about gay and lesbian students. And my history teacher who is just this guy who goes skiing, kind of a jocky guy, said, "That was a great article. I'm happy about you guys." I like the teachers who pay attention to what you're doing, no matter who you are. They're, like, "I saw you in the paper." They're not just there to give you a grade, like, "Here's a test." They actually get involved, not to the point of obsessed, but just enough. It was a great feeling because now I know he doesn't discriminate against me, and he accepts me and he thinks I'm a good person. That's incredible to have.

My psychology teacher's class . . . I'm the third [lesbian student], and we've opened his eyes. Now he's this amazing person. Before he was ignorant. Now he's incredible.

And all we can do is hope to educate teachers, because there's kids in middle school getting beat up in the hallways because of it, you know? I think with high school, it's just more accepting, and when you go to middle school before high school, it's awful for some reason. Kids are just more active.

The health class, at least in the high school, looks at same sex whatever or queer whatever in a derogative way. The curriculum says, "Here's these lesbian people, and we should accept them," something like that. It's not, like, "Here's the great things about being gay." It's, like, "Here's all the things that happen and that people think of them." And I don't even think it's that accepting. It's just, like, "There are people who are gay." And that's the whole curriculum.

So I think if you want to educate people better, it's get the health teachers to put better curriculum for teaching about same sex, transgender, anything, you know? Because it's looked at in a negative way instead of a positive way.

The psychology book refers to obese people as abnormal. Our teacher actually commented on that and said it was awful. But we don't have enough money for new books. So we can't get new ones. It makes a lot of rude comments. There's two things about homosexuality in the psychology book. One is we don't know if it's a choice or not, and I don't know what the other one is. You know, "There are these people" and that's it for psychology. It's sad.

I came out to my psychology class to make an educational thing out of it. Prior to that, they knew me . . . they're not my friends, but they've known about me. And then I told them this, so how can they judge me? I've got a lot of kids who—when my psychology teacher goes, "your little friend"—turn around and make a face at me and say [whispering] "Why can't he just say lesbian?" And I never had that before, and I think it's great. And I have people leaning across from me in the class say [whispering] "My mother's a lesbian." And I don't think they would do that without [my] coming out. And I think it's great that they can tell somebody. If I can help them, I think that's what I want to do. So if this makes things more normal for them, and more commonplace, then do it, you know?

My English teacher lets the kids read books that are very liberal and very queer friendly [for example, with lesbian characters]. And I think that's great . . . or a poem that's written by a lesbian author . . . and giving kids books . . . you know? But he's one [teacher] out of a lot.

[Advice for teachers?] Be open minded, I think, and be inclusive of everybody. It's hard to be politically correct in everything, every second, in every word you say. But there are some teachers you just don't want to approach sometimes because they are very closed.

Perseverance and Motivation

I like the fact that my mother said, "Do whatever you want as long as you are happy." Because even though I kind of messed up in high school and middle school and couldn't get into a really great college, I still was self-motivated, and I found it in myself to do what I wanted to do, instead of her telling me what to do. So I respect that. I think that's a great way to raise a kid.

[In elementary school] behavior-wise [I was good]. Interested in work, no. I wasn't interested in working hard. That didn't happen until later on in high school. That was always my issue. I was always in for recess because I didn't do my work.

I'm in ensembles outside of school, and I do all that. The school doesn't offer very much music education, so I kind of find my places elsewhere. Since that's what I'm interested in, rather than playing sports, I have to find [it] somewhere else.

Right now I'm looking at college. The only reason I started doing well in school was because I went to the state university and I heard their band. I realized that I wanted to do that. So in order for me to get there, I would have to pick up my academics. [I realized this] at the very beginning of my junior year. That was my fuel for getting through the next two years. If you want to play music, you need to do this. It's not me necessarily interested in academics, because I'm not. I just have a different mindset, you know? Artist-type people have that. And they'd rather be doing something else. Intellectual people would rather be sitting there with their books. And so, I see it as a way to do what I want, so I have to get through it in order to do it.

I think I did it on my own. I mean, if you go in the guidance office, they're like, "take the SATs, and do good in school, bye." Whatever happens, happens. Teachers at least in my high school, you get whatever grade you want. They don't care; if you get an F, you get an F. They're not saying, "You need to go to college. And you need to do this. Here's how much effort you put into this." I got scared about not being able to go to college. I knew I wasn't going to have much of a future if I didn't. So I scared myself.

And I did it all myself. I can honestly tell you that, cuz I did. And nobody told me I would get into the state university, but I did. Nobody told me I could get into the department of music, and I'm on the waiting list for that. I wasn't rejected. I did it myself because I wanted to. The school—it didn't help. The school says, "Do whatever you want. We're not responsible for you in that way. Get whatever grades you want. Let your parents deal with it." They're not, like, "Here's what has to happen." I don't know if they have the time, though. I don't know if I want to blame them for that. They have so many kids, you know?

[I'm successful] because I had a guidance counselor tell me, "There's no way in hell" basically—she didn't say that, but you could see it in her eyes—"You're never going to make it into the state university. You don't even have a shot. Go to community college." You could read it in her face. She was, like, "I don't think this is going to happen here." And from day one of junior year I said, "I'm going!"

[Recently] I called the admissions office, and they sent me a letter not rejecting me from the music department, which meant that I had to get into the university first, in order for them to send me that letter, so it means I got in. I haven't got my acceptance letter, but I basically know they're not messing with me. They sent that because I got in. And the second thing is that I wasn't supposed to walk into the music department at the state university, which is very, very good. And to be able to pull it off and be worthy of them at least putting me on the waiting list, because they can only take 12 people. They only took, like, five because they already had a certain amount in their studio. I wasn't supposed to do that. I've been playing for three and a half years. I've been playing seriously for nine months. And I did that, and I think that's cool, and I did it all by myself, and that's why [I'm proud] (*laughs*).

As my psychology teacher puts it, I'm very self-actualized. He said I'm one of the people he's ever met at my age who's so self-actualized. This shouldn't be happening. I should be conforming to everybody else. He admires me and tells me I'm great because I can be who I want to be and not care what anybody else thinks. I like that because I'm happier because of it. Everybody else is hiding something.

Ethnic Invisibility

[*How do you identify racially or culturally?*] White, or what are you talking about?

Well, my culture, I mean, I'm Italian. I don't know if you want that. I mean, that's important to me. It's important to me and my mother, and my grandfather. [But it's not important in my school]. [*Is there an Italian student group in your school?*] No! (*laughs*) Definitely not! You're not going to find something like that. (*pause*) I wish there was.

The only thing I can tell you is that when my psychology teacher told me—I told him that I was Italian—he told me he loved me because he's Italian! I mean he'll speak Italian in class.

[For holidays], we'll just make the basic eggplant parmesan, stuffed shells, or manicotti [*pronounced in a distinctly Italian accent*]. It's fun. My mom's into that.

My grandfather was a sheepherder in Italy for, like, seven years. He was an orphan, but then he came here.

[I admire] my grandfather because he was an orphan. Both of his parents died when he was, like, three. Put in an orphanage, never got a formal education, but still remained happy and healthy. He's still doing construction work at age 82. He made the best out of what he had. I'll always admire somebody for that. And he loves being Italian. He loves everything about his culture.

He's the only one in my family who would say, "I like your [green] hair." He's 82, and he's telling me that.

◆ ◆ ◆ # Commentary

Being gay or lesbian in school today is not as daunting a challenge as it once was. For one, more people are writing about what it means to be gay in school (as either a teacher or a student), and there are far more resources than ever.[7] Also, since the 1990s, there has been more legal recourse to counteract the discrimination faced by LGBT students.[8] This does not mean, however, that it is easy, and it is clear in Rebecca's case study that, no matter how "safe" and how "accepting" a school or even an entire town might be, there is ample reason for LGBT students to feel insecure or even in danger. For example, the Gay, Lesbian, and Straight Education Network (GLSEN), in its most recent report on safety in U.S. schools, found that anti-LBGT bullying and harassment are still common. On the other hand, they also reported that supportive school staff, more inclusive policies and practices, and Gay-Straight Alliances all made a positive difference, both in creating a safe environment and in promoting higher achievement among LGBT students.[9]

Rebecca's inconsistent comments about the use of slurs in her school are a good indication of mixed messages about safety. Although she felt she was quite privileged compared to LGBT students in other places, she was still careful about whom she came out to. She appreciated the efforts of some of her teachers to support gay and lesbian students and the GSA, but she was also clear that some teachers were "iffy" about supporting them. Additionally, although she mentioned that most people in her school were fairly nonchalant about LGBT students, she was aware of the strong negative feelings some of them had about gays and lesbians. Even in describing what was a relatively painless "coming out," Rebecca was quick to point out that she didn't lose *even one friend* as a result—something she wouldn't have to point out if she had "come out" as Italian, for example. So, in spite of her constant references to "It's West Blueridge, so it's accepting," Rebecca would tell a new student not to "broadcast it." Clearly, she knew that, in many ways, it was still unsafe to be a lesbian.

Related to the issue of LGBT identity in school was Rebecca's commitment to educate others. It was clear that Rebecca had reversed roles with some of her teachers, becoming in essence their teacher, at least as far as LGBT issues are concerned. One teacher, she said, was "ignorant," but he had become "incredible" and "amazing" because she and other lesbian students had been able to reach him.

Although it is admirable that Rebecca had taken on this role, it is also an indication of how far schools and teachers still need to go in understanding LGBT students. It is reminiscent of the role, often unwelcome, played by African American and other students of color who feel they must educate their teachers about their identities.

Calling herself "self-actualized," Rebecca was clearly proud of herself and of what she had accomplished. She got into the college of her choice by her own wits and determination. She didn't rely on teachers, guidance counselors, or anybody else to help her get where she wanted to go. In fact, it was precisely because of a guidance counselor's skepticism about her ability to get into college due to her grades that Rebecca had decided to prove the counselor wrong.

As in the case of Vanessa Mattison, whose case study follows Chapter 4, Rebecca was confused when asked about her cultural identity. "White, or what are you talking about?" was her initial response. Unlike Rebecca and Vanessa, all the other young people in our case studies immediately identified racially or culturally. In this, Rebecca is typical of many other White students who have not had to identify racially because they are perceived as "the norm." Nonetheless, as quickly became apparent later in the interview, Rebecca was proud of her Italian heritage and wished that it, too, could be part of her school experience demonstrating that being "safe" relates not just to sexual orientation but to all aspects of identity. Rebecca's interview, however, also underlined the complicated nature of ethnic identity. Half Italian and half Polish, Rebecca identified strongly as Italian; her sister, however, identified as Polish. In Rebecca's words, "She took to the Polish side, and I took the Italian side."

It is imperative that teachers develop a more nuanced understanding of culture in terms of sexual orientation, ethnicity, race, social class, disability, language, and other markers of identity. As in the case of Rebecca, it is evident that as our schools become more aware of the presence of LGBT students, we have a great deal to learn about being responsive to a large number of students who, until recently, have felt the need to remain "in the closet." Young people with courage and willpower like Rebecca's are making a difference in many schools. As more teachers become advocates for all students, we will not need to count as much on students like Rebecca to learn to do what is right.

◆◆◆ Reflect on This Case Study

1. What responsibilities do teachers have to their LGBT students? Does this responsibility extend to elementary schools as well? Why or why not? What do you, or would you, say to people who say that LGBT issues have no place in the school?

2. What are the advantages of a GSA? If you teach at a secondary school, is there a GSA at your school? If not, would you consider starting one? Why or why not?

3. Do you know of any LGBT students in your school? What is your perception of how they do academically? How do they feel? How do you know?

Notes to Chapter 6 Case Studies

Yahaira León

1. We appreciate the work of Dr. Jason Irizarry who interviewed Yahaira León. Dr. Irizarry is a faculty member in the School of Education at the University of Connecticut where his research focuses on multicultural teacher education and urban teacher recruitment and retention, with emphasis on increasing the number of teachers of color. He gave us additional information about the schools Yahaira attended and the cities in which she lived, including follow-up information about her summer program.

2. Elizabeth M. Grieco, *The Dominican Population in the United States: Growth and Distribution*. September 2004. Washington, DC: Migration Policy Institute, July 24, 2006. Available at: www.migrationpolicy .org/pubs/MPI_Report_Dominican_Pop_US.pdf; for more information, go to www.migrationpolicy.org and www.migrationinformation.org

3. Ramona Hernandez and Francisco L. Rivera-Batiz, *Dominicans in the United States: A Socioeconomic Profile, 2000*. (Dominican Research Monographs. October 2003.) New York: CUNY Dominican Studies Institute, July 1, 2006. Available at: www.earthinstitute .columbia.edu/cgsd/advising/documents/rivera_ batiz.pdf

4. *Ibid.*

5. *Ibid.*

6. Luis Guarnizo, Alejandro Portes, and William Haller, "Assimilation and Transnationalism: Determinants of Transnational Political Action among Contemporary Migrants." *American Journal of Sociology* 108 no. 6 (2003): 1211–48.

7. Peggy Levitt, "Salsa and Ketchup: Transnational Migrants Straddle Two Worlds." *Contexts* 3.2. (2004): 20–26; 20 (June 2006). Available at: www.ingenta connect.com/content/ucp/ctx/2004/00000003/ 00000002/art00004;jsessionid=142qtlj5iuasg.alice# avail

8. *Ibid.*

9. Francisco L. Rivera-Batiz and Carlos E. Santiago, *Island Paradox: Puerto Rico in the 1990s* (New York: Russell Sage Foundation, 1996).

10. Because Puerto Rico is under the political control of the United States, the term *migration* rather than *immigration* is ordinarily used to refer to the movement of Puerto Ricans to the United States, but this term is not quite accurate because it refers to movement within the same cultural and political sphere. Some writers have suggested that the term *(im)migration* is more suitable. See Roberto Marquez, "Sojourners, Settlers, Castaways, and Creators: A Recollection of Puerto Rico Past and Puerto Ricans Present." *Massachusetts Review* 36, no. 1 (1995): 94–118.

11. In 1974, the Decolonization Committee of the United Nations described Puerto Rico as a colony. For a number of years, the Committee consistently called on the United States to hand over sovereignty to the island. See Clara E. Rodriguez, "Puerto Ricans in Historical and Social Science Research." In *Handbook of Research on Multicultural Education*, 2nd ed., edited by James A. Banks and Cherry M. Banks (San Francisco: Jossey-Bass, 2004).

12. Carmen Rolón, "Puerto Rican Female Narratives about Self, School and Success," *Puerto Rican Students in U.S. Schools*, edited by Sonia Nieto (Mahwah, NJ: Lawrence Erlbaum, 2000): 141–165.

13. *Ibid.*, 149.

14. *Ibid.*, 149.

15. *Ibid.*, 154.

16. Jason G. Irizarry, "Representin' for Latino Students: Culturally Responsive Pedagogies, Teacher Identities, and the Preparation of Teachers for Urban Schools," diss., University of Massachusetts Amherst, 2005.

17. Jason G. Irizarry, "Ethnic Urban Intersections in the Classroom: Latino Students, Hybrid Identities and Culturally Responsive Pedagogy." *Multicultural Perspectives*. In press.

18. Patricia Bode, "Multicultural Art Education: Voices of Art Teachers and Students in the Postmodern Era," diss., University of Massachusetts Amherst, 2005.

19. Gilberto Q. Conchas, *The Color of Success: Race and High-Achieving Urban Youth* (New York: Teachers College Press, 2006): 113–115.

20. Paulo Freire, *Pedagogy of the Oppressed*, translated by Myra Bergman Ramos (New York: Continuum, 1970).

21. Ricardo D. Stanton-Salazar, *Manufacturing Hope and Despair: The School and Kin Support Networks of U.S.–Mexican Youth* (New York: Teachers College Press, 2001): 251.

22. *Ibid.*

23. For more information on the Junior Statesman Foundations's summer programs for high school students, see www.JSA.org.

James Karam

1. We want to thank Diane Sweet for the interviews with James as well as for transcripts and other extensive information she was able to find about the Arab American community.

2. U.S. Census Bureau, *Profile of Selected Social Characteristics: 2000* (Washington, DC: U.S. Government Printing Office, 2000). Data from the Arab American Institute is included in a PowerPoint presentation by Nader Ayish and Muna Shami, "Framing Arab American Issues Within Multicultural Education." National Association for Multicultural Education, 15th Annual International Conference, Atlanta, GA, November 2005.

3. Naseer H. Aruri, "The Arab-American Community of Springfield, Massachusetts." In *The Arab-Americans: Studies in Assimilation*, edited by Elaine C. Hagopian and An Paden (Wilmette, IL: Medina University Press International, 1969).

4. *Ibid.*

5. *Ibid.*

6. See especially the materials produced by the American-Arab Anti-Discrimination Committee. Their webpage (www.adc.org) is a rich source of information for educators. Also, Educators for Social Responsibility, or ESR (www.esrnational.org) has produced curriculum materials on the topic of discrimination against Arab Americans. See also Arab World and Islamic Resources (AWAIR) at www.awaironline.org; AMIDEAST (www.amideast.org); and the Arab American Institute, a Washington, DC–based organization that serves as a leadership group for Americans of Arab descent (www.aaiusa.org).

7. James J. Zogby, "When Stereotypes Threaten Pride." *NEA Today* (October 1982): 12.

8. See more information about Arab Americans at www.aaiusa.org

9. Laurie Olsen, *Made in America: Immigrant Students in Our Public Schools* (New York: New Press, 1997).

Hoang Vinh

1. We are grateful to Haydée Font for the interviews and transcripts for this case study. When she did these interviews, Haydée was a graduate student in multicultural education at the University of Massachusetts; she later worked in the development office at several universities. She is currently raising two sons and doing volunteer work but hopes to return to development work in the near future.

2. The Vietnamese use family names first, given names second. The given name is used for identification. In this case, Vinh is the given name and Hoang is the family name. According to the National Indochinese Clearinghouse (*A Manual for Indochinese Refugee Education*, Arlington, VA: National Indochinese Clearinghouse, Center for Applied Linguistics, 1976–1977), whereas in U.S. society John Jones would be known formally as Mr. Jones and informally as John, in Vietnam, Hoang Vinh would be known both formally and informally as Mr. Vinh or Vinh.

3. See Ronald Takaki, *Strangers From a Different Shore: A History of Asian Americans* (New York: Penguin Books, 1989); and Min Zhou and Carol L. Bankston III, "The Biculturalism of the Vietnamese Student." ERIC Clearinghouse on Urban Education *Digest*, no. 152 (March 2000).

4. Peter N. Kiang and Vivian Wai-Fun Lee, "Exclusion or Contribution? Education K–12 Policy." In *The State of Asian Pacific America: Policy Issues to the Year 2020* (Los Angeles: LEAP Asian Pacific American Public Policy Institute and the UCLA Asian American Studies Center, 1993): 25–48.

5. U.S. Census Bureau, *Profile of Selected Social Characteristics: 2000* (Washington, DC: U.S. Government Printing Office, 2000).

6. "A very rich man without a good education is not highly regarded by the Vietnamese," says Tam Thi Dang Wei, in *Vietnamese Refugee Students: A Handbook for School Personnel* (Cambridge, MA: National Assessment and Dissemination Center, 1980).

7. An excellent resource on the topic is the chapter "Asian Pacific American Students: Challenging a Biased Educational System" by Valerie Ooka Pang, Peter N. Kiang, and Yoon K. Pak, in *Handbook of Research on Multicultural Education*, 2nd ed., James A. Banks and Cherry A. McGee Banks, eds., (San Francisco: Jossey-Bass, 2004), 542–563.

8. Richard T. Schaefer, *Racial and Ethnic Groups*, 3rd ed. (Glenview, IL: Scott Foresman, 1988).

9. This and many related studies are documented in Alejandro Portes and Rubén G. Rumbaut, *Legacies: The Story of the Immigrant Second Generation* (Berkeley, CA: University of California Press; New York: Russell Sage Foundation, 2001).

Rebecca Florentina

1. We are grateful to John Raible who interviewed Rebecca and assisted in identifying the themes and analysis of the themes. He also provided the definitions in the glossary associated with LGBT issues. John is Assistant Professor, Department of Teaching, Learning, and Teacher Education at the University of Nebraska-Lincoln. His interests include exploring the intersections between identities, families, schools, and communities. We also wish to thank Stephen Pereira, Assistant Dean for Student Affairs at Hampshire College, for a number of resources related to LGBT teens.

2. For purposes of convenience, and because Rebecca most often identified simply as "lesbian," that is the term that is generally used in this case study. For other students who identify as lesbian, gay, bisexual, or transgender, the acronym LGBT is used.

3. Paul Gibson, "Gay Male and Lesbian Youth Suicide." In *Report of the Secretary's Task Force on Youth Suicide* (Washington, DC: U.S. Department of Health and Human Services, 1989).

4. Michael Sadowski, "Making Schools Safer for LGBT Youth." *Harvard Education Letter*, 22, no. 3 (May/June 2006): 1–3.

5. The Governor's Commission on Gay and Lesbian Youth, *Making Schools Safe for Gay and Lesbian Youth: Breaking the Silence in Schools and in Families* (Boston, MA: Massachusetts Department of Education, 1993).

6. Melinda Miceli, *Standing Out, Standing Together: The Social and Political Impact of Gay-Straight Alliances.* (New York: Routledge Falmer, 2005).

7. See, for example, David Campos, *Understanding Gay and Lesbian Youth: Lessons for Straight School Teachers, Counselors, and Administrators* (Lanham, MD: Scarecrow Education, 2005); Jean M. Baker, *How Homophobia Hurts Children: Nurturing Diversity at Home, at School, and in the Community* (San Francisco: Harrington Park Press, 2002).

8. David S. Buckel, "Legal Perspective on Ensuring a Safe and Nondiscriminatory School Environment for Lesbian, Gay, Bisexual, and Transgendered Students." *Education and Urban Education* 32, no. 3 (May 2000): 390–398.

9. Gay, Lesbian, and Straight Education Network (GLSEN), *National School Climate Survey 2005.* New York: Author, 2006. Also see a critique of Federal policy guidelines for LGBT students: Joan Doyle, "What's Safe in School? Contradictions and Inconsistencies in Federal Education Policy." *Progressive Perspectives* 4, no. 1 (Spring 2002): 1–3, 7, 10–13.

Linguistic Diversity in U.S. Classrooms

Sezin Ugor Aksoy. *They took it and only left this*. Collage mixed media, 2006.

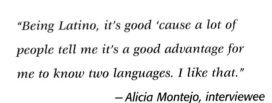

"Being Latino, it's good 'cause a lot of people tell me it's a good advantage for me to know two languages. I like that."

— *Alicia Montejo, interviewee*

L anguage is intimately linked to culture. It is a primary means by which people express their cultural values and the lens through which they view the world. This link was described by Henry Trueba in the following way:

> Whatever knowledge we acquire, it is always acquired through language and culture, two interlocked symbolic systems considered essential for human interaction and survival. Culture and language are so intricately intertwined that even trained scholars find it impossible to decide where language ends and culture begins, or which one of the two impacts the other the most.[1]

The language practices that children bring to school invariably affect how and what they learn, yet native language issues are frequently overlooked in multicultural education; race and ethnicity have been emphasized almost exclusively.[2] That language issues often go unaddressed in multicultural education is apparent in the lack of relevant terms concerning linguistic diversity. Terms that describe discrimination based on race, gender, and class are part of our general vocabulary (*racism, sexism, ethnocentrism, anti-Semitism, classism*), but until recently, no such term existed for language discrimination, although this does not mean that language discrimination did not exist. Tove Skutnabb-Kangas, by coining the term *linguicism* to refer to discrimination based specifically on language, has helped to make the issue more visible.[3]

This chapter explores the influence that language differences may have on student learning. How teachers and schools view language differences, whether and how they use these differences as a resource in the classroom, and different approaches to teaching language minority students, that is, those whose first language is not English, are all reviewed.

DEFINITIONS AND DEMOGRAPHICS

There are numerous terms to identify students who speak a language other than English as their native language. The term currently in vogue is *English Language Learners*, or *ELLs*. This term has become popular as a substitute for the more contentious *bilingual* (more information on the controversies surrounding bilingual education is given in a subsequent section of this chapter), although *bilingual* itself was a misnomer because most students to whom this label was applied were not really bilingual but rather *monolingual* in their native language, or *becoming bilingual* in their native language and English. (Nonetheless, the term usually was accurate for describing the *program* in which many of these students were placed.) The terms ELL or ESL (English as a Second Language), on the other hand, focus only on students' need to acquire English. Although *ELL* has become the preferred term in the current anti-bilingual education climate, a decade or two ago, the most common term was *limited English proficient*, or *LEP*, an unfortunate acronym to which many people objected. Another popular term used for these students is *language-minority students*, which reflects the fact that they speak a minority language in the United States. No term is completely accurate or appropriate. In this text, we have chosen to use either *ELL* or *language minority* to refer to students who are learning English as a second or additional language.

Who are the ELLs to whom we refer in this chapter? In the United States, the population of those who speak a language other than English as their native language has increased tremendously in the past several decades. By the 2000 census, nearly 46 million people, or about 18 percent of the total population, spoke a native language other than English. The number and variety of languages is over 450—from Urdu to Punjabi to Yup'ik—although by far the largest number (28 million) and percentage (about 60 percent) speak Spanish.[4] Table 7.1 enumerates the most widely

TABLE 7.1
United States—Ability to Speak English by Language Spoken at Home for the Population 5 Years and Over: 2000

Language Spoken at Home	Total Number	Speak English "very well" Number	Percent	Speak English "well" Number	Percent	Speak English "not well" Number	Percent	Speak English "not at all" Number	Percent
Population 5 years and over	262,375,150	(X)	(X)	(X)	(X)	(X)	(X)	(X)	(X)
Speak only English	215,423,555	(X)	(X)	(X)	(X)	(X)	(X)	(X)	(X)
Speak language other than English	46,951,595	25,631,190	54.6	10,333,555	22.0	7,620,720	16.2	3,366,130	7.2
Spanish or Spanish Creole	28,101,055	14,349,795	51.1	5,819,410	20.7	5,130,400	18.3	2,801,450	10.0
Other Indo-European languages	10,017,975	6,627,685	66.2	2,091,450	20.9	1,078,915	10.8	219,925	2.2
French (incl. Patois, Cajun)	1,643,840	1,228,800	74.8	269,460	16.4	138,000	8.4	7,580	0.5
French Creole	453,365	245,855	54.2	121,915	26.9	70,960	15.7	14,635	3.2
Italian	1,008,370	701,220	69.5	195,900	19.4	99,270	9.8	11,980	1.2
Portuguese or Portuguese Creole	564,630	320,445	56.8	125,465	22.2	90,410	16.0	28,310	5.0
German	1,383,440	1,079,695	78.0	219,465	15.9	79,560	5.8	4,720	0.3
Yiddish	178,940	123,160	68.8	35,455	19.8	17,295	9.7	3,030	1.7
Other West Germanic languages	251,135	182,050	72.5	58,290	23.2	9,420	3.8	1,375	0.6
Scandinavian languages	162,255	137,615	84.8	19,110	11.8	5,165	3.2	365	0.2
Greek	365,435	262,850	71.9	65,025	17.8	33,345	9.1	4,215	1.2
Russian	706,240	304,890	43.2	209,055	29.6	148,670	21.1	43,625	6.2
Polish	667,415	387,695	58.1	167,235	25.1	95,030	14.2	17,455	2.6
Serbo-Croatian	233,865	119,270	51.0	61,255	26.2	42,970	18.4	10,370	4.4
Other Slavic languages	301,080	176,715	58.7	72,945	24.2	41,860	13.9	9,560	3.2
Armenian	202,710	108,555	53.6	48,470	23.9	31,870	15.7	13,815	6.8
Persian	312,085	198,040	63.5	70,910	22.7	32,960	10.6	10,175	3.3
Gujarathi	235,985	155,010	65.7	50,635	21.5	22,520	9.5	7,820	3.3
Hindi	317,055	245,190	77.3	51,930	16.4	16,680	5.3	3,255	1.0
Urdu	262,900	180,020	68.5	56,735	21.6	20,815	7.9	5,330	2.0
Other Indic languages	439,285	274,140	62.4	108,510	24.7	43,395	9.9	13,240	3.0
Other Indo-European languages	327,945	196,470	59.9	83,685	25.5	38,720	11.8	9,070	2.8
Asian and Pacific Island languages	6,960,070	3,370,045	48.4	2,023,310	29.1	1,260,260	18.1	306,455	4.4
Chinese	2,022,140	855,690	42.3	595,330	29.4	408,595	20.2	162,525	8.0
Japanese	478,000	241,705	50.6	146,615	30.7	84,020	17.6	5,660	1.2

(continued)

TABLE 7.1 (CONTINUED)

Language Spoken at Home	Total Number	Speak English "very well" Number	Speak English "very well" Percent	Speak English "well" Number	Speak English "well" Percent	Speak English "not well" Number	Speak English "not well" Percent	Speak English "not at all" Number	Speak English "not at all" Percent
Korean	894,060	361,165	40.4	268,475	30.0	228,390	25.6	36,030	4.0
Mon-Khmer, Cambodian	181,890	77,620	42.7	51,650	28.4	41,460	22.8	11,160	6.1
Miao, Hmong	168,065	65,865	39.2	55,910	33.3	34,405	20.5	11,885	7.1
Thai	120,465	57,630	47.8	43,250	35.9	17,635	14.6	1,950	1.6
Laotian	149,305	67,565	45.3	43,175	28.9	32,100	21.5	6,465	4.3
Vietnamese	1,009,625	342,595	33.9	340,060	33.7	270,950	26.8	56,020	5.6
Other Asian languages	398,440	282,565	70.9	81,740	20.5	28,000	7.0	6,135	1.5
Tagalog	1,224,240	827,560	67.6	311,465	25.4	79,720	6.5	5,495	0.5
Other Pacific Island languages	313,840	190,085	60.6	85,640	27.3	34,985	11.2	3,130	1.0
Other languages	1,872,485	1,283,660	68.6	399,395	21.3	151,125	8.1	38,305	2.0
Navajo	178,015	115,025	64.6	42,975	24.1	14,390	8.1	5,625	3.2
Other Native North American languages	203,465	149,020	73.2	41,010	20.2	12,430	6.1	1,005	0.5
Hungarian	117,975	79,600	67.5	28,310	24.0	9,005	7.6	1,060	0.9
Arabic	614,580	403,395	65.6	140,055	22.8	58,595	9.5	12,535	2.0
Hebrew	195,375	158,450	81.1	28,575	14.6	7,770	4.0	580	0.3
African languages	418,500	294,455	70.4	87,135	20.8	30,875	7.4	6,035	1.4
Other and unspecified languages	144,575	83,715	57.9	31,335	21.7	18,060	12.5	11,465	7.9

[Data based on a sample. For information on confidentiality protection, sampling error, nonsampling error, and definitions, see http://www.census.gov/prod/cen2000/doc/sf3.pdf]

(X) Not applicable.

Source: Anneka L. Kindler, *Survey of the States' Limited English Proficient Students and Available Educational Programs and Services, 2000–2001 Summary Report.* (Washington, DC: National Clearinghouse for English Language Acquisition and Language Instruction Educational Programs, October 2002).

spoken languages in the nation's schools. The growth of the population that speaks native languages other than English is also reflected in public school enrollments. While the national growth of the school-age population—that is, those from 5 to 17 years of age—increased by 17 percent from 1990 to 2000, during the same time period, the percentage of English-language learners increased by a staggering 46 percent.[5] Even more dramatic, the growth of this population, compared to that during the previous decade, was over 100 percent (see Figure 7.1).

The demographic changes indicated by these statistics are part of a larger trend of immigration to the United States, which, since the late 1970s, has been responsible for a remarkable shift in our population. (Some of these data were presented in Chapter 1.) The reasons for this trend are varied, from a worsening economic situation in many countries, to a rise in the number of refugees from countries where the United States was involved in aggression (as was the case in Central America and

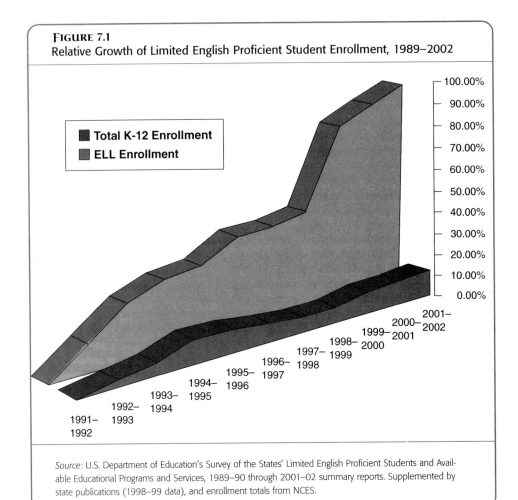

FIGURE 7.1
Relative Growth of Limited English Proficient Student Enrollment, 1989–2002

Source: U.S. Department of Education's Survey of the States' Limited English Proficient Students and Available Educational Programs and Services, 1989–90 through 2001–02 summary reports. Supplemented by state publications (1998–99 data), and enrollment totals from NCES.

Southeast Asia), to the loosening of immigration restrictions for some parts of the world. Unlike the earlier massive wave of immigration at the turn of the 20th century, the greatest number of immigrants are now from Asia and Latin America. All the states have felt the impact of this immigration, but the states with the largest enrollment of language-minority students are California (with over one-third of all students for whom English is a second language), Texas, Florida, New York, Illinois, and Arizona. At the same time, the greatest growth in the percentage of students with limited English proficiency were in states that had previously had very low numbers of such students. Georgia topped the list with a 113 percent increase, followed by Mississippi with a 79 percent increase.[6]

These changes in the population of the United States have profound implications for education. For one, approaches and programs to teach language-minority students need to be expanded. Most states have legislative provisions for students with limited English proficiency. However, although these services may include English as a second language (ESL) instruction, bilingual or dual language instruction, or both, the number of students in bilingual classrooms has decreased in the past several years. In 2000, for instance, only 22 percent of language minority students were receiving any instruction in their native language, although this does not mean that they were in bilingual programs.[7] The reasons for the decline of bilingual education programs also vary, from an ideological resistance to approaches based on native language instruction to legislative changes (bilingual education, for instance, has been eliminated in a number of states since the late 1990s). Finding qualified personnel has been another major problem. For instance, a survey of teachers concerning their preparedness to teach language-minority students found that only 20 percent of teachers felt "very well prepared" to teach them.[8]

A Brief Overview of the History of Language Diversity in U.S. Schools

The notion that children who do not yet speak English lack language altogether is a prevalent one in the United States, and it is linked with the mainstream perception that cultures other than the dominant one lack significance. In our nation, linguistic diversity has commonly been viewed as a temporary, if troublesome, barrier to learning. After students learn English, the thinking goes, learning can then proceed unhampered. Forgetting their native language is seen as a regrettable but necessary price to pay for the benefits of citizenship. As a result of this thinking, the traditional strategy in most schools has been to help students rid themselves as quickly as possible of what is perceived as the "burden" of speaking another language. Yet we lose a valuable resource, on both a personal and a national level, when we pressure students who speak a language other than English as their native language to drop that language and replace it with English. A far more productive strategy would be to encourage the maintenance of heritage languages while also promoting the learning of English.

Entire communities have been denied the use of their native language, not only for instruction in schools but also for social communication of all kinds. Throughout our history, the language rights of substantial numbers of people have been violated, from prohibiting enslaved Africans from speaking their languages to the recent imposition of "English Only" laws in a growing number of states.[9] Joel Spring provides many compelling historical examples of the strategy of linguistic "deculturalization" used in the schooling of Native Americans, Puerto Ricans, Mexican Americans, and Asian Americans.[10]

U.S. language policies and practices have by no means been uniform. Rather, they have ranged widely from "sink or swim" policies (i.e., immersing language-minority students in English-only classrooms to fend on their own) to the imposition of English as the sole medium of instruction, to allowing and even encouraging bilingualism. By 1900, for example, at least 600,000 children, or about 4 percent of students enrolled in public and parochial elementary schools, were being taught in bilingual German/English bilingual schools. Smaller numbers were taught in Polish, Italian, Norwegian, Spanish, French, Czech, Dutch, and other languages.[11]

The zigzag of support and rejection of languages other than English demonstrates the ambivalence with which language diversity has been viewed in the United States. Today, misgivings concerning native-language maintenance, particularly bilingual education, still exist. The public has always been deeply divided over bilingual education, and this is more true today than ever before. There is a general reluctance to support bilingual education because it involves the use of not only English but also a language other than English for instruction. The fact that bilingual education has as one of its fundamental goals the *learning of English* often goes unmentioned by opponents. They focus their opposition on the practice of using students' native language in instruction because they perceive it to be a threat to national unity. But it is a myth that English has been a unifying force. In the words of James Crawford, who has exhaustively researched language policies in the United States, "Such notions obscure a multilingual tradition that is unsurpassed in its variety and richness, while inventing for English a unifying role that it rarely enjoyed."[12]

In the United States, language use and patriotic loyalty have often been linked, and patriotism has been measured by how quickly one abandons his or her native language and replaces it with English. Such views hold sway today for any number of reasons, from the massive number of new immigrants crossing our borders, to the incidents of September 11, 2001. Being fluent in another language, even if one is also fluent in English, is often viewed with suspicion, at least in the case of immigrants. Consequently, where language issues are concerned, everyone has gotten into the fray. As President Theodore Roosevelt, a spokesperson for the restrictive language policies at the beginning of the 20th century that were a response to the huge influx of primarily East European immigrants to the United States, said: "We have room for but one language here, and that is the English language; for we intend to see that the crucible turns our people out as Americans, of American nationality, and not as dwellers in a polyglot boardinghouse."[13] Roosevelt's views were widely shared by many people who felt threatened by the new wave of immigrants.

At times, restrictive views of language have resulted in counterproductive policies that inhibit or even prohibit the learning of foreign languages, as was the case with the teaching of German in the period between World War I and World War II. More recently, in 1998, the controversy surrounding native-language use resulted in the passage of California's Proposition 227, in which bilingual education was weakened considerably. Arizona followed suit in 2000, and Massachusetts in 2002. (A similar proposition failed in Colorado in 2002.) The implications of these measures for the rest of the country need to be considered within the context of U.S. Society, which is becoming *more*, not *less*, linguistically diverse. That our society continues to be ignorant of other languages and cultures is self-evident. That it is now jeopardized by this monolingualism and monoculturalism in a world becoming increasingly interdependent is also becoming more and more apparent.

LINGUISTIC DIVERSITY AND LEARNING

All good teachers know that learning builds on prior knowledge and experiences. In the case of language-minority students, we seem to forget this truth as we effectively rob students of access to their prior learning, thus contradicting how learning takes place and the crucial role of language in the process. One's native language is a foundation for future learning. If we think of language development as the concrete foundation of a building, it makes sense that it needs to be strong to sustain the stress of many tons of building materials that will be erected on top of it. This is analogous to what takes place when students enter school in the United States: They use the language they know as a foundation for learning the content of the curriculum. For English speakers, this is a seamless process. For English-language learners, however, not knowing English is a tremendous disadvantage, not because their native language is ineffectual for learning, but because it is not usually viewed by their teachers and schools as a resource for learning. Extending the metaphor further, it would be as if the strong foundation that had been created were abandoned and the building materials were placed on top of a sand lot across the street. Needless to say, the building would crumble in short order.

According to Jim Cummins, "There is general agreement among cognitive psychologists that we learn by integrating new input into our existing cognitive structures or schemata. Our prior experience provides the foundation for interpreting new information. No learner is a blank slate."[14] As a rule, however, teachers and schools disregard language-minority students' native languages and cultures for what they believe to be good reasons: Because they link students' English-language proficiency with their prospective economic and social mobility, they may view English language learners as "handicapped" and thus urge students, through both subtle and direct means, to abandon their native language. For example, teachers and administrators ask parents to speak English to their children at home, they punish children for using their native language, or they simply withhold education until the children have mastered English, usually in the name of protecting students' futures.

Even if they have gifted and caring teachers, language-minority students may experience trauma when learning their new language. No doubt, the stress of immigration and the reasons for leaving their home countries play a part in this trauma for some of them, but just the process of learning a new language can be a devastating experience for many. In recounting her extensive experience teaching immigrant children, Cristina Igoa suggests that sheer weariness is one consequence: "A recurring theme regarding the inner world of the immigrant child is a feeling of exhaustion, not only from the sounds of a new language but also from the continual parade of strange sights and events in a new culture."[15]

Although some teachers may treat the fact that students speak a language other than English as a problem, lack of English skills alone cannot explain the poor academic achievement of language minority students. It is tempting to point to English "sink or swim" programs as the solution to the problem of academic failure, but confounding English-language acquisition with academic achievement is simplistic at best. For example, a study of a rural high school in northern California by Rebecca Callahan found that issues other than English proficiency were much more salient influences on the academic achievement of language-minority students. Specifically, track placement proved to be more significant because many English learners were enrolled in low-track curricula that do little to prepare them for college and other post-secondary school opportunities. More than anything, then, teachers' and schools' perception of the abilities of English-language learners get in the way of student achievement. In Callahan's words, "Constructions of English learners as deficient, bilingual programs as compensatory, and ESL classrooms as linguistic rather than academic speak to the marginalization of English learners in U.S. schools."[16]

In contrast to negative perceptions of bilingualism, a good deal of research confirms the positive influence of knowing more than one language. Native-language maintenance may act as a buffer against academic failure by simply supporting literacy in children's most developed language. For example, Lourdes Díaz Soto's research among 30 Hispanic families of young children with low and high academic achievement found that the parents of the higher achieving children favored a native-language environment to a greater extent than those of the lower achieving youngsters.[17] Patricia Gándara, in analyzing the impressive academic achievements of 50 Mexican American adults who grew up in poverty, found that the largest percentage of these successful adults grew up in households where *only* Spanish was spoken, and a remarkable two-thirds of them began school speaking *only* Spanish.[18]

That students' native language is an asset that can enhance their academic achievement was also found to be true by Ana Celia Zentella in a study of 19 families in El Barrio, a low-income, predominantly Puerto Rican community in New York City. In her research, the most successful students were enrolled in bilingual programs and were the most fluent bilinguals.[19] Also, in their review of research studies concerning the adaptation and school achievement of immigrants of various backgrounds, Alejandro Portes and Rubén Rumbaut came to a striking conclusion: Students with limited bilingualism are far more likely to leave school than those fluent in both languages. Rather than being an impediment to academic achievement, bilingualism can act to promote learning.[20]

Conclusions such as these contradict the common advice given to language minority parents to "speak English with your children at home." In contrast, Catherine Snow, a respected researcher in literacy and language acquisition, suggests that "the greatest contribution immigrant parents can make to their children's success is to ensure they maintain fluency and continue to develop the home language."[21] This makes sense, of course, and it leads us to reflect on the innate wisdom of many immigrant mothers, including my (Sonia's) mother, who ignored teachers' pleas to speak to us in English. Had it not been for my mother's quiet but obstinate resistance, my sister and I would probably now be monolingual English speakers rather than fluent bilinguals.

The problem of language-minority children has often been articulated as a problem of not knowing English. But the real problem may be what Luis Moll has labeled the "obsession with speaking English,"[22] as if learning English is the solution to all the other difficulties faced by language-minority students, including poverty, racism, poorly financed schools, and lack of access to excellent education. Learning English is, of course, important and necessary for all students; this is a given. But, rather than supporting the suppression or elimination of native language use at home and school, the research reviewed here supports promoting native-language literacy as a way to promote learning English more effectively. If this is the case, the language dominance of students is not the real issue; rather, *the way in which teachers and schools view students' language may have an even greater influence on their achievement.*

The way in which languages other than English are perceived by the schools and teachers, and whether modifications in the curriculum are made as a result, are therefore crucial issues to keep in mind. For this reason, language diversity needs to be placed within a sociopolitical context to understand why speaking a language other than English is not itself a handicap. On the contrary, it can be a great asset to learning. The myths regarding language use are part of the sociopolitical context. For example, in the United States, the prevailing view about knowing languages other than English is that, among culturally dominated groups, bilingualism is a burden, yet among middle-class and wealthy students, it is usually seen as an asset. It is not unusual to find in the same high school the seemingly incongruous, ironic situation of one group of students having their native language wiped out while another group of students struggles to learn a foreign language, a language they will never be able to use with any real fluency. There are more affirming approaches to teaching language-minority students, and they need to be used more widely than is currently the case. Recent research on how to build on students' languages and literacies provide a more hopeful direction in the education of language-minority students.[23]

APPROACHES TO TEACHING LANGUAGE-MINORITY STUDENTS

Given the dramatic increase in the number of English-language learners in our country in the past several decades, every classroom in every city and town has already been, or will soon be, affected. This reality is in stark contrast to the conventional wisdom that only specialists teach these children. For instance, a 2002 survey reported that *more than 40 percent* of all teachers in the nation reported that they taught students who were limited in their English proficiency, yet only 12 percent of these teachers had eight or more hours of training in how to teach these students.[24] More recently, in 2005, a survey of over 5,000 California teachers found that they were largely ill prepared to meet the needs of the state's nearly 1.6 million ELLs because they had received little professional development geared specifically to the task of teaching these students.[25] It is clear that the responsibility for educating language-minority students can no longer fall only on those teachers who have been trained specifically to provide bilingual education and ESL services. This responsibility needs to be shared

SNAPSHOT

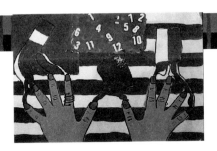

Liane Chang

Liane is a ninth-grade student at a comprehensive high school in a midsize town in the Northeast. Her father is European American, and her mother is Chinese. Liane is fortunate because her efforts to learn Chinese, her mother's native language, are supported in the school system. Her pride and excitement in developing fluency in Chinese speaks to the affirmation she experiences in both her school and home settings. Liane's experience points to the power of a school experience that can support students in maintaining or reclaiming their family language.

If I look at how my different ethnicities have influenced my education, I would have to say that it has impacted my confidence in expressing my cultures to others. When people ask me to tell them how I identify, I reply, "Eurasian" [and] their reaction is always a very positive comment, the sort of thing that could start a whole conversation. I think that being Eurasian is about the coolest identity a person could have. Many might think that it would be embarrassing to be anything other than what is said to be "American" but through my teachers' and peers' influence, I see it as an opportunity to be an individual.

Now I am learning Chinese in school (with the help of my mom). I felt that, since I am Chinese, I should learn the language so that, when my mom and I go to China, I can understand and speak the language also. My love of the Chinese language has always been great throughout my childhood. I used to dream and wonder what it would be like for me to speak a different language, and my inspiration came from my mother's conversations with her Chinese friends, either on the phone or in person. Late at night, right before I was tucked into bed, my mother would always say goodnight to me in Chinese.

My lesson on how to say "Thank you" in Chinese was useful when I went to Chinese restaurants or people's homes. Many trips yearly to New York City's Chinatown were also a great inspiration in my early childhood. This language and culture inspired me to choose to learn the language through my middle and high school world-language programs. Now that I'm learning Chinese, it's like I'm more

related to my mom. It gave me more of a personal connection with my mom . . . something that I'll always share with her. She can help me because she understands it, and [it is] just something between her and me . . . very special. It can be very, very difficult at times because, when she corrects me, it doesn't seem like I know the language very much. But she helps me in a way that I can't be helped at school, and she gives me a new outlook on the language. It's a neat experience.

My grandparents on the European side of me are the only grandparents I have ever known. They have taught me hard work ethics and frugality that they learned through their daily lives. From these cultures, I have received what my grandparents learned through generations and have passed down to my parents and myself. And because these were the only grandparents I have ever known during my life, their stories and memories were also passed to me to treasure and to pass on to other generations. Through their hardships growing up in Europe during World War II and their few choices, I feel that I can appreciate my opportunities here to receive a good education. During World War II, my grandpa in Poland was captured by the Germans and forced to do manual labor, but he did not have to go to a concentration camp. When he got out, he went to France, because he couldn't return to Poland. Then he married my Grandma, so my dad is French-Polish.

Somewhere else, people might think I'm not American because I don't look like the typical American, but here, in this school system, it's sort of the opposite. Being different makes you cool, and you can have your own individuality and you can differentiate yourself from different people. It's sort of a good thing, here, to be different—and I've never had someone be racist about my different cultures—except when you are really little, you know, the rhyme when they pull back their eyes? But that's little-kid stuff.

In seventh grade, I went to China with my Chinese teacher. It was a really good chance to see it . . . to be in an environment where I was actually a minority—being American—instead of being in an environment where everybody's similar, you feel not part of their culture, because it is so different from what you are used to. My language skills were new then. I knew basic questions of survival. The experience was really overwhelming at times, but really exciting too. We went to visit a Chinese high school, and we were

(continued)

each set up with a Chinese student, and we tried to communicate with, and ask them about their life. Actually it was the school that my mom's dad went to when he was in China. Isn't that neat?

In seventh grade art, I completed a project about myself, expressing various symbols that had meaning [for me]. Though I did not have many symbols, each of them represents a lot about my life and heritage. For example, the flags that I put on my collage symbolize more than my heritage. They symbolize the people who come from there and are a big part of my life.

In my picture, I have the flags of my heritage flowing out of my fingernails like smoke. There are a total of three: the Chinese, French, and Polish flags. The Chinese flag represents my heritage on my mom's side. Both of her parents were born in China and immigrated to Taiwan during the Chinese Revolution. On the other hand, in my painting, my dad is both French and Polish. Polish and French are a big part of my family. Last of all, I have an American flag for the background of my project. This, of course, represents the place my sister Jillian and I were born. Since it is the biggest part of my life, it is the largest in the collage. I am proud to be American and that is the most important thing of all that I symbolized in the project.

COMMENTARY

Liane's snapshot can help us think about what it might mean to have more school systems support students' identities by offering language courses from various language groups and even trips to the countries where those languages are spoken. Although not every language can be offered and trips are out of the question for many schools, it is intriguing to see how Liane's experience was made so much more positive by studying Chinese. Not only was Chinese one of the languages of her heritage, but it also promoted a closer relationship with her mother. We can adapt this approach for language-minority students in our schools: those who enter school without English but are our future citizens.

by *all* teachers and *all* schools, yet most teachers have had little training in language acquisition and other language-related issues.

What do all classroom teachers need to know to help them be better teachers of language minority students? How can they best prepare to teach students of different language backgrounds and varying language abilities? Fortunately, more attention is being paid to these questions than has been the case in the recent past.[26] In the following sections, we suggest a number of steps that teachers and schools can take to effectively educate English-language learners. Before doing so, however, we want to emphasize that we are not suggesting that teachers will automatically produce results by simply following a set of prescribed strategies. Although learning new approaches and techniques may be very helpful, teaching students successfully means, above all, changing one's attitudes toward the students, their languages and cultures, and their communities. Anything short of this will result in repeating the pattern of failure that currently exists.[27] As Jim Cummins has eloquently stated, "Fortunately, good teaching does not require us to internalize an endless list of instructional techniques. Much more fundamental is the recognition that human relationships are central to effective instruction."[28]

UNDERSTANDING LANGUAGE DEVELOPMENT, SECOND-LANGUAGE ACQUISITION, AND THE SOCIOPOLITICAL CONTEXT OF EDUCATION

All teachers need to understand how language is learned—both native and subsequent languages. This knowledge is often reserved for specialists in bilingual and ESL education, but it should become standard knowledge for all teachers. For example,

Stephen Krashen's significant theories of second-language acquisition and his recommendations that teachers provide students for whom English is a second language with *comprehensible input*—that is, cues that are contextualized in their instruction—is useful for all teachers who have language-minority students in their classrooms.[29] Likewise, related knowledge in curriculum and instruction, linguistics, sociology, and history are all helpful for teachers of language-minority students. Consequently, all teachers should have:

- Familiarity with first- and second-language acquisition
- Awareness of the sociocultural and sociopolitical context of education for language-minority students
- Awareness of the history of immigration in the United States, with particular attention to language policies and practices throughout that history
- Knowledge of the history and experiences of specific groups of people, especially those who are residents of the city, town, and state where they are teaching
- The ability to adapt curriculum for students whose first language is other than English
- Competence in pedagogical approaches suitable for culturally and linguistically heterogeneous classrooms
- Experience with teachers of diverse backgrounds and the ability to develop collaborative relationships with colleagues that promote the learning of language-minority students
- The ability to communicate effectively with parents of diverse language, cultural, and social class backgrounds[30]

According to Lily Wong Fillmore and Catherine Snow, besides appropriate preservice experiences and positive attitudes about ELL students, basic coursework in educational linguistics is "the bare minimum" for preparing teachers for today's schools.[31] Unfortunately, however, many teachers have not had access to this kind of knowledge during their teacher preparation or even in their professional development after becoming teachers. Consequently, they may need to acquire this knowledge on their own. They can do this by attending conferences in literacy, bilingual education, multicultural education, and ESL; participating in professional development opportunities in their district and beyond; subscribing to journals and newsletters in these fields; setting up study groups with colleagues to discuss and practice different strategies; and returning to graduate school to take relevant courses or to seek advanced degrees.

DEVELOPING AN ADDITIVE BILINGUAL PERSPECTIVE

Additive bilingualism refers to a framework for understanding language acquisition and development that *adds* a new language rather than *subtracts* an existing one.[32] This perspective is radically different from the traditional expectation in our society that immigrants need to exchange their native language for their new language, English. Many educators and others are now questioning whether it needs to be this way.

WHAT YOU CAN DO

ACCEPT STUDENTS' IDENTITIES

Learn to say each child's name correctly. Don't change *Marisol* to *Marcy* or *Vinh* to *Vinny*. As simplistic as it may sound, this basic rule of respect is violated daily in classrooms around the nation. Given the pressure to conform that all students face, some of them readily accede to having their names changed so that they can fit in. Although learning many names in different languages may be time consuming for teachers, it is a first step in affirming who students *are* rather than who we may want them to become.

Abandoning one's native language leads not only to individual psychological costs but also to a tremendous loss of linguistic resources to the nation. Additive bilingualism supports the notion that two is better than one—that English *plus* other languages can make us stronger individually and as a society.

The challenge is that many teachers do not speak the native languages of their students. Nevertheless, all teachers, even those who are monolingual English speakers, can create a learning environment that supports and affirms the native languages of their students. A good example comes from researchers David Schwarzer, Alexia Haywood, and Charla Lorenzen, who described their collaborative work within a multiliterate preschool classroom in Central Texas.[33] They suggest, for example, that teachers can tap into some of the resources available in students' native languages by creating a multiliterate learning community with the help of students, their families, elders, and other community members. Some of the ideas they suggest for doing this are creating a multiliterate print environment in the classroom; using literature in students' native languages; learning some key words in students' first languages; creating audiotapes of greetings, simple conversations, songs, and stories in students' first languages; and so on. It is clear that teachers—even those who do not speak the native languages of their students—can demonstrate an appreciation and support for these languages in numerous ways. There are many reasons for doing so, including the affirmation it gives students who do not yet speak English. Even more important, nurturing native-language literacy is supported by research demonstrating that the skills students develop in their native language are usually easily transferred to a second or third language.[34] This being the case, how can we continue to view bilingualism as a deficit?

CONSCIOUSLY FOSTERING NATIVE-LANGUAGE LITERACY

As we saw in the previous examples, developing an additive approach to language acquisition counters the false assumption that students must forget their native language. Even small gestures in the classroom can convey this message of inclusion of native languages. In her work with immigrant students, for instance, Cristina Igoa reserved the last period of the day, three times a week, for students to listen to stories or to read in their native languages. Because she did not speak all the languages of her many students, she recruited college students who were fluent in various languages to help out.[35]

Teachers can also make a commitment to learn at least one of the languages of their students. When they become second-language learners, teachers develop a new appreciation for both the joys and the struggles experienced by language-minority students—including exhaustion, frustration, and withdrawal—when they are learning English. This was what happened to Bill Dunn, a veteran teacher who decided to, in his words, "come out of the closet as a Spanish speaker." He realized that, after teaching for 20 years in a largely Puerto Rican community, he understood a great deal of Spanish, so he decided to study it formally and to keep a journal of his experiences. Although he had always been a wonderful and caring teacher, putting himself in the place of his students helped him understand a great many things more clearly—from students' grammatical errors in English to their boredom and misbehavior when they could not understand the language of instruction.[36] As a result, he developed more targeted pedagogical strategies for teaching them as well as a renewed respect for the situation of students who are learning English.

The responsibility to create powerful learning environments for English-language learners should not rest on individual teachers alone, however. Entire schools can also develop such environments: They can, for instance, make a conscious effort to recruit and hire bilingual staff members who can communicate with parents in their native languages. A major challenge, however, is that few teacher-preparation programs are currently preparing teachers and administrators to create positive conditions for English-language learners. Programs that do so are based on the premise that diversity is a resource to be cherished. Consequently, they provide a number of elements for preservice teachers and administrators: courses in language acquisition and development, field placements in schools that are successful with English-language learners, experiences in a second language, and others.[37]

These recommendations are based (1) on the assumption that all students come to their learning with skills and talents that can be used as resources and (2) on the notion that biliteracy is a value in itself, a case that has been made by numerous researchers including María de la Luz Reyes, John Halcón, María Fránquiz, María Torres-Guzmán, and many others.[38] Native-language literacy is a resource that should be cherished, and it is the basis for bilingual education, which we consider next.

LANGUAGE DIVERSITY AND THE CASE FOR BILINGUAL EDUCATION

The freedom to maintain and use one's native language is thought by some linguists and human rights advocates to be a basic human right. The proposal for a Declaration of Children's Linguistic Human Rights, for instance, places linguistic rights on the same level as other human rights.[39] This proposal includes the right to identify positively with one's mother tongue, to learn it, and to choose when to use it. Although these rights may be self-evident for language-majority children (in the United States this means native English speakers), they may not be so apparent for those who speak a language that carries a stigma, as is the case with most language-minority students in the United States.

Just as racial integration was considered a key civil right for those who were forcibly segregated, bilingual education is viewed by many language-minority communities as equally vital. There is a significant link between bilingual education and equity. Although frequently addressed as simply an issue of language, it can be argued that using students' native language in instruction is a civil rights issue. Doing this provides some measure of assurance that children who do not speak English will be educated in a language they understand. Without it, millions of children may be doomed to a future of educational underachievement and limited occupational choices.

In 1974, the U.S. Supreme Court recognized the connection between native-language rights and equal educational opportunity. In 1969, plaintiffs representing 1,800 Chinese-speaking students had sued the San Francisco Unified School District for failing to provide students who did not speak English with an equal chance to learn. They lost their case in San Francisco, but by 1974 they had taken it all the way to the Supreme Court. In the landmark *Lau v. Nichols* case, the Court ruled unanimously that the civil rights of students who did not understand the language of instruction were indeed being violated. Citing Title VI of the Civil Rights Act, the Court stated, in part:

> There is no equality of treatment merely by providing students with the same facilities, textbooks, teachers, and curriculum; for students who do not understand English are effectively foreclosed from any meaningful education. Basic skills are at the very core of what these public schools teach. Imposition of a requirement that, before a child can effectively participate in the educational program he must already have acquired those basic skills is to make a mockery of public education.[40]

Although the decision did not impose any particular remedy, its results were immediate and extensive. By 1975, the Office for Civil Rights and the Department of Health, Education, and Welfare issued a document called *The* Lau *Remedies*, which served as the basis for determining whether or not school systems throughout the United States were in compliance with the *Lau* decision. This document provided guidance in identifying students with limited proficiency in English, assessing their language abilities, and providing appropriate programs. Bilingual programs became the common remedy in most school systems.

The Equal Educational Opportunities Act (EEOA) of 1974 has also been instrumental in protecting the language rights of students for whom English is not their native language. This law interprets the failure of any educational agency to "take appropriate action to overcome language barriers that impede equal participation by its students in its instructional programs" as a denial of equal educational opportunity.[41] In both the *Lau* decision and the EEOA, bilingual education emerged as a key strategy to counteract the language discrimination faced by many students in our schools.

There is a dizzying array of program models and definitions of bilingual educa-tion,[42] but in general terms, *bilingual education* can be defined as an educational program that involves the *use of two languages of instruction* at some point in a stu-dent's school career. This definition is broad enough to include many program vari-ations. For example, a child who speaks a language other than English, let's say, Vietnamese, may receive instruction in content areas in Vietnamese while at the same time learning ESL. The cultures associated with both the native language and English are generally part of the curriculum as well. This approach, sometimes called *bilingual/bicultural education*, is based on the premise that the language and culture children bring to school are assets that must be used in their education.

In the United States, a primary objective of bilingual education is to develop pro-ficiency and literacy in the English language. As such, ESL is an integral and neces-sary component of all bilingual programs because it goes hand in hand with native-language instruction in content areas. When provided in isolation, however, ESL cannot be called *bilingual* education because the child's native language is not used in instruction. Although they are learning English, students in ESL programs may be languishing in their other subject areas because they do not understand the language of instruction. Their education usually consists only of learning English until they can function in the regular English-language environment.

In spite of opposition to bilingual education in many places, various models of bilingual education can still be found in schools throughout our nation. *Transitional bilingual education* is probably the most common model of bilingual ed-ucation in the United States. In this approach, students receive their content-area instruction in their native language while learning English as a second language. As soon as they are deemed ready to benefit from the monolingual English-language curriculum, they are "exited" or "mainstreamed" out of the program. The rationale behind this model is that native-language services should serve only as a transition to English. Therefore, there is a limit on the time a student may be in a bilingual program—usually three years. This limit was established in 1971 by Massachusetts, the first state to mandate bilingual education, and although bilin-gual education, as such, no longer exists in Massachusetts (it was replaced by a one-year English immersion program in 2002 through a ballot initiative), it has served as a model for other states.

Developmental or *maintenance bilingual education* can be characterized as a robust version of bilingual education because it provides a more comprehensive and long-term approach. As in the transitional approach, students receive content-area in-struction in their native language while learning English as a second language. The difference is that generally no limit is set on the time students can be in the program. The objective is to develop students' fluency in both languages, or *biliteracy*, by using both for instruction. The longer the students remain in the program the more func-tionally bilingual they become and therefore the more balanced the curriculum to which they are exposed. That is, the students can potentially receive equal amounts of instruction in English and their native language.

Two-way bilingual education, also called *two-way immersion*, is another model. This approach integrates students whose native language is English with students for whom English is a second language. The goal of this approach is to develop bilingual proficiency, academic achievement, and positive cross-cultural attitudes and behaviors among all students. The approach lends itself to cooperative learning and peer tutoring because all students have considerable skills to share with one another. There is generally no time limit, although some two-way programs are part of existing transitional programs and therefore have the same entrance and exit criteria, at least for the students who are learning English. Two-way programs hold the promise of expanding our nation's linguistic resources and improving relationships between majority and minority language groups.

A variety of approaches and strategies are used in two-way programs, depending on the students enrolled, the program design, and the particular community. Most two-way programs use students' native or second language at different stages, and most are Spanish-English programs. Results of the two-way model have been very positive. In a longitudinal study of students who had been in two-way immersion (TWI) Spanish/English programs, researchers Elizabeth Howard, Donna Christian, and Fred Genesee found impressive levels of performance in reading, writing, and oral language in both English and Spanish. Students, both native English speakers and native Spanish speakers, had very high levels of English fluency, and while native English speakers scored lower on reading Spanish than native Spanish speakers, their oral Spanish proficiency was quite high.[43] Another study of a two-way program found that a high number of high school students who had been enrolled in a two-way program throughout elementary school had positive attitudes toward school and expectations of attending college. Many of the Hispanic students in the study credited the two-way program with keeping them from dropping out of high school. The researchers, Kathryn Lindholm-Leary and Graciela Borsato, pointed to the development of a sense of "resiliency" among the Hispanic students in the study, especially those who were from low-income families.[44]

The fact is that bilingual education is generally more effective than other programs such as ESL alone, not only for learning content through the native language but also for learning English. This finding has been validated by many studies and meta-analyses throughout the years, most recently by a comprehensive summary of research conducted by the National Literacy Panel on Language-Minority Children and Youth.[45] This apparently counterintuitive finding can be understood if one considers that students in bilingual programs are educated in content areas *along with* structured instruction in English. Students in bilingual education programs are building on their previous literacy, but this may not be the case in ESL programs that concentrate on English grammar, phonics, and other language features out of context with the way in which real, day-to-day language is used.

Bilingual programs may have secondary salutary effects. These include motivating students to remain in school rather than dropping out, making school more meaningful and, in general, making the school experience more enjoyable. This was certainly true for Manuel Gomes, whose case study follows this chapter. Because of the close-knit relationships between his Crioulo-speaking teachers and their students, Manuel's transition to English was far easier than it might otherwise have been. A related phenomenon may be that bilingual education reinforces close relationships among children and their family members, promoting more communication than would be the case if they were instructed solely in English.

WHY THE CONTROVERSY OVER BILINGUAL EDUCATION?

Why is there such controversy over bilingual education despite research findings of its effectiveness? The truth is that bilingual education has always been controversial. Both its proponents and its opponents have long recognized its potential for empowering traditionally powerless groups. Thus, the issue is not so much whether bilingual education works, but rather the real possibility that it *might*. Bilingual education challenges conventional U.S. educational wisdom that native language and culture need to be forgotten in order to be successful students and "real Americans." Bilingual education continues to be controversial because it generally represents the class and ethnic group interests of traditionally subordinated groups and it comes out on the side of education as an emancipatory proposition. In the end, children who could benefit from bilingual education are, as Jim Cummins asserts, caught "in the crossfire."[46]

In spite of its sound pedagogical basis, bilingual education is, above all, a political issue because it is concerned with power relations in society. Understanding the political nature of bilingual education, and of multicultural education in general, is therefore essential if we are to develop effective programs for all students. For example, through an extensive review of programs for ELLs, the 2006 National Literacy Panel report concerning literacy for English language learners—a panel hand-picked and appointed by President George W. Bush—found that good bilingual programs produce faster results in developing English fluency than good English-only programs. Because this finding contradicted the administration's English-only agenda, it was not made public through official government channels. In an unusual move, both the *New York Times* and the *Los Angeles Times* urged the government to release the findings. Ultimately, the report was published privately.[47]

Nevertheless, although bilingual education is a political issue, we need to emphasize that it is *also* a pedagogical issue. Successful bilingual programs have demonstrated that students can learn through their native language while learning English *and also* achieving academically. This achievement contradicts the conservative agenda, which calls for a return to traditional curriculum and pedagogy. Successful bilingual education threatens to explode the myth of the "basics" if the basics means only valuing a Eurocentric curriculum and the English language. In fact, fluency in English, although necessary, is no guarantee that students of language-minority backgrounds will succeed in school or later in life. If this were the case, all language-minority students who have never been in bilingual programs or who were mainstreamed into regular classes years ago, would be doing quite well academically, but as we know, this is far from the case. Additionally, research by Alejandro Portes and Rubén Rumbaut found that the students they studied from nationalities that speak English best (including West Indians and Filipinos) are not necessarily those who earn the highest incomes or have the highest number of managers and professionals among their ranks. On the other hand, Chinese and other Asians and Colombians and other Latin Americans, with relatively low fluency in English, earn considerably more. English-language fluency, then, is not the only explanation. In some cases, according to Portes and Rumbaut, the way in which immigrants have been received and incorporated into the society also matters a great deal.[48]

PROMISING PRACTICES FOR LANGUAGE-MINORITY STUDENTS

Although bilingual education represents a notable advance over monolingual education, it is unrealistic to expect it to work for all English-language learners. It is often perceived as a panacea for all the educational problems of language-minority students, but even with bilingual education, many children are likely to face educational failure. No approach or program is a panacea for all the problems, educational and otherwise, facing young people. Essential issues such as poverty, racism, reception and incorporation into the society, and structural inequality also need to be faced. Simply substituting one language for another, or using books in Spanish with Dick and Jane in brownface, will not guarantee success for language-minority students. Expecting too much of even good programs is counterproductive because, in the absence of quick results, the children are again blamed.

As we have seen, effective pedagogy is not simply teaching subject areas in another language, but instead finding ways to use the language, culture, and experiences of students meaningfully in their education. Even when bilingual programs are more effective than ESL or immersion programs, the pedagogy in such classrooms all too frequently replicates the traditional "chalk and talk" or "transmission" methods found in most classrooms. If bilingual education is to challenge this kind of pedagogy, a far different and more empowering environment needs to be designed.

Another problem with bilingual programs has to do with the manner in which they usually define success. Bilingual programs, particularly weak models with a transitional focus, are meant to self-destruct within a specified time, generally three years. Success in these programs is measured by the rapidity with which they mainstream students. Therefore, their very existence is based on a compensatory-education philosophy, whereby students who enter school knowing little or no English are regarded as needing compensation. Their knowledge of another language is considered a crutch to use until they master what is considered the real language of schooling. Little wonder, then, that such programs are often viewed by parents and educators alike as ineffectual. In addition, because most bilingual programs are for poor children who attend high-poverty schools, they suffer from the same lack of adequate resources as other programs for poor children, including poorly trained teachers and few curricular materials.

Given this reality, it is not surprising that some parents do not want their children in bilingual programs or that these programs are often isolated and ghettoized in the schools. The message underlying this reality is not lost on students either. As a result, some language-minority children unconsciously jeopardize their language development by refusing to speak their native language in school: They stop using a language that could benefit their academic achievement by allowing them to access higher level cognitive skills than they employ when they use English, which they do not speak as well.

Contrary to the "quick exit" philosophy that undergirds most bilingual programs, research has documented that students generally need a minimum of five to seven years to develop the level of English proficiency needed to succeed academically in school.[49] Because most programs permit students to remain a maximum of just three to four years, only partially positive results can be expected. In spite of this, many programs are successful because they are better than programs that provide no native-language support at all.

Equally troublesome for some school districts is that in their student population, they have numerous language groups called *low incidence populations* (i.e., students who speak a particular language for which there may not be sufficient speakers to entitle them legally to a bilingual program). This is often the case with Asian languages and some European languages. Providing a bilingual program for each of these small groups would be not only impractical but impossible. In this situation, the most common programmatic practice is some kind of ESL approach.

The fact that most bilingual programs are based on the need to separate students is also problematic. Bilingual education has been characterized by some as tracking because students are separated from their peers for instruction. Although the reasons for this separation are legitimate and based on sound research and pedagogy, tracking as a practice flies in the face of equal educational opportunity. This makes it a particularly thorny issue in a democratic society. Add the research evidence suggesting that students should remain in bilingual classrooms until they develop sufficient academic competency in English, and we are left with some students in segregated language settings for a major part of their schooling. Nevertheless, it must be remembered that a great deal of segregation of language-minority students took place *before* there were bilingual programs (and it continues even more strongly today in sheltered English and ESL pullout-type programs). Yet very little criticism has been lodged against segregation in these cases.

In fact, Latino students, who represent by far the highest number in bilingual programs, are now the most segregated population in U.S. schools, and bilingual education has nothing to do with this.[50] Instead, "White flight," a retrenchment in busing policies, and segregated residential housing patterns are largely to blame. We must conclude that sometimes criticisms that students in bilingual programs are unnecessarily segregated are based more on an ideological opposition to bilingual education than concern about protecting students' civil rights.

It is also true, however, that every bilingual program has numerous opportunities for integrating students more meaningfully than is currently the case. Students in bilingual programs can take art, physical education, and other nonacademic classes with their English-speaking peers. Bilingual programs can also be more structurally integrated into the school, instead of separated in a wing of the building, so that teach-

WHAT YOU CAN DO

ACCEPT STUDENTS' LANGUAGE

Accept students' language, including language used by both new speakers of English and those who speak another variety of it, without overcorrection. Overcorrecting can jeopardize learning. Although all students need to learn Standard English, especially those who have been traditionally denied access to higher status learning, it is equally crucial that teachers accept and value students' native languages or dialects. Rather than always directly correcting students' language, model Standard English in your responses or statements. Students soon pick up the message that there are different ways of saying the same thing and that some are more appropriate in certain settings. Linda Howard's case study, which follows Chapter 4, provides a powerful example of this code switching.

ers from both bilingual and nonbilingual classrooms can collaborate. This seldom happens because bilingual teachers bear the burden of the "bilingual" label in the same way as their students. These teachers are suspected of being less intelligent, less academically prepared, and less able than nonbilingual teachers—this in spite of the fact that those who have been adequately prepared are fluent in two languages and have developed a wide range of pedagogical approaches for teaching a diverse student body. Because many bilingual teachers are from the same cultural and linguistic backgrounds as the students they teach, they bring a necessary element of diversity into the school, but most schools have not found a way to benefit from their presence.

Two-way bilingual programs provide another opportunity for integration and heightened academic achievement. As we have seen, children at all grade levels and from all ethnic, linguistic, and social class backgrounds can benefit from two-way programs, thus fulfilling both social and educational goals.

Finally, a word about the need to differentiate between *language-minority* students and the larger category of *immigrant* students. As Lin Goodwin rightfully has pointed out, it is often the case that these are conflated, as if all immigrant students are limited in their English proficiency or all students who are English-language learners are immigrants.[51] Neither of these is the case. In fact, there are many English language learners who are citizens (Puerto Ricans, for example, or others who are second or even third generation); there are also immigrants for whom English is a native language (Jamaicans, for instance). It is necessary, therefore, for teachers to understand that native language and national origin are different.

SUMMARY

There are numerous ways in which language differences may affect students' learning. These differences are not necessarily barriers to learning, but the history of linguicism in our society has resulted in making them so. Language policies and practices in the United States have ranged from a grudging acceptance of language diversity to outright hostility. We have seen the positive impact that recognizing and affirming students' native languages can have on their learning. Even teachers who do not speak the languages of their students can successfully teach them. In fact, they must be successful with them, because English language learners are found in all classrooms throughout the nation. As such, these students are the responsibility of all teachers, not just specialists in ESL and bilingual education. This requires that all teachers become familiar with theories and pedagogical approaches to second-language acquisition and development and have, or develop, positive attitudes about their language-minority students.

Bilingual education cannot completely reverse the history of failure for linguistic minority students; it is both unreasonable and naive to expect it to do so. Nevertheless, bilingual education has proved to be an effective program for students for whom English is a second language, because it is based on a fundamental critique of the "assimilation equals success" formula on which much of our educational policy and practice is based. The fact that it, alone, cannot change the achievement of students is an indication of the complexity of factors that affect learning.

We have also pointed out some of the problems that arise when programs for English language learners have low status and when these students are separated from other students for instruction. Even in bilingual programs, for example, when there is an emphasis on low-level rote and drill and there are low expectations for students, little learning takes place. In contrast, researcher Luis Moll has suggested that when schools exemplify "educational sovereignty"—that is, when they challenge the arbitrary authority of the dominant power structure, in this case manifested through English-only and high-stakes testing policies—English language learners will be successful. In a longitudinal study of a dual-language school in the Southwest, he found that all students in the school, regardless of their sociocultural characteristics, became literate in both languages. This success was due to several factors, including a highly qualified and diverse teaching staff, close and caring relationships between teachers and students, and the teachers' ideological clarity in understanding that teaching is above all a political activity. Moll concludes,

> The school, consequently, is not only successful in producing biliterate students, a rare achievement in U.S. schools, but also successful despite the heavy ideological and programmatic pressures of the state to dismantle bilingual education, a consequence of the state's English-only policy, and the current emphasis on high-stakes testing, also conducted only in English.[52]

Moll's study makes it clear that, while there is no magic solution for all the educational problems of English language learners, a good place to begin would be to honor and affirm students' native languages, their families, their communities, and the resources they bring to their education.

◆◆◆ To Think About

1. Research the English-only movement. Do you consider it an example of linguicism? Why or why not?

2. Why do you think bilingual education has been less controversial at some times than at others? Review the cases of referenda in California, Arizona, Colorado, and Massachusetts as examples.

3. The argument "My folks made it without bilingual education; why give other folks special treatment?" has often been made, particularly by descendants of European American immigrants. Is this a compelling argument? Why or why not?

4. If you were the principal of a school with a large population of language-minority students, how would you address this situation? What if you were a parent of one of those children? A teacher?

5. Some people are offended when the term *English as a Second Language (ESL)* is used. They believe that English should be the *first* language of everyone who lives in the United States. Why do people react in this way? What would you say to someone who said this?

◆◆◆ **Activities** for Personal, School, and Community Change

1. If you do not currently speak a language other than English, enroll in a course to learn one (preferably a language spoken by a number of your students). Keep a journal of your reflections, noting what you're learning; what it feels like to be a learner of another language; whether or not your relationship with your students changes; and if and how your teaching strategies change as a result.

2. Ask your students to do a "language inventory"—that is, ask them to find out how many members of their families speak or used to speak another language; what language or languages they speak or spoke; and, if they no longer speak it, why they do not. Encourage them to interview family members and even to audiotape them, if possible. Have them bring the results to class and use them as the basis for a lesson or unit on language diversity in the United States.

3. Find out what policies your school has concerning the use of languages other than English in the classroom, on the playground, and in other areas of the school. If there is an "English Only" policy in any of these, find out how it came about. Ask other staff members and families what they think about it. If you disagree with the policy, develop an action plan to address it.

◆◆◆ **Companion Website**

For access to additional case studies, weblinks, concept cards, and other material related to this chapter, visit the text's companion website at **www.ablongman.com/nieto5e**.

Notes to Chapter 7

1. Henry T. Trueba, "Culture and Language: The Ethnographic Approach to the Study of Learning Environments." In *Language and Culture in Learning: Teaching Spanish to Native Speakers of Spanish*, edited by Barbara J. Merino, Henry T. Trueba, and Fabián A. Samaniego (Bristol, PA: Falmer Press, 1993): 26–27.

2. This is changing as more authors are beginning to include language as an important component of multicultural education. See, for example, James A. Banks and Cherry McGee Banks (eds.), *Handbook of Research on Multicultural Education*, 2nd ed. (San Francisco: Jossey-Bass, 2004). Language issues are included in several chapters of the handbook. Donna Gollnick and Philip Chinn also include linguistic diversity as a separate issue in their conceptualization of multicultural education: Donna M. Gollnick and Philip C. Chinn, *Multicultural Education in a Pluralistic Society*, 7th ed. (New York: Prentice-Hall, 2006).

3. By *linguicism*, Skutnabb-Kangas means "ideologies and structures which are used to legitimate, effectuate and reproduce an unequal division of power and resources (both material and nonmaterial) between groups which are defined on the basis of language." See Tove Skutnabb-Kangas, "Multilingualism and the Education of Minority Children." In *Minority Education: From Shame to Struggle*, edited by Tove Skutnabb-Kangas and Jim Cummins (Clevedon, England: Multilingual Matters, 1988): 13.

4. U.S. Census Bureau, *Ability to Speak English by Language Spoken at Home for the Population 5 years and Over: 2000*. Census 2000, released October 29, 2004 (Washington, DC: Author, 2004).

5. *English Language Learners and the U.S. Census, 1990–2000*. These and many other data are available from the National Clearinghouse for English Language Acquisition and Language Instruction Educational Programs (NCELA) at www.ncela.gwu.edu

6. Anneka L. Kindler, *Survey of the States' Limited English Proficient Students and Available Educational Programs and Services: 1999–2000 Summary Report* (Washington, DC: U.S. Department of Education, Office of English Language Acquisition, Language Enhancement, and Academic Achievement for Limited English Proficient Students [NCELA], 2002).

7. *Ibid.*

8. National Center for Education Statistics, *Indicator of the Month: Teachers' Feelings of Preparedness*. Available at: nces.ed.gov/pubs2000/qrtlyspring/4elem/q4-6.html

9. James Crawford, *Hold Your Tongue: Bilingualism and the Politics of "English Only"* (Reading, MA: Addison-Wesley, 1992); see also James Crawford, *At War with Diversity: U.S. Language Policy in an Age of Anxiety* (Clevedon, England: Multilingual Matters, 2000).

10. Joel Spring, *Deculturalization and the Struggle for Equality: A Brief History of the Education of Dominated Cultures in the United States*, 5th ed (New York: McGraw-Hill, 2006).

11. Crawford, *Hold Your Tongue: Bilingualism and the Politics of "English Only."*

12. Crawford, *Hold Your Tongue*, 11.

13. As quoted in Crawford, *Hold Your Tongue*, 59.

14. Jim Cummins, *Negotiating Identities: Education for Empowerment in a Diverse Society* (Ontario, CA: California Association for Bilingual Education, 1996): 75.

15. Cristina Igoa, *The Inner World of the Immigrant Child* (New York: St. Martins Press, 1995): 50.

16. Rebecca M. Callahan, "Tracking and High School English Learners: Limiting Opportunity to Learn." *American Educational Research Journal* 42, no. 2 (Summer 2005): 305–328, p. 322.

17. Lourdes Díaz Soto, *Language, Culture, and Power: Bilingual Families and the Struggle for Quality Education* (Albany: State University of New York Press, 1997).

18. Patricia Gándara, *Over the Ivy Walls: The Educational Mobility of Low-Income Chicanos* (Albany: State University of New York Press, 1995).

19. Ana Celia Zentella, *Growing Up Bilingual: Puerto Rican Children in New York* (Malden, MA: Blackwell, 1997).

20. Alejandro Portes and Rubén G. Rumbaut, *Legacies: The Story of the Immigrant Second Generation* (Berkeley: University of California Press, and New York: Russell Sage Foundation, 2001).

21. Catherine Snow, "The Myths Around Bilingual Education." *NABE News* 21, no. 2 (1997): 29.

22. Luis C. Moll, "Bilingual Classroom Studies and Community Analysis: Some Recent Trends." *Educational Researcher* 21, no. 2 (1992): 20–24, p. 20.

23. Ana Celia Zentella, ed., *Building on Strengths: Language and Literacy in Latino Families and Communities* (New York: Teachers College Press, 2005).

24. National Center for Education Statistics, *Schools and Staffing Survey, 1999–2000: Overview of the Data for Public, Private, Charter, and Bureau of Indian Affairs Elementary and Secondary Schools* (Washington, DC: U.S. Department of Education, 2002): Table 1.19, pp. 43–44. Available at: nces.ed.gov/pubsearch/pubsinfor.asp?pubid + 2002313

25. Patricia Gándara, Julie Maxwell-Jolly, and Anne Driscoll, *Listening to Teachers of English Learners*

(Santa Cruz, CA: Center for the Study of Teaching and Learning, 2005).

26. Following are two excellent resources that focus on strategies and approaches for nonspecialist teachers who have ELLs in their classrooms: Carolyn Temple Adger, Catherine E. Snow, and Donna Christian, eds., *What Teachers Need to Know About Language.* Washington, DC: Center for Applied Linguistics, 2002; and Zeynep Beykont, ed., *The Power of Culture: Teaching Across Language Difference* (Cambridge, MA: Harvard Education Publishing Group, 2002).

27. Sonia Nieto, *The Light in Their Eyes: Creating Multicultural Learning Communities* (New York: Teachers College Press, 1999).

28. Jim Cummins, *Negotiating Identities: Education for Empowerment in a Diverse Society* (Ontario, CA: Cal-fornia Association for Bilingual Education, 1996): 73.

29. Stephen Krashen, *Second Language Acquisition and Second Language Learning* (New York: Pergamon Press, 1981).

30. For a more in-depth discussion of this issue, see Sonia Nieto, "Bringing Bilingual Education Out of the Basement, and Other Imperatives for Teacher Education." In *Lifting Every Voice: Pedagogy and Politics of Bilingual Education,* edited by Zeynep Beykont (Cambridge, MA: Harvard Educational Review, 2000).

31. Lily Wong Fillmore and Catherine E. Snow, "What Teachers Need to Know About Language." In *What Teachers Need to Know About Language,* edited by Carolyn Temple Adger, Catherine E. Snow, and Donna Christian (Washington, DC: Center for Applied Linguistics, 2002): 7–43, p. 43.

32. For early research on additive and subtractive bilingualism, see Wallace E. Lambert, "Culture and Language as Factors in Learning and Education." In *Education of Immigrant Students,* edited by A. Wolfgang (Toronto, Canada: Ontario Institute for Studies in Education, 1975).

33. David Schwarzer, Alexia Haywood, and Charla Lorenzen, "Fostering Multiliteracy in a Linguistically Diverse Classroom." *Language Arts* 80, no. 6 (July 2003): 453–460.

34. Terrence G. Wiley, *Literacy and Language Diversity in the United States,* 2nd ed. (Washington, DC: Center for Applied Linguistics, 2005).

35. Igoa, *The Inner World of the Immigrant Child.*

36. For a more extensive discussion of Bill Dunn's experience, see Nieto, *The Light in Their Eyes: Creating Multicultural Learning Communities.*

37. See, for example, Meg Gebhard, Theresa Austin, Sonia Nieto, and Jerri Willett, " 'You Can't Step on Someone Else's Words': Preparing All Teachers to Teach Language Minority Students." In *The Power of Culture:*

Teaching Across Language Difference, edited by Zeynep Beykont (Cambridge, MA: Harvard Education Publishing Group, 2002).

38. See, for instance, María de la Luz Reyes and John Halcón, eds., *The Best for Our Children: Critical Perspectives on Literacy for Latino Students* (New York: Teachers College Press, 2001); Berta Pérez and María E. Torres-Guzmán, *Learning in Two Worlds: An Integrated Spanish/English Biliteracy Approach,* 3rd ed. (Boston: Allyn and Bacon, 2002); and María E. Fránquiz and María de la Luz Reyes, "Multicultural Language Practices: Opportunity, Inclusion and Choice." *Primary Voices* 8, no. 4 (2000): 3–10.

39. Skutnabb-Kangas, "Multilingualism and the Education of Minority Children." In *Minority Education: From Shame to Struggle,* edited by Tove Skutnabb-Kangas and Jim Cummins (Clevedon, England: Multilingual Matters, 1988).

40. *Lau v. Nichols,* 414 U.S. 563 (1974).

41. *Equal Educational Opportunities Act of 1974,* 20 U.S.C. ¶ 1703(f).

42. For in-depth descriptions of the many program models and their implications, see Terrence G. Wiley, *Literacy and Language Diversity in the United States,* 2nd ed. (McHenry, IL: Center for Applied Linguistics and Delta Systems, 2005).

43. See Elizabeth R. Howard, Donna Christian, and Fred Genesee, *The Development of Bilingualism and Biliteracy From Grade 3 to 5: A Summary of Findings From the CAL/CREDE Study of Two-Way Immersion Education* (University of California, Santa Cruz: Center for Research on Education, Diversity, and Excellence, 2004).

44. Kathryn J. Lindholm-Leary and Graciela Borsato, *Impact of Two-Way Bilingual Education Programs on Students' Attitudes Toward School and College* (Santa Barbara, CA: Center for Research on Education, Diversity, and Excellence, 2001).

45. Diane August and Timothy Shanahan, eds., *Developing Literacy in Second-Language Learners* (Mahwah, NJ: Lawrence Erlbaum; and Washington, DC: Center for Applied Linguistics, 2006). See also Wayne Thomas and Virginia Collier, *National Study of School Effectiveness for Language Minority Students' Long-Term Academic Achievement* (Santa Cruz, CA: Center for Research on Education, Diversity, and Excellence, 2003); Kellie Rolstad, Kate Mahoney, and Gene V. Glass, "The Big Picture: A Meta-Analy-sis of Program Effectiveness Research on English Language Learners." *Educational Policy* 19, no. 4 (September 2005): 572–594; and Stephen Krashen, "Bilingual Education Accelerates English Language Development." Available at: www.nabe.org/documents/krashen_intro.pdf.   James

Crawford also does an excellent job of summarizing the research on the effectiveness of bilingual education. See James Crawford, *Educating English Learners: Language Diversity in the Classroom*, 5th ed. (Los Angeles: Bilingual Education Services, 2004).

46. Jim Cummins, *Language, Power, and Pedagogy: Bilingual Children in the Crossfire* (Clevedon, England: Multilingual Matters, 2000).

47. See Editorial, "Tongue-Tied on Bilingual Education." *The New York Times*, September 2, 2005; and Bruce Fuller, "Good Bilingual Education Programs Produce Faster Results Than Good English-Only Programs." *Los Angeles Times*, August 24, 2005.

48. Portes and Rumbaut, *Legacies: The Story of the Immigrant Second Generation*.

49. Wayne Thomas and Virginia Collier, *National Study of School Effectiveness for Language Minority Students' Long-Term Academic Achievement* Santa Cruz, CA: Center for Research on Education, Diversity, and Excellence, 2003).

50. Gary Orfield and John T. Yun, *Resegregation in American Schools* (Cambridge, MA: Civil Rights Project at Harvard University, 1999).

51. A. Lin Goodwin, "Teacher Preparation and the Education of Immigrant Children." *Education and Urban Society* 34, no. 2 (February 2002): 156–172.

52. Luis C. Moll, "Sociocultural Competence in Teacher Education," *Journal of Teacher Education* 56, no. 3 (May/June 2005): 242–247.

CHAPTER 7 CASE STUDIES

MANUEL GOMES

It's kind of scary at first, especially if you don't know the language.

The first thing you would notice about Manuel was that he was constantly on the move, as if the engine had started and he was ready to shift to fourth without moving through the other gears. Of slight stature and with a somewhat rumpled look, Manuel had an infectious and lively sense of humor and a generally positive attitude about life.

Manuel Gomes[1] had emigrated to Boston with his family from Cape Verde when he was 11 years old. When he was first interviewed, Manuel was 19 years old and was to graduate from high school that year. In many urban high schools, 19 is no longer a late age to graduate. In fact, many immigrant students graduate quite late. Immigrant and refugee students are more likely to be retained in-grade, to be inappropriately placed in special education, and to be at risk for being placed in low academic tracks on the basis of language differences or slow academic progress. That Manuel was soon to graduate from high school is noteworthy because the dropout rate for foreign-born students is close to 70 percent.[2]

Even before gaining its independence from Portugal in 1975, Cape Verde, an archipelago of ten large and several smaller islands off the West Coast of Africa, had a huge out-migration of its population. Official documents estimate that close to 180,000 Cape Verdeans emigrated voluntarily between 1970 and 1973, some 20,000 to the United States alone. The process of emigration had begun with the arrival of North American whaling boats from New England in the late 17th century. By the end of the 19th century, there was already a sizable Cape Verdean community in Massachusetts.

Currently, well over twice as many Cape Verdeans reside abroad than live at home. The 325,000 who live in the United States (about equal to the number who reside on the islands) represent the largest Cape Verdean community outside of Cape Verde.[3]

Having suffered from more than 400 years of colonial neglect under Portugal, Cape Verde was left in poor economic and social condition. For example, the literacy rate in 1981 was 14 percent, a dramatic indication of the lack of educational opportunities available to the majority of the people. Since independence, the situation improved remarkably, and the literacy rate in 1987 was more than 57 percent.[4] Although the official language of the islands is Portuguese, the lingua franca is Crioulo, an Afro-Portuguese Creole.

Most Cape Verdeans in the United States live in New England, primarily in Rhode Island and Massachusetts. Manuel's family, like most, came to the United States for economic reasons. Although formerly farmers in Cape Verde, they quickly settled into the urban environment. Manuel's father found a job cleaning offices downtown at night, while his mother stayed home to take care of their many children. They came to Boston, which has a large Cape Verdean community, and they lived in a three-decker home with apartments occupied by other members of the large family. The neighborhood, once a working-class Irish community, had become multiracial, with a big Catholic church close by and Vietnamese and Cape Verdean restaurants up the street. The older homes, the din on the street, and the crowding all created to the sense of an aging but still vibrant urban community.

Manuel was the youngest of 11 children, and he would be the first in his family to graduate from high school. He had been in a bilingual program for several years after arriving in Boston. The language of instruction in the program was Crioulo. The State Assembly of Massachusetts passed legislation in 1977 distinguishing Crioulo as a language separate from Portuguese and required that Crioulo-speaking students be placed in separate programs from those for Portuguese-speaking students. The result was a scramble to find Crioulo-speaking teachers and aides and to develop appropriate materials, because few or none existed. The rationale for placing Cape Verdean students in a separate program, notwithstanding the administrative problems it could create, was pedagogically sound because students should be taught in the language they speak and understand, not in their second or third language.

A benefit of separating the program was that a strong sense of community among teachers, students, and parents developed. Some of the teachers and other staff in the program were intimately involved in the life of the community, and the separation that often exists between school and home, especially for immigrant children, was alleviated. Manuel's participation in the bilingual program proved to be decisive in his education because it allowed a less traumatic transition to the English language and U.S. culture. Nevertheless, he constantly referred to how hard it had been to "fit in," both in school and in society in general.

Boston, like most big cities in the United States, is a highly diverse metropolitan area. It is not unusual to walk from street to street and hear languages from all over the world, smell the foods of different continents, and hear the music of a wide variety of cultures. In spite of this diversity, and perhaps in part because of it, the city is not without its tensions, including diverse economic vested interests and interethnic hostility. These tensions are evident in many arenas, including the schools. The attendant problems of segregation, with a long and tumultuous history in the city, are still apparent. The city's schools, for example, have experienced a vast decrease in the percentage of White and middle-class students since court-ordered desegregation and, although once highly regarded, have lost both resources and prestige.

Manuel's plans for the future were sketchy, but when interviewed, he was working in a downtown hotel and wanted to use the accounting skills he learned in high school to find a job at a bank. His positive experience in a theater class as a sophomore, along with his great enthusiasm and expressiveness, also sparked a desire to continue in the acting field. He had also talked of continuing his education by attending a community college.

Manuel was excited and proud of graduating from high school but reflected on the pain and fear of immigration. This is the major theme that characterized Manuel's experiences, both as a student and as an immigrant to this society. The role reversals within his family is another central theme that emerged. Finally, the *mediating role of bilingual education* in his success as a student was evident. Each of these themes is further explored in the following sections.

The Pain and Fear of Immigration

We have a different way of living in Cape Verde than in America. Our culture is totally different, so we have to start a different way of living in America. It's kind of confusing when you come to America, you know.

I liked going to school in Cape Verde, you know, 'cause you know everybody and you have all your friends there. In our country, we treat people different. There's no crime. You don't have to worry about people jumping you, taking your money, or walking at night by yourself. There's no fear for that, you know. In Cape Verde, you don't have to worry about something happening to your child, or you don't have to worry about using drugs.

My father and mother used to work on plantations. We used to grow potatoes; we used to grow corn; we used to grow beans and stuff like that. We had a lot of land. Every season, we farmed. We had cows. Me and my brother used to feed the cows and take them to walk and give them water to drink and stuff like that. We used to sell our milk to rich folks, and I used to deliver [it]. It was kinda fun. These rich people, every time I'd go there, they'd feed me, which I liked very much [*laughs*]. They used to give me cake and stuff like that, cookies. I liked that. We'd have a lot of crops and we'd give some away to poor people, those that don't have any. We had a lot of friends and stuff like that.

When we came to America, it was totally different.

In Cape Verde, they have this rumor that it's easier to make a living up here. So everybody wants to come up here. They have this rumor that once you get here, you find money all around you, you know. So, when you're, like, coming up here, they make a big commotion out of it: "Oh, you're going to America, rich country", and stuff like that. So they think once you come here, you got it made . . . you're rich. People in our country actually think that we're rich here, that we are filthy rich, that money surrounds us—we eat money!

I was disappointed in a lot of ways [when we came here], especially with the crime, especially with the kids. They don't respect each other; they don't respect their parents. It's very different here. It's very tough.

I was afraid. I had people jumping me a few times, trying to take my wallet and stuff like that. It's a scary situation. It didn't really bother me, but like what got to me, is, if they try to start a fight with you, you go to tell, like, a teacher, they couldn't do nothing about it. That's what got to me, you know?

It was a few students. I know this kid, this big Black kid. He tried to fight me, like, three times. Then I had a brother that was going to the same middle school, so he had a fight with my brother, my big brother. After that, it calmed down a little bit, you know?

Kids might try to stab you if you probably step on them. That happened to me once. I stepped on this kid's sneaker once, and he tried to fight me. He said, "What you doing?" I said that I'm sorry and he said, "That's not enough," and he tried to punch me. He didn't, but he was very furious.

You gotta get used to it. That's why a lot of Cape Verdean kids, when they get here, they change. They become violent, like some of the kids in America. So, it's sad. It's very hard for the parents. The parents are not used to that, and it's happening [to] a lot with parents in our neighborhood. It's happening to our family. I have a cousin, and his mother tried to commit suicide because her son was dealing drugs and hanging with the wrong crowd, with all these hoods. The son almost died because someone beat him up so bad. And it's sad, you know?

They try to be strict about it, you know. But with kids, they try to copy kids that were born here. They try to be like them. They try to go out and do the stuff that *they're* doing. It's like teen pressure, you know? So, it's very hard, you know? You want to fit in. You like to fit in with the crowd. If you hang with the wrong crowd, you're going to be in big trouble. You just change . . . and you're going to be a person that you don't want to be. You'll probably end up in jail.

I been here eight years, and I never hang with the wrong crowd. I've never used drugs in my life. I've never *smelled* cigarettes. So, I really hate when I see other kids doing it. It's sad when you see especially your friends doing it. So I had to say, "Go away. I don't want that life." So I had to separate from them. I had a hard time finding friends that wasn't doing that stuff like they were doing. It's very hard if you hate what your friends are doing.

Start learning the language was hard for me. And then start making friends, because you gotta start making new friends. When American students see you, it's kinda hard [to] get along with them when you have a different culture, a different way of dressing and stuff like that. So kids really look at you and laugh, you know, at the beginning.

It was difficult like when you see a girl at school that you like. It's kind of difficult to express yourself and tell her the way you feel about her, you know? When you don't even know the language, it's kind of hard. I had a hard time. It's kind of scary at first, especially if you don't know the language and, like, if you don't have friends there. Some people are slow to learn the language and some just catch it up easy. It wasn't easy for me . . . like, the pronunciation of the words and stuff like that. Like, in Portuguese and in English, they're different. It's kinda hard, you know?

I don't think I want to be an American citizen. To tell you the truth, I don't like America at all. [Well], I *like* it, but I don't like the lifestyles. It's different from my point of view. What I'm thinking of doing is work in America for 10 years and go back to my country, because America's a violent country. It's dangerous with crime, with drugs.

Role Reversals Within the Family

I took [my father] to the hospital. Then I found out that he had cancer. I didn't wanna tell him. The doctor told me that he had cancer. I didn't wanna tell him because he hates to get sick and he hates to die! He hates to die. If you tell him he's gonna die, he'll kill you before he dies!

This happened when I was in school, so I was missing school a lot. I was the only one that was able to understand the language and stuff like that. It actually got to the point that I had to tell him. It was, like, sad when I had to tell him because it's very hard to tell him that he had cancer.

Because they don't speak English, I have to go places with them to translate and stuff like that. So I'm usually busy. We have a big family, you know. I have to help them out.

If I felt like I had support from my family, if they only knew the language. . . . If they were educated, I could make it big, you see what I'm saying? I would've had a better opportunity, a better chance.

I'm very happy about [graduating]. It means a lot to me. It means that I did something that I'm very proud [of]. It feels good, you know? And I'd really like to continue in my education because, you know, I'm the first one. And I want to be successful with my life. I just wanted to help them, you know? I wanted to be the one to help them. They didn't support me, but I wanted to support them.

My mother's proud of me. My father is too. It was tough for me when I found out that my father had cancer because, you know, I really wanted to graduate. I just want to show him that I can be somebody, you know? I actually did this, try to graduate from high school, for him, you know?

Bilingual Education as Linguistic and Cultural Mediator

A Cape Verdean person is usually, he looks like he's a nice person, educated, you know? Not all of them, but like 70 percent of Cape Verdeans, they look educated. They're not violent. You can tell someone is Cape Verdean . . . if he starts pointing at you. That's a sign that he's Cape Verdean automatic. If he starts staring at you, he's Cape Verdean. We have problems when we look at American people. They might think we are talking about them and stuff like that, so we have to change that behavior. We have to get used to not pointing at people and not looking at them very much, because American people are not used to people staring at them.

What we do in our country, we *observe* people. It don't mean nothing to us Cape Verdeans. It's just normal. But if we do it to an American person, it makes that American person nervous, I guess, and he would ask you, "What are you looking at?" or "Why are you looking at me?" and start questioning and probably start trouble with you.

It's normal to us. That's why other people got to understand that not everybody has the same culture; not everybody is the same. So some people don't understand.

Like a Spanish [Hispanic] person, what he usually do, they use their body in a different way. With [Hispanic people], what they do, they point with their lips. They go [*demonstrates puckering of the lips*]. So, that's different. Other cultures, they might use their head; they might use their eyebrows.

It's good to understand other people's culture from different countries. America is made up of different countries, and we all should know a little bit about each one's cultures.

I think [teachers] could help students, try to influence them . . . that they can do whatever they want to do, that they can be whatever they want to be, that they got opportunities out there. Most schools don't encourage kids to be all they can be.

What they need to do is try to know the student before they influence him. If you don't know a student, there's no way to influence him. If you don't know his background, there's no way you are going to get in touch with him. There's no way you're going to influence him if you don't know where he's been.

You cannot forget about [your culture], you know? It's part of you. You can't forget something like that. . . . You gotta know who you are. You cannot deny your country and say "I'm an American; I'm not Cape Verdean." That's something that a lot of kids do when they come to America. They change their names. Say you're Carlos—they say, "I'm Carl." They wanna be American; they're not Cape Verdean. That's wrong. They're fooling themselves.

I identify myself as Cape Verdean. I'm Cape Verdean. I cannot be an American because I'm not an American. That's it.

[*Describe yourself as a student*] I'm not a genius [*laughing*]! [But] I know that I can do whatever I want to do in life. Whatever I want to do, I know I could make it. I believe that strongly.

 # Commentary

Manuel was eloquent in expressing his concerns as an immigrant and student, concerns related to his academic success and his motivation for graduating and possibly continuing his education. But, behind the sometimes forced enthusiasm he displayed, Manuel's voice was also tinged with sadness at what might have been. His expression changed when talking about his early experiences in Cape Verde. In spite of the obviously difficult circumstances of going to school—where he was in a crowded, one-room schoolhouse with many other students of all ages and where corporal punishment was a common practice—over the years, Manuel had idealized his experiences there. He seemed to have forgotten the harsh life he had in Cape Verde, although he did admit that he did not like farming. In spite of the difficulties, life there was, at least when he reflected on it years later, easier and more familiar. Manuel often contrasted the crime and violence in the United States with his romanticized memories of a bucolic childhood in Cape Verde.

With obvious pain, Manuel described what it was like being perceived as different by his peers when he first arrived in the United States. For example, other kids would call him names (" 'foreigner' and stuff like that") and ridicule him ("It really gets to a student when other students make fun"). The situation had changed after he reached high school, but those first years were indelibly etched in his memory.

The distress caused by immigration is multifaceted. Not only do immigrants leave behind a country that is loved and an existence that is at least familiar, if not comfortable, but they also leave a language and culture that can never find full expression in their adopted country. In addition, they are coming into a situation that, although it may offer many exciting possibilities, nonetheless is often frightening and new. Manuel was ambivalent about his experience in the United States.

Several of the painful incidents described by Manuel focus on interethnic rivalries and violence. This situation is a guarded secret, especially at many urban schools. School officials, perhaps fearful of being labeled racists, are reluctant to confront the prejudicial behaviors and actions of one group of students toward another, whether they involve conflicts between Black and White students or between different students of color, yet the issue is real and is becoming more apparent all the time. Racial stereotypes and epithets are commonplace, voiced by even the most seemingly sensitive students. For example, Manuel's comment about a "big Black kid" reinforces the negative stereotype of African American as frightening and violent.

Many immigrant children experience role reversals with their parents as a result of their parents' lack of English fluency as well as their lack of knowledge of U.S. customs. Based on their extensive studies of immigrant children, Alejandro Portes and Rubén Rumbaut explain: "This role reversal occurs when children's acculturation has moved so far ahead of their parents' that key family decisions become dependent on the children's knowledge."[5] Manuel had the role of "language broker" in his family because his was the public face that interacted with the greater community. Manuel's role as translator was especially prominent when his father developed cancer a few years before. Because his parents spoke little English, Manuel was placed in the extraordinary position of being the one to tell him that he had cancer. This experience had a great impact on Manuel, especially because the cancer was considered terminal. He also had to tell his father that he needed an operation, not an easy task given his father's memories of Cape Verde, where surgery was used only as a last resort and where, according to Manuel, the chances of recovery were slim. Although his father recovered from the cancer against all the odds, the experience left Manuel shaken. His grades also suffered during that period.

Many immigrant students play the role of family interpreter and arbiter, resulting in the transfer of authority and status from parents to children, which in turn can lead to further conflicts at home. In addition, teachers not accustomed to this kind of adult responsibility often interpret students' absences and lateness as a sign that their parents do not care about education or that the students are irresponsible. Frequently, just the opposite is true. Immigrant parents are not oblivious to the benefits of education, but they often need support in attending to their basic needs. Here is where the school, as an advocate of children and their families, can come in. The school can help by finding needed services or by helping parents devise ways to attend to family needs without keeping their children out of school.

There may also be different perceptions of family involvement among immigrant parents. Manuel's parents, for example, rarely visited his school. This is not surprising: Parent involvement in schools in most countries is minimal because, in these countries, the feeling is that, after children begin school, it is the school's responsibility to educate them. The parents, in essence, hand over their children to the school, trusting that the school will educate them. To jump to the conclusion that these parents do not care about education is to miss the mark. On the contrary, most economically oppressed parents see the role of education as extremely important and stress this to their children constantly.

By the time he got to high school, Manuel had learned enough English to be able to speak up. He said that the bilingual program at the high school provided a safe environment for him and other Cape Verdean students. It was a rather large program, much larger than the one at the middle school, and most of the teachers and some of the other staff were Cape Verdean as well. Cape Verdean students in the city had a strong identification with this high school and looked forward to attending it. In fact, it was always one of the more constructive and distinguishing characteristics of this particular urban school. That the bilingual program acted as a linguistic and cultural mediator was evident in many of Manuel's comments. For example, he was extremely perceptive about culture and its manifestations. This perceptiveness is a common by-product of bilingual programs, in which culture and language become a natural aspect of the curriculum. The description of how his Latino classmates use their lips to point rather than their fingers demonstrates Manuel's sensitivity and sophistication in understanding nonverbal cues. Many teachers, even those who work with students from different cultures, fail to pick up these sometimes subtle cues.

Manuel spoke fondly of his experiences with the teachers and students in the program. He said that it was "more comfortable" for him there. The program also helped mediate his experiences in the rest of the school and in his community in general. For example, he remembered the theater workshop that he took as a sophomore (a project that was unfortunately eliminated shortly thereafter). Although it was not part of the bilingual program and all the skits were in English, it focused on issues that were relevant to immigrant and language-minority students. Manuel recalled with great enthusiasm a monologue he did about a student going to a new school, a situation he could identify with because it was so reminiscent of his own experiences.

The significance of the bilingual program in Manuel's life cannot be overemphasized, and this has been true for many Cape Verdean and other language-minority students in Massachusetts. It is especially ironic, then, that Massachusetts became one of the latest casualties in the national attacks against bilingual education. Massachusetts, the first state to pass legislation mandating bilingual education in 1971, became one of the states to eliminate it in 2002. The bilingual program helped Manuel retain his language and culture and, with it, his ties to his family and community. It gave him something to "hold onto." Even this kind of program, however, is not enough if it is not part of a larger whole that affirms the diversity of all within it. It and other bilingual programs like it become tiny islands in a sea of homogeneity and pressure to conform.

One of the ways Manuel dealt with finding a place to fit in was by joining and becoming very active in a fundamentalist Christian church. As Manuel so eloquently expressed it, "That's the place I belong to. I fit there. I felt that God had moved there. Jesus got hold of me. He said, 'Calm down.' " A number of issues were apparently influential in leading Manuel to this particular church. It was about this time that his father developed cancer and Manuel was immersed in his role as "the man of the family." It was also around the time that he decided to drop some of his friends (as he said, "It's very hard if you hate what your friends are doing"). In looking for something to keep him on track, as the bilingual program and other cultural supports had done previously, he looked toward the community. Although Manuel had been raised a Catholic, the local Catholic church was completely unappealing to him. This, too, became an issue of "fitting in." Manuel said that the Catholic church had made few accommodations to its newest members, many of whom were immigrants who spoke little or no English. His new church, however, seems to have gone to great lengths to welcome Cape Verdeans, and Manuel felt he had finally found a place to fit in.

The tension of fitting in was well articulated by Manuel when he pitted being Cape Verdean against being American. He did not perceive the possibility that he could be *both* Cape Verdean *and* American as an option. That is, if he identified with being American, he felt he was abandoning his culture and country; on the other hand, if he chose to remain Cape Verdean, his possibilities in this society might be limited. These are hard choices for young people to make and are part of the pain of living in a culture that has a rigid definition of "American."

◆◆◆ Reflect on This Case Study

1. Considering some of the ways in which Manuel's experiences as an immigrant were frightening and painful, what can teachers and schools do to help?
2. Why do you think Manuel idealized his former life on the Cape Verde Islands?

3. What can account for Manuel's highly developed sensitivity to cultural differences? What can teachers and schools learn from this?

4. Given Manuel's many absences from school during his father's illness, it is probable that school authorities and teachers assumed that his family was wrong in keeping him home to attend to family business. What do you think? What could the school have done to accommodate his family's needs?

5. Why was it important for Manuel to graduate "for" his father?

6. How do you think the bilingual program acted as a linguistic and cultural mediator for Manuel? What can teachers in nonbilingual programs learn from this?

7. Do you understand why Manuel felt reluctant to identify himself as "American"? How would you approach this issue if he was one of your students?

ALICIA MONTEJO

My sister uses the word Hispanic or Latino; I'm Mexican:
I am really Mexican.

When she was first interviewed, Alicia Montejo[1] was finishing ninth grade at Red Rock High School in greater Denver, Colorado. Alicia's mother had died three years earlier and she had moved a few times since then. She was born and raised in a mid-size Texas border city and had been living there with her stepdad. His family served as her legal guardians for about 18 months. Then she moved to Colorado with her older sister, who became her legal guardian just six months before this interview.

Alicia attended preschool through sixth grade in a South Texas school district where school records cite the student population as 98 percent Hispanic and 93 percent economically disadvantaged. The district also lists the K–12 population as 51 percent Limited English Proficient. Being Mexican, speaking Spanish, and experiencing economic struggles were inseparable realities central to Alicia's life, both at home and school.

The school that Alicia attended for her freshman year is a public high school that had been created during massive district-wide reform as part of the Colorado Small Schools Initiative (CSSI),[2] which was funded by a grant from the Bill & Melinda Gates Foundation.[3] The school district, serving 5,700 students, transformed one large high school into seven distinct, small high schools, offering students a choice of enrollment. In Alicia's case, Red Rock High School met some of the district's objectives to create "personalized secondary learning environments that challenged and engaged students, supporting high standards for all."[4] However, it fell short in challenging Alicia to her fullest potential. The built-in option to transfer to one of the seven new high schools within the district appealed to Alicia, who said that she hoped to transfer to another school where she "could be pushed harder."

A 2006 report from the National Research Council on the perils of underinvestment in U.S. Hispanic youth paints a distressing portrait of Mexican American students' academic achievement and the difficulties they face.[5] According to the report, in 2003, the poverty rate for Mexican origin children was estimated at 28 percent, well above the national average of 17 percent for those under age 18.[6] Complex socioeconomic circumstances, combined with severely unequal schooling conditions from preschool through high school, create devastating and enduring consequences for Mexican American youth.[7] Among many factors that conspire to perpetuate this situation are low expectations of teachers and brutally under-resourced schools.[8] In a 20-year comparison of test scores reported in the National Assessment of Educational Progress, Hispanic students continue to lag behind Whites throughout middle and high school. These gaps are widest for Mexican Americans, the fastest-growing segment of the elementary school population.[9]

Even though the number of Hispanic college graduates has reached an all-time high, too many students of Mexican origin are still not completing high school.[10] When examining data on those who make it through high school, the dropout rate—or what some activists and researchers have called the *pushout rate*—is holding steady.[11] Tara J. Yosso's analysis of the data on the "K–12 educational pipeline" revealed that for every 100 Chicana/o students entering elementary school, only 44 graduate from high school. Her study also showed that for every 100 Chicana/o students, only 7 graduate with a bachelors degree, 2 earn a masters, and 1 earns a doctorate degree.[12]

Within this sociopolitical context, three themes emerge from Alicia's case study; she tells us a great deal about her perspective on her Mexican heritage and education. The role of Spanish language in shaping her identity is pervasive throughout these themes: *desire for academic challenge; family, respect, and expectations;* and *interconnectedness of language, identity, and learning,*with which we begin.

Interconnectedness of Language, Identity, and Learning

My dad and my mom, they came from Mexico. They moved here before I was born, but I was born here; Mexican American. All I say is that I am Mexican; my sister uses the word *Hispanic* or *Latino*; I'm Mexican. I am really Mexican.

Being Latino, it's good 'cause a lot of people tell me it's a good advantage for me to know two languages. I like that. Sometimes it's frustrating. I know English, but not perfect English. Sometimes it gets frustrating that you don't know what something's called in English.

By the time I was in first grade, I already had all my English. The school did have a program [for English language learners], but I didn't have to go to it. It worked out for me pretty good. Nobody at home taught me. I just learned from my friends in preschool and my teachers. My parents, they didn't speak English, so I guess I pushed myself really hard to learn English. My parents were pushing me really hard to learn English, they were, like, "You gotta learn it!"

I remember my pre-K teacher 'cause she helped me a lot. She taught me English. She spent time with me after school and everything. I had no friends then, and my teachers made me feel good. They were there for me and they helped me out. There was this one time where I didn't really know much English, but my friend next to me, she had to do her homework and she spoke pure Spanish, and I helped her out. That made me feel really good that I helped other people out with what they didn't know and what they did know. But still, I get frustrated sometimes when my friends need help or whatever and I don't know to help them out.

Now, in Colorado my friends are a little different. There are a lot of Mexican people here, but not as much as there were in Texas. There's mountains. You could see some of the mountains from here. There's different kinds of people, like African Americans, Latinos, White people, Asians. In Texas, I had friends from other kinds of groups, but mostly Mexican. In Texas, almost everybody spoke Spanish. Here in Colorado, some people speak Spanish, but lots don't. Here the Mexicans come from lots of different [regions in Mexico]. In Texas, everybody was from the same place. Here, even some of the Mexicans don't speak Spanish.

A lot of White people do not know Spanish. White people don't know how to pronounce stuff in Spanish, or they don't know Spanish at all. And they have a hard time communicating. Then there's some kids at our school that know pure Spanish, and they want to communicate with them but they can't. It's probably frustrating for them to not be able to talk to each other—communicate to other people that know a different language or something. But I can talk to everybody.

[If I could give advice to the school] I would tell teachers to help the Mexican kids who don't speak English. Help them a little but don't leave them behind, and don't do the work for them. Have a special class for them at one point in the day at least, but mostly regular classes. Then have a time when they can learn and use Spanish, and flash cards with the different languages—and learning how to speak better English—and learn in English and Spanish, both languages in school.

If a new Latino student came to our school, I would tell them not to give up. I mean, if they only know Spanish, not to give up. Just to try and understand as much as you can, or try to ask somebody that speaks both languages. It might be frustrating for them not to understand what their teachers are saying, but don't give up.

What I would advise teachers is to learn Spanish so they can teach [ELL Latino students]. Latinos that know pure Spanish, they get frustrating just to sit there and not be able to know what the teacher's talking about. They just sit there and they get a worksheet. They don't know what to do with it and they have to ask somebody. It would be frustrating. And then the [bilingual] students might not be able to explain to them right, and they get frustrating. Tell teachers just not to get frustrated with students that speak Spanish or other languages. Just try your best to communicate with them. The school does have teachers come in and translate the lessons for the Mexican kids, but all I saw was one for that one class.

When teachers understand our culture they speak to us in Spanish. Mr. Thomas, my humanities teacher, he knows Spanish 'cause he's married to a Mexican woman. He talks to everybody in Spanish! The people that know Spanish come to him and he tells me to translate to them something that I need to help them with, like a worksheet. You can tell if a teacher understands our culture by other stuff, too. Like in the art room, there's, like, Mexican stuff put up and all that: Mexican flag, Mexican paintings.

To get to know my culture, I would tell teachers to understand my language. Take a course or something; take courses. The other way they can learn about our culture is by asking us about it. Ask us.

Family, Respect, and Expectations

The person that I most admire is my sister. She went through a lot when she was small. She married a good husband. He doesn't do drugs, he don't cuss, he don't smoke or nothing. He's got a nice job. He's respectful to her. She made a lot of good choices. Like when she was a teenager, she didn't get pregnant or anything 'til now that she's married and she got a nice job. She really made a lot of good choices. Her and her husband. They act like my parents.

My mom talked to me about me growing up and having a good life. Not to let myself go with any guy or whatever, not to have sex: to protect myself. Nothing is holding me back from getting a good education, unless I get pregnant, which I probably won't. I'm scared for that. But, nothing's keeping me back. I'm more into school than that. Right now, I wouldn't be ready for a kid. I want to go on in school. I want to go straight to college and get a career and after I have a career and then maybe have children. One of my friends just had a baby and she's really struggling. I wouldn't want to be like that. I'm gonna do the same thing my sister did. I'm gonna wait till I grow up, have a nice job, and then think about babies.

My family taught me just to value school. Value what I have. All my family is positive about school. Since my dad was Mexican, he didn't really have many chances—he's like a construction [worker] or something like that. He told me that Mexicans don't have a lot of choice in work 'cause they're not legal from the United States. Doing good in school is to get a chance to do stuff that most of my family hasn't been able to do; to get a good job and have money, be able to raise a family.

From my family, I learned respect and manners. Well, my mom passed away in 2002; she's not here with us anymore. But she was really positive about school. My dad, he works—he's still alive but he's working off in a place [far from here]. They just tell me to get an education, to grow up and have a good job and a good family.

I was a good student when I was younger and I still am. My family, they taught me well. How to be respectful and everything, and how much school is important. Sometimes I think about ditching, but I don't, 'cause I'm a really good student. I have to do my work 'cause school is important to me. I know I complain a lot, but it is important to me. I'm friendly. I am respectful, most of the time. I help other people when they need help and if I know how, I'll help them. Pretty much, I'm responsible. Not all the time, but I'm responsible. But, when I'm having a bad day, or when teachers really get on my nerves, that's when I'm not that respectful. I talk back or I ignore them. I just tell them "Leave me alone," "Don't talk to me," or I'll just don't talk to them. I'll listen to them, but I won't talk to them. And you can tell right away whenever I have that look or whenever I roll my eyes.

My sister, she's very positive about me going to school. She wouldn't want me to drop out or anything like that. Her husband, he's the same way. They're really positive about school. He tells me stories, like, to get a good job. 'Cause not a lot of people have that chance to get an education and have a good job. People [who drop out] are usually [working] at Burger King or McDonalds or something, or a grocery store.

My sister is involved in the school. She works at a school. She's a teacher's aide with four-year-olds in the . . . pre-school. She likes it. She's thinking of getting a degree and her own job, I mean her own classroom for herself where she's teaching. She wants me to go to college. She's told me before and she talks to me about it a lot. [She asks about] what colleges do I want to go into, or whatever. My sister and her husband, they're there whenever I need help. They're fun to be around. But, my sister's a little bit uptight because she's never had to take care of a teenager.

Grades are important to me. I don't like a C or below. I love to make my family happy. Making them feel good, letting them know that I do good in school and that I try to keep my grades up high. Grades are important at home. My sister and her husband, they would want a B or above. They would prefer an A. They'll talk to me and they'll help me out with whatever I need, but they would rather an A. But they're not too happy with the C's. I mean they're OK with it, but they would rather an A.

Desire for Academic Challenge

School ended up pretty good freshman year [at Red Rock High School]. It was pretty good; it could have been a lot better. I liked how we actually could go out in fieldwork and actually learn stuff, not in school but the actual place where history happened. I wouldn't mind getting pushed a little bit harder. When there was a little bit more of a challenge, I did good. I got As, Bs, and Cs. I only got one D in my whole life. When I got that D, me and the teacher, we kinda knocked heads. We didn't work together. I could do better. I could be pushed more.

I want to go to Mountain Academy—they push you a little harder there. They don't really get to go out on field trips as much, but I want a new environment. I want something that's going to help me a little bit more—push me a little harder. Mountain Academy is more challenging. I want to be pushed harder. I want to meet new people. I want to see what's better for me.

I think [the teachers at Red Rock High School should] maybe get it to the next level. Mainly, when we wrote stuff, they don't push you hard. For your last final grade for the trimester, they would just pick your highest grade and give you that. Other kids passed when they were just not really doing the work in class. I feel like I slacked off a bit. I am a talkative person and sometimes I talked too much.

[In school] we have talked about what we want to do or be, but we don't talk much about college. In the future, I see me being a person that actually has nice work that's got money. I could support my kids that I have and the family. Help my family out and everything. Just a nice future. I am thinking of going into the medical field when I graduate, or the law enforcement field. Nobody is talking with me about helping me choose classes. [I am hoping to become] a doctor for children, a pediatrician or else law enforcement, border patrol . . . I am not interested in law enforcement as much as I was when I lived in Texas, but I am still thinking about it. When I lived in Texas, I lived near the border, and I saw the border patrol trucks all over the place. Now I am thinking a doctor—helping children.

◆ ◆ ◆ Commentary

The fusion of language and cultural identity became obvious during Alicia's interview. Her family and home community deeply influenced the intertwined relationship of her mother tongue and distinctive ways of life. She seemed shocked to discover that in Colorado, there are Mexicans who don't speak Spanish. As she changed communities and geographic region, the role of her bilingualism changed. Her perspective grew from taking her bilingualism for granted as intrinsic to everyday life, to perceiving her language skills as a precious asset, realizing that "some kids lose their Spanish, their own language." Although she had been academically bilingual since first grade, Alicia referred to Spanish as her language and equated knowing it with knowing her culture.

Notably, Alicia referred to the monolingual Spanish-speaking Mexican students as "knowing pure Spanish." At no time in the interview did she use deficit labels commonly heard in school policies and practices such as "non-English speaking"; "students without English"; or "limited English proficient." She consistently referred to those peers as "pure Spanish speakers" and supported bilingual education even though she herself did not participate in such a program.

In terms of advice for teachers, Alicia urged them to get to know her culture by learning to understand her language. She emphasized the importance of being patient with pure Spanish speakers and recommended offering support while still providing challenge. In addition, she encouraged teachers to "ask the kids." Her statements echo my (Patty's) research findings that urban students continually urge teachers to "just ask kids about their culture."[13] Alicia's insistence on being challenged academically also resonates with a great deal of other research that has found that many students view school curriculum as not challenging enough, contributing to decisions to drop out.[14] In a broad survey of more than 500 students who did not complete high school, 47 percent cited boredom and irrelevant curriculum as reasons for dropping out, challenging the myth that these students may be incapable of the work.[15]

Carlos Cortés points out that negative societal views and racial stereotypes are pervasive in mass media and popular culture.[16] Alicia's refusal to settle for limited opportunities and to accept stereotypical messages contributed to the construction of a "counterstory." Moreover, Alicia's words resonate with the work of researcher Tara J. Yosso who writes about the "very serious leaks" in the Chicana/Chicano educational pipeline. The harmful stereotypes stem from a "majoritarian story" that assumes all people enjoy access to equal education, faulting Chicana/o students for not taking advantage of that equal opportunity. In Yosso's work, counterstories point out the bias in the majoritarian story and reveal the structural, practical, and discursive influences that facilitate the high dropout (pushout) rates along the Chicana/o educational pipeline.[17]

Supporting and working for family and strong identification with, and solidarity among, family members are qualities that are held in high esteem in most Mexican communities.[18] Because of the centrality of the role of family in Mexican culture, and Alicia's perspective as a contemporary Latina and an academic high-achiever, she may have been zig-zagging through multiple cultural intersections in trying to negotiate statements about what is expected of Mexicans. Straddling the realms of race, class, and gender are especially challenging for a youth in her position.

Despite the various social and institutional structures that can impede academic success, Alicia was committed to continuing her academic achievement by trying to enroll in a different high school that would offer "more of a push." Her statements about the importance of school and grades express her family's values and teachings of *respeto*. Linking the completion of high school with a "nice future," she said she had aspirations to go to college and become a professional: either a medical doctor or a border patrol officer. While the latter may seem an ironic choice for a first-generation Mexican American, the social context reveals a great deal. In her economically strapped community on the Texas border, one of the only professional opportunities to which she was exposed was driving a border patrol truck. Her imagined engagement in border patrol also indexes what Ricardo D. Stanton-Salazar refers to as "playing host to the system." He argues, following the work of Bowles and Gintis, as well as Freire, that for many Mexican-origin urban youth, the diminished pool of resources, lack of institutional support, structured segregation, and cultural alienation lead community members to reproduce the unequal, hierarchical relations of the racialized, patriarchal capitalist society.[19]

Alicia's goals are visibly tied to making her family proud and her hope to adequately provide for a future family. These perspectives point to the urgency of wide-ranging curriculum choices and the role of expansive career and college counseling, especially for youth who are first-generation college-bound students, as their parents/guardians may be unfamiliar with the complexities of the U.S. educational system.[20] The cultural capital and social fluency required to be admitted to, and eventually succeed in, a quality college cannot be underestimated.

Alicia certainly demonstrated agency (i.e., her role as an agent in her own success). She was actively seeking supportive institutional structures. It remains to be seen if the structures and cultural processes at her new school provide the robust academic challenge and collaborative relationships that would help her succeed. With the median age of the Chicana/o population at 24 years and the Mexican and Mexican American community as the largest growing students of people of color in U.S. schools, the educational opportunities available to Alicia and her peers is a matter of moral urgency.

Notes to Chapter 7 Case Studies

Manuel Gomes

1. We are grateful to Carol Shea for the interviews and transcriptions and for many valuable insights in the development of this case study. After over 30 years in urban education, mostly at Madison Park High School in Boston as an English and theatre arts teacher and then as a school counselor, Carol is now involved in counselor training and in developing resources and support programs that assist young women in meeting their personal and educational needs.

2. Gary Orfield, ed., *Dropouts in America: Confronting the Graduate Rate Crisis* (Cambridge, MA: Harvard Education Press, 2004): 1–11.

3. Colm Foy, *Cape Verde: Politics, Economics, and Society* (London: Pinter, 1988).

4. Foy, *Cape Verde.*

5. See Alejandro Portes and Rubén Rumbaut, *Legacies: The Story of the Immigrant Second Generation* (Berkeley, CA: University of California Press; and New York: Russell Sage Foundation 2001).

Alicia Montejo

1. We appreciate the work of Stephanie Schmidt, an art teacher at Bear Creek High School in Colorado, who interviewed Alicia and helped us with many details for the case study.

2. For more information about the Colorado Small Schools Initiative (CSSI), see www.coloradosmall schools.org.

3. The Bill & Melinda Gates Foundation states on its website, www.gatesfoundation.org/Education, that "the Bill & Melinda Gates Foundation is committed to raising the high school graduation rate and helping all students—regardless of race or family income—graduate as strong citizens ready for college and work." The Gates Foundation has made a positive impact in many urban communities, yet questions remain about the use of private money for funding public schools. For a critique of the current movement to privately fund school reform, using the "small schools" banner, and a cautionary statement about abandoning the social justice concerns of the early small schools movement, see Michelle Fine, "Not in Our Name: Reclaiming the Democratic Vision on Small School Reform." *Rethinking Schools* 19, no. 4 (Summer 2005).

4. To protect the participant's anonymity, the school documents are not disclosed here.

5. See Marta Tienda and Faith Mitchell, eds., *Multiple Origins, Uncertain Destinies: Hispanics and the Ameri-*

can Future: Panel on Hispanics in the United States. Committee on Population, Division of Behavioral and Social Sciences and Education (Washington, DC: The National Academies Press, 2006). Electronic PDF version, accessed July 2006. http:fermat.nap.edu/catalog/11314.html

6. Tienda and Mitchell, eds., *Multiple Origins, Uncertain Destinies: Hispanics and the American Future*, 97. Also see U.S. Census Bureau, Hispanic Population Passes 40 Million, 2005. Available at: www.census.gov/PressRelease/www/releases/archives/population/005164.html; accessed July, 2006.

7. On the topic of unequal schooling, numerous studies provide data on the structural and institutional inequalities of the schooling of children of Mexican origin, noting the detrimental outcomes as well as the resilience of many students. See, for example, Robert Crosnoe, "Double Disadvantage or Signs of Resilience? The Elementary School Contexts of Children from Mexican Immigrant Families." *American Educational Research Journal* 42 no. 2 (2005): 269–303; and Robert Crosnoe, Monica Kirkpatrick, and Glen H. Elder, Jr., "School Size and the Interpersonal Side of Education: An Examination of Race/Ethnicity and Organizational Context." *Social Sciences Quarterly* 85 no. 5 (2004): 1259–1274. For more context, also see Richard R. Valencia, *Chicano School Failure and Success: Past, Present, and Future* (New York: Routledge/Falmer Press, 2002).

8. See, for example, B. Schneider, S. Martinez, and A. Owens, "Barriers to Educational Opportunities for Hispanics in the United States." In *National Research Council, Hispanics and the Future of America"* by Panel on Hispanics in the United States, Committee on Population, Division of Behavioral and Social Sciences and Education (Washington, DC: The National Academies Press, 2006): Chap 6.

9. National Center for Education Statistics, *Status and Trends in the Education of Hispanics*. NCES 2003-008. (Washington, DC: U.S. Department of Education, 2003).

10. Tienda and Mitchell, eds., *Multiple Origins, Uncertain Destinies: Hispanics and the American Future*, 87.

11. For more about "pushouts," see Tara J. Yosso, *Critical Race Counterstories Along the Chicana/Chicano Educa-*tional Pipeline (New York: Routledge, 2006): 4; and Daniel G. Solórzano, Maria C. Ledesma, Jeanette Pérez, Maria R. Burciaga, and Armida Ornelas, "Latina Equity in Education: Gaining Access to Academic Enrichment Programs." In *Latino Policy & Issues Brief, 4* (Los Angeles: UCLA Chicano Studies Research Center 2003).

12. Yosso, *Critical Race Counterstories, Along the Chicana/Chicano Educational Pipeline*, 2–3.

13. Patricia Bode, "Multicultural Art Education: Voices of Art Teachers and Students in the Postmodern Era," diss., University of Massachusetts Amherst, 2005.

14. John M. Bridgeland, John J. Dilulio, Jr., and Karen Burke Morison, *The Silent Epidemic: Perspectives of High School Dropouts*. A Report by Civic Enterprises with Peter D. Hart Research Associates for the Bill & Melinda Gates Foundation (Washington, DC: Civic Enterprises: March 2006). Available at: www.gatesfoundation.org/nr/downloads/ed/TheSilentEpidemic3-06FINAL.pdf; accessed June 2006.

15. Bridgeland, Dilulio, Jr., and Burke Morison, *The Silent Epidemic: Perspectives of High School Dropouts*.

16. Carlos E. Cortés, *The Children are Watching: How the Media Teach about Diversity* (New York: Teachers College Press, 2000).

17. Yosso, *Critical Race Counterstories Along the Chicana/Chicano Educational Pipeline*.

18. Nitza M. Hildago, "Latino/a Families' Epistemology." In *Latino Education: An Agenda for Community Action Research*, edited by Pedro Pedraza and Melissa Rivera (Mahwah, NJ: Lawrence Erlbaum, 2005): 375–402; and Tienda and Mitchell, *Multiple Origins, Uncertain Destinies: Hispanics and the American Future*, 19.

19. Ricardo D. Stanton-Salazar, *Manufacturing Hope and Despair: The School and Kin Support Networks of U.S.–Mexican Youth* (New York: Teachers College Press, 2001): 252. Also see Paulo Freire, *Pedagogy of the Oppressed*, translated by Myra Bergman Ramos (New York: Continuum, 1970) and Samuel Bowles and Herbert Gintis, *Schooling in Capitalist America: Education Reform and Contradictions of Economic Life* (New York: Basic Books, 1976).

20. Tienda and Mitchell, *Multiple Origins, Uncertain Destinies: Hispanics and the American Future*, 85.

Toward an Understanding of School Achievement

Paul Quackenbush, Khalea Glasgow, and Alexander Sasi Wallace in Tara Farley's art class. *Collaborative poetry painting.* Tempera, 2005.

"There's so much to learn and that's all I want to do is just learn, try to educate my mind to see what I could get out of it."

—*Paul Chavez, interviewee*

As improbable as it might sound, the words quoted on the previous page are those of a young man who was suspended and expelled from school on many occasions. A gang member with a difficult family life, Paul Chavez had managed to be accepted into an alternative school, where he was experiencing academic success for only the second time in his life. As you will see in his case study, which follows this chapter, Paul was resolute about continuing his education and becoming a teacher or counselor in order to help young people like himself. However, given his background and experiences, few people would have believed that he was capable of learning. Conventional theories of academic success or failure do not explain cases such as Paul's.

The simplistic dichotomy traditionally used to explain the school failure of students, particularly those from culturally diverse and poor backgrounds, can be summarized as follows: School failure is the fault either of the students themselves, who are genetically inferior, or of the social characteristics of their communities, which suffer from economic and cultural disadvantages and thus are unable to provide their children with the necessary preparation for academic success.[1] Alternative explanations are that school failure is caused by the structure of schools, which are static, classist, and racist and represent the interests of the dominant classes, or it is caused by cultural incompatibilities between the home and the school.[2]

This chapter reviews these and other theories about the complex conditions that may affect school achievement and then considers how these conditions may collectively influence the academic success or failure of students. After the discussion of these theories, the case studies of two students who have not been successful in school, Paul Chavez and Latrell Elton, are presented. Both of these young men were written off by their respective schools and teachers as incapable of becoming successful students. Their cases demonstrate that learning can take place even in the most difficult personal and societal circumstances.

DEFICIT THEORIES REVISITED

The theory that genetic or cultural inferiority is the cause of academic failure has been a recurrent theme in U.S. educational history. Throughout the past half century, much of the research on school failure has focused on the inadequacy of students' home environment and culture. In an early review of research concerning the poor achievement of Black children, for instance, Stephen and Joan Baratz found that most of the research was based on the assumption that Black children were deficient in language, social development, and intelligence. This assumption resulted in blaming students' failure to achieve on their so-called deficits. Singled out for blame were children's *poorly developed language* (more concretely, the fact that they did not speak Standard English); an *inadequate mother* (the assumption being that low-income Black mothers were invariably poor parents); *too little stimulation* in the home (that their homes lacked the kinds of environments that encouraged learning); *too much stimulation* in the home (their homes were too chaotic and disorganized or simply not organized along middle-class norms); and a host of other, often contradictory hypotheses. Baratz and Baratz found that the homes and backgrounds of Black children and poor children, in general, were classified in the research as "sick, pathological, deviant, or underdeveloped."[3] Such caricatures, which continue to exist, are of little value to teachers and schools who want to provide their students with a high-quality education.

The case studies of Paul and Latrell that follow this chapter are compelling examples of life in difficult circumstances: Both lived in poverty with families headed by single mothers; both had been involved in antisocial and criminal behavior; and both had had negative school experiences. One might be tempted to write them off because of these circumstances, but, as their case studies demonstrate, both Paul and Latrell had begun achieving academic success in alternative schools. Deficit explanations of school achievement cannot explain their success.

Although more comprehensive explanations of academic achievement have been proposed in recent decades, the theories of genetic inferiority and cultural deprivation popularized during the 1960s have left their mark on the schooling of children living in poverty and children of color. These theories are not only classist and racist but are also simply inadequate in explaining the failure of so many students. Although the social and economic conditions of their communities and families *can* be significant contributing factors in the academic failure of students, they alone are not the cause of student failure or success. As an early critic of deficit theories, the late William Ryan turned the argument of cultural deprivation on its head by claiming that it was a strategy to "blame the victim." In a book that had a great impact in challenging the theory of cultural inferiority during its heydey in the 1960s, Ryan was eloquent in his critique:

> We are dealing, it would seem, not so much with culturally deprived children as with culturally depriving schools. And the task to be accomplished is not to revise, amend, and repair deficient children, but to alter and transform the atmosphere and operations of the schools to which we commit these children.[4]

Students' identities—that is, their sense of self based in part on their race, ethnicity, social class, and language, among other characteristics—can also have an impact on their academic success or failure, but it is not these characteristics per se that *cause* success or failure. Rather, it is the school's *perception* of students' language, culture, and class as *inadequate* and *negative*, and thus the devalued status of these characteristics in the academic environment, that help explain school failure. In Paul Chavez's case, his early gang affiliation had had a decided negative effect on teachers' academic expectations of him. Teacher and author Linda Christensen provides another powerful example. Christensen, a talented high school teacher of students of diverse background, describes how she helps her students understand the power of their own language patterns *while at the same time* they learn Standard English without humiliation. Christensen recalls her own painful experiences as a working class child in the classroom of Mrs. Delaney, her ninth-grade English teacher, who taught her to be ashamed of her language, something that Christensen refuses to do with her own students:

> For too long, I felt inferior when I spoke. I knew the voice of my childhood crept out, and I confused that with ignorance. It wasn't. I just didn't belong to the group who made the rules. I was an outsider, a foreigner in their world. My students won't be.[5]

That the behaviors of middle-class parents of any race or ethnic group tend to be different from those of poor parents is amply documented. Parents living in poverty may be either unaware of the benefits of what middle-class parents know by experience or may be unable to provide certain activities for their children. Middle-class parents, for example, usually speak Standard English. They also tend to engage in school-like prereading activities much more regularly than working class parents. Schools deem other activities in which middle-class parents and their children participate as essential to educational success: going to the library on a consistent basis, attending museums and other cultural centers, and providing a host of other experiences that schools and society have labeled "enriching."

Whether these activities are, in fact, enriching is not in question; the problem is that the activities of poor families, some of which may also be enriching, are not viewed in the same way. For example, many poor families travel either to their original home countries or to other parts of the United States from where they originally came. Children may spend summers "down South" or in Jamaica or Mexico, but what they learn on these trips is usually ignored by the school in spite of its potentially enriching character. I (Sonia) recall, for example, that it never occurred to me that my own experience of visiting family in Puerto Rico between fifth grade and sixth grade might be of interest to my teacher or classmates. My teachers never told me this directly, but I had already gotten the message that issues of consequence to my family carried no great weight in school. When I think of the giant tarantula I caught, froze, and brought home, or of the many things I learned about living on a farm, or of how my Spanish substantially improved that summer, I can only conclude that these things might have been as interesting to my teacher and classmates as they were enlightening for me.

Students' ability to develop literacy and other academic skills, as traditionally defined by schools, is necessary for academic success, but if defined only in this way, academic success is limited because it encourages students to abandon part of their identity in the process. Students' abilities to use the skills, talents, and experiences learned at home and in the community to further their learning must *also* be included in a definition of academic success.

Shirley Brice Heath's classic research with a Black community that she called "Trackton" is a persuasive example. She found that the kinds of questioning rituals in which parents and other adults engaged with children were not preparing the children adequately for school activities.[6] In observing the White middle-class teachers of these children, she found that the questions they asked the students were qualitatively different from the kinds of questions the children were accustomed to being asked at home. Teachers' questions, for example, concerned pulling attributes of things out of context and naming them (e.g., to identify size, shape, or color). In contrast, in their homes the children were asked questions about whole events or objects as well as about their uses, causes, and effects. The questions their parents asked them often required the children to make analogical comparisons and understand complex metaphors. These questions frequently were linguistically complex, and they required a sophisticated use of language on the part of the children. Usually, there was no one "right" answer because answers involved telling a story or describing a situation.

Heath discovered that the result of the different kinds of questions asked in the different contexts was a perplexing lack of communication in the school: Normally communicative students were silent and unresponsive to teachers' questions, and teachers assumed that their students were deficient in language or were unintelligent. There was nothing wrong with the questions asked by the families in Trackton. They were simply different from those asked in school and therefore placed the children at a disadvantage for school success.

Through a research project with Heath, the teachers became aware of the differences in questioning rituals, and they began to study the kinds of questions that adults in Trackton asked. Some of these could be called *"probing questions,"* and teachers began using them in their school lessons as a basis for asking more traditional "school" questions, to which children also needed to become accustomed if they were to be successful in school. The results were powerful. Children became active and enthusiastic participants in these lessons, a dramatic change from their previous passive behavior.

This fortuitous example of learning to use the culture of students in their education contradicts the scenario of failure in many schools, where parents are expected to provide help in ways they may be unable to do. Some parents are unaware of how to give their children concrete support in areas such as homework, but this lack of support, in itself, does not necessarily produce school failure. Blaming parents or children for academic failure begs the question, for the role of schools is to educate *all* students from all families, not only the most academically gifted students from economically advantaged, mainstream, English-speaking, European American families. Moreover, students' home and family situations are seldom subject to change by the school. Because schools cannot change the living conditions of students, the challenge is to find ways to teach children effectively in spite of the poverty or other disabling conditions in which they may live. Instead of focusing on students' life circumstances, it makes sense for schools to focus on what they *can* change: themselves. As we discussed in Chapter 7, schools sometimes view children living in poverty and children of color as if they were blank slates, in effect tearing down the building blocks the children already have in order to start from a middle-class foundation. School-related skills are, of course, necessary for academic success, but there is no reason why they cannot be built on the linguistic, cultural, or experiential foundation that children already have. The fact that some children come to school with a rich oral tradition is a case in point. Perhaps their parents never read stories to them but instead *tell* them stories. This experience can either be dismissed by schools as trivial, or it can be used as the basis for learning.

Genetic and cultural inferiority theories are not a thing of the past. As recently as 1994, Richard Herrnstein and Charles Murray resurrected the argument that genetic inferiority was the root cause of the academic failure among African American students.[7] Although widely discredited by serious scholars as both ethnocentric and scientifically unfounded, genetic and cultural inferiority theories have survived because they provide a simplistic explanation for complex problems.[8] That is, by accepting theories of genetic and cultural inferiority, the detrimental effects of structural inequality, racism, and poverty on student learning do not have to be considered.

We also need to understand the power of what has been called the *cultural capital* of dominant groups. According to Pierre Bourdieu, cultural capital can exist in three forms: dispositions of the mind and body; cultural goods, such as pictures, books, and other material objects; and educational qualifications. In all three forms, transmission of cultural capital is, according to Bourdieu, "no doubt the best hidden form of hereditary transmission of capital."[9] That is, the values, tastes, languages, dialects, and cultures that have most status are invariably associated with the dominant group. As a consequence, the weight of cultural capital cannot be ignored. To do so would be both naive and romantic because it would deny the reality that power, knowledge, and resources are located in the norms of dominant cultures and languages. To imply that working class students and students from dominated groups need not learn the cultural norms of the dominant group is effectively to disempower the students who are most academically vulnerable. However, the curriculum should also be relevant to the cultural experiences and values of students from subordinated groups. A complete education needs to include *both* the norms and canon of the dominant culture and those of the dominated cultures. Including diverse culturally relevant curriculum is a valuable way to challenge a monocultural canon.

ECONOMIC AND SOCIAL REPRODUCTION REVISITED

The argument that schools reproduce the economic and social relations of society and therefore tend to serve the interests of the dominant classes, articulated first during the 1970s by scholars such as Samuel Bowles, Herbert Gintis, and Joel Spring, placed schools squarely in a political context.[10] According to this theory, the role of the schools was to keep the poor in their place by teaching them the proper attitudes and behaviors for becoming good workers, and to keep the dominant classes in power by teaching their children the skills of management and control that would presumably prepare them to manage and control the working class. Schools, therefore, reproduced the status quo and not only reflected structural inequalities based on class, race, and gender but also helped to maintain these inequalities.

Economic and social reproduction theorists maintain that the *sorting function of schools*, to use a term coined by Spring, is apparent in everything from physical structure to curriculum and instruction. For example, the schools of the poor are generally factory-like fortresses that operate with an abundance of bells and other controlling mechanisms, whereas the schools of the wealthy tend to be much more "open" physically and psychologically, allowing for more autonomy and creative thinking on the part of students. Likewise, relations between students and teachers in poor communities reflect a dominant–dominated relationship much more so than in middle-class or wealthy communities. The curriculum also differs. More sophisticated and challenging knowledge is generally taught in wealthy schools, whereas the basics and rote memorization are the order of the day in poor schools. The sorting function of the schools results in an almost perfect replication of the stratification of society. Although the theories of the economic and social reproduction theorists generally concerned the United States, they are true of all societies.

This thinking revolutionized the debate on the purposes and outcomes of schools and placed the success or failure of students in a new light. The benign, stated purpose of U.S. schooling to serve as an "equalizer" is seriously questioned by these theories. For example, following the logic of this thinking, it is no accident that so many students in urban schools drop out; rather, it is an *intended outcome* of the educational system. That is, some students are intentionally channeled by schools to be either fodder for war or a reserve uneducated labor force. Schools do just exactly what is expected of them: They succeed at school failure.

The arguments of the social reproduction theorists are compelling, and they have had an enormous impact on educational thinking since the 1970s. However, by concentrating on the labor-market purpose of schooling, these theories tend to offer static, oversimplified explanations of school success or failure. According to these theories, school life is almost completely subordinated to the needs of the economy, leaving little room for the role that students and their communities have in influencing school policies and practices. These analyses assume that schooling is simply imposed from above and accepted from below. In reality, schools are complex and perplexing institutions, and things are not always this neat or apparent.

While economic and social reproduction theories provide a more persuasive analysis of academic failure than either genetic and cultural inferiority or cultural incompatibility theories by placing schools in a sociopolitical context, these analyses are incomplete. They can fall into mechanistic explanations of dynamic processes, assuming a simple cause–effect relationship. Such theories fail to explain why students from some culturally dominated communities have managed to succeed in school or why some schools in poor communities are extraordinarily successful in spite of tremendous odds. By emphasizing only the role of social class, these social and economic reproduction theories fail to explain why schools are also inequitable for females and for students of racially and culturally subordinated communities. In addition, these theories overlook the lengthy struggles over schooling in which many communities have been historically involved: the desegregation of schools, bilingual education, multicultural education, and access to education for students with special needs as well as for females. If education were simply imposed from above, these reforms would never have found their way, even imperfectly, into schools. Some theorists, such as Michael Apple, have suggested that schools are a product of conflicts among competing group interests and that the purposes of the dominant class are never perfectly reflected in the schools but, rather, are resisted and modified by the recipients of schooling.[11]

Economic and social reproduction theories help explain how academic failure and success are not unintended outcomes but rather are logical results of differentiated schooling. They also help remove the complete burden of failure from students, their families, and communities to the society at large, and they provide a macroanalytic, or societal, understanding of schooling. Social reproduction theories, however, are incomplete because they generally fail to take cultural and psychological issues into account.

Cultural Incompatibilities Revisited

Another explanation for school failure is that it is caused by cultural incompatibilities—that is, because school culture and home culture are often at odds, the result is a "cultural clash" that produces school failure. According to this explanation, it is necessary to consider the differing experiences, values, skills, expectations, and lifestyles children have when they enter school and how these differences, in being more or less consistent with the school environment, affect their achievement. The more consistent that home and school cultures are, the reasoning goes, the more successful students will be. The opposite is also true. The more that students' experiences, skills, and values differ from the school setting, the more failure that they will experience.

This explanation makes a great deal of sense, and it explains school failure more convincingly than simple deficit theories. That some students learn more effectively in cooperative settings than in competitive settings is not a problem per se. What makes it a problem is that many schools persist in providing competitive environments *only*. Given this reality, cultural differences begin to function as a risk factor. This reasoning turns around the popular concept of "children at risk" so that the risk comes not from within the child, but develops as a result of particular school policies, practices, and structures.

Likewise, the fact that some students enter school without speaking English is not, itself, a satisfactory explanation for why some of them fail in school. Rather, the interpretation of their non-English speaking status and the value, or lack of value, given to the child's native language also matter. Whereas in some schools a student might be identified as *non–English speaking*, in another school that same child might be called *Khmer speaking*. The difference is not simply a semantic one. In the first case, the child is assumed to be missing language, but in the second case, the child is assumed to possess language already, even if it is not the majority language. And because language ability is the major ingredient for school success, how schools and teachers perceive children's language is significant.

The cultural mismatch theory is more hopeful than deterministic explanations such as genetic inferiority or economic reproduction theories because it assumes that teachers can learn to create environments in which all students can be successful learners. It also respects teachers as creative intellectuals rather than as simple technicians. Teachers are expected to be able to develop a critical analysis of their students' cultures and to use this analysis to teach all their students effectively. In terms of the kind of knowledge teachers need to know about their students' realities, the late Paulo Freire eloquently described their responsibility:

> Educators need to know what happens in the world of the children with whom they work. They need to know the universe of their dreams, the language with which they skillfully defend themselves from the aggressiveness of their world, what they know independently of the school, and how they know it.[12]

WHAT YOU CAN DO

EXPAND PERSPECTIVES OF SUCCESS

In conversation with fellow teachers—both casual chats and formal faculty meeting discussions—the topic of childrens' family life frequently arises. Too often these comments link family culture to underachievement. These statements are often made with an air of authority or by people in positions of authority, making them difficult to challenge and confusing to understand. There are ways to challenge prejudicial assumptions without alienating yourself from your peers or losing your job.

While other chapters, especially Chapters 6 and 9, focus on what you can do to get to know more about families' and students' cultural identities, this chapter focuses more on what you can do through your own reading and research. Teachers are smart and intellectually curious by nature. Their intellectual prowess deserves to be cultivated and supported. Teachers may also be overworked and have too much to read, so finding ways to integrate the most current research into school discussions can be helpful. Some strategies are described below.

BUILD RELATIONSHIPS FOR SOLIDARITY

The PERSONAL level: A colleague says something that rings of stereotyping and misinformation, for example, "Well, you know, Puerto Ricans, as a culture, do not value education." As upset as you may be, it is guaranteed that a full-blown confrontation will not have positive results. Let your colleague know that you are uncomfortable, but that you want to talk more. Their perspective has been developed over time and thus will take some time to change. It is also unlikely that any single retort or conversation will change their view, so start out with little things, such as "Oh, I am surprised to hear that point of view. It doesn't match up with the families that I know. Did you read about that somewhere? Because I would like to know more."

Try to keep your conversations rooted in research. For example, at an opportune moment, share some anecdotes about your positive experiences with Puerto Rican families in the school. At another time, share your excitement about, for example, the children's literature and cultural resources created by Edwin Fontánez of Exit Studio as great curriculum supplements.* Many teachers learn a great deal of cultural information from the children's resources they use in their classrooms. At another time, bring up some educational research that helps teachers support the academic achievement of Puerto Rican students, for example, such as the book *Puerto Rican Students in U.S. Schools* I (Sonia) edited.† Also refer to work that examines the education of Latinos more broadly, for example, *Latino Education: An Agenda for Community Action Research* edited by Pedro Pedraza and Melissa Rivera.‡

HONOR AND SUPPORT TEACHERS AS SCHOLARS AND INTELLECTUALS

The SCHOOL-WIDE level: Follow up your personal relationship building with school-wide action. Suggest to your principal, department chair, or curriculum director that a forthcoming faculty or department meeting be dedicated to reading some educational research about student achievement. A meeting that allows time for reading and discussion is the most effective, since many teachers may not have time to read in preparation for the meeting. This chapter is filled with citations of books, chapters, and articles about particular topics. You may choose a single article or a book chapter. Or, for a more comprehensive view, such as that which this chapter provides, break the faculty into small groups and assign each group a short article or portion of a chapter to read. Regroup the whole faculty and ask each group to have a member report on the findings of the article or chapter section and what the implications may be for your particular school community, thereby co-constructing a wider range of group knowledge.

Even if this seems like an untenable request of your administration, ask anyway. How do you know unless you try? If the first level of administration, let's say the principal, rejects the idea, try another level (department head, grade-level chair, team leader, district-wide curriculum director, or superintendent). If all else fails in your attempts to organize "sanctioned" in-school study-group discussions, try an after-school voluntary group. Whether the study groups are voluntary or as-

signed, be sure you document the time and get professional development points or credits for all participants. These strategies may be applied to a range of educational research topics.

*See www.exitstudio.com for books, CDs, and videos about Puerto Rican culture.

†Sonia Nieto, ed., Puerto Rican Students in U.S. Schools, (Mahwah, NJ: Lawrence Erlbaum, 2000).

‡Pedro Pedraza and Melissa Rivera, eds., Latino Education: An Agenda for Community Action Research (Mahwah, NJ: Lawrence Erlbaum, 2005).

Gloria Ladson-Billings, in coining the term *culturally relevant teaching*, has suggested that this kind of pedagogy is in sharp contrast to "assimilationist" teaching, whose main purpose is to transmit dominant culture beliefs and values in an uncritical way to all students. In the same vein, Geneva Gay's work in defining and explicating what she calls *culturally responsive teaching* has also been tremendously significant.[13]

Although the cultural mismatch theory is more comprehensive than the cultural or genetic deficit theories and is without their implicit racist and classist overtones, the cultural mismatch theory, too, is insufficient to explain why some students succeed and others fail. The extraordinarily high dropout rates among American Indian and Alaska Native students (higher than all other racial or ethnic groups in the United States) is a case in point. According to Richard St. Germaine, addressing cultural discontinuities through the curriculum can help, but this strategy alone is only a partial solution because the structural inequality that produces enormous poverty is left untouched.[14]

Newer research points to a major weakness in the theory of cultural discontinuity: Insufficient attention is given to cultural accommodation or biculturation, just to mention two responses to cultural diversity experienced by immigrants. No culture exists in isolation, and a rigid interpretation of the theory of cultural discontinuity presupposes that all children from the same cultural background experience school in the same way, yet we know this is far from true. The result of a cultural discontinuity perspective is that individual and family differences, school conditions, or the broader sociopolitical context that can also influence learning may be disregarded. In fact, a rigid interpretation of this theory hovers dangerously close to stereotyping students from particular cultural groups, resulting in *limiting* views of them and thus *limited* educational opportunities for them.

For instance, Gloria Ladson-Billings notes that the way the concept of culture is used by some teachers and students in preservice teacher education can exacerbate the problem and perpetuate stereotypes. These constructed meanings have evolved from notions such as "the culture of poverty" asserted by Oscar Lewis and Michael Harrington in the 1960s.[15] Ladson-Billings points out that a growing number of teachers use the term *culture* as a catchall for a wide variety of behaviors and characteristics when discussing students and parents who are not White, not English speaking, or not native-born U.S. citizens. For example, some teachers muse that "maybe it is part of their culture" for groups of students to be noisy or for parents to be absent from Open House night. Not only are these assessments inaccurate, they turn attention away from socioeconomic reasons or school practices that precipitate these behaviors. Parents may be absent from Open House night for any one of a number of reasons: For example, they may be working night shift or caring for younger children; they may have no transportation; they may feel isolated or unwelcome in the school; or they may not have had a translation of the Open House information into their language. Groups of children may be loud simply because they are groups of children, not because of their skin color or another reason related to "their culture."[16]

Another problem with the cultural discontinuity theory is that it cannot explain why students from some cultural groups are academically successful, even though, by all indications, they should not be. For example, Margaret Gibson's ethnographic research has documented that although Punjabi students are culturally very different from most of their peers, they have been quite successful in U.S. schools.[17] Their grades and high school graduation rates equal or surpass those of their classmates in spite of severe handicaps: Their families are primarily farm laborers and factory workers, and many are illiterate and speak little or no English. They generally have to become fluent in English in nonbilingual settings, very few of them have received any special assistance, and they have been subjected to tremendous discrimination by both peers and teachers. Also, their home values and the values practiced by the school are in sharp contrast. Given this situation, their cultural background should predispose them to school failure. That this is not the case leads us to other explanations, some of which may be the combination of social, economic, and cultural compatibility theories and others that are subsequently described in this chapter.

COMBINING PERSPECTIVES OF SOCIAL, ECONOMIC, AND CULTURAL COMPATIBILITY THEORIES

Examining cultural incompatibilities as well as social and economic inequities, and their resulting negative educational consequences, can assist in ascertaining how schools are effective or ineffective within the broader social picture. Richard Rothstein's research asserts that, outside of school, myriad factors related to social class and how families in some groups are stratified in society, profoundly influence learning in school.[18] Robert Evans extrapolates further on social and economic conditions, pointing to a "crisis in childrearing" that negatively affects school achievement.[19] These researchers' conclusions are double edged. They emphasize the powerlessness of schools to achieve educational equity without massive social reforms, while they also argue that educational reform efforts that do not take into account the social and economic conditions outside of schools can be only partially successful. At the same time, these researchers' frameworks are beneficial in their investigations of ways in which lack of health care, inadequate nutrition, inadequate housing, and unstable family life impinge on school experiences. Their writings assertively address social supports that are required for schools to be successful in educating all children. However, some argue that isolating social and economic reforms from school reform unnecessarily shifts the attention for resources and action away from schools. Pedro Noguera challenges this implication and argues that since poor children typically attend schools that are overcrowded, underfunded, and staffed by inexperienced teachers, schools need to be viewed as an integral part of social solutions. Noguera points out that "reducing poverty and improving schools should not be treated as competing goals."[20]

Moreover, both Rothstein and Evans stress the sociological backgrounds of families in poverty as risk factors for failure, exposing what some may unfortunately interpret as a shadow of the notion of cultural inferiority. Evans' theory is at particular risk for being reduced to the simplistic conclusion that families are to blame, which will certainly not advance social or educational reforms. Nevertheless, because both Rothstein and Evans shine light on the ways in which dominant cultural practices, specifically racial discrimination, perpetuate structural inequities, their work contributes to the overall efforts of multicultural school reform. They elaborate on how systemic biases, particularly institutionalized racism, influence family life, shape parents' preparation of children for school, and eventually affect students' attachment to school.

In the current environment of No Child Left Behind and high-stakes testing, these theories make a compelling case for examining and reforming social structures outside of the institution of the school in order to promote academic achievement for all children, especially those from low-income families. Specifically, these perspectives support teachers, particularly those who work in the most economically strapped neighborhoods, by widening the lens through which their communities of teaching and learning are viewed. Mark Simon reports on members of a teachers' study group who were inspired to take further action in response to Rothstein's book. They took walking tours of their students' neighborhoods and got to know families, fought for expansion of Head Start and other preschool programs, and initiated district conversations to reconsider the overemphasis on testing, which they viewed as devaluing many noncognitive aspects of their students' performance.[21]

Bearing in mind the insights and cautions about theories that focus on the interactive characteristics of social class, racial identity, culture, and academic achievement, we now move to another theory that has had a great impact on educational thinking in the past three decades.

CULTURAL-ECOLOGICAL THEORY: THE IMMIGRANT EXPERIENCE VERSUS THE "MINORITY" EXPERIENCE

A traditional argument used to explain differences in academic achievement is that it takes students from certain cultural groups who are not doing well in school a generation or two to climb the ladder of success, just as it took all other immigrants to do so. While this argument may largely be true for European immigrants (but by no means for all), it is a specious argument for others because it fails to explain the educational and historical experiences of African Americans, American Indians, Asian Americans, and Latinos, which are markedly different from those of European ethnic groups. For one, American Indians, African Americans, and many Mexican Americans can hardly be called new immigrants. Many have been here, on U.S. soil, for generations, and some for millenia. Furthermore, some Asians have been here for four or five generations, and although many do well in school, others are not as successful.

It is clear that certain groups represent unique cases of subjugation in U.S. history. This is true of American Indians, who were conquered and segregated on reservations; African Americans, who were enslaved and whose families were torn apart; Mexican Americans, whose land was annexed and who were then colonized within their own country; and Puerto Ricans, who were colonized and whose country is still under the domination of the United States. In addition, and probably not incidentally, they are all people of color, and the issue of race remains paramount in explaining their experiences.

In an alternative explanation of school failure and success, John Ogbu developed what he called the *cultural-ecological* theory that goes beyond cultural discontinuities. Ogbu with Herbert Simons suggested that it is necessary to look not only at a group's cultural background but also at its situation in the host society and its perceptions of opportunities available in that society.[22] Ogbu classifies most immigrants in the United States as *voluntary immigrants*, and racial minority group immigrants as either *voluntary* or *involuntary minorities*, that is, those who come of their own free will as compared with those who were conquered or colonized.[23] The latter groups were incorporated into U.S. society against their will. These included American Indians, Africans, Mexicans, and Puerto Ricans, among others. According to Ogbu, voluntary immigrants include all European and some Asian, African, and Central American immigrants, among others. The distinction is not always true, of course, because those who appear on the surface to be voluntary immigrants may not be so at all, and vice versa. Witness, for example, the current situation of millions of Mexicans who not only come voluntarily but risk their lives to do so. Nevertheless, the categories, imperfect as they are, help explain the present condition and educational experiences of some groups.

Ogbu concluded that students from particular backgrounds experience a great variability in academic performance and this variability often can be explained by the sociopolitical setting in which they find themselves. These students are not always racially d ifferent from the dominant group in a society, but they have lower social and political status. Other differences may also help explain their marginal status, especially their social class, gender, and native language. It is not their differences that make them marginal but rather the value placed on those differences by the dominant society. Several extensive reviews have documented that socially and politically dominated groups have experienced the most severe academic disadvantage.[24] In Japan, for instance, students of Korean descent and students from the Buraku caste tend to do quite poorly in Japanese schools because both are perceived in Japan as less valued than the majority population. When they emigrate to the United States, however, they are equally successful in school as immigrants from the Japanese majority. In addition, their IQ scores, a supposedly immutable indication of intelligence, also rise when these children emigrate to another society. Their dominated and devalued status in their home country seems to be the deciding factor because those who are in minority positions in their own countries are not subject to the same castelike status in another society and may therefore be more successful in school.

The same phenomenon has been found among Finns, who do poorly in Swedish schools but quite well in schools when they emigrate to Australia. Their history of colonization and subsequent low status in Swedish society seems to be the key ingredient. In New Zealand, the native Maori perform less well in school than immigrant Polynesians (who share a similar language and culture), and the Samis in Norway and Irish Catholics in Belfast also do less well than their dominant-group peers.

Similar results have been found closer to home. For example, in the United States, newly arrived immigrants tend to do better in school and have higher self-esteem than those born here.[25] Their self-esteem and school success depend not just on their ethnicity but also on their interaction with U.S. society and on the strength of the self-concepts they have developed in their home countries, where they are not seen as "minorities." Similarly, some research has concluded that American Indian students, especially those in urban settings who are almost completely cut off from their tribal roots, suffer negative consequences both for their self-esteem and their staying power.[26] Again, the differences in these situations seem to be the sociopolitical context of schooling.

The visions, hopes, dreams, and experiences of voluntary and involuntary minorities also need to be kept in mind. According to Ogbu, most voluntary minorities have a "folk theory" of school success: They see the United States as a land of opportunity where one gets ahead through education and hard work. According to this view, even a relative newcomer with few skills and little education can succeed economically, and their children can experience even more success if they work hard in school, largely because these immigrants have great faith in the "American Dream." As a result, they apply themselves to achieve it. They understand that, in order to achieve success, they may have to endure, for example, racism, economic hardships, and working at several menial jobs at the same time. These are accepted as the price

SNAPSHOT

Nini Rostland

Nini Rostland[1] is a fifteen-year-old freshman at Avery High School in a mid-size college town in the Midwest. She describes herself as racially and ethnically mixed. Her mother is Black South African and her father is Polish American. Her family moved from South Africa to the United States when she was in kindergarten, so most of her education has been in U.S. public schools. This snapshot of Nini emphasizes that many students of mixed heritage negotiate labels, assumptions, and expectations with friends and teachers in school settings.

It kind of makes me mad that they always try to put people into a certain box. You have to check a box every time you fill out a form. I don't fit in a box. Especially these days, more people are getting more and more racially mixed. I don't identify myself as Black or as White. I usually put "both" or "other", because I'm not either; I'm both.

My cultural identity is really important to me. It makes me mad when people say, "Oh, you are not White." Well, I know I'm not White. I'm not Black either. People automatically assume that I'm not Caucasian, and they are automatically, "You're Black". And I'm, like, "Not necessarily". It makes me mad sometimes.

Being of mixed heritage is kind of difficult sometimes because it's hard finding where you fit in. For me, for a while I didn't really know what kind of people would accept me. Now I find people who accept me just as I am, not for trying to be like them. Now I try to hang out with people who are of all different races. I hang out with the Black people, the mixed people, the White people, Asian, everything. I don't like to be classified as a certain thing. The Black people treat me like I'm one of them. I find that Black people are more accepting of people in their group. More of the White people are, like, "You're not rich and you're not White, so you can't be in our group". Most likely, if you are mixed with some Black, the group of Black people will accept you.

Some of my friends would say that you can be attracted to both, that White people can like you, mixed people can like you, and Black people can like you. My closest group of friends, there's a foursome of us, and we all became really close over the summer at this camp for people of mixed heritage or of other ethnic backgrounds. And over

that camp we have become really, best friends. That was in seventh grade. So for two years now, we've all been really close. And three of my friends are both like me: mixed with Black and White, and my other friend is African.

It's difficult because you don't really fit anybody's expectation. I think expectations may be holding me back a little bit. I think when people see me, they assume, "Oh, she's Black". They automatically assume, "Oh, she's not going to achieve well". That is kind of holding me back because it's sort of like a psychological thing where you think, "Well, if that's what people expect you to achieve", then you kind of think, "Oh, I might achieve that". I'm trying to turn that around, and be, like, "Well I can achieve anything I want to."

I think school in some ways is kind of like mainstreaming. It's what we are all forced into doing when we're young. You have to go to school, you have to get an education, you have to go to college so you can get a good job. But really, I think if you look back at history, the people who went out of the way of the expectations of society, they were the ones who went on to be really great. I understand that there is a good reason why I should go to school, because I don't want to be working at McDonald's my entire life. But I also think that it's important that I be able to explore other things.

School's really not that challenging to me. One of the classes that I actually learn something in and enjoy is art class because I am learning a lot of new techniques. But most of my other classes are just memorization, and I'm really not learning anything from it. I have found very few teachers who actually teach classes in an interesting way that makes me really want to work. But, when I see all the stuff that my mom did, it makes me feel like my mom went through a lot harder stuff than I have ever went through, so I should try my hardest at what I'm doing right now. One way that I think school is really important is through my mom. Because I have seen that to get to where she came from, she had to put in a lot of effort and go through a lot of high-level schooling just so that she could come to the U.S.

Both of my parents taught me about each of their heritages. I can just identify with that because that's me. I learned about my dad's Polish background because his parents are Polish and they make a lot of Polish dishes. We even went to a traditional Polish dinner where they made Polish meals and stuff like that. My dad has told me about some of the traditions they had when he was younger. Also, from my dad I've learned about social issues and what's going on in the world. I learn so much about government and that kind of stuff from my dad. From my mom I've learned ethnic pride. I'm really proud of my heritage. My mom is South African and she came through a lot just so that she could be here. I know a lot of history about what happened in South Africa and what my mom and my brother both lived through. They've told stories about what happened to them and stuff like that. But my parents don't really know what it's like to be of mixed heritage.

COMMENTARY

Racial, ethnic, and cultural identities are constantly under construction, and adolescence is an especially vulnerable time for this formation. Messages from peers, family, popular culture, and school strongly influence a young person's perspectives on their cultural heritages, identities, and school engagement. Nini appears to possess a strong sense of identity and she articulates an appreciation for her mixed heritage. Her parents provide her with familial, historical, and cultural

appreciation, and she has formed powerful bonds, through a summer camp experience, with a small group of peers with similar roots. Simultaneously, she struggles with feelings of acceptance within certain groups and the threat of negative anticipations. The tensions she experiences around racial identity extend beyond peer groups and are felt in teacher expectations as well. Can schools offer the level of affirmation that the summer camp provided while simultaneously creating a robust academic atmosphere? Can we develop learning communities that help students and teachers cross racial boundaries to cultivate more full individual selves within deeply connected communities? If, as Nini says, "These days, more people are getting more and more racially mixed," what are the implications for developing learning communities that affirm multiple histories and multiple forms of cultural knowledge?

1. We appreciate the work of Dr. Carlie Tartakov, who interviewed Nini and provided background information for the snapshot, and that of John Raible, who helped transcribe the interview.

they have to pay for success. Immigrants coming from war-torn countries or refugee camps and those who have experienced the death of loved ones may not consider living in an urban ghetto and engaging in backbreaking work to be a severe hardship. Marcelo Suarez-Orozco, for example, documents the extraordinary success of many Central Americans, who go to the same schools and live in the same impoverished and crime-filled neighborhoods as Mexican Americans who have been much more unsuccessful in school.[27]

For Ogbu, the major problem in the academic performance of children from what he calls *castelike minorities* is not that they possess a different language, culture, or cognitive or communication style. The problem lies instead in the nature of the history, subjugation, and exploitation they have experienced, together with their own responses to their treatment. Castelike minorities in the United States tend to perceive schooling as providing unequal returns: In their communities, the children do not see their elders getting jobs, wages, or other benefits commensurate with their level of education.

Also, according to Ogbu, because of the long history of discrimination and racism in U.S. schools, involuntary minority children and their families are often distrustful of the educational system. Children in these communities have routinely been subjected to what Jim Cummins calls *identity eradication*,[28] whereby their culture and language have been stripped away as one of the conditions for school success. These negative experiences result in their perception that equal educational opportunity and the folk theories of getting ahead in the United States are myths. The folk theories, however, are readily accepted by immigrants who have not had a long history of discrimination in this country. Given this situation, Ogbu claims that it is not unusual for students from castelike minorities to engage in what he calls *cultural inversion*, that is, to resist acquiring and demonstrating the culture and cognitive styles identified with the dominant group. He asserts that these behaviors are considered "White"; include being studious and hardworking, speaking standard English, listening to European classical music, going to museums, getting good grades, and so on. Instead, involuntary minority students may choose to emphasize cultural behaviors that differentiate them from the majority and are in opposition to it—that is, demonstrate what Ogbu calls *oppositional behavior*. Such behaviors include language, speech forms, and other manifestations that help to characterize their group but are contrary to the behaviors promoted by the schools.

Even extremely bright students from involuntary minority groups may try just to "get by" because they fear being ostracized by their peers if they engage in behaviors that conform to the mainstream culture. They must cope, according to Signithia Fordham and John Ogbu, "with the burden of acting White."[29] These students, assert Fordham and Ogbu, see little benefit from academic success, at least in terms of peer relationships. Those who excel in school may feel both internal ambivalence and external pressures not to manifest such behaviors and attitudes. In research conducted in a predominantly African American school, Fordham and Ogbu found that successful students who were accepted by their peers also were either very successful in sports or had found another way to hide their academic achievement. According to Ogbu, involuntary minority parents, who themselves have a long history of discrimination and negative experiences at school, may subconsciously mirror these same attitudes, adding to their children's ambivalent attitudes about education and success.

Newer Perspectives About Cultural-Ecological Theories and Immigrant and "Minority" Experiences

Cultural-ecological theories have been helpful in explaining differences in the school experiences of students of various backgrounds. But the theories have also come under great scrutiny and criticism for being incomplete, ahistorical, and inflexible in allowing for individual differences. For example, Ogbu's theory may result in placing an inordinate responsibility on students and families without taking into account conditions outside their control that also affect learning. In addition, Ogbu's theories do not explain the long struggle of African American and other involuntary minorities for educational equality, nor do they explain the tremendous faith so many of these communities have had in the promise of public education. His explanation of oppositional culture has been criticized as being dangerously close to the old concept of the "culture of poverty," a deficit theory developed by Oscar Lewis in the 1960s that persists even today, and has been roundly criticized for its racist and ethnocentric overtones.[30]

More recent research has posed a direct challenge to Ogbu's framework, especially because of its inability to account for intragroup variability (see the section "Complicating Theories of Identities and Cultures Within School Structures" on page 289). That is, why do some involuntary minorities do well in school while others do not? Some scholars and educators have found Ogbu's theories too dichotomous and deterministic. For example, the typology does not neatly fit all groups, such as Mexican Americans, who share elements of both voluntary and involuntary minorities. Also, recent studies—most notably, one by Margaret Gibson—have found that the second generation of voluntary minorities is experiencing as much school failure as more established involuntary minorities because they do not wholeheartedly accept the folk theory of success as did their parents. They are also less likely to perceive the long-term benefits of hard work and study.[31]

Another criticism has to do with the role and influence of oppositional culture. As viewed by Ogbu, oppositional culture is detrimental to academic success because, in rejecting behaviors and attitudes that can lead to success, students are, in effect, jeopardizing their own futures. The possibility that African American students could be *both* oppositional *and* academically successful is not presented as a possibility in Ogbu's theory. David Gillborn, who has studied youths of various backgrounds in Great Britain, suggests that the dichotomy between resistance and conformity is too simplistic because it overlooks the great complexity of students' responses to schooling. That is, accommodation does not guarantee that success will follow, nor is it the only way to be academically successful; similarly, opposition does not necessarily lead to failure.[32] To understand this process more clearly, we now turn to a consideration of the concept of resistance.

RESISTANCE THEORY

Resistance theory, as articulated by scholars such as Henry Giroux, Jim Cummins, and Herbert Kohl, adds another layer to the explanation of school failure.[33] According to this theory, not learning what schools teach can be interpreted as a form of political resistance. Frederick Erickson maintains that, whereas cultural differences may cause some initial school failures and misunderstandings, it is only when they become entrenched over time that *not-learning*, a consistent pattern of refusing to learn, becomes the outcome of schooling.[34]

Resistance theory is helpful because it attempts to explain the complex relationship between disempowered communities and their schools. Students and their families are not only victims of the educational system but also actors. They learn to react to schools in ways that make perfect sense, given the reality of the schools, although some of these coping strategies may in the long run be self-defeating and counterproductive. On the other hand, Herb Kohl, describing *not-learning* as the response of students who refuse to learn, has concluded, "Over the years I've come to side with them in their refusal to be molded by a hostile society and have come to look upon not-learning as positive and healthy in many situations."[35]

There are numerous examples of students' resistance and they range from innocuous to dangerous: Inattention in class, failure to do homework, negative attitudes toward schoolwork, poor relationships with teachers, misbehavior, vandalism, and violence are all illustrations of students' resistance. We see many of these manifestations of resistance in the case studies of Paul Chavez and Latrell Elton that follow this chapter.

Students who develop a critical consciousness may also end up resisting education. Such students are often branded and punished as loudmouths and troublemakers. Although some drop out, others choose to no longer actively participate in the "game" of school. They might still show up, but they may adopt a passive or passive-aggressive stance. Others end up cutting many of their classes. Students who do continue coming to class may "dumb down" their own critical responses to the curriculum or to their teachers' pedagogy because they know instinctively that being seen as too critical or too much of a leader is potentially dangerous. Teachers, on the other hand, are often frustrated by apparently disinterested youth, even in honors classes, who look bored and disengaged or who allow themselves to engage only minimally and only with the more interesting and inventive strategies used by creative teachers. As a result, many capable and critically aware students are intellectually "on strike" even though they may be physically present in school.[36]

Dropping out is an extreme form of refusing education. Michelle Fine's 1991 study of a large urban school found two major reasons for students' decisions to leave: a political stance of resistance and disappointment with the "promise of education." Many of the students she spoke with were articulate in their resistance to school; even some of those who stayed in school were unsure about what benefits they would derive from their education.[37]

What causes students to resist education and otherwise engage in behaviors that might ultimately jeopardize their chances of learning? There is no simple answer to this question, but one probable element is a school climate that rejects students' identities. This is nowhere more evident than in the case studies that follow this chapter. Both Paul and Latrell were eloquent in describing how their backgrounds were not reflected in the school structures and curriculum. Latrell, especially, had perceived few positive messages in his school experience.

The nature of teachers' identities is also important. For example, in his research among Yup'ik students and teachers, Jerry Lipka found that resistance was virtually nonexistent, and he concluded that resistance theory "makes much less sense in a classroom where the teacher is your uncle or your aunt and where most of the school employees come from your community."[38] This being the case, what are the implications for students from culturally dominated groups? Does it mean that they always need to be taught by teachers from their own cultural communities? This might be appropriate in some situations, but it is untenable and unrealistic in others. Moreover, believing this to be the case would imply that teachers can never be successful with students of backgrounds different from their own. This is not true, as we have seen in much of the literature cited, and as you will also see in the case studies of Paul and Latrell, both of whom had some caring and respectful teachers who did not share their ethnicity. Furthermore, in a society that claims to be democratic and pluralistic, believing that only teachers of particular backgrounds can teach students of the same background is unacceptable. A more comprehensive view of students' academic success or failure is needed.

COMPLICATING THEORIES OF IDENTITIES AND CULTURES WITHIN SCHOOL STRUCTURES

Dissatisfied with the cultural-ecological explanations of school failure like those derived from Ogbu and Fordham's theories on "acting White," and likewise unconvinced by resistance theories such as those previously described, some alternative theories are emerging from scholars such as Prudence Carter, Gilberto Conchas and D. Bruce Jackson.[39] These researchers present research in which students' perspectives, voices, and experiences are centered. Both Conchas and Carter take a sociological view of the ways in which culture and identity are discussed and enacted by urban students. Jackson, speaking from his experience as a high school teacher, focuses on the academic identities and agency—that is, self-advocacy and proactive engagement—of students. Conchas warns, for example, that minority group categories used in cultural-ecological theoretical frameworks do not allow for variations in the school experiences of racial minorities.[40]

Likewise, Carter cautions against creating master narratives that try to speak of all members of "involuntary minority groups" as if each student in these groups had identical experiences and perspectives.[41] For instance, she points out that recent research has shown that African Americans subscribe to the basic values of education as much as Whites do, or in some case, even more so. Nearly all of the participants in Carter's study agree that education is the key to success. They believe in the so-called American Dream that education may bring good jobs, home and car ownership, and intact families.

To more fully discuss what results in academic achievement, Carter points to *attachment to* and *engagement in* school, as explained by Monica Johnson, Robert Crosnoe, and Glen Elder.[42] *Attachment* is the affective component, or the degree to which students feel a sense of belonging and feel welcome and a part of school. *Engagement* is the behavioral component: whether students put in effort, are attentive, complete their homework, and so on. While attachment and engagement are conceptually distinct, they are often confused with valuing education. Carter maintains this distinction while allowing that both attachment and engagement influence achievement.

By interviewing 68 youths from low-income communities who identified as African American or Latino/Latina, Carter challenges the framework of "oppositional culture." She pays close attention to the ways in which culture is discussed influence student engagement and achievement:

> Students use culture as a vehicle to signal many things, ranging from the stylistic to the political. The oppositional culture framework, however, ignores the full spectrum

of why and how culture becomes a social and political response to schooling by discounting the positive values and functions of these students' culture.[43]

Carter highlights youths' positive cultural assertions that contribute to their success, and she argues that their ethno-racial cultures are not adaptations to the limits created by a dominant culture. She maintains that focusing on a student's culture as a maladaptive response to social marginalization ignores the roles and values of nondominent cultural practices in the lives of minority youth.

Carter also found that gender is enacted in specific ways that affect school achievement within the lives of female and male students in marginalized communities. That girls and boys take up academic achievement by developing attachment, and committing to engagement, in differing ways, is often ignored in research about low income students of color. So much of the focus has been on disparities among racial and ethnic groups that the gender story *within* the groups has gone untold. Furthermore, the students, both girls and boys, in Carter's study did not equate academic achievement with "acting White." Instead, students recognized the unfairness in, and were critical of, the representation of what counts as knowledge, and the linking of intelligence (or what it means to be smart) with certain styles that acculturate toward "White" middle class ways.

Within the ethno-racial groups in her study, Carter noted three categories of characteristics that describe how students manage their identities: *noncompliant believers, cultural mainstreamers*, and *cultural straddlers*. Of these three, the noncompliant believers were found to have the widest disparity in their belief in the benefits of school, their engagement, and their achievement. The cultural mainstreamers embrace the dominant cultural repertoire, although they also express their own racial or ethnic background as a central part of their identity. Cultural straddlers obey school rules just as the cultural mainstreamers do, but they navigate between multiple cultures, including ethnic groups, peer groups, communities and schools, to simultaneously create meanings with their co-ethnic peers. According to Carter, cultural straddlers critique the school's cultural exclusivity and "negotiate schooling in a way that enables them to hold onto their native cultural styles and also embrace dominant cultural codes and discourses," making them more successful with their African American and Latino peers than cultural mainstreamers.[44]

Carter asserts that culture *does* matter in the achievement of African American and Latino students. She notes that students draw upon both dominant cultural capital and nondominant cultural capital to construct academic success. Three forces—race/ethnicity, class, and gender—dictate much about how "acting Black," "acting Spanish," or "acting White" get integrated into the identities of students. She is clear that African American and Latino students need tools to make them literate, self-sufficient, politically active, and economically productive. Educators cannot disregard the values of different groups' cultural repertoires; they need to build upon the powerful cultural dynamics permeating the school.

Conchas's study also holds implications for how educators address the cultural identities within schools. He focused on a group of students, most of whom identified as African American, Latino, and Vietnamese. Conchas is emphatic about the different ways that these students embraced and asserted their cultural and academic identities within and between groups. By examining and comparing specific programs that follow the structural model of "school-within-a-school," Conchas addressed the institutional mechanisms of programs that create alienation among some successful students of color. Examining students' ideology in such programs revealed that they "embraced the importance of individualism and meritocracy, while simultaneously downplaying the significance of race, class, and gender equity."[45] Conchas found mechanisms in some programs that acted as a "mediating force against racial disparity."[46] Some programs supplied youth with both cultural and social capital, and encouraged cooperative experiences of academic achievement.

Conchas found that nurturing, mentoring relationships within schools are significant for students' development of multiple forms of social capital that may contribute to educational success. As such, he suggests that concentrated efforts are needed to reduce ethnic segregation and equalize all students' access within schools to mentoring and encouragement. Conchas also points to structural models supporting sociocultural processes that can develop a high-achieving academic culture of success. He cites the benefits of smaller, intimate school-within-a-school structures or small learning communities. His findings note that school structures directly contribute to differing patterns of school adaptation within and between racial groups. Moreover, some institutional arrangements are much better at creating a supportive cross-ethnic community of learners, while the sense of exclusion and competition in some programs contributes to racial tensions in schools.

Conchas's description of a culture of academic achievement, the social capital created by school relationships, and the call for small learning communities reverberate with some assertions made by D. Bruce Jackson. Jackson points out that students who are successful in school take on and sustain what he calls *academic identity*. Academic identity is an understanding of self within the context of school, in which intellectual activities within and outside of school are valued. Jackson acknowledges the many forces that influence student identity but argues that, despite the range of theories about student success or failure, success depends on what students decide to do or not do. Although teachers can influence those decisions, ultimately it is students who really direct how they spend their time. They are critical agents in their own education.

Although the theories developed by Carter, Conchas, and Jackson stem from a range of research projects conducted from diverse perspectives, they share a concern for the ways in which students' identities intersect with school cultures. They all maintain that while sociocultural factors and discriminatory histories may influence students' perception of their academic identities and their academic achievement, these factors do not *predetermine* academic success. These scholars are optimistic about the opportunity to tap into youths' dynamic, multiple ways of shaping self and their diverse means of expressing cultural identities. Within this lively interplay lies the potential for taking up academic identity and all the strategies for success that comprise it. It would be simple-minded to assert that simply wanting to succeed magically grants one an academic identity. That is why the focus of these theories holds particular promise: Rather than designing a particular roadmap to success, their focus is more like a global positioning system for teachers and students to view the multifaceted aspects of identity and the web of structures that support academic achievement.

THE IMPACT OF EDUCATORS' CARING

Another essential component in promoting student learning that has received great attention in the past two decades is what Nel Noddings has called the "ethic of care."[47] Noddings's impressive contribution to the conversation concerning student engagement with schooling cannot be overemphasized. For her, educators' caring is just as important—and in some cases, even more so—than larger structural conditions that influence student learning. Noddings postulates that whether and how teachers and schools care for students can make an immense difference in how students experience schooling. Her research is corroborated by a nation-wide survey of several hundred 13- to 17-year-old students who were asked whether they work harder for some teachers than for others. Three out of four said "yes" and that the reason was that these were the teachers who cared most for them. The survey authors concluded that effective schooling relies almost entirely on creative and passionate teachers.[48] Angela Valenzuela, in a three-year investigation of academic achievement among Mexican and Mexican American students in a Texas high school, provides compelling examples of care among a small number of teachers.[49] Teachers showed they cared through close and affirming relationships with their students, high expectations for students' capabilities, and respect for their students' families. This was the case in spite of the general context of the school that provided what Valenzuela called *subtractive schooling*, that is, a process that divested students of the social and cultural resources they brought to their education, making them vulnerable for academic failure. Her research led Valenzuela to locate the problem of "underachievement" not to students' identities or parents' economic situation but to school-based relationships and organizational structures. Nilda Flores-Gónzales, in a study among Latino students in Chicago, came to similar conclusions.[50] For both of these researchers, care was of immense significance.

The problem is that educators sometimes think of caring only as outward shows of affection—something that teachers might find difficult or even inappropriate. Hugging students, however, is not the only way to demonstrate care. One parent described a teacher to us who loved her students but did not hug them. She explained, "She loves them with her eyes!" She went on to say that this teacher also loved her students with her encouragement, her demands, and her expectations. Hence, *care* does not just mean giving students hugs or pats on the back. Care means loving students in the most profound ways: through high expectations, great support, and rigorous demands.

Another example comes from Susan Roberta Katz in research done among Central American and Mexican immigrant students in a California high school. Exploring the tensions between these students and their teachers, she found striking differences in the perceptions of each. Although teachers felt they were doing their best under difficult circumstances, students described these same teachers as racist and uncaring. Katz's analysis was that students' perceptions may have been linked to structural conditions in the school such as rigid ability tracking and high teacher turnover, conditions that contributed to rendering the possibility of consistent caring relationships remote. She found that both teachers' caring and high expectations were essential in fostering positive learning outcomes for students. Specifically, Katz concluded,

> High expectations can result in setting goals that are impossible for the student to reach without adult support and assistance. On the other hand, caring without high expectations can turn dangerously into paternalism in which teachers feel sorry for "underprivileged" youth but never challenge them academically.[51]

A further example comes from a study that also focused on students of Mexican descent in California. Here, too, the climate of the educational program was found to influence students' engagement with learning. In this migrant-education program, researchers Margaret Gibson and Livier Bejínez discovered that staff members facilitated students' learning in various ways: caring relationships, access to institutional support, and activities based on students' cultural backgrounds. The researchers concluded that caring relationships were at the very heart of the program's success. Specifically, in spite of students' vulnerable status (including their migrant status, poverty, and the fact that only 7 percent had parents who had completed high school), there was a remarkably high degree of school persistence. Nearly halfway through their senior year, amazingly, 75 percent were still attending high school. As in other research highlighted here, the researchers explain *caring* not just as affection but as close and trusting relationships that, most importantly, create a sense of *belonging* in the school community. This sense of belonging is especially meaningful, they conclude, for Mexican American and other students of color because of the power differential that exists between them and people of the dominant society. Specifically, Gibson and Bejínez state that "students who feel they can bring their whole selves to school and have their multiple identities affirmed, or at the very least allowed, are more likely to feel they belong in school and are more likely to engage with the schooling process than those who do not."[52]

These ideas resounded in two distinct recent research projects we (Sonia and Patty) each conducted. In my (Sonia's) research with teachers, when I asked them to explain why they teach, I found five qualities that describe caring and committed teachers: *a sense of mission; solidarity with and empathy for students; the courage to challenge mainstream knowledge; improvisation; and a passion for social justice.*[53] All of these are rooted in caring and committed practices, but here we focus on the second quality: *solidarity with and empathy for* students. Solidarity and empathy can also be described as love, although love is not a word that one hears very often when discussing teaching. Within the context of schools, love means that teachers have genuine respect, high expectations, and great admiration for their students. *Solidarity* means remembering what it was like to be a child, and forming a community of learners. The combination of empathy and solidarity is demonstrated in numerous ways, including valuing students' families, understanding what life is like for different children, and anticipating the diverse worlds they encounter.

Patty's study echoed Sonia's. When I (Patty) interviewed students in urban schools, I asked them what teachers needed to know to be effective in diverse classrooms. Their answers consistently pointed to solidarity with, and empathy for, students. One of the implications that my study asserts is that reconceptualized multicultural teacher education may need to consider ways to teach what were previously called *unteachable qualities* such as solidarity, empathy, and compassion to influence high academic achievement.[54]

Another theory closely connected with the ethic of caring is described by Ricardo Stanton-Salazar as a "social capital networks framework." This theory focuses on the centrality of social relations and networks between adults and youth, particularly vulnerable youth who rarely have access to the social capital that more privileged students take for granted. According to Stanton-Salazar, these networks function to reproduce or deny privilege and power. In the end, Stanton-Salazar argues, it is the power of institutional agents, such as teachers, counselors, and other adults who can manipulate the social and institutional conditions in and out of school, that determines who "makes it" and who doesn't. What exactly are the kinds of networks and institutional supports to which he refers? As examples, he cites various kinds of knowledge, including particular discourses and social capital: *bridging* (i.e., providing access to gatekeepers and to other opportunities usually closed to disenfranchised students), advocacy, role modeling, emotional and moral support, and advice and guidance.[55] These supports are linked with caring because it is only through trusting and close relationships with teachers that some students gain access to such networks. Through these networks, students can learn to "decode the system" and to participate in power while that they continue to honor their identities. In turn, these networks provide students with the skills and resources they will need to successfully navigate the broader society.

DEVELOPING A COMPREHENSIVE UNDERSTANDING OF STUDENT LEARNING

No simple explanation accounts for student achievement or failure. As we have seen in this chapter, most explanations have been inadequate or incomplete. Some have failed to consider the significance of culture in learning; others have not taken into account the social, cultural, and political context of schooling; and still others have placed all the responsibility for academic failure or success on students and their families. Even the persistence of racism and discrimination, the presence of unjust policies and practices in schools, and the role that schools play in reproducing existing societal inequities do not fully explain school failure.

Broad societal structures, for instance, make a difference in student learning. Newer perspectives concerning the education of new and old immigrant groups of color in the United States have emerged in the past several years, and they add significantly to our understanding of the achievement of these groups. For example, Alejandro Portes and Rubén Rumbaut, in a series of long-term, comprehensive studies of immigrant families of various backgrounds, conclude that the process of "growing up American," in their words, "ranges from smooth acceptance to traumatic confrontation depending on the characteristics that immigrants and their children bring along and the social context that receives them."[56] Portes and Rumbaut found that race is a paramount factor in whether and how groups are accepted into the mainstream, and it can overpower the influence of other factors such as social class, religion, or language.

In addition, the context of immigrants' arrival is also consequential. Portes and Rumbaut suggest that immigrants fleeing from communism are received more favorably than those fleeing economic exploitation. As examples, they cite the case of Haitian, Nicaraguan, and Mexican immigrants, who have significantly lower earnings than Cubans and Vietnamese, even after controlling for level of education, knowledge of English, and occupation. Also, no matter how long they have been here, the earnings of Mexicans, Nicaraguans, and Haitians remain flat, while those of Vietnamese and Cubans increase each additional year of residence in the United States. Portes and Rumbaut come to this astonishing conclusion: "Hence, no matter how educated a Mexican or Haitian parent is, his or her chances of moving ahead economically are significantly constrained by the social environment in which his or her group has become incorporated."[57] Thus, for these groups, a college degree yields no improvement in earnings. This conclusion flies in the face of conventional wisdom that education equals economic advancement. Clearly, additional factors—race, context of incorporation, and others—are at work here.

Even in the face of these larger structural conditions, however, the school context *can* make a difference. Underachievement, as Jim Cummins has suggested, is also the result of the interactions between teachers, students, and their families.[58] When teachers respect and affirm the identities and experiences of students and their families, they also change the nature of the interactions they have with them, and this can help promote student achievement. In Paul Chavez's case, for instance, the staff's closeness with him and his family paid off in his growing association with school and learning.

Also, how students and communities *perceive* and *react* to schools is another consideration in explaining school achievement. However, in spite of the perceptions and reactions of particular groups to schools, there are always individual exceptions. The students in Prudence Carter's and Gilberto Conchas's studies make clear that not all African American students, even those from economically oppressed communities, fail; many do not see school success as "acting White"; and not all voluntary immigrants are successful in school. Unless we look at individual cases as well as at entire groups, we fall into rather facile, inaccurate explanations of failure. These can lead to stereotypes and inappropriate educational expectations.

School climate makes a difference in other ways as well. When teachers and schools believe their students are capable learners and they create appropriate learning environments for them, young people are given a clear and positive message about their worth and abilities. The policies and practices of schools, and the hopes and expectations they have for students, are also key variables in explaining student academic achievement. In Paul's case study, you will see the positive effect that participating in developing the school rules had on him. In the case of Latrell, he characterized the atmosphere in his school as negative: "Like I'm just a prisoner, like I'm a bad person." On the other hand, he described the school's teachers as supportive: "They've been helping me out a lot, a way, way lot. 'Cause I've got after-school tutorial, and we got more help after school. I'm a good student right now". Latrell's case illustrates that school policies are not always consistent with teachers' practices, presenting the student with a challenging landscape to navigate.

Looking beyond just cultural and social class characteristics as determinants of school achievement can be empowering because it shines light on what teachers and schools can do to improve student learning. As we saw in Chapter 5, characteristics of the school environment and culture that make a positive difference include an enriched and more demanding curriculum, respect for students' languages and cultures, high expectations for all students, and encouragement of parental involvement. However, reforming school structures alone will not lead to substantive improvement in student achievement if such changes are not accompanied by profound changes in what we believe students deserve and are capable of learning. In short, changing school policies and practices is a necessary but insufficient condition for improving academic achievement. As we have seen in the discussion about care, the nature of the relationships among students, teachers, and schools also matter a great deal. This is where the issue of caring and mentoring matter most.

Learning environments that may seem at first glance to be totally culturally inappropriate for some students can in fact be effective. The so-called "Catholic school effect" is a case in point. In some ways, nothing seems more culturally incompatible for African American and Latino students than a Catholic school: Bilingual programs are usually unavailable, classes tend to be overcrowded, and formal environments that stress individual excellence over cooperation are common. In spite of these conditions, Catholic schools have been successful environments for many Latino and African American children, especially those from poor communities. The literature points to the fact that Catholic schools, because of restricted resources, tend to offer all students a less differentiated curriculum, less tracking, and more academic classes. They also have clear, uncomplicated missions and strong social contracts.[59] What may at first glance appear to be incongruous in terms of cultural compatibility is explained by school structures that imply high expectations for all students.

This discussion leads us to the conclusion that school achievement can be explained only by taking into account multiple, competing, and dynamic conditions: the school's tendency to replicate society and its inequities; cultural and language incompatibilities; the unfair and bureaucratic structures of schools; the nature of the relationships among students; students' multiple and dynamic ways of asserting ethno-racial, gender and cultural identities; teachers' relationships with the communities they serve; and the political relationship of particular groups to society and the schools. It is tricky business, however, to seek causal explanations for school success and failure. Understanding how numerous complex conditions are mediated within the school and home settings can also help explain students' academic success or failure. Understanding all these conditions contributes to a more comprehensive explanation of the massive school failure of many students. This is the sociopolitical context of multicultural education, and it forms the basis for the conceptual framework that has been developed in this book.

SUMMARY

In this chapter, we have explored a number of theories regarding conditions that influence school failure and success. The deficit theories popularized in the 1960s were responsible for much of our educational policy during that era; their influence has continued into the present. These theories assumed that children from families whose cultural backgrounds differed from the majority, or from poor neighborhoods, were either genetically or culturally inferior to culturally dominant children from the middle class.

An alternative explanation developed during the 1970s was that schools were responsible for school failure because they reproduced the existing economic and social inequities, and therefore, replicated structural inequality. During this time, the cultural mismatch theory was also developed. According to this theory, schools are unsuccessful in educating a substantial number of students because there is a mismatch between their home cultures and the culture of the school. Social class and family background have re-emerged in recent research as forces outside of schools that influence underachievement. These theories argue for the necessity of changing social policy in order to support achievement among students marginalized by race and class. The theories of John Ogbu and others, developed during the late 1970s, argue that there is a crucial distinction between castelike minorities and immigrant minorities. These theorists argue that cultural differences alone cannot explain the differential school achievement of distinct "minority" groups.

Resistance theory also has helped us understand that students and their families are frequently engaged in some form of resistance to the education to which they are exposed. Resistance may be either passive or active, and it may have consequences that are counterproductive to the interests of the students who engage in it. Alternatively, resistance can lead to a critical awareness of structural inequality and a desire to succeed academically in order to make change, as we shall see in both case studies that follow this chapter illustrate.

Challenges to Ogbu's cultural-ecological theories and to resistance theories come from Prudence Carter and Gilberto Conchas. The majority of low-income students of color in urban schools who participated in their studies did not equate "acting White" with high academic achievement. The students were critical of social and education stratification that devalued expressions of knowledge differing from middle-class White norms. Carter and Conchas cited ways in which the students constructed academic identities that intersected with their ethno-racial cultures, gendered selves and socioecomnic experiences. These theories refute labeling nondominant school behaviors and academic performance as maladaptive responses to the dominant framework.

Finally, the significance of caring relationships among students and their teachers has taken on great significance in the recent past. There is a growing awareness of the tremendous difference that teachers—and the school climate in general—can make in the lives and futures of young people. Teachers and schools that affirm students' identities, believe in their intelligence, and accept nothing less than the best have proved to be inspirational for young people, even if they live in otherwise difficult circumstances. In fact, the case can be made that such relationships are one of the most important elements of student learning.

We have attempted to develop a comprehensive view of school achievement by providing an analysis and critique of a number of theories. It is clear that no single explanation of academic achievement is sufficient to explain why some students succeed in school and others fail. Rather, we need to understand school achievement as a combination of *personal, cultural, familial, interactive, political, relational*, and *societal* issues, and this requires an understanding of the sociopolitical context in which education takes place.

◆ ◆ ◆ To Think About

1. What did William Ryan mean by "culturally depriving schools"? Can you give some examples?

2. Think of your own students. How accurate do you think John Ogbu's classification of "voluntary" and "involuntary" minorities is? Consider both the advantages and disadvantages of this theory.

3. Think about schools and classrooms with which you are familiar. Have you noticed examples of student resistance? If so, what are they, and what is their effect?

4. Consider Prudence Carter's categories: cultural mainstreamers, cultural straddlers, and noncompliant believers. How can these categories help you understand your students and their achievement? Does your teaching style and philosophy support one of these categories more than another? Is there a category you would like to support more?

5. You and a group of your colleagues need to determine why a particular student has been doing poorly in your classes. What will you look at? Why?

◆ ◆ ◆ Activities for Personal, School, and Community Change

1. If you teach in an elementary school, plan a visit to the homes of your students to get to know their families. Use the occasion to find out about the children: what they like and what motivates them to learn. Ask the families about some of the culturally enriching activities they are engaged in within their communities. If you teach in a middle or high school class in which you have many students, making home visits unlikely, ask students to describe some of the activities they do with their families. How can you use what you've learned to create a more culturally affirming classroom?

2. Think about a teacher who has made a difference in your life. Try to get in touch with her or him. Tell that person how he or she influenced you, and ask for advice on how you can have the same impact on your students. How can you apply what you have learned from this to your own teaching?

3. Get together with a group of colleagues to discuss how students in your school display "resistance" behaviors. What exact behaviors are they? Are these behaviors getting in the way of their engagement with school? If so, what can you do about them? You may also want to visit one another's classrooms to lend a pair of "fresh eyes" to the situation. Decide on a plan of action for your classrooms, and come together again to talk about the results.

 ## Companion Website

For access to additional case studies, weblinks, concept cards, and other material related to this chapter, visit the text's companion website at **www.ablongman.com/nieto5e**.

Notes to Chapter 8

1. For full expositions of these arguments, see, for example, Carl Bereiter and Siegfried Englemann, *Teaching Disadvantaged Children in the Preschool* (Englewood Cliffs, NJ: Prentice-Hall, 1966); Arthur R. Jensen, "How Much Can We Boost IQ and Scholastic Achievement?" *Harvard Educational Review* 39 no. 1 (1969): 1–123; Frank Reissman, *The Culturally Deprived Child* (New York: Harper & Row, 1962).

2. See Samuel Bowles and Herbert Gintis, *Schooling in Capitalist America: Educational Reform and the Contradictions of Economic Life* (New York: Basic Books, 1976); Joel Spring, *The Rise and Fall of the Corporate State* (Boston: Beacon Press, 1972).

3. Stephen S. Baratz and Joan C. Baratz, "Early Childhood Intervention: The Social Science Base of Institutional Racism." In *Challenging the Myths: The Schools, the Blacks, and the Poor*, Reprint Series no. 5 (Cambridge, MA: Harvard Educational Review, 1971).

4. William Ryan, *Blaming the Victim* (New York: Vintage Books, 1972): 61.

5. Linda Christensen, "Whose Standard? Teaching Standard English." In *Language Development: A Reader for Teachers*, edited by Brenda Miller Power and Ruth Shagoury Hubbard (Englewood Cliffs, NJ: Merrill, 1996).

6. Shirley Brice Heath, *Ways with Words* (New York: Cambridge University Press, 1983).

7. Richard J. Herrnstein and Charles Murray, *The Bell Curve: Intelligence and Class Structure in American Life* (New York: Free Press, 1994).

8. Steve Fraser, ed., *The Bell Curve Wars: Race, Intelligence, and the Future of America* (New York: Basic Books, 1995) provides a collection of essays by leading scholars that refute the assertions of Herrnstein and Murray. Also see "The Bell Curve: Laying Bare the Resurgence of Scientific Racism." *American Behavioral Scientist* 39, no. 1 (September/October 1995).

9. Pierre Bourdieu, "The Forms of Capital." In *Handbook of Theory and Research for the Sociology of Education*, edited by John G. Richardson (New York: Greenwood Press, 1986): 246.

10. See Bowles and Gintis, *Schooling in Capitalist America: Educational Reform and the Contradictions of Economic Life*, and Spring, *The Rise and Fall of the Corporate State*.

11. Michael W. Apple, *Teachers and Texts: A Political Economy of Class and Gender Relations in Education* (Boston: Routledge and Kegan Paul, 1986).

12. Paulo Freire, *Teachers as Cultural Workers: Letters to Those Who Dare Teach* (Boulder, CO: Westview Press, 1998): 72–73.

13. Gloria Ladson-Billings, *The Dreamkeepers: Successful Teachers of African American Children* (San Francisco: Jossey-Bass, 1994). See also Geneva Gay, *Culturally Responsive Teaching: Theory, Research, and Practice* (New York: Teachers College Press, 2000).

14. Richard St. Germaine, "Drop-out Rates Among American Indian and Alaska Native Students: Beyond Cultural Discontinuity." In *ERIC Digest, Clearinghouse on Rural Education and Small Schools* (Charleston, WV: Appalachia Educational Laboratory, November 1995).

15. Oscar Lewis, *La Vida: A Puerto Rican Family in the Culture of Poverty—San Juan and New York* (New York: Random House, 1965); and Michael Harrington, *The Other America: Poverty in the United States* (New York: Scribner, 1997/1971).

16. Gloria Ladson-Billings, "It's Not the Culture of Poverty, It's the Poverty of Culture: The Problem with Teacher Education." *Anthropology and Education Quarterly* 37, no. 2 (June 2006): 104–109.

17. Margaret A. Gibson, "The School Performance of Immigrant Minorities: A Comparative View." *Anthropology and Education Quarterly* 18, no. 4 (December 1987): 262–275.

18. Richard Rothstein, *Class and Schools: Using Social, Economic and Education Reform to Close the Black–White Achievement Gap* (New York: Economic Policy Institute, Teachers College, 2004).

19. Robert Evans, *Family Matters: How School Can Cope With the Crisis in Childrearing* (San Francisco: Jossey-Bass, 2004); also see Robert Evans, "Reframing the Achievement Gap." *Phi Delta Kappan* 86, no. 8 (April 2005): 582–589.

20. Pedro Noguera, "Social Class, But What About Schools?" *Poverty & Race* 13, no. 5. Washington, DC: Poverty & Race Research Action Council, (September/October 2004): 11–12.

21. Mark Simon, "What Teachers Know." *Poverty & Race* 13, no. 5. Washington, DC. Poverty & Race Research Action Council (September/October 2004): 16.

22. John U. Ogbu and Herbert D. Simons, "Voluntary and Involuntary Minorities: A Cultural-Ecological Theory of School Performance with Some Implications for Education." *Anthropology & Education Quarterly* 29, no. 2 (1998): 155–188.

23. John U. Ogbu, "Variability in Minority School Performance: A Problem in Search of an Explanation." *Anthropology & Education Quarterly* 18, no. 4 (December 1987): 312–334.

24. For a more extensive discussion, see Evelyn Jacob and Cathie Jordan, eds., *Minority Education: Anthropological Perspectives* (Norwood, NJ: Ablex, 1993).

25. María E. Matute-Bianchi, "Situational Ethnicity and Patterns of School Performance Among Immigrant and Nonimmigrant Mexican-Descent Students." In *Minority Status and Schooling*, edited by Margaret A. Gibson and John U. Ogbu. Also, research by Susan Katz with Central American and Mexican immigrants found that those who were born in the United States or who had arrived here before the age of 5 had the most difficulties at school in terms of both academics and behavior. See Susan Roberta Katz, "Where the Streets Cross the Classroom: A Study of Latino Students' Perspectives on Cultural Identity in City Schools and Neighborhood Gangs." *Bilingual Research Journal* 20, nos. 3, 4 (Summer/Fall 1995): 603–631.

26. Donna Deyhle and Karen Swisher, "Research in American Indian and Alaska Native Education: From Assimilation to Self-Determination." In *Review of Research in Education* 22, edited by Michael W. Apple (Washington, DC: American Educational Research Association, 1997): 113–194.

27. Marcelo M. Suarez-Orozco, " 'Becoming Somebody': Central American Immigrants in the U.S." *Anthropology & Education Quarterly* 18, no. 4 (December 1987): 287–299.

28. Jim Cummins, *Negotiating Identities: Education for Empowerment in a Diverse Society* (Ontario, CA: California Association for Bilingual Education, 1996).

29. Signithia Fordham and John U. Ogbu, "Black Students' School Success: Coping with the 'Burden of Acting White.' " *Urban Review* 18, no. 3 (1986): 176–206.

30. For Oscar Lewis's theory of the culture of poverty, see *La Vida: A Puerto Rican Family in the Culture of Poverty—San Juan and New York* (New York: Random House, 1965).

31. Margaret A. Gibson, "Conclusion: Complicating the Immigrant/Involuntary Minority Typology." *Anthropology and Education Quarterly* 28, no. 3 (September 1997): 431–454.

32. David Gillborn, "Ethnicity and Educational Performance in the United Kingdom: Racism, Ethnicity, and Variability in Achievement." *Anthropology & Education Quarterly* 28, no. 3 (September 1997): 375–393.

33. Henry A. Giroux, *Theory and Resistance in Education: A Pedagogy for the Opposition* (South Hadley, MA: Bergen & Garvey, 1983); see also Cummins, *Negotiating Identities: Education for Empowerment in a Diverse Society*; and Herbert Kohl, *'I Won't Learn From You' and Other Thoughts on Creative Maladjustment* (New York: New Press, 1994).

34. Frederick Erickson, "Transformation and School Success: The Politics and Culture of Educational Achievement." In *Minority Education*, edited by Evelyn Jacob and Cathie Jordan.

35. Kohl, *'I Won't Learn From You' and Other Thoughts on Creative Maladjustment*, 2.

36. We are grateful to John Raible for these insights.

37. Michelle Fine, *Framing Dropouts: Notes on the Politics of an Urban Public High School* (Albany: State University of New York Press, 1991).

38. Jerry Lipka, "Toward a Culturally-Based Pedagogy: A Case Study of One Yup'ik Eskimo Teacher." In *Transforming Curriculum for a Culturally Diverse Society*, edited by Etta R. Hollins (Mahwah, NJ: Lawrence Erlbaum, 1996).

39. Prudence L. Carter, *Keepin' It Real: School Success Beyond Black and White* (New York: Oxford University Press, 2005); Gilberto Q. Conchas, *The Color of Success: Race and High-Achieving Urban Youth* (New York: Teachers College Press, 2006); D. Bruce Jackson, "Education Reform as if Student Agency Mattered: Aca-

demic Microcultures and Student Identity." *Phi Delta Kappan* 84, no. 8 (April 2003): 579–585.

40. Conchas, *The Color of Success: Race and High-Achieving Urban Youth*, 12–13.

41. Carter, *Keepin' It Real: School Success Beyond Black and White*, 8.

42. Monica K. Johnson, Robert Crosnoe, and Glen H. Elder, Jr. "Students' Attachment and Academic Engagement: The Role of Race and Ethnicity." *Sociology of Education* 74, no. 4 (2001): 318–334.

43. Carter, *Keepin' It Real: School Success Beyond Black and White*, 8.

44. Carter, *Keepin' It Real*, 30–31.

45. Jackson, "Education Reform as if Student Agency Mattered: Academic Microcultures and Student Identity."

46. Conchas, *The Color of Success: Race and High-Achieving Urban Youth*, 115.

47. Nel Noddings, *The Challenge to Care in Schools: An Alternative Approach to Education* (New York: Teachers College Press, 1992).

48. S. Crabtree, "Teachers Who Care Get the Most from Kids." *Detroit News*, June 4, 2004, 9.

49. Angela Valenzuela, *Subtractive Schooling: U.S.-Mexican Youth and the Politics of Caring* (Albany: State University of New York Press, 1999).

50. Nilda Flores-González, *School Kids, Street Kids: Identity and High School Completion Among Latinos* (New York: Teachers College Press, 2002).

51. Susan Roberta Katz, "Teaching in Tensions: Latino Immigrant Youth, Their Teachers, and the Structures

of Schooling." *Teachers College Record* 100, no. 4 (Summer 1999): 809–840.

52. Margaret A. Gibson and Livier F. Bejínez, "Dropout Prevention: How Migrant Education Supports Mexican Youth." *Journal of Latinos and Education* 1, no. 3 (2002): 155–175.

53. Sonia Nieto, *Why We Teach* (New York: Teachers College Press, 2005): 204.

54. Patricia Bode, "Multicultural Art Education: Voices of Art Teachers and Students in the Postmodern Era," diss., University of Massachusetts Amherst, 2005.

55. Ricardo Stanton-Salazar, "A Social Capital Framework for Understanding the Socialization of Racial Minority Children and Youth." *Harvard Educational Review* 67, no. 1 (Spring 1997): 1–40.

56. Alejandro Portes and Rubén Rumbaut, *Legacies: The Story of the Immigrant Second Generation* (Berkeley: University of California Press, and New York: Russell Sage Foundation, 2001). Valerie E. Lee, Linda F. Winfield, and Thomas C. Wilson, "Academic Behaviors Among High-Achieving African-American Students." *Education and Urban Society* 24, no. 1 (November 1991): 65–86.

57. *Ibid.*, 80.

58. Cummins, *Negotiating Identities: Education for Empowerment in a Diverse Society*.

59. See, for example, Anthony S. Bryk, Valerie E. Lee, and Peter B. Holland, *Catholic Schools and the Common Good* (Cambridge, MA: Harvard Educational Review Press, 1993) and Jacqueline Jordan Irvine and Michele Foster, *Growing Up African American in Catholic Schools* (New York: Teachers College Press, 1996).

CHAPTER 8 CASE STUDIES

PAUL CHAVEZ

I don't want to speak too soon, but I'm pretty much on a good road here.

Speaking in an earnest and intense tone, Paul Chavez[1] thought carefully before sharing his thoughts about the importance of school, the "hood," and his family. Paul was 16 years old at the time of his interview, and he had already lived a lifetime full of gang activity, drugs, and disappointment. The signs were evident, from his style of dress to the "tag" (tattoo) on his arm, to his reminiscence of "homeboys" who had been killed. Describing himself as Chicano and Mexican American, Paul's was the third generation in his family to be born in Los Angeles. He did not speak Spanish but said that both his mother and grandmother did, even though they too were born and raised here.

Paul lived with his mother, two brothers ages 19 and 9, and two younger sisters. Another brother, 21, was not living at home. His mother was trying to obtain her high school equivalency diploma; she had failed the test once, but was studying hard to try to pass it the next time. She and Paul's father had been separated for about four years, and Paul described the entire family as "Christian." His mother was a church leader, and his brother was a Bible study leader. Even his father, a recovering alcoholic, who had lived on the streets for years and spent time in prison, was living in what Paul called a "Christian home," probably a halfway house.

The one-family homes in Paul's East L.A. neighborhood mask the poverty and despair that are easier to see in other urban ghettos, with their high-rise tenements and projects. Here, the mostly Latino families struggle to maintain a sense of community in the well-kept homes on small lots. However, signs of gang activity are apparent in the tags on buildings and walls. Paul said that an outsider suspected of belonging to another gang was likely to get jumped merely for walking down the street.

School problems began for Paul when he was in third or fourth grade, and he had been suspended on numerous occasions for poor behavior. The problem was not lack of ability (his teachers always felt he was smart) but rather lack of interest. He was more interested in belonging to a "school gang," a group of young boys looking for boys in other classes to fight. In spite of the lure of gangs, he remembered fifth grade as the best year he had had in school, and he attributed this to Ms. Nelson, the most caring teacher he had until he went to his current school. Paul already wore gang-affiliated attire, and he had a reputation as a troublemaker, but she did not let this get in the way of her high expectations of him. It was in her class that he became interested in history, and he recalled being fascinated by the American Revolution.

By the time Paul began junior high school, peer pressure, family problems, and street violence brought the situation to a head. Seventh and eighth grades were his worst years. He was expelled in eighth grade, and although he was told by school authorities to attend an alternative school in another district, he refused to go and instead stayed home for six months. By ninth grade he was heavily involved in gang activity, joining the 18th Street Gang, a gang with thousands of members not only in L.A. but also in other cities and even in other states. Thirteen of his cousins were or had been in the same gang, as was an older brother, so the role of gang as "family" was even more revelant in his case. An uncle and a cousin had both been killed as a result of their gang activity.

Encouraged by his mother, Paul tried to enroll in another program but was again expelled after a few months. Then he heard about and applied to the Escuela de Dignidad y Orgullo (School of Dignity and Pride), a high school for students who had dropped out of other schools. With a large Chicano population, the school was characterized by a multicultural curriculum with a focus on Chicano history, and it relied on student and staff involvement in its day-to-day operations. All talk of gangs was discouraged, and the staff tried hard to create a different kind of community here, one not affiliated with gang culture. The staff included counselors, a psychologist, a probation officer, and several teachers. Although Paul had not formally been arrested, because of his previous problems, he agreed to a voluntary placement with the probation officer, just to "keep me on the right road," he said.

The new road Paul had taken was far from easy for him, however. He had also been expelled from Escuela de Dignidad y Orgullo, and it was only after trying another program and then spending several months on the street that he had realized he wanted to return. All of his friends had quit school, and he feared ending up like them. He had been accepted at Escuela once again and had done well since returning two years before. At the time he was interviewed, Paul was spending most of his time at school, doing homework every day when he got home, and working after school at the local city hall, a job the school found for him. Paul described Escuela as different from any other he had attended because the entire staff cared about and encouraged the students and because Chicano culture and history were central to the curriculum, making it a more exciting place to learn.

Paul's philosophy at this point was to take life one day at a time because the lure of gang life was still ever-present. He had not yet quit the gang, and it was obvious that he was at a crossroads in his life. The next several months might determine which direction his life would take: either an escalating life of crime on the streets or a promising future of education and work.

Paul's case study highlights two goals he had had for a long time: *to be respected* and to make something of himself, two goals that are frequently at odds. Another theme is his determination to *"make it better,"* and the third is the *importance of family support.*

"Everybody's Gotta Get Respect"

I grew up ditching school, just getting in trouble, trying to make a dollar, that's it, you know? Just go to school, steal from the store, and go sell candies at school. And that's what I was doing in the third or fourth grade. I was always getting in the principal's office, suspended, kicked out, everything, starting from the third grade.

My fifth grade teacher, Ms. Nelson, she put me in a play and that, like, tripped me out. Like, why do you want *me* in a play? Me, I'm just a mess-up. Still, you know, she put me in a play. And in fifth grade, I think that was the best year out of the whole six years [of elementary school]. I learned a lot about the Revolutionary War, you know? The fifth grade was a grade I'll always remember. Had good friends. We had a project we were involved in. Ms. Nelson was a good teacher. She just involved everyone. We made books, this and that. And I used to like to write, and I wrote two . . . three books. Was in a book fair and this and that. She did pretty nice things. She got real deep into you, just, you know, "Come on, you can do it." That was a good year for me, the fifth grade.

My most troubled years was my junior high years. Seventh grade, first day of school, I met this guy and then, from there, we started to form. And every junior high, you're gonna have a group, okay? You're gonna have a group that you hang around with. And it got to we just started always starting trouble in classes. Whatever period we had, we just started trouble in. And me, I have a great sense of humor, right? I can make people laugh a lot. So then I was always getting kicked out of the classroom. And so what that got me was kind of, I guess popular, right? Where girls were always around me. I had a big group. But, like, I was always the one clowning, getting in trouble. So it kind of like set a path for me where I was, like, all right, so I clown and get popularity. All right, I understand now the program.

I [wasn't] in a gang, but I was dressing pretty . . . still gang affiliated. And so people looked like, "Well, where you from?" "I ain't from nowhere." And that kind of like got me to want to be from somewhere so I could tell 'em, "Well, I'm from here. . . ." Those were the years in seventh grade, and I was fighting with eighth graders. I'd be in a dance, a little Oriental kid would come up to me and she goes, "I know you, you're Paul," this and that. They would know me. It made me feel good.

Being in a gang, you think about who you're retaliating, you know, just another Chicano brother. And that's kind of deep. Well, why you're gonna be from a neighborhood [gang], have pride, this and that, and take out your own *Raza*, you know?[2] So that kind of always caught me in my mind. You see a lot of your own people just going down because of your neighborhood. And it's a trip. And you got a lot of homeboys that come out from the system, the jails, and it's real segregated in there, you know, the Blacks and Chicanos. And they even got the border brothers, the ones from Mexico who don't speak no English. They're even separated from the Chicanos, the Sureños, that's right from South L.A. Okay, they're paranoid in there, and everybody is, like, "What's up with the Blacks? It's on, it's on. We're gonna have a war." And everybody, then they turn little things into big things. So it's really just a race war going on in the inside, and they bring it out to us.

It has a great hold on you, and it's, like, I talk to my cousin. He's still into it real deep. I'm not really. Don't get me wrong: I'm from the neighborhood, but I'm not really deep into it. You know what I mean? But it's, like, I talk to 'em. "Yeah, we were with the homeboys on the Eastside, blah, blah, blah, this and that," and I'll be like, "Damn," and I think, "I wish I was there getting off on drinking and shit."

I had a cousin, he was 16 in '89 when he passed away. He was my cousin . . . family . . . from 18th Street, too. And what happened, see, he passed away and that's another tragedy. It's just, you see so much. I'm 16, and I see so much. First his dad passed away and then my cousin . . . my uncle and my cousin. And you think, "Man, all this because of a gang!" And there's times when you just sit and you think, you sit and you think, and you say, "Why? Why? Why? What is this?" But you don't know why, but you have it so much inside of you. It's hard, it's not easy to get rid of. I don't want to get rid of, but you just got to try to focus on other things right now. I'm from a gang and that's it, and just 'cause I'm from a gang doesn't mean I can't make myself better.

But me, I do care. I have a life, and I want to keep it. I don't want to lose it. I have two little sisters, and I want to see them grow up too, and I want to have my own family. So, I got the tag. I got a big 18 on my arm where everybody could see it, and that's the way I was about a year ago. You know, man, if you would be talking a year ago I'd be, like, "I'm from the neighborhood." I'd be talking to you in slang street all crazy, you know? Now I'm more intelligent.

I try not to get influenced too much . . . pulled into what I don't want to be into. But mostly, it's hard. You don't want people to be saying you're stupid. "Why do you want to go to school and get a job?" I was talking to my homeboy the other day, so [he said] ". . . school? Drop out, like. . . ." "Like, all right, that's pretty good. Thanks for your encouragement" [*laughs*]. See, they trip like that, but they just mess around. That's just a joke, but it's, like, you just think about things like that. I guess your peers, they try to pull you down and then you just got to be strong enough to try to pull away.

I got to think about myself and get what I got to get going on. Get something going on, or else nobody else is going to do it. It's where you're starting to think a little different. You sort of know what's happening. All they're thinking about is partying, this and that. Nothing wrong with it, but I got to try to better myself.

Making It Better

I guess in a lot of ways, I am [successful] . . . a lot of things I'm trying to achieve. Starting something, already you're successful, you know? But finishing it, it's gonna make you more complete . . . successful and complete. Got to have your priorities straight. Get what you got to get done, and get it done, and just be happy when you're doing something.

I came to this school, and it was deep here. They got down into a lot of studies that I liked, and there was a lot going on here. But see, I was me, I was just a clown. I always liked to mess around, so they gave me chance after chance. I took it for granted, and they kicked me out. They booted me out, right? So I went back to that other school and it was like, "This thing is boring. Nothing going on." And so I called over here and I go, "I need another chance," this and that, to get back into school. So they gave me another chance and that's why I'm here right now, 'cause they gave me a chance.

They get more into deeper Latino history here, and that's what I like. A lot of other, how you say, background, ethnic background. We had even Martin Luther King. We had Cesar Chavez. We had a lot of things.

I never used to think about [being Chicano] before. Now I do . . . being Brown and just how our race is just going out. You know, you don't want to see your race go out like that.

[Mexican American], it's what you make it, you know? Let's say I'm Chicano and I dress like a gang member. They're gonna look at you like one of those crazy kids, you know, Mexican kid, Chicano kid. But if you present yourself nice or whatever, it really depends how your outer appears. Like, people say it's just *from the inside*, but it's really what's *on the outside* . . . how you look on the outside, like tattoos and that. So it's, like, I get discriminated because of a lot of things, and I can't really pinpoint it. So it's, like, I don't really know if it's 'cause I'm Brown or if it's 'cause of my gang tattoo, so I can't really pinpoint. But for me, as far as me being Chicano, it's prideful, it's pride of your race, of what you are.

[Chicano young people] have some pretty trippy insights of life. It's like they know how to talk to people, and they know how to give presentations, you know what I mean? Like what we're doing right now [*referring to the interview*]. A lot of the things they say is pretty deep.

[In this school], they just leave the killings out and talk about how you can make it better, you know what I'm saying? Try to be more of the positive side of being a Brown person, that's what I'm talking about. A lot of the other alternative schools you can't go because of your gang. It's all gang affiliated. Every single alternative school is gang affiliated. This is the only one where it's all neutral.

[To make school better I would] talk about more interesting things, more things like what *I* would like, students would like. And I would just get more involved . . . get more people involved. Get things going, not just let them vegetate on a desk and "Here's a paper," . . . teach 'em a lesson and expect them to do it. You know, get all involved.

Put some music in the school. I mean, put some music and get some like drawings. Get a better surrounding so you feel more like the 'hood, you could learn more, you'll feel more comfortable. This [school] is pretty good, but if you had somebody kicking it, put like a character on the wall of something . . . yeah, like a mural or something, it would be more like a more comfortable setting to work.

Try to find out what we think is important. Try to do the best you can to try to get it. The kids want it. They're gonna use it. If they don't want it, they're not, so. . . . I remember the *Diary of Anne Frank*. I was pretty deep into the Nazis and Jews, and so that was pretty cool.

I think [multicultural education] is important because that goes back to segregating. You got to get to know everybody more better. If you understand them better, you're gonna get along better. So, yeah, I think that would be good.

I'm getting out all I can get out [from this school]. There's so much to learn and that's all I want to do is just learn, try to educate my mind to see what I could get out of it. Anything I can, I'm gonna get out of it.

I was here when they barely opened this school. I brought my mom and my dad, and we had a couple of kids here and the staff here. What we did was wrote all the rules, just made an outline of how the school was gonna be: People are gonna get treated right, what you could wear. Everything was done with each other, you know? It wasn't just talked about with the staff and brought to the students. It was the students *and* the staff.

[*What would have made school easier for you?*] If you had asked me that question a year ago, I would have said, "No school!" School would have been made easier if it wasn't so early in the morning [*laughs*]. But school, it will be better if more activities [are] going on. People wouldn't just think of it as a routine. People got into it really where it really meant something. But it's both on the students' part and the teachers' part. It takes both.

The classes [should have] more better learning techniques. It's an advanced age. We got a lot of computer things going on. Get a lot of things going with computers and a lot of things that are going to draw the eye. Catch my eye and I'm gonna be, "Oh, all right," and gonna go over there and see what's up.

I think they should get more of these aides, assistants, to be parents, okay? 'Cause the parents, I notice this: A parent in a school is more, like, they got love. That's it, they got love and they give it to you. They give it back to more students. I think they should get more, like, parents involved in the school, like, to teach this and that. Get more parents involved in the classroom, too. Parents have a lot of things to say, I would think, about the schools.

[Teachers should] not think of a lesson as a lesson. Think of it as not a lesson just being taught to students, but a lesson being taught to one of your own family members, you know? 'Cause if it's, like, that they get more deep into it, and that's all it takes. Teach a lesson with heart behind it and try to get your kids to understand more of what's going on. And don't lie to your kids . . . like, to your students, saying "Everything is okay and 'just say no to drugs'; it's easy." Let them know what's really going on. Don't beat around the bush. Let them know there's gangs, drugs. "You guys got to get on with that. That's for kids. Do what you got to do and stay in education." They're starting to do that more now. Try to get a dress code going on. I never used to like that, but that's a pretty good idea, you know? But not really a strict dress code, but just where you can't wear gang attire.

It just catches up to you later on. It does because when you're in the 10th grade and you sit down to do fractions and you can't do a problem 'cause you didn't really learn the basics, it all catches up. When I was in junior high, I didn't do math the whole seventh and eighth grade. I never did a math paper. Maybe turned one or two in, but it was, like, I don't like math, and it all catches up to you.

Now I take every chance I get to try to involve myself in something. Now it's like I figure if I'm more involved in school, I won't be so much involved in the gang, you know? . . . It's what you put into it, what you're gonna get out of it. And you know, sometimes I tell myself, like, accountants are always working with numbers, and I say, "I want to be an accountant because I want to do something where I got to work hard to try to get it, and show that I could learn math and do it real good." That's just the kind of person I am, where if I can't do something, like, just to trip myself up, I want to do this. You know, just so I can learn it more real good and show 'em that I can . . . try to make an example out of myself, of everything I do.

[Good grades] make you feel good, getting A's. See this gang-member-type man getting A's. I get pretty good grades. I get A's, B's, and C's. That's better than all F's on report cards that I used to get, all failures in all six subjects.

After when I get my diploma, it's not the end of school, it's the beginning. I still want to learn a lot more after that. I basically want to go to college. That's what I want to do. Get more schooling so I could learn more.

Probably I would want to be either a teacher, a counselor, something like working with youngsters to share my experience with them, you know? 'Cause I know there's a lot of people out there who talk down to youngsters, you know what I'm saying? Instead of talking *with* them. And just try to understand what they're going through.

I mean, you can't get a teacher, put 'em in a classroom with a bunch of kids from the neighborhood, and the teacher lives in [another neighborhood] and expect to understand. I have problems at home, a lot of problems. And to come into school and for a teacher to come with a snotty attitude, I'm gonna give it back. That's the way it is.

I don't want to speak too soon, but I'm pretty much on a good road here. I'm pretty much making it. Trying to make something out of myself. I'm on that way, you know . . . I'm going that way.

You can't talk about next month, at least at this time. I'm just today, get it done. That's it. The best I can.

And I just, I'm tripping out on myself. I don't believe I'm doing this. But I don't really like to build myself too high . . . because the higher you are the harder you're gonna fall. I don't want to fall.

Family Support: "I Had a Love That Kept Me Home"

I like kids. I like kids a lot. They see me and, "Gee, that guy is scary. He's a gang member. . . . " This experience the other day when I was at work: I was working in [a daycare center], and I walked in and the kids were looking at me like and whispering. And this one kid, this Oriental kid, came up and we started playing. The next thing I know, she was sitting on my lap and all these kids just started coming towards me. And they know: They could feel I love kids.

You need to educate your mind. Somebody gets born and throw 'em into the world, you know, they're not gonna make it. You get somebody, you born 'em, you raise 'em, you feed 'em and encourage 'em, and they're gonna make it. That's what the reason for going to school is. A lot of it, of my going to school, is 'cause of my mom. I want her to be proud and her to say that I made it and this and that.

My mom used to run with gangs when she was young. My mom and my father both belonged to gangs. They're out of it. They don't mess around no more.

I learned a lot of morals from my mother. Respect, how to respect people. If my mom wasn't in church, she wouldn't be there for us, I don't think. She would be trying to find a way to seek to comfort herself, you know what I mean?

My mom, she's real strong and real understanding. Not strict, but more understanding, you know? She don't really compromise with me. Usually what she says is what she says, that's it. My mom, I wouldn't change nothing, nothing [about her]. My dad, I would . . . just have him be there for me when I was younger. I could have turned out different if he was there, you never know.

It's hard for me to talk to my mom or my dad, but I talk to my mom about a lot of things like girlfriends, things that happen. Like when homeboys die, I don't go talking to nobody else but my mom. My homeboy just passed away about a month ago or two months ago, and I just remember I was in my mom's room. My mom was ironing and I just started crying, and I don't cry a lot. I started crying and I started telling her, "I hurt, Mom. I don't know why, but I hurt so much." 'Cause I had been trying to, how do you say, run from it, I'd been trying to put it off, like my homeboy's gone, 'cause we were pretty close. So I was like, "It hurts, Mommy." She said, "I know, in your gut," like this and that. So we talked. We get pretty much into it.

She dropped out in the tenth grade, and she was pregnant. And she says, "I want you to do good. Don't be like me, going back to school when it's already kind of late, you know." It's never too late, but you know what I'm saying. She was like, "Just learn now, Paul. Do it the first time right and you won't have to do it again."

My mom wants me to go to school basically so I could have a good house and home when I build up my family, and so we won't have to be five people living in a three-bedroom home, with not that much money to live on, you know?

My mom makes a good living, not in money but in moral standards. We're happy with what we've got and that's just the bottom line. So I go to school for my mom, try to help her and try to help me.

My mom, she's not really [involved in school]. She's too busy doing her own thing. She gets out of school, makes dinner, cleans the house, goes to church, comes home, irons for my two sisters. She doesn't really have time for all this. She'll come in and she'll talk to my probation officer, talk to Isabel [*a staff member*], different people, yeah, pretty much involved when she can be.

You're gonna realize that you got to learn from day one and education will never end. It's only when you stop it. I realize that now. But see, me, I never really had somebody to push me. My mother pushed me, and my mom, she just got tired. "Paul, you're too much for me." My father, he never really pushed me. He talked to me. That was, like, "Education, Paul, education," you know? And getting letters from my dad in jail, "Stay in school," and that's all. He said some pretty deep things, understanding things to me. And my dad always knew the right words to say to me that kind of encouraged me. And my mom. They both encouraged me.

If it wasn't for the family, the love I get from my family, I would look for it in my homeboys. I never had to do that. I just wanted my homeboys to party. A lot of my friends, they go to homeboys to look for just to kick it with somebody. See, me, I had a love that kept me home, that kept me in my place.

I remember I used to just take off from Friday night to Monday morning, come home. My mom be worrying all night, "Where is this guy?" and I was in the street. And that was like every weekend. 'Til now, I stay home every day and I'm just going to school. . . . I come from work, do my homework, whatever. Go to work, come home, go to church, 'cause I go to church with my mother.

My mom, she's really proud of me. My friend was telling me that she was at church, at Bible study, a gathering at home of church people. And [my mom] was crying. She was proud. [My friend] said, "Your mom was talking about you, and she was crying. She's real proud." And that's my mom, she's real sensitive. I love my mom so much it's even hard to explain. And she thinks . . . she tells me, "You don't care about me, Paul," this and that, 'cause like it's hard for me. . . . It's hard for me to show my feelings.

◆ ◆ ◆ Commentary

Luis Rodríguez, author of *Always Running, La Vida Loca: Gang Days in L.A.*, whose experiences parallel Paul's in many ways, describes gangs as young people's search for a sense of belonging.[3]

Looking back on his own youth and fearing for the future of his son, who was following the same path, Rodríguez wrote his book to encourage people to understand that gangs, in spite of providing belonging, respect, and protection to their members, represent an unhealthy and self-destructive response to oppression. Gangs emerge when communities are deprived of basic human rights. According to Rodríguez, few young people would choose gangs if they were given decent education, productive jobs, and positive channels for social recreation.

Schools may unwittingly contribute to young people's gang involvement by failing to provide the strong cultural identity and support that students need. In fact, James Diego Vigil has suggested that neighborhoods (streets) and schools interact in ways that can interfere with the learning of many Chicano students. According to him, understanding this connection can help educators create a more positive school experience for Chicano students. Vigil suggests that schools can develop a balanced strategy of *prevention, intervention,* and *suppression.*[4] For example, *prevention* would focus on strengthening families and addressing some of the conditions that lead children to street life and gangs. *Intervention* would address students' behavioral problems, and *suppression* would confront the most destructive behavioral aspects of gang culture. However, suppression can also unintentionally lead to creating school dropouts, for instance, when dress codes that may appear to be neutral rather than targeted at only gang members, drive gang members out of school. Even in the early grades, when Paul began to dress like a gang member, teachers' negative reactions—if not specific dress codes—made him feel that school was not a place for him. That is why he so vividly remembered Ms. Nelson, the one teacher who treated him kindly despite his attire.

The yearning for respect, which is, after all, just another word for a sense of competence, is what Paul described when he talked about joining first what he called a "school gang" and later the full-fledged street gang. Young men and women in desperate economic straits are turning in ever larger numbers to *"la vida loca,"* or the crazy life of gangs. In 1991, when Paul was interviewed, Los Angeles alone was estimated to have 100,000 gang members in 800 gangs. In that peak year for gang activity, nearly 600 youths were killed, mostly by other youths.[5]

The rage felt by young people when their dreams are denied or suppressed is turned inward, resulting in such things as drug abuse or suicide, or turned outward. The unspeakably violent actions of Chicanos against their own *Raza,* so poignantly expressed by Paul, is an example of the latter. Rodríguez describes this violence as emanating too often from the self-loathing that is the result of oppression: "And if they murder, the victims are usually the ones who look like them, the ones closest to who they are—the mirror reflections. They murder and they're killing themselves, over and over."[6]

Nevertheless, blame for gangs and for other manifestations of oppression in our society cannot be placed on schools. The issues are too complicated for simplistic scapegoating; they include massive unemployment, a historical legacy of racism and discrimination, and a lack of appropriate housing and health care, among others. In addition, families struggling to survive on a daily basis can seldom do much to counteract the lure of gangs and drugs, with their easy money and instant popularity, that influences so many of their children. As Paul said, his mother, try as she might, just got tired: "Paul, you're too much for me," she said.

Although schools can neither do away with gangs nor put a stop to the violence taking place in communities across the United States every day, they can make a difference. Paul was quick to place the responsibility for his past on his own shoulders rather than blaming teachers. However, when he thought more deeply about it, he also recognized that particular teachers and schools *did* make a difference. This is nowhere more evident than in the case of Ms. Nelson or, years later, the teachers in his alternative school.

Chicano parents and their children often have high aspirations, but, unless these are somehow incorporated into the culture of schools, they will make little difference. For instance, Alejandro Portes and Rubén Rumbaut, in their extensive research on various immigrant communities, found that the strengths of these communities are frequently disregarded by schools. In the specific case of Mexican Americans, they concluded that "In many Mexican families, the *only* thing going for the children is the support and ambition of their parents. These aspirations should be strengthened rather than undermined."[7] This finding compels us to shift the focus to the context and structure of schools rather than to focus only on the shortcomings of students and their families. In other words, policies and practices need to be reviewed to make education more engaging and positive for all students. In this regard, schools need to develop strategies that use a more culturally congruent approach rather than an approach based on culture as a deficit.

Paul's suggestion that his school hire more parents as school aides because they "got love and they give it to you" reminds us of the powerful influence of family on Hispanic/Latino culture. Even families in difficult circumstances want the best for their children but often are unaware of how to provide it for them. His father's insistence on "Education, Paul, education," if unaccompanied by structural support to help him stay in school, is of little help. Paul clearly understood this when he said that, although his parents supported him, they never really pushed him.

Paul Chavez was fortunate to be in the alternative school he was attending, and it seemed to be serving as a safeguard to keep him at some distance from his gang. The policies and practices of his school were geared toward creating a positive learning environment. There was no tracking; staff interactions with students were positive and healthy; students were involved in the school's governance; there were high expectations and demanding standards of all students; and their languages and cultures were an integral part of the school's curriculum. Nevertheless, an insightful observation by Vigil is worth noting here. Alternative schools, he says, may replicate street gang culture by concentrating a critical mass of gang members in one place. Thus, these schools can act as "temporary warehouses," or in the words of some of the gang members quoted by James Vigil, as "preparation for prison."[8]

One cannot help but remember, however, that at the time of his interview, Paul was only 16 years old, a tender age, and he had so many difficult situations and easy temptations still facing him. In spite of Paul's strong motivation and eloquent insights, his school's caring, his mother's love and strict discipline, and his growing realization that gang life is no solution to the problems facing Chicano youth, he still had a long and hard road ahead of him.

◆ ◆ ◆ Reflect on This Case Study

1. What can teachers and schools learn from Paul's fifth-grade teacher, Ms. Nelson? Give specific suggestions.
2. What support services do you think are needed in schools such as those in Paul's neighborhood? Why?
3. Take a look at the recommendations that Paul made to improve schools. Which do you think make sense? Why?
4. Why do you think Paul never thought about being Chicano before? What kinds of ethnic studies would be important for students at different levels?
5. How can schools use the tremendously positive feelings about family that Paul and other Latinos have?

LATRELL ELTON

I wanna do positive stuff now. I wanna do something positive with my life.

At the time he was interviewed, Latrell Elton,[1] a 16-year-old African American young man, was finishing his sophomore year of high school in Atlanta, Georgia. After starting at his local high school, the district transferred him to Bowden County Alternative High School, a school for students who had been expelled from their home schools. While the alternative school claimed to develop self-esteem, self-discipline, trust, lifelong learning, and respect for others, Latrell's description of his experience there raises many concerns about the gaping divide between a school's missions and the messages, both explicit and implicit, that students receive from the school's policies and practices.

Latrell reported that the alternative school is 100 percent segregated: "The school is—all it is—is Black. The students are all Black and the teachers are all Black," aligning it with Jonathon Kozol's description of apartheid schools.[2] Within this environment, Latrell's narrative pointed to three distressing themes: *his school experience as resembling prison; the detrimental messages about his racial identity;* and his *low expectations for the future.*

Prison Analogy

We're in school; but it ain't like the regular school. When you go in the school, they check you tucked in your shirt. And then you gotta go through the metal detectors. When you go through the metal detectors, they search you. After they search you, you go on to the cafeteria—you sit down. Goin' through metal detectors at school, I don't feel uncomfortable with it. Well, truly it shouldn't be happenin' but I don't be feelin' uncomfortable with it, you know what I'm saying? Every day we go in school, they searchin' us like we prisoners and stuff. I put my own self in a predicament to go to that school. I didn't really wanna go. But they were, like, "Well Mr. Elton, we can't let you in school until you go and do a year in there." And I was, like, "All right. I'll do what I gotta do." The main thing I'm focused on is trying to get up out that school. As soon as I get up out that school I'll be a happy person.

We ride on a bus that have two Bowden County motorcycle mans right here. They have marked police in the front, one in the middle and one in the back, and they have each marked police on each bus. Man, make me feel like I'm in jail. Like I'm just a prisoner, like I'm a bad person. My bus have burglary bar windows. They got cameras on there. You can't get up out your seat.

Detrimental Messages and Racial Identity

I'm African American. Y'all don't want to hear what I got in my blood. I got the N-word in my blood. 'Cause I'm just, I just don't like sitting down, I can't stay seated. I just wanna run around, get my energy out. It's negative. Right now I'm trying to control it at school. When I was in [my previous] school, I used to run around, can't sit down in class, sit on top of the desk, cut. But now I don't. I sit down.

I feel like Black folk these days, we doin' stupid stuff, we wanna kill each other over little stupid stuff like a car. We wanna go out here and break into houses. To tell you the truth, the whole jail system is made for us only. That's why they build jails and welfare: for Black people. 'Cause they know what we're gonna do. [Black people] put themselves in a predicament. I ain't gonna lie.

Say, for instance, a Black person would have got shot right here and we call the ambulance. You know how long it's gonna take them? About an hour to 35 minutes just to come. Just to come. Oh, this Black person, they got shot. That's one less Black person we got to worry about on the street. One person we ain't got to do nothing for. But if it's like a mixed person being shot, they be on the scene in less than five minutes. You hear the sirens and everything. You got helicopter, news, and everything.

About my neighborhood, I would tell you: Be safe. Be careful. Don't trust nobody around here. People around here, they steal, they'll lie to you. Everything. They'll do everything around here. People around here, they just don't care. Like, you trying to cross the street, they won't slow down. They'll just keep flying by you. Just go on.

The community people are all Black folk. That's what all it is. That's what I said, nothing but black folks all on the street. They like this because they ain't been in no real life, you know what I'm saying? With people who got quieter streets, who like respect, like neighborhood watch. We ain't got no neighborhood watch. It's just people out there doing stupid stuff. Where I'm from, when we had neighborhood watch, they wouldn't be doing what they doing now.

Future Expectations

I hope when I get out of Bowden Alternative School, I can go ahead and go back to regular school. And when I get on to regular school, first thing I'm gonna be looking for is basketball tryout. When I find out when they having basketball tryout, I'm gonna stay after school. I'm just gonna play basketball. And when I play basketball, I'm gonna try and go pro. I'm trying to go to the top. Trying to be the best I can be in basketball. My teacher told me I could be a comedian. I got jokes. I got some jokes. I could joke. I'm gonna try and be a comedian too if basketball don't happen.

I see all these folks out here, they be like, "Yeah cous', do this, selling drug gonna get money." Selling drugs ain't gonna get you nowhere. Drug money don't last long. And then drugs get you locked up and stuff. I wanna do positive stuff now. I wanna do something positive with my life. I don't wanna keep on doing no negative stuff. Can't keep on doing that. It just ain't right. 'Cause I see all this money, there's money out here. I tell people, there's money out here. You got cars you can wash—you even got—even yards to cut . . . cut grass all day, you know what I'm saying? I don't like cutting yards, but I cut 'em. Only why I cut 'em is because, sometimes when I'm feeling broke and I got more to cut.

It make me feel good about myself [to have a job cutting grass] 'cause I know I ain't gotta go out here and ask nobody for no money, you know what I'm saying? 'Cause I don't want my momma see me in a couple more years on the street asking folks for 50 cents. I want her to see me coming in a car. So clean. With a big old house, with a bag full of money. Just say, "Momma, for all the years of hard work you put me through, there you go, right there. There you go, a brand new set of car keys, there go you some house keys, there you go." See my momma there, up in the house. I got big plans for when I get out of school.

'Cause if I keep on putting my mind on right things, positive things, I ain't got to worry about no niggaz' still trying to get through my brain and trying to make me mess up. 'Cause right now, since I been in these sports and stuff, it's helped me out a lot. Because I know I'm with safe people. People who I really can trust. People who I ain't gotta worry about got illegal drugs. I know I ain't gotta worry about all that. I'm on the right track. I can do this and that to make my life positive.

Now, since I'm in the alternative school, they've been helping me out a lot, a way, way lot. 'Cause I've got after-school tutorial, and we got more help after school. I'm a good student right now. I consider myself a good student. [What makes me a good student right now is] my behavior, the way I done calmed down. Going to school on time. Getting A's. Passing all my classes. I ain't got to worry about none of this. Last year, [at my previous school] I didn't have nothing but stress. I didn't know what to do with my work. Until I met this lady named Miss Kathy. So when I met her, I showed her my report card and I talked to her about getting me a mentor. And then when she had found me this mentor, and ever since, I been coming home with good grades, passing. Look, yo, I show her every Tuesday, look at my progress report. You see, I done did good. I done finally learned something. I don't worry about falling asleep in class, not doing no work. I used to fall asleep everyday in class.

In literature class now my average is a D. It's between a C and a D. By the end of the semester, I'm hoping to have A's, A's, A's, A's, A's by paying attention, doing what I'm doing every day all day. Working. Trying not to go to sleep.

The school I went to before, I went there and I just kept causing trouble. I had so many friends that I knew from middle school, you know what I'm saying? They trying to tell me, "Do that. Go do that, mess with that right there". But like I told my mom when I get out that school system and stuff I ain't got to worry about it. Gotta be a grown man. I can make my own decisions, do what I wanna do. I ain't gotta worry about people telling me what to do, and I just be free.

◆ ◆ ◆ Commentary

Latrell is a bright, perceptive young man who was painfully aware of the ravages of institutionalized racism in his community. His poignant comments point to both the responsibilities of school structures and the limits of the school's reach within under-resourced and over-exploited communities. Latrell said he was "not uncomfortable" about entering the school house through metal detectors, implying that he viewed it as a necessary reality.

He equated having the "N-word in my blood" with struggling to conform to classroom expectations, apparently having absorbed the message that staying seated and overcoming restlessness are racial traits. It is evident that Latrell's perspective of his racial identity and cultural group had become skewed by experiences of racism, marginalization, and violence.

While Latrell's hopeful outlook on the future was courageous, it also pointed to a lack of adequate guidance and academic preparation for professional goals. In the overwhelming shadow of American popular culture, it has become the norm for many young people, especially young men, to dream of becoming professional athletes or entertainers. While these are noteworthy possibilities that should not be dismissed, both are exceptionally competitive careers, considering the percentage of individuals who actually secure personal and financial success in such pursuits. Strong guidance and career counseling services in some schools help students with such aspirations follow their hearts *and* prepare for a collegiate trajectory that supports their vision. For example, thoughts of pursuing a career in sports medicine, sports management, physical education, theater studies, entertainment management, or entrepreneurial endeavors did not even appear in Latrell's vocabulary. Regrettably, he is not alone.

In Gilberto Conchas's research of successful programs for urban youth of color, he found a common thread among the low-income African American males in the school that he studied. Even in a highly successful program that boasted strong graduation rates and consistent levels of matriculation into two- and four-year colleges, low-income African American males placed higher value on athletic fame than on their collegiate path. Conchas writes, "They knew college was important but they really wanted to play football or basketball or perhaps become entertainers."[3] Conchas's research illustrates that although these particular low-income African American males were provided with the social and academic support systems essential for college, "their perceptions of social mobility were seemingly no different than the general stereotype."[4] Despite the tenacious power of negative stereotypes, Conchas concludes that schools can take steps to counteract the negative consequences of linking racial identity and academic performance. He insists, "We must remain critical of larger historical and structural forces that impact African American youth's perceptions of the opportunity structure."[5]

By indicting systemic social injustices, Latrell was perceptive about the opportunity structures that limit students' life options. He linked standard-of-living disparities to institutionalized oppression. In his daily life, he witnessed the slow response of emergency services as a reflection and reinforcement of the pervasive messages about the disposability of Black people. He perceived the lack of cooperation among members of his community as a response to the constraints of living immensely unequal lives.

Many urban schools recognize the toll that inhumane socioeconomic conditions have taken on minority students' perceptions of themselves and their racial identities. Some school administrations have implemented self-esteem programs and attempted to include culturally affirming curriculum. While such efforts may be commendable, they are insufficient shields against the forces of historically rooted racist beliefs and structures of racism. Reflecting on the myriad methods of self-esteem-building tactics that have become commonplace in many urban schools, Jonathon Kozol asserts,

> We are in a world where hope must be constructed therapeutically because so much of it has been destroyed by the conditions of internment in which we have placed these children. It is harder to convince young people that they "can learn" when they are cordoned off by a society that isn't sure they really can.[6]

Kozol's assessment concurs with Latrell's: "They like this because they ain't been in no real life." Yet, this *is* Latrell's real life, as it is the real life of his family, his peers, and his neighbors.

The poetic nuance of Latrell's phrase exposes his feeling that having a different kind of life was unrealistic or even other-worldly. However, despite his indictment of institutional inequities and community challenges, Latrell's perspective is explicitly hopeful. He recognized that mowing lawns pays less than selling drugs, but he deliberately chose cutting grass as a means of resisting the prevalent opportunities for drug dealing. He saw the analogies to prison in his school structures but yearned for academic success. He revealed his awareness of his responsibility in achieving higher grades, but it is unclear whether the adults in his world were hearing his hopeful voice. What will it take for Latrell and his peers to attend a U.S. urban school where the notion of metal detectors seems foreign and out of place? Why does it seem only imaginary for Latrell to engage in a rigorous curriculum that promotes fluency in multiple academic disciplines, with participation in co-curricular activities that promote healthy athleticism and artistic accomplishments and with teachers and guidance counselors supporting achievable, fulfilling goals?

◆◆◆ Reflect on This Case Study

1. Latrell's racial identity was continually developing, especially as a young adult. Given the negative perceptions of school that Latrell articulated, what can you, as an individual teacher, do, and what can the school, as an institution, do to positively influence Latrell's racial identity development?
2. Conchas's research suggests ways that schools can create structures to counteract the negative consequences of the linkage between racial identity and academic performance. How might a small group of dedicated teachers embark on changing structures in schools? Identify the stakeholders the group would have to bring on board to effect change.
3. What perceptions do you think most teachers would have of Latrell? What information would you share with those teachers to advocate for Latrell's participation in rigorous academics, arts, and athletics? What support structures would you build to help Latrell be successful?
4. What do you think about Latrell's assessment of having metal detectors in his school entrance and bars on the bus windows? Do you think such measures are necessary? Might there be alternative safety strategies?

5. Imagine you are Latrell's teacher. How does your memory of your high school experience compare to Latrell's? How do the communities and neighborhoods in which you grew up compare to Latrell's? What can you do as a teacher to come to know the realities of your students' daily lives? Does it matter?

Notes to Chapter 8 Case Studies

Paul Chavez

1. We are grateful to Dr. Mac Lee Morante for the interview and background information for Paul's case study. Dr. Morante is a bilingual school psychologist for the Anaheim City Schools and also works as a counselor at Santa Ana College in California.

2. *Raza* refers to the people of Mexican and Mexican American origin.

3. Luis J. Rodríguez, *Always Running, La Vida Loca: Gang Days in L.A.* (New York: Simon & Schuster, 1993): 250.

4. James Diego Vigil, "Streets and Schools: How Educators Can Help Chicano Marginalized Gang Youth." *Harvard Educational Review* 69, no. 3 (Fall 1999): 270–288.

5. Rodríguez, *Always Running, La Vida Loca: Gang Days in L.A.*

6. Rodríguez, *Always Running, La Vida Loca*, 9.

7. Alejandro Portes and Rubén Rumbaut, *Legacies: The Story of the Immigrant Second Generation* (Berkeley, CA: University of California Press and New York: Russell Sage Foundation, 2001), 280.

8. James Diego Vigil, "Streets and Schools: How Educators Can Help Chicano Marginalized Gang Youth." *Harvard Educational Review* 69, no. 3 (Fall 1999): 270–288.

Latrell Elton

1. We want to thank Vera Stenhouse for conducting the interview with Latrell. Vera is currently a doctoral candidate at Emory University where her research explores how new teacher preparation programs educate teachers to work with diverse students. Vera also provided follow-up information about Latrell's school to add depth to the case study.

2. Jonathon Kozol, *Shame of the Nation: The Restoration of Apartheid Schooling in America* (New York: Crown, 2005).

3. Gilberto Q. Conchas, *The Color of Success: Race and High-Achieving Urban Youth* (New York: Teachers College Press, 2006): 113–115.

4. Conchas, *The Color of Success*, 56.

5. Conchas, *The Color of Success*, 59.

6. Kozol, *Shame of the Nation*, 37.

PART 3

IMPLICATIONS OF DIVERSITY FOR TEACHING AND LEARNING IN A MULTICULTURAL SOCIETY

Alexandra Ekstein-Konin in Ben Sear's art class. *Self-portrait.* Relief print, 2005.

"We want our classrooms to be just and caring, full of various conceptions of the good. We want them to be articulate, with the dialogue involving as many persons as possible, opening to one another, opening to the world."

—*Maxine Greene*

"The Passions of Pluralism: Multiculturalism and the Expanded Community," *Educational Researcher,* 1993.

Part 3 analyzes the experiences of the young people in the case studies and snapshots by placing their stories in the broader sociopolitical context of schools and society. It also reviews some of the changes that can be made in schools and classrooms, based on the lessons young people can teach us through their experiences and insights. Students, although rarely consulted, are eloquent in expressing their own needs, interests, and concerns. It is in this spirit that their stories, desires, hopes, and goals are presented.

Chapter 9 explores conditions and experiences that students in the case studies and snapshots perceived as central to academic and social success. This exploration describes how young people, in their own words, define success; what they believe helped them achieve; and what held them back. The major purpose of this discussion is to explore what teachers and schools can do to provide successful academic environments for all students.

Chapter 10 presents three case studies of curriculum in a wide array of structural models that deal with a range of grade levels, content, topics, and skills. The chapter honors teachers' ingenuity and intellectual prowess in developing curriculum specific to their learning communities. Rather than advocating any one single model, the examples are presented in the hope that educators will find inspiration from which to design their own units. An additional curriculum case is on the companion website at www.ablongman.com/nieto5e.

Chapter 11 concerns three major conditions that promote learning among students: maintaining and affirming cultural connections, supporting extracurricular activities and experiences, and developing positive learning environments in schools. In this chapter, the seven characteristics that define multicultural education are developed further in a model ranging from *tolerance* to *affirmation, solidarity, and critique.*

Three major ideas are addressed in Part 3. One is that *complete assimilation as a prerequisite for success in school or society is a dubious notion at best, and a counterproductive one at worst.* The stories of the students in the case studies and snapshots are striking examples of this tension. These young people embody tremendous strength and resilience, and they want to do well and succeed in spite of sometimes overwhelming odds. But the conflicting experiences they have had in school also attest to the difficulties they have encountered.

A second significant idea discussed in Part 3 is that *schools need to accommodate their policies and practices to students' needs and realities if they are to be safe and nurturing learning environments.* When schools do not provide the structures needed for learning and affirmation, they can become places of defeat and despair.

The third significant idea illustrated in Part 3 is that *classroom curriculum can affirm students' identities while rigorously advancing academic achievement in preparation for life in a multicultural society.* Myriad models of curriculum design can be adapted within the multicultural perspectives asserted in this text, as demonstrated by the four curriculum examples described in Chapter 10.

Learning from Students

Timothy Burbank, Nyima Smith, Ben Hastings in Ben Sear's art class. *Self-portrait*. Relief print. 2005.

"To keep us from forgetting our culture's language, schools could still have reading sessions in our culture's language. I think that would help the Asian students."

— *Savoun Nouch, interviewee*

The voices of the students in the case studies and snapshots in this book are testimony to the vitality and spirit of youth. Despite a variety of conditions that might severely test the mettle and aspirations of others in similar circumstances, these youths have demonstrated a staunch determination to succeed in school and in life. Most define themselves as successful students, and they are proud of this fact, so understanding the insights of these particular students can be enlightening for educators interested in providing effective learning environments for all young people. Students who have not been as fortunate also have important messages for us, for they challenge our prevailing assumptions about learning and teaching.

In this chapter, four major issues that emerged from the case studies and snapshots are reviewed:

- A redefinition of success and achievement
- The conflicted nature of culture and language
- The key role of activities outside of academics in sustaining students' enthusiasm and motivation for school
- The central role of family, community, and school in providing environments for success

THE MEANING OF SUCCESS

Many young people have a conception of education that is distinct from that commonly held by schools. For instance, the role of hard work in becoming educated was mentioned by most of the students. During his interview, for instance, Kaval Sethi, whose snapshot appears in Chapter 4, said that intelligence rather than hard work was rewarded in his school. He said, "I don't think school is fair for people who are not as intelligent as other people. . . . It is very rigid." Others also made it clear that intelligence is not an innate ability or immutable quality—something that one is born with—as it often is defined in U.S. society. Intelligence is, in fact, something that one cultivates, studies hard to attain, and eventually achieves. Being smart is a goal, not a characteristic. Being smart is also the result of family and community support and the quality of care shown by teachers and schools. In this sense, intelligence is within everyone's reach.

Grades are a major indicator of academic success in our schools, and their importance is increasing in the current climate of accountability and high-stakes standardized tests. Grades were significant for most of the students we interviewed, but contrary to what many teachers and schools might believe, academically successful students may not consider grades to be as meaningful as other manifestations of their success. Many of the students we interviewed mentioned being satisfied with a grade for which they worked hard even if it was not the best grade. On the other hand, Fern Sherman's A's in English were not particularly satisfying to her because the class was neither engaging nor challenging. Fern's and Yahaira Léon's science classes, which were far more demanding classes in which they did not get as high a grade, were nevertheless their favorites.

The purposes of education are much broader and more noble for many students than the limited goals schools often set. Thus, although teachers often talk in terms of future employment and career goals, many of the students interviewed saw education as far more. While some did mention hope for a good job in the future (certainly a positive aspiration), a more nuanced interpretation of their words reveals deeper goals. More than a concern about the quality of their future job, many students exhibited a desire to fulfill their potential as human beings and as family members. For Hoang Vinh, going to school had one purpose: to become educated. He considered a good job to be secondary. Yahaira said, "The reason for going to school is to educate your mind."

A word needs to be said, however, about the vague or romantic ideals some female students tend to have regarding their future. Alicia Montejo, Fern Sherman, and Linda Howard all talked about dual and seemingly contradictory career goals. Alicia wanted to be either a medical doctor or a border patrol officer; Fern, a fashion lawyer or U.S. president; and Linda, a teacher or a world famous singer. Particularly for females, the reality of limited choices in the past, and the continuing sexualization of their identities, have an impact. Most of these young women selected what seems to be a glamorous choice or one that appears to wield social power. Besides culture, language, and social class, gender also mediates what students may consider realistic goals for their future.

But females' ethnic cultures not only *limit* their choices; they may also *expand* them. Girls are often subject to limited role expectations and gender stereotyping, but they may also receive affirming and powerful cultural messages about being female. A study done by Pilar Muñoz and Josette Henschel illustrates this seeming contradiction. They interviewed ten Puerto Rican women to determine what messages these women had received during their childhood regarding their future role in society. All the women reported that they had been taught to be submissive, quiet, long-suffering, and patient by their mothers and grandmothers. These were the *verbal* messages they heard throughout their youth. However, they also learned *nonverbal* attitudes and behaviors from their mothers and grandmothers—that women need to be resourceful, intelligent, and stronger than men. These dual and apparently conflicting messages were not lost on the women interviewed, all of whom were extraordinarily strong and resilient and had learned to "take care of themselves."[1]

PRIDE AND CONFLICT IN CULTURE

One of the most consistent, and least expected, outcomes to emerge from our interviews was the resoluteness with which young people maintained pride and satisfaction in their culture and the strength they derived from it. This does not mean that their pride was sustained without great conflict, hesitation, or contradiction. Because young people's positive sense of cultural identification challenges the messages and models of an essentially assimilationist society, it creates its own internal conflicts, but the fact that almost all of the students mentioned a deep pride in their culture cannot be overlooked. Students volunteered that their culture helped them in many ways and that they felt proud of who they were. Vanessa Mattison was an exception; she was uncomfortable even describing herself in ethnic terms. She reflected pride and shame in her cultural background, but for a different reason: because of the unfair privilege she derived from it as a white person.

Moreover, many of them understood that their culture was not what they *do*, but who they *are*. These young people seemed to understand intuitively that their heritage informed and enriched them, but they were also clear that it did not define them. For many, strong self-identification was understood as a value. "You gotta know who you are," is how Manuel Gomes expressed it. At the same time, they resisted essentialist notions of identity. Instead, they understood, to a much greater extent than most adults, that they were *cultural hybrids*. "I mix a lot of American values into my culture" is how Kaval described this hybridity.

We have written elsewhere, with colleagues Eugenie Kang and John Raible, about young people's growing awareness of the multiple influences on their identities and cultures. These influences draw from categories of race and identity but do not adhere to stable, fixed notions or labels.[2] Likewise, Nadine Dolby questions formulations of identity that rely on absolute categories and argues that multicultural education must embrace a more dynamic and nuanced notion of self. In her one-year ethnographic study of a multiracial high school in Durban, South Africa, she found that students "actively produce self" as a "changing, not reified, formation".[3] The young people described in this book's case studies and snapshots defined culture as an active, dynamic interplay of their home, school, youth, traditional and contemporary cultures, and more, as they created and recreated identities.

CONFLICT AND AMBIVALENCE

Pride in culture was neither uniform nor easy for these young people. Eugene Crocket, whose snapshot appears at the end of Chapter 10, spoke about the difficulty of being "out" concerning his gay dads when he was in middle school: "I wasn't ashamed, but more embarrassed. I don't know . . . I didn't want people to think of me as different." He went on to explain the conflict: "At home everything is normal, like everyone else's family. Going out in public is a little more different." The experiences of other students in the case studies and snapshots are similar in their negotiation between love for family and comfort in family culture, and confrontation with mainstream expectations.

Pierre Bourdieu's theory of *cultural capital* and of the role of schools in determining what knowledge has greatest status is helpful here.[4] This theory postulates that because schools primarily reflect the knowledge and values of economically and culturally dominant groups in society, they validate and reinforce the cultural capital that students from such groups already bring from home. This validation takes place through the overt and covert curriculum and the school climate. According to Bourdieu, the confirmation of the dominant culture's supremacy results in a *symbolic violence* against groups that are devalued. The cultural model held up for all is not within easy reach of all, and only token numbers of students from less-valued groups can achieve it. If they learn and take on this cultural capital—abandoning their own culture, language, and values—they may succeed. In this way, although few students from dominated groups are permitted to succeed, the myth of a meritocracy is maintained.

Some examples of the symbolic violence suffered by the students we interviewed help illustrate this point. James Karam's Lebanese culture was missing from all school activities, although other, more "visible" cultures were represented. Rashaud Kates longed for the presence of African American historical figures in his school curriculum. Nadia Bara, a Muslim American, and Kaval, a Sikh, both mentioned that their cultures were virtually nonexistent in their schools before September 11, 2001. After that date, they became visible, but mostly in negative ways. The invisibility of Native American content in Fern's schools and in the school's books and curriculum is another example of the devaluation of knowledge. Students may perceive that what is not taught is not worthy of learning.

In contrast, the language and culture of Manuel was highly evident in his schools, and teachers often referred to them explicitly both in curricular and extracurricular activities, giving them even more status. Liane Chang, whose middle school offers classes in Chinese, felt affirmed in her desire to become fluent in the native language of her mother. The schools of these two students demonstrate, in a concrete way, respect for students' identities. In the case of Manuel, the bilingual program was at least partly responsible for his success. In Liane's case, teaching a language visible in the community makes a statement about the importance of that language to the *entire* community. Savoun Nouch, whose case study is at the end of this chapter, and Paul Chavez, although not previously successful in school, became empowered by the multicultural curriculum at their alternative schools.

It is hardly surprising that symbolic violence causes conflict in students from devalued groups. This problem is not unique to the United States; it is evident wherever one group is dominant and held up as the appropriate model. The Finns, who were formerly colonized by the Swedes, and who live in Sweden are a case in point. Finns who emigrate to Sweden are often perceived in negative and sometimes hostile ways. In the words of a young Finn who was educated in Sweden and experienced this firsthand, "When the idea had eaten itself deeply into my soul that it was despicable to be a Finn, I began to feel ashamed of my origins." The result can be a conflict that is difficult to resolve. This particular young man concluded that such conflict was the price he had to pay: "In short, in order to live in harmony with my surroundings, I had to live in perpetual conflict with myself."[5]

The painful alienation from family and culture is not inevitable, although it is a particularly difficult dilemma for first-generation immigrants. Even though the task of trying to fit together what are, at times, contradictory values takes its toll, it need not always result in the complete loss of language and culture. The case studies and snapshots in this book demonstrate that students struggle to maintain both, in spite of the difficulty of doing so.

Although they learned to feel proud of themselves for many things, including their culture, their dexterity in functioning in two worlds, and their bilingualism, several of the students interviewed also learned to feel ashamed of their culture and of the people who reflect it. They faced what they saw as irreconcilable choices: denying or abandoning their identity to succeed, or holding onto it and failing in school and society. Sometimes, students blame their families and communities for perceived failures while absolving the school of almost all responsibility.

Latrell Elton sometimes used words to describe his community that either victimized or blamed people for their failure: "They [Black people] put themselves in a predicament," and "doin' stupid stuff," some of the very words used by those outside the African American community to criticize it. Although demanding accountability from one's own community is necessary, the critical analysis that must accompany it is missing. Latrell's case, however, is complex. For instance, he did not place all of the responsibility on his own community. He also considered the role that social structures, schools, and teachers play by having low expectations of Black students. Nini Rostland's comments concurred with Latrell's perspective: "I think expectations may be holding me back a little bit. I think when people see me, they assume, "Oh, she's Black." They automatically assume, "Oh, she's not going to achieve well.""

Nini's snapshot provides a window into negotiating identity as a multiracial youth. In school, she often felt that neither her Polish American identity nor her African heritage were recognized. Assumptions based on her appearance were exacerbated by institutional racism. The strong influence of her family, friends, and summer camp environment supported her assertions of multiple perspectives, but her interview also revealed the weight of always being a boundary crosser and cultural bridge between groups. Some students who are not supported as strongly as Nini may try to ignore or disregard cultural identity, an unfortunate and ultimately counterproductive strategy.

Vanessa's case is especially notable and poignant. Because she was actively opposed to racism and other forms of discrimination (note her actions beginning in elementary school and her stand against heterosexism), she attempted to distance herself from the privileges she earned simply as a result of her ethnic background. Vanessa knew that she had benefited because of being White, but she thought this was unfair. Consequently, she took the position that one's culture and race are unimportant, accepting colorblindness as the ultimate expression of fairness.

Others for whom the conflict is simply too great are expelled or drop out, either physically or psychologically. This was the case with Paul and Savoun. For many students who drop out of school, the reason is not that they are incapable of doing the work, but that the school is an unaffirming place. For example, in an extensive review of literature on the education of American Indian students, Donna Deyhle and Karen Swisher concluded that the major reason for leaving school was students' perceptions that the school curriculum was not connected to their lives.[6] More recent research by Sandy Grande on the education of American Indians proposes *red pedagogy*, that is, paying particular attention to contemporary students' multifaceted identities in order to assertively address their realities.[7]

As we have seen, most of the young people in the case studies have struggled to remain true to themselves, but the process of fitting into a culture different from their family culture is a complex one. Moreover, the students are also challenging the dichotomy between being culturally different from the majority and succeeding academically. This dilemma has been aptly described by Laurie Olsen in her comprehensive study of a highly diverse urban high school in California. One young woman interviewed by Olsen talked about the pressure from peers and teachers to stay within strictly defined cultural borders. She observed, "They want to make you just their culture and if you try to be who you are, and try to be both American and yourself, forget it. It won't work. It's not allowed."[8]

SELF-IDENTIFICATION AND CONFLICT

Like the student in Olsen's study, another conflict that some of the students in the case studies and snapshots felt was expressed as an inability to identify both as "American" and as belonging to their cultural group. Their sense of pride in culture precluded identification with the United States because, for these students, claiming both meant denying their background or being a traitor to it. Why some young people make this choice is no mystery. Ethnicity in the United States, according to Stanley Aronowitz, has been "generally viewed as a temporary condition on the way to assimilation."[9] This being the case, it is no surprise that Manuel, for example, was emphatic about saying "I'm Cape Verdean. I cannot be an American because I'm not an American. That's it."

Later in this chapter, Christina Kamau marked out her identity when she said, "I'm not Black American, I'm African and I came from Kenya." Yahaira, who was born in the United States, as were her parents, stated, "I'd say I'm Puerto Rican and Dominican" with no reference to the American context. Our society has forced many young people to make a choice, and the students in the case studies and snapshots sometimes made it in favor of their heritage and family culture. Considering their youth and the negative messages about ethnicity around them, this is a courageous stand, but it can also be a limiting one. The consequences of such a choice probably affect what they think they deserve and are entitled to in our society. Having no attachment to the dominant society, they may also feel they have no rights. That is, they may feel they have no right to claim their fair share of society's power and resources or even to demand equality within it. Exclusive identification as a member of their cultural group may also exacerbate the conflict of feeling separate, different, and, consequently, powerless.

But are these the only choices? Fortunately, recent research is pointing in a healthier direction. In their longitudinal research among young people of various immigrant backgrounds, Alejandro Portes and Rubén Rumbaut came to the conclusion that the most positive path to identity was what they called *selective acculturation*, that is, a process by which children of immigrant backgrounds acculturate to the host society in a measured and careful way while at the same time maintaining ties with their ethnic communities. Portes and Rumbaut state,

> This path is closely intertwined with preservation of fluent bilingualism and linked, in turn, with higher self-esteem, higher educational and occupational expectations, and higher academic achievement . . . Children who learn the language and culture of their new country without losing those of the old have a much better understanding of their place in the world. They need not clash with their parents as often or feel

embarrassed by them because they are able to bridge the gap across generations and value their elders' traditions and goals.[10]

The preservation and intersection of languages, cultures, and identities were also salient themes advanced by the 26 immigrant youth interviewed by Judith Blohm and Terri Lapinsky. Their book emphasizes the diverse ways in which students claim their identities inside and outside the home, and it offers curriculum and activities to affirm them.[11] Another example of the tension felt in making choices can be seen in the following snapshot of Gamini Padmaperuma, who sometimes felt pressure to identify in one way or the other. Gamini wrote about his identity for a project done in my (Patty Bode's) art class, in which students developed *identity portraits*, both in writing and graphically. Gamini's portrait accompanies his words.

The way the young people in our case studies and snapshots sustained culture is fascinating. In more than one case, they maintained their "deep culture," particularly values and worldviews, although they may have abandoned more superficial aspects such as food and music preferences. These modifications are a function not only of clashing messages from school and home but also of young peoples' involvement with a peer culture with its own rituals and norms. Although peer culture acts as a primary assimilating structure of our society, we should not assume that individuals have completely abandoned their family's culture simply because they act like other young people their age.

CREATING NEW CULTURES

Identity is constantly being negotiated and renegotiated by young people. Gamini Padmaperuma presents a good example of this negotiation. His snapshot demonstrates in a graphic way how complicated identity can be, but even adolescents of similar backgrounds have starkly different senses of their personhood. For instance, a recent volume co-edited by Clara Park, A. Lin Goodwin, and Stacey Lee advances a comprehensive perspective of how "American identities" are shaped by Asian and Pacific Americans.[12] Similarly, an exploration of how adolescents negotiate their multiple identities, and what teachers and schools can learn from them, is described in a book edited by Michael Sadowski.[13] Throughout the chapters in the book, various authors demonstrate why identity matters so much to adolescents.

That young people are involved in creating new cultures is evident in the remarks of the students in the snapshots and case studies. Their native cultures do not simply disappear, as schools and society might expect or want them to. Rather, aspects of the native culture are retained, modified, reinserted into different environments, and recast so that they are workable in a new society. Yahaira, for instance, loved rap and hip hop music, not salsa. Nevertheless, the influence of the Latino culture (as well as other cultures) on these musical forms cannot be denied.

Fashioning a new culture is no easy task. It involves first the difficult and painful experience of learning to survive in an environment that may have values and behaviors at polar extremes from those in the home, for instance, the often-cited example of Latino children looking down when being reprimanded. Whereas these children have been taught in their homes to look down as a sign of respect, in U.S.

SNAPSHOT

Gamini Padmaperuma

At the time of his interview, Gamini was an eighth-grade student in a midsize town in the Northeast. His parents speak Singhalese, their native Sri Lankan language. In spite of his youth, Gamini powerfully articulated the struggle to learn Singhalese in the United States, a society with a strong and growing monolingual stance. In his snapshot, he pondered the problems and promises of crossing cultures in U.S. schools.

In art class, we have been working on A Portrait of Our Hands as a painting, in unison with curriculum of other classes. Our hand paintings are supposed to give a visual image of how we identify ourselves.

As one first looks at my painting, they will see the following: an American flag on the left side of a road, on the other side of the road is the Sri Lankan flag, and handle bars of a bike with my hands on it. The handlebars of the bike with my gloved hands on it represent my passion for biking. I like biking because it's a place where I can get away from everything and just concentrate on one thought, whatever that may be, while still paying attention to the road ahead.

My cultural background has played an influence on my educational experience since the beginning of my schooling: Sri Lankan by nationality, I have seen how it has made me more conscious about my culture. I realize who I am,

what makes me different from many of my peers, and how that relates me to my surroundings.

Being Sri Lankan hasn't really affected how my teachers treat me but rather what is expected of me from myself and my family. In Sri Lanka, when I was traveling there, I realized how valued academics and an education are. There, it is the highest priority of any child, not sports, not being popular, but totally focused on learning. My parents didn't leave those values behind; they still would expect me to succeed in school, which is an expectation of myself as well. But in Sri Lanka, a given student's social status, in school (that is, how "cool" or popular), isn't important. But in the American culture, kids tend to take school for granted, and they're more concerned about what they wear and how popular they are.

When I look at my parents, I see how far they have come. Coming from Sri Lanka to America is a big thing, so I should not shame my parents—they've worked so hard. If I blow off school, it would really upset them. This poses a problem between myself and my parents, for they have trouble understanding how important it is to spend time with friends, and doing school work. Well, I can do both. The schools my parents had gone through—the school that my dad went to was an all boys' school since he was in kindergarten through high school, and the school that my mom went to was an all girls' school. So my parents aren't so comfortable with how in America we have boys and girls going to the same school. Like, sometimes when I have a girl over, just like as a friend, they aren't as comfortable as the other American parents. But my parents are working really hard for us. My mom has a long ride to work because the job is better paying so she and my dad can earn enough to send me and my other two brothers to go to college. They work so hard for us.

I've lived in the U.S. all of my life, and I consider myself an American, but the Sri Lankan culture has been weaved into my life since I was young. Every so often my family will have religious ceremonies so my brothers and I can experience the traditions from the "Old Country." I can't speak Singhalese, which is the official language of Sri Lanka, so when I travel there I generally can't speak to some of the kids who haven't learned English yet. When I traveled there two summers ago, it was the first time I was surrounded by people who are like me, but I could not really communicate with them. I got to stay with my relatives, and I actually spent a day in the Sri Lankan school where my mom had

(continued)

gone [co-ed now]. It is a very big difference. I really noticed how teaching is a lot stricter there and the kids take it a lot more seriously. But I also now see how we take for granted the things we have in our school here, like lots of textbooks, and even the classroom and the building. It also taught me so much about cultures and societies. Educationally, I feel like I should start working harder and live up to my parents' expectations. It made me think a lot.

I have been trying to learn the language. I can understand what my parents are saying because they talk to one another, and I have picked up words, but I feel ashamed that I can't speak Singhalese. Especially when I see some of my other friends who speak their language with their parents. It makes me feel that I should really work on that. There are kids who are born here, and they can speak their parents' language.

See, when I was younger, I knew English, and I didn't care about my parents' language. I wouldn't want to go to the grocery store and start talking to my mom in Singhalese, like if she asked me to go get milk. I knew what she was talking about, but I felt embarrassed, I felt weird because people start looking at you and wonder about your language and stuff. But now I see my cousin, who lives in England, but he lived in Sri Lanka for a year, and he is learning the language. I am pretty amazed because he can come back and speak Singhalese. It makes me wish I could do something like that. A lot of Sri Lankan kids tend to lose the language when they go to American, English-speaking schools. You speak it at home, but then you go to school in kindergarten and it just goes out the window.

But if you look at my painting, you see that the road I'm headed on splits, one towards America, one to Sri Lanka, and one in the middle. It represents a choice I have to make. Should I turn onto the road and take a bite of Americana? Should I turn towards Sri Lanka, continue Buddhism, learn about the language, have the culture take a larger portion of me? Or should I take the middle path? I don't know where it leads. Is it rough? Is it tough? I don't know.

COMMENTARY

Most students, particularly adolescents, make choices about how much of their culture and language to embrace and how much to be influenced by those around them while shaping a self-image. They may do so consciously or subconsciously, but they do choose. Do Gamini's choices have to be "rough" or "tough"? Can we create a school environment and a society where Gamini and other students like him feel proud to speak their family's language—where they can create a new road rather than face difficult choices of "American" or home culture?

mainstream society, such behavior is generally interpreted as disrespectful. Children who misbehave are expected to "take their medicine"; they are told "Look me straight in the eye." This is an example of how the behaviors expected at home and at school may be diametrically opposed. Even five-year-old children are expected to understand the subtle nuances of these behaviors. They usually do, although their teachers may be completely unaware of the conflicts involved or of the great strain students may experience because of such competing expectations. This example only scratches the surface of cultural clashes.

On the other hand, even knowing about such "cultural behaviors" may lead teachers to have stereotypical expectations of all students of a particular background. For instance, expecting that all Latino students will look down as a sign of respect is unrealistic because Latinos are a heterogeneous group. Some Latinos have been in this country for a few days, while others have been here for many generations; some have been raised in more traditional ways and some in less traditional ways; they come from various social and economic backgrounds; and they may speak Spanish only or English only, or a combination of the two. In addition, their individual differences also make each person a unique individual. Because of all these differences and others, teachers should be cautious about expecting students of the same background to behave in the same way.

In creating new cultures, young people also need to choose from an array of values and behaviors, selecting those that fit in the new society and discarding or transforming others. The process is neither conscious nor planned. Those whose values and behaviors differ from the mainstream's are inevitably involved in this transformation every day. Whether children or adults, students or workers, they are directly engaged in changing the complexion, attitudes, and values of our society. In the process, they may experience the pain and conflict that the young people in our case studies and snapshots articulated so well.

The point to remember is that U.S. society does not simply impose its culture on all newcomers. The process is neither as linear nor as straightforward as those who claim complete success for the process of *anglo-conformity* might have us believe,[14] but neither has the result been a truly pluralistic society. Although the United States is, in fact, multicultural, it is sometimes so in spite of itself, that is, it is not always the result of a conscious goal. For the most part, our society still reflects and perpetuates European American values and worldviews, but it has always also reflected, albeit at times poorly or stereotypically and against its will, the values of less respected and dominated groups as well. Latino heritage, for instance, can be seen in innumerable ways, from architecture in the Southwest to the myth of the cowboy. Jazz, widely acknowledged to be the greatest authentic U.S. music, is primarily African American in origin rather than European American.

What is "American" is neither simply an alien culture imposed on dominated groups nor an immigrant culture transposed indiscriminately to new soil. Neither is it an amalgam of old and new. What is "American" is the result of interactions of old, new, and created cultures. These interactions are neither benign nor smooth. Often characterized by unavoidable tension and great conflict, the creation of new cultures takes place in the contexts of the family, the community, and the schools.

Creating new cultures is made even more complicated by schools which, consciously or not, perceive their role as needing to shape all students to fit the middle-class, European American model. "They want to *monoculture* us," says a student in a video of successful Hispanic students in a Boston high school speaking about their identities and their schooling.[15] As we can see in the case studies and snapshots, students of diverse backgrounds respond in numerous ways to the pressures of an assimilationist society that is attempting to do away with differences. By refusing to accept either assimilation or cultural rejection, they force us to look at new ways of defining success.

IDENTITY AND LEARNING

Students pick up competing messages about language and culture from teachers, schools, and society. This was evident in the remarks of the students in our case studies and snapshots. One of the messages to emerge can be stated as follows: *Culture is important*, something that most of the students are proud of and maintain, However, students also learn that *culture is unimportant* in the school environment.

WHAT YOU CAN DO

ENCOURAGE THE EXPRESSION OF MULTIPLE IDENTITIES IN THE CLASSROOM

Design some classroom activities to help students express themselves as cultural beings and to provide opportunities for you to learn from, and affirm, those expressions. An example follows.

With your students, make a classroom list of the many different group affiliations that students move in and out of throughout their school week: family, neighborhood, sports teams, faith communities, hobby groups/clubs, performing arts groups, lunch groups, locker buddies, after-school classes, chat rooms, various classrooms/course activities, circles of friends, and so on. Make another list of the behaviors that "go with" each of these group affiliations. Make another list of how some behaviors may

clash or cause tension if they are demonstrated in a different setting. Make a list of behaviors that are transferable and useful across multiple settings. Discuss what this means for cultural identities. Help students understand that most of us are influenced by multiple cultures and have more than one way of identifying ourselves. Brainstorm how you may learn from one another, as a classroom community, about affiliation groups that are less visible in your school.

From time to time, revisit this activity to help you and your students delve deeper into identity. Play the card game "Go Fish" and pretend that each card represents an aspect of identity. Keep written journals about what it is like to have somebody "fish away" an aspect of your identity and what it feels like to "fish away" somebody else's identities. Don't be surprised if your students decide to change the rules of the game.

Research corroborates the perspectives of many of the case study students, that is, that culture is significant and that it can support learning. One intriguing lesson that can be gleaned from the case studies and other related research is this: The more that students are involved in resisting complete assimilation while maintaining ties to their ethnic and linguistic communities, the more successful they will be in school. There are, of course, many examples to the contrary, that is, of people who have assimilated in order to succeed in school. Nevertheless, based on the case studies and snapshots in this book, as well as recent research highlighted here, we can legitimately ask whether it is necessary to abandon one's identity to be successful. That is the question that young people are asking themselves and us, as educators.

In our case studies and snapshots, most students suggest an alternative route to academic success. For them, maintaining cultural connections seems to have had at least a partially positive influence on academic achievement. Although it is important not to overstate this assertion, it is indeed a real possibility and one that severely challenges the "melting pot" ideology that has dominated U.S. schools and society into the 21st century. As discussed in Chapter 7, similar findings in terms of language maintenance have been consistently reported by researchers. That is, when students' language is used as the basis for their education—when it is respected and valued—students tend to succeed in school.

The notion that assimilation is a prerequisite for success in school or society is contested both by the research reviewed here and by the case studies and snapshots.

The experiences of these young people call into question the often-cited claim that students who are not from European American backgrounds have poor self-images and low self-esteem. It is not that simple. In fact, schools and society may be complicit in *creating* low self-esteem. That is, students do not simply develop poor self-concepts out of the blue; self-concepts are also the result of policies and practices of schools and society that respect and affirm some groups while devaluing and rejecting others. Although young people might partially internalize some of the many daily negative messages about their culture, race, ethnic group, class, and language, they are not simply passive recipients of such messages. They also actively resist negative messages through more positive interactions with peers, family, and even school. The mediating role of families, communities, teachers, and schools helps to contradict detrimental messages and to reinforce more affirming ones.

The conclusion that sustaining native language and culture nurtures academic achievement turns on its head not only conventional educational philosophy, but also the policies and practices of schools that have done everything possible to eradicate students' identities in order, they maintain, for all students to succeed in school. We suggest that the opposite is true: School policies and practices that stress cultural knowledge, build on students' native-language ability, and emphasize the history and experiences of the students' communities would be much more productive.

BEYOND ACADEMICS

In nearly all the case studies and snapshots of students who were successful in school, significant involvement in activities beyond academics emerged as a key component. Whether through school-related organizations, hobbies, religious groups, or other activities, students found ways to support their learning. Often, although the activities promoted learning, they had little to do with academics. These activities had several important roles, both academic and nonacademic: keeping students on track, removing them from negative peer pressure, developing leadership and critical thinking skills, and giving them a feeling of belonging.

While such activities take place in a range of settings, from organized or structured formal programs to extended family or neighborhood settings, the role of organized after-school programs for youth development cannot be overstated. A burgeoning field of research is documenting the influence of these community activities on young people's lives. Robert Halpern's research describes the historical development of after-school programs and emphasizes their critical role, especially in the lives of children from economically strapped communities.[16] In another study, Barton J. Hirsch studied six Boys and Girls Clubs across the country and, through the voices of students, documented how recreation and relationship building create a "second home" for these urban youth.[17] Similarly, in a study of a math and science enrichment program, Annie Bouie outlined the successes that can spring from focusing on the inherent strengths and resilience of young people's cultures and communities.[18] The research and practice of these community workers and others points to the growing importance of after-school programs and their relationships to schooling.

WHAT YOU CAN DO

WIDEN HORIZONS BY ACKNOWLEDGING WHAT YOU DO NOT KNOW

Study your list of students who you are currently teaching. Do any of them have cultural experiences or backgrounds with which you are unfamiliar? Pick two students who may represent groups of which you have little knowledge. For the purpose of example, we'll use two groups that Eugene mentions in his snapshot in Chapter 10: Tibetans and lesbian, gay, bisexual, and transgender (LGBT) people.

Assignment for the Teacher: Make a KWL chart for each of the two students you have selected: what I KNOW, what I WANT to know, What I LEARNED). Make a plan to fill in the charts within one month. Use at least one print source as resources: Read a book or an article. Also, take at least one field trip that immerses you in each family's culture: Visit a community event, a performance, or the students' family. Perhaps you can also visit an arts event, go to a Tibetan cultural gathering, attend a political rally or meeting to support gay marriage rights, or take each student's family out for ice cream.

After you fill in "what I learned," choose two other students' families and start with two new KWL charts. Continue throughout the year.

KEEPING ON TRACK

One way in which activities other than school help is by keeping students "on track." That is, nonschool activities focus students' attention on the importance of school while simultaneously providing some relief from it. This finding is consistent with other research. For instance, Jabari Mahiri's research on the literacy activities of 10- to 12-year-old African American males during participation in a neighborhood basketball association found that this sport had immense motivational value in inspiring them to engage in literacy activities.[19]

In the case studies and snapshots, extracurricular activities also had a definitive influence, and these extended beyond simply sports. Rashaud, for example, spoke about his membership in Future Business Leaders of America. This after-school group engaged in community service in children's hospitals and nursing homes. In addition to a sense of fulfillment, these activities provided a framework for understanding the role of the business leader beyond that as somebody who focuses on making money. Involvement in the Gay-Straight Alliance was significant in carving out a place where Rebecca Florentina and other LGBT students could feel at home. Melinda Miceli's research documents the social and political impact of the Gay-Straight Alliance. She emphasizes the role of the first student leaders who create these organizations within their communities as vehicles of change within schools.[20] Such after-school activities taught Rashaud, Rebecca, and their peers essential life skills, and it also gave them the impetus and energy to educate others.

Many researchers have documented the important role of the arts in cocurricular, extracurricular, and out-of-school activities in developing rich multicultural student expression. A collection of essays by Maxine Greene provides a critical account of the role of the arts in social change. She argues that releasing students' imagination and artistic expression asserts multicultural student voices while developing skills in academic disciplines.[21] To illustrate the power of arts in after-school communities, Shirley Brice Heath and Laura Smyth, in collaboration with researcher Milbrey Mclaughlin, created a documentary film and guidebook. The film and book present four case studies of high-quality after-school arts programs that defy stereotypical public perceptions of urban youth.[22]

SHIELDS AGAINST PEER PRESSURE

The negative peer pressure to which students are subjected can be very difficult to resist, but most of the students in the case studies were successful in doing so. One reason was the activities in which they were involved, which for some, shield them against negative influences. This was described vividly by Paul, who had not yet totally succeeded in resisting the pressure to be in a gang but nevertheless said, "Now it's like I figure if I'm more involved in school, I won't be so much involved in the gang, you know?" As you will see, Savoun also explained the role of peers in his former choices: "I was unwilling to focus on my education life. I chose friends over education, and one thing led to another and I dropped out there."

For other students as well, involvement in these school-related and community activities took up nonschool time, acting as a preventive strategy for discouraging less productive, although at times more alluring, activities. This was the reason, for example, that Manuel dropped some of his friends; at just about the same time, he joined a church in which he became deeply involved. Linda's devotion to music and Avi's insistence on honoring the Sabbath can probably be understood in this way as well.

DEVELOPING CRITICAL THINKING AND LEADERSHIP SKILLS

Extracurricular and after-school activities also contribute to the development of important skills such as critical thinking and leadership qualities. Through a theater workshop based on students' experiences and ideas, Manuel was able to analyze critically his own experience as an immigrant to this country. This workshop gave him a place to reflect on his experiences more deeply and to articulate consciously and clearly the pain and fear that he felt in his first years here.

James's involvement with bicycle racing, his self-acclaimed first love, consumed both his time and attention. Before his bike accident, he was riding 40 miles per day. James's involvement in bicycling extended beyond racing itself, however. He subscribed to all of the related magazines, got his racing license, and was actively recruiting others interested in the sport to start a biking club. He was also planning to approach local bicycle merchants with the idea of obtaining financial support to sponsor the team. Gamini expressed a similar attachment to biking, an activity that helped him sort out his thoughts.

Avi's work in the synagogue is another powerful example of how extracurricular activities can develop leadership skills. Not only did his involvement in the temple require a great deal of study and sacrifice, but it also made him a role model for others in his community. The same was true of Nadia's involvement in her mosque and of Kaval's work in the Gurudwara, the Sikh house of worship. Vanessa's work with a peer education group helped her develop important leadership qualities and a growing critical awareness and sensitivity to issues of exclusion and stratification.

BELONGING

The feeling of belonging, so important for adolescents, is also a benefit of participating in extracurricular activities. Young people seek to fit in and belong in any way they can. Some meet this need by joining gangs or taking part in other harmful activities in which they feel part of a "family." For many young people, the satisfaction of belonging is particularly evident in activities related to their ethnic group. Paul and Savoun were notable exceptions to participation in out-of-classroom activities. Transportation, finances, and obligations to care for his sisters prevented Savoun from joining the football team at his former school. Paul and Savoun succumbed to the lure of some of the only "extracurricular" activities in their neighborhoods—gangs and criminal activity—yet, when provided with more positive outlets, they blossomed.

Manuel, James, Kaval, Nadia, and Avi found their niche through, among other things, their houses of worship. In these cases, their religious commitment affirmed their ethnicity as well. For Manuel, a Protestant sect was much more in tune with his culture than the Catholic church typically associated with Cape Verdeans. As he so dramatically stated during one of his interviews, "I felt that God had moved there," implying that a cultural resonance was missing in the local Catholic church. Combining his cultural and religious activities, Rashaud was active in a local Black church. Kaval not only attended the Sikh Gurudwara, but he also helped out in the soup kitchen. Nadia not only attended her mosque to pray, but she also was considering teaching Arabic to some of the younger children whose families attended.

The role of faith communities in young people's lives also needs to be understood in a cultural context. For many people with deep connections to religion, their spiritual lives are not an add-on or an extracurricular activity. The youth groups or committees that emerge from religious communities may be extracurricular, but in many cases, they have inextricable connections with cultural identities. Khyati Y. Joshi's research on the experiences of second-generation Indians offers a framework for understanding the relationships of ethnicity and race to religion in America. Joshi argues for educational curricular reforms and, more broadly, for recognition of religion as a form of social identity.[23] In this context, young people's activities in their religious communities may be significant factors in their identity development.

These are valuable illustrations of how extracurricular activities in school, as well as activities outside school, including hobbies and religious and cultural organizations, support student learning. Rather than detracting from students' academic success by taking time away from homework or other school-related activities, such involvement helps young people by channeling their creative and physical energy. In some cases, the activities may also have academic benefits.

FAMILY, COMMUNITY, AND SCHOOL ENVIRONMENTS FOR SUCCESS

Successful students are surrounded by messages that encourage success, including direct and indirect support from family and friends, activities that enhance, rather than detract from, success, and teachers and other school staff who demonstrate their care.

THE CRUCIAL ROLE OF FAMILY

The ways families support children in their learning are complex and sometimes not what one might expect. Non–middle-class families, in particular, may not have much experience with academic involvement or achievement, but they do what they can to help their children in other ways. One way that families demonstrate their support for academic success is through high expectations. Education was highly valued by the families of all these students, regardless of their economic background. In fact, in some instances, working class parents and parents living in poverty had even *more* hope in education than middle-class parents, for obvious reasons.[24] They could not always help their children with homework or in learning English, and because they often lacked the "cultural capital" valued in society at large, they could not pass it down to their children. As a result, the ways they manifested high expectations were sometimes indirect, but the messages they verbalized to their children were clear. Vinh said his uncle supported him by saying, "Next time, you should do better." Alicia explained, "Doing good in school is to get a chance to do stuff that most of my family hasn't been able to do." Rashaud told us about his parents' concern: "It matters to me, because if they didn't care, I wouldn't care. Since they do, I really do. I really want to make them proud."

Family messages that communicate high expectations, although powerful, are not always enough. Many of the young people described in the case studies and snapshots had great respect and appreciation for their families and understood the sacrifices that had been made on their behalf. Nevertheless, this appreciation did not always make their school experiences any easier or more tolerable. Because their parents were not always able to give them concrete help and tangible guidance, students sometimes lacked a sense of direction. Manuel put it most poignantly when he said, "If I felt like I had support from my family, if they only knew the language . . . If they were educated, I could make it big, you see what I'm saying?" Although parents' inability to speak English is not a liability in itself, it can become one if the school does not provide alternative means for student learning through such structures as bilingual programs and homework centers.

Given the kind of help middle-class parents are able to provide for their children, Manuel was absolutely right when he concluded, "I would've had a better opportunity, a better chance." A good example comes from Barbara Comber's research that focused on early literacy experiences of children in Australia. Comber explains that children's families do not just "disappear" when the children start school. On the contrary, children bring with them their privileges and disadvantages and everything they have learned prior to beginning school. Discussing three specific children, she argued that children's lives aren't simply "background" information for teachers, and, in describing Mark, one of the children, she explained:

> At home, Mark did not have a collection of books and nobody read him bedtime stories. But he did have knowledge and dispositions which counted for quite a lot in making the transition to school. He knew how to be a "good boy." He knew what counted as important practices in the classroom (e.g., looking after books, answering questions).[25]

Even families who lack formal education and have limited experience with the means for achieving academic success frequently do a great deal to prepare their children for school. They often compensate by providing other critical support to their children. In the case of students from different linguistic backgrounds, parents and other family members frequently maintain native language use in the home, despite contrary messages from school and society. Such language use helps students develop literacy and prepares them for school. The more students are able to use language in a variety of ways and in diverse contexts, the more they replicate the literacy skills necessary for successful schoolwork.

This is a crucial message for teachers to understand. Although the children in their classrooms might not have the specific skills called for in school, they *do* have attitudes, skills, and capabilities that can be tapped to advance their learning.

Maintaining native-language communication at home also implies nurturing cultural connections through such activities as family rituals and traditions, not to mention the even more meaningful underlying cultural values that help form young people's attitudes and behaviors. Savoun put it plainly: "I would never want to leave my culture or my language; I always want to learn more." "Apprenticeship" in their families, and the consequent learning of culture, language, and values, is a primary way in which children receive and internalize the message that they are important.

Encouraging communication within the family is another way parents support the academic success of their children. The importance of talking with their parents about issues central to their lives was mentioned by a number of young people. Alicia recalled significant conversations with her mother, when she was still alive, about "protecting herself," sexual responsibility, and the importance of school. Yahaira stated that she talked to her mother about "almost everything," including school achievement. As you will see in Nadia's case study, she described each member of the family as forming a piece of the "puzzle" and communication as central to maintaining this close connection. For Vinh, even long-distance communication was meaningful. He wrote to his parents weekly and was in turn revitalized by their messages. Linda's description of shared dinnertime in her family is a moving expression of the value of communication.

In numerous ways, academically successful students in the case studies and snapshots made it clear that they dedicated their school success to their parents, almost as a way of showing their gratitude for the sacrifices their parents made for them. These young people frequently mentioned that their parents were the motivating force behind their success, even if the parents did not always completely understand or appreciate what it meant. For example, Paul was inspired to return to school by his mother's own return to school. Gamini said that he wanted to do well for his family because of all they had sacrificed for him and his brothers. More than one student mentioned making her or his parents *happy*. This focus on parents' happiness, not what one might expect from modern, sophisticated adolescents, is a theme that emerged time and again.

Students in the case studies and snapshots often described their parents in remarkably tender and loving ways. From Yahaira's "my mom is the person I admire the most in the world," to Vanessa's "they're caring and they're willing to go against the norm," students made it clear that they had warm, close-knit relationships with their parents, which had a significant influence on their lives and the formation of values. Savoun described his affection for his family thus: "It's been great to be a member of my family. Sometime they don't understand me, but I still love them." Linda said that her parents were "always there for me, all the time" and even that she understood the "twisted reasons" for their rules and limits.

This is not to say that parents whose children are not successful in school have *not* provided affirming environments. There are a multitude of complex reasons why students are successful in school, and a close and warm relationship with parents is only one of them. Notwithstanding the caring and loving environments that parents may provide their children, their children may still be rebellious, alienated, or unsuccessful in school. A good example is Paul, who maintained that, "If it wasn't for the family, the love I get from my family, I would look for it in my homeboys. . . . I had a love that kept me home." While earnestly stating this, Paul was still engaged in the gang. Latrell expressed his earnest desire to avoid drug dealing and "negative stuff" so he could make his mother proud. His interview demonstrated the many forces that he had to negotiate to accomplish his goal of a positive future.

Other issues also influence academic success. What Carlos Cortés called *the societal curriculum*, that is, influences of the general society—including the mass media, gender-role expectations, anti-immigrant hysteria, and rampant violence—are another layer of the sociopolitical context of education that needs to be considered.[26] Other influences may also affect school achievement: rank within family; other family dynamics, including relationships among siblings; and simple personality and idiosyncratic differences. It appears, however, that a close and open relationship between children and their parents or guardians is a necessary but incomplete element of school success.

Although their relationships with their parents and other family members were obviously prominent in the academic success of these students, with some exceptions, the family was uninvolved in the school, according to the traditional definition of parent involvement: Most of the students' families did not go to school unless called, did not attend meetings or volunteer in school activities, and were not members of parent organizations. This was somewhat surprising, considering the research on the relationship between parental involvement and their children's academic achievement, which is reviewed in Chapter 5. The fact that some of these parents did not speak English, that they themselves had not always had positive experiences in schools, and that they were inhibited by the impersonal and unreceptive nature of many schools may be partial explanations. Conflicting work schedules, child care needs, and other situations also help explain their noninvolvement.

TEACHERS, SCHOOLS, AND CARING

Many of the students in the case studies and snapshots mentioned particular teachers, programs, or activities in school that helped them succeed. The key role teachers play in the achievement of their students is not surprising. The most important characteristic students looked for in their teachers was "caring." Students evaluated their teachers' level of caring by the amount of time they dedicated to their students, their patience, how well they prepared their classes, and how they made classes interesting.

For Manuel, caring came in the form of an entire program. The bilingual program, in his case, was critical to his eventual school success. For Liane, the fact that her school offered Chinese as a language of study was a powerful message that the language was valued in the school community. In many ways, students remembered the teachers who had affirmed them, whether through their language, their culture, or their concerns.

Students are empowered not only by studying about their *own* culture but also by being exposed, through a variety of pedagogical strategies, to different perspectives. Numerous students mentioned this, including Paul, who was empowered when he read *The Diary of Anne Frank* in elementary school. It was not only the subject matter but also how it was taught that made history come alive for him. Several students mentioned the desire to learn more about world regions and the cultural groups involved in current events. Several mentioned wishing they were taught more about the war in Iraq and expressed a desire to learn about Iraqi experiences and Islamic traditions.

Teachers of the same background as students also make a difference. Several recent studies have pointed to the positive influence that same-group identity among a teacher and students can have. A study by Sabrina Zirkel, for instance, found that students with race- and gender-matched role models had better academic performance, had more achievement-oriented goals, and thought more about their future, compared to students who did not have such matched role models.[27] However, the fact that the teachers and other staff members who understand and call on the students' cultures are often from the same background does not mean that only educators from the students' ethnic group can teach them or be meaningful in their lives.

WHAT YOU CAN DO

EXPAND THE "COMFORT ZONE" FOR YOU AND YOUR STUDENTS

The students in the snapshots and case studies told us about crossing cultural boundaries and negotiating multiple worlds. How often do you consider the many realms that students are required to juggle to meet school success? Here is a little experiment to help you consider life through the eyes of students whose lives may not be easily integrated into mainstream cultures.

YOUR COMFORT ZONE: TWO WEEKS IN THE LIFE OF A TEACHER

Week One: Consider your daily routines, environments, and communications as a teacher and also as a member of your community. For one week, keep brief journal entries that describe these experiences: What is your usual journey to and from work? Where do you purchase your food? How do you take care of your laundry? Who are the people you see in these events? Do you have a regular "pit-stop" in your weekly routine: visiting a neighbor or family member, stopping at a coffee shop, an exercise class, a library, escorting young ones to activities or elders to appointments? In what language do you speak when you engage in these activities? Write down the mundane and the ordinary.

Week Two: Change your daily routine. Try a different route to get to work. Purchase your food from a merchant you have never or rarely visited. Cook a recipe or purchase prepared food you have never tasted. Fold your laundry in a different way. Travel to an unfamiliar neighborhood. Change the day of some routines that do not have prescribed schedules. Learn at least two sentences in a language you have never spoken. Keep brief journal entries. What did you notice? How did you feel? How well did you function? Did these changes have positive aspects? Were there negative aspects?

Everyday experiences such as getting to work, purchasing food, and folding laundry are not necessarily cultural events, but cultural life *is* enacted and comprised of everyday experiences. To cultivate empathy for, and solidarity with, students who are perceived as different—or perceive themselves as different—it is useful to reflect on how familiarity and routine create comfort. You don't have to plan a heritage festival to develop awareness of how identities are asserted and affirmed in our daily lives.

This exercise will help you imagine how students may feel when their perspectives and identities are negated or ignored. In turn, the significance of the little things that make a difference in students' school day, such as a warm smile, an extra moment of patience in an explanation, or acknowledgement for "little" accomplishments, take on fresh meaning. Imagine a classroom where all the students and teachers work from such a perspective.

Your Students' Comfort Zones: Adapt this activity for your classroom but do not assign it until you have done it yourself!

Having teachers from students' ethnic backgrounds cannot be underestimated, but students in the case studies also named teachers *not* from the same background who had made a difference in their lives. These teachers had either learned the students' language or were knowledgeable about, and comfortable with, the students' cultures, or they were simply sensitive to the concerns of young people.

What can teachers and other educators learn from these examples? For one, it is apparent that how educators view their role in relation to their students can make a powerful difference in the lives of students. This role definition is not about strategies as much as it is about attitudes. In the words of Jim Cummins, "The interactions that take place between students and teachers and among students are more central to student success than any method for teaching literacy, or science or math."[28]

In a related area, the lesson that *relationships* are at the core of teaching and learning is reinforced through these case studies. Students mentioned teachers who cared about them and how these teachers helped to make them feel that they belonged. When students feel connected to school, they identify as *learners*, and they have a far greater chance of becoming successful students. When they feel that they do not belong, identifying as a learner is more difficult.

Finally, educators can learn that there are many ways to show caring. Accepting students' differences is one way; another is to have rigorous and high expectations of them. Also, becoming what Ricardo Stanton-Salazar has called *institutional agents*, providing social networks for students, is equally meaningful. These networks, from information on college admissions, to securing needed tutoring services, are generally unavailable to culturally marginalized students or those living in poverty, but they can make the difference in achieving academic success.[29] Prudence Carter builds on that notion by calling for "multicultural navigators" who are fluent in the social and cultural capital of college admissions, scholarship acquisition, and the like, yet do not totally acculturate, or give in, to the establishment. According to Carter, navigators are needed who can demonstrate:

> how to overcome poverty with critical, self-loving, and other respecting perspectives, who do not make them ashamed of who they are but rather proud of how far they will go.[30]

Whether they are in traditional or alternative schools, whether they are from mainstream or non-mainstream backgrounds, whether they speak students' native languages or not, *all* teachers can make a significant difference in their students' lives. The young people in our case studies and snapshots have provided much food for thought in how this can happen.

SUMMARY

In this chapter, we reviewed the major themes that emerged in the case studies, with particular attention to four themes related to academic achievement:

- A redefinition of education and success
- Pride and conflict in culture and language
- The role of activities not related to academics in sustaining school success
- The important support of family, community, and teachers

Cultural, linguistic connections can play a key role in students' academic success. In most of these cases, language and culture have been reinforced in the home and sometimes in the school as well. When reinforced in both settings, the message that language and culture are valued is clear and powerful. If they are valued only in the home, students may develop conflicted feelings about them.

The larger society also plays a key role in student learning. If young people see their culture devalued in such things as political initiatives (e.g., propositions to abolish bilingual education or to ban gay marriage), they are certain to develop conflicted attitudes concerning their ethnic group and family culture. However, in spite of sometimes harsh attacks on their culture, successful students have been able to maintain considerable pride in their ethnic group, family culture, and community. In the process, they reject both the pressure to assimilate and the pressure to give up. They are transforming culture and language in order to fit in, but on their own terms.

Involvement in activities outside the classroom also plays a part in promoting students' academic achievement. Most successful students we interviewed were involved successfully in extracurricular activities and other activities outside of school. Whether such activities are sports, social clubs, religious groups, or other community activities does not seem to matter. Students' involvement in such activities may help them develop a sense of fulfillment, leadership, and other skills that reinforce academic achievement and remove them from possible negative peer pressures.

Finally, families, communities, and schools work in different, complementary ways to motivate students to succeed. Although families from culturally nondominant and economically poor communities are sometimes unable to give their children the tangible help and support that dominant and economically secure families are able to, they serve an indispensable role in their children's school accomplishments. The families of all the successful students we have studied—from middle class to low-income families—have provided support in the following ways:

- Maintaining native language and ethnic connections in the home
- Having high expectations of their children at all times
- Providing loving and supportive home environments
- Communicating with their children on a consistent basis

Teachers and schools also play an essential role in students' success. We have seen that teachers who care, who take time with students, and who affirm their students' identities are the most successful. School policies and practices that support students in their learning are also critical. Students were explicit in pointing out the classroom activities and school practices that helped them learn from help after school to small-group work. As the students pointed out, when schools and families work together, school success can become a reality.

◆◆◆ To Think About

1. What characteristics do you think define academic success? Do they differ from how you think most teachers define it? Do you think your cultural values influence your definition? How?

2. If it is true that pride in culture and language is important for academic success, what does this mean for school policies and practices? Discuss policies and practices related to culture and language that you think schools should consider to promote educational equity for all students.

3. Caring on the part of teachers, schools, and parents was highlighted by a number of students. What might schools do to give students the message that they care? How would these practices compare with current practices?

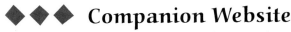 ## Activities for Personal, School, and Community Change

1. The crucial role of families in providing environments for success was highlighted by many of the students in the case studies, but their families' role was often different from that which schools traditionally define as *involvement*. Come up with an action plan for working with parents to develop environments for success while also respecting their specific contexts. For example, not all families have computers, so requiring that they provide them for their children is unrealistic. Likewise, not all families speak English fluently, and asking them to do so might be counterproductive. What can you do in such cases to encourage families to motivate their children to become academically engaged?

2. Involvement in school and community activities emerged as a major support for the academic success of students in the case studies. Brainstorm some ways that your school can promote such activities. Be specific, citing concrete examples.

3. If you don't already do so, begin a weekly "Letter to Parents" in which you highlight some of the classroom activities their children have been doing. You can ask for their advice on curriculum issues, encourage them to volunteer in the classroom, and so on. You might also include children's work in the letters from time to time.

◆◆◆ Companion Website

For access to additional case studies, weblinks, concept cards, and other material related to this chapter, visit the text's companion website at **www.ablongman.com/nieto5e**.

Notes to Chapter 9

1. Pilar Muñoz and Josette Henschel interviewed ten Puerto Rican women who differed in age, social class, marital status, and length of stay in the United States. I am grateful to Josette and Pilar and to the women they interviewed for this example.

2. Sonia Nieto, Patty Bode, Eugenie Kang, and John Raible, "Pushing the Boundaries of Multicultural Education: Retheorizing Identity, Community and Curriculum." In *Handbook of Curriculum and Instruction*, edited by F. Michael Connelly, Ming Fang He, and Joanne Phillion (Thousand Oaks, CA: Sage, 2007).

3. Nadine Dolby, "Changing Selves: Multicultural Education and the Challenge of New Identities." *Teachers College Record* 102, no. 5 (2000): 898–912.

4. Pierre Bourdieu, "The Forms of Capital." In *Handbook of Theory and Research for the Sociology of Education*, edited by John G. Richardson (New York: Greenwood Press, 1986). Also see David Halpern, *Social Capital* (Cambridge, England: Polity Press, 2005) for a review of the burgeoning literature and definitions of social capital.

5. Antti Jalava, "Mother Tongue and Identity: Nobody Could See That I Was a Finn." In *Minority Education: From Shame to Struggle*, edited by Tove Skutnabb-Kangas and Jim Cummins (Clevedon, England: Multilingual Matters, 1988): 164–165.

6. Donna Deyhle and Karen Swisher, "Research in American Indian and Alaska Native Education: From

Assimilation to Self-Determination." In *Review of Research in Education*, vol. 22, edited by Michael W. Apple (Washington, DC: American Educational Research Association, 1997): 113–194.

7. Sandy Grande, *Red Pedagogy: Native American Social and Political Thought* (Lanham, MD: Rowman & Littlefield, 2004).

8. Laurie Olsen, *Made in America: Immigrant Students in Our Public Schools* (New York: New Press, 1998): 55.

9. Stanley Aronowitz, "Between Nationality and Class." *Harvard Educational Review* 67, no. 2 (Summer 1997): 188–207.

10. Alejandro Portes and Rubén Rumbaut, *Legacies: The Story of the Immigrant Second Generation* (Berkeley, CA: University of California Press; and New York: Russell Sage Foundation, 2001): 274. Also see Alejandro Portes and Rubén Rumbaut, *Immigrant America: A Portrait*, 3rd ed. (Berkeley: University of California Press, 2006).

11. Judith M. Blohm and Terri Lapinsky, *Kids Like Me: Voices of the Immigrant Experience* (Boston: Intercultural Press, 2006).

12. Clara C. Park, A. Lin Goodwin, and Stacey J. Lee, *Asian American Identities, Families, and Schooling: Research on the Education of Asian and Pacific Americans.* (Charlotte, NC: Information Age, 2003).

13. Michael Sadowski, ed., *Adolescents at School: Perspectives on Youth, Identity, and Education* (Cambridge, MA: Harvard Education Press, 2003).

14. *Anglo-conformity* refers to the pressures, both expressed and hidden, to conform to the values, attitudes, and behaviors representative of the dominant group in U.S. society.

15. The excellent video *How We Feel: Hispanic Students Speak Out* was developed by Virginia Vogel Zanger and is available from Landmark Media, Falls Church, VA. The contact information is www.landmarkmedia.com and (800)342-4336.

16. Robert Halpern, *Making Play Work: The Promise of After-School Programs for Low-Income Children* (New York: Teachers College Press, 2003).

17. Barton J. Hirsch, *A Place to Call Home: After-school Programs for Urban Youth* (New York: Teachers College Press, 2005).

18. Annie Bouie, *After-School Success: Academic Enrichment with Urban Youth* (New York: Teachers College Press, 2006).

19. Jabari Mahiri, *Shooting for Excellence: African American and Youth Culture in New Century Schools* (Urbana, IL: National Council of Teachers of English; and New York: Teachers College Press, 1998).

20. Melinda Miceli, *Standing Out, Standing Together: The Social and Political Impact of Gay-Straight Alliances* (New York: Routledge, 2005).

21. Maxine Greene, *Releasing the Imagination: Essays on Education, the Arts, and Social Change* (San Francisco: Jossey-Bass, 2000).

22. Art*Show*, to be understood as "arts show how," comprises a dual package of resource guide and documentary video. The resource guide summarizes the project from which a focus on the linguistic and cognitive aspects of learning in the arts emerged. The project and the guide–video package are the culmination of ten years of research on youth organizations by Shirley Brice Heath, Laura Smyth, and Milbrey W. McLaughlin. See the book: Laura Smyth and Shirley Brice Heath, *ArtShow: Youth and Community Development* (Washington, DC: Partners for Livable Communities, 1999). Also see the documentary film *ArtShow* directed by Shirley Brice Heath. The documentary video was produced for Partners for Livable Communities and for distribution to PBS, 1999. (Winner of Gold Award, Worldfest Video and Film Festival, Houston, 2000; Winner of Chris Award, 2000.) For more information see www.shirleybriceheath.com

23. Khyati Y. Joshi, *New Roots in America's Sacred Ground: Religion, Race, and Ethnicity in Indian America* (New Brunswick, NJ: Rutgers University Press, 2006).

24. See Alejandro Portes and Rubén Rumbaut, *Legacies*. Also see Prudence Carter, *Keepin' It Real: School Success Beyond Black and White* (New York: Oxford University Press, 2005).

25. Barbara Comber, "What *Really* Counts in Early Literacy Lessons." *Language Arts* 78, no. 1 (September 2000): 39–49.

26. Jim Carnes, "Searching for Patterns: A Conversation with Carlos Cortés." *Teaching Tolerance* no. 16 (Fall 1999): 10–15.

27. Sabrina Zirkel, " 'Is There a Place for Me?' Role Models and Academic Identity Among White Students and Students of Color." *Teachers College Record* 104, no. 2 (March 2002): 357–376.

28. Jim Cummins, *Negotiating Identities: Education for Empowerment in a Diverse Society, 2nd ed* (Ontario, CA: California Association for Bilingual Education, 2001).

29. Ricardo D. Stanton-Salazar, *Manufacturing Hope and Despair: The School and Kin Support Networks of U.S.-Mexican Youth* (New York: Teachers College Press, 2001).

30. Carter, *Keepin' It Real: School Success Beyond Black and White*, 155–156.

CHAPTER 9 CASE STUDIES

NADIA BARA

I could never really stand in other people's shoes but now . . .
I kind of feel for the people that had racists against them
because now I kind of know how they feel.

In some ways, it's hard to believe that Nadia Bara[1] was just 14 years old when she was first interviewed. Talking about school, her family, her religion, or the joys and difficulties of being different, she was at once a wise older spirit and a teenager.

A ninth grader in a high school known throughout the state as an excellent school, Nadia lived with her mother and father in Linden Oaks, a comfortable, upper middle-class suburb in the Midwest that boasts the highest yearly median income in the state. Her sister Layla, 18, was a first-year student at the state university, also a well-regarded institution in the Midwest. Layla lived on campus a couple of hours from home but frequently returned home on weekends. Nadia's mother, Sarah, and her husband, Omar, both physicians, had lived in the United States for nearly two decades. Sarah was born in the United States, but while still a child, she had returned with her family to Syria, where she was raised and completed her education, including her medical training. Omar was born in Kuwait and attended medical school in Egypt. They met and married in Kuwait and came to live in the United States shortly before the birth of their first daughter, Layla.

The entire family visits Syria for at least two weeks every year to see family and friends and reconnect with their roots. During these trips, they usually visit at least one new place, too. They had recently been to Holland, Germany, Austria, and Maui. These trips had increased Nadia's motivation to travel, which she loved because, as she said, "I love seeing all the different types of people anywhere." During her interview, Nadia spoke fondly about her experiences in Syria, while also describing her status as an insider/outsider both in Syria and the United States.

The Bara family is a close-knit and fairly religious one. They belong to a relatively sizable Muslim community in Linden Oaks, and they try, in the midst of the fast-paced and postindustrial society of the United States, to live as Syrians and Muslims. This is not always possible, and Nadia and her sister both spoke of the tribulations they've faced because of their identities.

Nadia and her family are part of a growing Arab and Muslim presence in the United States. In 2000, the U.S. Census Bureau counted 1.2 million Arabs in the United States, or about 0.4 percent of the U.S. population, although Muslims continue to arrive in the United States, and a growing number of non-Arabs in the United States are converting to Islam.[2] Arabs are a remarkably diverse group, hailing from some 20 countries in the Middle East and Northern Africa. Most Arabs in the world are Muslims, but Arabs are only 20 percent of all Muslims in the world (estimated to be more than 1 billion in number). In fact, Islam is the fastest growing religion in the world.[3] Nevertheless, as we saw in Chapter 6, only a quarter of Arabs in the United States are Muslim. Arabs live in many parts of the United States, settling in places that would surprise many people. According to Diana Eck, for example, about a century ago, three small communities in North Dakota were home to an early group of Muslim immigrants, and one of the first mosques in the country was built in 1920 in the town of Ross, North Dakota. In addition, the Muslim community in Cedar Rapids, Iowa, goes back more than 100 years. Thus, from the start, the Midwest has been a destination for Muslims from various countries.[4]

Reasons for making the United States their destination vary greatly, but economic and political reasons account for why many come. Although Arabs are not new to the United States, the challenges they face have become more apparent in the recent past. These include negative stereotyping, racism, discrimination, and misinformation about their history and culture, a theme echoed by Nadia. Schools are some of the places where these problems are most visible.

The Bara family chose public schools for their daughters. This decision was not an easy one to make, particularly because of differences in religion and religious practices. Both Nadia and Layla have done very well in school. Layla, for instance, graduated with a 4.0 grade-point average from the same high school that Nadia was attending. Nadia loved school and was also doing well academically, having received a special award for earning straight A's in eighth grade. She was involved in many nonschool activities, especially sports (soccer, tennis, track, and volleyball), as well as school activities, including student council, theater productions, and the school newspaper.

As pointed out in the case of James, the Christian Maronite student whose case study appears after Chapter 5, until recently, Arabs and Arab Americans were often "invisible" in schools. This invisibility disappeared after the events of September 11, 2001, when they became all too visible. Nevertheless, Arabs are still frequently invisible in curricula and in other school policies and practices. Consequently, Islam is the religion about which most Americans have the least information and the most biases.[5]

In the case study that follows, we see a young woman who reflects on these issues in a thoughtful and mature way. The major themes that surfaced in Nadia's interviews were *belonging and the challenge of difference, the call to activism,* and *the centrality of family.*

"I'm Torn Right in the Middle": Belonging and the Challenge of Difference

I'm Nadia. I'm fourteen years old, and I am a freshman at Linden Oaks High School. I speak Arabic, English, and I've been in Spanish since first grade. One of my best friends is Jewish, and a lot of my friends are Protestant and Catholic, and I have many Black, White, everything [background of friends] . . . it's good.

I think the thing I like the most about myself is, I guess, how I can be funny and make people feel better. All my friends, they say I can cheer people up. I would much rather be laughing than thinking about bad stuff. I think that's a good thing, being optimistic.

I'm Arabic, and my parents are both Syrian. When I come here, you know I feel like I belong and . . . I mean I feel American, but I also go back to my race, you know? But when I go to Syria, for some strange reason, I feel like I belong even more. I'm, you could say, the only Syrian at my school right now, but there's lots of other people from the Middle East. But it's never been a problem, and I don't know, at first, after September 11th it was a little shaky, and I didn't want to tell people that I was Arabic because you got the weird looks, or when I went to camp someone asked me, they said, "Are you . . . you kind of look Afghani?" That's when it's a bit of a burden, just when you get singled out. People look at you different when they find out you're Arabic, especially now. Before [before] it wasn't [that way] at all. But now, especially when we're in restaurants or something as a family, my parents are talking Arabic, the waitresses will come and [ask] "Where are you from?" My parents will tell them, and they all give us weird looks like it's scary.

But I love going back to Syria. It's one of the greatest places in the world, and I love to be there, and I love my religion. I love it. I mean it's just there's times when it's a little hard, but it's no big deal. Before, I never thought about it very much. Going to Syria makes it all much better. It's so fun because you don't have to hide anything about your religion there, and you can be completely religious. It's great because everyone's the same.

Being Muslim and being American is hard because, here, I guess you know how the traditional Muslims, they wear the *hajab* over their head? There's a lot of stuff that I guess we're not too religious about, and it's really hard to be that religious here when you have friends. I mean, I don't have a boyfriend. Lots of my friends are dating, and they all go and that's what's a little hard about it. You feel kind of different and singled out. Sometimes if I wanna go out with friends and stay 'til eleven [my parents] won't let me. All my friends stay out 'til twelve, and I come home at ten. My parents are a lot stricter than all my other friends' [parents] and I don't date and I don't talk to boys on the phone. I'm not allowed to do that. Like, it's a lot stricter, but sometimes I think it's for the better but other times . . . I mean, I get frustrated a lot with it because these are the times when everyone is dating and everyone is going out, and I'm not allowed to go out, like, every day of the weekend. But I pray and I fast during Ramadan, and we give to charity and everything like that. It's just lots of stuff is hard to keep up with when you're a teenager growing up in America, trying to be Muslim, and trying to be Arabic, and trying to be American. Sometimes it's a lot but . . . I love everything.

A lot of my friends or just people at my school, they're not that religious, and they don't really have much to fall back on. And I guess it's very humbling maybe, just to go back and be at home and know that, even if you don't belong at school or even if that didn't work out, you have your religion and you have your culture and you know that *that's* never gonna change. And that makes you who you are.

Going back to Syria, I feel very much at home. But there's also times in Syria when I feel like I don't know as much as everyone there knows and I guess especially now, this year, when I went back there's a little more hostility towards . . . I mean, not my family, but people that we would see on the street if they heard us talking English. Just because of everything that's going on in Palestine, there's a little more hostility towards Americans I guess. And that's when it becomes a little hard, because I'm torn right in the middle, you know? But going to Syria, being Muslim, in a Muslim group, I'm not the strongest, most religious Muslim, but I have the beliefs. When you're in Syria, sometimes it makes you feel bad because I look around I'm like "Wow, I'm not religious enough and when I go home I'm going to be very good," but then, when you get home, you don't know what to do because it's a back and forth thing really.

[In school], the weird thing was they never really asked us our nationality or anything until [after 2001]. They would ask you in every class, and you had to raise your hand [saying] what you were and they went through every culture except they didn't have Middle Eastern. And so I never raised my hand, and they're, like, "What *are* you?" And I [would say] "Arabic" and then they would um . . . I mean the teachers, they never gave me, like, weird looks or anything like that. It's just sometimes kids are . . . especially after September 11th, everyone's shaky.

The thing that was really cool is my friends have stuck with me through and through. They know who I am and they know my family and they've known I'm Arabic and they haven't changed at all. My friends have stayed the same. My teachers don't care at all. It's just every now and then you'll get a weird look or you'll get a weird feeling . . . kind of feel singled out sometimes, but it's nothing too big at all.

We were on a field trip one time. We were coming back on the bus, and there's another boy who goes to my mosque, and he's made fun of a lot. I don't really know why. And a boy that's normally my friend, he made fun of the other boy that's Muslim and he told him (this is after September 11th), he told him something like "Well at least, I don't believe in blowing planes into buildings" and I felt bad because Khallid, the boy that goes to my mosque, he didn't really say anything, and I was infuriated, so I yelled at my friend. Which was really an uncomfortable feeling because I hated to yell at my friend, but I was so sad and hurt that he would say something like that. And I just told him "How could you say something when you don't know?" Now he kind of held a grudge about it, and we're kind of friends, but it was just really an uncomfortable feeling to be in that situation because Khallid didn't say anything, and I think he was really just too scared to get into it.

Most of the time I just tell myself, especially with that boy, he doesn't know any better. I feel bad because he's uneducated . . . it's kind of like looking at a German and saying "Oh, they're a Nazi." It's just stereotypes, and I think that's horrible and I just try to tell myself "Don't get mad, don't let it get to you. Just tell him that that's not right and try to educate him that that's completely wrong."

I think now, after the events of September 11th, it's become more of an issue. And the weird thing was when we would learn about racism and just stuff like that, I never really knew what it felt like, and I could never really stand in the people's shoes, but now I kind of feel for the people that had racists against them. People that I know have been discriminated against, but I haven't myself as much. I think now I just have a bigger . . . I'm trying to think of the word, like I feel for them, I guess, a little more. I kind of know how they feel, and I'm more understanding because I've been through it, I guess.

I know adults are a lot more smart about the whole thing, and they know that not all Arab people are terrorists, and I just wouldn't want [teachers] to associate everything that I say or do with my ethnicity or with my religion, and I'm not a representative of it. I know I'm a representative of it *to an extent*, but what I do does not portray what every other Arabic Muslim would do. We're all different, and no one is the same.

My friend Chelsea, she's Jewish, Russian. All our lives we never even *thought* about me being Muslim and her being Jewish and how anywhere else that would have been such a big deal, and we never thought about it, and we've been best friends since, like, second grade, and she's such a great person. Now, after September 11th, when we hear about all this stuff and when we hear about the fights going on in Israel and Palestine, it's really hard. But her mom is so open-minded. I love our friendship because it's against what everyone would say in the Middle East. It proves that it doesn't matter where you're from or what religion you are, you can still be getting along well.

The Call to Activism

Just a couple of weeks ago I was confronted by one of the leaders of the mosque to see if I could teach the little kids, the ones that don't know . . . like the ones from Bosnia and the ones that don't know Arabic hardly at all, if I could teach them Arabic. I haven't heard from the lady again, but that sounds like fun. My sister did that before she went off to college, and she said it was really fun. I like kids.

My dad came to me, and one of his friends had asked him [to speak to me]. They were having a rally for peace in the Middle East. It was just a lot of people from our mosque trying to put something together, and they wanted a youth speaker, and I jumped at the chance 'cause I like speaking and I like writing. So I wrote a speech up in, like, the end of May, and the rally was in the beginning of June, and so I went and I gave a speech, and it was really great. I got interviewed for the newspaper, and a different lady came from this world newspaper. She interviewed me, and so we got a copy of those. It was really fun. I like to get really involved.

Most of the time I hate hearing about what's going on in Palestine, [and] Israel you know, 'cause it's heart wrenching. We can't do much over here to help, and I feel like the littlest thing [can help]. Just do whatever you can to help, so I jumped at the chance to do that.

I love being in front of people. Like I love doing speeches, and just being in front of a crowd is fun for me. When they asked me if I would do that speech, I wanted to do it so bad, but then I was also, like, "This could be kind of weird, if I'm in the newspaper and someone sees it." And I was really hesitant sometimes, but just to give people a good feeling of what it is to be Arabic and what it is to be Muslim. And just to show them that we're not all terrorists and we're not all radicals.

The Centrality of Family

My parents are very family oriented, and they always want us to have a family dinner hour. Like, especially on Sundays, we all come together, and we just do something together just like how they grew up. Everything's family oriented. We celebrate [holidays], especially since there's not very much of our family here. Everyone's in Syria. We get as much as we can, especially during our holiday. My parents try to make it a very big deal, since me and my sister aren't that religious. They try and make it a very big deal, so we can get close to our religion, at least for that part of time. A while ago we had to drive to Florida, and it was a 17-hour drive, very long drive. I learned so much in that 17 hours in the car with my parents, them talking about their backgrounds with their families and everything. I guess they taught [my culture] to me in a way that I think I won't ever forget it. Instead of a teacher teaching it to you. They love their culture, and they love going back to Syria, as do I. And so, pretty much everything I know came from them, and all my religious beliefs came from them.

My sister, I followed in her footsteps a lot. Pretty much, we're almost the exact same, but there's so many things about her that I love. . . . I'm pretty good at looking at the bright side of things, especially with my sister. So if I'm having a horrible day, she can just cheer me up right away and the same with [me]. I can cheer her up in a second. [My parents] want to hear about friends. It's good to tell them, but once again you can't tell your parents everything . . . I tell lots of stuff to my parents, and I tell lots of stuff to my sister. It's good to have that, I guess.

I have learned lots of things [from my parents], most of them when I was younger, but one of the main ones was be proud of who you are and be confident. Because when I was younger . . . I mean now I'm starting to not have as much insecurities, but I've always had lots of insecurities, and they were always there just to make me feel a lot better about myself and bring the self-esteem up and just make you feel very good. You know, they always say, "Don't be afraid of who you are—be confident. No one's better than you, but you're not better than anyone else."

I can sit with my dad on the couch for like ten hours just watching TV and just joking around. He's the biggest joker, and we have so much fun, and I guess when I want something, I go to my dad and, you know, it's kind of like "daddy's girl." We have a lot of fun; we both have the same interest in sports, and so we connect like that, and he's very good at boosting self-esteem and all that, and he's the best compliment giver. And also with my mom, I guess, mom and daughter always have a little harder time, but my mom is great. She's always so busy; I don't think any of my friend's moms work as much. . . . But she always has time to come home and drive me to places I need to go, and she's always there for advice. And I feel for her because I know it's hard because sometimes she doesn't understand. That's what I tell her when I'm upset with her, I say, "You don't understand." But she really does, I guess.

I'm the youngest and I've always had my spot. I guess we're all like a puzzle. Without one of us, it's not the same. Like especially now with my sister gone, it's a little harder, so we're all trying to make up for it, and so I'm trying to mature a little more because I know that my mom, especially my mom, she's having the hardest time with it. They're not used to that 'cause, where they grew up, you go to college [and] you come home at the end of the day and you stay at your house. So they're not used to this at all, and so it's hard on them. I guess, like I said, without every piece of the puzzle, it doesn't go together. So we're all trying to work together a bit more, and I'm sympathizing with my parents more, and I'm not fighting with them as often. I know that I'm needed in the family just as everyone else is. It really feels good to have that spot, and you know it's never gonna go away . . . We all make a difference.

When we're all together, we talk about pretty much anything, especially now we mostly talk about, like, my sister's college and how everything's changing. A lot of the times we talk about what's going on in the Middle East, although it hurts. I don't like to talk about that stuff very much because I feel so helpless, and I can't do anything, and my parents get so frustrated, and they watch like the Arabic news 'cause we have Arabic channels. Arabic news show a lot more. They show like a dead person, and they show like what happened when someone got shot. It's so, so heart wrenching, and you feel so helpless, and it's horrible. So sometimes I get very frustrated, and I don't want to talk about it, but it's always gonna be there, I guess, and so you have to face it. And we talk about school and we talk about doctor stuff a lot. My parents always have funny stories about patients, and so it's fun.

I think that lots of happiness doesn't just come from grades, but [from being] with friends and with family.

◆ ◆ ◆ Commentary

In Nadia's voice, we hear some of the complexities involved in finding a way to manage family, school, religion, and other activities. Nadia wore a necklace with "God is good" written on it; at the same time, she played soccer and spoke publicly against racism and bigotry. This is a complex balancing act for a young person of Nadia's age, but she was nevertheless managing admirably.

It was clear throughout the interview with Nadia and her family that she was deeply attached to her religion and culture. She was simultaneously living with the challenges of fitting in and belonging in two very distinct cultural worlds. As a result, she felt, at times, both comfortable and uncomfortable in one or the other. Generally, Nadia was comfortable in her school and in her city. At other times, she felt the sting of discrimination, something that, prior to September 11, 2001, she said she had not really experienced. When she and her family traveled to Syria, Nadia sometimes was more at home there than here, while at other times, she felt like an outsider. Her musings about fitting in were poignant, and they reflect the experiences of a growing number of young people of diverse backgrounds in our society.

School could be a place where these differences are negotiated, but this has not been the case for Nadia. She mentioned that, before September 11th, no one had even mentioned Syria or Muslims. Afterward, being Muslim became a negative thing. When she said "teachers don't care" that she's Muslim, she said it in a positive way, meaning that they didn't discriminate on the basis of her background. But neither did they make it part of the curriculum, something that might have helped Nadia feel more included while also educating other students about her community.

There are several ways in which Nadia was negotiating these dilemmas of diversity. For one, as we saw, diversity was not an empty concept to Nadia. Her best friend was Jewish, and she also had an African American friend who was teaching her to cook soul food. In addition, even at this young age, Nadia was becoming outspoken about justice and fair play. This was evident in her participation in Heart Connection at school. She had also agreed to teach Arabic to young Muslim children. Her willingness, even eagerness, to speak publicly at a rally condemning bigotry against Muslims was another indication of her commitment to social justice.

But it was in her strong family connection that Nadia and her sister were able to negotiate their identities most powerfully. The Bara family was a close-knit and loving family, a family that insisted on maintaining certain cultural and religious values as a foundation for their daughters' futures. Nadia didn't like all their rules, but it was obvious that she appreciated them nevertheless. Although she would rather have stayed out later with her friends, or she might have liked the opportunity to talk to boys on the phone, she was grateful for her parents' values. The metaphor of a puzzle, and of each piece having a particular and crucial place in the puzzle, is a fitting one. She wanted to "fit in" but not in a cookie-cutter way. Nadia is a unique piece of our American puzzle, and it is young people like her who can make it work.

Reflect on This Case Study

1. What do you think Nadia meant when she said that she was "torn right in the middle"? As a teacher, what could you do about this?

2. Since 9/11, have you noticed any changes in your students' perceptions or actions concerning Muslim students? What are some ways to address these issues in the curriculum?

3. Nadia said that her parents weren't very involved in her school (in such activities as PTA, for instance) because they were very busy. Can you think of some ways they might be "brought into" the school by becoming involved at some level? How? What might you ask them to do?

4. If you were one of Nadia's teachers and had seen the newspaper article in which she was featured, would you have said or done anything about it? Why or why not? If so, what would you do?

SAVOUN NOUCH

When people look at me as an Asian I say, "No I'm not Asian, I'm Cambodian." There are other Asian kids, but I am the only Khmer kid.

Savoun Nouch[1] said that he had "traveled quite a distance" to start to his senior year at Watershed High School in Providence, Rhode Island. His mother arrived in New England as a refugee from Cambodia. Savoun was born in New England, but he and his mother migrated to California when he was a small child. He said, "I think of California as my actual home." His mom chose Stockton, California, because of its sizable Cambodian community (over 10,000 in a city of 285,000 in 1990). A friend welcomed them into her home there.

In Stockton, Savoun attended a large city high school with 2,500 students. The student population was diverse, and according to Savoun, almost 25 percent of the student body was Asian, primarily Cambodian. The school also included a small percentage of Native American and Filipino students and more sizable percentages of White, African American, and Latino students. About 8 percent of the students were English Language Learners. Furthermore, just over half the students participated in meal-assistance programs.

The school community struggled with racial tensions that played out in harmful ways. Savoun described how school gangs dominated his early high school experiences: "My school was very segregated, basically Asians. We Cambodians, we were the Asians. We got together and we were feuding with other nationalities. Almost every single day we would get into arguments and it would escalate into a fight with Blacks and Latinos. Every day. Mostly fist fights, but a few times there were some weapons. Some people outside of school got wounded or lost their lives."

The Cambodian population in U.S. schools today is a diverse group in terms of religious practices, language, education, and more. Some are first-generation immigrants, recently arrived from Cambodia or Thailand, where many refugee camps were located. Others are second- and third-generation Americans, with the perspectives and languages common to mainstream American teens. Some Cambodian families hold Buddhist beliefs close to their daily lives, others are secular, and still others practice Christianity or other religions.[2] In spite of their varied experiences, the Khmer community shares a common tormented history and a determined resiliency.

Thirty years have passed since the genocide carried out by Pol Pot's regime of the Khmer Rouge. The four years from 1975 through 1979 saw the death of 1.7 million people by execution, starvation, disease, and overwork in labor camps. The Khmer Rouge's "Democratic Kampuchea," a horrific campaign of social, ethnic, and racial cleansing wiped out a large percentage of Cambodia's population (estimates range from 20 percent to 48 percent). Pol Pot tried to exterminate the Cham, Vietnamese, Thai, and Lao minorities in Cambodia.[3] For many Cambodians in America, the tragedies of that holocaust and the efforts to sustain cultural memory persistently influence daily life.[4]

The political struggles that created the Cambodian diaspora and the resulting widespread post-traumatic stress among Cambodians are notable. Political analysts from the 1970s through today assert that President Richard M. Nixon's bombing campaign of Cambodia, which was implemented without Congressional approval, set the stage for civil-war-torn Cambodia to be relinquished to Pol Pot's regime.[5] Estimates are that between 100,000 and 600,000 civilians lost their lives and two million were rendered homeless by the United States bombings, ostensibly done to push the communist North Vietnamese away from the Cambodian border. Instead, the Vietnamese moved deeper inside Cambodia, and the U.S "carpet bombings" followed, inflicting greater devastation on the peasant civilians. To escape the violent chaos of internal civil war and the bombings, hundreds of thousands of Cambodian people fled their country to seek refuge in neighboring countries. These horrendous experiences led to more than 235,000 Cambodian refugees' resettling overseas between 1975 to 1992, including 180,000 in the United States.[6]

Escaping violence was a theme that shaped Savoun's life in many ways. His parents' escape from the Khmer Rouge in Cambodia was echoed by his deliberate break away from racially motivated gang violence in California. He dropped out of the large high school and twice made efforts to re-enter school through different alternative programs. But the gang activity persisted, and as he explained,

> [I]t was a very rocky road, and I decided that this was not the way life should be for me. I realized if I stayed, there was nothing there for me. I finally decided to drop everything and leave.

With the company and moral support of a good friend, Savoun got on a bus headed for the East Coast and got off by mistake in Providence, Rhode Island. Since he had a cousin in Providence who welcomed him "with open arms," he stayed with her and enrolled in a new high school, with a fresh start.

Because of the history of violence that had affected Savoun and his family, the major theme that reappeared many times in his interview was a *determination to escape violence*. Yet, just as powerful were the themes of *family pride and academic achievement* as well as *cherishing culture and language*.

Cherishing Culture and Language

It's great to be Cambodian; I'm proud of it. I love this culture, love everything about it. You have your culture to 'represent'—to cherish. I am different from somebody in Cambodia; I have the opportunity to learn English and to have more hope and to have a better life, but I have not been to Cambodia. Identity and culture is important to me. I am proud of my culture because of where I was born from. Being Khmer has been a big part of my upbringing. I have learned from my parents my culture, how I was brought up, everything. They have been through a whole lot of devastating moments back in Cambodia. So what we have now, we should cherish it. The people in Cambodia don't have what we have now. [My parents] really don't talk about it, because it brings bad memories for them. So I ask them myself, so they answer my questions, but I have to ask.

My mother carried the Cambodian culture a lot with her when she came to the United States. They worked in the past, grew crops back in Cambodia, near Phenom Penn. But there's not a lot of Khmer farmers around here. She wanted to stay in the Cambodian environment; my neighborhood in California was all Cambodian people. Every single day she could be there and talk with her friends, just chat with Cambodian people. They are very isolated from the world. They don't really go out that much unless they go to their friends. Mostly all their friends are Cambodian. They do not interact with other cultures very much.

We are different from other American families. We don't celebrate holidays as much as other cultures. That's a big difference. We do celebrate some, like Thanksgiving and Christmas, now—and birthdays. Cambodian New Year is the only Khmer holiday. For me, for my birthday, I would just get a present—no cake; no friends come over; I did not invite people over. My parents were not into inviting people over. It was like, "We keep it really simple. Here's your gift and don't ask for more." We have our family—we have how our family acts—how we are brought up different ... So, we act different, we cook different, things like that. For Thanksgiving, my parents do cook American food. So on a Thanksgiving dinner table, it is a mixture of Cambodian food and American food: Turkey, with stuffing, and we have mashed potatoes, Cambodian soup ... all those things together.

When I was in California, my parents take me to temple [to] get some blessings, and we participate in Cambodian activities. My parents would take me there, see the monks to get my blessings. I would ask them why. They would tell me to "vanish all the bad things." I went to temple once a year. My parents would go much more often to the temple. I did not like to go for the prayers that much when I was younger, but when it was Cambodian New Year, I was always there! In the future, definitely, I would like to go to the temple more on my own, to be more involved in my parents, to get a good feel for why they go to the temple ...

The first person I learned from was my parents ... to speak Cambodian. I don't know that much, but I know enough to speak it. Mom speaks Khmer at home. When I got to school, [learning English] was a process between elementary school and toward junior high. I just had to figure out. There were teachers' assistants who translated English for kids who did not know English. At times, we had reading sessions where she would actually read in Cambodian, teach the lessons so we could learn in Cambodian *and* English. There was a balance of Cambodian and English when I was growing up. I would never want to leave my culture or my language; I always want to learn more.

I got the hang of English ever since I hit junior high. I was speaking, like, intermediate English. I was actually speaking a balance of Cambodian and English, but at junior high there was no more reading sessions, no more culture lessons. None of it. Basically, I was speaking all English throughout the junior high and the high school. There was no more of my culture's language in the school. The only time I would speak my language was to my family members and with some friends.

As I learn more and more English, I am forgetting my culture's language right now. To keep us from forgetting our culture's language, schools could still have reading sessions in our culture's language. I think that would help the Asian students. Reading sessions would help ... because a lot of the students right now, they are forgetting their culture's language and they really do not know how to speak as much as they used to. We would love to learn more. We wish we would. I just try to speak as much Cambodian at home as possible. When I am at home and speak to the other people and older people, I only speak Cambodian.

When I lived with my parents, I did a lot of translation. It was hard for me because I don't speak Cambodian that well, and when you translate back and forth, there are words in English that do not translate into Cambodian. I talked to my parents pretty well. They can understand me. It's been great to be a member of my family.

Sometime they don't understand me, but I still love them. Growing up, it was a problem. It was hard for them to know what I've been through. They think it is very easy for me because I was born in America, I had the opportunity to go to school. [But] I had to deal with all these peer pressures. Gang stuff. Stuff they don't know anything about. They think it's a perfect world out there. They seen hard stuff back in Cambodia.

Determination to Escape Violence

I would describe my neighborhood I live in now [in Rhode Island] as a pretty good community ... no violence, a lot of nice people, a lot of Hispanic. But at my old school [in California] what I remember most was—there was a lot of violence. A lot of racial issues between we Asians and other cultures such as African American and Hispanics. You can say that it was gang related. It's more about who is the boss of the school, who won the school. I was part of a gang. It's all about what you are going to say and who is going to kick whose ass. I had my peers with me. I had my friends, so I felt very comfortable. I would say 90 percent of my friends in California dropped out of school because of gangs and violence. A few got shot, a few ended up in the hospital, a few got locked up. Only a few are still thinking about life.

Everything got rough for me because I was in a gang. I did not really have the support that I needed. I was the type of kid . . . I always wanted to play sports, but, money wise, the football uniform, and transportation from practice . . . it was very hard, it would be too hard, and my sisters, I had to look after them after school. I didn't have the support from my family, so everything was a big whole downfall for me because, during my junior year my average was like less than a 2.0 GPA. I stopped going to school. One thing led to another and I dropped out of my junior year at Avery High School.

I wouldn't say [the school administrators and teachers] didn't try to help me. It wasn't really that. They didn't really have any interventions to help students with the whole bureaucracy to get kids through. All you had to do was go to the guidance counselor and they would transfer you. I went to two different high schools. The first one was a model alternative school. The same thing happened. My friends were there, and there wasn't a lot of support. I was unwilling to focus on my education life. I chose friends over education, and one thing led to another and I dropped out there.

They are my friends, but they have different goals in life. I feel bad for them. I moved out here to change. I would hope the same thing for them. I would hope they could move out here with me. I can't control another person's life. When you are in the gang, [you don't realize there are] more things than being in a gang. I think about the future. Like what does life bring to you. There are things like life and education. You got to get your education, think more about life . . . than gang bangin' 'cause that's not gonna get you nowhere in life.

To get to Watershed High School now, in Providence, my cousin talked to the co-founder of the school and asked for me to get an interview. I went there and they interviewed me and ever since then, I fell in love with it. I fell in love with it because [of] the diversity, how personal the teachers get with you. It is no typical school. At the interview there are not teachers who interview you; it was students. That breaks that barrier, like kids-to-kids. I talked to a few kids. There was no Asians at all, only one girl. Everyone else was different nationalities and I was so surprised and the way they welcomed me, I was like "this school must be very great and there is no one feuding or fighting or nothing." I was so surprised there was no one feuding or anything. I was the only Asian kid, and the diversity was really great because even though I was the only Asian (and lots of—majority was Spanish and African American), [there were] no racial problems at all. Nobody feuding. I just loved it!

It has changed my whole perspective about school. Going to school here, because the teachers are so involved with you either at school or at home—always there for you, ready to talk to you and everything—about your education. They call me up at home to talk to me.

Family Pride and Academic Achievement

You got to have an education. It is important. In order to pursue your dream, what you want in life, get your education first. For my family, my parents, it is important for other people to see their reputation, how they raised their child to be, to go to school, and it is the opportunity America gives to you, so get that opportunity and make it useful. They make a great deal about their reputation, their reputation for the son they're raising. They don't want to have a son who is a bad kid, with other people talking about them. They want you to be good. If you do bad things, the community will hear about you. They will often spread rumors, the gossip in the Khmer community.

My parents support me being here in Providence 100 percent, and my cousin supports me being here with her 100 percent. My cousin welcomed me with open arms. I believe in education 100 percent. My parents want to hear good things, like if I'm getting my work done, how I'm getting my work done, all the details. My advisor contacts them and tells them the things they need to know and what I need to know. I never had my parents back in California participate in what the teachers had to offer, so this is a very new experience.

It is important to me to be Cambodian in my school. Definitely I stand out from the crowd because I am the only Cambodian person at my school. One of the teachers, she tried to learn more about my culture, so then I did a book report and everything. I wanted to do it on Cambodian and Khmer, on my culture. She tells me she is very fascinated by my culture. She knows something about the Khmer Rouge genocide, a little something about it.

The way the school works, they wouldn't just pass out work and have it just turned in. It has to be completed and 100 percent revised. So every time she handed out an assignment, we would continually revise it until it reached its perfection. We went through that whole process for the whole entire junior year and senior year. The way she was, the way she treated us, the way she made that connection—it made me work. She would contact me, out of school, to see what I was doing. We would have conversations, like friend to friend. That made us bonded very well and then I opened up.

To improve schools, if they could change the system the way they teach, that would be great idea, but even if they can't change the system, have a good relationship with the students and be in contact with them, always be in contact with them. Call them up. And, of course, I would love to learn more about my culture. If the teachers would make, like, an elective about my culture, that would be it. Learn more about the history, the war, the whole South East Asian history. The politics, who and what—a lot of information that is hard to get if you don't learn it in school. My mother told me about her escape from Cambodia. It was hard living in Cambodia. She lived in a refugee camp for awhile. That's about it. But she did not tell me much about the war.

My advisor helped me plan my future—give me prep for college, looking for scholarships, looking for college, everything—the whole 9 yards. What would help me be successful into the future is: Be more involved with me—I tend to procrastinate a lot. I need someone there telling me I need to get stuff done. My advisors are very hard on me. They call me up at home. But that makes me successful.

[In the future,] I definitely want to go back to California to be closer to my mom. The person I most admire is my mother because of what she's been through in the past and how she's got me here. I want to go to college first for four years. So I can at least support my mom when I go back. I don't want to leave with nothing and go back with nothing.

◆◆◆ Commentary

Maintaining and reshaping cultural traditions is a work in progress for Savoun. In Chapter 6 we cautioned about the pitfall of essentializing culture and the importance of understanding culture as an evolving process rather than as a static product. A cultural-historical approach, as defined by Kris Gutierrez and Barbara Rogoff, illustrates the flexibility of cultural identity in Savoun's life.[7] Savoun's identity evolves through a process of amalgamation of his parents' perspective as Cambodian farmers and refugees from civil and international warfare, transplanted to Stockton, California, living in a primarily Khmer-speaking neighborhood; of his multiple perspectives in urban youth cultures, with the expressiveness of hip-hop; and then of his experiences in and out of gang affiliations. For Savoun, his culture is something to be "cherished," yet its history, traditions, religious practices, and language appear to be elusive. While certain Cambodian practices and beliefs may be lost to Savoun, other new understandings are gained.

Nancy Smith-Hefner's research reveals the efforts of Khmer Americans to maintain and reinvent culture in the aftermath of the violence of the holocaust. In her ethnographic study of Cambodians residing in metropolitan Boston, Smith-Hefner portrays the attempts to preserve Khmer Buddhism by the elders in the community. Her study provides a context for understanding how cultural heritage may influence the performance of Khmer children in U.S. schools.[8] In a more recent study of Cambodian children, Roberta Wallitt suggests that, in addition to gaining insights from studies such as Smith-Hefner's, more contemporary studies are needed. As the Cambodian population in the United States ages, cultural values and influences will fluctuate.[9]

Issues of cultural identity dominated Savoun's school experiences. He moved from a school where about 25 percent of the student body was Cambodian, to being the only "Khmer kid" at Watershed High School. As much as Savoun appreciated his new school, with its personalized approach and supportive infrastructure, he was conscious of his isolation as the only Cambodian student. The isolation was underscored by his own—and his teachers'—lack of knowledge about his cultural history. His comments point out how the refugee experience is often invisible or misrepresented in school curriculum. Similarly, in Roberta Wallitt's study, she found that "one of the greatest sources of alienation was the absence of their history and culture in the curriculum."[10]

Despite the lack of Cambodians and the absence of a culturally specific curriculum in his current high school, Savoun was deeply affirmed and felt a strong sense of solidarity with his peers and teachers at Watershed. There, he was pleasantly surprised to learn that racial diversity does not necessarily lead to violence. The importance of cultivating a safe learning environment that develops racial inclusion is articulated in Savoun's affectionate description of his new school life: "No racial problems at all. Nobody feuding. I just loved it!"

In terms of academic achievement, Savoun compared his new school to his old school and explained, "They wouldn't just pass out work and have it just turned in." He proudly noted that his teachers expected nothing less than perfection in his final drafts of schoolwork. Teacher communication was another hallmark of his experience at Watershed. On multiple occasions, he mentioned that his teachers "call me up at home." Likewise, another recommendation from Wallitt's study concerned the essential role teachers, advisors, and mentors can play when they develop cultural competency and reach out to support students through home visits, phone calls, navigation of college applications, and attending cultural events.[11] The effort to reach out to Savoun outside of school hours left an enduring imprint of caring support and high expectations on him.

When we last checked in with Savoun, he had just graduated from Watershed High School. He was ecstatic about making his family proud through his accomplishments and was looking forward to starting community college in the fall "and then transferring credits to a bigger college." With the support of his advisor, he transformed his interest in car repair and auto mechanics to a goal of achieving a degree in business, with the hope of eventually opening his own car dealership. The outcome of this vision is still a few years away, but his willfulness to make sound educational choices, combined with his sincerity to "represent his culture" by providing for his mother and a future family of his own, appears to have pointed him toward success.

◆◆◆ Reflect on This Case Study

1. Savoun mentioned that his teacher "wouldn't just pass out work and have it just turned in. It has to be completed and 100 percent revised." How might teachers present the revision process as motivation of pride and accomplishment, as Savoun expressed?

2. Savoun said "To keep us from forgetting our culture's language, schools could still have reading sessions in our culture's language." That may not have been possible because Savoun was the only Cambodian student in his school, but what are some strategies that could have been implemented in the school to affirm and cultivate his language?

3. Receiving phone calls from teachers left a lasting impression on Savoun. What are the implications for your classroom practice? How can you integrate such personal communication with students outside of the school day?

4. In almost every school, there are students who may feel that they are "the only one" of a cultural, religious, ethnic, language, sexual orientation, class, or ability group. How can you and your colleagues affirm the students' identities in meaningful ways that make them feel more "visible" and understood while also challenging them academically?

5. Gang activity affects the school lives of countless students and families in U.S. schools. What can we learn from Savoun's case study about the teacher's role in helping students resist gang activity?

CHRISTINA KAMAU

If you could just go, to have a chance to go to some countries that are suffering and see the difference . . . you will be so shocked.

As a 16-year-old junior in high school, Christina Kamau[1] expressed viewpoints common to many immigrant teens in the United States. At the same time, her individual perspectives, based on personal life experiences, are evident. Christina's family is from Kenya where she attended school until fifth grade. They moved to Botswana, where she attended middle school in her early teens. At the beginning of her freshman year of high school, her family immigrated to the United States—to Shephardstown, a mid-size college town surrounding a large state university in the heart of the Midwest.

Christina's family is much like many of the over 1 million African immigrants currently living in the United States. The U.S. Census Bureau reports over 50 percent of this population arrived between 1990 and 2000, making African immigrants significantly more visible in U.S. schools in recent years.[2] In the 1990s, the highest numbers came from Nigeria, Ethiopia, and Ghana.

The influence of African immigrants in the United States is evident in the cultural, linguistic, political, business, and religious life of big cities and small towns throughout the country. Larger urban areas such as New York, Washington, DC, Houston, Atlanta, and Chicago are home to the largest numbers of recent African immigrants, but increasingly, small towns and suburbs, especially in the Midwest, are the destination for families such as Christina's.

Since culture, language, religion, and political frameworks are so diverse within the continent of Africa, the sociopolitical contexts of African immigrants vary greatly. Media coverage of African immigrants often focuses on refugees. The difficulties faced by immigrant refugees cannot be underestimated, but within the broad scope of African immigrant demographics, refugees account for only 10 percent of the immigrant population admitted to the United States in the 1990s. Of these, more than 40,000 were Somalis, and approximately 21,000 came from Ethiopia, while 18,500 arrived from the Sudan.[3] The children of refugee families bring values such as a vibrant connection to family and religious communities, steadfast determination to maintain multiple languages, and strong traditions. In addition, they often have vivid memories of human suffering in their homeland, which has continuing strife due to civil wars, human rights abuses, political unrest, corrupt governments, natural disasters, and the ravages of economic policies gone awry under globalization. The most recent difficulties in Sierra Leone, the Democratic Republic of Congo and Darfur, Sudan, attest to the widespread difficulties and challenges faced by many African states.

The detrimental effects of these struggles should not be diminished, but there is a propensity in the West, especially in the United States, to view Africa condescendingly and as if it were a monolith. The widespread misperceptions of Africa affect mainstream America's perspective on immigrants from the African continent. For instance, most people in the United States do not know that the majority of immigrants from Africa are highly skilled professionals who intend to establish permanent homes in the United States.[4] Christina's father, for example, is a university professor, and her mother is a medical student. While the influx of highly educated immigrants continues, their employment in the United States does not always match their talents. Their opportunities are limited for a variety of reasons, including immigration documentation and the fact that university degrees from oversees are often not recognized here. Many with prestigious credentials work as cab drivers, restaurant servers, or parking lot attendants, striving for the American Dream through any opportunity that may be available. Frequently, it is more than economics that motivates this community. In his comprehensive assessment of contemporary African immigrants, Joseph Takougang points out, "The new African immigrant is no longer just interested in making money; they are also interested in building stronger communities and organizing themselves in order to become a more powerful political and economic force in their respective communities."[5]

Racism also influences wages and job opportunities. Despite their hard work and determined outlook, Takougang reveals that, not surprisingly, many African immigrants encounter racism. Many do not have a history of experience with race relations in the United States and are naive about the confrontations with institutional racism and negative stereotypes.[6] A tragic illustration of racist violence, the 1999 killing of Amadou Diallo, an African immigrant from Guinea, by New York police officers, has become a metaphor for the way African immigrants are perceived and treated by some law enforcement authorities.[7]

Christina entered U.S. schools in ninth grade within this challenging yet hopeful and complex social, political, economic and cultural matrix. Relocating several times into vastly diverse cultures and language communities, she cultivated her perspectives on friendship, learning, and the meaning of academic achievement. The viewpoints she expressed during her interview highlight three themes: *adapting to new cultures and school structures*, *preconceptions and stereotypes*, and *educational achievement for social action*.

Adapting to New Cultures and School Structures

Just push yourself into being the best you can be, and try to strive the best you can be. Just remember where you came from. You know, remember your origin in Africa. You're not American; you're African first. Always keep that in mind.

After being in Kenya my whole life, Botswana was difficult. I started to go to a Christian, American type of school. And the school was way different for me, honor roll and all this stuff I didn't understand. There was no corporal punishment, you understand. [I did not know] what detention was. In Kenya, you get beaten by the teacher and you go home, even though you didn't do anything wrong. [Teachers] call your parents most of the times.

But I got used to Botswana. Our teacher was never like one-to-one, and she would teach a whole class and just gives you books to help yourself. Never checked to see who was correct, just give you points for completion. I didn't understand that, because in Kenya [there is] step by step and explaining. You know what to know. When I went to the American-type-school in Botswana, I found it very different to be trying all these different things. The funny thing was, in my math class, they let us use calculators, which I never did in Kenya. You had to know your time's tables and your subtraction and addition and all your facts. You have to do that on your paper. You can't use a calculator to solve those problems. So, in sixth grade I was introduced to a calculator. I was, like, "I don't know how to do this"! I found it strange and exciting too. It made my life easier in school terms because I can do homework much faster and go play and go do something else. So it was different for me for awhile.

Then, in seventh grade I moved to another school. It was, like, a private school and it had from elementary all the way to high school. That was different because I couldn't speak the same language as everybody else because each country in Africa has their own languages and their own native language. I spoke Swahili, and then in Botswana, you speak Botswanan. I couldn't speak Botswanan. I had to get used to learning how to interact with other students without them making fun of me trying say things. I had to speak in English all the time. That made me practice my English a lot because I couldn't communicate with them in any other way except in my English.

To make friends and do all those other things were hard for me because all the other students were, you know, cliquish. Because they had their own languages and they knew how to talk to each other without having to speak English, which I had to do all the time. But school became easier for me because my teacher could talk to me all the time in English and try to teach me a little bit of Botswana and interpret the other students. So that was pretty nice.

When I came here [to the United States] I was really shocked by the high school. We entered the parking lot, I kept asking Mom, "Are all these cars for the teachers or all for the students?" She was, like, "Yeah, all for the students." I couldn't believe how many students have such nice cars, so many cars, it was so crazy. Also the building was, like, wow, I always thought high school [was like] in TV and stuff in movies. I always wonder what it would be like to go to school in America.

School was crazy in the U.S. at first. First, projectors. I have never seen a projector before in my whole life. I got used to that, I guess, even the markers. Writing on the board in Africa, we used chalk, chalkboards in Africa. I miss that. I wish we had that here. Because markers smell strange, I don't know, it's hard for me to see up there with the projector. So I couldn't understand how you could look there at your answers, to check your answers to see if your answers are correct.

And at the beginning of the first semester, it was my world studies class, the teacher says we have to go to the media center, and I don't know where the media center is, and I didn't know what that was. So all of us go, open the door, and it's a bunch of kids and computers everywhere! I was, like, "cool", 'cause I never seen so many computers before! It was really hard for me to get used to going to Microsoft and going, oh, check tool, and check spell, check all these stuff. First day at school, my teacher said, "You have to research on different regions"; it's like research on Hinduism because we're studying India. He said, "OK, log on, get your password and get your stuff and get to the Internet and go to Google and start searching". I didn't know I *had* a log name. I could see other kids looking at me, wondering, "Why she is not knowing all these things?" We didn't have all these stuff. So I started looking for the Internet, so many programs—Microsoft Excel, PowerPoint, school printing, and all these stuff. All by myself, was trying to get to the Internet. So the other teacher kind of sees me sitting. "OK, I can help you." By the way, he is Laotian, he is from Laos, so he told me that he had a hard time. He knows how I feel.

I noticed that on the next day for my English class, all we did was type up papers, like every week. Every Friday, double-spaced page of essay. So I was used to writing with my hand, all my rough drafts, I could write them. Handwriting, you have really good handwriting, good grammar in Africa. But, the first paper, I didn't know how to type, so I asked. She, at least took half of the points off because it wasn't typed. I tried to explain to her, I was still learning. But she was, like, "You need to get a move on because you have to catch up with these people." Now I'm pretty good at typing and stuff and I'm trying to encourage my sister to get that stuff done because it's a big deal when it comes to high school. If you don't know how to use computers you are in a big trouble, because that's all we use all the time to research for classes. It is really big deal for us.

Preconceptions and Stereotypes

When I couldn't get that computer stuff, some girls were calling me an "African girl" because "an African girl doesn't know anything." That's not really nice of you to say that. Even the teacher went to her and said, "That's not really nice for you to say. It's not like you who have the privilege to go Internet everyday and get all these things. She's still getting accustomed to all these stuff."

I guess some other people really help me. Like the way my best friend was to the lunch lady. So I go to the line to get my food first day. I couldn't understand how this huge cafeteria, all of us could sit and talk, so noisy! Everybody's trying to get food and huge line. She told me,

"You gotta move on, you know, you have to get your food." I go to line and have my ID card and going to my line and get my food. She tells me to swipe my card so that we can get my food and get out. And I swiped my card and it didn't go through. She was like, "Wait, your card is not yet activated." I have no idea how to do that; it was my first day! She was really mean, I could tell. Maybe she didn't have a good day. So some girls behind me, some African girls behind me, heard my accent, "Oh are you from Africa?" I was, like, "Yes!" They say, "OK, we will pay for you." I am like, "Really? That's so sweet of you." They paid for me, and got out. We sat down and they were, like, "Is this your first day? We could tell, because the same thing happened to us!" I was like, "OK." [*giggle*]. So we have something common, that's only my best friends, they are from Ghana. We are good friends now.

I really have a big deal with people calling me *Black American*. I don't like being called that because I noticed that people in our school use that to get a sympathy from other people. "Oh yeah, my ancestors struggle for this and that" and you know what? That's gone. It's gone, so you can't use it now to defend yourself. Because you are creating another stereotype for you. In our school, there is very few Black people. And I'm sad for the fact that I'm not being able to interact with them that well 'cause they are not open to me. They always say, "Oh that's African culture." I think that I have more White friends than Black friends. I can still talk to them and I always say hi. I always say, "I'm not Black American, I'm African and I came from Kenya."

All the teachers are really nice to me. They all are interested about Africa. Africa is really cool. [They] always ask me, "Is it how we see on TV?" I tell them, "No, it's no way. [On TV] it's like a jungle place. We have CDs, we have cars and computers; it depends on what level class you come from." They all are interested, and for my English class that's all I did, my life comparing to American and African. Yeah, even in my speech class, that's all I did. My teacher was like, "Let's learn about Africa," all the time.

I joined track as an after-school activity. That's because my coach was, like, "Are you from Africa, from Kenya?" I was, like, "Yes." "Well, you have to join the track for me." The funny thing is that I have never run before. [*laughter*] He found out that I couldn't run that well, but he taught me, and pushed me, and it was fun. I met a lot of people; it was a good experience for me.

Educational Achievement for Social Action

Freshmen year, it was not good for me, even my GPA reflected that, and my parents were disappointed. I was really disappointed myself because less than 3.0 GPA was a really big shock for me. All my teachers told me, "You have a lot of potentials, just try to get used to the school." And so, in my sophomore year, I tried really hard; I did all my homework and always ask questions. Even after school—I went to school earlier and stayed later than everyone and my GPA was able to go higher to 3.8. That was really good thing for me. I'm hoping to do the same thing this year— try to even get 4.0 GPA.

I just want to get my degree and go help people somewhere. I want to be somewhere in Africa or somewhere in China. Somewhere where I know I am useful to help people. For me right now, going to school is a really big deal because I want to help people. That's the only way for me to get that education through school. For me, that is the reason for going to school. For me, it's getting a better education. I have seen in Africa that people give up. You know, here you can drop out of school and go to try your GED after a while. In Africa you don't get to do that. When you drop out of school, it's a failure; it's like an embarrassment to your family.

Also this year, Mr. Gervisay is recommending me to join the model UN, like a club. I'm really opinionated. Especially like in Mr. Gervisay's class, he encourages you to talk about politics, what's going in the world. Most people would be not interested, [they say] "Oh, the war, it's not in the U.S." How could you be so ignorant about something that happened to you? It's gonna affect you for the rest of your life, you know. If you could just go, to have a chance to go to some countries that are suffering and see the difference. You are so sheltered here that you can't step away; you will be so shocked.

I have the privilege of being here. For me, being here, my parents always say, "The land of opportunities, take them." You know, it's really hard, for many people dream to be here. And some of the best schools are here, like the state university. [My parents] want me to go to school because I can be a better person. I can help them raise [my] little sisters, you know, when they are older, look after myself, and I wouldn't get that chance if I didn't have that education to be able to get a job. Be better myself and be independent.

[For my future] I'm really battling between being a doctor or UN advocate, like maybe a lawyer. To see the wrongs of all the countries' policies and those stuff. I wish I could be, not a secretary general of the United Nations, but just trying to see a way of being able to tell other countries, you know, if you did something wrong you have to face the consequences. Right now, in the world, any country, as long as you have the power, you don't face up to what you did wrong. Because my parents punish me, you know, when I get something wrong—always have the consequences, you always have to face it. I notice that other countries don't do that, and I always believe in the UN. Bunch of countries always together, you know, try to make the world a better place. But, being a doctor for me would be fine, to do like doctor's organizations, Doctors Without Borders. Maybe in Africa, help a bunch of orphan kids and that would be a good thing. I don't know—it's a hard one, maybe a pediatrician. Because I like kids, but I don't know.

I guess being the fact that I am an international student, I have to push myself harder. I have to work harder and to prove that I do have the intelligence as everybody else and I should get the same opportunity as everybody else, especially with college. You can be anything. It doesn't matter what color you are and what shape, what country, what language you speak.

◆ ◆ ◆ Commentary

Christina demonstrated remarkable resilience in adapting to school structures in various countries and cultures. When she described each school experience, she eloquently noted a range of approaches to curriculum, instructional methods, and homework practices. She compared administrative policies regarding student behavior, parent involvement, dress code, and more. She analyzed her school achievement the first year in Shepardstown High School, considering all those factors, and made explicit adjustments in her approach to her studies, such as staying after school for help and practicing technology skills.

The importance of having peers in school who share some perspectives was evident throughout Christina's interview. From her description of the language differences in Botswana to the lunch line rescue by the Ghanaian students in the U.S. high school, it was clear that immigrant students are often isolated in facing the academic and social realms of school. However, unlike many immigrant students, Christina already spoke English, which established a common ground in academics and social endeavors. Yet, Christina's language of origin, nationality, African identity, and more, influenced her integration into the school. She emphasized that there were very few Black students in her school, highlighting racial identity concerns. Some students feel desperately alone despite spending their day in a school building with hundreds, or even thousands, of other students and adults.

The issue of cultural isolation affects students' views of school life, and it has curricular and structural implications. The more teachers get to know students through the curriculum, the more insight they may gain into students' perspectives, thereby cultivating authentic connections in relationships and in curricular adaptations. Judith Blohm and Terri Lapinsky provide several examples of "linking classroom to community" in a book that includes interviews with more than 2 dozen teen immigrants.[8] As structural remedies, some schools create buddy systems, ambassador programs, and other "safety nets" to assist new students, especially immigrants, to navigate the mystifying structures of the school year. Too often, the quick-fix approach is used. For example, Christina told us, "I had an ambassador at the first day at school to show me all the classes, and she did help me, but, like, the second day of the school, she left."

In addition to the challenge of establishing peer groups, adapting to new technologies and teaching methods, and navigating surprising new institutional structures, fighting bias was a major theme in Christina's school life. The perceptions of some teachers and peers about the capabilities of an "African girl" did not sway Christina's determination to achieve academically, but it did make her feel that she had to prove herself. Simultaneously, she spoke affectionately of most teachers' efforts to learn about her heritage and to weave her experiences in Africa into her schoolwork. When confronted with a so-called positive stereotype—that all Kenyans are talented runners—she laughed out loud. She demonstrated a graceful capacity to recognize the damaging implications of stereotypes while overcoming the limits of prejudicial encounters. Such wisdom and stalwart determination is to be commended, but it most certainly added tremendous weight to the challenge of adapting to a new culture and new school.

By emphasizing markers of her identity as a Kenyan, and more broadly as an African, Christina distinguished her language and her continent of origin as powerful affinities, but she also differentiated herself from her African American counterparts. She stressed that she had a "big deal with people calling me Black American," pointing to the differences in historical heritage between recent African immigrants and African Americans. The dynamic between African American communities and African immigrant communities is a complex and multilayered phenomenon.[9] A report from the New York Public Library Schomberg Center for Research in Black Culture observes that for many immigrants from Africa,

> [I]dentity as "black" is often perceived as a negation of culture and origin, which Africans regard as the most important elements of identity. They are keenly aware that they encounter racism and discrimination as black people; but they generally reject the imposition of an identity they feel does not completely reflect who they are.[10]

Despite confronting racism and the implications of being Black in America, Christina holds a classic view of the American dream. "You can be anything. It doesn't matter what color you are and what shape, what country, what language you speak," she asserts. For Christina, this may well be true because of the combination of many dynamics. Her family's social class advantage and their expectations that education will make her a better person are undergirded by Christina's and her parents' models of academic achievement. Her peer support helps navigate the confusing cultural conflicts, and the dedication of many teachers advances her academic achievement. From these sources, and clearly from within her own strength, Christina had resolved to get her degree and "go help people somewhere." Christina's accomplishments and determination raise the question about how schools may support rigorous academic engagement of students who are culturally, linguistically, and racially different: Specifically, how might schools influence *all* students to view successful education as a means to serve others and to help fight injustice?

◆◆◆ Reflect on This Case Study

1. Christina described some examples of teachers' and students' demonstrating solidarity with, and empathy for, her. How do these scenarios change her school experience? Imagine her school experience without these demonstrations of solidarity and empathy. How might a school encourage a mindset that manifests these gestures by staff members and students, especially toward students who are culturally, racially, and linguistically different?

2. In her new school, several assumptions were made about Christina's prior knowledge and skills, ranging from technology to athletics. When do preconceived notions become damaging stereotypes? Give examples of how teachers can explore the prior knowledge of students and build on it in an affirming way to engage students in academic rigor.

3. What do you think about Christina's differentiation between African Americans and Africans? What tensions are revealed in her statements? What is the role of the school in recognizing and taking action regarding these tensions?

4. The practical aspects of daily school life can be a struggle for any new student. What makes some of these challenges particularly difficult for international students? How could Christina's first experiences with the media center, cafeteria, locker combinations, and the like, be made more welcoming? If such welcoming strategies are not in place in your school, what might you and your colleagues do to call attention to the need for them and what suggestions for effective change might you make?

5. Christina brings a critical and international perspective to current events and political struggles that appears to differ from the viewpoint of many of her fellow students who were born and raised in the midwestern college town. How can a teacher integrate diverse voices in classroom discussions to co-construct knowledge? What is the teacher's responsibility in framing multiple perspectives while cultivating socially responsible student understanding?

Notes to Chapter 9 Case Studies

Nadia Bara

1. We appreciate Dr. Carlie Tartakov, who located the Bara family and spent a day interviewing the daughters Nadia and Layla, and Sarah, their mother. Dr. Tartakov also sent information about the city in which they live and the Muslim community there. In addition, she transcribed all the interviews, going above and beyond our expectations. All of these things made the job of developing this case study a great deal easier than it might have been.

2. U.S. Census Bureau, *Census 2000*. Table DP-2. "Profile of Selected Social Characteristics: 2000." (Washington, DC: U.S. Department of Commerce, 2000).

3. P. Hajar, "Arab Americans: Concepts, Strategies, and Materials." In *Teaching Strategies for Ethnic Studies*, 7th ed., edited by James A. Banks (Boston: Allyn and Bacon, 2003).

4. Diana L. Eck, *A New Religious America: How a "Christian Country" Has Become the World's Most Religiously Diverse Nation* (New York: HarperCollins, 2001).

5. Eck, *A New Religious America*.

Savoun Nouch

1. We appreciate the work of Keonilrath Bun, who interviewed Savoun for this case study. Keo is a graduate of Rhode Island School of Design, currently preparing to apply to architecture school.

2. See, for example, Stephanie St. Pierre, *Teenage Refugees from Cambodia Speak Out: In Their Own Voices* (New York: Rosen, 1995); see also Ji-Yeon O. Jo, "Neglected Voices in the Multicultural America: Asian American Racial Politics and Its Implication for Multicultural Education." *Multicultural Perspectives* 6, no. 1 (2004): 19–25.

3. Ben Kiernan, *The Pol Pot Regime: Race, Power, and Genocide in Cambodia Under the Khmer Rouge, 1975–79*, 2nd ed. (New Haven, CT: Yale University Press, 2002).

4. For a study that focuses on resilience and Cambodian life in the United States, see Nancy Smith-Hefner, *Khmer American: Identity and Moral Education in a Diasporic Community* (Berkeley: University of California Press, 1999); also, for a first person account of survival of the Khmer Rouge and resilience, see Chanrithy Him, *When Broken Glass Floats: Growing Up Under the Khmer Rouge* (New York: W. W. Norton, 2001).

5. Ben Kiernan, *How Pol Pot Came to Power: Colonialism, Nationalism, and Communism in Cambodia*, 2nd ed. (New Haven, CT: Yale University Press, 2004).

6. United Nations, High Commission for Refugees Report, *The State of The World's Refugees 2000: Fifty Years of Humanitarian Action*, "Chapter 4: Flight from Indochina," 79–103. (Accessed June 2006 at www.unhcr.org/cgibin/texis/vtx/publ/opendoc.pdf?tbl=PUBL&id=3ebf9bad0); also see W. Courtland Robinson, *Terms of Refuge: The Indochinese Exodus and the International Response* (London, England: Zed Books, 1998).

7. Kris Gutierrez and Barbara Rogoff, "Cultural Ways of Learning: Individual Traits or Repertoires of Practice." *Educational Researcher* 32, no. 5 (July 2003): 19–25.

8. For considerations of how Khmer culture may influence children's school engagement, see Smith-Hefner, *Khmer American: Identity and Moral Education in a Diasporic Community*. For more context on Cambodian youth and school engagement, see Margaret E. Goldberg, "Truancy and Dropout among Cambodian Students: Results from a Comprehensive High School." *Social Work in Education* 21, no. 1 (January 1999): 49–63.

9. Roberta Wallitt, "Breaking the Silence: Cambodian Students Speak Out About School, Success, and Shifting Identities," diss. University of Massachusetts Amherst, 2005.

10. Wallitt, "Breaking the Silence," 296.

11. Wallitt, "Breaking the Silence."

Christina Kamau

1. We appreciate the work of Dr. Carlie Tartakov, who interviewed Christina and provided support for this case study. Dr. Tartakov is Professor Emerita at Iowa State University.

2. U.S. Census Bureau. Available at: www.census.gov/; see also Baffour Takyi, "The Making of the Second Diaspora: On the Recent African Immigrant Community in the United States of America." *Western Journal of Black Studies* 26, no. 1 (2002): 32–43.

3. U.S. Census Bureau. Available at: www.census.gov/. For a more in-depth analysis of the Sub-Sahara African Diaspora, see John Arthur, *Invisible Sojourners: African Immigrant Diaspora in the United States* (Westport, CT: Greenwood Press, 2000).

4. Gumisai Mutume, "Reversing Africa's 'brain drain': New initiatives tap skills of African expatriates." *Africa Recovery* 17, no. 2 (July 2003): 1. See also the United Nations Web page www.un.org/ecosocdev/geninfo/afrec/vol17no2/172brain.htm

5. Joseph Takougang, "Contemporary African Immigrants to the United States." *Irinkerindo: A Journal of African Migration,* issue 2 (December 2003). Available at: www.africamigration.com/?CFID = 662515&CFTOKEN = 14479383

6. Xue Lan Do Rong and Frank Brown, "Socialization, Culture, and Identities of Black Immigrant Children: What Educators Need to Know and Do." *Education and Urban Society* 34, no. 2 (February 2002): 247–273.

7. Delario Lindsey, "To Build a More 'Perfect Discipline': Ideologies of the Normative and the Social Control of the Criminal Innocent in the Policing of New York City." *Critical Sociology* 30, no. 2 (2004): 321–353. See also Maxwell S. Hines, "Remembering Amadou Diallo: The Response of the New Teachers Network." *Phi Delta Kappan* 84, no. 4 (December 2002): 303–306.

8. Judith M. Blohm and Terri Lapinsky, *Kids Like Me: Voices of the Immigrant Experience* (Boston: Intercultural Press, 2006).

9. Mojubaolu Olufunke Okome, "Emergent African Immigrant Philanthropy in New York City." *Research in Urban Sociology* 7 (2004): 179–191. See also Takougang, "Contemporary African Immigrants to the United States." (December 2003).

10. Howard Dodson and Sylviane A. Diouf, eds., *In Motion: The African-American Migration Experience* (New York: The New York Public Library Schomberg Center for Research in Black Culture, August 2006). Available at: www.inmotionaame.org/migrations/landing.cfm?migration = 13

10

Adapting Curriculum for Multicultural Classrooms

Diana Corley, in Gina Simm's class.
Family portrait. Mixed media, 2005.

"The curriculum is never simply a neutral assemblage of knowledge, somehow appearing in the texts and classrooms of a nation. It is always part of a selective tradition, someone's selection, some group's vision of legitimate knowledge."

— *Michael Apple*

"The Politics of Official Knowledge," *Teachers College Record*, 1993.

A question that we hear time and time again is "What does a truly multicultural curriculum look like?" Teachers are swamped with data about achievement and models of so-called "best practices." It can be difficult to sort out trendy jargon from effective teaching.

When considering the implications of the previous chapters, it is clear that multicultural education is a multifaceted, complex process. Nowhere is this process more visible than in the curriculum teachers implement in their classrooms. Many teachers in PK–12 classrooms acknowledge the need to adapt the curriculum and their practices to meet the needs of their increasingly diverse student populations. However, there are many challenges they face in developing a multicultural curriculum.

In keeping with our commitment to making curriculum culturally relevant to specific learning communities, we do not provide specific lesson plans or "canned" curriculum in this book. Instead, we present three cases of curriculum with which teachers and students have demonstrated success. There are myriad ways in which curriculum may be conceived and designed. We do not advocate any one, single model. The three approaches described in this chapter include concrete, hands-on examples to provide educators with both inspiration and ideas for developing a parallel unit on a similar or different theme or to spin off an activity and add their own creative questions. The three cases include:

1. Studying specific cultures and geographic regions: a study of Cambodia and the Cambodian American experience

2. Transforming pedagogy: detracking math

3. A thematic approach: expanding definitions of Family

In addition to the three cases described here, a fourth example can be found on the Companion Website at www.ablongman.com/nieto5e. The curriculum case focuses on teaching about current events in a unit called "Hurricane Katrina and the Opportunity for Change."

One approach to transforming curriculum through a more multicultural perspective is the strategy of teaching about a specific geographical region and the cultural experiences of its people. This approach can develop rich, robust questions and understandings about specific groups, their histories, and their traditions. However, if the topic of a certain cultural group is approached as merely "adding color" to the curriculum, teachers run the risk of stumbling into any one of a number of pitfalls that run counter to the critical multicultural approach we have advanced in the previous chapters. Such pitfalls include perpetuating stereotypes by painting a group of people with a broad brush, "exoticizing" the "other" through a shallow "tourist" approach or, even more damaging, developing new pigeonholes by reinforcing a limited understanding of the experiences of a group of people. Out of concern for these pitfalls and fear of the unfamiliar, teachers may shy away from presenting a unit about specific cultural groups.

On the other hand, using a problem-posing approach and constructing curriculum with students on topics that both teachers and students want to explore creates an authentic learning experience. This is not to suggest that teachers enter blindly into creating curriculum on a random topic or subject area. Some preparation is always necessary. When teachers announce their own curiosity and model their own struggle with ignorance, students are empowered to ask previously hushed questions and uncover misconceptions. For instance, in a study of Cambodia and the Cambodian American experience, students who are unfamiliar with the topic may feel sanctioned to voice confusions that they might otherwise feel inhibited to ask—for example: "I thought Cambodians and Vietnamese kids were the same. How are they different?" "Why did Cambodian families move here to our community?" Or some students may point to social discrepancies that they feel uncomfortable about voicing: "I'm Cambodian and all my relatives are Cambodian, and we all live together with our relatives in the apartments at the edge of town. Why don't most White kids live with their relatives?"

Students' questions can reveal how social structures create stereotypes and lack of information that may lead to tension, alienation, and conflict. Attentive teachers can invite those questions and affirm a classroom culture that creates trustful, respectful dialogue. Such dialogue reveals that many of us are wondering about these things and why it is so crucial to use our academic skills to demystify the questions. By modeling an inquisitive mindset that takes a social justice stance, educators can encourage students to express their wonderment. Teachers can do this by making statements such as, "There is a growing Cambodian community here in our town. The first Cambodian families immigrated here in the 1970s, yet 30 years later, we study very little about the Cambodian culture or the experience of Cambodian American families in our school. Do you think it is worth exploring this community?" Dialogue can help promote academic rigor directed by a classroom community's curiosity.

Curricular Adaptation 1: A Study of Cambodia and the Cambodian American Experience

In what follows, we offer an example of a curriculum that was developed by a team of teachers of middle school students in an effort to stimulate intellectual growth, deepen understandings, support curiosity, and affirm the identities of students from all backgrounds. Besides describing the curriculum that the team of teachers developed, this example provides suggestions for expanding it.[1] We hope this sample curriculum will be viewed within the framework of critical pedagogy and multicultural education. It is one of many models that can be transferred and expanded to other curriculum units of regional studies and cultural groups, and it lends itself to continual adaptation by teachers for their specific learning communities.

What We Don't Know

A team of seventh grade teachers was concerned about the academic achievement of their Cambodian students, so they developed and implemented a curriculum about Cambodia. They called themselves *Team C* and included teachers of science, math, social studies, English, and art. These teachers noticed that while there was a small population of Cambodian students—an average of 8–10 in a school of about 630 students—the Cambodian students expressed their culture in several distinct ways. Team C teachers also noticed, with distress, that many of the Cambodian students in the school were experiencing low academic achievement. The individual teachers on the team brought a range of philosophies and perspectives to their classrooms, but something on which they all agreed was that they lacked knowledge about Cambodia and the Cambodian American experience.

PREPARATION

Supported by the school system's staff development funds, the team of teachers met during the summer to study the topic of Cambodia. They enrolled in a course called *Cambodian Culture, American Soil: Conflict, Convergence and Compromise* co-taught by a Cambodian teacher in their district, and his colleague, an activist in the community.[2] In addition to taking the course, the principal also provided each teacher with copies of the book *First They Killed My Father: A Daughter of Cambodia Remembers* by Loung Ung.[3]

While many school districts may not support such in-depth staff development, an alternative approach to a study group could be for teachers to read primary sources and have book discussions. Such an approach requires commitment of considerable time and energy, but the results can be transformative. Many appropriate books and resources are listed at the end of this case.[4]

Whether preparation for curriculum development comes through coursework, reviewing literature, or field research, there is rarely a moment when teachers think they know everything they should to embark on creating a curriculum. On the contrary, thoughtful teachers are intensely aware of the endless boundaries of knowledge on any given subject. Rather than avoid the unknown, a problem-posing teacher launches into the topic by asking the students stimulating questions. Herein lies the tension between over-preparing structured curriculum, which may exclude student voices, and including student questions in the actual development of the curriculum. Teacher preparation as a foundation is essential, and setting some goals for framing students' questions is helpful.

GOAL SETTING

When setting goals from a multicultural perspective for a curriculum unit about a geographical region or specific cultural group, teachers need to think beyond content, facts, and figures to consider the unit of study as intellectual and cultural work. Teachers who plan curriculum with a social justice mindset bring far-reaching goals to the curriculum design by considering what ideas will endure long after the books are closed and years after the students leave their classrooms. Grant Wiggins and Jay McTighe refer to these concepts as *big ideas* or *enduring understandings* and assert that depth of understanding is developed if these concepts are clearly articulated in the classroom when embarking on a unit of study, as opposed to content only to be tested at the end.[5]

A multicultural curriculum with enduring understandings based on a social justice perspective can help motivate teachers and students to work together toward social change. A unit about Cambodia and the Cambodian American experience could be designed with the following enduring understandings:

- Knowledge about historical events can help us understand current social conditions.
- War, genocide, and forced migration deeply influence people's lives for many generations.
- Recovering, preserving, and renewing cultural identity is an ongoing process of education, artistic expression, and cultural exchange.
- Awareness of the oppression and resistance experienced by a group of people can motivate them, and others, to work toward social change.

These enduring understandings could be taught through many content areas within a range of thematic topics, and they are transferable to other cases of war and displacement. Overarching goals such as the ones listed above can serve as guidelines when teachers get into the nitty-gritty work of planning objectives for their daily lessons and activities to uncover specific content. Team C teachers formulated the following specific objectives for the unit:

- All students will understand the history of Cambodia and its relationship with the United States.
- All students will develop inquiry about the Cambodian presence in western Massachusetts: What do we know? What do we wonder? (What is our knowledge? What are our questions?)
- All students will engage in direct involvement with the Cambodian community: at the Cambodian community garden, at the Buddhist temple with the monks, with high school "buddies" from the Cambodian club, and other community events.
- The curriculum will affirm identity of Cambodian students and families.
- The curriculum will build understanding among all students of all backgrounds.

The first two objectives are traditionally academic in nature, pointing to understanding history and current events. The academic achievement *embedded in* the overarching enduring understandings and in the specific objectives for the content underscores that multicultural education is *basic education*, as emphasized in Chapter 3. Likewise, the editors of *Rethinking Schools* have consistently asserted that multicultural curriculum and classroom practice must be academically rigorous.[6] The deliberate intellectual work of this unit disputes the misperception that multicultural curriculum is just about making people feel good, as detractors may claim. Each of the objectives addresses academic engagement in a variety of ways. Throughout this curriculum, you will see many opportunities for students to develop and increase skills.

THE WORK OF LEARNING

One of the first questions teachers often ask is, "How long should I spend on this unit?" The unit about Cambodia and the Cambodian American experience was developed and operated as three different schedule plans: (1) events throughout the school year, (2) intensive study for one to three weeks and (3) the focus group week. We will give examples of the activities for the three different schedule plans.

The School Year   While the major framework and implementation of the unit work happened within a one- to three-week schedule, many other experiences reinforced the overarching enduring understandings throughout the year. Team C teachers had a great deal of other curriculum on many other topics to teach, yet they viewed the entire school year as having opportunities for teaching and learning about the Cambodian experience unit. Some of the activities throughout the year included visitors and field trips.

Visitors

A Community Member   The social studies teacher invited a man who was a teacher in their school and a member of the Cambodian community (Mr. Mao) to visit her classes for four different sessions. The students were captivated by Mr. Mao's memories of his childhood, his family, his village, and his strategies for survival when captured by the Khmer Rouge. He showed the students how he had to trick the Khmer Rouge soldiers into believing he was a peasant farmer by demonstrating that he knew how to make rope from raw fibers. Mr. Mao's visits emphasized the grim tragedies of surviving genocide as well as the resilience of human nature. His warm nature and sparkling wit overcame the seventh graders' discomfort with the difficult topic of genocide, creating a community of honest questioners. The personal accounts Mr. Mao related to the class were reinforced by a series of videos about the history of Cambodia and the devastation caused by Pol Pot's regime, which the students had previously viewed.

High School Khmer Culture Club   Other guests included high school students from the district's Khmer Culture Club. The high school students shared their experiences as Cambodian American teenagers. They discussed the challenges of negotiating multiple cultural perspectives and the tension between traditional Cambodian family structure and mainstream U.S. teen culture. Many of the high school students had never been to Cambodia; they were born in the United States or had emigrated as very young children from refugee camps. Their experiences of Cambodia were vicarious, derived from collective memories of the elders in their families. Some teens were second-generation Cambodian Americans. Some were fluent in Khmer and English and some spoke no Khmer. They articulated the responsibilities of being bilingual youth in a culture in which most of the adults with literacy skills had been murdered in the genocide. The challenge of becoming assimilated into the U.S. mainstream while simultaneously maintaining cultural solidarity with their families had often been compounded by their struggles against institutionalized racism and poverty.

The teens also shared and taught traditional art forms, such as Cambodian folk dance and poetry, to the middle school youth. In addition, they talked about their favorite music and forms of entertainment in U.S. popular culture. The high school students' visits provided a dialogue and demonstration of the perspectives of many postmodern youth who are fluent in family language, Hip-Hop culture, Standard English, and multiple ways of expressing their academic and artistic knowledge. By making multiple perspectives visible and embodied, these encounters expanded the notion of what it means to be Cambodian American.

Master Musician   Another visitor, provided through the Cambodian Masters in the Classroom Program, played traditional Cambodian music and demonstrated traditional musical instruments to the whole team.[7]

Field Trips

Cambodian Community Garden   In the early fall, the entire team took a trip to the local Cambodian Community Garden. The vegetables grown in the garden were sold to restaurants and farmers' markets to raise funds for rebuilding temples and schools in Cambodia. The whole team picked vegetables to contribute to the community effort.

Khmer Dance Performance   A combination of serendipity and resourcefulness brought Team C to a performing arts event at a nearby university. The Asian Dance Program was hosting a performance of the award-winning Cambodian Angkor Dance Troupe from Lowell, Massachusetts.[8] Since the teachers were alert to gleaning from the community all available knowledge related to the Cambodian experiences, and energetic enough to write grants to fund the trip, all seventh graders, including Team C students, attended the dynamic dance performance. The Angkor Dance Troupe features teen Cambodian dancers who are mastering the classical Cambodian traditional dance forms as well as developing hybrid performances that integrate break dance and other Hip-Hop forms into their movements. One of the seventh graders, Eric, made this observation about the performance: ". . . I wish I was a Cambodian dancer. Those guys can break dance mad-cool and then they know their culture, too. I wish I had something like that."

In lieu of a lucky coincidence of a live performance within walking distance of one's school, teachers can use videos, DVDs, and websites projected onto a large screen to bring the performing arts to their students. For example, *Monkey Dance* is a recent documentary film about three teens from the Angkor Dance Troupe coming of age in Lowell, Massachusetts. The website about the film explains, "Children of Cambodian refugees inhabit a tough, working class world overshadowed by their parents' nightmares of the Khmer Rouge. Traditional Cambodian dance links them to their parents' culture, but fast cars, hip consumerism, and good times often pull harder."[9]

The Peace Pagoda and the Nipponzan Myohoji Sangha Buddhist Temple   Teachers made connections with the monks at the nearby Buddhist temple[10] in Leverett, Massachusetts, where many of the Cambodian families gather for prayer and meditation as well as for education and celebration. A field trip was planned in early April so that Team C students could help clean the grounds and plant flowers in anticipation of the annual Cambodian New Year celebration. As is not unusual during spring in New England, it had snowed several inches on the day of the field trip and the gardening plans turned into a snow-shoveling project, which also included a snowball battle with the monks! The monks taught Team C students about many of the symbols in the physical space of the temple as well as the role of Buddhism in many Cambodian families.

Team C scheduled these visitors and field trips between September and June. The teachers witnessed a sustained interest in the topic of Cambodia and the Cambodian experience long after the one- to three-week immersion study. Giving the students some breathing room to consider the topic, and the questions throughout the school year, reinforced the intellectual depth of the study.

One to Three Weeks   The teachers developed an intensive classroom unit of study that can last from one to three weeks. (These time frames are flexible, depending on how often teachers meet with their classes and the depth of study on the topic. Since this curriculum was enacted in a middle school, each Team C teacher taught in a specific discipline.)

English Class   The English teacher led an in-depth investigation of Cambodian and Southeast Asian folk tales. Students read from children's picture books (traditional prose translated into English from the Khmer source) and saw videos of storytellers. Specific attention was focused on how folktales use humor and metaphor to teach lessons. These activities met the state's framework standards and were integrated with a wider body of literature about cross-cultural folktales in the English department curriculum. Students could draw similarities and differences about the literature while viewing the Cambodian folktales as a means for reclaiming and reinvigorating cultural symbols that had been threatened by extinction in the aftermath of the genocide.[11]

Science Class   During the two years that this curriculum was implemented, there were two science teachers. One year, a science teacher led an investigation of endangered species in Southeast Asia. Students developed research projects on specific animals and species. They expressed their findings in text and artistic forms to create over-size classroom books. The books of illustrated scientific research were donated to the local elementary school, which served a large population of Cambodian students. In addition, the seventh graders created bookmarks depicting a synopsis of their research. They sold the bookmarks in a fund-raising effort to purchase protected areas of rainforest acreage in Southeast Asia.

Another year, a science teacher integrated his science curriculum with a study of the local Cambodian Community Garden. While at the garden, the science teacher led groups in measuring the space with global positioning satellite (GPS) devices; students worked in partner groups to map the surface area while learning about technology and computation. At school, they went to the computer lab and learned how to download and analyze the data. These science activities met the state's framework and standards for studying ecosystems and using technology for collection and analysis of data.

Social Studies Class   The social studies teacher engaged the students in an exploration of the refugee experience. They scrutinized the legal and social implications of refugee status, giving specific attention to the ravages of war and the conditions that cause a population to be forcibly displaced and become "refugees." They developed questions about the plight of people in many regions, from Afghanistan and Cambodia to the United States. In addition to studying groups from abroad who have been named political refugees under U.S. policy, they also critically examined the history of American Indian groups and compared their status in their native land as similar to the refugee experience.

Math Class   The math teacher worked with concepts of ratio, proportion, and scaling to compare and contrast the amount of space used in a typical house in Cambodia with the amount of space in a typical house in the United States. The math teacher worked with the Cambodian community teacher, who provided lots of photographs and illustrations of houses in Cambodian villages and cities. The students designed a scale model of a house that reflected the typical size and shape of a Cambodian house. Meeting the seventh grade math standards, they worked from their individual design of a flat net that could be folded into a three-dimensional structure.

The math teacher also worked closely with the science teacher on a map activity. Students divided the maps into sections and analyzed Cambodia's ecosystems in science class. In the math activity, they developed an analysis of the total Cambodian population compared to the population densities in specific areas of the country. Using computational skills, they created a visual graph to illustrate their understanding of how people are dispersed regionally. This activity was integrated with the social studies investigation of the refugee experience to learn what the population looked like before and after the war.

Art Class   In art class, the seventh graders studied the history, architectural design, and sculptural relief work of the temple of Angkor Wat. Studying the 12th century temple as an example of architectural accomplishment and cultural endurance helped bring alive the intersection of spiritual beliefs, political struggles, and environmental changes in Cambodia's history. Students explored Cambodia's cultural junctions of India and China through the presence of Hindu and Buddhist traditions, multiple language influences, and the stories illustrated by the seemingly endless sculptural murals of the temple.

By studying the symbolism, stories, and mind-boggling technical prowess demonstrated in the construction of the temple, the seventh graders gained insight into the depth of history and the significance of the temple in present-day Cambodia. One student exclaimed, "No wonder they put it in the middle of their flag!"

Continuing with the art exploration, the students, using clay and plaster, created their own relief sculptures depicting the animals they studied in science class and the folktales they explored in English. When some students asked about copying illustrations of the goddesses that are carved on Angkor Wat, they had a group discussion about religious iconography and who had the right to appropriate religious imagery. They imagined what it might be like for a classroom to produce 25 crucifixes or 25 images of the Star of David. They also looked at the work of some contemporary artists who use religious imagery in their work—whether reverently or irreverently—and noticed that most of these artists have a personal connection with the religious images they use. Such open discussions helped students make informed, deliberate decisions about whether or not they chose to imitate the statues of the goddesses of Angkor Wat.

Focus Groups   After their intensive one- to three-week studies in the separate disciplines—visiting each teacher throughout their school day as middle school students usually do—Team C students chose a focus group in which to work. Each focus group worked in a single discipline for a full school week. Students spent the entire day with one teacher, working in depth on a single project. As the seventh graders said, it was "just like elementary school!" Each focus group visited the art room daily to work on a visual art component of the focus group project. Students chose from the following focus group activities:

- The English teacher led a focus group of students to dramatize the folktales the team had studied. Students collaboratively made decisions while directing plays, memorizing lines, creating costumes, and managing props and scenery. In art class, they worked on scenery and props for the plays inspired by illustrations from the picture books and by their study of Angkor Wat.

- The science teacher led a focus group in the construction of a scale model of the Cambodian Community Garden. Students used the data from their GPS activity to re-create the plot of land they had visited on the field trip. To investigate how to grow certain vegetables, they compared the climate and environmental conditions in Cambodia with the conditions in their hometown. In art class, they used materials and techniques to develop the 3-D effect of the scale model garden.

- The math focus group expanded upon the scale-model house design and built three-dimensional houses to reflect their study of the typical architecture of Cambodian houses. They carried their house to and from the art room each day, adding structural and technical details, surface design, and texture to try to depict an authentic-looking Cambodian house. In art class, they compared U.S. houses to Cambodian houses and used images from the book *Material World: A Global Family Portrait* by Peter Menzel, Charles Mann, and Paul Kennedy[12] to consider the implications of consumerism in the United States.

- The social studies focus group decided to write and perform vignettes to demonstrate various refugee experiences throughout the world. Some students took on the role of the United Nations. Others took on the role of the Red Cross and the Red Crescent, while some wrote and performed the parts of the refugees and some took on the role of military guards in refugee camps. In art class, they worked on scenery, props, and costumes informed by their research projects and news media images.

Demonstration Day   At the end of the focus group week, Team C students and teachers hosted Demonstration Day to illustrate their knowledge, understandings, and questions about Cambodia and the Cambodian American experience. All families, friends, and school personnel were invited. On a rotating schedule, visitors could enter each classroom to get a sense of what the students had learned. The science focus group set up their garden model in the art room, and the math focus group placed their houses in the garden to create a scale model of a Cambodian village. The students welcomed visitors and held discussions about contrasting and comparing the environments and houses in Cambodia to those of the New England valley where they lived. The English focus group performed mini-plays inspired by the Cambodian folktales but adapted by the seventh graders as "fractured fairytales" to reflect the intersection of U.S. popular culture, ancient stories, middle school humor, and symbolism of the Cambodian tales. The social studies focus group also performed their vignettes to "pull" their audience into the experiences of refugees. After each vignette, the group held a question-and-answer session with the audience, drawing upon their research findings.

The seventh grade students of Team C completed Demonstration Day with a feeling of fulfillment and accomplishment. Each student participated fully in the work of the intensive unit and individually evaluated their work. Each seventh grader engaged in self-directed participation within a collective group goal in their focus group. The students increased their skills in every academic content area, yet the teachers and students realized that there was still much to learn. Team C teachers asked the students to evaluate the learning experiences. Students wrote many statements about their challenges, accomplishments, and achievements. One Cambodian student, Prasour, wrote, "I liked this part of school when we studied my own culture. I thought it was awesome. The kids who aren't Cambodian thought it was awesome. It just makes you feel awesome to be Cambodian."

RESOURCES FOR TEACHING ABOUT THE CAMBODIAN EXPERIENCE

These resources are listed in two categories: professional and classroom.

PROFESSIONAL RESOURCES from which to draw information or excerpts for classroom curriculum (for adult readers)

Altman, Linda: J., *Genocide: The Systematic Killing of a People* (Berkley Heights, NJ: Enslow, 1995).

"Pol Pot: Secret Killer" *A&E Biography* (New York: A. E. T. Networks, 1997). DVD.

Brown, Karen, *Trauma and Recovery* (Amherst, MA: WFCR, NPR, 2002). Radio broadcast.

Nath, Vann, *A Cambodian Prison Portrait: One Year in the Khmer Rouge's S-21* (Bangkok, Thailand: White Lotus, 1998).

Ung, Loung, *First They Killed My Father* (New York: HarperCollins, 2000).

Ung, Loung, *Lucky Child: A Daughter of Cambodia Reunites with the Sister She Left Behind* (New York: HarperCollins, 2005).

CLASSROOM RESOURCES suitable for student use, including folktale picture books

Bartok-Baratta, Mira, and Roberta Dempsey, *Stencils Indonesia, Cambodia, and Thailand* (Glenview, IL: Scott Foresman, 1996).

(continued)

Canesso, Claudia, *Cambodia* (New York: Chelsea House, 1989).

Carrison, Muriel P., *Cambodian Folk Stories from the Gaitloke* (Rutland, VT: Charles E. Tuttle, 1987).

Chamrouen, Yin, *In My Heart. I Am a Dancer* (Philadelphia: Philadelphia Folklore Project, 1996).

Chiemruom, Sothea, *Dara's Cambodian New Year* (Cleveland, OH: Modern Curriculum Press, 1992).

Coburn, Jewell, *Khmers, Tigers and Talismans from the History and Legends of Mysterious Cambodia* (Thousand Oaks, CA: Burn, Hart, 1994).

Coburn, Jewell, *Angkat, The Cambodian Cinderella* (Auburn, CA: Shen's Books, 1998).

Criddle, Joan D., *Bamboo and Butterflies: From Refugee to Citizen* (Davis, CA: East/West BRIDGE, 1992).

Criddle, Joan D., and Thida Mam, *To Destroy You Is No Loss* (New York: Doubleday, 1987).

Dagens, Bruno, *Angkor: Heart of an Asian Empire* (New York: Harry Abrams, 1995).

De Silva, Dayaneetha, *Cambodia* (Milwaukee: Gareth Stevens, 2000).

Ho, Minfong, *The Clay Marble* (New York: Farrar, Straus and Giroux, 1991).

Ho, Minfong, and Saphan Ros, *Brother Rabbit* (New York: Morrow, 1997).

Knight, Margy Burns, *Who Belongs Here? An American Story* (Gardiner, ME: Tilbury House, 1993).

Kodish, Deborah, and Deborah Wei, *Teacher's Guide to In My Heart, I Am a Dancer* (Philadelphia: Philadelphia Folklore Project, 2001).

Lipp, Fred, *The Caged Birds of Phnom Penh* (New York: Holiday House, 2001).

Maryknoll World Productions, *Beyond the Killing Fields* (Maryknoll, NY: Author, 1993). Video Magazine.

Norton, Ann W., *The Spirit of Cambodia . . . a Tribute* (Providence, RI: Providence College, 2002).

Pastore, Clare, *Journey to America: Chantrea Conway's Story: A Voyage from Cambodia in 1975* (New York: Berkley Jam Books, 2001).

Ray, Nick, *Cambodia* (Melbourne, Australia: Lonely Planet, 2000).

Sam, Sam-Ang, and Patricia S. Campbell, *Silent Temples, Songful Hearts: Traditional Music of Cambodia* (Danbury, CT: World Music Press, 1991).

St. Pierre, Stephanie, *Teenage Refugees from Cambodia Speak Out* (New York: Rosen, 1995).

Ung, Loung, *First They Killed My Father* (New York: HarperCollins, 2000).

Ung, Loung, *Lucky Child: A Daughter of Cambodia Reunites with the Sister She Left Behind* (New York: HarperCollins, 2005).

Wall, Lina Mao, and Cathy Spagnoli, *Judge Rabbit and the Tree Spirit* (San Francisco: Children's Book Press, 1991).

CURRICULAR ADAPTATION 2: TRANSFORMING PEDAGOGY BY DETRACKING MATH

As established in Chapter 5, the structural and organizational issues in schools greatly influence student learning. Educational researcher Jeannie Oakes has consistently reported evidence that the practice of tracking negatively influences most students. Her research findings regarding tracking, especially how tracking in schools stratifies students by race and social class, have been confirmed by many others. This example of a curricular adaptation demonstrates the challenge of taking up the tracking issue in a middle school math department by following the work of a school principal and some determined teachers to transform the groupings of students for math classes.[13]

BELIEF SYSTEMS

When considering the sociopolitical context of multicultural education to create change—as discussed in Chapter 1—we need to go beyond the classroom to confront the school's policies and practices as well as the societal ideologies that support them. The perspective that some kids can "handle" more abstract thinking and that others must be relegated to "skill and drill" is undergirded by a long-held math-instruction belief that students cannot learn about one concept until they master the "previous" concept. This belief system reinforces roadblocks to a fully integrated math curriculum for heterogeneous groups of students.

In U.S. schools, it is well documented that in kindergarten and first grade, most of the math material that students are learning is new information.[14] Yet, from kindergarten through seventh grade, there is a gradual but steady decline in new information that is introduced. By seventh grade, the larger piece of the math "pie" is review work, while a tiny percentage is new material. This remains the case until a student takes eighth grade algebra, when, rather suddenly, the abstract thinking and symbol manipulation introduced is almost entirely new. This, in turn, creates an even wider chasm if some students have greater access and opportunity to enroll in the algebra course, while others remain in "regular" math, consisting mostly of reviewing old concepts and revisiting skills.

THE PROCESS OF CHANGE

Changing this middle school math department's practices was a long process. To create effective change, it was necessary for the principal and the teachers to be critically cognizant of the belief system on which the old practices had been built. The former practice at the school in the seventh and eighth program segregated students by so-called ability. Students could sign up for "accelerated" math or "regular" math in seventh grade, which would feed into the eighth grade programs of algebra for the "accelerated" students and regular math for the "regular" students.

The principal of the school, who was a former math teacher, initially created structural change within the seventh grade math curriculum. As one step in the gradual process, the administration changed the way in which students would enter their seventh grade math classes. Instead of entering the seventh grade as either an "accelerated" math student or a "regular" math student (which was based on test scores and recommendations from sixth grade teachers), the students would enter seventh grade math curriculum in fully integrated, heterogeneous groups. At the end of the first quarter, after nine weeks of curriculum study and some testing, they would be re-grouped, dividing them into accelerated and regular classes for the second quarter. This was a strategic step in an attempt to meet students' needs in a more equitable way, but there were several pitfalls with the practice.

During the first quarter, the math teachers presented an equally challenging curriculum to all students. They also frequently offered "extensions" or an extra challenge as a choice for various assignments. During the first quarter, the seventh grade math teachers noted that most students took up the challenge and tried to solve the extensions with spirited enthusiasm. However, they witnessed a marked difference during the second quarter, after the classes had been designated "accelerated" or "regular." It comes as no surprise that most of the students in the "regular" math class stopped engaging in the extension lessons, while the students in the accelerated classes regularly pursued the extensions. For many students in the regular math class, it took less than one day's time to shift their perceptions about their possible math achievements from feeling capable of accomplishing the extensions to feeling incapable of meeting the challenge.

The practice of entering seventh grade as an integrated group and then shifting to accelerated and regular classes went on for a few years as the math department continued to struggle with how to make the curriculum more equitable while maintaining a rigorous academic program.

It's Not Only What We Teach; It's How We Teach

An eighth grade teacher, Mr. Mike Hayes, who at the time worked in the math department at the middle school, took note of the inequities. He witnessed that the accelerated curriculum engaged students in more abstract work and problem solving and the regular math curriculum offered more work on developing concrete skills at a lower level. Mr. Hayes critiqued the practice by noting, "This practice said that we believed kids needed different things to achieve in mathematics. The structures in place sent the message '*You* ["advanced" math students] should get an interesting, rich problem to work on and *you* ["regular" math students] should do fractions.' It said a lot about what we were communicating to students, parents, and guardians. It's not only what we teach; it's how we teach".

Mr. Hayes was inspired by the work of Robert Moses and Charles Cobb documented in the book: *Radical Equations: Civil Rights from Mississippi to the Algebra Project*.[15] In that text and in Moses' continuing work in public schools, he asserts, "The ongoing struggle for citizenship and equality for minority people is now linked to an issue of math and science literacy." Moses argues that in the 21st century, the unfinished work of the Civil Rights Movement is economic access. Moreover, economic access is critically dependent on science and math literacy. Mr. Hayes found that reading the work of Moses and Cobb transformed his teaching. He reported, "Reading that book gave my life's work a new sense of meaning." In addition to inspiration, the book gave theoretical substance and practical application to the questions about the pedagogy of the math department that Mr. Hayes had been asking and trying to solve.

While the adjustments were evolving in the seventh grade structure, Mr. Hayes was teaching eighth grade math. Building on the momentum of his principal's vision to detrack the math curriculum, he launched an effort to try to create more access to algebraic ideas for more eighth graders. He teamed up with fellow math teacher Alan Dallmann.[16] The two teachers piloted an approach they called *conceptual algebra*. This approach, which was directly inspired by the work of Robert Moses, strived to bridge the gap for students who were not enrolled in algebra. It offered students in the regular eighth grade math program the opportunity to participate in abstract symbol manipulation while continuing to develop their computation and arithmetic skills. In part, this teaching strategy built the challenges of more concrete math problems into more abstract-thinking challenges. This approach helped construct a scaffold of success for students who had not previously engaged in algebra. As a teaching strategy, this method also helped Mr. Hayes and Mr. Dallman assess their own teaching and get a sense of where the students were in terms of abstract thinking. The success of the conceptual algebra curriculum convinced these teachers that all students would benefit from engaging in algebraic thinking, regardless of their computational and technical skills. While a responsible curriculum would need to ensure that basic skills were constantly developed, such skill development would no longer be an impediment to participating in more theoretical ideas. These teachers believed and witnessed that students can learn about abstract concepts even when they are struggling with fractions.

This curricular change in the eighth grade math curriculum was one step to opening doors for more students to engage in higher level thinking. While the formal algebra class was still exclusive to about one-fourth of the students, the conceptual algebra approach in the regular math classes shifted practices throughout the math department. The teaching of conceptual algebra in eighth grade took hold throughout the math department as a structural change.

Beyond Math Class   While these math teachers were posing problems about the traditional structure of their department, other teachers in the school, outside the math departments, were raising questions about it as well. Teachers in the art, English, science, and social studies departments all noticed that the team of students was grouped by specific classes that reflected the enrollment in the accelerated math class. For example, even though there were no ability groups or "tiered" classes by achievement level in science and English departments, the science and English classes were populated in ways that accommodated the accelerated math schedule. Therefore, the practice of one department was influencing the learning and the administrative structure of all the content-area classes, resulting in what were, for all intents and purposes, tracked classes.

The English and science teachers brought questions to the school governing board called the *Leadership Council*, where issues were discussed and debated. The teachers asked, "Why do we have accelerated math classes in our school? Does the practice of accelerated math match the mission of our school?" Within this wider school discussion, the math department proposed that it was time to detrack the seventh grade math classes.

At the same time, another school structure was undergoing change. The school was adopting the policy of teams of teachers "looping" with students so that one team of students and teachers would remain together as a consistent learning community throughout seventh and eighth grade. Mr. Hayes would be teaching seventh grade the following year and remaining with that team of kids for their eighth-grade year. Envisioning an opportunity, he proposed to the principal that he pilot a completely heterogeneous, untracked seventh grade math program only for his team of students.

Mr. Hayes emphasized that rather than eliminating accelerated math curriculum, the fully integrated program would offer every student an opportunity to participate in accelerated math.

Support for All Students   Mr. Hayes realized he and his students would need support to make his plan work. He was determined to increase the skill level of students who would have been left out of the traditional accelerated program and to challenge the students who were already demonstrating strengths. The special education teacher, Blanca Zelaya, co-taught the math classes with Mr. Hayes.[17] They partnered on teaching strategies and techniques. The students viewed Mr. Hayes and Ms. Zelaya as co-teachers rather than perceiving each as the teacher of a certain group. By sharing the classroom and curriculum, they offered a richer curriculum to every student.

The following year, the school followed Mr. Hayes's pilot model and embarked on the practice of every seventh grade student's participating in the full math curriculum. The accelerated component was offered in completely heterogeneous groupings for all students.

The math teachers and administrators realized the importance of the community's support to create sustainable change. Before launching the new seventh grade math approach, they held meetings to discuss every aspect of the change. They knew that each component of the community would need to be included in the dialogue. They met with math teachers from the elementary schools and high school to clarify the goals of the changes within the broader scope of the math curriculum in the school district. At their middle school, they held a faculty meeting that engaged every teacher in the school in a dialogue about the implications of the structural change within the math department, that is, how the change would affect the whole school. The math teachers and administrators also held meetings for the parents and guardians.

The decision to detrack the math curriculum did not reflect a unanimous community vision. Within each of these community groups, there was some support for the new model and some dissent. The most common concern of detractors was that heterogeneous groupings might "water down" the curriculum. This common concern often leads to amplification of voices representing high-achieving students and muting of the concerns of students who have traditionally been marginalized. The public meetings emphasized that by offering accelerated math curriculum to all students, the children who have consistently achieved would continue to engage in robust, creative problem solving and skill development. Simultaneously, the children who had previously been relegated to regular math would be able to participate in higher level thinking and skill development. Moreover, students who need additional support to meet the highest challenge would also be buttressed by a team teaching approach to the curriculum. While disagreements continued, it became evident that most people were eager to get on board when they realized that all children would be more challenged within the new structure.

With every seventh grade math class adopting a heterogeneous approach, the special education teachers co-taught lessons with the math teachers. For students needing to hone certain competencies, the school provided extra support for sharpening skills in a program called *math tune-up*. The math tune-up class was not a special education program. A teacher of regular math taught the tune-up class during slots in the students' schedules that did not "pull out" the students from their regular math classes. The entire school schedule was examined creatively to create these possibilities.

More Work Ahead   The detracking of one seventh grade math curriculum is an ongoing process. The teachers described several promising developments, as well as pitfalls in their department's effort, that generated school-wide implications. The positive aspects were many: Students from all backgrounds, regardless of previous accomplishments, engaged in rigorous math curriculum that pushed the edges of student potential. Academic achievement increased for many students. Perceptions on who gets to be included were expanded by school discourses about "smartness", "intelligence", "good students," and "talent". The teachers reported feeling invigorated by the continual challenge to creatively present material to make it more engaging, understandable, and achievable to a wide range of learners. The limits of the change became clearer as students moved from seventh grade to eighth grade and then from eighth grade to the high school. When the seventh grade students moved to eighth grade, they were grouped into algebra groups or regular math groups. The eighth grade curriculum had changed significantly to offer more abstract thinking and symbol manipulation to the regular math groups, but the course offerings were separate, with little "wiggle room" to move from one course to the other during the eighth grade year.

Additionally, in an effort to create more access to a rigorous curriculum for a wider range of learners, the structure of the high school math department had shifted in configuration. Yet, while the high school math curriculum offered a wide range of courses for math credit, the classes that held more academic sway, such as honors and AP credit, continued to be "gated" by the eighth grade algebra requirements, thus perpetuating implicit messages about who belongs where. Even within a math department and school district committed to making serious structural change to achieve multicultural goals, external forces choke off much of the progress toward equitable change. Teachers who are supported by principals and curriculum directors are still pressured by *perceptions* of what a rigorous math curriculum should look like. College entrance requirements and state and national testing policies shape a great deal of high school math curricula. This middle school math department made significant change within the structures of the school and the wider school district. Yet the struggle to create a more inclusive math curriculum that asserts academic challenge remains contained mostly within the seventh grade program. The forces at play within the broader math department in this school district mirror the struggles of most math departments in U.S. schools concerning math ability and achievement.

The perimeters of social change at the macro level, that is, U.S. public schools, did not prevent Mr. Hayes and his colleagues from pursuing social justice at the micro level, that is, within his department. They looked at the structural limitations

RESOURCES FOR TEACHING AND DETRACKING MATH

Gutstein, Eric, *Reading and Writing the World with Mathematics: Toward a Pedagogy for Social Justice* (New York: RoutledgeFalmer, 2005).

Gutstein, Eric, and Bob Peterson, *Rethinking Mathematics: Teaching Social Justice by the Numbers* (Milwaukee: Rethinking Schools, 2005).

Moses, Robert, and Charles Cobb, *Radical Equations: Civil Rights from Mississippi to the Algebra Project* (Boston: Beacon Press, 2002).

Nasir, Na'ilah Suad, and Paul Cobb, eds., *Improving Access to Mathematics: Diversity and Equity in the Classroom* (New York: Teachers College Press, 2006).

Oakes, Jeannie, *Keeping Track: How Schools Structure Inequality*, 2nd ed. (New Haven, CT: Yale University Press, 2005).

Sinclair, Nathalie, *Mathematics and Beauty: Aesthetic Approaches to Teaching Children* (New York: Teachers College Press, 2006).

Stavy, Ruth, and Dina Tirosh, *How Students (Mis)Understand Science and Mathematics: Intuitive Rules* (New York: Teachers College Press, 2000).

Webb, Norman L., and Thomas A. Romberg, eds., *Reforming Mathematics Education in America's Cities: The Urban Mathematics Collaborative Project* (New York: Teachers College Press, 1994).

of their K–12 program and made changes specifically within their spheres of influence: the grades they taught at the middle school. The determination and achievements of these students and teachers demonstrate the qualities of social justice education that we outlined in Chapter 1. The ongoing efforts of the math department provided all students with the *material resources* necessary to learn to their full potential. The changes in the seventh grade math curriculum also provided students with *emotional resources* by demonstrating a belief in students' ability and worth; maintaining high expectations of them; imposing rigorous academic standards; and providing essential social and cultural capital to negotiate the world. By transforming the way in which students perceive themselves and their peers as mathematical thinkers, this case also exhibits a social-justice learning environment that promotes critical thinking and agency for social change.

CURRICULAR ADAPTATION 3: EXPANDING DEFINITIONS OF FAMILY

Another approach to transforming a curriculum is the strategy of examining a particular theme from a variety of perspectives. In the case study that follows, we offer a glimpse into a study of *family* as the theme. The concept of family has always been both deeply political and intimately personal. The political framework for defining family has become a contentious issue in recent years because of the lesbian, gay, bisexual, transgender (LGBT) community's struggle to gain legal marital status. The voices of political parties and special interest lobbying groups that claim ownership of the definition of *family values* have punctuated the controversy.

This case is divided into descriptions of three approaches to curricular adaptation. The first two examine the topic of family in two settings: first grade and middle school. These two approaches set the stage for an innovative approach to curricular adaptation in a third setting: a high school English literature course.

WHY THE TOPIC OF FAMILY?

The topic of family is an attractive theme for teachers because it offers many promising possibilities. The promise lies in the idea that every student from preschool through high school may be able to tell a story about family and relate to ideas about family change. Such stories and ideas provide ways for teachers and students to collaborate and involve every student in the curriculum. Yet, if these attributes are not approached with a problem-posing multicultural perspective, a curriculum about family can prove to be problematic—and even damaging to students. What is often thought to be a "universal" theme requires acknowledgement of multiple experiences and perspectives, with specific attention to deep-seated myopic views of the definition of *family* that may work to support institutional oppression of some people.

WHO IS INCLUDED?

For example, families who are headed by lesbian, gay, bisexual, and transgender people have been the specific target of recent oppressive political campaigns, and they are frequently ignored or deliberately silenced in school curricula. Also, families who are headed by adults who are not married, whether homosexual or heterosexual, are excluded from traditional definitions of family, and the children of these families may be questioned about the validity of their family structure. Families headed by single parents are still not affirmed in many curricula. Students who have family members who are incarcerated rarely see a welcome opportunity to share their story, and they are silenced by some teachers if they attempt to raise the topic. Families caring for members with mental illness may be reluctant to participate in a classroom invitation to share stories from home. The perspective of children of adoption is frequently omitted in classroom discussions about heredity and family trees. There are as many pitfalls in approaching family as a theme as there are families in our schools, so how does a teacher develop a curriculum about family that embraces the potential to draw from the strength of one of the most elemental human experiences and simultaneously lead students to fight oppression, develop critical thinking skills, and affirm all community members?

When teachers embark on the study of family with clarity about the long-term goals of the unit, it helps students tap into the shared understanding of human experience. Long-term goal setting may help avoid activities that exclude some students from the classroom community. In its most effective form, a curriculum rooted in big ideas or enduring understandings will lead students to actively pursue human rights for all families.

AVOIDING PITFALLS

A common activity in curriculum about family includes students' researching the history of their names. While this can be a powerful community-building activity, it is also rife with difficulties, especially when it is not grounded by an overarching long-term goal. Many students may know the family story of their name or may have easy access to it by asking family members who are eager to share the story. However, many children may not. Children of adoption and children in foster care may not know the origin of their name and may feel that such an assignment will lower their status as a classroom community member. Other students may have painful associations with the history of their name, such as one student we met who reported that he was named after a family member who had been incarcerated for abusing him.

Rather than discard the assignment about researching one's name and relegate such potentially robust activities to the "untouchable" category, teachers may develop a menu of various assignments from which students can choose. For example, if the big idea of the assignment is to *engage in research skills related to naming and personal history*, the menu of activities might include:

- Research the name of the street on which you live (or the name of the building, housing community, neighborhood, the name of the building in which your faith community, or the land on which your tribal community lives). Find out when it was named and why. Tell us something about its history, and if you choose the place where you live (building, street, housing community, or tribal community land), find out when your family moved there or started living there. Some "family moves" are exciting and celebratory. Other "family moves" may be a response to family and community difficulties such as economic strife, natural disasters, or political oppression. Tell us only what you and your family would like to share.
- Research the name of our school and compare it to the name of another school in our district that you have never attended. Tell us something about the history of the school between the time it was named and the time you began attending the school.
- Research the name of an important person in your family, your religious community, your tribal community, or your cultural community. Tell us something about what the name means. Tell us something about the history of the person between the time she or he was named and the time you were born.
- Research your name and its origins. Find out who chose your name and why. Tell us something about what your name means. Tell us something about the history of your family between the time you were named and the time you began attending this school.

A culminating activity may involve each student's creating an artistic representation of his or her own name to display as a heading for his or her research presentations. The artistic representations may provide another way for students to demonstrate knowledge while simultaneously bringing a unifying activity to a classroom where students have been engaged in an assortment of research projects.

The pitfalls and promises of the history-of-your-name activity are examples of why it is critical to begin a curriculum with big ideas or enduring understandings rather than simply planning activities. This curricular activity also exemplifies the delicate balance inherent in a teacher's role. Even the most thorough multicultural curriculum cannot solve personal crises that some children face. When students reveal painful memories or dangerous situations, it is critical that teachers tap into the resources in the school and community through guidance counselors and social workers to keep their students healthy and safe.

What follows are examples of curriculum for three different grade levels: one created by first grade teachers and students, another created by a middle school team of teachers, and the last developed by a high school English teacher.

First Grade Curriculum Based on Big Ideas

The first grade curriculum about family stems from the following four big ideas—or enduring understandings and essential questions:

1. There are all kinds of families.
   - What is a family?
   - How do we know a group of people make up a family?
2. Families have "wants & needs":
   - What do families need? (Food, water, clothing, shelter, love).
   - What is the difference between a need and a want?
   - What are some things that you must have to survive?
   - Is money a want or a need? Are some things "in between"? Do all families need a way to exchange goods?
3. Responsibilities
   - What are the responsibilities that parents and guardians attend to while kids are at school?
   - What are the responsibilities of each child in the family?
4. Experiencing *change* is common to all families. (Examples of change: marriage, divorce, getting older, moving, illness, getting well, death, birth.)
   - Does change happen in all families?
   - Why do we like or dislike change?
   - Can we prepare for change in families?

With these enduring understandings in mind, the first grade teachers start each school year with the integrated social studies unit on family and spend approximately six weeks incorporating these big ideas into all aspects of the curriculum. Additionally, as the year unfolds, they study other units in specific content areas that reinforce and revisit many of the enduring understandings that were established during the unit on family. The other units in the social studies and science curricula throughout the year are anchored in the big ideas concerning the family unit.

All Kinds of Families   The teachers deliberately take an anti-bias approach throughout the six-week unit on family as well as through the school year, by teaching first graders that there are all kinds of families. Through children's literature, the daily calendar, math problems, and other activities of classroom life, the students consistently see images of, and learn about, family diversity. Specific attention is given to affirming the particular families of the children in the classroom while simultaneously expanding the students' views of what family can be. Some of the many examples of "all kinds of families" include families headed by gay dads and lesbian moms, families experiencing divorce, families created or expanded through adoption, single-parent families, families struggling with financial resources, multiracial families, foster families, families experiencing illness or death, families in which the grandparents are raising the children, families with stepparents and step siblings, families from a wide range of different racial, ethnic, and religious backgrounds as well as those that may be defined as *nuclear* or *traditional families*.

Families in the Classroom   In many schools, the practice of bringing family members from all walks of life into the classroom as helpers and experts has had more support in recent years. In a unit about family, this is certainly a dynamic component. Teachers can develop many creative means for parents, guardians, and extended family members to be present. However, making *all* families "visible," and the diversity of their life experiences honored, is a challenging endeavor. To explore the big idea about families and responsibilities, one teacher developed an activity that rises to the challenge.

At the beginning of this activity, the classroom community discusses the idea of responsibilities. The students complete a series of assignments to explore and document the responsibilities of adults and children in the family. The assignments are designed to raise awareness of responsibilities but also to make every child's family visible in the classroom. The students in the class make a list of responsibilities that they have in school or "jobs" they need to accomplish. This simple task expands the notion of what it means to have a "job" beyond a place of work where one gets paid money. Especially for children in families struggling with unemployment, this wide view of jobs and responsibilities affirms the work of all family members. The class also makes a list of jobs that kids do at home such as making their beds, walking the dog, carrying their plates to the sink, helping to carry groceries, folding towels, etc.

After developing their understandings of responsibilities, each first grader conducts a family survey by interviewing the adults in the family, asking questions such as: What responsibilities do you have while I am at school? What jobs do you do, either at home or away from home? These interview questions allow for a range of replies to be respected, as opposed to the more narrow question that children frequently hear: "Where do your parents work?" The first graders learn more about what their caregivers are doing and about the assortment of possibilities of adult responsibilities, and the teacher gains an intimate view into the complex workings of each student's family. The assignment results in adult replies such as caring for younger children or elders, searching for employment, cleaning or fixing up the home, taking care of the yard, volunteer work, going to school, resting to go to the night shift at work, and much more. The students hear about a variety of places that people call *work*: the office, the school, the fire station, the bakery, the construction site, the chemistry lab, the home, the sandwich shop, the hospital, grandma's house, the cafeteria, the hotel, and more.

Part of the interview requires the students to ask the adults what they have to be "good at" to accomplish their responsibilities. This kind of questioning affirms the multiple intelligences required for everyday life. Children hear about skills such as talking to people, knowing when the baby is hungry, using special tools, keeping things organized, being a good listener, making food taste good, knowing different kinds of plants, figuring out when a burning building might fall down (in the case of a parent who is a firefighter), etc. The assignment continues with students' researching the jobs for which all the children in their home have responsibility. Eventually, they investigate what the adults in their families imagined they would be when they grew up and how this compares to the adult responsibilities they now have.

Finally, the students spend time drawing, writing, and presenting their investigations, culminating in imagining several kinds of responsibilities they would like to have when they grow up.

The work of multicultural education is not only to affirm students about who they are, but also to challenge them about who they may become. This variation on a common early childhood activity of "What do you want to be?" is designed to provide multiple models, unleash imaginations, and expand the possibilities these first graders imagine for themselves. All the while, every family "comes to life" in the class, even if the adults in the family could not enter the classroom door.

Children's Literature   The first grade teachers use children's literature to emphasize that there is not one "normal" way to experience family, but rather that diversity *is* normal. While reading lively and engaging children's literature such as *1,2,3: A Family Counting Book* by Bobbie Combs and illustrated by Dannamarie Hosler, students see paintings that depict families headed by gays and lesbians, including two dads reading a bedtime story to their kids, two moms sharing popsicles with their kids on the porch, and several families gathered in community activities.[18] Using children's literature that includes encounters with families with same-sex parents deliberately combats heterosexism in early childhood and provides opportunities to teach explicitly about human rights for all families. When students learn accurate, respectful language and vocabulary regarding the LGBT community, they may ask questions that uncover anti-LGBT perspectives.

While the selection of children's literature that depicts families headed by LGBT people is still limited, it has grown significantly in breadth and depth since 1989, when Leslea Newman wrote and self-published *Heather Has Two Mommies*.[19] With the 20th anniversary of that book approaching, Newman and many other authors and publishers have expanded children's literature selections with texts that affirm families headed by gay and lesbian couples, single people, and LGBT parents who have separated. Some recent titles for early childhood literacy activities that include a more inclusive definition of family and affirm families headed by lesbian, gay, bisexual, and transgender people are listed on the GLSEN website.[20]

There is a growing list of titles in children's literature that affirm LGBT identity. Early childhood teachers and students who are engaging in the "dangerous discourse" we discussed in our assertion of multicultural education as education for social justice in Chapter 3, use these books and other similar resources.[21] Dangerous discourse becomes common practice and unthreatening when these books are integrated into daily literacy activities that develop reading and listening skills, motivate class discussion, and make interdisciplinary connections. Along with books that depict many other kinds of families, a rich children's literature collection affirms diverse family structures and questions those who exclude families headed by gay, lesbian, bisexual, and transgender parents from fully participating in a democracy.

Early childhood is an essential phase of development in which to address heterosexism by integrating this literature. Children are on the cusp of what Louise Derman-Sparks calls *pre-prejudice*. They are asking questions that may be naive about society's oppressions or they may be ventriloquating social epithets without understanding the meaning behind the words. First grade is an educational stage ripe with opportunity to expand a child's world.[22]

Problem-posing teachers realize that developing a children's literature collection is an ongoing, organic process. We are not suggesting that a first grade book shelf or a unit about family diversity should focus only on families headed by lesbian, gay, bisexual, and transgender people. Such an approach would obviously not affirm the families of all students in the class. However, given the sociopolitical context of the human rights struggles of the LGBT community, a critical component of a multicultural curriculum confronts the negative ways that LGBT people are depicted by the popular media. An expanding children's literature collection may act as a counternarrative to oppressive acts and highlight the positive role of LGBT-headed families in the classroom. These books broaden the scope of a curriculum that also includes quality literature depicting families with diverse ethnic and racial identities, religious practices, socioeconomic situations, disabilities/abilities, languages, and so forth, as well as the myriad ways that families are shaped through birth, adoption, foster care, extended families, and more.

Daily Calendar and Family Concepts   Every day in these first grade classrooms starts with a morning meeting and calendar activity. Using a model created by teacher Val Penniman and parent Debbie Shumway, the teachers introduce alphabet skills, vocabulary, math patterns, and concepts about the current unit through the calendar activity.[23] For the family unit, the teachers designed daily calendar pieces (using clip art) to delve into concepts and vocabulary with which the children are familiar but which they may not always have the opportunity to use to develop academic knowledge.

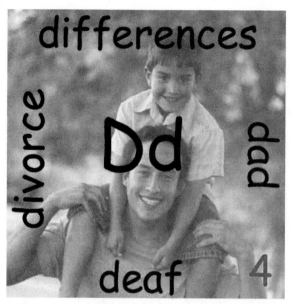

Calendar piece from Gina Simm's and Susie Seco's first grade class. Design inspired by Val Penniman's and Debbie Shimway's *Calendar Connections*. www.calendar-connections.com

For example, on calendar day number 4, the alphabet letter is D and the vocabulary words are *difference, dad, divorce, deaf*. By including words such as *divorce, difference*, and *deaf* along with words that may be more typical of a family unit such as *dad*, the classroom curriculum is normalizing experiences so children may engage in academic skill development while some who are usually marginalized are being affirmed in their family experiences. Simultaneously, other children are challenged to expand their perspective of families. Integrating vocabulary words such as *divorce* and *deaf* provides a means for students to ask questions and share stories in an emotionally safe and academically rigorous environment. Abilities, disabilities, and family change are studied through stories and studying vocabulary.

All Kinds of Family Portraits   Artistic expression is honored in these classrooms as a form of sharing knowledge. Every student creates a family portrait. By studying various examples of family portraits from contemporary and historical artists, the first graders gain a panoramic view of the multitude of ways that the concept of family can be expressed. A curriculum that expands the definition of *family* also expands the notion of what is included in a family portrait. The book *Honoring Our Ancestors: Stories and Pictures by Fourteen Artists*, edited by Harriet Rohmer, is illustrated with lively paintings by various artists who depict "ancestors" in poetic and metaphorical ways.[24] The paintings in this book represent family memories, spiritual stories, family quotes, and even a room with nobody in it to remind the viewer of the loss of a loved one. Each painting is accompanied by an artist's narrative in very "kid-friendly" language, which leads first graders through robust literacy activities that integrate the visual image with the written word.

In another strategy to connect visual imagery and text, teachers and students study the books created by *Family Diversity Projects*, in which many different kinds of families are portrayed in captivating photographs with accompanying interviews of family members. Resources that use photography and interview text to depict the true stories of real families are powerful tools for developing critical thinking. In addition to using the books as curriculum resources, many teachers and schools display the touring photo-text exhibits, which can be rented from the Family Diversity Projects collection. Currently there are four traveling exhibits:[25]

- *In Our Family: Portraits of All Kinds of Families*
- *Love Makes a Family: Portraits of Lesbian, Gay, Bisexual and Transgender People and Their Families*

I like to play sports with my family. I like when my dad plays baseball with me. I like it when my mom tucks me in bed.

Michael Warren, in Gina Simm's class. *Family portrait.* Mixed media, 2005.

- *Nothing to Hide: Mental Illness in the Family*
- *Of Many Colors: Portraits of Multiracial Families*

Throughout the study of family, first graders see images and hear stories of families that remind them of their own. These images and stories serve the concurrent purpose of stretching their understanding of what other families are like. The work of multicultural education for social justice begins in the earliest grades with the most elemental of human experience to help students imagine a fair world for "all kinds of families."

MIDDLE SCHOOL INTEGRATED CURRICULUM

The exhibits and books of the Family Diversity Projects also serve as an anchor for the integrated middle school curriculum about family. The middle school teachers developed big ideas to expand skills and inquiry across all content areas. The enduring understanding is that *oppression and resistance are experienced and acted upon in diverse ways by families in our society*, the essential questions are:

- How do we create an inclusive definition of family?
- What is family?
- Where do I belong?

Bearing in mind the difficulties that some students may encounter with a curriculum about families, the teachers did not ask students to bring in family photographs. They knew that many children would not have family photos and that some children would feel uncomfortably exposed by a requirement to share family photos. Instead, the team focused on the materials in the Family Diversity Projects photo-text exhibit *In Our Family* and on books as points of departure for research, as well as the discussions about the teachers and staff members' families. Thus, all teachers brought their own family photos to share with the students at the beginning of the unit. These family photos provided opportunities to discuss the various ways of defining family and to share with the middle school students some aspects of the teachers' lives beyond the classroom walls.[26]

Diversity Within Groups   At first glance, it would appear that the team of teachers who undertook this unit was a group of middle class White people. This is true, but it is not the whole story. The teachers were critically aware of the dominance of their identities and asserted that their students deserved to see many different kinds of families modeled in class discussions. So the team presented their family photos to the students, and the classroom community discussions pointed out the many ways in which the teachers' families were different.

In this case, one female teacher was married to a man who had children from a previous union, so she had stepchildren. One male teacher was married to a woman and had no children. One female teacher had three sons: one from her first marriage, one from her second marriage in which she was still partnered, and one foster son who was different racially from her other family members. One female teacher lived with her lesbian partner and was adopting a child of a different race. One White male teacher was married to a White woman and they had two biological children—the only "nuclear" or "traditional" family among the teaching team.

These differences opened up opportunities for considering other kinds of diversity. Teachers invited other school faculty and staff members to visit their classrooms and bring some of their family photos. The faculty and staff visitors included a Jewish woman who told the story of her parents' surviving the Holocaust and the loss of her husband to cancer, as well as the triumph of her niece over cancer; an African American man who is married to a woman and raising their grandson; and a biracial gay man who had been adopted by a white family.

These conversations about the families in which the adults live provided models for students' consideration of the topic of family as an academic subject, rich with research possibilities. The students saw the teachers as full participants in the unit of study rather than simply as "deliverers" of information. The unintended consequence of this activity was that students witnessed different adults sharing their family experiences at varying levels of disclosure with distinct styles of storytelling. It gave students a range of models from which to embark on their academic work.

Studying Our Own Assumptions   The social studies teacher launched the study by bringing each class to the Family Diversity Projects photo exhibit before the accompanying text was installed in the display. (A similar activity could be designed by looking at books and photocopies of pictures of families.) The students examined each photograph and wrote responses to prompts such as:

- Find a family with whom you think you have something in common.
- Find a family with whom you think you have nothing in common.
- Pick a photo that makes you curious; write your questions.
- Pick a photo that makes you smile; tell us why.
- Pick a photo that makes you sad; tell us why.

The social studies students compared each other's responses to the photos. They began to look critically at assumptions they were making on the basis of a photograph. Then the teachers added the companion text to each photograph, and the students revisited the exhibit, with plenty of time to read the text.

The reading and analysis of the text pointed to the sociological objectives of the unit. Students uncovered ways in which they made assumptions about some families and how those assumptions may stem from, or lead to, stereotypes. Students also learned ways in which they made accurate guesses about some of the families. For example, Jeffrey pointed out a family of four—comprised of a mom, a dad, and two sons who were both wearing baseball caps—as one that was similar to his own family. The family structure and the love of baseball were similar traits to those of Jeffrey's family. Upon reading the text, Jeffrey learned that all four people in the photo are deaf and communicate in American Sign Language, which is different from Jeffrey's family's hearing and language abilities.

Group Membership and Responsibility   These activities eventually led to a study of how people group themselves and how society groups people. The students started with examining their membership roles in family and then expanded to examining their membership in other groups such as basketball teams, lunch-table groups, after-school clubs, religious communities, racial groups, ability groups, and so forth. This examination included analyzing group behavior and social influences on groups. When juxtaposed with the histories of various groups, these analyses helped to flesh out stories of historical oppression and resistance in the minds of these middle school students. Rather than demonizing one group or romanticizing another, students began to see the links of social power, social position, and group power. Ultimately, the students critically analyzed their own group membership and their social responsibilities within groups. They worked cooperatively to develop strategies to take responsibility when these groups dominate other groups in the microcosm of the middle school as well as in the larger society.

Reading, Writing, Researching, and Reflecting   The language arts curriculum explored the experiences of diverse families through a range of literature. The middle school students selected books from an array of titles. Like photo-text exhibits, literature offers students an opportunity to engage in other families' experiences, some that may resonate with their own and some that may open new worldviews to their early adolescent minds.

Poetry was a central vehicle for expression and questioning in the English class. Building on the curriculum advanced by Linda Christensen in *Reading, Writing and Rising Up*, each student composed a poem called "I am From" to articulate the multiple dimensions of identity within family.[27]

While the work of poetry writing and literature circles was evolving in the English classroom, the students embarked on homework research projects to investigate their family histories. Again, if such a project is undertaken, it is advisable to provide a menu of assignments from which every student may choose to find meaningful, affirming work that also expands their academic skills. For example, a common project may be to assign students to research and report on when their family immigrated to this country. But when a teacher approaches the curriculum with the big idea in mind (*Oppression and resistance are experienced and acted upon in diverse ways by families in our society*), the exclusion of Native American children in an assignment about immigration becomes more obvious. Approaching the big ideas with critical pedagogy, the classroom considers multiple views of what immigration means to various families. This array of perspectives may include the forced migration and extermination of Native Nations, the forced immigration of enslaved people, immigration to escape war and political oppression, refugee experiences, the circular migration/immigration families in U.S. territories (called colonies by some) such as Puerto Rico, and the ongoing political oppression and resistance of families caught in the crossfire of U.S. immigration restrictions. When research findings based on each student's own family's perspective are integrated in a critical classroom context, voice is given to stories that have been silenced, encouraging students to question narratives that exclude some family experiences.

Measuring, Reflecting, and Representing   In math class, the middle students spent a two-week period that the math teacher called *A Day in the Life*, carefully measuring how their time was spent. They created circle graphs ("pie charts") and bar graphs to analyze the percentage of time spent with family, comparing this percentage to time spent on homework, extracurricular events, friends, and other details such as grooming. (Grooming was a substantial piece of most middle school students' pie charts and graphs!) Students learned critical time-management skills as well as gained an understanding of the diverse ways that their peers' families spend time.

Genetics, Probability, and Critical Pedagogy   Starting with two essential questions—*What is family?* and *Where do I belong?*—the science curriculum was integrated with math to study probability equations related to genetics and human traits such as eye color. By studying the science of genetic structure and the mathematical strategies to predict human traits, students of all family backgrounds and configurations are affirmed. Rather than starting with what each student knows about their heritage, teachers can start with what they *do not* know and what they are curious about to form hypotheses about their ancestor's genetic composition. Science teachers can pose a variety of examples from which students may choose to develop their equations and predictions. This activity is more welcoming to children of adoption and others who may have no information about their biological heredity. The students learn academic skills for analyzing data and pursuing deeply personal questions.

Old Arguments, New Knowledge, and Social Justice   A scientifically grounded study of genetics also provides well-informed arguments against racism and ethnic oppression. A critical pedagogy examines misinformation about intelligence and ability and replaces it with methodologically rigorous academic knowledge. With race-based and ethnic-based hate crimes and genocides across the globe, from the United States to Rawanda, Darfur, and Iraq, students can develop accurate, rational, and scientifically sound refutations to historically and ethnically rooted oppressions. By integrating their sociological research findings on group behavior and group membership with scientific and mathematical skills, middle school students can make assertive choices about human rights issues that affect their own families. They can become activists about global concerns.

Research Questions   The development of students as activist scholars was woven throughout each subject, and social studies objectives were evident in all content areas. In one of the final social studies assignments, students chose a research question to pursue through a variety of methods. For example, one student's question was "What gets families through hard times?" She practiced social science research methodologies such as reading the photo-text exhibit, interviewing her own family members, and interviewing friends and neighbors. She contrasted these real-life families' experiences with those of families she saw on TV. Many students were compelled to compare their research data with the representation of families in the media. Students learned how to organize their data by themes and write essays with a critical eye toward the media's representation of family.

Visual Art and Visual Culture   To address the many visual and verbal messages regarding what families look like in visual culture, the interdisciplinary art curriculum was integrated with the social studies skills the students had developed. By examining images of families in film, web media, print media, and various expressions of popular culture, students can develop skills in critical and visual literacy. Within this dialogue, the middle school students consciously drew a self-portrait in the context of a family portrait. By developing confidence in art-making skills, this lesson encouraged student expressions about diverse families while expanding concepts about art and the powerful role of visual culture.

Identity and Beauty   Critical understanding of facial features and value systems was underscored in the context of a visual arts drawing lesson stemming from the big idea of the unit. The art teacher and social studies teacher integrated concepts surrounding physical anthropology that also drew upon the math and science research in genetics. They studied skin color and other various human traits. They asked why certain groups in specific geographic locations developed unique adaptations that we see today in the diversity of the human form, which is most obvious in facial features, hair texture, and skin color. Exploring these concepts in the process of self-portrait drawing deepened students' critical perceptions. The class discussion sharpened analytical questions about who gets to define *beauty* and how judgments about physical appearances in U.S. society may be shaped by commercially driven aims and conformist values. The culminating works of art created by the students communicated many messages that stemmed from their understanding of oppression and resistance based on discussions throughout the unit. Students used layers of collage, glue, papers, paint, and oil pastel to express academic research, scientific and mathematical skills, poetic insights, and socially active engagement with their multiple and inclusive definitions of family.

A Family Celebration   As a culminating event, a celebration of the students' accomplishments and a demonstration of their knowledge was held, and every student on the team invited their families to school for the event. A huge art and text display was mounted wherein each student exhibited a collaged frame of three items: a self-portrait, a family portrait, and an "I am From" poem. Every social studies essay, mathematical graph, and scientific research project was on display. Parents, grandparents, caregivers, guardians, and siblings listened intently as students read poetry and excerpts of essays. Many family members who had never before entered the school building attended the event. Students grabbed the hands of loved ones to escort them to each exhibit. The teachers noticed how students proudly "showed off" their work to their visitors, but on a surprising note, many students were eager to point out the work of their classmates as well. Teachers overheard students telling the stories of their peers' families and how they related to the research assignments.

The most popular display was the dessert table; every family had contributed a favorite family dessert! Excited students urged peers and teachers to taste the snacks such as Jalissa's grandmother's flan or Ari's uncle's favorite chocolate-chip concoction. After the families and children went home and the last paper plates were cleaned up, teachers reported a feeling of transformation precipitated by the Family Dessert and Demonstration Day that closed the unit. Teachers described knowing their students more deeply and intimately.

Students wrote self-assessments of their work and told of making connections with teachers and peers in unexpected ways, "wanting to work [their] hardest," and feeling that the project was "awesome". The sense of accomplishment and community bond among the team of teachers and students continued to grow throughout the school year. Teachers talked about their growing knowledge about oppression and resistance as well as their expanding definitions of family, and students and teachers cultivated an enduring sense of belonging.

CURRICULAR CHANGE IN HIGH SCHOOL LITERATURE

This portion of the case presents another example for multicultural changes in the curriculum. The deliberate anti-bias work that we saw in the first grade and middle school unit on family paves the way for students to engage in inclusive high school curriculum. The following example is the curriculum for a high school English literature course called *Gay and Lesbian Literature*.[28]

SNAPSHOT

Eugene Crocket

Usually I think of my family as an adoptive family more than a gay family.

Eugene Crocket,[1] a soft-spoken Irish American ninth grader, carries himself in a poised manner that commands respect. He has a slight build and longish brown hair that falls into his eyes, which become animated and sparkle as he speaks. Eugene grew up in the rural New England community of Hilton and attends a regional high school in nearby Howardstown, with students from a variety of backgrounds. Eugene spoke at length about his best friend, a Tibetan student, and described how they are both active in an after-school club, Students for a Free Tibet.[2] In this snapshot, Eugene focuses on his experience of being adopted and raised by two gay dads.

There are six people in my family. I have three brothers and two dads. [Both dads are European American]. One of my dads, Tom, lives in Puerto Rico right now and sells real estate. My other dad, Ted, cleans houses. I call Tom *Dad* and Ted *Poppy*, like *Pop* but *Poppy*.

I am the youngest in the family. My oldest brother Ronnie is 21. Then there's Michael. He's 19. Mark, he's 17, and I'm 15. Ronnie lives in Howardstown and has his own apartment. Michael is getting his own apartment soon. Mark is going away to college, so pretty soon it's going to be just me at home. Ronnie and Mark are more into sports, but me and Michael like to play video games more.

Most people, if they look at my family, they might think it's weird or something. They might think it's odd because it's not the so-called ordinary family. Personally, I don't see being in my family as too much different, because it's my family and I've known them my whole life. It's just regular to me, being in my family.

All four of my brothers are biological brothers. My dads adopted all of us at the same time. I was six months old, and the others were three years old, four, and six. Ronnie probably remembers it most. Basically, our parents were getting into drugs, and not able to take care of us. My oldest brother Ronnie was pretty much, like, he would feed me the bottle and change my diaper and stuff. My parents just weren't able to take care of us. I'm not really sure if they

sought the adoption agency, or if they were reported by a neighbor or something. We were foster kids and then we got adopted. There was a whole controversial thing in the community, because my dads were in the newspaper a lot. They had to argue for being two gay men to get us. I guess they got threatened sometimes. I know they were in the newspaper a lot. This was in the early 1990s.

These days, I'm pretty comfortable talking about it. Not too many people ask, but my close friends pretty much already know about my two dads. I've told them why we were adopted. If I make friends with someone, and they get to know my family, then they might ask questions.

When I was around the age of 11 or 12, I would notice people looking at us. They could probably put together what our family is, like, "Huh, look at that." I felt different, and I didn't like it. Now if that happens, I don't really care.

Usually I think of my family as an adoptive family more than a gay family. In Hilton, there were three adoptive families in my grade, including me. I did feel different, because the three of us were adopted, but I was the only one that had two dads. I didn't really mind that people knew I was adopted and stuff. But sometimes it was a little awkward telling them about my parents. So I felt different, and I didn't like having both my parents come to school. I wasn't ashamed, but more embarrassed. I don't know, I didn't want people to think of me as different. Now, my dad Tom, he lives in Puerto Rico, and Ted, he's not really involved with school or the PTA or whatever. Usually Ted is the one who goes to parent night. I know one other kid at my school now who has two moms, and I know this other girl who was adopted who also has lesbian moms.

At home everything is normal, like everyone else's family. Going out in public is a little more different. I was going to have a class get-together one time, in seventh grade. I wanted to have a bunch of friends over, but I was, like, "How about not at my house, guys," just because I didn't want them to see pictures or something. The sense of stress was only for that moment, so I just kept it to myself. If we're ever talking about family, I usually just say "my dad," rather than "my dads." Usually I try to get to know people well before I tell them that I have two dads, so I already know what their opinions are, and stuff. I have to be pretty sure I can trust them before I can tell them. I did have one friend who was Christian. I used to be better friends with him, but now I'm not as good friends with him. I made sure not to tell him, because of the Bible and all that. I don't know what he would have done, so I thought it best not to tell him.

At my high school, there's lots of using the word *gay* and the f-a-g word, like, "That's so gay." They don't actually mean it, but it's become like an insult or something. So homophobia isn't that bad in our school. It doesn't make me too uncomfortable, but it bothers me a little bit, though. If I know the person saying it, I might say something. It matters who says it.

At our school, we have a gay and lesbian literature class. We also have a Gay-Straight Alliance.[3] I think it's a good idea. I know some people in it. People might assume you were gay or lesbian if you joined it. I don't really know what the GSA does. It has maybe ten people in it, maybe more.

One time in Spanish class, we were doing the family words. My teacher was asking everyone about their mother and their father, and I didn't want to get called on. I didn't want her to be, like, "Oh, what does your mom do?" "I don't have a mom, I don't know." I didn't get called on; I lucked out. I probably would have just said, "I don't have a mom." Another time in high school, we had to do a family tree. The teacher said we didn't have to do our parents, we could do our grandparents and our aunts and stuff. I only put in one of my parents. But in fourth grade, when we had to do a family tree, I did put in both my dads. I always felt more comfortable in elementary school. We were doing the family tree on our heritage, and I did it based on my adoptive parents, because they're the parents that I know.

Being in this family, I have learned to, if I see someone who is different, to not think of them as odd or weird, but to accept people for who they are. I try not to make stereotypes, like not ask people about their mom's name and their dad's name, because I know that not everyone has a mom and a dad. Stuff like that. If I have to fill out a form at school and it says "mother's name," I just cross that out and write "father's name." I haven't ever seen a teacher react to that.

My sixth grade teacher, Ms. Kamp, she really helped me a lot. She made me more comfortable. I was really shy and she made me a lot more comfortable speaking to groups. Academically, I got better. If we had a topic like this, she would ask me if I felt comfortable with it, like if we talked about gay/lesbian stuff. She would ask me in private—like when people were talking, she would come over and whisper it to me. She was also my neighbor.

COMMENTARY

Eugene's snapshot raises the issue of how children of gay and lesbian parents must negotiate "outing" themselves—and their parents—as mem-

bers of families headed by gay parents. Even in liberal Howardstown, with its GSA and gay and lesbian literature class, issues of homophobia and limited understanding of what makes a family arise in school, causing students like Eugene to feel uncomfortable, if not unsafe. At the same time, Eugene reported feeling particularly supported by one teacher, Ms. Kamp, who perhaps knew him better than most, since she was also his neighbor in their small town.

As one of four brothers who were all adopted as a sibling group, Eugene benefited from built-in emotional support at home. Other adopted children may feel more isolated, particularly if they are the only adopted child in their family. Even with his family support and his relatively tolerant school environment, Eugene's anecdotes about offensive put-downs and questions from insensitive teachers and classmates sharpens the discussion of homophobia in schools. Teachers can do a better job of monitoring the school environment for offensive language that sets students apart. They can take care to incorporate flexibility, openness, and inclusivity in their approaches to both the pedagogy and curriculum.

Finally, Eugene's participation in the Tibetan club underscores the importance of choice. Whereas, concerned adults might assume that students like Eugene would be better served by joining the Gay-Straight Alliance or even a group specifically for children of gay/lesbian parents,[4] in this case, Eugene took comfort in his close friendship with a Tibetan student and preferred to join Students for a Free Tibet as one of only two white students in the group. Perhaps as he progresses through high school, Eugene may be drawn to GSA or another student group. The important note for school officials is making certain that schools provide a variety of outlets that address diverse student interests and various comfort levels.

NOTES

1. We appreciate the work of our friend and colleague Dr. John Raible, who interviewed Eugene and developed the introduction and commentary for the snapshot.

2. Students for a Free Tibet is an international organization on college and high school campuses committed to nonviolent direct action

(continued)

in solidarity with the Tibetan people. For more information go to www.studentsforafreetibet .org/

3. The Gay-Straight Alliance Network provides resources and information on how to start a Gay-Straight Alliance in your school or com-

munity group at www.gsanetwork.org/index .html

4. One such group for children of gay/lesbian parents is GLSEN (Gay, Lesbian, Straight Education Network).

The course was conceived and designed by an English teacher, Ms. Sara Barber-Just. Initially, it was Ms. Barber-Just's research, creativity, and commitment to education for social justice—backed by a supportive department chair, principal, and superintendent—that brought the curriculum to the classroom. Eventually the English department at the high school and the school board approved this course as an integral part of the school curriculum.

Imagining Possibilities Ms. Barber-Just was teaching in the English department of a high school that offered a range of familiar high school literature courses such as Foundations of American Literature, Masterpieces of Ancient and Medieval Worlds, and Masterpieces of the Renaissance and Modern Worlds as well as more assertively multicultural courses such as Women in Literature and African American Literature. Teachers in the department had developed these courses over the years and they had become integrated into the school's course offerings. Ms. Barber-Just imagined that the models in place for the African American Literature and Women in Literature courses could be applied to a course called *Gay and Lesbian Literature*. Both of the former courses dealt with identity issues, and the African American Literature course was organized chronologically by historical time periods.

Ms. Barber-Just developed a proposal for a course combining a wealth of research from her graduate studies and her experiences with the department's curriculum. Her research portfolio reflected an extensive review of gay and lesbian literature with a theoretical grounding in social justice education. In planning the Gay and Lesbian Literature course, she used a course structure that paralleled those of the two courses that were already offered, focusing on group-specific content from a social justice perspective. Her course mirrored the high academic standards within the department, with expectations for students to read thoroughly and critically, write expressively and analytically, and discuss the work passionately and fairly. The following is an excerpt from the proposal she wrote, which became part of the course description:

Students in public schools have been reading literary classics by gay, lesbian, and bisexual authors for more than a century; however, gay authors' lives are often concealed rather than rightfully explored. This course closely examines the struggles and triumphs of these artists—as well as the historical periods during which they wrote—allowing readers to more deeply analyze their diverse literary contributions. *Gay and Lesbian Literature* is split into five major sections, moving in chronological order from the early 1900s to the 1990s. Class readings include works written by gay and lesbian authors during eras of severe legal and social oppression; conformity and self-loathing; anger, activism, and radicalism; and, finally, pride and acceptance. The course focuses on renowned modern and contemporary American authors such as Willa Cather, James Baldwin, Rita Mae Brown, and Michael Cunningham, and concludes with an examination of Sri Lankan author Shyam Selvadurai and a study of short stories from around the world. Each unit includes a combination of critical essays, poetry, short story, and/or film, providing a rich cultural and historical context for the featured literature.[29]

Sara Barber-Just explained that for purposes of this course, she would base the definition of *gay and lesbian literature* on two criteria: (1) literature written by LBGT people and (2) literature including gay themes in the content. (A list of some texts, films, and websites from the course is included in the resource section at the end of this chapter section.)

With several caveats, the curriculum director and the principal quietly agreed to offer this course during the pilot model. It would be offered for independent study credit only. Students could sign up for the course if their schedules allowed and they would acquire credit for it, but the credit would not count toward the English credits required to graduate. To teach the course, Ms. Barber-Just would need to fit it into her free period and continue to carry a regular English teacher's course load. She would not earn any additional pay. That is how the course was offered during its first term. As a matter of fact, Ms. Barber-Just dropped her teaching contract down to less than fulltime to make space for the Gay and Lesbian Literature course in her schedule. She was teaching the same amount of courses and numbers of students for less pay.

Student Requests and Requirements   Word spread like wildfire among the student body about the new Gay and Lesbian Literature course, and the class quickly filled up, with a waiting list of students eager to take the course. During the first term that the course was offered, the students were excited and engaged in the work. They began to question why they were not gaining English department credit for the rigorous academic work. By the second term that the course was offered, the students urged Ms. Barber-Just to appeal for English credit on their behalf. It did not seem fair to them that they were reading five major novels, producing high-level writing, attending all the classes, and yet not being awarded department credit. After reviewing the syllabus and the impressive academic accomplishments of the students in the class, the English department voted unanimously to award English department credit for the course.

A vote by the school board was needed to add a new class to the program of studies. Ms. Barber-Just compiled portfolios of student work to be reviewed by the school board. The student portfolios included analytical and reflective writing about the five major units of study and the accompanying five books, short stories, poetry, essays, films, and course discussions. The board approved the addition of the course to the official English department's study program.

Student Voices   The literary products in the student portfolios were superior by many standards. The knowledge of historical events, social influences on literature, and writing techniques that they reflected were remarkable. But the most compelling facet of the students' work was the consistency with which they mentioned the power of giving voice to unspoken realities. Students wrote about their own biases and their own sexual orientations: gay, straight, and bisexual. They reflected on the importance of this course to support LGBT and questioning youth and build understanding among heterosexual teens. They spoke of lack of information about the LGBT community and critiqued the misinformation of the mass media. Consistently, student reflections mentioned the safety of their classroom community and their commitment to be engaged in social justice. In some of the most moving pieces, students wrote their reflections in the form of letters to their parents.

EVOLUTION OF CURRICULUM

Multicultural curriculum is a process, as we described in Chapter 3; it grows organically along with the needs and struggles of the community. This is true of the Gay and Lesbian Literature course launched by Ms. Barber-Just. In response to student demands, the school added an extra section of the course each year. Moreover, advanced placement recognition (AP credit) may now be achieved through the Gay and Lesbian Literature course. What started out as an independent study offering became socially sanctioned knowledge—a school course—as English department credit, and optional AP credit, through the determination of high school students and the courage of a teacher.

One teacher and her students could not have made these changes in isolation, however. As Christine Sleeter points out, "While teachers have varying degrees of agency to construct multicultural curriculum, teachers also work in systems that institutionalize particular concepts of curriculum, learning, teaching and relationships."[30] While maintaining high academic standards, a stalwart department chair, a supportive principal, and ultimately a visionary school board recognized the needs of a community and acted with resolve to reshape the school curriculum, which continues to become more just and inclusive.

The Gay and Lesbian Literature course reflects the needs and identities of students and families in the immediate community of the school, including LGBT and their straight allies. Perhaps more significantly, the curriculum is responding to the urgency of nation-wide social change. Melinda Miceli's statement affirms this reality: "Today, LGBT and straight ally students are in a position to imagine the possibilities of change that they can accomplish by capitalizing on the progress made by the gay rights movement."[31] The "imagined possibilities of change" accomplished by Sara Barber-Just with so many students, families, colleagues, administrators, and school board members provides a model of fierce hopefulness in the ongoing process of making school curriculum—and society—more changeable.

RESOURCES FOR TEACHING ABOUT EXPANDING DEFINITIONS OF FAMILY

These resources are divided into three categories: early childhood, middle school, and high school.

Children's Literature Resources for Early Childhood*

Combs, Bobbie, *ABC: A Family Alphabet Book* (Ridley Park, PA: Two Lives, 2001).

de Haan, Lisa, *King and King* (Berkeley, CA: Tricycle Press, 2002).

Elwin, Rosamund, and Michele Plause, *Asha's Mums* (London, England: Women's Press, 2000).

Garden, Nancy, *Molly's Family* (New York: Farrar, Straus and Giroux, 2004).

Hoffman, Eric, *Best Colors/Los Mejores Colores* (St. Paul, MN: Redleaf Press, 1999).

Newman, Leslea, *Felicia's Favorite Story* (Ridley Park, PA: Two Lives, 2002).

Newman, Leslea, and Diana Souza, *Heather Has Two Mommies* (Boston: Alyson Publications, 2000).

Parr, Todd, *The Family Book* (New York: Little, Brown Young Readers, 2003).

Richardson, Justin, and Peter Parnell, *And Tango Makes Three* (New York: Simon & Schuster, 2005).

Setterington, Ken, *Mom and Mum Are Getting Married* (Toronto, Canada: Second Story Press, 2004).

Simon, Norma, *All Families Are Special* (Morton Grove, IL: Albert Whitman, 2003).

Skutch, Robert, *Who's in a Family?* (Berkeley, CA: Tricycle Press, 1997).

Valentine, Johnny, *The Duke Who Outlawed Jelly Beans and Other Stories* (Boston: Alyson Publication, 2004).

Wickens, Elaine, *Anna Day and the O-Ring* (Boston: Alyson Publications, 1994).

*Special thanks to Nancy Alach from Cambridge Friends School in Cambridge, MA, for this suggested bibliography of children's literature.

Resources Used in the Middle School Curriculum

Beard, Jean J., Peggy Gillespie, Kay Redfield Jamison, Kenneth, Duckworth, and Gigi Kaeser, *Nothing to Hide: Mental Illness in the Family* (New York: New Press, 2002).

Gillespie, Peggy, and Gigi Kaeser, *Of Many Colors: Portraits of Multiracial Families* (Amherst: University of Massachusetts Press, 1997).

Kaeser, Gigi, and Peggy Gillespie, *Love Makes a Family: Portraits of Lesbian, Gay, Bisexual and Transgender Parents and Their Families* (Amherst: University of Massachusetts Press, 1999).

Kaeser, Gigi, and Peggy Gillespie, *In Our Family: Portraits of all Kinds of Families* (with Curriculum Guide). (Amherst, MA: Family Diversity Projects, 2003).

Rohmer, Harriet, ed., *Honoring Our Ancestors: Stories and Pictures by Fourteen Artists* (San Francisco: Children's Book Press, 1999).

Rohmer, Harriet, ed., *Just Like Me: Stories and Self-Portraits by Fourteen Artists* (San Francisco: Children's Book Press, 1997).

Film and Literature Resources Used in the High School Gay and Lesbian Literature Course

Baldwin, James, *Giovanni's Room* (New York: Dial, 1956).

Brown, Rita Mae, *Rubyfruit Jungle* (Plainfield, VT: Daughters Inc., 1973).

Cather, Willa, *A Lost Lady* (New York: Alfred A. Knopf, 1923).

Cunningham, Michael, *The Hours* (New York: Farrar, Straus and Giroux, 1998).

Far from Heaven, Dir. Todd Haynes, 2002.

Forster, E. M., *Maurice* (New York: Norton, 1971).

(continued)

Ma Vie en Rose, Dir. Alain Berliner, 1997.

Shyam Selvadurai, *Funny Boy* (Harvest Books, 1997).

The Celluloid Closet, Dir. Rob Epstein and Jeffrey Friedman, 1995.

The Trial of Oscar Wilde, Dir. Ken Hughes, 1960.

Woolf, Virginia, *Mrs. Dalloway* (Richmond, England: Hogarth Press, 1925).

◆◆◆ To Think About

1. What is the difference between discussing the facts and descriptions of current events in the classroom and cultivating a critical perspective on the power structures that surround current events? Consider these two approaches in the context of a current event in the news this week.

2. When you hear a student use the word *gay* as a put down (or pejorative term sometimes invoked to insult LGBT identity), what is your response? What does that student learn from your response? What do other students learn from your response? How can you make it a teachable moment about vocabulary, human rights, and courage?

3. Many school structures that divide students by so-called ability appear to be impenetrable to a single teacher's efforts. If such structures are in place in your school, how can you adapt your curriculum to challenge those structures? Do you have to do it alone? What will be the long-term effects of the changes you make to your approach, your classroom, and your curriculum?

4. When students name racism that they see in society, mass media, curricular materials, or the school hallways, how do you respond? How can you affirm and make student voices audible while cultivating a classroom discussion around social justice in which all students feel welcome to participate?

5. Do you call on families to participate in the curriculum? When does it happen? Is it around holiday celebrations? Heritage festivals? How can you expand the role of families in your classroom while including and honoring the families who may not be able to participate in school activities?

◆◆◆ Activities for Personal, School, and Community Change

1. Study the demographics of your classroom, your grade level, your team, or your school. Think about students' heritages and cultural backgrounds. Take note of a specific group about which you may have little knowledge or experience and commit to implementing some curriculum about it. How might you create a unit of study to deepen the understanding of this group's experience? How can you do this in such a way that does not "exoticize" the group or create greater isolation for the members of that group? The teachers of the unit about Cambodia started by educating themselves; they also realized that they would learn more by diving in, researching, and teaching with their students. Where will you begin in your own

classroom? Draw in colleagues for support, co-teaching, content integration, and expansion of this idea.

2. Many teachers are challenged by the notion of implementing multicultural curriculum in the current standards-based climate. Start a teacher book-discussion group based on Christine Sleeter's book *Un-Standardizing Curriculum: Multicultural Teaching in the Standards-Based Classroom* (see note 18). Ask your principal, superintendent, curriculum director or PTO to purchase the books. Meet at least once a month throughout the school year with the end goal of each teacher designing a new unit, or re-designing a former curriculum unit with their fresh ideas inspired by Sleeter's practical, yet revolutionary approach.

3. LGBT identity continues to be a target of institutional and personal oppression. Collaborate with colleagues to make your school a "safe zone" for LGBT students and their families. Collect resources from GLSEN and PFLAG (see appendix) and create an action plan in your school for students to feel affirmed and protected. Educate yourself, colleagues, students, and administrators. Plan curriculum and community events to welcome, affirm and express solidarity with LGBT students, family and communities members.

 # Companion Website

For access to additional case studies, weblinks, concept cards, and other material related to this chapter, visit the text's companion website at **www.ablongman.com/nieto5e**.

Notes to Chapter 10

1. We would like to thank the teachers of Amherst Regional Middle School, Amherst, Massachusetts: Margarita Bonifaz, Sarah Lange Hayes, Gale Kuhn, Lynn Podesek, Sokhen P. Mao, Paul Plummer, and Maura Neverson, whose work and dedication made this unit of study about Cambodia a success for all of their students. Patty also worked on this curriculum team as the art teacher.

2. Ronnie J. Booxbaum, PhD, and Sokhen P. Mao, MEd, developed this staff development course and wrote a handbook to accompany it.

3. Loung Ung, *First They Killed My Father* (New York: HarperCollins, 2000).

4. See Luong Ung, *Lucky Child: A Daughter of Cambodia Reunites with the Sister She Left Behind* (New York: HarperCollins, 2000) and Molyda Szymusiak, Jane Hamilton-Merritt (translator), and Linda Coverdale, *The Stones Cry Out: A Cambodian Childhood, 1975–1980* (Bloomington: Indiana University Press, 1999).

5. Grant Wiggins and Jay McTighe, *Understanding by Design*, 2nd ed. (Alexandria, VA: Association for Supervision and Curriculum Development (ASCD), 2005).

6. Bill Bigelow, Brenda Harvey, Stan Karp, and Larry Miller, eds., *Rethinking Our Classrooms: Teaching for Equity and Justice*, vol. 2 (Milwaukee, WI: Rethinking Schools, 2001).

7. The Cambodian Masters Program supports revival of the traditional art forms of Cambodia and inspires contemporary artistic expression. They have visiting artists, lecturers, and performances. Available at: www.cambodianmasters.org/masters/index.htm

8. The Angkor Dance Troupe helps Cambodian young people navigate the balance between contemporary youth culture and their cultural heritage. See www.angkordance.org

9. *Monkey Dance* is a documentary film by Julie Mallozzi about three teens coming of age in Lowell, Massachusetts. See www.monkey-dance.com/ and www.juliemallozzi.com/monkey.html

10. The Peace Pagoda Nipponzan Myohoji Sangha Buddhist temple was created as a collaborative effort by Vietnam Veterans Against the War and

the Cambodian American Community. See www.peacepagoda.org

11. See the Resources for Teaching About Cambodia at the end of this case study, which includes many of the folktales that Margarita Bonifaz used in this unit.

12. Peter Menzel, Charles C. Mann, and Paul Kennedy, *Material World: A Global Family Portrait* (San Francisco: Sierra Club Books, 1995).

13. We are grateful to Michael Hayes for being so generous with his time to help us create this case study. Michael recently left the classroom and became a co-principal at Amherst Regional Middle School, Amherst, Massachusetts.

14. See National Council of Teachers of Mathematics (NCTM) at www.nctm.org. Also see Jeannie Oakes, *Keeping Track: How Schools Structure Inequality*, 2nd ed. (New Haven, CT: Yale University Press, 2005).

15. Robert Moses and Charles Cobb, *Radical Equations: Civil Rights from Mississippi to the Algebra Project* (Boston: Beacon Press, 2002).

16. We are grateful for Alan Dallmann's role in the transformation of this curriculum and in this case study.

17. We are grateful to Blanca Zelaya for her critical role in the math curriculum and the development of this case study.

18. Bobbie Combs and Dannamarie Hosler, illus., *1,2,3: A Family Counting Book* (Ridley Park, PA: Two Lives, 2001).

19. Leslea Newman and Diana Souza, Illustrator, *Heather Has Two Mommies* (Boston: Alyson, 2000).

20. GLSEN (Gay, Lesbian, Straight Education Network) is a national organization working to end anti-gay biases in schools. The group is striving to assure that each member of every school community is valued and respected regardless of sexual orientation or gender identity/expression. GLSEN's website (www.glsen.org) has innumerable resources for teachers of students of all ages.

21. Ellen Bigler, *American Conversations: Puerto Ricans, White Ethnics and Multicultural Education* (Philadelphia: Temple University Press, 1999).

22. Louise Derman-Sparks, *Teaching/Learning Anti-Racism: A Developmental Approach* (New York: Teachers College Press, 1997).

23. Val Penniman and Debbie Shumway's "Calendar-Connections," which helps teach critical thinking in a classroom curriculum, may be found at www.calendar-connections.com

24. Harriet Rohmer, ed., *Honoring Our Ancestors: Stories and Pictures by Fourteen Artists* (San Francisco: Children's Book Press, 1999).

25. Family Diversity Projects is a nonprofit organization co-founded by Peggy Gillespie and Gigi Kaeser. It produces and circulates photo-text exhibits to educate people about the many facets of diversity. The exhibits tour nationally and internationally. See www.familydiv.org

26. We are grateful to the teachers who developed this curriculum and gave it their heartfelt attentions for three years at Amherst Regional Middle School. They are Beth Adel Wohlleb, social studies teacher; Phil Covelli and Gale Kuhn, science teachers; Mari Hall, health teacher; Esther Haskell, English teacher; and Robert Lord, math teacher. Dr. John Raible worked as a consultant on the curriculum. Patty worked as an art teacher with the team. Also, Kristen French provided feedback with a critical multicultural perspective for the unit.

27. Linda Christensen, *Reading, Writing and Rising Up* (Milwaukee: Rethinking Schools, 2000).

28. We are grateful to Sara Barber-Just for her inspiring contributions to the field of high school English language arts teaching, and for the time she spent helping us to develop this case study.

29. Sara Barber-Just, "Curriculum Proposal for Amherst Regional High School" 2001.

30. Sleeter, *Un-Standardizing Curriculum: Multicultural Teaching in the Standards-Based Classroom*, 179.

31. Melinda Miceli, *Standing Out, Standing Together: The Social and Political Impact of Gay-Straight Alliances* (New York: Routledge, 2005): 12.

11

Affirming Diversity: Implications for Teachers, Schools, and Families

Sedrick Gary, in Julie Sawyer's art class. *Self-portrait*. Acrylic painting and photograph, 2005.

"I think [teachers] could help students, try to influence them, that they can do whatever they want to do, that they can be whatever they want to be, that they got opportunities out there. . . . Most schools don't encourage kids to be all they can be."

—*Manuel Gomes (interviewee, Chapter 7)*

In spite of the fact that Manuel Gomes, whose case study appears at the end of Chapter 7, came from a large immigrant family that was struggling to make ends meet and survive in a new country, he had great faith in education. The youngest of 11 siblings, he was the first to graduate from high school. Manuel was facing the future with determination and hope. His story can serve as a lesson that students who live in even the most difficult circumstances can succeed academically. In particular, the above statement that Manuel made during his interview speaks volumes:

The case studies and snapshots you have read provide concrete evidence that academic success and failure defy easy categorization and the conventional expectations that teachers, schools, and society may have of students from particular backgrounds. The experiences of these young people also point to specific conditions in home, school, community, and societal contexts that may contribute to learning. In reality, students do not achieve academic success on their own, but in conjunction with family, peers, teachers, schools, and society. This being the case, in this chapter we return to the themes discussed in Chapter 9, with an eye toward understanding how supportive learning environments can be promoted. This chapter also considers what it means to be an American and suggests a model of multicultural education that emerges from the seven characteristics defined in Chapter 3.

LESSONS FROM STUDENTS: MAINTAINING AND AFFIRMING IDENTITY

The racism and other forms of discrimination to which students are subjected in school and society are evident in several of the case studies. Discrimination is either overt—for example, when Kaval Sethi felt singled out for wearing a turban—or more subtle, as when James Karam's culture was invisible in school activities or as Gamini Padmaperuma had felt intimidated about speaking Singhalese in public when he was younger. Rashaud Kates, Nini Rostland, and Latrell Elton expressed the weight of low expectations felt by many African American and multiracial students. Yet, in spite of overpowering and sometimes demoralizing attitudes, behaviors, policies, and practices, most of these students chose not to deny or abandon their culture or language. Instead, they tended to rely on them even more firmly, although with more nuanced and dynamic ideas about identity, and not necessarily in the school setting. These young people's reliance on their native culture and language may shield them from the devaluation of their identities by schools and society.

A few of the students had supportive school environments that accepted and built on their identities. In Savoun's case, teachers in his elementary schools supported his language through what he called *culture lessons*. Manuel felt that his bilingual program was an oasis of cultural support. Liane felt supported by her school in her effort to learn Chinese, her mother's native language. Their experiences reinforce the findings of extensive research by Alejandro Portes and Rubén Rumbaut that a pervasive and positive sense of cultural heritage is unmistakably related to mental health and social well-being.[1] Therefore, the first lesson for schools would seem to be that bilingual and multicultural programs must become integral to the learning environment.

SUPPORTING NATIVE LANGUAGE APPROACHES

Bilingual education has been a vital part of the educational landscape in the United States for nearly four decades. In spite of growing linguistic diversity, however, approaches that use students' native languages have always been accompanied by great controversy, as we saw in Chapter 7. During the past several years, negative attitudes about bilingual education on the part of the general public have resulted in ballot questions in several states that have eliminated these programs. Too often, also, if bilingual programs survive political contempt, they have been relegated, metaphorically speaking, to the space next to the boiler room in the basement or to large unused closets.[2] In addition, bilingual teachers have been segregated programmatically and physically from other staff, making both teachers and students feel isolated from the school community.

There needs to be a rethinking of the place for native-language use for language-minority students. Promoting students' native language—whether through bilingual or ELL programs, or even in nonbilingual settings in which teachers encourage students to use it among their peers and in their learning in general—helps make language-minority students visible and respected in the school environment. Valuing their language made a difference for the young people in our case studies and snapshots, as they mentioned time and again. Some ways in which teachers and schools can support students for whom English is not a native language include the following:

- Encouraging parents to use the native language at home, by both speaking and reading it to their children
- Allowing students to work in same-language groups for some cooperative learning activities
- Encouraging students to use words in their native language when they don't know the equivalent word in English and to explain what they mean
- Asking students who are English Language Learners to teach other students some of their home language
- Making multilingual word charts in the classroom of commonly used words and phrases such as *pencil, crayon, book, please,* and *thank you* and asking students to list translations from their home language
- Encouraging and allowing students to use their native language in the classroom and on the playground and school grounds
- Promoting the learning of second languages among teachers by providing language classes in the school[3]

Where bilingual programs are available, students who do not yet speak English and those who are most proficient in a language other than English should have first priority for placement in these programs. But students from homes where a language other than English is spoken, even if they themselves seem fluent in

SNAPSHOT

David Weiss

When he was interviewed, David Weiss was 13 years old and a student in middle school. Adopted from Chile by a White Jewish family in the United States when he was just a few months old, he talked about what it meant to be adopted, biethnic, and bicultural. David was from the Mount Puche tribe of Native Americans, and he identified as Latino. He spoke English as his native language and learned to read Hebrew for his recent bar mitzvah. He wanted to learn Spanish, which he planned to take in school the next year because, as he said, "I was born in Chile, and I should know Spanish." David described some of the dilemmas and complexities of his hybrid identity.

My birth mother left a letter for me, which I have in the bank. I saw a picture of her. She said she didn't have enough money to raise two children and couldn't take care of me. That's why I was adopted.

Most people don't recognize me as Latino or Native American. They think I'm American and White. In looks, I am White, but inside, no. My blood is Chilean and Native American.

A teacher at school told me about another boy who's also from Chile and also adopted. Now we're friends. At first, I was surprised. It's kind of a coincidence, because we were in Santiago at the same time. At first I didn't tell him I was from Chile. I got to know him, and then I told him. He said I didn't look like it. We used to talk about being adopted.

Most people know I'm adopted. I tell them. People think I look different from my mom. People notice my older brother's color more than mine. [His brother, also adopted, is darker.] One time in Health class, the teacher asked kids if they had any stories about their birth. Most kids had something to say. I didn't—I wouldn't share it, anyway.... Well, it depends.

If I could, I would join a school club for adopted kids and for different racial people. That way, I'd know more adopted people.

COMMENTARY

David's snapshot presents a poignant example of the dilemmas inherent in issues of both hybrid identities and adoption. For example, David was clear about the fact that race and ethnicity are not so easy to determine. He said that what he looks like is not necessarily what he is inside. This is an important insight for teachers to remember and understand, and it is especially crucial in the case of adopted children, who may not have any information about their ethnic backgrounds or birth parents. David's statement that he would join a school club for adopted kids if there were one is a reminder that not all school clubs should be based on ethnicity, race, or hobbies. Having a place to "belong" is a need for all young people.

English, should also be given the opportunity to participate. The seeming conversational English fluency of some students often misleads teachers into believing that they can handle the academic rigors of cognitively demanding work in English. This is not always the case. For example, a major finding of researchers K. Tsianina Lomawaima and Teresa McCarty on Navajo bilingual programs found that students in grades K–6 who had the benefit of cumulative, uninterrupted initial literacy experiences in the Navajo language made the greatest gains on local and national measures of achievement.[4]

The case studies and snapshots make abundantly clear the positive results of maintaining native-language fluency in promoting the academic success of students, but bilingualism is also a worthy goal on its own and a valuable resource that should be supported. Doing away with precisely the kinds of programs needed in a society with growing linguistic and cultural diversity and international interdependence is foolhardy at best. Certainly, the events of September 11, 2001, and the United States war on Iraq are powerful reminders that we live in a global context and need to understand people in the international community. Language is one significant way to achieve this understanding. Thus, space and funds permitting, monolingual speakers of English can and should also be included in bilingual programs. As discussed in Chapter 7, a growing body of research on two-way programs, in which English speakers and speakers of another language are integrated in one classroom and learn both languages, confirms that these programs are a powerful way for both groups to develop bilingualism and favorable attitudes toward diversity.

DEVELOPING COMPREHENSIVE MULTICULTURAL PROGRAMS

Another key lesson from the case studies and snapshots is that multicultural education should be an integral part of the school experience of all students. This is not to imply that the interviewed students themselves recommended multicultural education. On the contrary, if they mentioned it at all, it was usually in the context of fairs, cookbooks, or other more superficial aspects and was certainly not in the comprehensive way it has been defined in this text. The students were generally unaware of what multicultural education might be if it were approached more comprehensively and of how it could help them. When students are asked specifically about addressing diversity in the schools, however, they tend to be supportive of such efforts. For instance, a survey concerning multiculturalism conducted among almost 2,500 middle and high school students found that a majority were interested in learning more about cultural differences. Among those who were dissatisfied with the extent to which they were learning about multiculturalism in the school, most wanted their school to place more emphasis on it rather than less.[5] In the same way, the yearning in the voices of the students in our case studies and snapshots make it clear that they wanted closer connections with their cultural identities, from Rebecca Florentina's gratitude for some of her teachers' support of the Gay/Straight Alliance (GSA) in her school, to Savoun Nouch's wish for continued "reading groups" in his language, to the case of David Weiss, whose snapshot follows. David longed to learn Spanish, the language of his ancestry.

Multicultural education can help new students adjust to the community and school and can also address issues of interethnic prejudice and hostility that are not new to most schools. With the influx of large numbers of new immigrants, and with few appropriate programs to prepare either communities or schools for them, the problem is becoming more serious. Students' lack of understanding of cultures different from their own, the preconceptions about diverse groups of people they and their families may have brought from other countries, their internalizing of the negative ways in which differences are treated in our society, and the lack of information provided in the schools all serve to magnify the problem. Add to this the peck-ing order established in schools among different social and cultural groups and the general reluctance of schools to deal with such knotty issues, and we are left with unresolved but unremitting interethnic hostility.[6] This was poignantly illustrated by Savoun's descriptions of the violent racial tensions at his former school and his astonishment at the absence of gangs and feuding among racial groups at his new school.

A growing body of research on multicultural education suggests that only by reforming the entire school environment can substantive changes in attitudes, behaviors, and achievement take place.[7] Most schools have not undertaken such a comprehensive approach. When they do, they find that they need to modify the school culture itself. As a result, they may include in their plans such strategies as conflict resolution, cooperative learning, multicultural curriculum development, parent and community involvement, and the elimination of tracking. Such a comprehensive approach is necessary but also fraught with difficulty because it challenges traditions and ideologies that are at the very heart of schooling in the United States.

SUPPORT BEYOND ACADEMICS

When young people are involved in meaningful activities outside of an academic context, whether in the school or community or in a combination of activities, including school clubs and sports, religious groups, and out-of-school hobbies, they find support that helps protect them from negative peer pressure and helps develop and reinforce their leadership and critical thinking skills. What are the implications of this kind of involvement for schools and communities?

INCLUSIVE AND MEANINGFUL ACTIVITIES

All schools, but particularly those at the secondary level, need to provide inclusive and meaningful activities that attract a wide range of students. Given the renewed emphasis on "the basics" that resulted from the educational reform movement that began in the 1980s and continues today, many schools drastically cut or eliminated arts programs and minimized extracurricular activities. Some reforms, particularly those focusing on "raising standards"—such as longer school days and fewer so-called frills such as music and art—have been felt most profoundly at schools serving economically deprived and culturally marginalized students. The negative results of eliminating arts programs in urban schools in the most economically strapped communities have been thoroughly documented in the reported results of Jonathan Kozol's research.[8] Also, in an edited volume about the critical and necessary role of the arts, Nick Rabkin and Robin Redmond advance the explicit connection of arts education to all other school subject areas and to academic achievement. Rabkin, Redmond, and their colleagues call for an urgent reinvestment of resources and development of policies that recognize the arts as integral to effective education and school improvement.[9]

Some schools that cut arts education from the school day attempt to add arts activities to extracurricular and after-school programs. Even in schools that provide extracurricular activities, a majority of students are not involved; this is so for many reasons, ranging from lack of funds to schedule conflicts. For example, some sports programs, although presumably open to all, are in effect restricted to the students most able to afford them. Other programs meet after school and, because they provide no transportation, are available only to those who can get home on their own or who can rely on family or friends for transportation. Students who work after school are also unable to take part in these activities. In some cases, extracurricular activities reflect only one culture or language—although that may not be the intent of the programs—leading students of other backgrounds to perceive that they are not welcome. For example, Cambodian students who are interested in joining the soccer team may feel excluded because there are no other Cambodian students on the team, or Mexican American students in a bilingual program may want to work on the school newspaper but may not even attempt to join if the newspaper is written entirely in English.

The main issue here is equal access. A school may claim that its activities are open to all students, but a policy statement is meaningless unless backed up in practice. Equal conditions of participation need to be established for all students. For instance, if a sports program is costly because of the required equipment, it is reasonable for the school to provide such equipment for those who cannot afford it. The same is true of transportation. If some students are excluded from participating in activities because they do not have the same opportunity as others to get home from school, alternative means of transportation must be provided. There is also something seriously wrong if the newspaper staff in a culturally pluralistic school consists of only European American students. In these cases, broad-based and intentional recruitment of a diversity of students is necessary. This can be done not only by posting announcements but also by making more earnest efforts to involve previously uninvolved students, such as making announcements in every language spoken in the school, delivering special invitations to students during homeroom, having students from various backgrounds involved in the recruiting program, and providing alternative meaningful activities. For the newspaper, for instance, a project in which students interview their families and neighbors concerning a particular issue of importance to the community might be the incentive. Providing help to translate articles into English and promoting the publication of some articles in languages other than English would also help.

Schools could do a lot more to embrace the interests and experiences of their students than they currently do. Students may be involved in many activities that influence their learning and could contribute to their peers' school lives. For example, studying for a bat mitzvah, caring for a family member with disabilities, rehearsing for a community play, singing in a faith-community choir, and working a part-time job are activities that could be shared in the classroom as part of the curriculum. Cultivating experiences, both during school and after school, that reveal student strengths may support student attachment and engagement while contributing to the whole learning community. Looking for ways in which students can make their voices heard is more likely to result in the participation of a broader range of young people. Neglecting these opportunities will result in the continuation of segregated and restricted school activities.

IMPLICATIONS FOR FAMILIES AND COMMUNITIES

Families and communities also have a responsibility to provide meaningful outlets for young people. This responsibility is carried out by families, for example, when they give their children chores at home. Having family responsibilities can help students in classroom situations that require behaviors such as diligence, independence, and commitment. As exemplified in the first grade curriculum about family described in Chapter 10, even the youngest family members can make meaningful contributions. Teachers can encourage parents to give their children jobs at home and then support them when they do.

Communities can use the creative energy and enthusiasm of young people by including them in volunteer work at elementary schools or day care centers, work with the elderly, or activities in social service agencies. Opportunities for after-school community service can be provided in much more meaningful ways than they currently are. Through community service, students can develop their cognitive abilities, cooperative team-mindedness, leadership and research skills, and critical thinking, especially because many of them are genuinely interested in, and concerned about, the issues affecting their communities. A moving example of such concern is evident in research reported by Mavis Sanders and Adia Harvey. They describe how one urban elementary school developed strong connections with community businesses and organizations as part of its program of school, family, and community partnerships. Through observations and interviews with the principal, parents, students in grades 3, 4, and 5, and community partners such as businesses, places of worship, private foundations and health care institutions, they developed a case study of successful school-community partnerships. They point to the essential role of the principal's leadership and the school's initiative by identifying four factors that built successful bridges to the school's community: the school's commitment to learning; the principal's support and vision for community involvement; the school's receptivity and openness to community involvement; and the school's willingness to engage in two–way communication with potential community partners about their level and kind of involvement.[10] Other research focusing on secondary students engaged in activism and community change is documented by Ernest Morrell, who described a summer institute where Los Angeles teens were apprenticed as critical researchers to carry out research projects in urban schools and communities. Morrell demonstrates how the students researched the conditions of Los Angeles area schools by using the Educational Bill of Rights and a school accountability Report Card as assessment tools. The student research findings led to structural changes in policy, beneficial relations with the community, and a transformative experience for the youth.[11]

DEVELOPING ENVIRONMENTS FOR SUCCESS

The students in our case studies and snapshots sought and participated in environments in which they would fit in. These environments can be positive, as in the case of Yahaira Leon's work with the Mock Trial Club that led to her summer engagement in the Junior Statesman Foundation, or the GSA for Rebecca, or they can be negative, as in the case of gang involvement for Savoun and Paul Chavez. There are several implications concerning what schools and families can do to provide positive environments that promote the achievement of all students. The following section explores what educational researchers have called *mutual accommodation*.[12]

MUTUAL ACCOMMODATION

A key question teachers and schools must ask themselves in their interactions with students—particularly those from diverse racial, ethnic, and linguistic backgrounds—is this: *Who does the accommodating?* This question gets to the very heart of how students from nondominant groups experience school every day. Unlike students from nondominant groups, dominant-group students rarely have to consider learning a new language to communicate with their teachers because they already speak the acceptable school language. The same is true of culture. Dominant-group students generally do not have to think about their parents' lifestyles and values because their families are the norm, as was seen in Vanessa Mattison's case. Students from other groups, however, have to consider such issues every single day.

Some accommodation is, of course, necessary. If students and teachers spoke different languages at all times, operated under different goals and assumptions, and in general had varying expectations from the schools, chaos would result. Students from nondominant groups and their families always expect to make some accommodations, which is clear in their willingness to learn English, their eagerness to participate in school life, and their general agreement with the rules of the game implicit in their social contract with the schools.

But when does accommodation become acquiescence? The problem is that usually *only* students from nondominant groups and their families are asked or forced to do the accommodating, as pointed out by Irma M. Olmedo's interviews of Puerto Rican and Mexican mothers and grandmothers regarding their children's schooling in low-income high-crime neighborhoods in Chicago. The Latina participants in her study confronted many cultural conflicts with the expectations of North American institutions, especially schools. An important theme that emerged was the concept of *respeto*—in particular how the women defined it, the importance they attached to it, and the conflicts that arose in their efforts to pass these values onto the new generation. Yet, Olmeda found that these women constructed new identities and modes of behavior that included *accommodation and resistance*. Their strategies of resistance demarcated the private sphere, or the home, from the public sphere, or the school.

Olmeda argues that accommodation and resistance are not dichotomous phenomena but rather are interwoven strategies developed "in response to the challenges of raising children in a different cultural environment and from a precarious social position. What may appear to be accommodation to mainstream expectations is also accompanied by resistance, a strategy for creating a space where familial values can be supported and nourished."[13]

Hence, although nonmainstream students acknowledge the need to do some accommodating, they also recognize the benefits that accompany the affirmation of their languages and cultures. A good example comes from a study by Steven K. Lee in which he surveyed 280 Latino students in seven urban middle schools in Southern California. All the students were enrolled in bilingual classes, including Spanish maintenance and sheltered classes, and the majority of students surveyed "supported the use of two languages in the classroom, hoped to develop fluency in two languages, and thought that bilingual education facilitated their educational experience and helped to increase their cognitive and emotional well-being."[14]

How can we address this issue of who does the accommodating? In their early research on this question—research that is worth remembering in the present anti-bilingual education context—Estéban Stephan Díaz, Luis Moll, and Hugh Mehan found that when teachers used the social and linguistic resources of their Mexican American students, they helped their students learn. In reading, teachers coordinated aspects of English reading lessons by using both English and Spanish in the classroom. Rather than focusing on which language was used, teachers made comprehension their lessons' primary goal, and what previously had been a painful and slow process for students was transformed into a successful learning environment. The result was a three-year leap forward in English reading skills. Similar findings were reported in a writing group. The researchers concluded that a model of "mutual accommodation" is called for. That is, teachers and schools, as well as students, need to modify their behaviors in the direction of a common goal: "academic success with cultural integrity."[15]

The lesson for teachers and schools is that contrary to conventional wisdom and practice, it is not students and their families who must always do the accommodating. The misguided belief in one-way accommodation explains the tendency among educators to view unsuccessful students as either genetically inferior or culturally deprived. When students do not automatically accommodate to the school (or other) system, their intelligence or ability or that of their families or communities is questioned. The perspective of mutual accommodation allows schools and teachers to use the resources all students already have to work toward academic success. In this model, neither the student nor the teacher expects complete accommodation. Rather they work together, using the best strategies at the disposition of each. In the process of mutual accommodation, teachers and students are equally enriched. Using students' language, identities, and experiences as the basis for student learning might mean that teachers have to expand their own repertoires of teaching. Doing so is an advantage for everyone. For example, using various communication styles can result in all students becoming more flexible in their learning. Reorganizing the social structure of classrooms can facilitate significant improvements in prosocial development, academic achievement, and interethnic relations. Even students' attitudes and behaviors toward one another can be influenced in a positive way. Moreover, providing alternative means for learning is an essentially equitable endeavor, and it strengthens the democratic purposes of schooling.

For schools and teachers, mutual accommodation means accepting and building on students' language, culture, and family knowledge as legitimate expressions of intelligence and as the basis for learning. For students and families, mutual accommodation means accepting the culture of the school in areas such as expectations about attendance and homework and learning the necessary skills for academic achievement. Through this process, students, their families, teachers, and schools all benefit. Students and their families, while being respected and accepted, can proceed with learning. At the same time, teachers expand their teaching skills and their way of looking at both ability and intelligence.

TEACHERS' RELATIONSHIPS WITH STUDENTS

Most teachers enter the teaching profession because of a profound belief in young people and an eagerness to help them learn. However, many obstacles—including a lack of respect for teachers, teachers' limited power, unresponsive administrators, classes that are too large, and the challenges of reaching students from a dizzying variety of backgrounds—make teaching a very difficult job indeed. In spite of these challenges, developing healthy relationships with students is one way to maintain the hope and joy that drew teachers to education in the first place.

Students in our case studies talked at length about teachers who made a difference in their attitudes about school and their engagement with learning. Sometimes these teachers were from the same racial or ethnic background as the students themselves. Linda Howard spoke emphatically about the support she got from both her first grade teacher, who was Black, and Mr. Benson, who was "mixed" like her. Given the general invisibility of many students' cultures and languages in the school environment, this kind of connection is healthy. One implication for schools is that more teachers who share the cultural background of students must be recruited.

Teachers from students' racial, cultural, and ethnic backgrounds can make a significant contribution to the school, enriching both the environment and the curriculum, but an undue burden is placed on these teachers when they are seen as the representative of their entire racial, ethnic, or linguistic group. Not only are they expected to be role models for students, but also they are increasingly called on to solve problems of cultural misunderstanding, translate letters, visit homes, begin the school's multicultural committee, and so on—usually with no extra compensation or recognition. The situation not only is unfair to these teachers but also may result in absolving the school of responsibility for meeting the needs of all its students. Schools have an obligation to aggressively recruit teachers who are as diverse as the student body, but this is something that, until now, has not been given national priority. When faculty members are from a variety of cultural backgrounds and are multilingual, students are more likely to perceive the significance of intellectual pursuits in their own lives. Nevertheless, all teachers, regardless of background, need to develop skills in multicultural communication and understanding. Their cultural knowledge and awareness, and their curricular and instructional accommodations, can make a major difference in student learning and engagement.

All teachers can become role models for all students as long as they are caring and knowledgeable about their students. One way in which teachers can build substantial relationships with students is by offering help to those who do not seek their aid. This issue arose numerous times during our interviews for the case studies. The number of students who had absolutely no guidance in school was astonishing. For students who are the first in their families to go to college, such help is indispensable because their families often have no prior experience from which to draw in guiding their children. Students who are most vulnerable in terms of having access to college frequently receive the least help in schools, even when they are successful and have high aspirations for continued schooling. Research has confirmed the significance of teachers' support of their students' aspirations and goals. In a study using longitudinal data of a cohort of 11,000 adolescents, Robert Croninger and Valerie Lee investigated the benefits of teachers' guidance and support for students at risk for dropping out of high school. The researchers concluded that positive relations with teachers reduce the odds of dropping out, as do informal interactions with teachers outside the classroom. Even more significant, Croninger and Lee found that such guidance was especially crucial for students who have a history of difficulties at school. They concluded, "When adolescents trust their teachers and informally receive guidance from teachers, they are more likely to persist through graduation."[16]

The detrimental role that low expectations play in the school achievement of students, particularly those from nondominant groups, was reviewed in Chapter 4. The young people in our case studies and snapshots frequently pointed this out as a problem in their classrooms and schools. They said that they and their classmates were treated like babies; that the work teachers gave them was undemanding; and that any work, no matter how poor, was accepted. The attitude that students are incapable of performing adequately because they happen to be Black, speak a language other than English, or come from a poor family is widespread, but lowered expectations are not always conscious or based on negative intentions. Sometimes, lowering expectations is a teacher's way of adapting their instruction to accommodate student differences. Good intentions, however, do not always lead to positive results. Because such accommodations are based on the presumption that particular students are incapable of high-quality work due to language and cultural differences, they are patronizing at best.

The key lesson for schools and educators is that teachers need to raise expectations and standards for all students. High standards can be achieved in a great variety of ways, and not only through the standardized tests that are increasingly being used as the sole way to measure student learning. Multicultural education means finding and using culturally, multiculturally, and linguistically relevant materials to develop students' cognitive skills. It also means using a variety of approaches in instruction. Raising standards and expectations does not require homogenizing instruction, but rather creating new and different opportunities for learning for all students. In the end, however, it is students' relationships with their teachers that matter most.

Family Environments for Learning

Very few of the parents mentioned in the case studies and snapshots were involved in school in any but the most superficial way, at least according to the way that parent involvement is usually defined. Few of them volunteered their time in school, went to meetings, or even visited the school on a consistent basis. The reasons for this lack of involvement were many, ranging from inability to speak English, to limited funds, to lack of previous experience with such activities, to their own negative experiences with schooling.

Consequently, we need to explore the activities in which these parents *were* involved in order to develop a more hopeful and democratic model of parent involvement, one that is within the reach of all students, despite the level of their parents' schooling, their socioeconomic background, or the language spoken at home. First, most of the parents of the students interviewed for the case study and snapshots, whether successful or not, stressed the importance of going to school and going on to college. Many of the students mentioned that their parents wanted them to have a better chance, to do better than they had done, and to have the opportunity for a good job.

How did these parents support their children's learning? Although most did not help with homework, they monitored it and asked questions that demonstrated an interest in what their children were doing in school. They also provided support in other ways. James talked about how his mother removed his brother from a class because she was unhappy with the way the teacher was treating him. Yahaira explained her mother's tenacious efforts to move the family into a better school district. Fern Sherman described the time her father had a flat tire and flagged down a car to take him to her school so that he would not miss a class play she was in. It is clear that these parents were willing to go to great lengths to support their children.

Another way in which the parents of the students we interviewed supported their children's academic success was through continued use of their native language and reliance on family cultural values. When students came from a family in which a language other than English was spoken, it was maintained as the language of communication in the home. Although English was also used in most of the homes, the salience of the native language was evident. In all cases, the cultural values of the family were emphasized, whether through religious observance, important family rituals, or deep-seated values such as family responsibility, respect for elders, or high academic aspirations. Rather than obstructing academic success, reliance on native language and culture promoted it.

Home activities as well as school activities need to be considered in an expanded definition of parent involvement. If schools and teachers perceive parent involvement as simply involvement in what occurs in the school, the vital role parents can have in their children's academic success is denied. Educators must be concerned not just with the kinds of activities traditionally equated with school success, that is, having many books and toys in the home or attending cultural centers such as museums or going to plays. These are worthwhile activities for families, but not all families have access to them, nor are they part of every family's repertoire. All families, however, *are* capable of providing intangibles such as consistent communication, high expectations, pride, understanding, and enthusiasm for their children's school experiences.

The view that parents of families living in poverty and those who speak another language or come from a non-dominant culture are unable to provide environments that promote learning can lead to condescending practices that reject the skills and resources that these families already have. Practices such as "top-down" classes on parenting, reading, nutrition, and hygiene taught by "experts" are the result of this kind of thinking. A humorous example of patronizing attitudes such as these can be found in Esmeralda Santiago's novel *When I Was Puerto Rican*. Santiago recounts how the mothers of the children in Miss Jiménez's class in Puerto Rico were asked to attend a meeting with experts from the United States who would teach them "all about proper nutrition and hygiene, so that we would grow up as tall and strong as Dick, Jane, and Sally, the *Americanitos* in our primers." At the meeting, the experts brought charts with foods, most of which, at the time, were unknown in the tropics, such as carrots and broccoli, iceberg lettuce, apples, pears, and peaches. On the other hand, the "experts" did not bring any of the staples with which the mothers were familiar. "There was no rice on the chart, no beans, no salted codfish. There were big white eggs, not at all like the small round ones our hens gave us. . . . There were bananas but no plantains, potatoes but no *batatas* [sweet potatoes], cereal flakes but no oatmeal, bacon but no sausages." At the end of the meeting, the mothers received peanut butter, cornflakes, fruit cocktail, peaches in heavy syrup, beets, tuna fish, grape jelly, and pickles—none of which formed part of the Puerto Rican diet—and the mother of the protagonist, Negi, concluded, "I don't understand why they didn't just give us a sack of rice and a bag of beans. It would keep this family fed for a month."[17]

Such scenes, although humorous, are not uncommon. On the other hand, when parents are perceived to have skills, strengths, and resources that can aid their children's learning, the results are different. There is nothing wrong with information to help parents with the upbringing and education of their children when it is given with mutual respect, dialogue, and exchange. Parenting is hard work, and any help that teachers and schools can give parents is valuable, but it needs to be offered through two-way communication that inspires confidence and trust.

EXPANDING DEFINITIONS: WHAT IT MEANS TO BE AMERICAN

As movingly expressed by students in some of the case studies and snapshots, a number of young people had great difficulty accepting a split concept of self (what has commonly been called the *hyphenated American*). In our society, this dichotomy is common: One is either American or foreign, English-speaking or Spanish-speaking, Black or White. The possibility that one could at the same time be Spanish-speaking and English-speaking, Vietnamese and American, or Black and White is hardly considered. A case study of Lowell, Massachusetts, by Peter Kiang quotes a

Cambodian who expressed this sentiment with obvious pain: "When they say 'American,' they don't mean us—look at our eyes and our skin."[18]

What does it mean to be an American? This is, in many ways, the quintessential American dilemma, yet historically it has not invited a deep or sustained critical conversation. Throughout our history, with successive generations of newcomers and conflicts with old-timers, either easy speculation or pat answers have been offered because there is an unstated assumption of what it means to be an American. Questioning the assumed definition seems almost heretical because a number of troubling contradictions emerge, particularly questions of equality and social justice.[19]

The designation of American has generally been reserved for those who are White and English speaking. Others, even if they have been here for many years, have still been seen as separate. As the previous example of the Cambodian demonstrates, no matter how many generations of an Asian family have been here and regardless of whether they speak only English and have little contact with their native heritage, they are not generally considered American. Conversely, the same is usually *not* true for European Americans, even recent arrivals. Even Blacks who have been in this country for hundreds of years are sometimes seen as quite separate. When one is not White, being accepted as a "real" American is far more difficult despite years of residence or even language spoken. Racism has always been implicated in the acceptance or rejection of particular groups in U.S. society.

CHALLENGING "HEARTBREAKING DILEMMAS"

As we can see then, for a variety of reasons, the definition of *American,* as currently used, may effectively exclude those who are least powerful. As such, it legitimates the cultural, economic, and political control and hegemony of those who are already dominant in U.S. society. Our present and future diversity demands an expanded and inclusive definition—not hyphenated Americans, implying split and confused identities. *African-American* might imply a bifurcated identity, whereas *African American* signifies that a new definition is possible—one that emphasizes not confusion or denial, but the transformation of what it means to be an American.

In the past, *Americanization* always implied Anglocization. To become Americanized meant not only learning English but also forgetting one's native language and not only learning the culture but also learning to eat, dress, talk, and even behave like the European American model. As so movingly expressed by a writer describing the experience of Jews in New York about 100 years ago, "The world that we faced on the East Side at the turn of the [20th] century presented a series of heartbreaking dilemmas."[20] To go through the process of Americanization has meant the inevitable loss of a great part of oneself in the bargain.

These heartbreaking dilemmas still exist today, as we have seen in the case studies and snapshots. A hundred years ago, the choice was generally made in favor of assimilation. Although no less difficult today, the choices are not as limited as they once were. There are two major reasons for this. First, the Civil Rights Movement and related movements for women's, ethnic, and LGBT rights, among others, have led to more freedom in asserting one's identity because they have transformed the sociopolitical and historical contexts in which such decisions are made. Second, the number and diversity of immigrants in the United States in the past three decades has been unequaled in our history. These changes are profoundly affecting the meaning of assimilation.

A Different Approach

In some ways, the students currently enrolled in our schools are more fortunate than previous students because they have more freedom to determine what to do about their language and culture, but the choice may still be a painful one. On one hand, if they choose to identify with their ethnic background, they may feel alienated from this society; on the other hand, if they identify with U.S. (generally meaning mainstream White) culture, they feel like traitors to their family and community.

As they currently exist, these choices are clear-cut and rigid: One is either true to oneself and family, or one is an American. This can be compared to what Wallace Lambert has called *subtractive bilingualism*, that is, the kind of bilingualism that develops at the expense of one's native language.[21] This kind of bilingualism means that one does not really become bilingual at all but rather goes from being monolingual in one language to being monolingual in another, although sometimes vestiges of the original language may remain. Multiculturalism, too, is subtractive if it allows only a transition from being monocultural in one culture to being so in another. Ned Seelye describes this dilemma: "One can escape appearing culturally different by forfeiting one of the two cultures—and there is always considerable pressure on economically and politically subservient groups to make this sacrifice—but trading one brand of monoculturalism for another seems an unnecessarily pallid business."[22]

The opposite of subtractive multiculturalism can be called *additive multiculturalism*. Just as we have seen that children who achieve fuller bilingual development enjoy cognitive advantages over monolinguals, we can speculate that those who reach a state of additive multiculturalism also enjoy advantages over monoculturals, including a broader view of reality, feeling comfortable in a variety of settings, and multicultural flexibility.

Expanding the definition of American may help students and others facing the dilemma of fitting into a multicultural society by providing alternatives to self-identification and expanding the choices in making accommodations between cultural and linguistic as well as social and national identification. The students in our case studies and snapshots, as well as many others, would have more choices than before and would no longer face such "heartbreaking dilemmas" to the same extent that they currently do. European Americans would no longer be considered the only true Americans. *E pluribus unum* can no longer mean that cultural differences have to be denied in order to foster a false unity. Neither is complete cultural maintenance a realistic choice, since it implies that native traditions should be preserved in a pure and idealized state without the interdependence that is so necessary in a pluralistic society.

No longer a choice of whether one should assimilate or not, the question now is "How far can society, and the institutions of society such as schools, be pushed to accommodate the changing definition of American?" It is probably the first time in our history that this question has been asked in more than a rhetorical way. The view of the United States as a monolithic, monocultural, and monolingual society is being challenged daily, as seen in the wide use of languages other than English by an increasing percentage of the population, and by the ease and conviction with which growing numbers of people are claiming their identities as vital resources to be nurtured and maintained. The fact that this question can even be posed places us in a unique historical moment; in the past, such possibilities could not be seriously considered. Therefore, the view that schools must be the obligatory assimilators of students, needs to be disputed. The boundaries of pluralism, formerly delimited by an Anglocentric definition, were being vigorously questioned during the last quarter of the 20th century. Since September 11, 2001, there has been some backsliding on the issue of what it means to be an American, with more rigid views expressed than we have seen in some time. Policies such as "English only" and anti-immigrant sentiments are gaining strength, and there is less patience with diversity in some quarters. However, because of the social and historical global context in which we are living, these policies are, in the long run, ineffective.

In an insightful essay on assimilation written three decades ago, William Greenbaum proposed two reasons why assimilation occurred so quickly in the past: one was hope, and the other was *shame*. Hope contributed in a major way by holding out the promise of equality, economic security, and a safe haven from war and devastation. However, according to Greenbaum, shame was the "main fuel" for the American melting pot: "The immigrants were best instructed in how to repulse themselves; millions of people were taught to be ashamed of their faces, their family names, their parents and grandparents, and their class patterns, histories and life outlooks."[23]

Shame is no longer acceptable to a growing number of people. The students in the snapshots and case studies, for example, challenge what it means to be an American. Not content to accept past limitations, they provide evidence that an evolution of meaning is taking place. They are still caught in the conflict and uncertainties of how to expand their possibilities, but these young people are increasingly sure of who they are. They are determined to define their own identities—identities that are different from their parents but not restricted to the old, static definition of *American* that has up to now been available.

As long as there are newcomers and as long as there are those who refuse to be included in a definition that denies them both their individual and group identities, the question of what it means to become American will be with us. The challenge for us as a society is to make room for everyone. Maxine Greene refers to those among us who are marginalized, both newcomers and old-timers, when she says, "There are always strangers, people with their own cultural memories, with voices aching to be heard."[24]

LEVELS OF MULTICULTURAL EDUCATION AND SUPPORT

If indeed we reject past limits on what it means to be an American, we need to consider how multicultural education can be incorporated in a natural and inclusive way into curricula and instruction.

STARTING OUT

How does a school or a teacher achieve a multicultural perspective? To say that multicultural education must be comprehensively defined, pervasive, and inclusive is not to imply that only a full-blown program qualifies. Because multicultural education is a process, it is always changing and never quite finished. Because multicultural education is critical pedagogy, it is necessarily dynamic. A static "program-in-place" or a slick-packaged program is contrary to the very definition of multicultural education.

We illustrate with an example from Susan Barrett, who was a talented high school English teacher in a community of European American (primarily Irish, French, and Polish) and Puerto Rican students. Many years ago, when asked how she included a multicultural perspective in her teaching, Susan replied that she had not yet reached that level; rather, she said, her classroom had what she called *bicultural moments*. As a proponent of multicultural education, she used inclusive curriculum and instructional strategies that emerged from this perspective. However, because she felt that the children in her classes did not even know about their own or one another's backgrounds, let alone about the world outside their communities, her curriculum focused on exploring the "little world" of her students' community before venturing beyond it.

In our enthusiasm to incorporate a multicultural philosophy in our teaching, we can sometimes forget that our classrooms are made up of young people who usually know very little about their own culture or those of their classmates. The students themselves are a gold mine of resources for teaching and learning. *Starting out small,* then, means being sensitive to bicultural moments and using them as a beginning for more wide-ranging multicultural education.

BECOMING A MULTICULTURAL PERSON

Developing truly comprehensive multicultural education takes many years, in part because of our own monocultural education. Most of us, in spite of our distinct cultural or linguistic backgrounds, were educated in monocultural environments. We seldom have the necessary models for developing a multicultural perspective. We have only our own experiences, and no matter what our background, these have been overwhelmingly Eurocentric and English-speaking.

Becoming a multicultural teacher, therefore, means first becoming a multicultural person. Without this transformation of ourselves, any attempts at developing a multicultural perspective will be shallow and superficial. However, becoming a multicultural person in a society that values monoculturalism is not easy. It means re-educating ourselves in several ways.

First, *we simply need to learn more*. We need to be involved in activities that emphasize pluralism. We also need to look for books and other materials that inform us about people and events we may know little about. Because of the multicultural nature of our society, these materials are widely available, although sometimes we have "learned" not to see them.

Second, *we need to confront our own racism and biases*. It is impossible to be a teacher with a multicultural perspective without going through this process. Because we are all products of a society that is racist and stratified by gender, class, and language, among other differences, we have all internalized some negative messages in one way or another. Sometimes, our biases are unconscious, as in the case of a former student who referred to Africans as *slaves* and Europeans as *people* but was horrified when this was pointed out to her. Sometimes the words we use convey deep-seated stereotypes, as when a student who does not speak English is characterized as "not having language," as if they did not speak any language. Our actions also carry the messages we have learned, for example, when we automatically expect that our female students will not do as well in math as our male students. Our own re-education means not only learning new things but also *unlearning* some of the old. In the case of LGBT students, for example, it is common for both teachers and students to make statements such as "I don't care what they are, as long as they don't bring it into the classroom," as if the identities of LGBT students should be erased because they make other people uncomfortable. In all these cases, the process of confronting our own racism and biases can be difficult and painful, but it is a necessary part of becoming multicultural.

Third, *becoming a multicultural person means learning to see reality from a variety of perspectives*. Because we have often learned that there is only one "right answer," we have also developed only one way of seeing things. A multicultural perspective demands just the opposite. Reorienting ourselves in this way can be exhausting and difficult because it requires a dramatic shift in our worldview.

Researcher John Raible has developed a theory of identity that is informative. Through his study of White siblings in families with transracially adopted brothers and sisters, Raible advances the constructs of *transracial identity* and *post-White identity* by viewing how some individuals from dominant groups develop nondominant perspectives. According to Raible, transracialized individuals develop more complex understandings of social practices, and they learn to view them from multiple perspectives. He explains the related notion of post-White identity as an active personal effort to redefine what it means to be White in the context of transracialization. He goes on to say,

> Rather than implying an "after-white" or "no longer white" identity, post-white identifications signal an intentional break with racialization based, in the case of these individuals, on their unconventional familial circumstances *and* on their ongoing intimate involvement with people of color outside the family and culturally delineated mainly by racialization.[25]

Although the transformation of individuals from being monocultural to being multicultural will not, by itself, guarantee that education will become multicultural, it will lay the groundwork for it.

A MODEL OF MULTICULTURAL EDUCATION

A monocultural perspective reflects a fundamentally different framework for understanding differences than does a multicultural one. Even multicultural education, however, has a variety of levels of support for pluralism. We classify them into at least four levels: *tolerance; acceptance; respect;* and *affirmation, solidarity, and critique*. In the process of becoming multicultural, we need to consider these levels of multicultural education and how they might be operationalized in our schools. These categories should be viewed as dynamic and as having penetrable borders. Our purpose in using them is to demonstrate the various ways in which multicultural education can be implemented in schools. Please keep in mind, however, that whenever we classify and categorize reality, as we do in this model, we run the risk that it will be viewed as static and arbitrary rather than as messy, complex, and contradictory, which we know it to be.

In what follows, we propose a model, ranging from monocultural education to comprehensive multicultural education, based on the seven characteristics of multicultural education described in Chapter 3. This model explores how multicultural education pays attention to many components of the school environment and takes different forms in different settings.[26]

Tolerance is the first level of support for pluralism. To be tolerant means to have the capacity to bear something, although at times it may be unpleasant. To tolerate differences means to endure them, although not necessarily to embrace them. We may learn to tolerate differences, but this level of acceptance can be shaky because what is tolerated today can be rejected tomorrow. Tolerance, therefore, represents the lowest level of multicultural education in a school setting, yet many schools have what they consider very comprehensive mission statements that stress tolerance in striving for diversity. Although the schools may believe that these are adequate expressions of support, they do not suffice. In terms of school policies and practices, tolerance may be viewed as having to bear linguistic and cultural differences as the inevitable burden of a culturally pluralistic society. When this is the perspective, programs that do not build on differences but rather replace them—for example, ELL programs—may be superficial at best. Black History Month might be commemorated with an assembly program and a bulletin board, but would stop there. The lifestyles and values of students' families, if different from the majority, may be considered by schools to require modification.

Acceptance is the next level of support for diversity. If we accept differences, at the very least, we acknowledge them without denying their importance. In concrete terms, programs that acknowledge students' languages and cultures are visible in the school if diversity is accepted. These programs might include a transitional bilingual program that uses the students' primary language, at least until they are "mainstreamed" into an English-language environment. Acceptance of diversity might also be reflected in the celebration of some differences through activities such as multicultural fairs and cookbooks. In a school with this level of support for diversity, time might be set aside weekly for "multicultural programs," and parents' native languages might be used for communicating with them through newsletters.

Respect is the third level of multicultural education. To *respect* means to admire and hold in high esteem. When diversity is respected, it is used as the basis for much of the education offered. This might mean offering programs of bilingual education that employ students' native language not only as a bridge to English but also throughout their schooling. Frequent and positive interactions with parents would take place. In the curriculum, students' values and experiences would be used as the basis for their literacy development. Students would be exposed to different ways of approaching the same reality, and as a result, they would expand their way of looking at the world. *Additive multiculturalism* would be the ultimate goal for everybody.

Affirmation, solidarity, and critique, which we consider the highest level of support for diversity, is based on the premise that the most powerful learning happens when students work through their differences, even if it is sometimes difficult and challenging. This means accepting the different cultures and languages of students and their families as legitimate and embracing them as valid vehicles for learning. It also means understanding that culture is not fixed or unchangeable and that it can be held up to scrutiny and criticized. Because multicultural education is concerned with equity and social justice for all people, and because basic values of different groups are often diametrically opposed, conflict is inevitable. What makes this level different from the others is that conflict is not avoided but accepted as an inescapable part of learning.

Passively accepting the status quo of any culture is inconsistent with multicultural education. Simply substituting one myth for another contradicts the basic tenets of multicultural education because no group is inherently superior or more heroic than any other. At this level, students not only "celebrate" diversity, but also they reflect on and challenge it as well. As expressed by Mary Kalantzis and Bill Cope, multicultural education "needs to consider not just the pleasure of diversity but more fundamental issues that arise as different groups negotiate community and the basic issues of material life in the same space—a process that equally might generate conflict and pain."[27] Such fundamental issues may be difficult and even impossible, to reconcile, and they might include different values about respect, authority, family, and gender roles, to name just a few.

Multicultural education without critique keeps cultural understanding at the romantic or exotic stage. If we are unable to transcend our own cultural experience through reflection and critique, we cannot hope to understand and critique that of others. For students, this process begins with a strong sense of solidarity with others who are different from themselves. When based on deep respect, critique is not only necessary but also, in fact, healthy. Without critique, the danger that multicultural education might be used to glorify myths into static "truth" is very real.

In the school, affirmation, solidarity, and critique mean using students' identities in a consistent, critical, comprehensive, and inclusive way. This goes beyond creating ethnic enclaves, which can become exclusionary and selective, although for disenfranchised communities, this might certainly be a step in the process of implementing multicultural education. To achieve the highest level of support for diversity (affirmation, solidarity, and critique) schools must develop *multicultural* settings in which all students feel reflected and visible, for example, through two-way bilingual programs in which the languages of all students are used and maintained meaningfully in the academic setting. The curriculum would be characterized by multicultural inclusiveness, offering a wide variety of content and perspectives. Teachers' attitudes and behaviors would reflect only the very highest expectations for all students. Instructional strategies would also include a range of means to teach students. Families would be welcomed and supported in the school as students' first and most important teachers. Their experiences, viewpoints, and

TABLE 11.1
Levels of Multicultural Education

		Characteristics of Multicultural Education	
	Monocultural Education	**Tolerance**	
Antiracist/Antidiscriminatory	Racism is unacknowledged. Policies and practices that support discrimination are left in place. These include low expectations and refusal to use students' natural resources (such as language and culture) in instruction. Only a sanitized and "safe" curriculum is in place.	Policies and practices that challenge racism and discrimination are initiated. No overt signs of discrimination are acceptable (e.g., name calling, graffiti, blatantly racist and sexist textbooks or curriculum). ESL programs are in place for students who speak other langauges.	
Basic	Defines education as the 3 R's and the "canon." "Cultural literacy" is understood within a monocultural framework. All important knowledge is essentially European American. This Eurocentric view is reflected throughout the curriculum, instructional strategies, and environment for learning.	Education is defined more expansively and includes attention to selected information about other groups.	
Pervasive	No attention is paid to student diversity.	A multicultural perspective is evident in some activities, such as Black History Month and Cinco de Mayo, and in some curriculum and materials. There may be an itinerant "multicultural teacher."	
Important for All Students	Ethnic and/or women's studies, if available, are only for students from that group. This is a frill that is not important for other students to know.	Ethnic and women's studies are only offered as isolated courses.	
Education for Social Justice	Education supports the status quo. Thinking and acting are separate.	Education is somewhat, although tenuously, linked to community projects and activities.	
Process	Education is primarily content: who, what, where, when. The "great White men" version of history is propagated.	Education is both content and process. "Why" and "how" questions are tentatively broached.	
Critical Pedagogy	Education is domesticating. Reality is represented as static, finished, and flat.	Students and teachers begin to question the status quo.	

suggestions would be sought out and incorporated into classroom and school programs and activities. In turn, families would be exposed to a variety of experiences and viewpoints different from their own, which would help them expand their horizons as well.

Other ways in which these four levels might be developed in schools are listed in Table 11.1. Of course, multicultural education cannot be categorized as neatly

Characteristics of Multicultural Education		
Acceptance	**Respect**	**Affirmation, Solidarity, and Critique**
Policies and practices that acknowledge differences are in place. Textbooks reflect some diversity. Transitional bilingual programs are available. Curriculum is more inclusive of the histories and perspectives of a broader range of people.	Policies and practices that respect diversity are more evident, including maintenance bilingual education. Ability grouping is not permitted. Curriculum is more explicitly antiracist and honest. It is "safe" to talk about racism, sexism, and other examples of discrimination.	Policies and practices that affirm diversity and challenge racism are developed. There are high expectations for all students; students' language and culture are used in instruction and curriculum. Two-way bilingual programs are in place wherever possible. Everyone takes responsibility for challenging racism and discrimination.
The diversity of lifestyles and values of groups other than the dominant one are acknowledged in some content, as can be seen in some courses and school activities.	Education is defined as knowledge that is necessary for living in a complex and pluralistic society. As such, it includes much content that is multicultural. *Additive multiculturalism* is the goal.	Basic education *is* multicultural education. All students learn to speak a second language and are familiar with a broad range of knowledge.
Student diversity is acknowledged, as can be seen not only in "Holidays and Heroes" but also in consideration of different learning styles, values, and languages. A "multicultural program" may be in place.	The learning environment is imbued with multicultural education. It can be seen in classroom interactions, materials, and the culture of the school.	Multicultural education pervades the curriculum; instructional strategies; and interactions among teachers, students, and the community. It can be seen everywhere: bulletin boards, the lunchroom, assemblies.
Many students are expected to take part in curriculum that stresses diversity. A variety of languages are taught.	All students take part in courses that reflect diversity. Teachers are involved in overhauling the curriculum to be more open to such diversity.	All courses are completely multicultural in essence. The curriculum for all students is enriched.
The role of the schools in social change is acknowledged. Some changes that reflect this attitude begin to be felt: Students take part in community service.	Students take part in community activities that reflect their social concerns.	The curriculum and instructional techniques are based on an understanding of social justice as central to education. Reflection and action are important components of learning.
Education is both content and process. "Why" and "how" questions are stressed more. Knowledge of, and sensitivity to, students of all backgrounds are more apparent.	Education is both content and process. Students and teachers begin to ask, "What if?" Teachers build strong relationships with students and their families.	Education is an equal mix of content and process. It is dynamic. Teachers and students are empowered. Everyone in the school is becoming a multicultural person.
Students and teachers are beginning a dialogue. Students' experiences, cultures, and languages are used as one source of their learning.	Students and teachers use critical dialogue as the primary basis for their education. They see and understand different perspectives.	Students and teachers are involved in a "subversive activity." Decision-making and social action skills are the basis of the curriculum.

as this chart would suggest. This model simply represents a theoretical way of understanding how different levels of multicultural education might be visible in a school. It also highlights that, to be most effective, multicultural education needs to be a pervasive philosophy and practice. Although any level of multicultural education is preferable to the education offered by a monocultural perspective, each level more vigorously challenges a monolithic and ethnocentric view of society and education. As such, the fourth level is clearly the highest expression of support for multicultural education.

The fourth level—affirmation, solidarity, and critique—is also the most difficult to achieve for some of the reasons mentioned previously, including the lack of models of multicultural education in our own schooling and experiences. It is here that we educators are most confronted by values and lifestyles different from our own and with situations that severely test the limits of our tolerance. Interacting with people who are different from us in hygienic practices, food preferences, and religious rites can be trying. It is also extremely difficult, and at times impossible, to accept and understand cultural beliefs and practices that run counter to our most deeply held beliefs. For example, if we believe strongly in equality of the sexes and have in our classroom children whose families value males more highly than females; if we need to communicate with parents who believe that education is a frill and not suitable for their children; or if we have children in our classes whose religion forbids them to take part in any school activities except academics—all of these situations test our capacity for affirmation and solidarity.

Culture is not static, nor is it necessarily positive or negative. The cultural values and practices of a group of people reflect their best strategies for negotiating their environment and circumstances at a particular historical moment. What some groups have worked out as appropriate strategies may be considered unsuitable or even barbaric and uncivilized by others. Because each cultural group has developed in a different context, we can never reach total agreement on the best or most appropriate ways in which to lead our lives.

One way to tackle this dilemma is to emphasize the human and civil rights of all people. These rights guarantee that all human beings are treated with dignity, respect, and equality. Sometimes the values and behaviors of a group so seriously challenge these values that we cannot accept or tolerate them. If the values we, as human beings, hold most dear are based on extending rather than negating rights, we believe we must decide on the side of these more universal values.

This brings us to a final consideration: *Multicultural education is not easy. If it were, everyone would be doing it.* Resolving conflicts about cultural differences is difficult and sometimes impossible. The extent to which our particular cultural lenses may keep us from appreciating differences can be very great. Also, some values are simply irreconcilable, and we need to accept this fact. Usually, however, accommodations that respect both cultural values and basic human rights can be found. Because societies have generally resolved such conflicts in only one way, that is, favoring the dominant culture, few avenues for negotiating differences have been in place. Multicultural education, although at times difficult, painful, and time consuming, can provide one way of attempting such negotiations.

BALANCING HOPE AND DESPAIR

Anything less than a program of comprehensive multicultural education will continue to short-change students in our schools. Beginning with the Common School Movement in the late 19th century and stretching into the present, our society has promised all students an equal and high-quality education, but teachers who began teaching after the Civil Rights Movement came to an end have not heard this message proclaimed very loudly. Moreover, educational results have belied the promise of educational equality. Students most victimized by society, that is, those from economically poor and culturally and linguistically dominated groups, are also the most vulnerable in our schools. Their status in society tends to be replicated in the schools. Unless our educational system confronts inequity at all levels and through all school policies and practices, we will simply be proceeding with "business as usual."

The case studies and snapshots in this book underscore the central role of schools in promoting academic success for all students and multicultural education as a promising means to achieve this goal. *Affirming Diversity*, the title of this book, is at the core of multicultural education. It implies that cultural, linguistic, and other differences can and should be accepted, respected, and used as a basis for learning and teaching. Rather than maladies to be cured or problems to be confronted, differences are a necessary starting point for learning and teaching, and they can enrich the experiences of students and teachers.

Affirming diversity is not enough unless we also challenge inequitable policies and practices that grant unfair advantages to some students over others.[28] But simply tackling issues of racism and discrimination at the school level does little to change the broader context. Although improvement in education must take place at the school level, changing the school alone will not lead to substantive changes in society. Schools have often been sites of protest, resistance, and change, and their role in influencing public policy has sometimes been significant. However, racism, classism, ethnocentrism, sexism, linguicism, ableism, heterosexism, religious oppression and other forms of discrimination exist in schools because they exist in society. To divorce schools from society is impossible. Although schools may, with all good intentions, attempt to provide learning environments free from bias, after students leave the classroom and building, they are again confronted with an unequal society.

Teachers, schools, and students engaged in challenging social inequities need to understand that they are involved in a struggle that critiques and questions the status quo not only of schools but also of society. They will inevitably be involved in what Mildred Dickeman, more than three decades ago, described as "a subversive task" if they are serious about facing issues of cultural pluralism in schools.[29] Her perspective defies the simple definition of multicultural education as celebratory, implying a more complex understanding of differences.

A balance between hope and despair is difficult to maintain, yet that is precisely what is required. Multicultural education is not a remedy for social inequality, and it cannot guarantee academic success. At the same time, if one of the primary purposes of education is to teach young people the skills, knowledge, and critical awareness to become productive members of a diverse and democratic society, a broadly conceptualized multicultural education can have a decisive influence. Although racism cannot be wiped out by schools, the role that schools can play should not be underestimated: By developing antiracist and affirming policies and practices, schools can make a genuine difference in the lives of many students.

SUMMARY

In this final chapter, we have reviewed the responsibility of schools to strengthen bilingual and multicultural education. The role of meaningful extracurricular activities was also considered, with examples of what schools and communities can do. Suggestions concerning the role of teachers and families in providing environments for success for all students were presented, specifically, *mutual accommodation, teachers' relationships with students, and family environments for learning.*

We also addressed two additional issues that have implications for multicultural education: the definition of *American* and how various levels of multicultural education affect the learning environment. If we begin with the premise that what it means to be an American must be continuously renegotiated, there is ample room for promoting a society characterized by inclusiveness.

◆◆◆ Final Thoughts

The student body in U.S. schools is becoming more diverse than ever before, reflecting more racial, cultural, linguistic, and social class differences. But our ability to understand these differences and to use them in constructive ways is still quite limited. Multicultural education is one significant way to address differences, but we should not think of it as a superficial set of activities, materials, or approaches. Although it would have been easy to do in this book, we have resisted presenting cookie-cutter lesson plans because such an approach can overlook or downplay the school conditions that produce unequal academic outcomes in the first place. In fact, we would go so far as to say that a prepackaged series of lesson plans is in direct conflict with the goals of a comprehensive multicultural education. If the purpose of education is to prepare young people for productive and critical participation in a democratic and pluralistic society, then the activities, strategies, and approaches we use in their instruction need to echo these concerns. Schools, as currently structured, do little to prepare students for such a future because the curriculum and instruction tend to contradict these goals.

In addition to recognizing the growing diversity of the student body, educators cannot overlook the stratification of society, which profoundly affects the schooling of students. The cultural and linguistic differences students bring to school, along with how these differences are perceived, also need to be addressed through the curriculum and instruction. To act as if race, social class, ethnicity, native language, sexual orientation, and other differences are immaterial to schooling is disingenuous. It is only by addressing all these issues in a systematic way through the curriculum, instruction, and other practices that real change will happen.

In the final analysis, multicultural education is a moral and ethical issue. The current conditions in our world call for critical thinkers who can face and resolve complex issues—problems such as war, ethnic polarization, poverty, contamination of our natural resources, and rampant racism—in sensitive and ethical ways. We need all the help we can get to solve these problems, and using the talents and strengths of all young people is crucial. If we believe that all students are capable of brilliance, that they can learn at high levels of achievement, and that the cultural and linguistic resources they bring to school are worthy of respect, affirmation, and solidarity, then multicultural education represents a far more principled approach for our schools than does monocultural education.

◆◆◆ To Think About

1. Three different models for understanding pluralism (or the lack of it) are the following:

   - *Anglo-conformity:* All newcomers need to conform to the dominant European-American, middle-class, and English-speaking model.
   - *"Melting pot":* All newcomers "melt" to form an amalgam that becomes American.
   - *"Salad bowl":* All newcomers maintain their languages and cultures while combining with others to form a "salad," which is our unique U.S. society.

   Form three groups, with each group taking one of the previous options and arguing that it represents the dominant ideology in U.S. society. Have each group give concrete examples. Afterward, in a large group, decide if one of these ideologies is really the most apparent and successful. Give reasons for your conclusions. How would you critique each of these ideologies? What are the advantages and disadvantages of each?

2. What are schools for? To determine the *function* of schools, investigate the *structure* of schools. Given the following objectives of education, work in small groups to design a school to achieve each one:

   - The purpose of schools is to "Americanize" or assimilate all students to the American way of life.
   - The purpose of schools is to prepare a few good managers and a lot of good workers.
   - The purpose of schools is to develop critical thinkers.
   - The purpose of schools is to prepare citizens of all backgrounds for active participation in a democratic society.

   Explore how a school founded on one of these goals might function. Describe the curriculum, materials, administration, community outreach, and structure in the school you design. Working together, compare the differences among the four hypothetical schools. Then compare each of these schools to schools with which you are familiar. What can we learn from these comparisons?

3. Define *American*.

4. How would you identify a person who has developed what we have called *additive multiculturalism*? How might that individual be different from one who is monocultural? Give some examples.

5. Mildred Dickeman (see Note 29) has suggested that teachers are engaged in "a subversive task" if they challenge the monocultural curriculum and other inequities of schools. What does she mean? Do you agree?

◆◆◆ Activities   for Personal, School, and Community Change

1. With a group of colleagues, think about some of the ways extracurricular activities in your school limit the participation of students. Consider sports, the newspaper, the student government, and other activities. How can your school become more inclusive? Share your ideas with the parent/teacher organization (PTO) and ask for their input and advice. Then present your suggestions to your principal.

2. Ask your principal to set up a study group to determine how well your school is fulfilling its responsibility to educate a diverse population. Use the guidelines in *Diversity Within Unity: Essential Principles for Teaching and Learning in a Multicultural Society* by James A. Banks, et al.[30] Evaluate your school to see how effective it is in meeting these guidelines. Consider the curriculum; materials; interactions among staff, students, and community; and the entire environment for living and learning in the school.

3. Develop a curriculum in which your students can learn specific ways of *accommodating* without *acquiescing*. You may want to read Bob Fecho's book *"Is This English?" Race, Language, and Culture in the Classroom* or Vivian Vasquez's *Negotiating Critical Literacy with Young Children* for specific ideas. Fecho and Vasquez both use language arts primarily, but you can develop similar lessons for other subject areas.[31]

◆◆◆ Companion Website

For access to additional case studies, weblinks, concept cards, and other material related to this chapter, visit the text's companion website at **www.ablongman.com/nieto5e**.

Notes to Chapter 11

1. Alejandro Portes and Rubén G. Rumbaut, *Legacies: The Story of the Immigrant Second Generation* (Berkeley, CA: University of California Press; and New York: Russell Sage Foundation, 2001). Also see the special issue (November 2005) of *Ethnic and Racial Studies* that presents original results from the third wave of the Children of Immigrants Longitudinal Study (CILS), a decade-old panel that followed a large sample of second-generation youths from early adolescence to early adulthood. Portes and Rumbaut, with other colleagues, articulate this extensive research in the results of the third survey, conducted in 2001–2003. Take special note of Alejandro Portes and Rubén G. Rumbaut, "Introduction: The Second Generation and the Children of Immigrants Longitudinal Study." *Ethnic and Racial Studies* 28 no. 6 (November

2005): 983(17). Also see Alejandro Portes, Rubén G. Rumbaut, *Immigrant America: A Portrait*, 3rd ed. (Berkley, CA: University of California Press, 2006).

2. For further development of this idea, see Sonia Nieto, "Bringing Bilingual Education Out of the Basement, and Other Imperatives for Teacher Education." In *Lifting Every Voice: Pedagogy and Politics of Bilingual Education*, edited by Zeynep Beykont (Cambridge, MA: Harvard Educational Review, 2000). Also see Theresa Montaño, Sharon H. Ulanoff, Rosalinda Quintanar-Sarellana, and Lynne Aoki, "The Debilingualization of California's Prospective Bilingual Teachers." *Social Justice* 32 no. 3 (Fall 2005): 103–119.

3. For more insights on this issue, see Zeynep Beykont, *The Power of Culture: Teaching Across Language Difference* (Cambridge, MA: Harvard Education Publishing Group, 2002).

4. K. Tsianina Lomawaima and Teresa L. McCarty, *"To Remain an Indian": Lessons in Democracy from a Century of Native American Education* (New York: Teachers College Press, 2006). Also see Teresa L. McCarty, "Reclaiming the Gift: Indigenous Youth Counter-Narratives on Native Language Loss and Revitalization." *American Indian Quarterly* 30, Nos. 1, 2 (Winter/Spring 2006): 28–48. For more on Navajo culture and educations, see Kathryn Manuelito, "The Role of Education in American Indian Self-Determination: Lessons from the Ramah Navajo Community School." *Anthropology & Education Quarterly* 36, no. 1 (March 2005): 73–87.

5. *Metropolitan Life Survey of the American Teacher 1996*. A survey conducted by Louis Harris and Associates, as cited in G. Pritchy Smith and Deborah H. Batiste, "What Do Students Think About Multiculturalism?" *Multicultural Education* 4, no. 4 (Summer 1997): 45–46.

6. Laurie Olsen, "Learning English and Learning America: Immigrants in the Center of a Storm." *Theory Into Practice* 39, no. 4 (2000): 196–202.

7. For a review, see Sonia Nieto, *The Light in Their Eyes: Creating Multicultural Learning Communities* (New York: Teachers College Press, 1999).

8. Jonathon Kozol, *The Shame of the Nation: The Restoration of Apartheid Schooling in America* (New York: Brown, 2005).

9. Nick Rabkin and Robin Edmond, *Putting the Arts in the Picture: Reframing Education in the 21st Century* Chicago: Columbia College Chicago, 2004).

10. Mavis G. Sanders, and Adia Harvey, "Beyond the School Walls: A Case Study of Principal Leadership for School–Community Collaboration." *Teachers College Record* 104 no. 7 (2002): 1345–1368.

11. Ernest Morrell, "Youth-Initiated Research as a Tool for Advocacy and Change in Urban Schools." In *Beyond Resistance! Youth Activism and Community Change*, edited by Shawn Ginwright, Pedro Noguera, and Julio Cammarato (New York: Routledge, 2006): 112–128.

12. Stephan Díaz, Luis C. Moll, and Hugh Mehan, "Sociocultural Resources in Instruction: A Context-Specific Approach." In *Beyond Language: Social and Cultural Factors in Schooling Language Minority Students* (Los Angeles: Office of Bilingual Education, California State Department of Education, Evaluation, Dissemination and Assessment Center, 1986).

13. Irma M. Olmedo, "Accommodation and Resistance: Latinas Struggle for Their Children's Education." *Anthropology & Education Quarterly*, 34, no. 4 (December 2003): 374.

14. Steven K. Lee, "The Latino Students' Attitudes, Perceptions, and Views on Bilingual Education." *Bilingual Research Journal* 30, no. 1 (2006): 107–122. Available at: http://brj.asu.edu/vol30_no1/art6.pdf

15. Stephan Díaz, Luis C. Moll, and Hugh Mehan, "Sociocultural Resources in Instruction: A Context-Specific Approach." *In Beyond Language: Social and Cultural Factors in Schooling Language Minority Students.*

16. Robert G. Croninger and Valerie E. Lee, "Social Capital and Dropping Out of High School: Benefits to At-Risk Students of Teachers' Support and Guidance." *Teachers College Record* 103, no. 4 (August 2001): 548–581.

17. Esmeralda Santiago, *When I Was Puerto Rican* (Reading, MA: Addison-Wesley, 1993): 64, 66, 68.

18. Peter Nien-Chu Kiang, *Southeast Asian Parent Empowerment: The Challenge of Changing Demographics in Lowell, Massachusetts*. Monograph no. 1. (Boston: Massachusetts Association for Bilingual Education, 1990).

19. For a more complete treatment of this idea, see Sonia Nieto, "On Becoming American: An Exploratory Essay." In *A Light in Dark Times: Maxine Greene and the Unfinished Conversation*, edited by William Ayres and Janet L. Miller (New York: Teachers College Press, 1998).

20. Words of Morris Raphael Cohen, quoted in Stephan F. Brumberg, *Going to America, Going to School: The Jewish Immigrant Public School Encounter in Turn-of-the-Century New York City* (New York: Praeger, 1986): 116.

21. Wallace Lambert and Donald Taylor, *Coping with Cultural and Racial Diversity in Urban America* (Westport, CT: Praeger, 1990).

22. H. Ned Seelye, *Teaching Culture: Strategies for Intercultural Communication* (Lincolnwood, IL: National Textbooks, 1993).

23. William Greenbaum, "America in Search of a New Ideal: An Essay on the Rise of Pluralism." *Harvard Educational Review* 44, no. 3 (August 1974): 411–440.

24. Maxine Greene, *The Dialectic of Freedom* (New York: Teachers College Press, 1988): 87.

25. John Raible. "Sharing the Spotlight: The Non-adopted Siblings of Transracial Adoptees," diss., University of Massachusetts Amherst, 2005.

26. See Sonia Nieto, "Affirmation, Solidarity, and Critique: Moving Beyond Tolerance in Multicultural Education." *Multicultural Education*, 1, no. 4 (Spring 1994): 9–12, 35–38 for an expansion of this model, with scenarios for each level.

27. Mary Kalantzis and Bill Cope, *The Experience of Multicultural Education in Australia: Six Case Studies* (Sydney: Centre for Multicultural Studies, Wollongong University, 1990): 39.

28. I (Sonia) have written on this issue in more detail in "Profoundly Multicultural Questions." *Educational Leadership* 60, no. 4 (December 2002/January 2003): 6–10.

29. Mildred Dickeman, "Teaching Cultural Pluralism." In *Teaching Ethnic Studies: Concepts and Strategies*, 43rd Yearbook, edited by James A. Banks (Washington, DC: National Council for the Social Studies, 1973).

30. See James A. Banks, Peter Cookson, Geneva Gay, Willis D. Hawley, Jacqueline Jordan Irvine, Sonia Nieto, Janet Ward Schofield, and Walter W. Stephan, *Diversity Within Unity: Essential Principles for Teaching and Learning in a Multicultural Society* (Seattle, WA: Center for Multicultural Education, University of Washington, 2001).

31. Bob Fecho's book is *"Is This English?" Race, Language, and Culture in the Classroom* (New York: Teachers College Press, 2003), and Vivian Vasquez's is *Negotiating Critical Literacy with Young Children* (Mahwah, NJ: Lawrence Erlbaum, 2004).

Bibliography

Adams, David W., *Education for Extinction: American Indians and the Boarding School Experience, 1875–1928* (Lawrence: University Press of Kansas, 1995).

Adger, Carolyn Temple, Catherine E. Snow, and Donna Christian, eds., *What Teachers Need to Know About Language* (Washington, DC: Center for Applied Linguistics, 2002).

Allport, Gordon W., *The Nature of Prejudice* (Reading, MA: Addison-Wesley, 1954).

Amrein, Audrey I., and David C. Berliner, "High-Stakes Testing, Uncertainty, and Student Learning," *Education Policy Analysis Archives* 10, no. 18 (2002). Available at: http://epaa.asu.edu/epaa/v10n18/

Antrop-González, René, and Anthony De Jesús, "Toward a Theory of *Critical Care* in Urban Small School Reform: Examining Structures and Pedagogies of Caring in Two Latino Community-Based Schools." *International Journal of Qualitative Studies in Education* 19, no. 4 (2006): 409–433.

Anyon, Jean, "Inner Cities, Affluent Suburbs, and Unequal Educational Opportunity." In *Multicultural Education: Issues and Perspectives*, 4th ed., edited by James A. Banks and Cherry A. McGee Banks (New York: Wiley, 2003).

Anyon, Jean, *Radical Possibilities: Public Policy, Urban Education, and a New Social Movement* (New York: Routledge, 2005).

Anzaldúa, Gloria, *Borderlands/La Frontera: The New Mestiza* (San Francisco: Aunt Lute Press, 1987).

Apple, Michael W., *Teachers and Texts: A Political Economy of Class and Gender Relations in Education* (Boston: Routledge and Kegan Paul, 1986).

Apple, Michael W., *Identity and Curriculum*, 3rd ed. (New York: RoutledgeFalmer, 2004).

Aronowitz, Stanley, "Between Nationality and Class." *Harvard Educational Review* 67, no. 2 (Summer 1997): 188–207.

Arthur, John, *Invisible Sojourners: African Immigrant Diaspora in the United States* (Westport, CT: Greenwood, 2000).

Aruri, Naseer H., "The Arab-American Community of Springfield, Massachusetts." In *The Arab-Americans: Studies in Assimilation*, edited by Elaine C. Hagopian and Ann Paden (Wilmette, IL: Medina University Press International, 1969).

Ashton-Warner, Sylvia, *Teacher* (New York: Simon & Schuster, 1963).

Au, Katherine H., and Alice J. Kawakami, "Cultural Congruence in Instruction." In *Teaching Diverse Populations: Formulating a Knowledge Base*, edited by Etta R. Hollins, Joyce E. King, and Warren C. Hayman (Albany: State University of New York Press, 1994).

August, Diane, and Timothy Shanahan, eds., *Developing Literacy in Second-Language Learners* (Mahwah, NJ: Lawrence Erlbaum; and Washington, DC: Center for Applied Linguistics, 2006).

Ayish, Nader, and Muna Shami, "Framing Arab American Issues Within Multicultural Education." PowerPoint

Presentation, National Association for Multicultural Education, 15th Annual International Conference, Atlanta, GA, November 2005.

Ayres, Ian, and Jennifer Gerarda Brown, *Straightforward* (Princeton, NJ: Princeton University Press, 2005).

Ayvazian, Andrea, "Interrupting the Cycle of Oppression: The Role of Allies as Agents of Change." In *Race, Class, and Gender in the United States*, 4th ed., edited by Paula S. Rothenberg (New York: Worth, 2001).

Baker, Jean M., *How Homophobia Hurts Children: Nurturing Diversity at Home, at School, and in the Community* (San Francisco: Harrington Park Press, 2002).

Ballenger, Cynthia, *Teaching Other People's Children: Literacy and Learning in a Bilingual Classroom* (New York: Teachers College Press, 1999).

Ballentine, Darcy, and Lisa Hill, "Teaching Beyond *Once Upon a Time*." *Language Arts* 78, no. 1 (September 2000): 11–20.

Banks, James A., *An Introduction to Multicultural Education*, 4th ed. (Boston: Allyn and Bacon, 2007).

Banks, James A., "Multicultural Education: Historical Development, Dimensions, and Practice." In *Handbook of Research on Multicultural Education*, 2nd ed., edited by James A. Banks and Cherry A. McGee Banks (San Francisco: Jossey-Bass, 2004).

Banks, James A., *Teaching Strategies for Ethnic Studies*, 7th ed. (Boston: Allyn and Bacon, 2003).

Banks, James A., and Cherry McGee Banks (eds.), *Handbook of Research on Multicultural Education*, 2nd ed. (San Francisco: Jossey-Bass, 2004).

Banks, James A., Peter Cookson, Geneva Gay, Willis D. Hawley, Jacqueline Jordan Irvine, Sonia Nieto, Janet Ward Schofield, and Walter W. Stephan, *Diversity Within Unity: Essential Principles for Teaching and Learning in a Multicultural Society* (Seattle: Center for Multicultural Education, University of Washington, 2001).

Baratz, Stephen S., and Joan C. Baratz, "Early Childhood Intervention: The Social Science Base of Institutional Racism." In *Challenging the Myths: The Schools, the Blacks, and the Poor*. Reprint Series no. 5 (Cambridge, MA: Harvard Educational Review, 1971).

Bartolomé, Lilia I., "Beyond the Methods Fetish: Toward a Humanizing Pedagogy." *Harvard Educational Review* 64, no. 2 (Summer 1994): 173–194.

Bempechat, Janine, "Learning From Poor and Minority Students Who Succeed in School." *Harvard Education Letter* 15, no. 3 (May/June 1999): 1–3.

Bereiter, Carl, and Siegfried Englemann, *Teaching Disadvantaged Children in the Preschool* (Englewood Cliffs, NJ: Prentice-Hall, 1966).

Berger, Ron, "What is a Culture of Quality?" In *Going Public With Our Teaching: An Anthology of Practice*, edited by Thomas Hatch, Dilruba Ahmed, Ann Lieberman, Deborah Faigenbaum, Melissa Eiler White, and Desiree H. Pointer Mace (New York: Teachers College Press, 2005).

Berliner, David C., "Our Impoverished View of Educational Reform." *Teachers College Record*. Available at: www.tcrecord.org/content.asp?contentID+12106, August 2, 2005.

Beykont, Zeynep, ed. *The Power of Culture: Teaching Across Language Difference* (Cambridge, MA: Harvard Education Publishing Group, 2002).

Bigelow, Bill, Linda Christensen, Stanley Karp, Barbara Miner, and Bob Peterson, eds., *Rethinking Our Classrooms: Teaching for Equity and Justice*, vols. 1 and 2 (Milwaukee: Rethinking Schools, 1994).

Bigelow, Bill, Brenda Harvey, Stan Karp, and Larry Miller, eds., *Rethinking Our Classrooms: Teaching for Equity and Justice*, vol. 2 (Milwaukee: Rethinking Schools, 2001).

Bigelow, Bill, and Bob Peterson, *Rethinking Columbus: The Next 500 Years*, 2nd ed. (Milwaukee: Rethinking Schools, 1998).

Bigler, Ellen, *American Conversations: Puerto Ricans, White Ethnics, and Multicultural Education* (Philadelphia: Temple University Press, 1999).

Black, Susan, "The Roots of Vandalism." *American School Board Journal* (July 2002). Available at: www.asbj.com/current/research.html

Black, Susan, "Second Time Around." *American School* 191, no. 11 (November 2004). Available at: www.asbj.com/researcharchive/index.html

Blohm, Judith M., and Terri Lapinsky, *Kids Like Me: Voices of the Immigrant Experience* (Boston: Intercultural Press, 2006).

Boateng, Felix, "Combating Deculturalization of the African-American Child in the Public School System: A Multicultural Approach." In *Going to School: The African-American Experience*, edited by Kofi Lomotey (Albany: State University of New York Press, 1990).

Bochniek, Michael, and A. Widney Brown, *Hatred in the Hallways: Violence and Discrimination Against Lesbian, Gay, Bisexual, and Transgender Students in U.S. Schools* (New York: Human Rights Watch, 2001).

Bode, Patricia, "Multicultural Art Education: Voices of Art Teachers and Students in the Postmodern Era," diss., University of Massachusetts Amherst, 2005.

Books, Sue, ed., *Invisible Children in the Society and Its Schools*, 3rd ed. (Mahwah, NJ: Lawrence Erlbaum, 2007).

Bouie, Annie, *After-School Success: Academic Enrichment with Urban Youth* (New York: Teachers College Press, 2006).

Bourdieu, Pierre. "The Forms of Capital." In *Handbook of Theory and Research for the Sociology of Education*, edited by John G. Richardson (New York: Greenwood Press, 1986).

Bourdieu, Pierre, *Outline of Theory and Practice* (Cambridge, England: Cambridge University Press, 1977).

Bothelo, Maria Jose, and Marsha Kabakow Rudman,, *Mirrors, Windows, and Doors: Critical Multicultural Analysis of Children's Literature* (Mahwah, NJ: Lawrence Erlbaum, 2008).

Bowles, Samuel, and Herbert Gintis, *Schooling in Capitalist America: Educational Reform and the Contradictions of Economic Life* (New York: Basic Books, 1976).

Bridgeland, John M., John J. Dilulio, Jr., and Karen B. Morison, *The Silent Epidemic: Perspectives of High School Dropouts*. A Report by Civic Enterprises with Peter D. Hart Research Associates for the Bill & Melinda Gates Foundation (Washington, DC: Civic Enterprises, March 2006). Available at: www.gatesfoundation.org/nr/downloads/ed/TheSilent Epidemic3-06FINAL.pdf

Brumberg, Stephan F., *Going to America, Going to School: The Jewish Immigrant Public School Encounter in Turn-of-the-Century New York City* (New York: Praeger, 1986).

Bryk, Anthony S., Valerie E. Lee, and Peter B. Holland, *Catholic Schools and the Common Good* (Cambridge, MA: Harvard Educational Review Press, 1993).

Buckel, David S., "Legal Perspective on Ensuring a Safe and Nondiscriminatory School Environment for Lesbian, Gay, Bisexual, and Transgendered Students." *Education and Urban Education* 32, no. 3 (May 2000): 390–398.

Buckley, Jack, Mark Schneider, and Yi Shang, "Fix it And They Might Stay: School Facility Quality and Teacher Retention in Washington, DC." *Teachers College Record* 107, no. 4 (May 2005): 1107–1123.

Callahan, Rebecca M., "Tracking and High School English Learners: Limiting Opportunity to Learn." *American Educational Research Journal* 42, no. 2 (Summer 2005): 305–328, p. 322.

Campos, David, *Understanding Gay and Lesbian Youth: Lessons for Straight School Teachers, Counselors, and Administrators* (Lanham, MD: Scarecrow Education, 2005).

Carnes, Jim, "Searching for Patterns: A Conversation with Carlos Cortés." *Teaching Tolerance* no. 16 (Fall 1999): 10–15.

Carter, Prudence L., *Keepin' It Real: School Success Beyond Black and White* (New York: Oxford University Press, 2005).

Castor, Mei L., Michael S. Smyser, Maile M. Taualii, Alice N. Park, Shelley A. Lawson, and Ralph A. Forquera, "A Nationwide Population-Based Study Identifying Health Disparities Between American Indians/Alaska Natives and the General Populations Living in Select Urban Counties," *American Journal of Public Health* 96, no. 8 (2006): 1478–1484.

Center on Education Policy, *From the Capital to the Classroom: Year 4 of the No Child Left Behind Act* (Washington, DC: Author, 2006).

Children's Museum, Boston, *Many Thanksgivings: Teaching Thanksgiving—Including the Wampanoag Perspective* (Boston: The Children's Museum, 2002).

Christensen, Linda, Reading, *Writing and Rising Up* (Milwaukee, WI: Rethinking Schools, 2000).

Christensen, Linda, "Whose Standard? Teaching Standard English." In *Language Development: A Reader for Teachers*, edited by Brenda Miller Power and Ruth Shagoury Hubbard (Englewood Cliffs, NJ: Merrill, 1996).

Clewell, B. C., M. Puma, and S. A. McKay, *Does It Matter if My Teacher Looks Like Me? The Impact of Teacher Race and Ethnicity on Student Academic Achievement* (New York: Ford Foundation, 2001).

Cochran-Smith, Marilyn, "Blind Vision: Unlearning Racism in Teacher Education." *Harvard Educational Review* 70, no. 2 (Summer 2000): 157–190.

Cohen, Geoffrey L, Julio Garcia, Nancy Apfel, and Allison Master, "Reducing the Racial Achievement Gap: A Social-Psychological Intervention." *Science* 313, no. 5791 (September 2006): 1307–1310.

College Board, "2004 College Bound Seniors Test Scores: SAT." *College-Bound Seniors 2004: A Profile of SAT Program Test Takers* (New York: Author, 2005).

Colorado Small Schools Initiative (CSSI). Directed by Colorado Children's Campaign. Denver, Colorado. June 2006. Available at: www.coloradosmallschools.org

Comber, Barbara, "Critical Literacies and Local Action: Teacher Knowledge and a 'New' Research Agenda." In *Negotiating Critical Literacies in Classrooms*, edited by Barbara Comber and Anne Simpson (Mahwah, NJ: Lawrence Erlbaum, 2001): 271–282.

Comber, Barbara, "What *Really* Counts in Early Literacy Lessons." *Language Arts* 78, no. 1 (September 2000): 39–49.

Combs, Bobbie, Dannamarie Hosler, illus. *1, 2, 3 A Family Counting Book* (Ridley Park, PA: Two Lives Publishing, 2001).

Compton-Lilly, Catherine, *Confronting Racism, Poverty, and Power: Classroom Strategies to Change the World* (Portsmouth, NH: Heinemann, 2004).

Conchas, Gilberto Q. *The Color of Success: Race and High-Achieving Urban Youth* (New York: Teachers College Press, 2006).

Cortés, Carlos E., *The Children Are Watching: How the Media Teach About Diversity* (New York: Teachers College Press, 2000).

Cowhey, Mary, *Black Ants and Buddhists: Thinking Critically and Teaching Differently in the Primary Grades* (Portland, ME: Stenhouse, 2006).

Crabtree, Steve. "Teachers Who Care Get Most From Kids." *Detroit News*, June 4, 2004. Available at: www.detnews.com/2004/schools/0406/04/a09-173712.htm.

Crawford, James, *At War With Diversity: U.S. Language Policy in an Age of Anxiety* (Clevedon, England: Multilingual Matters, 2000).

Crawford, James, *Educating English Learners: Language Diversity in the Classroom*, 5th ed. (Los Angeles: Bilingual Education Services, 2004).

Crawford, James, *Hold Your Tongue: Bilingualism and the Politics of "English Only"* (Reading, MA: Addison-Wesley, 1992).

Croninger, Robert G., and Valerie E. Lee, "Social Capital and Dropping Out of High School: Benefits to At-Risk Students of Teachers' Support and Guidance." *Teachers College Record* 103, no. 4 (August 2001): 548–581.

Crosnoe, Robert, "Double Disadvantage or Signs of Resilience? The Elementary School Contexts of Children from Mexican Immigrant Families." *American Educational Research Journal* 42, no. 2 (2005): 269–303.

Crosnoe, Robert, Monica Kirkpatrick, and Glen H. Elder, Jr., "School Size and the Interpersonal Side of Education: An Examination of Race/Ethnicity and Organizational Context." *Social Sciences Quarterly* 85, no. 5 (2004): 1259–1274.

Cruz-Janzen, Marta I., "Curriculum and the Self-concept of Biethnic and Biracial Persons," diss., College of Education, University of Denver, April 1997.

Cummins, Jim, *Negotiating Identities: Education for Empowerment in a Diverse Society* (Ontario, CA: California Association for Bilingual Education, 1996).

Cummins, Jim, "Alternative Paradigms in Bilingual Education Research: Does Theory Have a Place?" *Educational Researcher* 28, no. 7 (October 1999): 26–32, 41.

Cummins, Jim, *Language, Power, and Pedagogy: Bilingual Children in the Crossfire* (Clevedon, England: Multilingual Matters, 2000).

D'Amico, Joseph J., "A Closer Look at the Minority Achievement Gap." *ERS Spectrum* (Spring 2001): 4–10.

Darling-Hammond, Linda, "New Standards and Inequalities: School Reform and the Education of African American Students." In *Black Education: A Transformative Research and Action Agenda for the New Century*, edited by Joyce E. King (Mahwah, NJ: Lawrence Erlbaum; and Washington, DC: American Educational Research Association, 2005).

David, Jane L., and Patrick M. Shields, *When Theory Hits Reality: Standards-Based Reform in Urban Districts, Final Narrative Report* (Menlo Park, CA: SRI International, 2001).

Dee, Thomas S., *Teachers, Race, and Student Achievement in a Randomized Experiment* (Cambridge, MA: National Bureau of Economic Research, 2000).

Delgado-Gaitan, Concha, *Involving Latino Families in Schools: Raising Student Achievement Through Home-School Partnerships* (Thousand Oaks, CA: Corwin Press, 2004).

Delpit, Lisa, and Joanne Kilgour Doudy, eds., *The Skin That We Speak: Thoughts on Language and Culture in the Classroom* (New York: New Press, 2002).

DeMarrais, Kathleen P., and Margaret LeCompte, *The Way Schools Work: A Sociological Analysis of Education*, 4th ed. (Boston: Allyn and Bacon, 2007).

Derman-Sparks, Louise, *Teaching/Learning Anti-Racism: A Developmental Approach* (New York: Teachers College Press, 1997).

Derman-Sparks, Louise, and the A.B.C. Task Force, *Anti-Bias Curriculum: Tools for Empowering Young Children* (Washington, DC: National Association for the Education of Young Children, 1989).

Derman-Sparks, Louise, Patricia G. Ramsey, Julie Olsen Edwards, and Carol Brunson Day, *What If All The Kids Are White?: Anti-Bias Multicultural Education With Young Children and Families* (New York: Teachers College Press, 2006).

Dershowitz, Alan M., *The Vanishing American Jew* (New York: Simon & Schuster, 1998).

DeVoe, Jill, Peter Katharin, Margaret Noonan, Thomas Snyder, and Katrina Baum, *Indicators of School Climate and Safety: 2005* (Washington, DC: Bureau of Justice Statistics, and the National Center for Education Statistics, 2005).

Dewey, John, *Democracy and Education* (New York: Free Press, 1916).

Deyhle, Donna, and Karen Swisher, "Research in American Indian and Alaska Native Education: From Assimilation to Self-Determination." In *Review of Research in Education*, vol. 22, edited by Michael W. Apple (Washington, DC: American Educational Research Association (AERA), 1997).

Díaz, Stephan, Luis C. Moll, and Hugh Mehan, "Sociocultural Resources in Instruction: A Context-Specific Approach." In *Beyond Language: Social and Cultural Factors in Schooling Language Minority Students* (Los Angeles: Office of Bilingual Education, California State Department of Education, Evaluation, Dissemination and Assessment Center, 1986).

Dickeman, Mildred, "Teaching Cultural Pluralism." In *Teaching Ethnic Studies: Concepts and Strategies*, 43rd Yearbook, edited by James A. Banks (Washington, DC: National Council for the Social Studies, 1973).

Dinnerstein, Leonard, *Anti-Semitism in America* (New York: Oxford University Press, 1994).

"Do Brighter Walls Make Brighter Students?" Available at: www.cnn.com/2005/EDUCATION/12/19/paint.in .schools.ap/index.html

Dodson, Howard, and Sylviane A. Diouf, eds., *In Motion: The African-American Migration Experience* (New York: The New York Public Library Schomberg Center for Research in Black Culture, August 2006). Available at: www.inmotionaame.org/migrations/ landing.cfm?migration=13

Dolby, Nadine, "Changing Selves: Multicultural Education and the Challenge of New Identities." *Teachers College Record* 102, no. 5 (October 2000): 898–912.

Donaldson, Karen B. McLean, *Through Students' Eyes: Combating Racism in United States Schools* (Westport, CT: Praeger, 1996).

Donaldson, Karen B. McLean, *Shattering the Denial: Protocols for the Classrooms and Beyond* (Westport, CT: Bergin and Garvey, 2001).

Donato, Rubén, *The Other Struggle for Equal Schools: Mexican Americans During the Civil Rights Era* (Albany: State University of New York Press, 1997).

DuBois, W. E. B., "Does the Negro Need Separate Schools?" *Journal of Negro Education* 4, no. 3 (1935): 328–335.

Eccles, Jacquelynne, and Lee Jussim, "Teacher Expectations II: Construction and Reflection of Student Achievement." *Journal of Personality and Social Psychology* 63, no. 6 (December 1992): 947–961.

Eck, Diana L., *A New Religious America: How a "Christian Country" Has Become the World's Most Religiously Diverse Nation* (New York: HarperCollins, 2001).

Editorial, "Tongue-Tied on Bilingual Education," *The New York Times*, September 2, 2005.

Education Trust, *The Funding Gap 2005* (Washington, DC: Author, 2005).

Eller-Powell, Rebecca, "Teaching for Change in Appalachia." In *Teaching Diverse Populations: Formulating a Knowledge Base*, edited by Etta R. Hollins, Joyce E. King, and Warren C. Hayman (Albany: State University of New York Press, 1994).

Elmore, Richard F., "Testing Trap." *Harvard Magazine* (September-October 2002). Available at: www .harvard-magazine.com/on-line/0902140.html

Epstein, Joyce L., *School, Family, and Community Partnerships: Preparing Educators and Improving Schools* (Boulder, CO: Westview, 2001).

Equal Educational Opportunities Act of 1974, 20 U.S.C. 1703(f).

Erickson, Frederick, "Transformation and School Success: The Politics and Culture of Educational Achievement." In *Minority Education*, edited by Evelyn Jacob and Cathie Jordan (Norwood, NJ: Ablex, 1993).

Erickson, Frederick, and Gerald Mohatt, "Cultural Organization of Participant Structures in Two Classrooms of Indian Students." In *Doing the Ethnography of Schooling: Educational Anthropology in Action*, edited by George D. Spindler (New York: Holt, Rinehart and Winston, 1982).

Evans, Robert, *Family Matters: How School Can Cope With the Crisis in Childrearing* (San Francisco: Jossey-Bass, 2004).

Evans, Robert, "Reframing the Achievement Gap." *Phi Delta Kappan* 86, no. 8 (April 2005): 582–589.

"Exit Exams Decrease Graduation Rates." *FairTest Examiner* (August 2006). Available at: www.fairtest.org

Fecho, Bob, *Is This English? Race, Language, and Culture in the Classroom* (New York: Teachers College Press, 2003).

Ferguson, Ann Arnett, *Bad Boys: Public School in the Making of Black Masculinity* (Ann Arbor: University of Michigan Press, 2001).

Fine, Michelle, *Framing Dropouts: Notes on the Politics of an Urban High School* (Albany, NY: State University of New York Press, 1991).

Fine, Michelle, "Not in Our Name: Reclaiming the Democratic Vision of Small School Reform." *Rethinking Schools* 19, no. 4 (Summer 2005): 11–14.

Finn, Jeremy D., Susan B. Gerber, Charles M. Achilles, and Jayne Byrd-Zaharias, "The Enduring Effects of Small Classes." *Teachers College Record* 103, no. 2 (April 2001): 145–183.

Flores-González, Nilda, "The Structuring of Extracurricular Opportunities and Latino Student Retention." *Journal of Poverty* 4, nos. 1, 2 (2000): 4(1/2), 85–108.

Flores-González, Nilda, *School Kids, Street Kids: Identity and High School Completion Among Latinos* (New York: Teachers College Press, 2002).

Fordham, Signithia, and John U. Ogbu, "Black Students' School Success: Coping With the 'Burden of Acting White.'" *Urban Review* 18, no. 3 (1986): 176–206.

Foster, Michele, *Black Teachers on Teaching* (New York: New Press, 1997).

Foy, Colm, *Cape Verde: Politics, Economics and Society* (London, England: Pinter, 1988).

Fránquiz, María E. and Reyes, María de la Luz, "Multicultural Language Practices: Opportunity, Inclusion and Choice." *Primary Voices* 8, no. 4 (2000): 3–10.

Fraser, Steve, ed., *The Bell Curve Wars: Race, Intelligence, and the Future of America* (New York: Basic Books, 1995).

Freire, Paulo, *Pedagogy of the Oppressed* (New York: Seabury Press, 1970).

Freire, Paulo, *The Politics of Education: Culture, Power, and Liberation* (South Hadley, MA: Bergen & Garvey, 1985).

Freire, Paulo, *Teachers as Cultural Workers: Letters to Those Who Dare Teach* (Boulder, CO: Westview Press, 1998).

Fuller, Bruce, "Good Bilingual Education Programs Produce Faster Results Than Good English-Only Programs." *Los Angeles Times*, August 24, 2005.

Future of the First Amendment. John S. and James L. Knight Foundation. Available at: http://firstamendmentfuture.org

Gándara, Patricia, *Over the Ivy Walls: The Educational Mobility of Low-Income Chicanos* (Albany: State University of New York Press, 1995).

Gándara, Patricia, Julie Maxwell-Jolly, and Anne Driscoll, *Listening to Teachers of English Learners* (Santa Cruz, CA: Center for the Study of Teaching and Learning, 2005).

Gardner, Howard, *Frames of Mind* (New York: Basic Books, 1983).

Gardner, Howard, *Frames of Mind: The Theory of Multiple Intelligences*, 10th Anniversary Issue (New York: Basic Books, 1993).

Gardner, Howard, *Intelligence Reframed* (New York: Basic Books, 1999).

Gardner, Howard, *Multiple Intelligences: New Horizons* (New York: Basic Books, 2006).

Gates Foundation (The Bill & Melinda Gates Foundation. Available at: www.gatesfoundation.org/Education; accessed July 2006.

Gay, Geneva, "Mirror Images on Common Issues: Parallels Between Multicultural Education and Critical Pedagogy." In *Multicultural Education, Critical Pedagogy, and the Politics of Difference*, edited by Christine E. Sleeter and Peter L. McLaren (Albany: State University of New York Press, 1995): 155–189.

Gay, Geneva, *Culturally Responsive Teaching: Theory, Research, and Practice* (New York: Teachers College Press, 2000).

Gay, Lesbian, Straight Education Network (GLSEN), *National School Climate Survey 2005* (New York: Author, 2006).

Gebhard, Meg, Theresa Austin, Sonia Nieto, and Jerri Willett, "'You Can't Step on Someone Else's Words': Preparing All Teachers to Teach Language Minority Students." In *The Power of Culture: Teaching Across Language Difference*, edited by Zeynep Beykont (Cambridge, MA: Harvard Education Publishing Group, 2002).

Gibson, Margaret A., "The School Performance of Immigrant Minorities: A Comparative View." *Anthropology & Education Quarterly* 18, no. 4 (December 1987): 262–275.

Gibson, Margaret A., "Conclusion: Complicating the Immigrant/Involuntary Minority Typology." *Anthropology & Education Quarterly* 28, no. 3 (September 1997): 431–454.

Gibson, Margaret A., and Livier F. Bejínez, "Dropout Prevention: How Migrant Education Supports Mexican Youth." *Journal of Latinos and Education* 1, no. 3 (2002): 155–175.

Gibson, Paul, "Gay Male and Lesbian Youth Suicide." In *Report of the Secretary's Task Force on Youth Suicide* (Washington, DC: U.S. Department of Health and Human Services, 1989).

Gillborn, David, "Ethnicity and Educational Performance in the United Kingdom: Racism, Ethnicity, and Variability in Achievement." *Anthropology & Education Quarterly* 28, no. 3 (September 1997): 375–393.

Gillespie, Peggy and Gigi Kaeser, *Family Diversity Projects: Diversity exhibits you can bring to your community*. August 2006 www.familydiv.org.

Gimenez, Martha E., "Latino/'Hispanic': Who Needs a Name? The Case Against a Standardized Terminology." In *Latinos and Education: A Critical Reader*, edited by Antonia Darder, Rodolfo D. Torres, and Henry Gutiérrez (New York: Routledge, 1997): 225–238.

Giroux, Henry A., *Theory and Resistance in Education: A Pedagogy for the Opposition* (South Hadley, MA: Bergen & Garvey, 1983).

Giroux, Henry, "Rewriting the Discourse of Racial Identity: Towards a Pedagogy and Politics of Whiteness." *Harvard Educational Review* 67, no. 2 (Summer 1997): 285–320.

Giroux, Henry A., "Democracy, Freedom, and Justice After September 11th: Rethinking the Role of Educators and the Politics of Schooling." *Teachers College Record* 104, no. 6 (September 2002): 1138–1162.

Goldberg, Margaret E., "Truancy and Dropout among Cambodian: Results from a comprehensive High School." *Social Work in Education* 21, no. 1 (January 1999): 49–63.

Gollnick, Donna M., and Philip C. Chinn, *Multicultural Education in a Pluralistic Society*, 7th ed. (New York: Prentice-Hall, 2006).

Gonzalez, Juan, "Schools Ruling Defies Logic." *Daily News, City Beat*, Thursday, June 27, 2002.

Gonzalez, Norma E., Luis Moll, and Cathy Amanti, eds., *Funds of Knowledge: Theorizing Practices in Households and Classrooms* (Mahwah, NJ: Lawrence Erlbaum, 2005).

Goodlad, John I., *A Place Called School* (New York: McGraw-Hill, 1984).

Goodwin, A. Lin, "Teacher Preparation and the Education of Immigrant Children." *Education and Urban Society* 34, no. 2 (February 2002): 156–172.

Gordon, David T., ed., *Minority Achievement* (Cambridge, MA: Harvard Education Letter Focus Series no. 7, 2002).

Gordon, Edmund W., "Bridging the New Diversity: The Minority Achievement Gap." *Principal* (May 2000): 20–23.

Gorski, Paul C., "Savage Inequalities: Uncovering Classism in Ruby Payne's Framework," diss., Hamline University, St. Paul, MN, 2005. Available at: www.EdChange.org

Gould, Stephen Jay, *The Mismeasure of Man* (New York: Norton, 1981).

Governors' Commission on Gay and Lesbian Youth, *Making Schools Safe for Gay and Lesbian Youth: Breaking the Silence in Schools and in Families* (Boston: Massachusetts Department of Education, February 25, 1993).

Grande, Sandy, *Red Pedagogy: Native American Social and Political Thought* (Lanham, MD: Rowman & Littlefield, 2004).

Greenbaum, William, "America in Search of a New Ideal: An Essay on the Rise of Pluralism." *Harvard Educational Review* 44, no. 3 (August 1974): 411–440.

Greene, Maxine, *The Dialectic of Freedom* (New York: Teachers College Press, 1988).

Greene, Maxine, "Reflections: Implications of September 11th for Curriculum." *Division B: Curriculum Studies Newsletter* (Washington, DC: American Educational Research Association, Fall 2001).

Greene, Maxine, *Releasing the Imagination: Essays on Education, the Arts, and Social Change* (San Francisco: Jossey-Bass, 2000).

Grieco, Elizabeth M., "The Dominican Population in the United States: Growth and Distribution." Migration Policy Institute, September 2004. Available at: www.migrationpolicy.org/pubs/MPI_Report_Dominican_Pop_US.pdf

Guarnizo, Luis, Alejandro Portes, and William Haller, "Assimilation and Transnationalism: Determinants of Transnational Political Action among Contemporary Migrants." *American Journal of Sociology* 108 (2003): 1211–1248.

Gutierrez, Kris D., and Barbara Rogoff, "Cultural Ways of Learning: Individual Traits or Repertoires of Practice." *Educational Researchers* 32, no. 5 (2003): 19–25.

Haberman, Martin, "The Pedagogy of Poverty versus Good Teaching." *Phi Delta Kappan* 73, no. 4 (December 1991): 290–294.

Haberman, Martin, "Selecting 'Star' Teachers for Children and Youth in Urban Poverty." *Phi Delta Kappan* 76, no. 10 (June 1995): 777–781.

Hajar, Paula., "Arab Americans: Concepts, Strategies, and Materials." In *Teaching Strategies for Ethnic Studies*, 7th ed., edited by James A. Banks (Boston: Allyn and Bacon, 2003).

Halpern, David, *Social Capital* (Cambridge: Polity Press, 2005).

Halpern, Robert, *Making Play Work: The Promise of After-School Programs for Low-Income Children* (New York: Teachers College Press, 2003).

Harris, Violet J., ed., *Using Multiethnic Literature in the K–8 Classroom* (Norwood, MA: Christopher-Gordon, 1997).

Harris Interactive, *Survey of the American Teacher: An Examination of School Leadership* (Rochester, NY: Author, 2003). Available at: www.metlife.com/Applications/Corporate/WPS/DCA/Pagegenerator/0,1674,P2315,00.htm/

Harry, Beth, and Janette Klingner, *Why Are So Many Minority Students in Special Education? Understanding Race and Disability in Schools* (New York: Teachers College Press, 2006).

Heath, Shirley Brice, *Ways with Words* (New York: Cambridge University Press, 1983).

Heath, Shirley Brice, "Ethnography in Communities: Learning the Everyday Life of America's Subordinated Youth." In *Handbook of Research on*

Multicultural Education, 2nd ed., edited by James A. Banks and Cherry A. McGee Banks (San Francisco: Jossey-Bass, 2004): 146–162.

Henderson, Anne T., and Karen L. Mapp, *A New Wave of Evidence: The Impact of School, Family, and Community Connections on Student Achievement* (Austin, TX: Southwest Educational Development Laboratory, 2002).

Herbst, Philip H., *The Color of Words: An Encyclopaedic Dictionary of Ethnic Bias in the United States* (Yarmouth, ME: Intercultural Press, 1997).

Hernandez, Ramona, and Francisco L. Rivera-Batiz, Dominican Research Monographs. October 2003. CUNY Dominican Studies Institute. Available at: www.earthinstitute.columbia.edu/cgsd/advising/documents/rivera_batiz.pdf; accessed July 1, 2006.

Herrnstein, Richard J., and Charles Murray, *The Bell Curve: Intelligence and Class Structure in American Life* (New York: Free Press, 1994).

Hidalgo, Nitza M., "Free Time, School Is Like a Free Time": Social Relations in City High School Classes, diss., Graduate School of Education, Harvard University, 1991.

Hildago, Nitza M., "Latino/a Families' Epistemology." In *Latino Education: An Agenda for Community Action Research*, edited by Pedro Pedraza and Melissa Rivera (Mahwah, NJ: Lawrence Erlbaum, 2005).

Him, Chanrithy, *When Broken Glass Floats: Growing Up Under the Khmer Rouge* (New York: W. W. Norton, 2001).

Hines, Maxwell S., "Remembering Amadou Diallo: The Response of the New Teachers Network." *Phi Delta Kappan* 84, no. 4 (2002): 303–306.

Hirsch, Barton J., *A Place to Call Home: After-school Programs for Urban Youth* (New York: Teachers College Press, 2005).

Hirsch, E. D., *Cultural Literacy: What Every American Needs to Know* (Boston: Houghton Mifflin, 1987).

Hirsch, E. D., ed., *What Your Fourth Grader Needs to Know: Fundamentals of a Good Fourth-Grade Education (The Core Knowledge)* (New York: Delta, 1994).

Hong, Guanglei, and Stephen W. Raudenbush, "Effects of Kindergarten Retention Policy on Children's Cognitive Growth in Reading and Mathematics." *Educational Evaluation and Policy Analysis* 27, no. 3 (Fall 2005): 205–224.

Hopstock, Paul J., and Todd G. Stephenson, *Descriptive Study of Services to LEP Students and LEP Students With Disabilities* (Arlington, VA: Development Associates, 2003).

Howard, Elizabeth R., Donna Christian, and Fred Genesee, *The Development of Bilingualism and Biliteracy From Grade 3 to 5: A Summary of Findings From the CAL/CREDE Study of Two-Way Immersion Education* (University of California, Santa Cruz: Center for Research on Education, Diversity, and Excellence, 2004).

Howard, Gary, "We Can't Teach What We Don't Know": White Teachers, Multiracial Schools, 2nd ed. (New York: Teachers College Press, 2006).

Howe, Irving, *World of Our Fathers* (New York: Simon & Schuster, 1983).

Hughes, Julie M. and Bigler, Rebecca S., "Addressing Race and Racism in the Classroom." In *Lessons in Integration: Realizing the Promise of Racial Diversity in American Schools*, edited by Erica Frankenberg and Gary Orfield. (Charlottesville: University of Virginia Press, 2007).

Huh, Nam Y., "Does Money Transform Schools?" *The Christian Science Monitor*, August 9, 2005. Available at: www.csmonitor.com/2005/0809/p01.S03-ussc.html

Igoa, Cristina, *The Inner World of the Immigrant Child* (New York: St. Martins Press, 1995).

Irizarry, Jason, "Ethnic and Urban Intersections in the Classroom: Latino Students, Hybrid Identities, and Culturally Responsive Pedagogy." *Multicultural Perspectives* (forthcoming).

Irizarry, Jason, "Representin' for Latino Students: Culturally Responsive Pedagogies, Teacher Identities, and the Preparation of Teachers for Urban Schools." diss., University of Massachusetts Amherst, 2005.

Irvine, Jacqueline Jordan, *Critical Knowledge for Diverse Teachers and Learners* (Washington, DC: American Association of Colleges for Teacher Education, 1997).

Irvine, Jacqueline Jordan, and Michele Foster, *Growing Up African American in Catholic Schools* (New York: Teachers College Press, 1996).

Irvine, Jacqueline Jordan, and James W. Fraser, "Warm Demanders." *Education Week* 17, no. 35 (May 1998): 56–57.

Jackson, D. Bruce, "Education Reform as if Student Agency Mattered: Academic Microcultures and Student Identity." *Phi Delta Kappan* 84, no. 8 (April 2003): 579–585.

Jacob, Evelyn, and Cathie Jordan, eds., *Minority Education: Anthropological Perspectives* (Norwood, NJ: Ablex, 1993).

Jalava, Antti, "Mother Tongue and Identity: Nobody Could See That I Was a Finn." In *Minority Education: From Shame to Struggle*, edited by Tove Skutnabb-Kangas and Jim Cummins (Clevedon, England: Multilingual Matters, 1988).

Jensen, Arthur R., "How Much Can We Boost I.Q. and Scholastic Achievement?" *Harvard Educational Review* 39, no. 2 (1969): 1–123.

Jo, Ji-Yeon O., "Neglected Voices in the Multicultural America: Asian American Racial Politics and its Implication for Multicultural Education." *Multicultural Perspectives* 6, no. 1 (2004): 19–25.

Johnson, Monica K., Robert Crosnoe, and Glen H. Elder, Jr., "Students' Attachment and Academic Engagement: The Role of Race and Ethnicity." *Sociology of Education* 74, no. 4 (2001): 318–334.

Jones, M. Gail, Brett D. Jones, and Tracy Hargrove, *The Unintended Consequences of High-Stakes Testing* (Lanham, MD: Rowman & Littlefield, 2003).

Joshi, Khyati Y., *New Roots in America's Sacred Ground: Religion, Race, and Ethnicity in Indian America* (New Brunswick, NJ: Rutgers University Press, 2006).

Kaeser, Gigi, and Peggy Gillespie, *Of Many Colors: Portraits of Multiracial Families* (Amherst: University of Massachusetts Press, 1997).

Kalantzis, Mary and Bill Cope, *The Experience of Multicultural Education in Australia: Six Case Studies* (Sydney: Center for Multicultural Studies, Wollongong University, 1990).

Kaplan, Jack, "The Effectiveness of SAT Coaching on Math SAT Scores." *Chance* 18, no. 2 (2005): Available at: www.fairtest.org.

Katz, Michael B., *Class, Bureaucracy, and the Schools: The Illusion of Educational Change in America* (New York: Praeger, 1975).

Katz, Susan Roberta, "Where the Streets Cross the Classroom: A Study of Latino Students' Perspectives on Cultural Identity in City Schools and Neighborhood Gangs." *Bilingual Research Journal* 20, nos. 3, 4 (Summer/Fall 1995): 603–631.

Katz, Susan Roberta, "Teaching in Tensions: Latino Immigrant Youth, Their Teachers, and the Structures of Schooling." *Teachers College Record* 100, no. 4 (Summer 1999): 809–840.

Keahi, Sarah, "Advocating for a Stimulating and Language-Based Education: 'If You Don't Learn your Language, Where Can You Go Home To?' " In *Indigenous Educational Models for Contemporary Practice: In Our Mother's Voice*, edited by Maenette Kape'ahiokalani Padeken Ah Nee-Benham and Joanne Elizabeth Cooper (Mahwah, NJ: Lawrence Erlbaum, 2000): 55–60.

Kelly, Karen, "Retention vs. Social Promotion: Schools Search for Alternatives." *Harvard Education Letter* 15, no. 1 (January/February 1999): 1–3.

Kiang, Peter Nien-Chu, *Southeast Asian Parent Empowerment: The Challenge of Changing Demographics in Lowell, Massachusetts*, Monograph no. 1 (Boston: Massachusetts Association for Bilingual Education, 1990).

Kiang, Peter Nien-Chu, and Vivian Wai-Fun Lee, "Exclusion or Contribution? Education K–12 Policy." In *The State of Asian Pacific America: Policy Issues to the Year 2020* (Los Angeles: LEAP Asian Pacific American Public Policy Institute and the UCLA Asian American Studies Center, 1993).

Kiernan, Ben, *How Pol Pot Came to Power: Colonialism, Nationalism, and Communism in Cambodia*, 2nd ed. (New Haven: Yale University Press, 2004).

Kiernan, Ben, *The Pol Pot Regime: Race, Power, and Genocide in Cambodia under the Khmer Rouge, 1975–79*, 2nd ed. (New Haven, CT: Yale University Press, 2002).

Kim, Heather, *Diversity Among Asian American High School Students* (Princeton, NJ: Educational Testing Service, 1997).

Kindler, Anneka L., *Survey of the States' Limited English Proficient Students and Available Educational Programs and Services 2000–2001 Summary Report* (Washington, DC: U.S. Department of Education, Office of English Language Acquisition, Language Enhancement, and Academic Achievement for Limited English Proficient Students [NCELA], October 2002).

King, Joyce, ed. Black Education: *A Transformative Research and Action Agenda for the New Century* (Washington, DC/Mahwah, NJ: AERA/Lawrence Erlbaum, 2005).

Kohl, Herbert, *"I Won't Learn From You" and Other Thoughts on Creative Maladjustment* (New York: New Press, 1994).

Kozol, Jonathon, "Great Men and Women (Tailored for School Use)." *Learning Magazine* (December 1975): 16–20.

Kozol, Jonathon, *The Shame of the Nation: The Restoration of Apartheid Schooling in America* (New York: Crown, 2005).

Krashen, Stephen, *Second Language Acquisition and Second Language Learning* (New York: Pergamon, 1981).

Krashen, Stephen, "Bilingual Education Accelerates English Language Development." Available at: www.sdkrashen.com/articles/krashen_immpersion.pdf

Kugler, Eileen Gale, *Debunking the Middle-Class Myth: Why Diverse Schools Are Good for All Kids* (Lanham, MD: Scarecrow Press, 2002).

Kymlicka, Will, "Foreword." In *Diversity and Citizenship in Education: Global Perspectives*, edited by James A. Banks (San Francisco: Jossey-Bass, 2004): xiii–xviii.

Ladner, Matthew, and Christopher Hammons, "Special But Unequal: Race and Special Education." In *Rethinking Special Education for a New Century*, edited by Chester E. Finn, Andrew J. Rotherham, and Charles R. Hokanson (Washington, DC: Thomas B. Fordham Foundation, 2001).

Ladson-Billings, Gloria, *The Dreamkeepers: Successful Teachers of African American Children* (San Francisco: Jossey-Bass, 1994).

Ladson-Billings, Gloria, *Crossing Over to Canaan: The Journey of New Teachers in Diverse Classrooms* (San Francisco: Jossey-Bass, 2001).

Ladson-Billings, Gloria, "It's Not the Culture of Poverty, It's the Poverty of Culture: The Problem with Teacher Education." *Anthropology & Education Quarterly* 37, no. 2 (June 2006): 104–109.

Lambert, Wallace E., "Culture and Language as Factors in Learning and Education." In *Education of Immigrant Students*, edited by A. Wolfgang (Toronto: Ontario Institute for Studies in Education (OISE), 1975).

Lambert, Wallace E., and Donald Taylor, *Coping with Cultural and Racial Diversity in Urban America* (Westport, CT: Praeger, 1990).

Larson, Joanne, and Patricia D. Irvine, " 'We Call Him Dr. King': Reciprocal Distancing in Urban Classrooms." *Language Arts* 76, no. 5 (May 1999): 393–400.

Lau v. Nichols, 414 U.S. 563 (1974).

Lawrence, Sandra M., and Beverly Daniel Tatum, "White Educators as Allies: Moving From Awareness to Action." In *Off White: Readings on Power, Privilege, and Resistance*, edited by Michelle Fine, Lois Weis, Linda Powell Pruitt, and April Burns (New York: Routledge, 2004): 363–372.

Lee, Carol D., "Why We Need To Re-Think Race and Ethnicity in Educational Research." *Educational Researcher* 32, no. 5 (2003): 3–5.

Lee, Carol D., "Intervention Research Based on Current Views of Cognition and Learning." In *Black Education. A Transformative Research and Action Agenda for the New Century*, edited by Joyce E. King (Washington, DC: American Educational Research Association; and Mahwah, NJ: Lawrence Erlbaum, 2005): 45–71.

Lee, Enid, "Equity and Equality." From a keynote speech at the annual Connecticut NAME Conference, October 2004.

Lee, Enid, Deborah Menkart, and Margo Okazawa-Rey, *Beyond Heroes and Holidays: A Practical Guide to K–12 Anti-Racist, Multicultural Education and Staff Development* (Washington, DC: Network of Educators on the Americas [NECA], 1998).

Lee, Jaekyung, *Tracking Achievement Gaps and Assessing the Impact of NCLB on the GAPS: An In-Depth Look into National and State Reading and Math Outcome Trends* (Cambridge, MA: The Civil Rights Project, 2006).

Lee, Steven K., "The Latino Students' Attitudes, Perceptions, and Views on Bilingual Education." *Bilingual Research Journal* 30, no. 1 (Spring 2006) 107–122. Available at: http://brj.asu.edu/vol30_no1/art6.pdf

Lee, Valerie E., and S. Loeb, "School Size in Chicago Elementary Schools: Effects on Teachers' Attitudes and Students' Achievement." *American Educational Research Journal* 37 (2000): 3–31.

Lee, Valerie E., and David T. Burkam, "Dropping Out of High School: The Role of School Organization and Structure." *American Educational Research Journal* 40, no. 2 (Summer 2003): 353–393.

Levin, Murray, *'Teach Me!' Kids Will Learn When Oppression Is the Lesson* (Lanham, MD: Rowman & Littlefield, 2001).

Levitt, Peggy, "Salsa and Ketchup: Transnational Migrants Straddle Two Worlds." *Contexts* 3, no. 2 (2004): 20–26.

Lewis, Oscar, *La Vida: A Puerto Rican Family in the Culture of Poverty—San Juan and New York* (New York: Random House, 1965).

Lindholm-Leary, Kathryn J., and Graciela Borsato, *Impact of Two-Way Bilingual Education Programs on Students' Attitudes Toward School and College* (Santa Barbara, CA: Center for Research on Education, Diversity, and Excellence, 2001).

Lindsey, Delario, "To Build a More 'Perfect Discipline': Ideologies of the Normative and the Social Control of the Criminal Innocent in the Policing of New York City." *Critical Sociology* 30, no. 2 (2004): 321–353.

Lipka, Jerry, "Toward a Culturally-Based Pedagogy: A Case Study of One Yup'ik Eskimo Teacher." In *Transforming Curriculum for a Culturally Diverse Society*, edited by Etta R. Hollins (Mahwah, NJ: Lawrence Erlbaum, 1996).

Lipka, Jerry, Gerald V. Mohatt, and the Ciulistet Group, *Transforming the Culture of Schools: Yup'ik Eskimo Examples* (Mahwah, NJ: Lawrence Erlbaum, 1998).

Lipman, Pauline, "Restructuring in Context: A Case Study of Teacher Participation and the Dynamics of Ideology, Race, and Power." *American Educational Research Journal* 34, no. 1 (1997): 3–37.

Lipset, Seymour Martin, and Earl Raab, *Jews and the New American Scene* (Cambridge, MA: Harvard University Press, 1995).

Loewen, James W., *Lies Across America: What Our Historic Sites Got Wrong* (New York: New Press, 2000).

Loewen, James W., *Lies My Teacher Told Me: Everything Your American History Textbook Got Wrong*, reissue ed. (New York: New Press, 2005).

Lomawaima, K. Tsianina, "Educating Native Americans." In *Handbook of Research on Multicultural Education*, edited by James A. Banks and Cherry A. McGee Banks, 2nd ed. (San Francisco: Jossey-Bass, 2004).

Lomawaima, K. Tsianina, and Teresa L. McCarty, "When Tribal Sovereignty Challenges Democracy: American Indian Education and the Democratic Ideal." *American Educational Research Journal* 39, no. 2 (Summer 2002): 279–305.

Lomawaima, K. Tsianina, and Teresa L. McCarty, *"To Remain an Indian": Lessons in Democracy From a Century of Native American Education* (New York: Teachers College Press, 2006).

Lopez, Alejandra, "Mixed-Race School-Age Children: A Summary of Census 2000 Data." *Educational Researchers* 32, no. 6 (August/September 2003): 25–27.

Love, Angela and Ann C. Kruger, "Teacher beliefs and student achievement in urban schools serving African American students." *The Journal of Educational Research* 99, no. 2 (Nov–Dec 2005): 87–112.

Maaka, Margaret J., "E Kua Takoto te Mānuka T~utahi: Decolonization, Self-Determination, and Education." *Educational Perspectives* 37, no. 1 (2004): 3–13.

Madaus, George, and Marguerite Clarke, "The Adverse Impact of High-Stakes Testing on Minority Students: Evidence From One Hundred Years of Test Data." In *Raising Standards or Raising Barriers? Inequality and High-Stakes Testing in Public Education*, edited by Gary Orfield and Mindy L. Kornhaber (New York: The Century Foundation Press, 2001).

Mahiri, Jabari, *Shooting for Excellence: African American and Youth Culture in New Century Schools* (Urbana, IL: National Council of Teachers of English; and New York: and Teachers College Press, 1998).

Mantsios, Gregory, "Class in America: Myths and Realities (2000)." In *Race, Class, and Gender in the United States*, 5th ed., edited by Paula S. Rothenberg (New York: Worth, 2001).

Manuelito, Kathryn, "The Role of Education in American Indian Self-Determination: Lessons from the Ramah Navajo Community School." *Anthropology & Education Quarterly* 36, no. 1 (March 2005): 73–87.

Marquez, Roberto, "Sojourners, Settlers, Castaways, and Creators: A Recollection of Puerto Rico Past and Puerto Ricans Present." *Massachusetts Review* 36, no. 1 (1995): 94–118.

Matute-Bianchi, María E., "Situational Ethnicity and Patterns of School Performance Among Immigrant and Nonimmigrant Mexican-Descent Students." In *Minority Status and Schooling*, edited by Margaret A. Gibson and John U. Ogbu (New York: Garland, 1991).

Maxwell-Jolly, Julie, Patricia Gándara, and Anne Driscoll, "Listening to Teachers of English Language Learners." *Newsletter of the U.C. Linguistic Minority Research Institute* 14, (Spring 2005) no. 3: 1–2.

McCarty, Teresa L., *A Place to Be Navajo: Rough Rock and the Struggle for Self-Determination in Indigenous Schooling* (Mahwah, NJ: Lawrence Erlbaum, 2002).

McCarty, Teresa L., "Reclaiming the Gift: Indigenous Youth Counter-Narratives on Native Language Loss and Revitalization." *American Indian Quarterly* 30, nos. 1, 2 (Winter/Spring 2006): 28–48.

McCaslin, Mary, and Thomas L. Good, "Compliant Cognition: The Misalliance of Management and Instructional Goals in Current School Reform." *Educational Researcher* 21, no. 3 (April 1992): 4–17.

McDermott, Ray P., "The Cultural Context of Learning to Read." In *Papers in Applied Linguistics: Linguistics and Reading Series 1*, edited by Stanley F. Wanat (Washington, DC: Center for Applied Linguistics, 1977).

McDermott, Ray P., "Social Relations as Contexts for Learning in School." *Harvard Educational Review* 47, no. 2 (May 1977): 198–213.

McIntosh, Peggy, "White Privilege and Male Privilege: A Personal Account of Coming to See Correspondences Through Work in Women's Studies." Working paper no. 189 (Wellesley, MA: Wellesley College Center for Research on Women, 1988).

McLaughlin, Milbrey W., and Joan E. Talbert, *Professional Communities and the Work of High School Teaching* (Chicago: University of Chicago Press, 2001).

McNeil, Linda, *Contradictions of School Reform: Educational Costs of Standardized Testing* (New York: Routledge, 2000).

Mead, S., "Schooling Crumbling Infrastructure: Addressing a Serious and Unappreciated Problem." Available at: www.edweek.org/ew/articles/2005/06/15/a40mead.h24.html

Meier, Deborah, *In Schools We Trust: Creating Communities of Learning in an Era of Testing and Standardization* (Boston: Beacon Press, 2003).

Meier, Deborah, " 'As Though They Owned The Place': Small Schools as Membership Communities." *Phi Delta Kappan* 87, no. 9 (May 2006): 657–662.

Meier, Deborah, and George Wood, eds., *Many Children Left Behind: How The No Child Left Behind Act is Damaging Our Children and Our Schools* (Boston: Beacon Press, 2004).

Meier, Kenneth J., Robert D. Wrinkle, and J. L. Polinard, "Representative Bureaucracy and Distributional Equity: Addressing the Hard Question." *Journal of Politics* 61 (November 1999): 1025–1039.

Menkart, Deborah J., "Deepening the Meaning of Heritage Months." *Educational Leadership* 56, no. 7 (1999): 19–21.

Menzel, Peter, Charles C. Mann, and Paul Kennedy, *Material World: A Global Family Portrait* (San Francisco: Sierra Club, 1995).

Mercado, Carmen I., and Luis Moll, "Student Agency Through Collaborative Research in Puerto Rican Communities." In *Puerto Rican Students in U.S. Schools*, edited by Sonia Nieto (Mahwah, NJ: Lawrence Erlbaum, 2000).

Merriam, Sharan B., *Qualitative Research and Case Study Applications in Education*, 2nd ed. (San Francisco: Jossey-Bass, 1998).

Merriam, Sharan B., *Case Study Research in Education: A Qualitative Approach* (San Francisco: Jossey-Bass, 1998): 27.

Merton, Robert, "The Self-Fulfilling Prophecy." *Antioch Review* 8, no. 2 (1948): 193–210.

Miceli, Melinda, *Standing Out, Standing Together: The Social and Political Impact of Gay/Straight Alliances* (London, England: Routledge, 2005).

Migration Policy Institute, *The Dominican Population in the United States: Growth and Distribution* (Washington, DC: Author, 2004). Available at: www.migrationpolicy.org/pubs/MPI_Report_Dominican_Pop_US.pdf

Miller, Robin Lin, and Mary Jane Rotheram-Borus, "Growing Up Biracial in the United States." In *Race, Ethnicity, and Self: Identity in Multicultural Perspective*, edited by Elizabeth Pathy Salett and Diane R. Koslow (Washington, DC: National Multicultural Institute, 1994).

Miner, Barbara, "Testing Companies Mine for Gold." *Rethinking Schools* 19, no. 2 (Winter 2004): 5–7.

Moll, Luis C., "Bilingual Classroom Studies and Community Analysis: Some Recent Trends." *Educational Researcher* 21, no. 2 (March 1992): 20–24.

Moll, Luis C., "Sociocultural Competence in Teacher Education." *Journal of Teacher Education* 56, no. 3 (May/June 2005): 242–247.

Monkey Dance. Dir. Julie Mallozzi. Documentary. Center for Asian American Media, 2004. www.monkeydance.

Montaño, Theresa, Sharon H. Ulanoff, Rosalinda Quintanar-Sarellana, and Lynne Aoki, "The Debilingualization of California's Prospective Bilingual Teachers." *Social Justice* 32, no. 3 (Fall 2005): 103–119.

Montgomery, Joan, "A Different Mirror: A Conversation with Ronald Takaki." *Educational Leadership* 56, no. 7 (April 1999): 9–13.

Moreno, José F., ed., *The Elusive Quest for Equality: 150 Years of Chicano/Chicano Education* (Cambridge, MA: Harvard Educational Review, 1999).

Morin, Richard, "The Color of Disaster Assistance." *Washington Post*, June 9, 2006. Available at: www.washingtonpost.com/wp-dyn/content/article/2006/06/08/AR2006060801768/html

Morrell, Ernest, *Becoming Critical Researchers: Literacy and Empowerment for Urban Youth* (New York: Peter Lang, 2004).

Morrell, Ernest, "Youth Initiated Research as a Tool for Advocacy and Change in Urban Schools." In *Beyond Resistance! Youth Activism and Community Change*, edited by Shawn Ginwright, Pedro Noguera, and Julio Cammarota (New York: Routledge, 2006): 112–128.

Morrell, Ernest, and Jeff Duncan-Andrade, "Promoting Academic Literacy With Urban Youth Through Engaging Hip-Hop Culture." *English Journal* 9, no. 6 (2002): 88–92.

Moses, Robert P., "Quality Education Is a Civil Rights Issue." In *Minority Achievement*, edited by David T. Gordon (Cambridge, MA: Harvard Education Letter Focus Series no. 7, 2002): 26–27.

Moses, Robert and Charles Cobb, *Radical Equations: Civil Rights from Mississippi to the Algebra Project* (Boston: Beacon Press, 2002).

Mutume, Gumisai, "Reversing Africa's 'Brain Drain': New Initiatives Tap Skills of African Expatriates." *Africa Recovery* 17, no. 2 (July 2003): 1. United Nations. Available at: www.un.org/ecosocdev/geninfo/afrec/vol17no2/172brain.htm

National Center for Children in Poverty, *Basic Facts About Low-Income Children* (March 2005). Available at: http://www.nccp.org

National Center for Education Statistics, *Indicator of the Month: Teachers' Feelings of Preparedness*. Available at: nces.ed.gov/pubs2000/qrtlyspring2005/4elem/q4-6.html.

National Center for Education Statistics, *Schools and Staffing Survey, 1999–2000: Overview of the Data for Public, Private, Charter, and Bureau of Indian Affairs Elementary and Secondary Schools* (Washington, DC: U.S. Department of Education, 2002): 43–44. Table 1.19.

National Center for Education Statistics, *State Nonfiscal Survey of Public Elementary/Secondary Education* (Washington, DC: U.S. Department of Education, 2001).

National Center for Education Statistics, *Status and Trends in the Education of Hispanics* (NCES 2003-008) (Washington, DC: U.S. Department of Education, 2003).

National Clearinghouse for English Language Acquisition and Language Instruction Educational Programs, *English Language Learners and the U.S. Census, 1990–2000*. Available at: www.ncela.gwu.edu

National Collaborative on Diversity in the Teaching Force, *Assessment of Diversity in America's Teaching Force: A Call to Action* (Washington, DC: Author, October 2004).

National Commission on Excellence in Education, *A Nation at Risk: The Imperative for Education Reform* (Washington, DC: U.S. Government Printing Office, 1983).

National Council of Churches, "Ten Moral Concerns in the Implementation of the *No Child Left Behind Act: A Statement of the National Council of Churches Committee on Public Education and Literacy* 2006. Available at: www.ncccusa.org

National Council of Teachers of Mathematics, NCTM, available at www.nctm.org.

National Indochinese Clearinghouse, *A Manual for Indochinese Refugee Education, 1976–1977* (Arlington, VA: Center for Applied Linguistics, 1976).

Neill, Monty, Lisa Guisbond, and Bob Schaeffer, with James Madison, and Life Legeros, *Failing Our Children: How "No Child Left Behind" Undermines Quality and Equity in Education* (Cambridge, MA: National Center for Fair and Open Testing, 2004).

Nelson-Barber, Sharon, and Elise Trumbull Estrin, "Bringing Native American Perspectives to Mathematics and Science Teaching." *Theory into Practice* 34, no. 3 (Summer 1995): 174–185.

Newman, Leslea, *Heather has Two Mommies* (Boston: Alyson Books, 2000).

Nichols, Sharon, and David C. Berliner, *The Inevitable Corruption of Indicators and Educators Through High-Stakes Testing* (Tempe, AZ: Educational Policy Studies Laboratory, Educational Policy Research Unit, Arizona State University, March 2005). Available at: http://edpolicylab.org

Nieto, Sonia, "Affirmation, Solidarity, and Critique: Moving Beyond Tolerance in Multicultural Education." *Multicultural Education* 1, no. 4 (Spring 1994): 9–12, 35–38.

Nieto, Sonia, "On Becoming American: An Exploratory Essay." In *A Light in Dark Times: Maxine Greene and the Unfinished Conversation*, edited by William Ayres and Janet L. Miller (New York: Teachers College Press, 1998).

Nieto, Sonia, *The Light in Their Eyes: Creating Multicultural Learning Communities* (New York: Teachers College Press, 1999).

Nieto, Sonia, "Bringing Bilingual Education Out of the Basement, and Other Imperatives for Teacher Education." In *Lifting Every Voice: Pedagogy and Politics of Bilingual Education*, edited by Zeynep Beykont (Cambridge, MA: Harvard Educational Review, 2000).

Nieto, Sonia, "Profoundly Multicultural Questions." *Educational Leadership* 60, no. 4, (Dec 2002/Jan 2003): 6–10.

Nieto, Sonia, *What Keeps Teachers Going?* (New York: Teachers College Press, 2003).

Nieto, Sonia, *Why We Teach* (New York: Teachers College Press, 2005).

Nieto, Sonia, Patty Bode, Eugenie Kang, and John Raible, "Pushing the Boundaries of Multicultural Education: Retheorizing Identity, Community and Curriculum." In *Handbook of Curriculum and Instruction*, edited by F. M. Connelly, M. F. He, and J. Phillion (Thousand Oaks, CA: Sage, 2007).

Nine-Curt, Carmen, *Nonverbal Communication* (Cambridge, MA: Evaluation, Dissemination, and Assessment Center, 1984).

No Child Left Behind Act of 2001, Public Law 107-110.

Noddings, Nel, *The Challenge to Care in Schools: An Alternative Approach to Education* (New York: Teachers College Press, 1992).

Noguera, Pedro, "Joaquin's Dilemma: Understanding the Link Between Racial Identity and School-Related Behaviors." In *Adolescents at School: Perspectives on Youth, Identity, and Education*, edited by Michael Sadowski (Cambridge, MA: Harvard Education Press): 19–30.

Noguera, Pedro, "Social Class, But What About Schools?" *Poverty & Race* 13, no. 5 (September/October 2004): 11–12.

Oakes, Jeannie, *Keeping Track: How Schools Structure Inequality* (New Haven, CT: Yale University Press, 1985).

Oakes, Jeannie, *Keeping Track: How Schools Structure Inequality*, 2nd ed. (New Haven, CT: Yale University Press, 2005).

Oakes, Jeannie, and Gretchen Guiton, "Matchmaking: The Dynamics of High School Tracking Decisions." *American Educational Research Journal* 32, no. 1 (Spring 1995): 3–33.

Oakes, Jeannie, Amy Stuart Wells, Makeba Jones, and Amanda Datnow, "Detracking: The Social Construction of Ability, Cultural Politics, and Resistance to Reform." *Teachers College Record* 98, no. 3 (1997): 482–510.

Oakes, Jeannie, Karen Hunter Quartz, Steve Ryan, and Martin Lipton, *Becoming Good American Schools: The Struggle for Civic Virtue in Education Reform* (San Francisco: Jossey-Bass, 2000).

Ogbu, John U., "Variability in Minority School Performance: A Problem in Search of an Explanation." *Anthropology & Education Quarterly* 18, no. 4 (December 1987): 312–334.

Ogbu, John U., and Herbert D. Simons, "Voluntary and Involuntary Minorities: A Cultural-Ecological Theory of School Performance with Some Implications for Education." *Anthropology & Education Quarterly* 29, no. 2 (September 1998): 155–188.

Okome, Mojubaolu Olufunke, "Emergent African Immigrant Philanthropy in New York City." *Research in Urban Sociology* 7 (2004): 179–191.

Olmedo, Irma M., "Accommodation and Resistance: Latinas Struggle for Their Children's Education." *Anthropology & Education Quarterly*, 34, no. 4 (December 2003): 373–395.

Olsen, Laurie, *Made in America: Immigrant Students in Our Public Schools* (New York: New Press, 1997).

Olsen, Laurie, "Learning English and Learning America: Immigrants in the Center of a Storm" *Theory Into Practice* 39, no. 4 (Summer 2000): 196–202.

Orfield, Gary, *Schools More Separate: Consequences of a Decade of Resegregation* (Cambridge, MA: The Civil Rights Project at Harvard University, June 2001).

Orfield, Gary, "Losing Our Future: Minority Youth Left Out." In *Dropouts in America: Confronting the Graduate Rate Crisis*, edited by Gary G. Orfield (Cambridge, MA: Harvard Education Press, 2004): 1–11.

Orfield, Gary, ed., *Dropouts in America: Confronting the Graduate Rate Crisis* (Cambridge, MA: Harvard Education Press, 2004): 1–11.

Orfield, Gary, and Mindy L. Kornhaber, eds., *Raising Standards or Raising Barriers? Inequality and High-Stakes Testing in Public Education* (New York: The Century Foundation Press, 2001).

Orfield, Gary and Chungmei Lee, *Why Segregation Matters: Poverty and Educational Inequality*. Available at: http://civilrightsproject.harvard.edu/research/deseg/deseg05.phpmimetext/

Orfield, Gary, and John T. Yun, *Resegregation in American Schools* (Cambridge, MA: Civil Rights Project at Harvard University, 1999).

Ortiz, Flora Ida, "Hispanic-American Children's Experiences in Classrooms: A Comparison Between Hispanic and Non-Hispanic Children." In *Class, Race and Gender in American Education*, edited by Lois Weis (Albany: State University of New York Press, 1988).

Pang, Valerie Ooka, Peter N. Kiang, and Yoon K. Pak, "Asian Pacific American Students: Challenging a Biased Educational System." In *Handbook of Research on Multicultural Education*, 2nd ed., edited by James A. Banks and Cherry A. McGee Banks (San Francisco: Jossey-Bass, 2004): 542–563.

Park, Clara C., A. Lin Goodwin, and Stacey J. Lee, eds. *Asian American Identities, Families, and Schooling: Research on the Education of Asian and Pacific Americans.* (Charlotte, NC: Information Age, 2003).

Payne, Ruby, *A Framework for Understanding Poverty* (Highlands, TX: aha! Process, 2001).

Pedula, Joseph J., Lisa M. Abrams, George F. Madaus, Michael K. Russell, Miguel A. Ramos, and Jing Miao, *Perceived Effects of State-Mandated Testing Programs on Teaching and Learning: Findings from a National Survey of Teachers* (Boston: National Board on Educational Testing and Public Policy, Boston College, 2003).

Pellegrino, James W., Naomi Chudowsky, and Robert Glaser, *Knowing What Students Know: The Science and Design of Educational Assessment* (Washington, DC: National Academy Press, 2001).

Pérez, Berta, and María E. Torres-Guzmán, *Learning in Two Worlds: An Integrated Spanish/English Biliteracy Approach*, 3rd ed. (Boston: Allyn and Bacon, 2002).

Perkins, Bruce K., *Where We Learn: The CUBE Survey of Urban School Climate* (Washington, DC: Urban Achievement Task Force, Council of Urban Boards of Education and the National School Boards Association, 2006).

Pewewardy, Cornel, "Will the 'Real' Indians Please Stand Up?" *Multicultural Review* 7, no. 2 (June 1998): 36–42.

Philips, Susan Urmston, *The Invisible Culture: Communication in Classroom and Community on the Warm Springs Indian Reservation* (reissued with changes) (Prospect Heights, IL: Waveland Press, 1993).

Phillips, D. C. (ed.), *Constructivism in Education*. National Society for the Study of Education Yearbook, vol. 99, issue 1 (Chicago: University of Chicago Press, 2000).

Phinney, Jean D., "A Three-Stage Model of Ethnic Identity Development in Adolescence." In *Ethnic Identity Formation and Transmission Among Hispanics and Other Minorities*, edited by Martha E. Bernal and George P. Knight (Albany: State University of New York Press, 1993).

Pizarro, Marcos, *Chicanas and Chicanos in School: Racial Profiling, Identity Battles, and Empowerment* (Austin: University of Texas Press, 2005).

Pollard, Diane S., and Cheryl S. Ajirotutu, *African-Centered Schooling in Theory and Practice* (Westport, CT: Bergin and Garvey, 2000).

Pollock, Mica, *Colormute: Race Talk Dilemmas in an American School* (Princeton, NJ: Princeton University Press, 2004).

Portes, Alejandro, and Rubén G. Rumbaut, "Introduction: The Second Generation and the Children of Immigrants Longitudinal Study." *Ethnic and Racial Studies* 28 no. 6 (Nov 2005): 983(17).

Portes, Alejandro, and Rubén G. Rumbaut, *Legacies: The Story of the Immigrant Second Generation* (Berkeley: University of California Press; and New York: Russell Sage Foundation, 2001).

Portes, Alejandro, and Rubén G. Rumbaut, *Immigrant America: A Portrait*, 3rd ed. (Berkeley: University of California Press, 2006).

Prah, Pamela M., "Schools With Poor, Minority Students Get Less State Funds." Available at: www.stateline.org, accessed October 29, 2003.

Provenzo, Eugene F., Jr., *Critical Literacy: What Every American Ought to Know* (Boulder, CO: Paradigm, 2005).

Public Education Network and *Education Week, Action for All: The Public's Responsibility for Public Education* (Washington, DC: Authors, April 2001).

"Public School Facilities: Providing Environments That Sustain Learning." *ACCESS* (Quarterly Newsletter of the Advocacy Center for Children's Educational Success With Standards) 4, no. 1 (Winter 2004): 1.

Quality Counts at 10: A Decade of Standards-Based Education, 2006. Available at: www.edweek.org/ew/articles/2006/01/05/17overview.h25.html

Rabkin, Nick, and Robin Edmond, *Putting the Arts in the Picture: Reframing Education in the 21st Century* (Chicago: Columbia College Chicago, 2004).

Raible, John, "*Sharing the Spotlight: The Non-adopted Siblings of Transracial Adoptees*, diss., University of Massachusetts Amherst, 2005.

Ramirez, Manuel, and Alfredo Castañeda, *Cultural Democracy, Bicognitive Development and Education* (New York: Academic Press, 1974).

Ramsey, Patricia G., *Teaching and Learning in a Diverse World: Multicultural Education for Young Children*, 3rd ed. (New York: Teachers College Press, 2004).

Reissman, Frank, *The Culturally Deprived Child* (New York: Harper & Row, 1962).

Reyes, María de la Luz, "Challenging Venerable Assumptions: Literacy Instruction for Linguistically Differ-ent Students." *Harvard Educational Review* 62, no. 4 (Winter 1992): 427–446.

Reyes, María de la Luz, and John Halcon, eds., *The Best for Our Children: Critical Perspectives on Literacy for Latino Students* (New York: Teachers College Press, 2001).

Reyhner, Jon, "Native American Languages Act Becomes Law." *NABE News* 14, no. 3 (December 1, 1990): 1, 8–9.

Reyhner, Jon, "Bilingual Education: Teaching the Native Language." In *Teaching the Indian Child: A Bilingual/Multicultural Approach*, edited by J. Reyhner (Billings, MT: Eastern Montana College, 1992).

Richardson, Virginia, "Constructivist Pedagogy." *Teachers College Record* 105, no. 9 (December 2003): 1623–1640.

Rist, Ray C., "Student Social Class and Teacher Expectations: The Self-Fulfilling Prophecy in Ghetto Education." In *Challenging the Myths: The Schools, the Blacks, and the Poor*, Reprint series no. 5 (Cambridge, MA: Harvard Educational Review, 1971).

Rist, Ray C., "Author's Introduction: The Enduring Dilemmas of Class and Color in American Education," *Harvard Educational Review*, HER Classic Reprint 70, no. 3 (Fall 2000): 257–301.

Rivera-Batiz, Francisco L., and Carlos E. Santiago, *Island Paradox: Puerto Rico in the 1990s* (New York: Russell Sage Foundation, 1996).

Rodriguez, Clara E., Irma M. Olmedo, and Mariolga Reyes-Cruz, "Deconstructing and Contextualizing the Historical and Social Science Literature on Puerto Ricans." In *Handbook of Research on Multicultural Education*, 2nd ed. edited by James A. Banks and Cherry A. McGee Banks (New York: Macmillan, 2004).

Rodriguez, Luis J., *Always Running, La Vida Loca: Gang Days in L.A.* (New York: Simon & Schuster, 1993).

Rolón, Carmen "Puerto Rican Female Narratives about Self, School and Success," In *Puerto Ricans in U.S. Schools* edited by Sonia Nieto. (Mahwah, NJ: Lawrence Erlbaum, 2000).

Rohmer, Harriet, ed., *Honoring Our Ancestors: Stories and Pictures by Fourteen Artists* (San Francisco: Children's Book Press, 1999).

Rolstad, Kellie, Kate Mahoney, and Gene V. Glass, "The Big Picture: A Meta-Analysis of Program Effectiveness Research on English Language Learners." *Educational Policy* 19, no. 4 (September 2005): 572–594.

Rong, Xue Lan Do, and Frank Brown, "Socialization, Culture, and Identities of Black Immigrant Children:

What Educators Need to Know and Do." *Education and Urban Society* 34, no. 2 (February 2002): 247–273.

Root, Maria P., "Multiracial Families and Children: Implications for Educational Research and Practice." In *Handbook of Research on Multicultural Education*, 2nd ed. edited by James A. Banks and Cherry A. McGee Banks (San Francisco: Jossey-Bass, 2004): 110–124.

Rosenberg, Pearl M., "Color Blindness in Teacher Education: An Optical Illusion." In *Off White: Readings on Power, Privilege, and Resistance*, edited by Michelle Fine, Lois Weis, Linda Powell Pruitt, and April Burns (New York: Routledge, 2004): 257–272.

Rosenthal, Robert, "Pygmalian Effects: Existence, Magnitude, and Social Importance." *Educational Researcher* 16, no. 9 (December 1987): 37–41.

Rosenthal, Robert, and Lenore Jacobson, *Pygmalion in the Classroom* (New York: Holt, Rinehart and Winston, 1968).

Rothenberg, Paula S., ed., *Race, Class, and Gender in the United States*, 5th ed. (New York: Worth, 2001).

Rothstein, Richard, *Class and Schools: Using Social, Economic, and Educational Reform to Close the Black-White Achievement Gap* (New York: Teachers College Press; and Washington, DC: Economic Policy Institute, 2004).

Roughgarden, Joan, *Evolution's Rainbow: Diversity, Gender, and Sexuality in Nature and People* (Berkeley: University of California Press, 2005).

Rumbaut, Rubén G., "The Crucible Within: Ethnic Identity, Self-Esteem, and Segmented Assimilation Among Children of Immigrants." In *Origins and Destinies: Immigration, Race, and Ethnicity in America*, edited by Silvia Pedraza and Rubén G. Rumbaut (Belmont, CA: Wadsworth, 1996).

Ryan, William, *Blaming the Victim* (New York: Vintage Books, 1972).

Sacchetti, Maria, and Tracy Jan, "High School Dropout Rate Reaches Highest in 14 Years." *The Boston Globe*, October 22, 2005. Available at: www.boston .com/news/local/massachusetts/articles/2005/ 10/22/high_school_dropout_rates_reaches_highest_ in_14-years?/mode + PF

Sadker, Myra, and David Sadker, "Gender Bias: From Colonial America to Today's Classrooms." In *Multicultural Education: Issues and Perspectives*, 5th ed., edited by James A. Banks and Cherry A. McGee Banks (New York: Wiley, 2005).

Sadowski, Michael, "Are High-Stakes Tests Worth the Wager?" In *Minority Achievement*, edited by David T. Gordon (Cambridge, MA: Harvard Education Letter Focus Series no. 7, 2002).

Sadowski, Michael, *Adolescents at School: Perspectives on Youth, Identity, and Education* (Cambridge, MA: Harvard Education Press, 2003).

Sadowski, Michael, "Making Schools Safer for LGBT Youth." *Harvard Education Letter* 22, no. 3 (May/ June 2006): 1–3.

Sanders, Mavis G., and Adia Harvey, "Beyond the School Walls: A Case Study of Principal Leadership for School–Community Collaboration." *Teachers College Record* 104, no. 7 (October 2007): 1345–1368.

Santiago, Esmeralda, *When I Was Puerto Rican* (Reading, MA: Addison-Wesley, 1993).

Schaefer, Richard T., *Racial and Ethnic Groups*, 3rd ed. (Glenview, IL: Scott Foresman, 1988).

Schneider, Barbara, Sylvia Martinez, and Ann Owens, "Barriers to Educational Opportunities for Hispanics in the United States." *National Research Council: Hispanics and the Future of America* (Chapter 6). Panel on Hispanics in the United States, Committee on Population, Division of Behavioral and Social Sciences and Education. (Washington, DC: The National Academies Press, 2006).

Schniedewind, Nancy, and Ellen Davidson, *Open Minds to Equality: A Sourcebook of Learning Activities to Affirm Diversity and Promote Equality*, 3rd ed. (Milwaukee, WI: Rethinking Schools, 2006).

Schofield, Janet Ward, "The Colorblind Perspective in School: Causes and Consequences." In *Multicultural Education: Issues and Perspectives*, 5th ed., edited by James A. Banks and Cherry A. McGee Banks (New York: Wiley, 2005).

"School Discipline: An Uneven Hand." *Seattle Post-Intelligencer*, July 1, 2002. Available at: seattlepi .nwsource.com/disciplinegap/

Schwarzer, David, Alexia Haywood, and Charla Lorenzen, "Fostering Multiliteracy in a Linguistically Diverse Classroom." *Language Arts* 80, no. 6 (July 2003): 453–460.

Seelye, H. Ned, *Teaching Culture: Strategies for Intercultural Communication* 3rd ed. (Lincolnwood, IL: National Textbook Company, 1993).

Selden, Steven, *Inheriting Shame: The Story of Eugenics and Racism in America* (New York: Teachers College Press, 1999).

Sheets, Rosa Hernández, "From Remedial to Gifted: Effects of Culturally Centered Pedagogy." *Theory Into Practice* 34, no. 3 (Summer 1995): 186–193.

Shin, Hyon B., "School Enrollment: Social and Economic Characteristics of Students—October 2003." In *Current Population Reports* (Washington, DC: U.S. Census Bureau, 2005).

Shor, Ira, *When Students Have Power: Negotiating Authority in a Critical Pedagogy* (Chicago: University of Chicago Press, 1996).

Simon, Mark, "What Teachers Know." *Poverty & Race* 13, no. 5 (September/October 2004): 16.

Singham, Mano, "The Achievement Gap: Myths and Realities." *Phi Delta Kappan* 84, no. 8 (April 2003): 586–591.

Skutnabb-Kangas, Tove, "Multilingualism and the Education of Minority Children." In *Minority Education: From Shame to Struggle*, edited by Tove Skutnabb-Kangas and Jim Cummins (Clevedon, England: Multilingual Matters, 1988).

Sleeter, Christine E., "White Racism." *Multicultural Education* 1, no. 4 (Spring 1994): 5–8, 39.

Sleeter, Christine E., *Multicultural Education and Social Activism* (Albany: State University of New York Press, 1996).

Sleeter, Christine E., *Un-Standardizing Curriculum: Multicultural Teaching in the Standards-Based Classroom* (New York: Teachers College Press, 2005).

Smerden, Becky A., David T. Burkham, and Valerie E. Lee, "Access to Constructivist and Didactic Teaching: Who Gets It? Where Is It Practiced?" *Teachers College Record* 101, no. 1 (Fall 1999): 5–34.

Smith, Fran, "Candor in the Class." Available at: http://edutopia.or/magazine/ed1article.php?id=Art_1499&issue_apr_06

Smith, G. Pritchy, and Deborah H. Batiste, "What do Students Think about Multiculturalism?" *Multicultural Education* 4, no. 4 (Summer, 1997).

Smith-Hefner, Nancy, *Khmer American: Identity and Moral Education in a Diasporic Community* (Berkeley: University of California Press, 1999).

Smyth, Laura, and Heath, Shirley Brice, *ArtShow: Youth and Community Development* (Washington, DC: Partners for Livable Communities, 1999).

Snow, Catherine, "The Myths Around Bilingual Education." *NABE News* 21, no. 2 (1997): 29, 36.

Snow, Richard E., "Unfinished Pygmalion." *Contemporary Psychology* 14, no. 4 (1969): 197–200.

Solórzano, Daniel G., Maria C. Ledesma, Jeanette Pérez, Maria R. Burciaga, and Armida Ornelas, "Latina Equity in Education: Gaining Access to Academic Enrichment Programs." *Latino Policy & Issues Brief* 4 (Los Angeles: UCLA Chicano Studies Research Center, February 2003).

Solsken, Judith, Jo-Anne Wilson Keenan, and Jerri Willett, "Interweaving Stories: Creating a Multicultural Classroom Through School/Home/University Collaboration." *Democracy and Education* (Fall 1993): 16–21.

Soto, Lourdes Diaz, *Language, Culture, and Power: Bilingual Families and the Struggle for Quality Education* (Albany: State University of New York Press, 1997).

Spring, Joel, *The Rise and Fall of the Corporate State* (Boston: Beacon Press, 1972).

Spring, Joel, *American Education*, 12th ed. (New York: McGraw-Hill, 2006).

Spring, Joel, *Deculturalization and the Struggle for Equality: A Brief History of the Education of Dominated Cultures in the United States*, 5th ed. (New York: McGraw-Hill, 2006).

St. Germaine, Richard, "Drop-out Rates Among American Indian and Alaska Native Students: Beyond Cultural Discontinuity." In *ERIC Digest, Clearinghouse on Rural Education and Small Schools* (Charleston, WV: Appalachia Educational Laboratory, November 1995).

St. Pierre, Stephanie, *Teenage Refugees from Cambodia Speak Out: In Their Own Voices* (New York: Rosen, 1995).

Stanton-Salazar, Ricardo D., "A Social Capital Framework for Understanding the Socialization of Racial Minority Children and Youth." *Harvard Educational Review* 67, no. 1 (Spring 1997): 1–40.

Stanton-Salazar, Ricardo D., *Manufacturing Hope and Despair: The School and Kin Support Networks of U.S.–Mexican Youth* (New York: Teachers College Press, 2001).

Steele, Claude M., "Race and the Schooling of Black Americans." *Atlantic Monthly* (April 1992): 68–78.

Suarez-Orozco, Marcelo M., " 'Becoming Somebody': Central American Immigrants in the U.S." *Anthropology & Education Quarterly* 18, no. 4 (December 1987): 287–299.

Swisher, Karen, and Dilys Schoorman, "Learning Styles: Implications for Teachers." In *Multicultural Education for the 21st Century*, edited by Carlos F. Díaz (New York: Longman, 2001).

Swope, Kathy, and Barbara Miner, *Failing Our Kids: Why the Testing Craze Won't Fix Our Schools* (Milwaukee: Rethinking Schools, 2000).

Szymusiak, Molyda, *The Stones Cry Out: A Cambodian Childhood, 1975–1980*. Trans. Jane Hamilton-Merritt and Linda Coverdale (Bloomington: Indiana University Press, 1999).

Takaki, Ronald, *Strangers From a Different Shore: A History of Asian Americans* (New York: Penguin Books, 1989).

Takougang, Joseph, "Contemporary African Immigrants to the United States." *Irinkerindo: A Journal of African Migration* Issue 2 (December 2003).

Takyi, Baffour, "The Making of the Second Diaspora: On the Recent African Immigrant Community in the

United States of America." *Western Journal of Black Studies* 26, no. 1 (2002): 32–43.

Tam, Thi Dang Wei, *Vietnamese Refugee Students: A Handbook for School Personnel* (Cambridge, MA: National Assessment and Dissemination Center, 1980). Available at: www.africamigration.com/?CFID = 662515&CFTOKEN = 14479383

Tatum, Beverly Daniel, *"Why Are All the Black Kids Sitting Together in the Cafeteria?" and Other Conversations About Race* (New York: HarperCollins, 1997).

Tatum, Beverly Daniel, "Talking About Race, Learning About Racism: The Application of Racial Identity Development Theory in the Classroom." *Harvard Educational Review* 62, no. 1 (Spring 1992): 1–24.

Taylor, Denny, and Catherine Dorsey-Gaines, *Growing Up Literate: Learning From Inner-City Families* (Portsmouth, NH: Heinemann, 1988).

Terman, Lewis, *The Measurement of Intelligence* (Boston: Houghton Mifflin, 1916).

Tharp, Roland G., "Psychocultural Variables and Constants: Effects on Teaching and Learning in Schools." *American Psychologist* 44, no. 2 (February 1989): 349–359.

Thomas, Wayne P., and Virginia Collier, *National Study of School Effectiveness for Language Minority Students' Academic Achievement* (Santa Cruz, CA: Center for Research on Education, Diversity, and Excellence, 2003).

Tienda, Marta, and Faith Mitchell, eds., *Multiple Origins, Uncertain Destinies: Hispanics and the American Future: Panel on Hispanics in the United States*. Committee on Population, Division of Behavioral and Social Sciences and Education (Washington, DC: National Academies Press, 2006). Electronic book PDF version available at: www7.nationalacademies.org/ocga/briefings/Hispanics_and_the_American_Future.asp; accessed July 2006.

Tomás Rivera Newsletter 2, no. 4 (Fall 1989)

Trueba, Henry T., "Culture and Language: The Ethnographic Approach to the Study of Learning Environments." In *Language and Culture in Learning: Teaching Spanish to Native Speakers of Spanish*, edited by Barbara J. Merino, Henry T. Trueba, and Fabián A. Samaniego (Bristol, PA: Falmer Press, 1993).

Tyack, David B., *The One Best System: A History of American Urban Education* (Cambridge, MA: Harvard University Press, 1974).

Tyack, David B., "Schooling and Social Diversity: Historical Reflections." In *Toward a Common Destiny: Improving Race and Ethnic Relations in America*, edited by Willis D. Hawley and Anthony W. Jackson (San Francisco: Jossey-Bass, 1995).

Ung, Loung, *First They Killed My Father* (New York: Harper Collins, 2000).

Ung, Luong, *Lucky Child: A Daughter of Cambodia Reunites with the Sister She Left Behind* (New York: Harper Collins, 2000).

United Nations, High Commission for Refugees Report, *The State of The World's Refugees 2000: Fifty Years of Humanitarian Action*, "Chapter 4: Flight from Indochina," pp. 79–103. Available at: www.unhcr.org/cgibin/texis/vtx/publ/opendoc.pdf?tbl = PUBL &id = 3ebf9bad0; accessed June 2006.

U.S. Census Bureau, *Profile of Selected Social Characteristics: 2000* (Washington, DC: U.S. Department of Commerce, 2000).

U.S. Census Bureau, *Profile of the Foreign-Born Population in the United States: 2000* (Washington, DC: U.S. Department of Commerce, 2002).

U.S. Department of Education, National Center for Education Statistics, *Status and Trends in the Education of Hispanics* (NCES 2003-008) (Washington, DC: Author, 2003).

U.S. Census Bureau, *Language Spoken at Home and Ability to Speak English for the Population 5 Years and Over: 2000*. Source: Census 2000, released October 29, 2004. Internet release date: February 25, 2003. Available at: www.census.gov/population/cen2000/phc-t20/tab04.pdf

U.S. Census Bureau, *Census 2000 Summary File 1* (Washington, DC: U.S. Department of Commerce, 2002).

U.S. Census Bureau, *Hispanic Population Passes 40 Million* (2005). Available at: www.census.gov/PressRelease/www/releases/archives/populatioon/005164.html; accessed July, 2006.

U.S. Census Bureau, *Income, Poverty, and Health Insurance Coverage in the United States, Current Population Survey, 2003 to 2005 Annual Social and Economic Supplements* (Washington, DC: U.S. Department of Commerce, 2005).

Valdés, Guadalupe, *Con Respeto: Bridging the Distance Between Culturally Diverse Families and Schools* (New York: Teachers College Press, 1996).

Valencia, Richard R., "Inequalities and the Schooling of Minority Students in Texas: Historical and Contemporary Conditions." *Hispanic Journal of Behavioral Sciences* 22, no. 4 (2000): 445–459.

Valencia, Richard R., *Chicano School Failure and Success: Past, Present, and Future* (New York: RoutledgeFalmer, 2002).

Valenzuela, Angela, *Subtractive Schooling: U.S.–Mexican Youth and the Politics of Caring* (Albany: State University of New York Press, 1999).

Valldejudi, Jorge M., and Juan Flores, "New Rican Voices: Un Muestrario/A Sampler at the Millennium." *Journal of the Center for Puerto Rican Studies*, 12, no. 1 (2000): 49–96.

Vasquez, Vivian, *Negotiating Critical Literacies With Young Children*. (Mahwah, NJ: Lawrence Erlbaum, 2004).

Vigil, James Diego, "Streets and Schools: How Educators Can Help Chicano Marginalized Gang Youth." *Harvard Educational Review* 69, no. 3 (Fall 1999): 270–288.

Vogt, Lynn A., Cathie Jordan, and Roland G. Tharp, "Explaining School Failure, Producing School Success: Two Cases." In *Minority Education: Anthropological Perspectives*, edited by Evelyn Jacob and Cathie Jordan (Norwood, NJ: Ablex, 1993).

Wallitt, Roberta, "Breaking the Silence: Cambodian Students Speak Out About School, Success, and Shifting Identities," diss., University of Massachusetts Amherst, 2005.

Walters, Laurel Shaper, "Putting Cooperative Learning to the Test." *Harvard Education Letter* 16, no. 3 (May/June 2000): 1–7.

Wehlage, Gary G., and Robert A. Rutter, "Dropping Out: How Much Do Schools Contribute to the Problem?" In *School Dropouts: Patterns and Policies* (New York: Teachers College Press, 1986).

Weinberg, Meyer, "Notes From the Editor." *A Chronicle of Equal Education* 4, no. 3 (November 1982): 7–8.

Weinberg, Meyer, *Because They Were Jews: A History of Anti-Semitism* (Westport, CT: Greenwood Press, 1986).

Weinberg, Meyer, *Racism in the United States: A Comprehensive Classified Bibliography* (Westport, CT: Greenwood Press, 1990).

Wheelock, Anne, *Crossing the Tracks: How "Untracking" Can Save America's Schools* (New York: New Press, 1992).

Wiggins, Grant and Jay McTighe, *Understanding by Design*, 2nd ed., (Alexandria, VA: Association for Supervision and Curriculum Development, 2005).

Wijeyesinghe, Charmaine L., and Bailey W. Jackson, III, eds., *New Perspectives on Racial Identity Development: A Theoretical and Practical Anthology* (New York: New York University Press, May 2001).

Wiley, Terrence G., *Literacy and Language Diversity in the United States*, 2nd ed. (Washington, DC: Center for Applied Linguistics, 2005).

Williamson, Joel, *New People: Miscegenation and Mulattoes in the United States* (New York: Free Press, 1980).

Willis, Arlette, ed., *Teaching and Using Multicultural Literature in Grades 9–12: Moving Beyond the Canon* (Norwood, MA: Christopher-Gordon, 1998).

Wilson, Bruce L., and H. Dickson Corbett, *Listening to Urban Kids: School Reform and the Teachers They Want* (Albany: State University of New York Press, 2001).

Wineburg, Samuel S., "The Self-Fulfillment of the Self-Fulfilling Prophecy: A Critical Appraisal." *Educational Researcher* 16, no. 9 (December 1987): 28–37.

Winerip, Michael, "One Secret to Better Test Scores: Make State Reading Tests Easier." *The New York Times*, October 5, 2005. Available at: www.nytimes.com/2005/10/05/education/05education.html

Witkin, Herman A., *Psychological Differentiation* (New York: Wiley, 1962).

Wong Fillmore, Lily, and Catherine E. Snow, "What Teachers Need to Know About Language," In *What Teachers Need to Know About Language*, edited by Carolyn Temple Adger, Catherine E. Snow, and Donna Christian (Washington, DC: Center for Applied Linguistics, 2002): 7–43.

Woodson, Carter G., *The Miseducation of the Negro* (Washington, DC: Associated Publishers, 1933).

Yearwood, Junia, "Words That Kill." In *What Keeps Teachers Going?*, edited by Sonia Nieto (New York: Teachers College Press, 2003).

Yon, Daniel A. *Elusive Culture: Schooling, Race, and Identity in Global Times* (Albany: State University of New York Press, 2000).

Yonezawa, Susan, Amy Stuart Wells, and Irene Serna, "Choosing Tracks: 'Freedom of Choice' in Detracking Schools." *American Educational Research Journal* 39, no. 1 (Spring 2002): 37–67.

Yosso, Tara J., *Critical Race Counterstories along the Chicana/Chicano Educational Pipeline* (New York: Routledge, 2006).

Zanger, Mark H., *The American Ethnic Cookbook for Students* (Phoenix, AZ: Onyx Press, 2001).

Zeichner, Kenneth, "Pedagogy, Knowledge, and Teacher Preparation." In *Closing the Achievement Gap: Reframing the Reform,* edited by Belinda Williams (Washington, DC: Association for Supervision and Curriculum Development, 2003).

Zentella, Ana Celia, *Growing Up Bilingual: Puerto Rican Children in New York* (Malden, MA: Blackwell, 1997).

Zentella, Ana Celia, ed., *Building on Strengths: Language and Literacy in Latino Families and Communities* (New York: Teachers College Press, 2005).

Zhou, Min, and Carol L. Bankston, III, "The Biculturalism of the Vietnamese Student." *Digest*, ERIC Clearinghouse on Urban Education, no. 152 (March 2000).

Zinn, Howard, *A People's History of the United States, 1492–Present* (New York: Harper Perennial, 2005; first edition 1980).

Zirkel, Sabrina, " 'Is There a Place for Me?' Role Models and Academic Identity Among White Students and Students of Color." *Teachers College Record* 104, no. 2 (March 2002): 357–376.

Zogby, James J., "When Stereotypes Threaten Pride." *NEA Today* (October, 1982): 12.

Index